Hikaru Nakamura

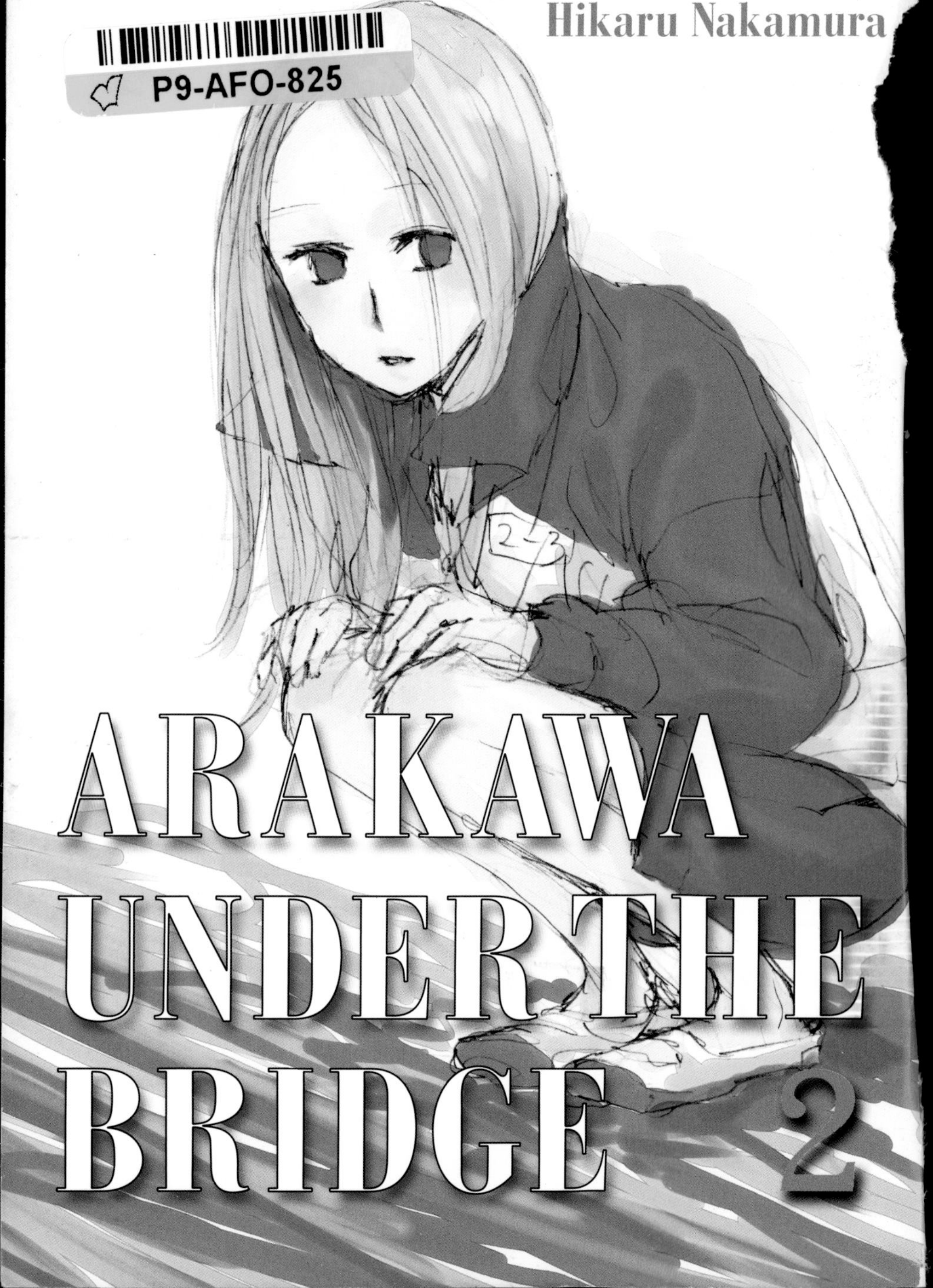

ARAKAWA UNDER THE BRIDGE 2

C O N T E N T S

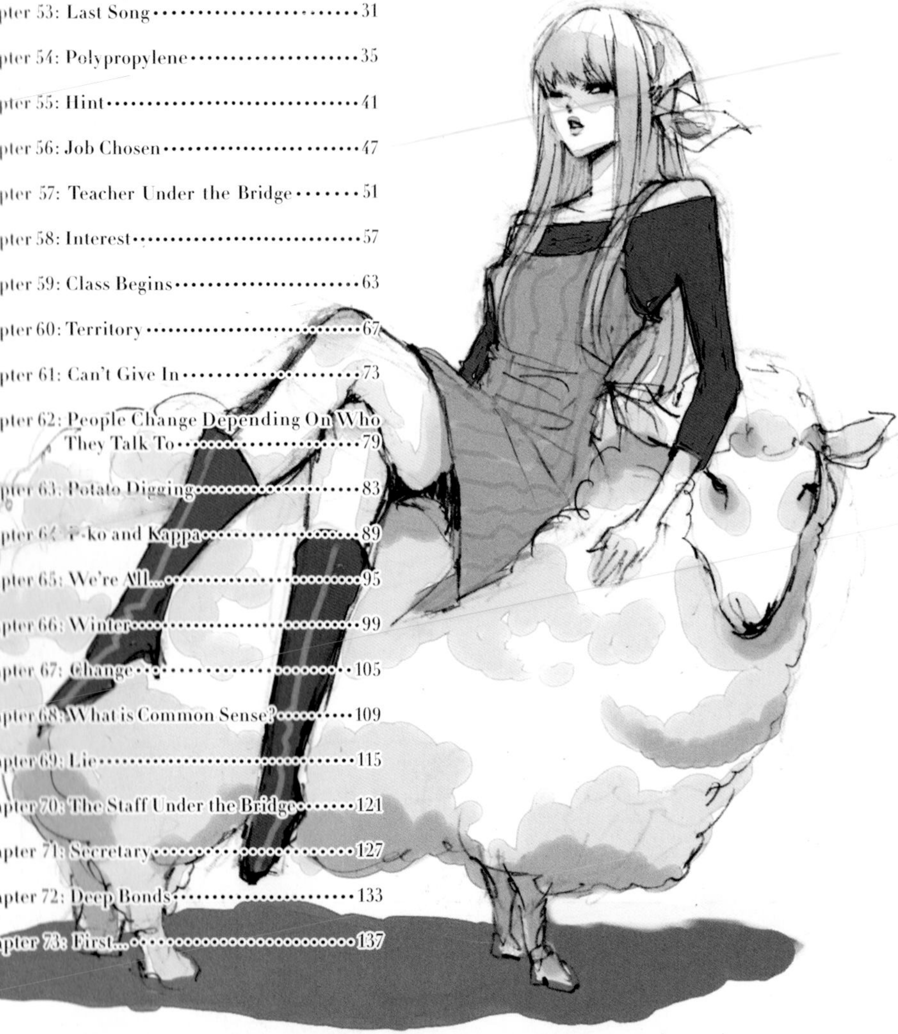

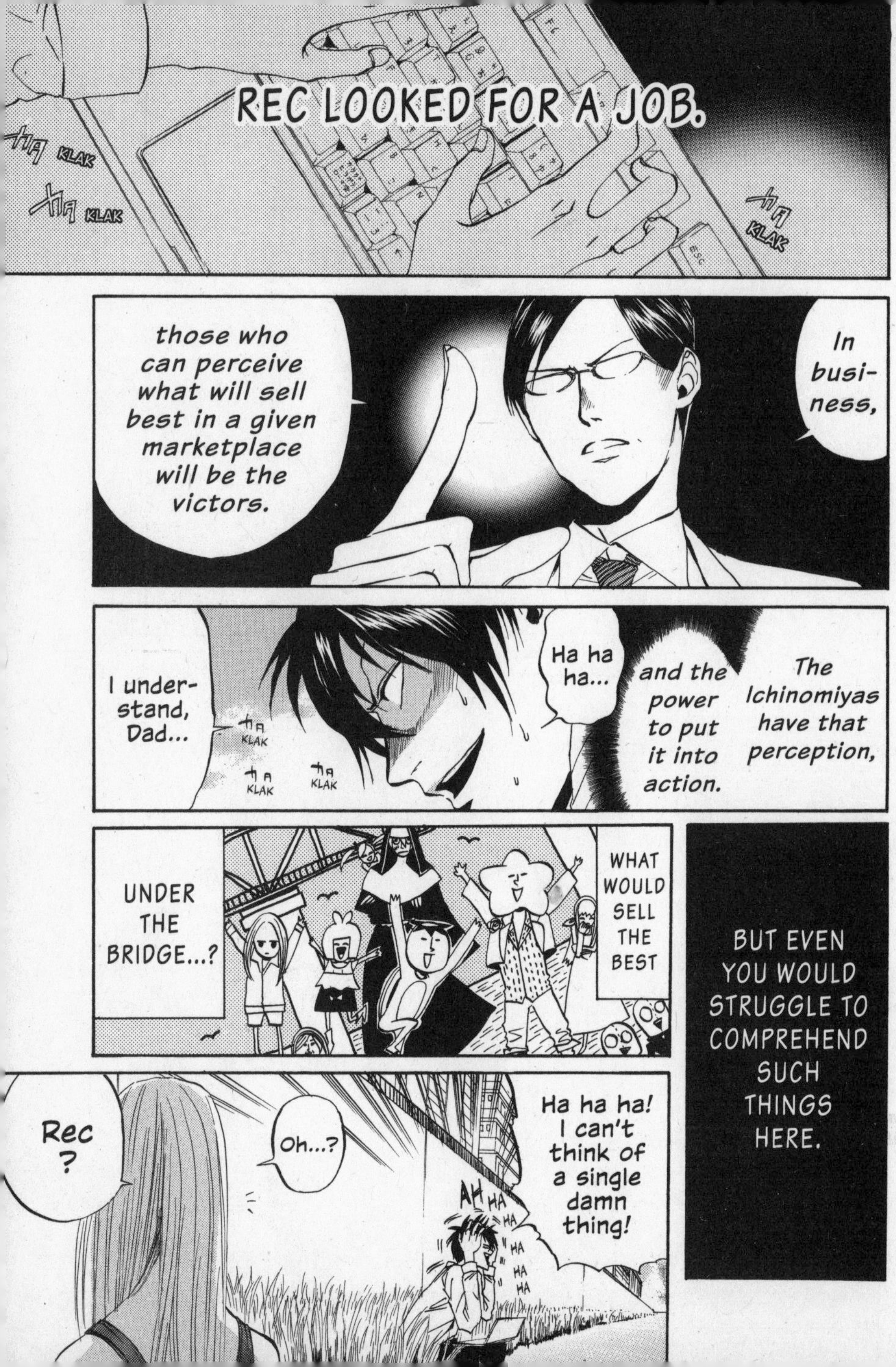
REC LOOKED FOR A JOB.
KLAK
KLAK
KLAK
In business,
those who can perceive what will sell best in a given marketplace will be the victors.
The Ichinomiyas have that perception,
and the power to put it into action.
Ha ha ha...
I understand, Dad...
KLAK
KLAK
KLAK
BUT EVEN YOU WOULD STRUGGLE TO COMPREHEND SUCH THINGS HERE.
WHAT WOULD SELL THE BEST
UNDER THE BRIDGE...?
Ha ha ha! I can't think of a single damn thing!
AH HA HA HA HA HA
Oh...?
Rec?

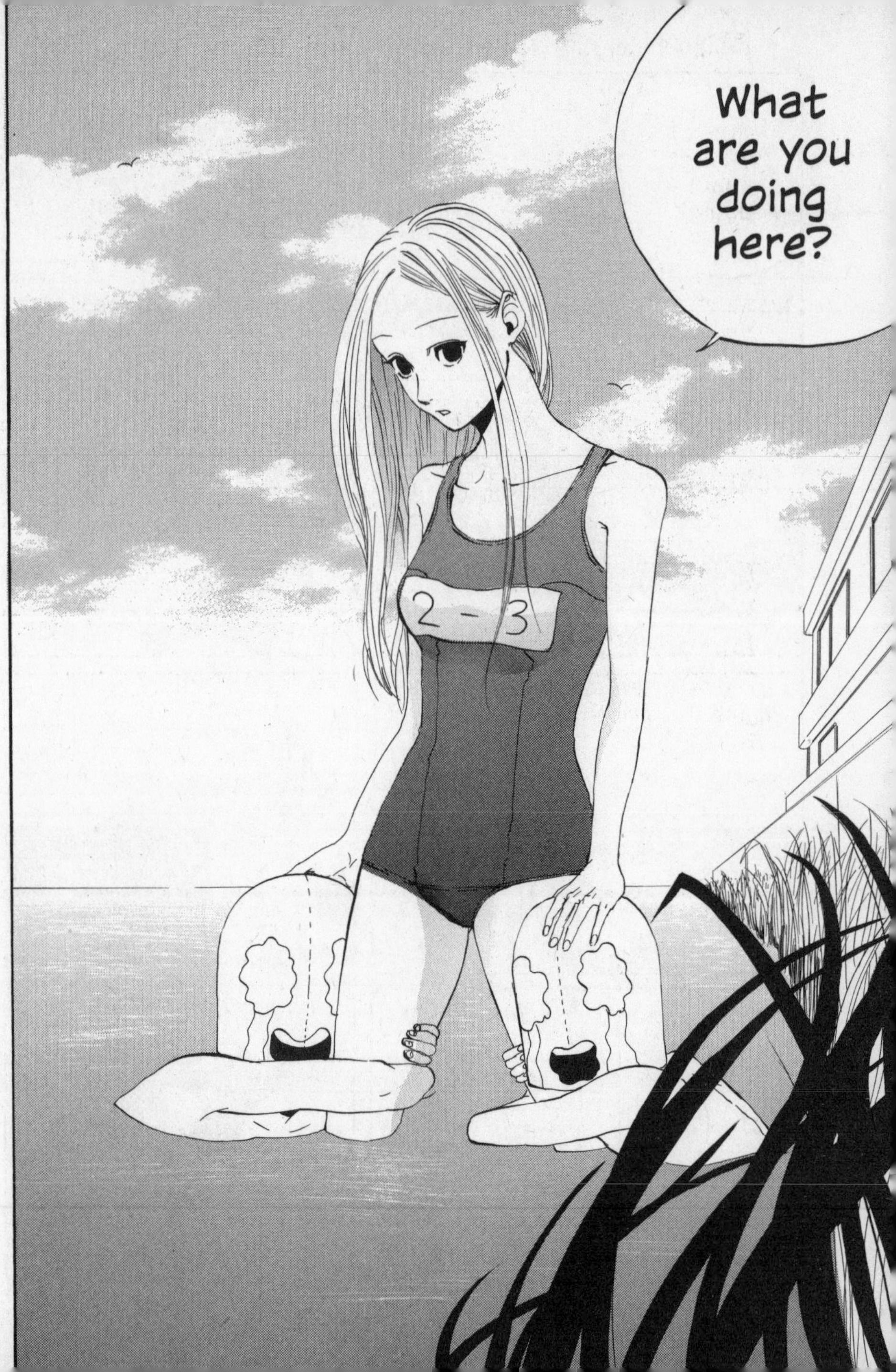
What are you doing here?
2-3

Chapter 48: If Fish Have Hearts So Does Water

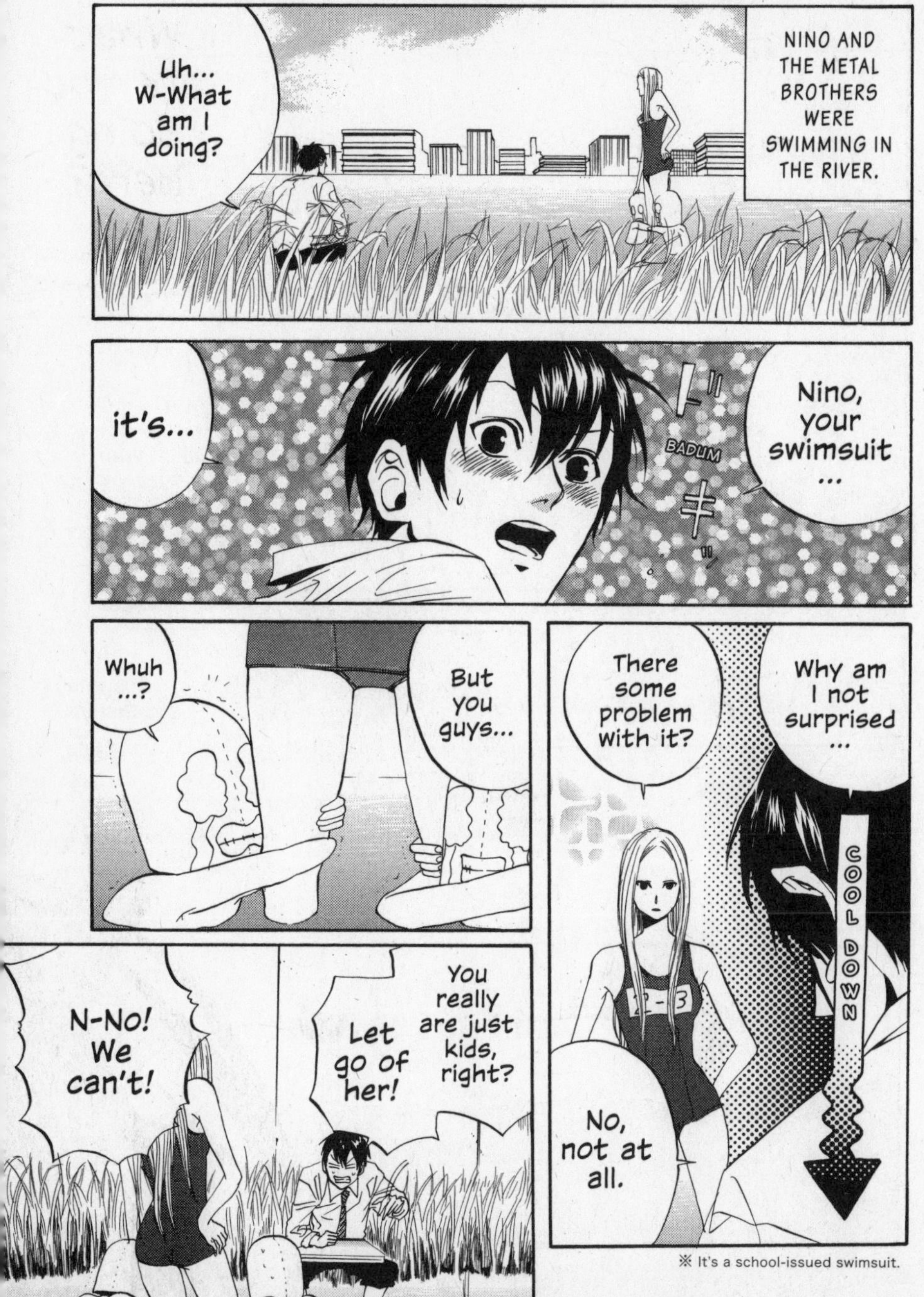
NINO AND THE METAL BROTHERS WERE SWIMMING IN THE RIVER.
Uh... W-What am I doing?
Nino, your swimsuit ...
BADUM
it's...
Why am I not surprised ...
COOL DOWN
There some problem with it?
No, not at all.
But you guys...
Whuh ...?
You really are just kids, right?
Let go of her!
N-No! We can't!

※ It's a school-issued swimsuit.

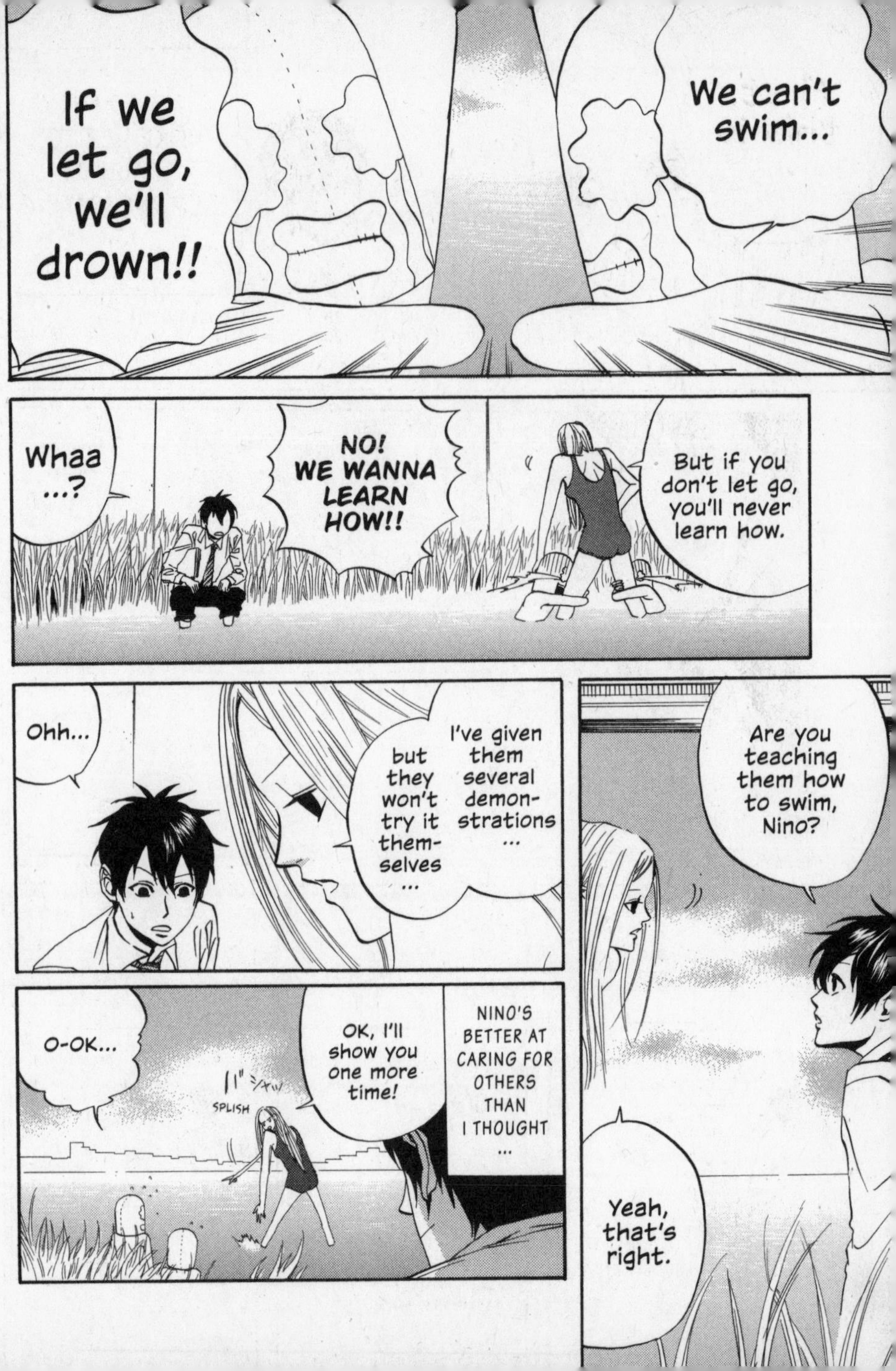
We can't swim...
If we let go, we'll drown!!
But if you don't let go, you'll never learn how.
NO! WE WANNA LEARN HOW!!
Whaa ...?
Are you teaching them how to swim, Nino?
Yeah, that's right.
I've given them several demonstrations ...
but they won't try it themselves ...
Ohh...
NINO'S BETTER AT CARING FOR OTHERS THAN I THOUGHT ...
OK, I'll show you one more time!
SPLISH
O-OK...

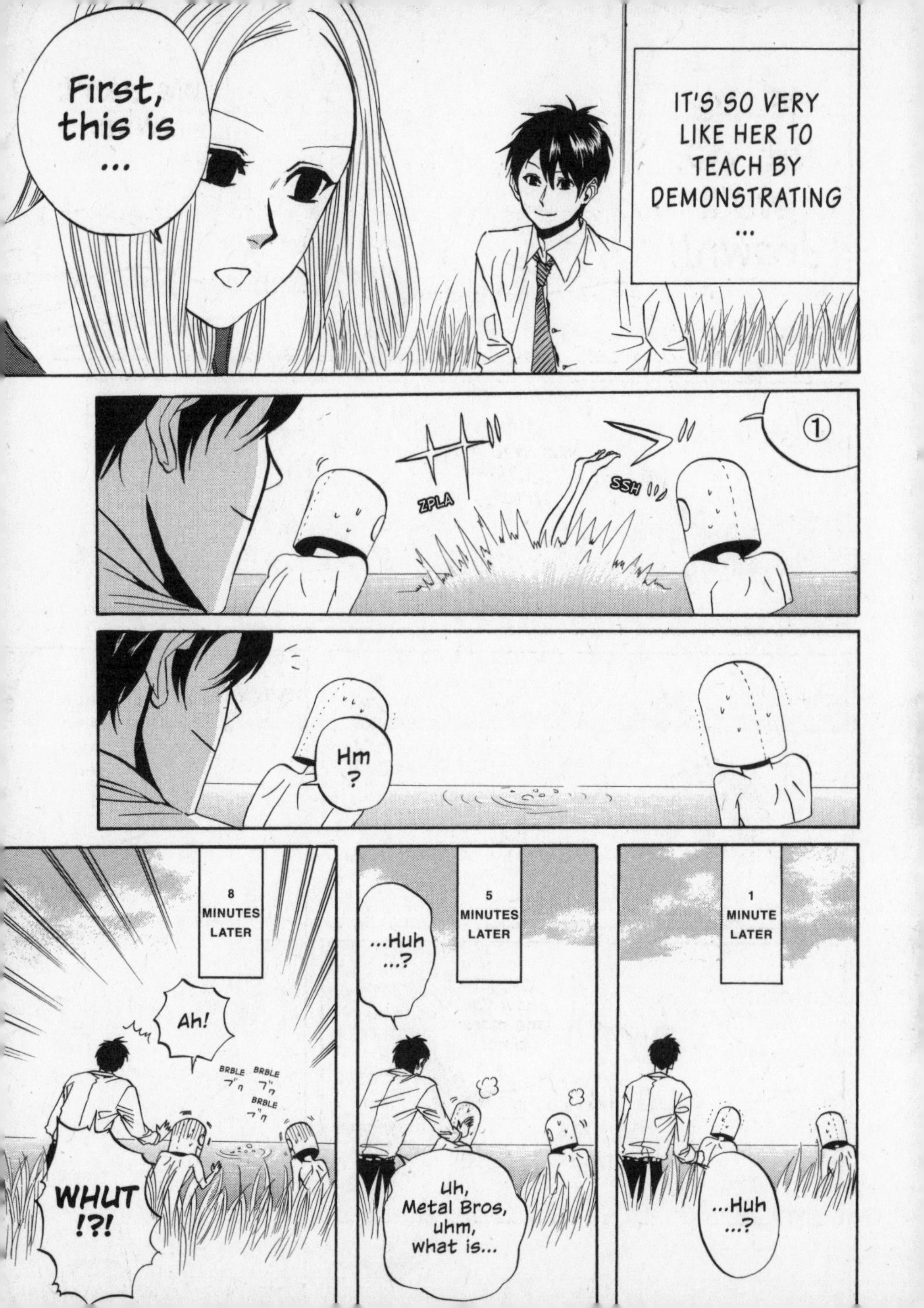
IT'S SO VERY LIKE HER TO TEACH BY DEMONSTRATING ...
First, this is ...
①
SSH
ZPLA
Hm ?
1 MINUTE LATER
...Huh ...?
5 MINUTES LATER
...Huh ...?
Uh, Metal Bros, uhm, what is...
8 MINUTES LATER
Ah!
BRBLE
BRBLE
BRBLE
WHUT !?!

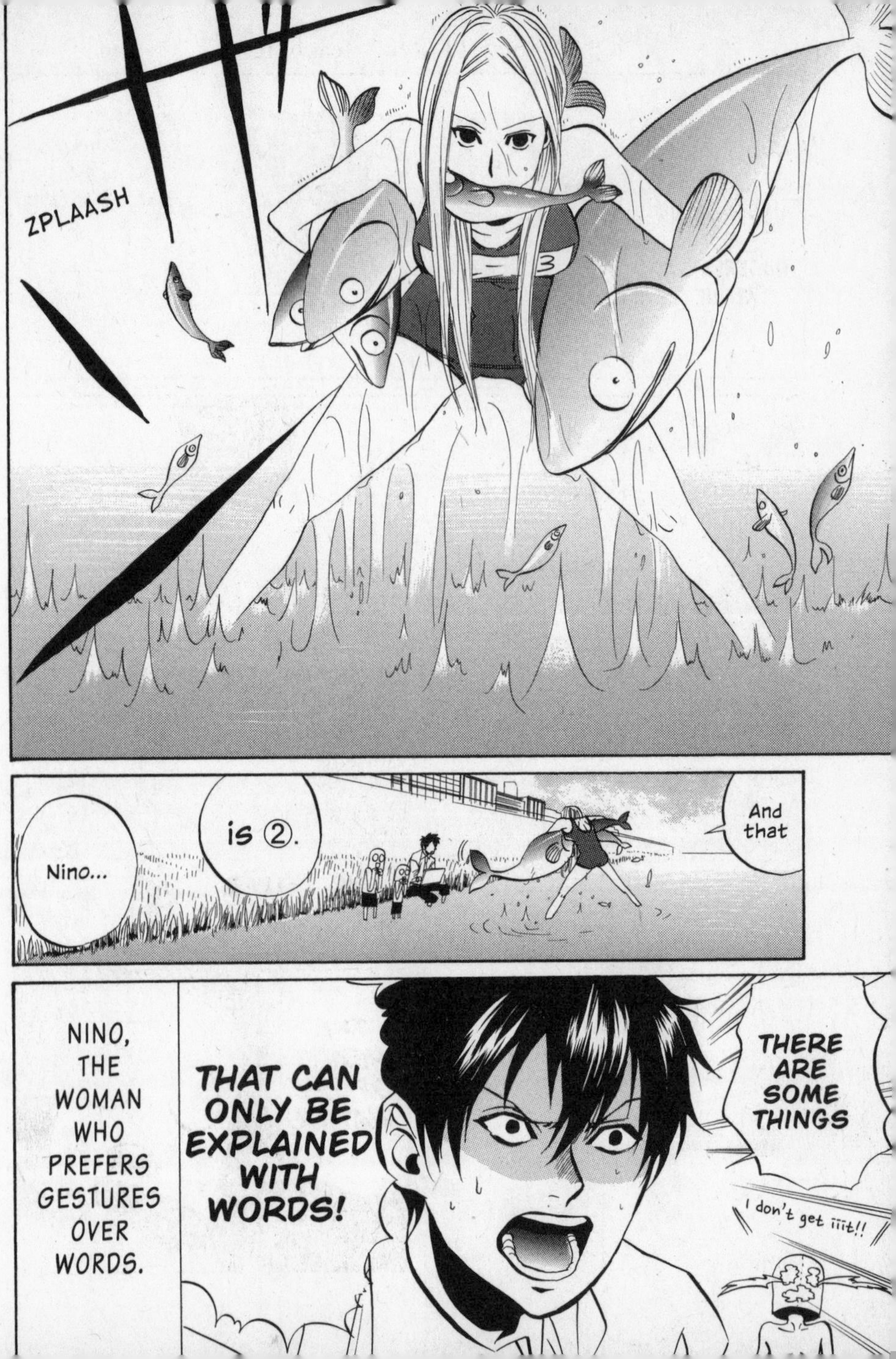

ZPLAASH
And that
is ②.
Nino...
THERE ARE SOME THINGS
THAT CAN ONLY BE EXPLAINED WITH WORDS!
NINO, THE WOMAN WHO PREFERS GESTURES OVER WORDS.
I don't get iiit!!

Chapter 49: Rec's Teachings

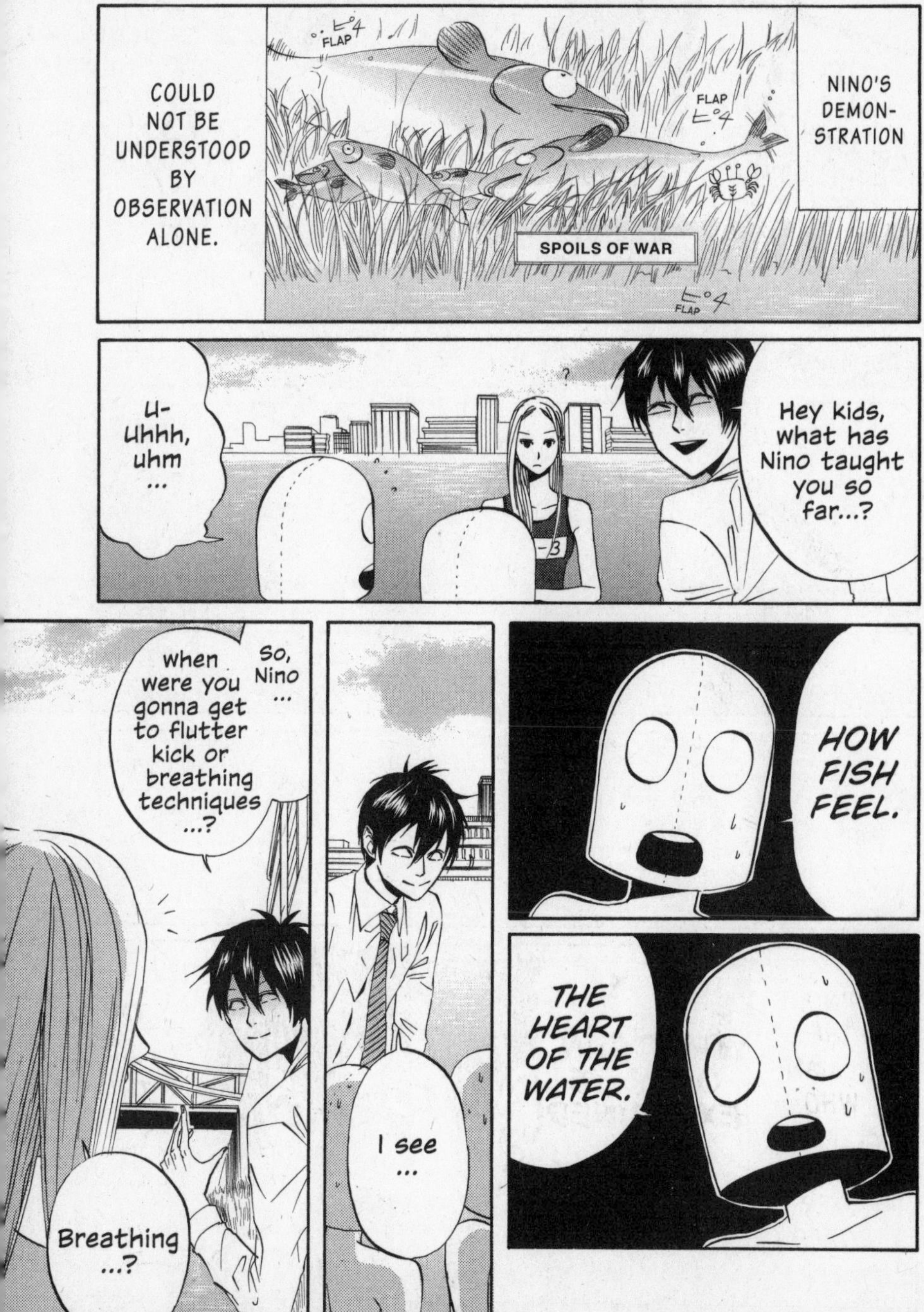
NINO'S DEMONSTRATION
FLAP
FLAP
SPOILS OF WAR
FLAP
COULD NOT BE UNDERSTOOD BY OBSERVATION ALONE.
Hey kids, what has Nino taught you so far...?
U-Uhhh, uhm ...
HOW FISH FEEL.
THE HEART OF THE WATER.
I see ...
So, Nino ...
when were you gonna get to flutter kick or breathing techniques ...?
Breathing ...?

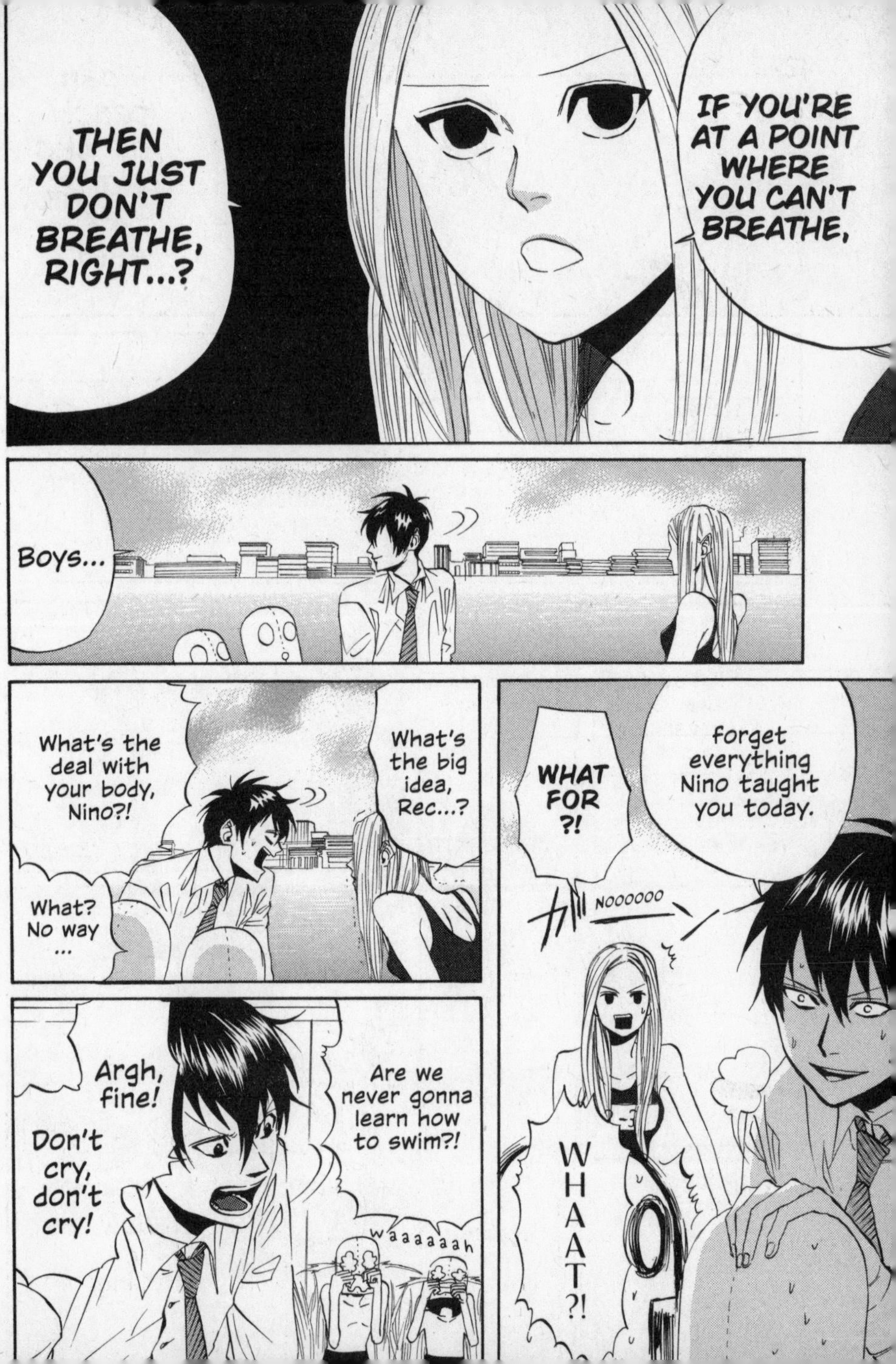
IF YOU'RE AT A POINT WHERE YOU CAN'T BREATHE,
THEN YOU JUST DON'T BREATHE, RIGHT...?
Boys...
forget everything Nino taught you today.
WHAT FOR?!
NOOOOOO
WHAAT?!
What's the big idea, Rec...?
What's the deal with your body, Nino?!
What? No way ...
Are we never gonna learn how to swim?!
Argh, fine!
Don't cry, don't cry!
waaaaaah

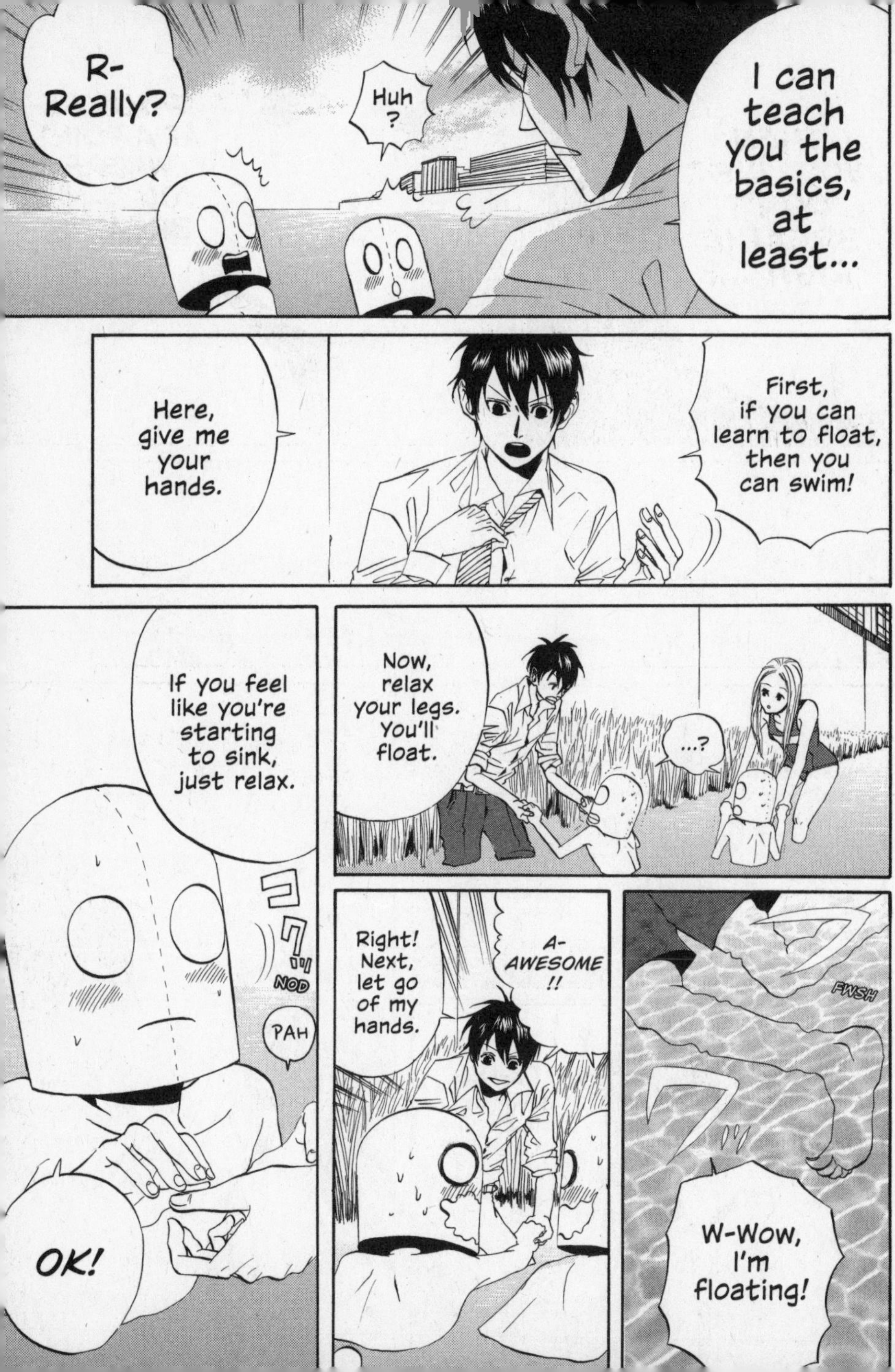
I can teach you the basics, at least...
Huh?
R-Really?
First, if you can learn to float, then you can swim!
Here, give me your hands.
Now, relax your legs. You'll float.
...?
FWSH
W-Wow, I'm floating!
A- AWESOME !!
Right! Next, let go of my hands.
If you feel like you're starting to sink, just relax.
NOD
PAH
OK!

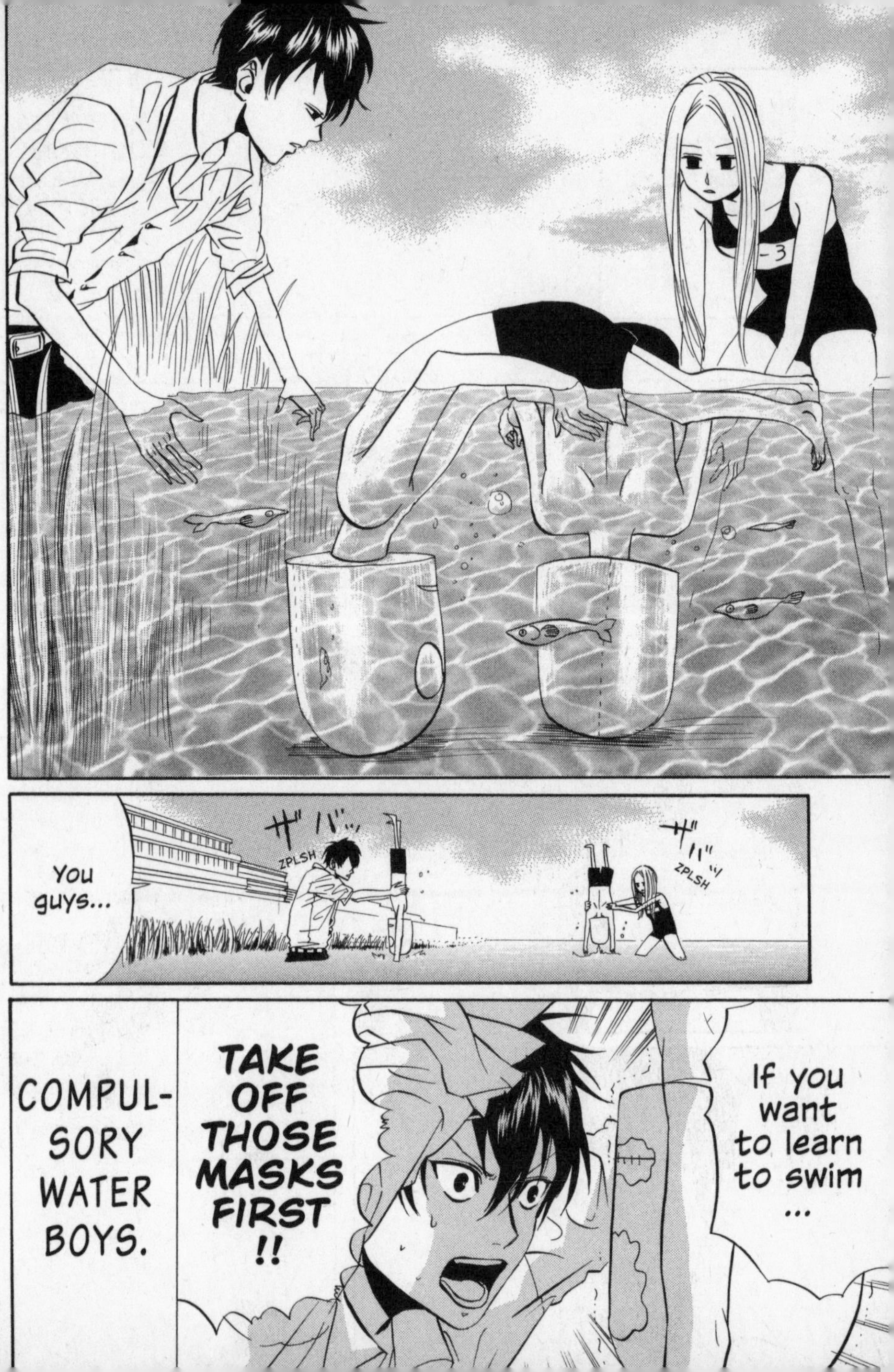
ZPLSH
ZPLSH
You guys...
If you want to learn to swim ...
TAKE OFF THOSE MASKS FIRST !!
COMPUL-SORY WATER BOYS.

Chapter 50: Impetus

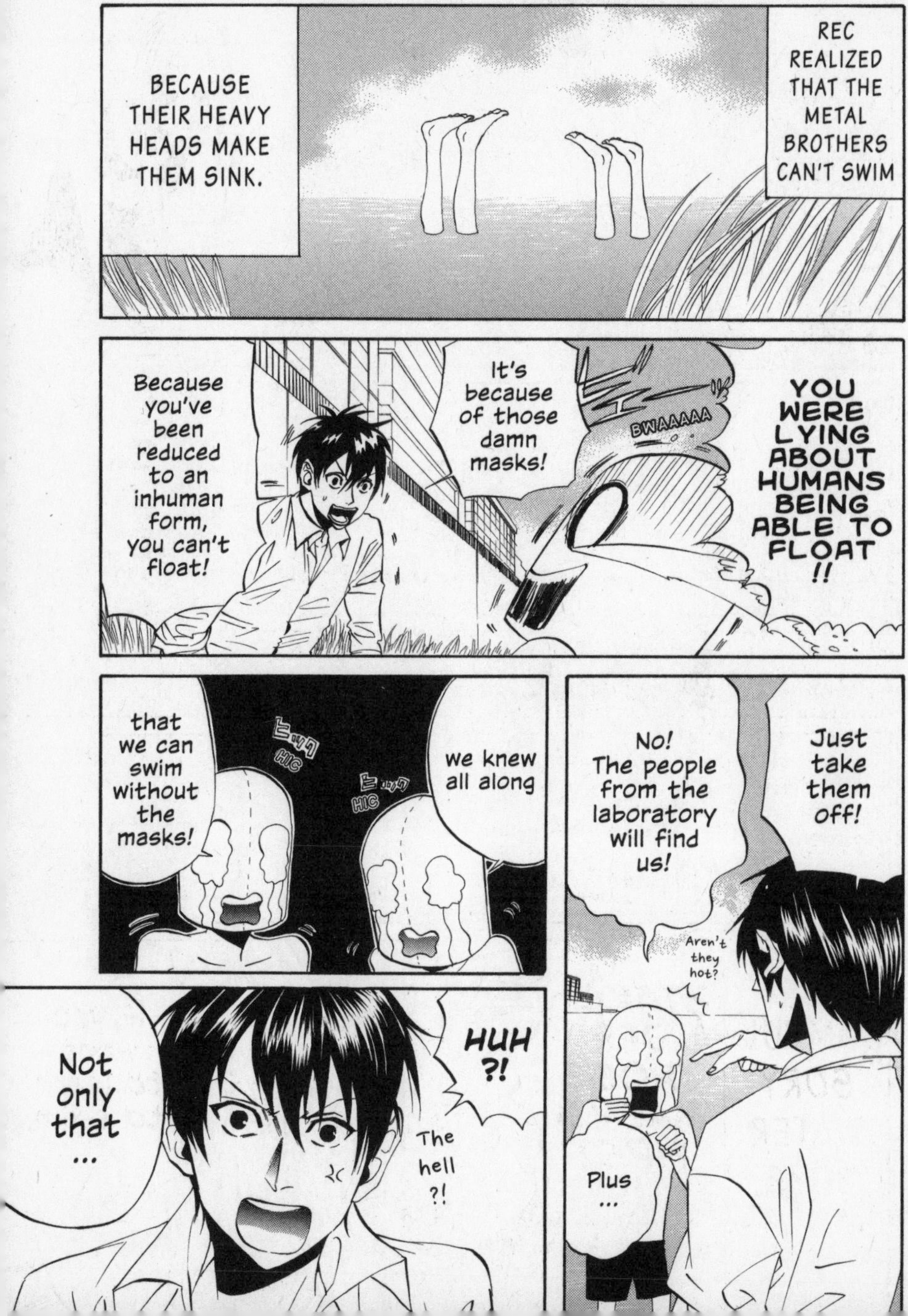
REC REALIZED THAT THE METAL BROTHERS CAN'T SWIM
BECAUSE THEIR HEAVY HEADS MAKE THEM SINK.
YOU WERE LYING ABOUT HUMANS BEING ABLE TO FLOAT !!
BWAAAAA
It's because of those damn masks!
Because you've been reduced to an inhuman form, you can't float!
Just take them off!
No! The people from the laboratory will find us!
Aren't they hot?
Plus ...
we knew all along
HIC
HIC
that we can swim without the masks!
HUH ?!
The hell ?!
Not only that ...

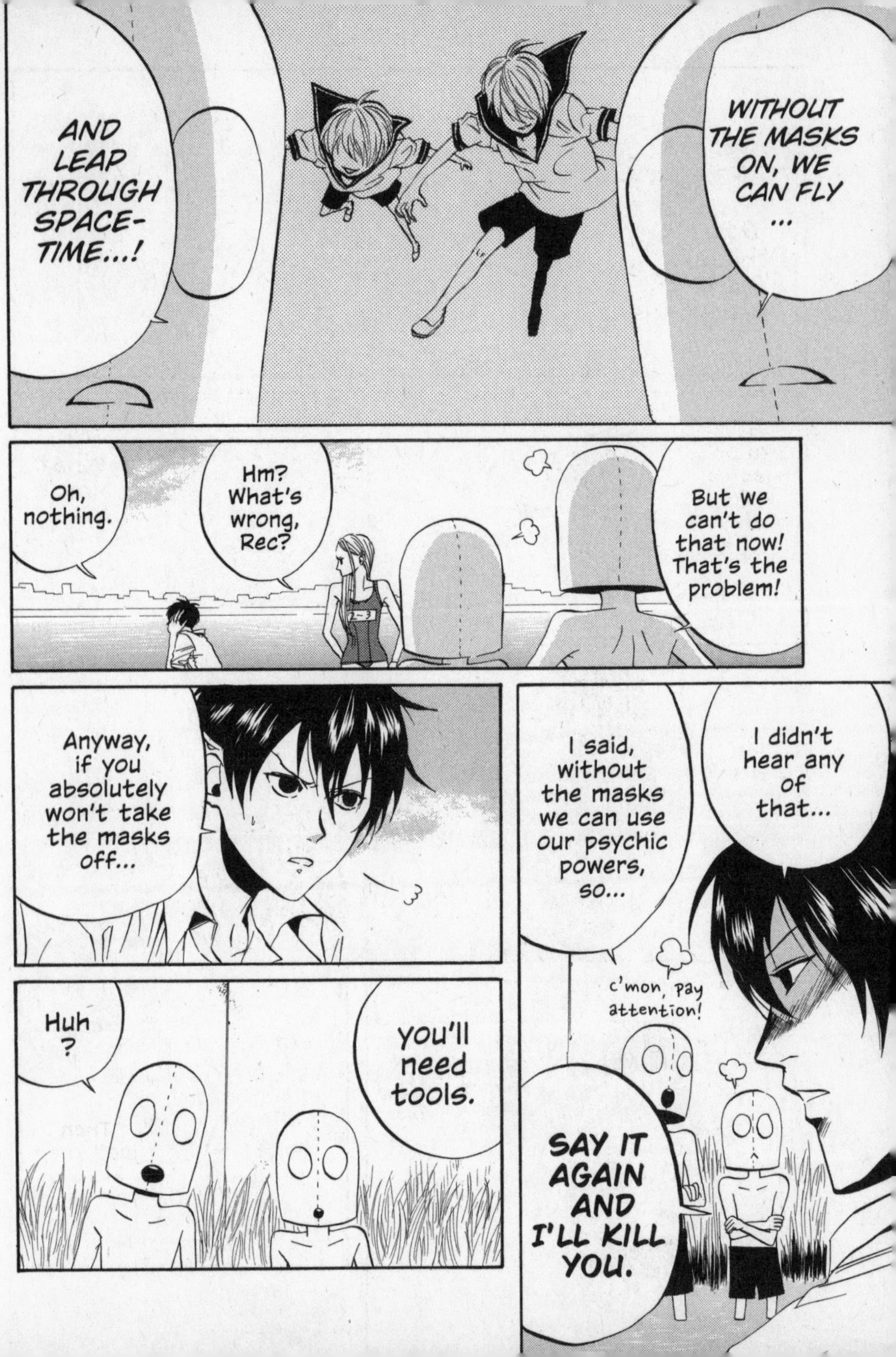
WITHOUT THE MASKS ON, WE CAN FLY ...
AND LEAP THROUGH SPACE-TIME...!
But we can't do that now! That's the problem!
Hm? What's wrong, Rec?
Oh, nothing.
I didn't hear any of that...
I said, without the masks we can use our psychic powers, so...
c'mon, pay attention!
SAY IT AGAIN AND I'LL KILL YOU.
Anyway, if you absolutely won't take the masks off...
you'll need tools.
Huh ?

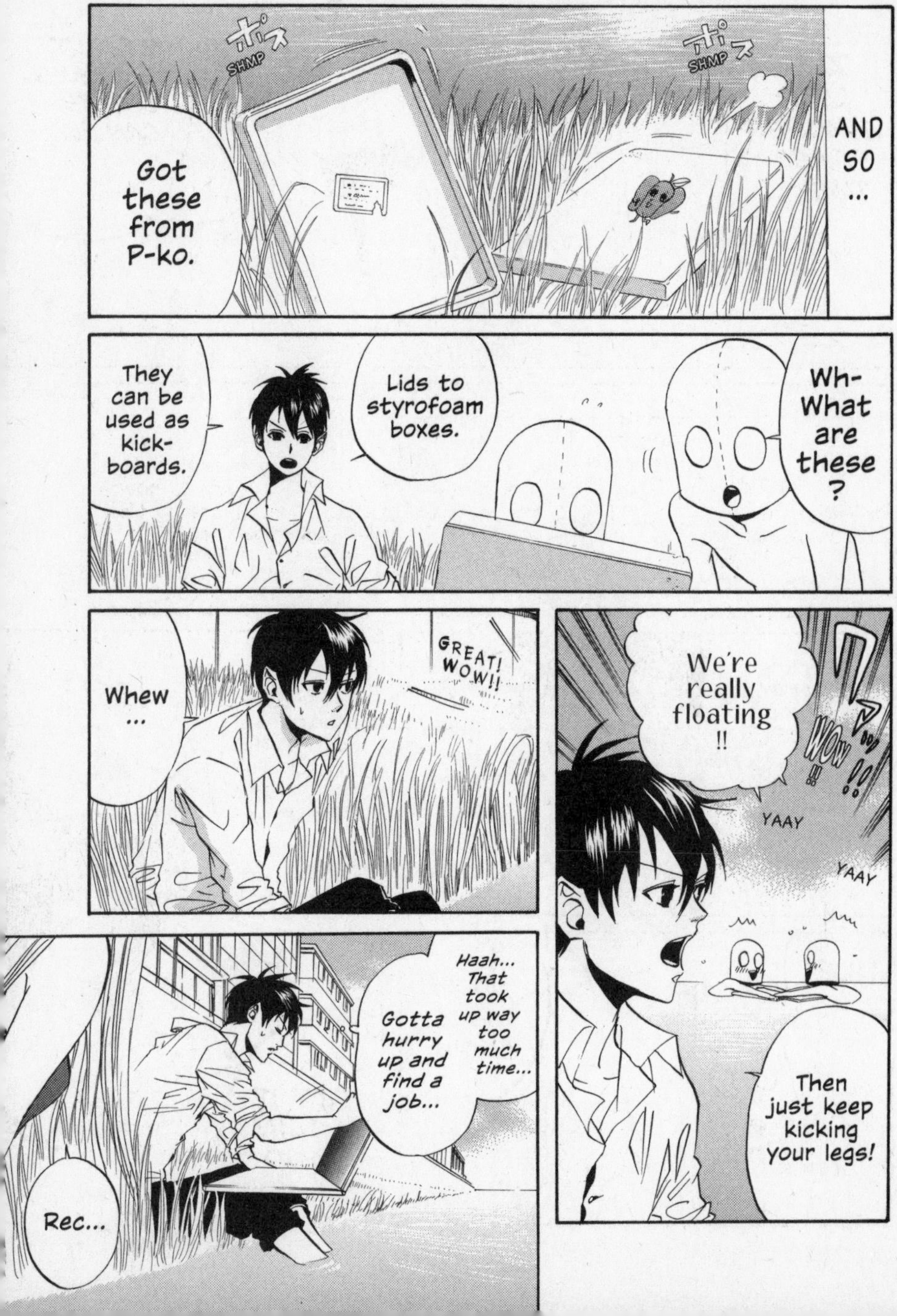
AND SO ...
SHMP
SHMP
Got these from P-ko.
Wh- What are these?
Lids to styrofoam boxes.
They can be used as kick-boards.
We're really floating !!
WOW !!
YAAY
YAAY
Then just keep kicking your legs!
GREAT! WOW!!
Whew ...
Haah... That took up way too much time...
Gotta hurry up and find a job...
Rec...

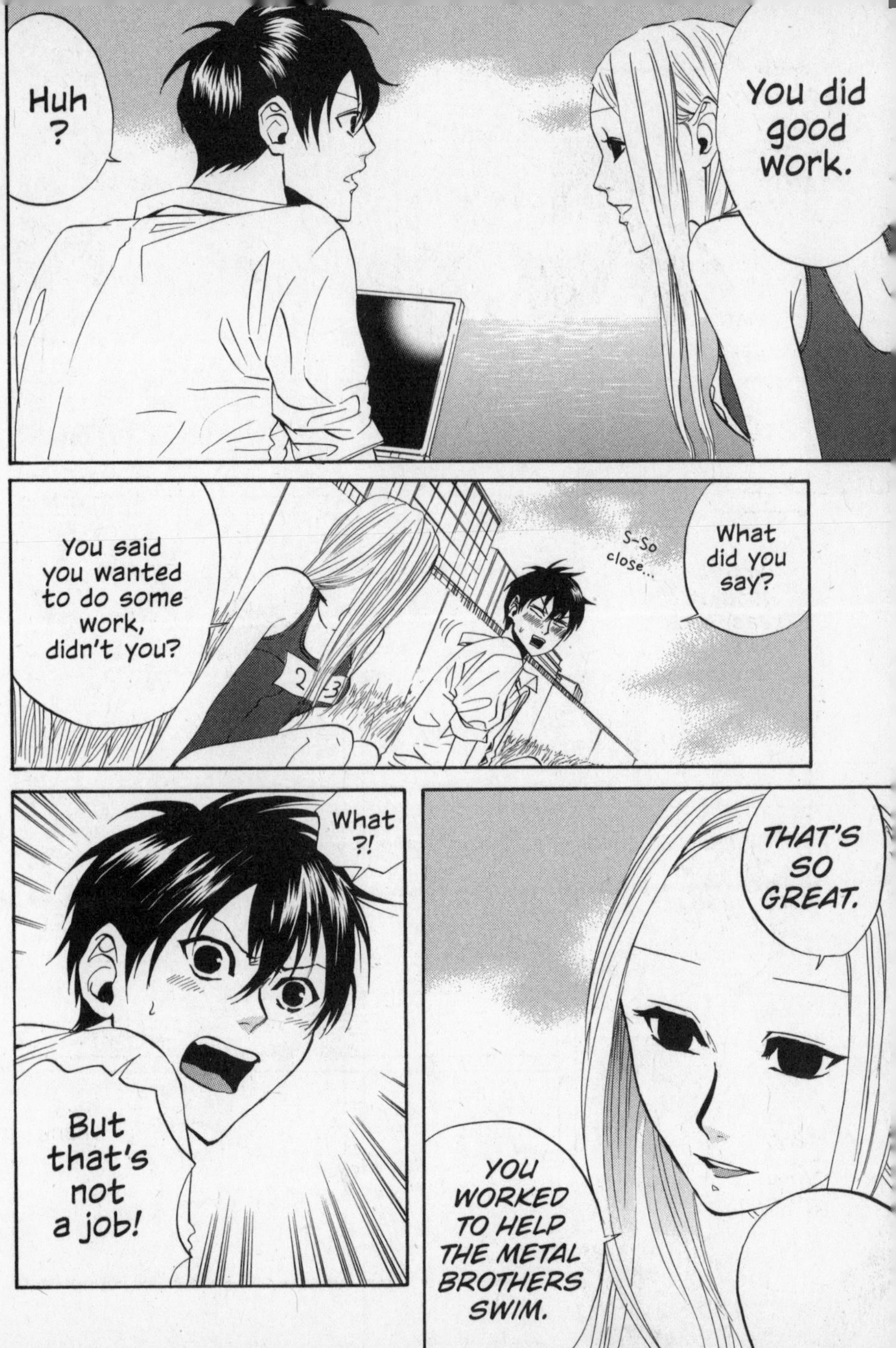
You did good work.
Huh?
What did you say?
S-So close...
You said you wanted to do some work, didn't you?
THAT'S SO GREAT.
YOU WORKED TO HELP THE METAL BROTHERS SWIM.
What?!
But that's not a job!

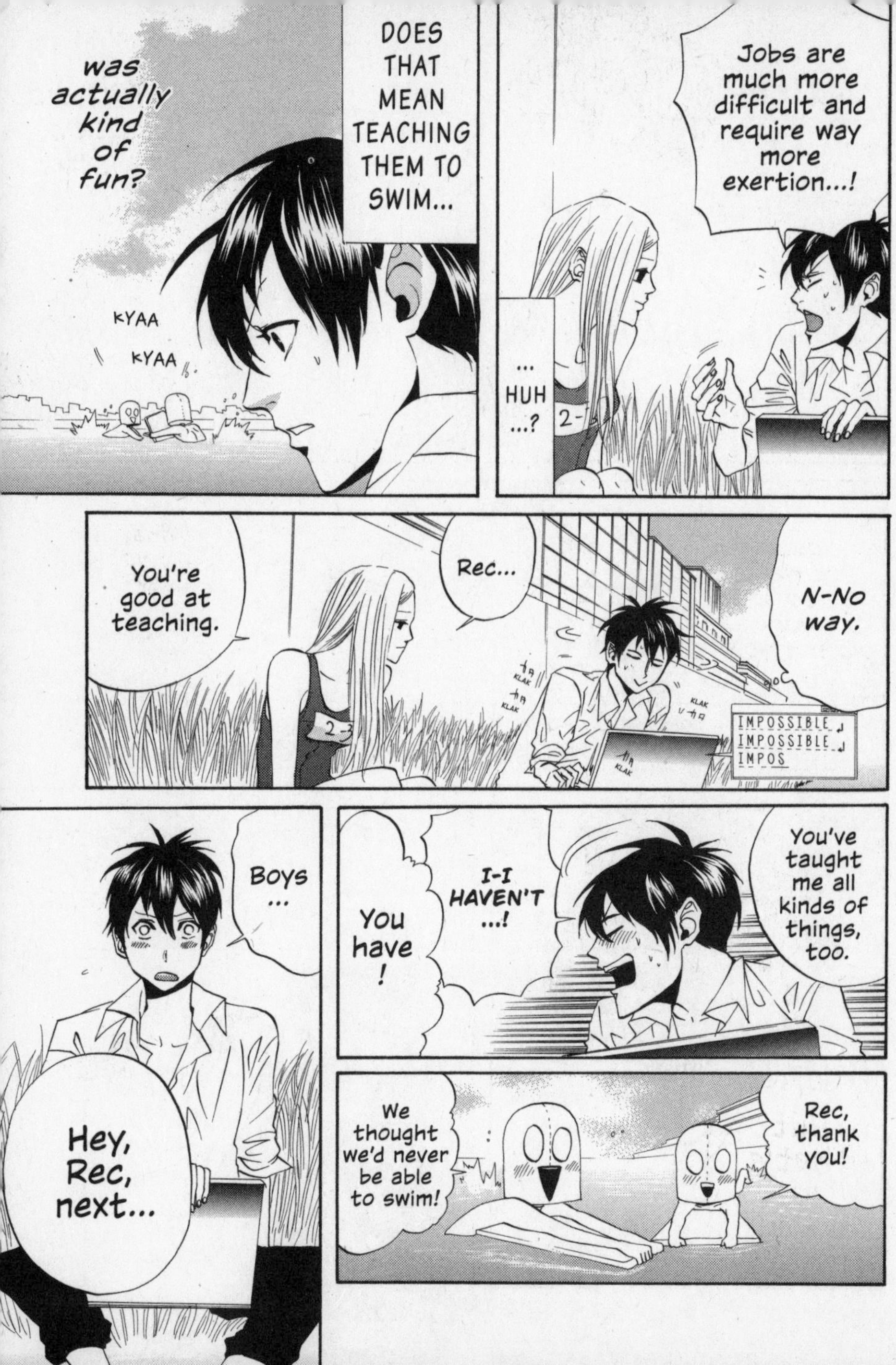
Jobs are much more difficult and require way more exertion...!
... HUH ...?
DOES THAT MEAN TEACHING THEM TO SWIM...
was actually kind of fun?
KYAA
KYAA
N-No way.
IMPOSSIBLE
IMPOSSIBLE
IMPOS
KLAK
KLAK
KLAK
KLAK
Rec...
You're good at teaching.
You've taught me all kinds of things, too.
I-I HAVEN'T ...!
You have !
Rec, thank you!
We thought we'd never be able to swim!
Boys ...
Hey, Rec, next...

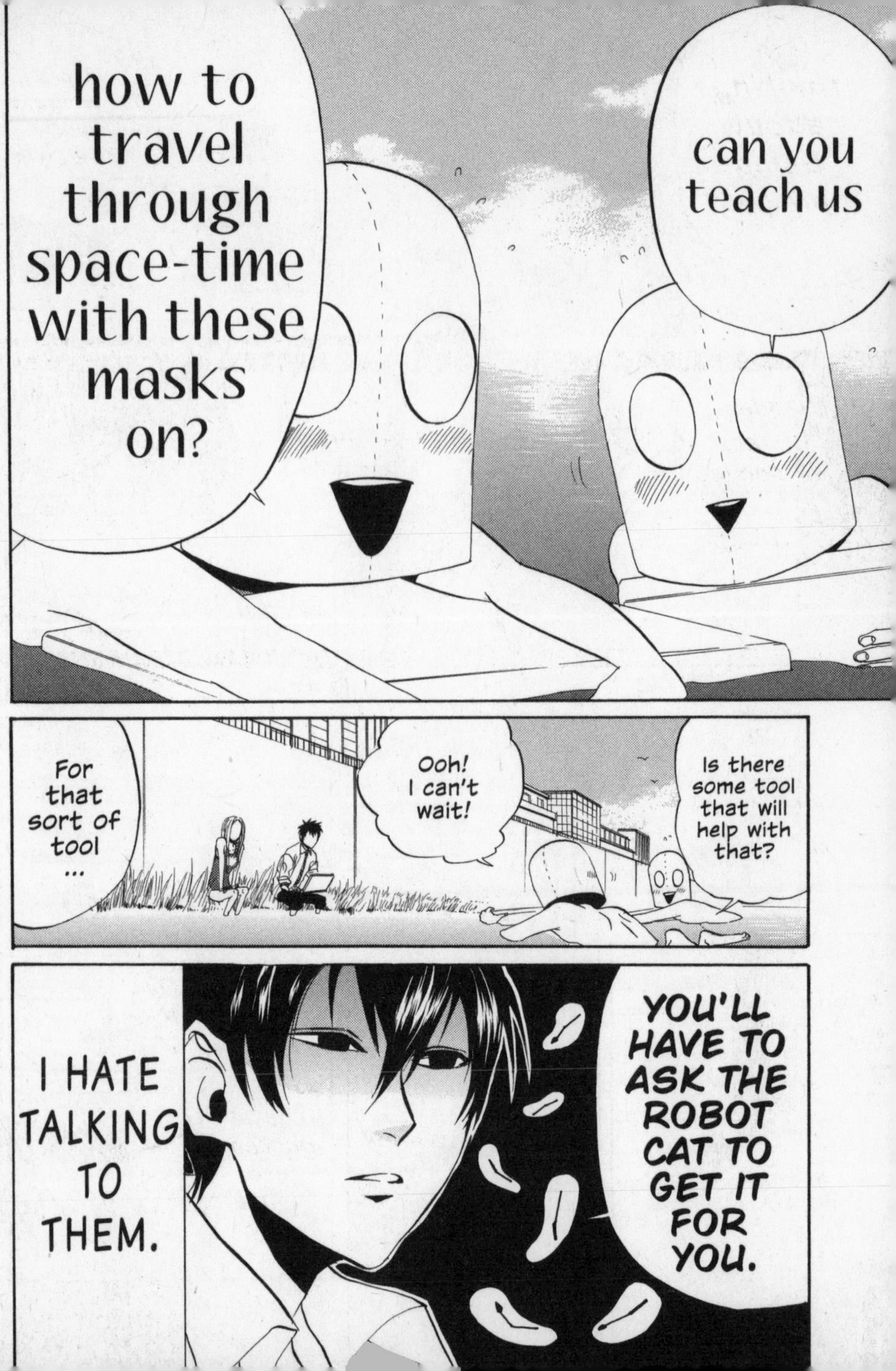
can you teach us
how to travel through space-time with these masks on?
Is there some tool that will help with that?
Ooh! I can't wait!
For that sort of tool ...
YOU'LL HAVE TO ASK THE ROBOT CAT TO GET IT FOR YOU.
I HATE TALKING TO THEM.

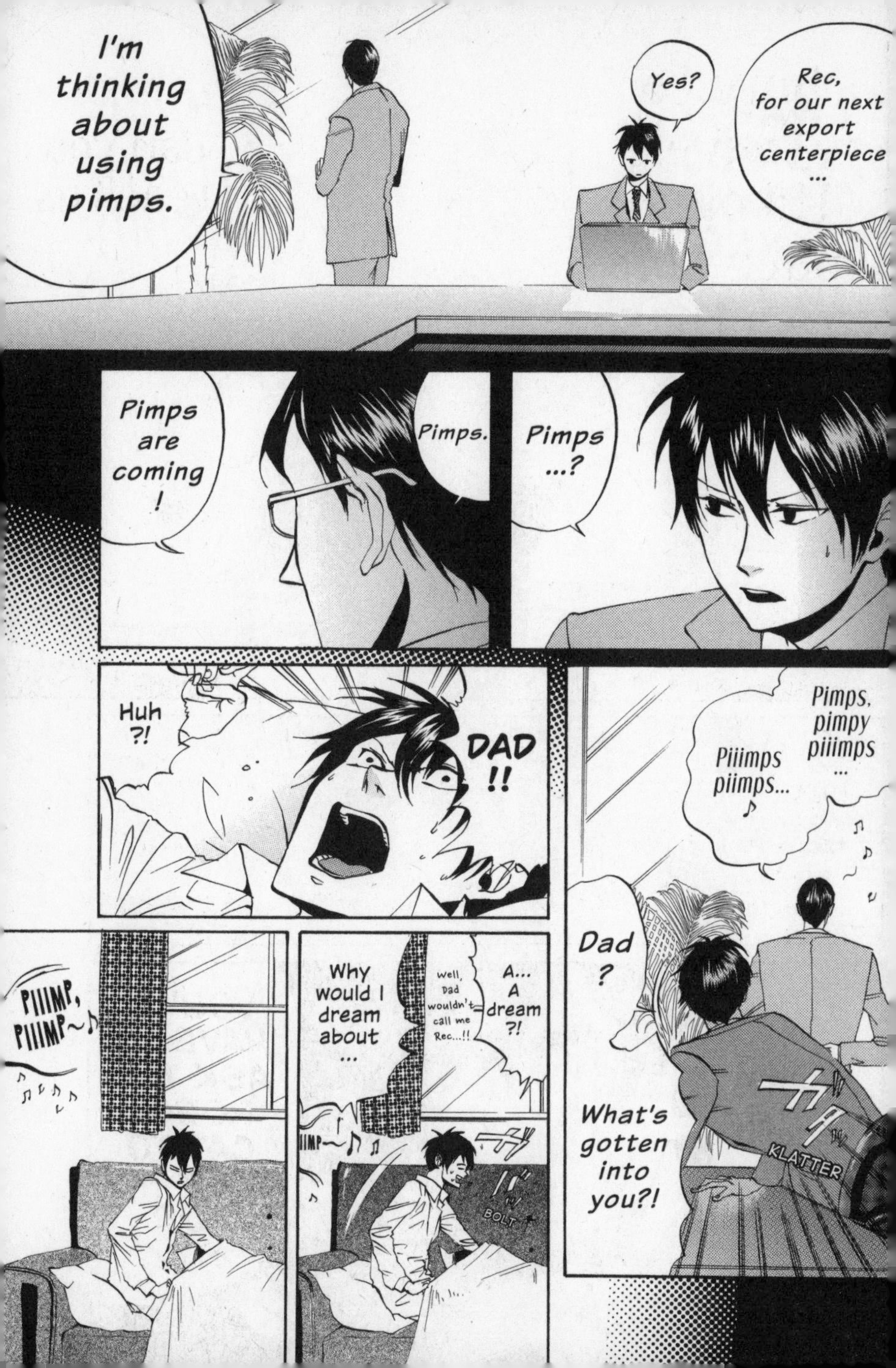
Rec, for our next export centerpiece ...
Yes?
I'm thinking about using pimps.
Pimps ...?
Pimps.
Pimps are coming !
Pimps, pimpy piiimps ...
Piiimps piimps... ♪
Dad ?
What's gotten into you?!
KLATTER
DAD !!
Huh ?!
A... A dream ?!
Well, Dad wouldn't call me Rec...!!
Why would I dream about ...
IIIMP~♪
BOLT
PIIIMP, PIIIMP~♪

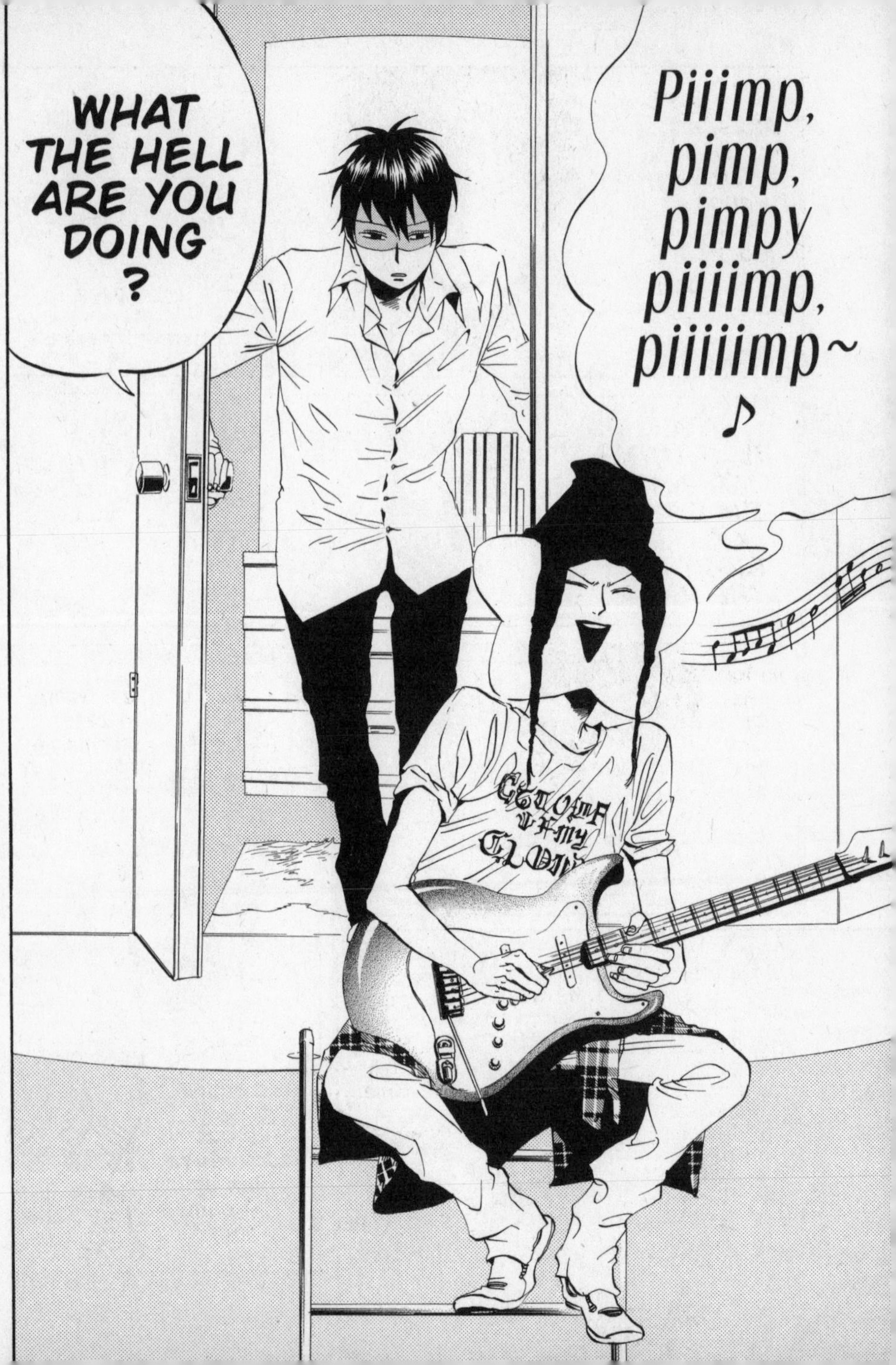
Piiimp, pimp, pimpy piiiimp, piiiiimp~ ♪
WHAT THE HELL ARE YOU DOING ?

Chapter 51: Music Battle

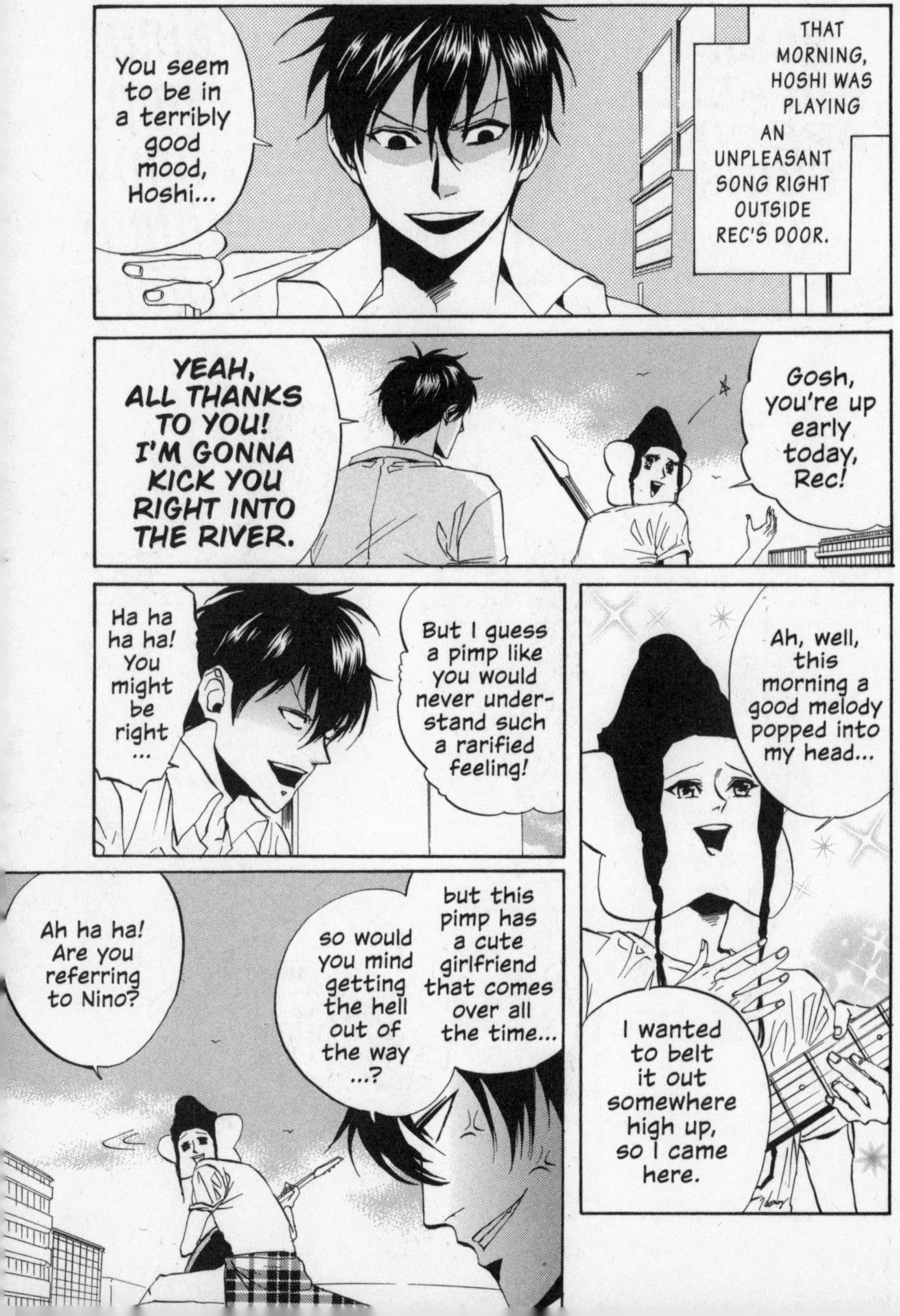
THAT MORNING, HOSHI WAS PLAYING AN UNPLEASANT SONG RIGHT OUTSIDE REC'S DOOR.
You seem to be in a terribly good mood, Hoshi...
Gosh, you're up early today, Rec!
YEAH, ALL THANKS TO YOU! I'M GONNA KICK YOU RIGHT INTO THE RIVER.
Ah, well, this morning a good melody popped into my head...
I wanted to belt it out somewhere high up, so I came here.
But I guess a pimp like you would never under-stand such a rarified feeling!
Ha ha ha ha! You might be right ...
but this pimp has a cute girlfriend that comes over all the time...
so would you mind getting the hell out of the way ...?
Ah ha ha! Are you referring to Nino?

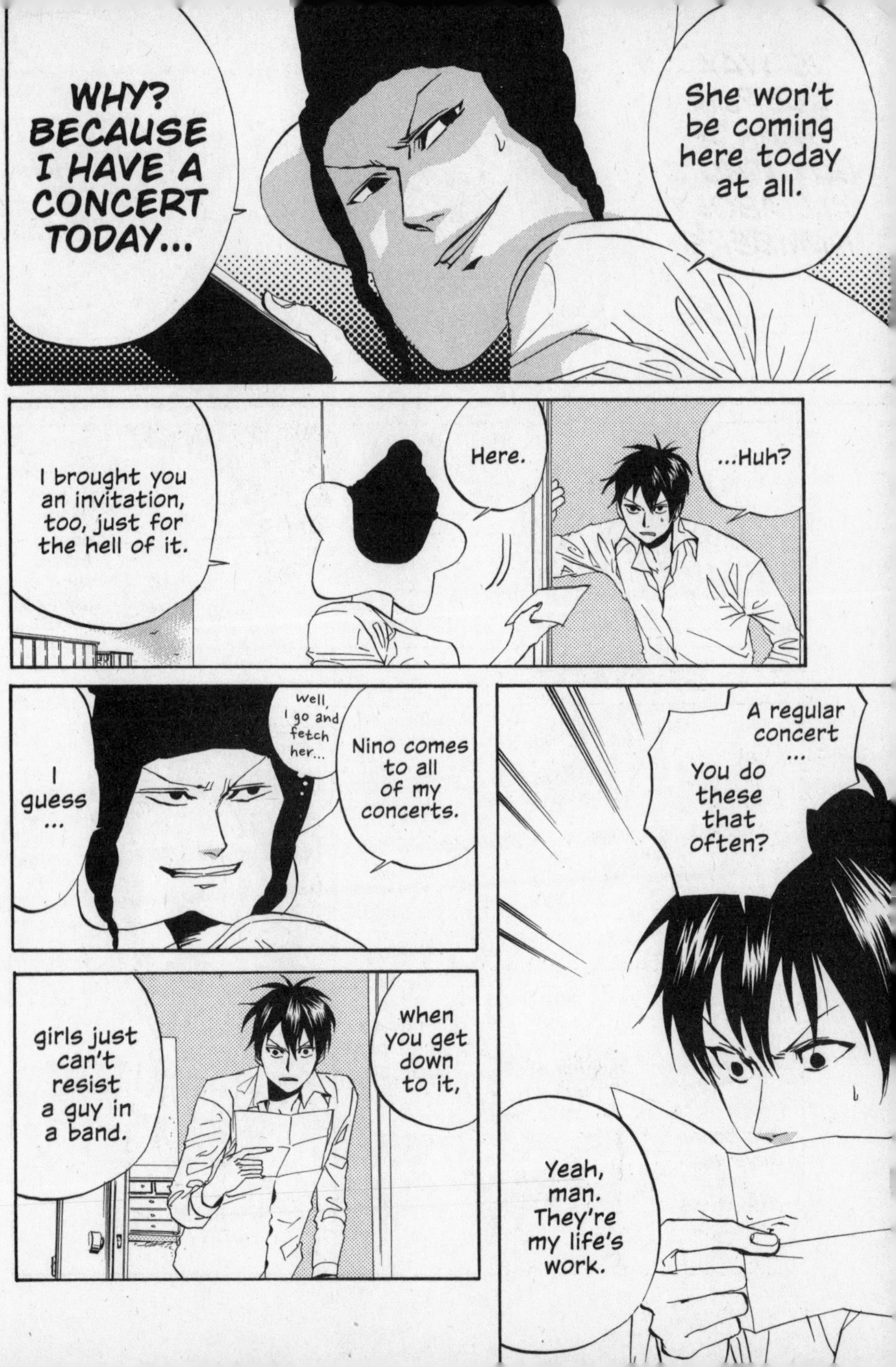
She won't be coming here today at all.
WHY? BECAUSE I HAVE A CONCERT TODAY...
...Huh?
Here.
I brought you an invitation, too, just for the hell of it.
A regular concert ... You do these that often?
Yeah, man. They're my life's work.
Nino comes to all of my concerts.
Well, I go and fetch her...
I guess ...
when you get down to it,
girls just can't resist a guy in a band.

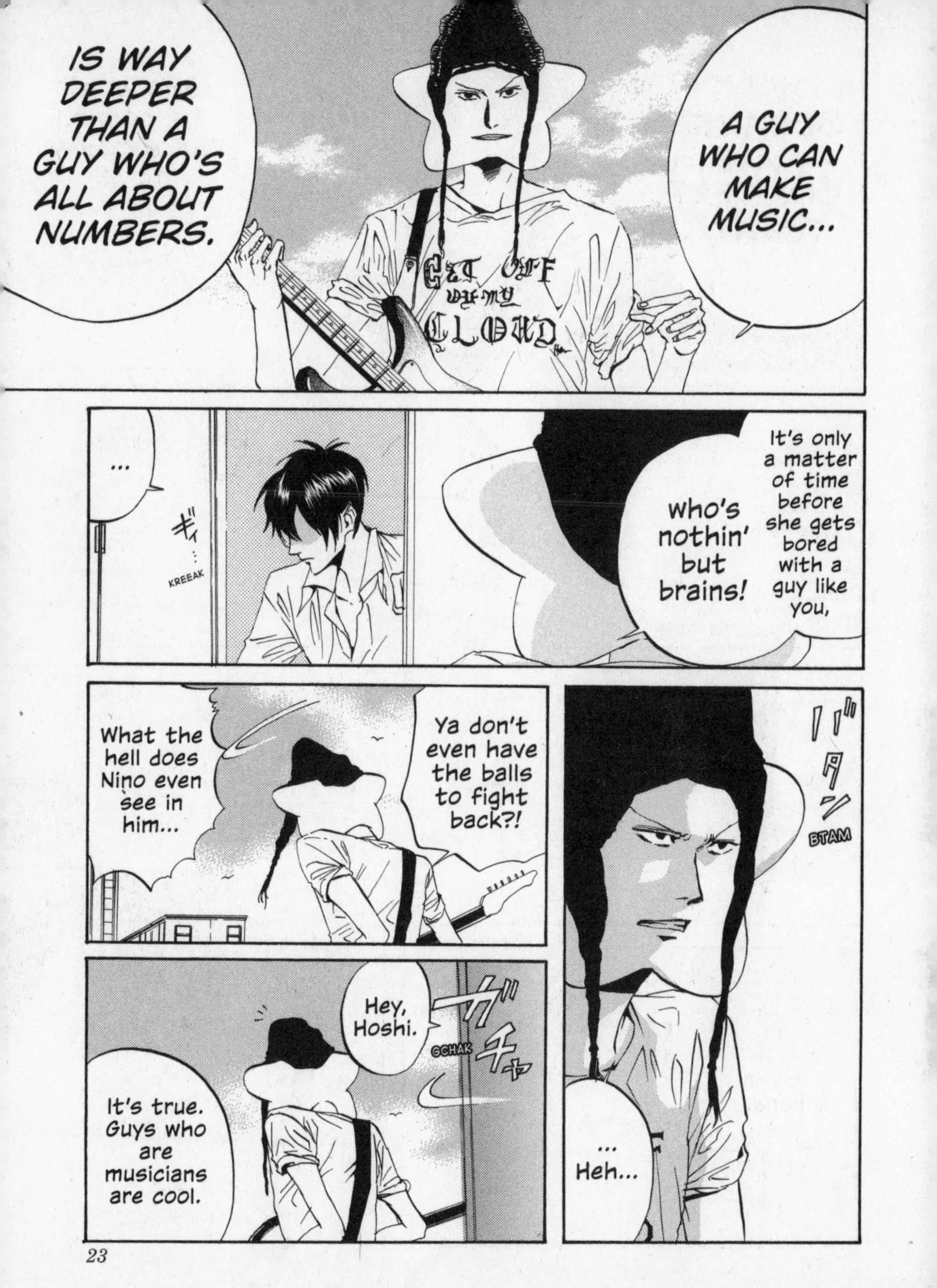
A GUY WHO CAN MAKE MUSIC...
IS WAY DEEPER THAN A GUY WHO'S ALL ABOUT NUMBERS.
It's only a matter of time before she gets bored with a guy like you,
who's nothin' but brains!
KREEAK
...
BTAM
... Heh...
Ya don't even have the balls to fight back?!
What the hell does Nino even see in him...
Hey, Hoshi.
GCHAK
It's true. Guys who are musicians are cool.

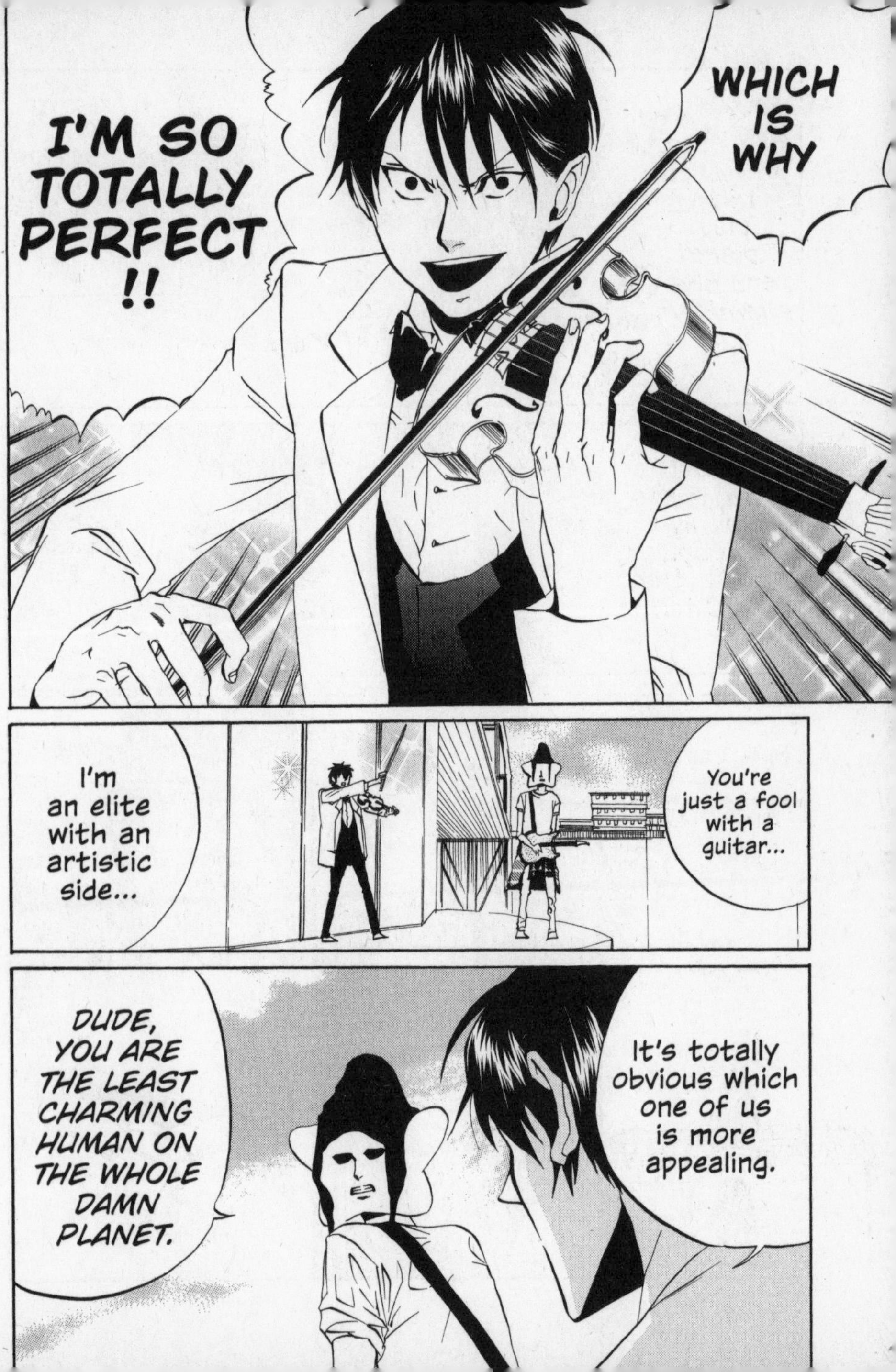
WHICH IS WHY
I'M SO TOTALLY PERFECT!!
You're just a fool with a guitar...
I'm an elite with an artistic side...
It's totally obvious which one of us is more appealing.
DUDE, YOU ARE THE LEAST CHARMING HUMAN ON THE WHOLE DAMN PLANET.

Chapter 52: Wonderful Music

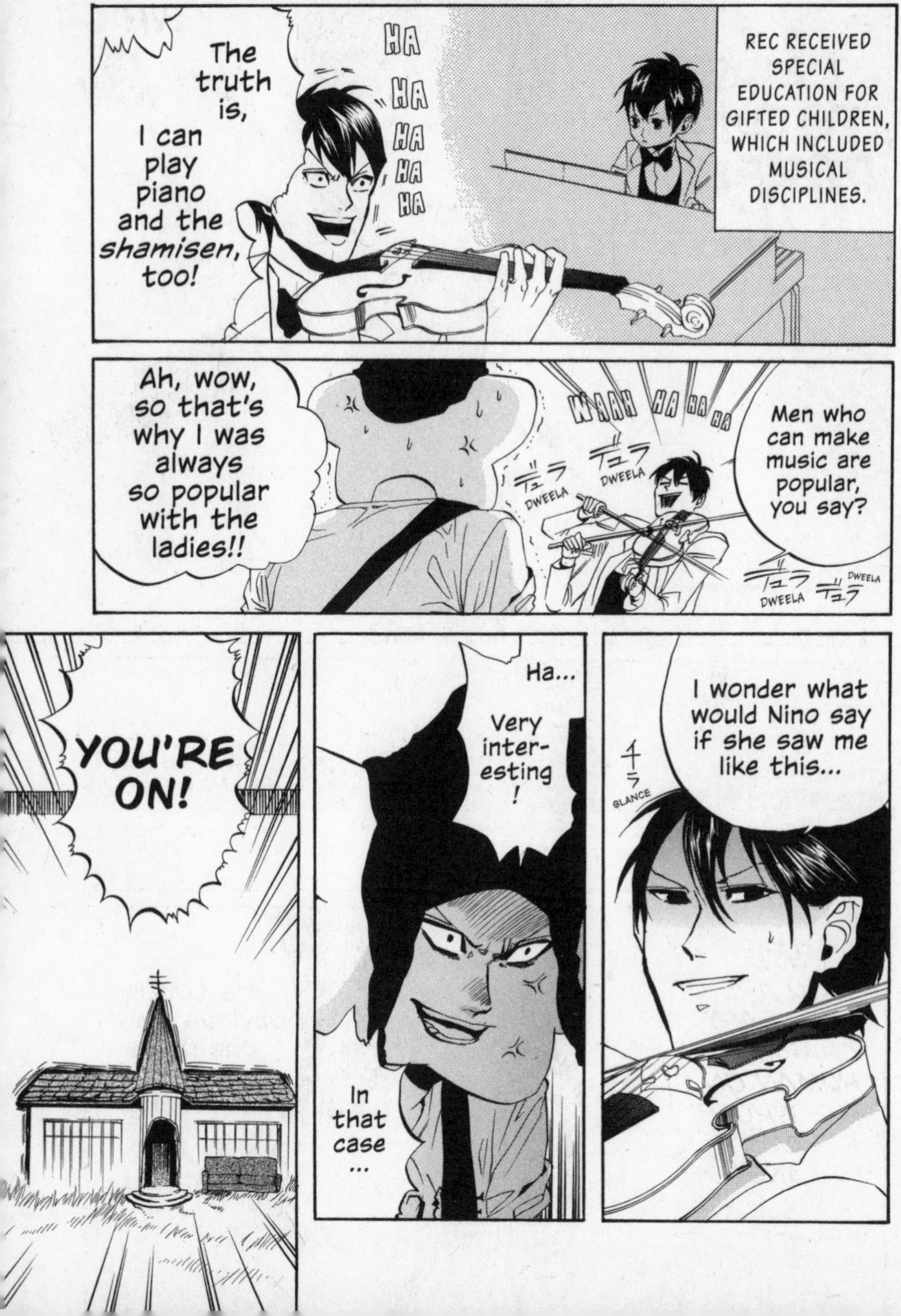
REC RECEIVED SPECIAL EDUCATION FOR GIFTED CHILDREN, WHICH INCLUDED MUSICAL DISCIPLINES.
HA HA HA HA HA
The truth is, I can play piano and the *shamisen*, too!
Men who can make music are popular, you say?
DWEELA DWEELA
WAAAH HA HA HA HA
DWEELA DWEELA
Ah, wow, so that's why I was always so popular with the ladies!!
I wonder what would Nino say if she saw me like this...
GLANCE
Ha...
Very inter-esting!
In that case...
YOU'RE ON!

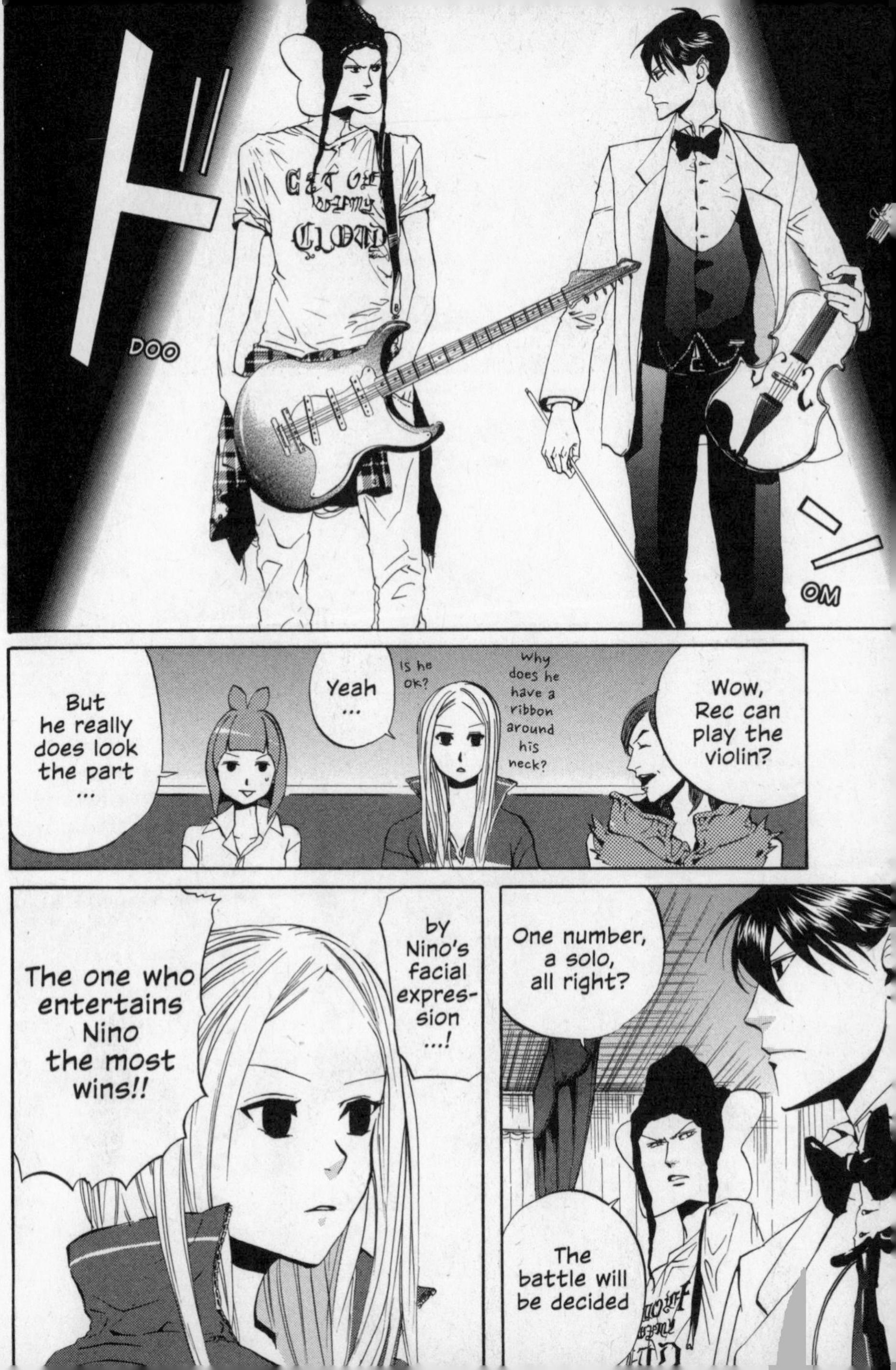
DOO
OM
Wow, Rec can play the violin?
Why does he have a ribbon around his neck?
Is he OK?
Yeah ...
But he really does look the part ...
One number, a solo, all right?
The battle will be decided
by Nino's facial expres- sion ...!
The one who entertains Nino the most wins!!

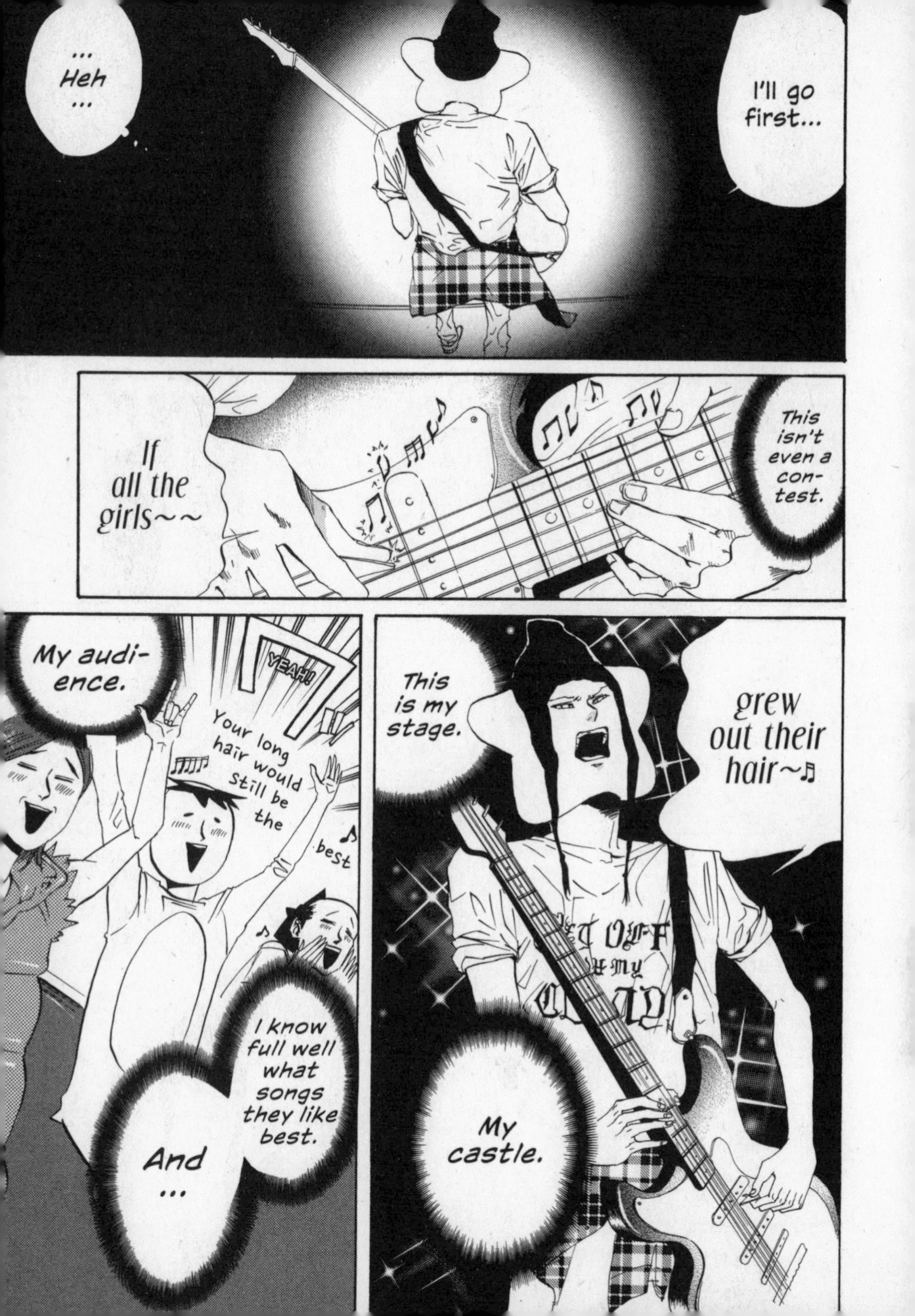
I'll go first...
... Heh ...
This isn't even a con-test.
If all the girls~~
grew out their hair~♫
This is my stage.
My castle.
YEAH!!
Your long hair would Still be the best
My audi-ence.
I know full well what songs they like best.
And ...

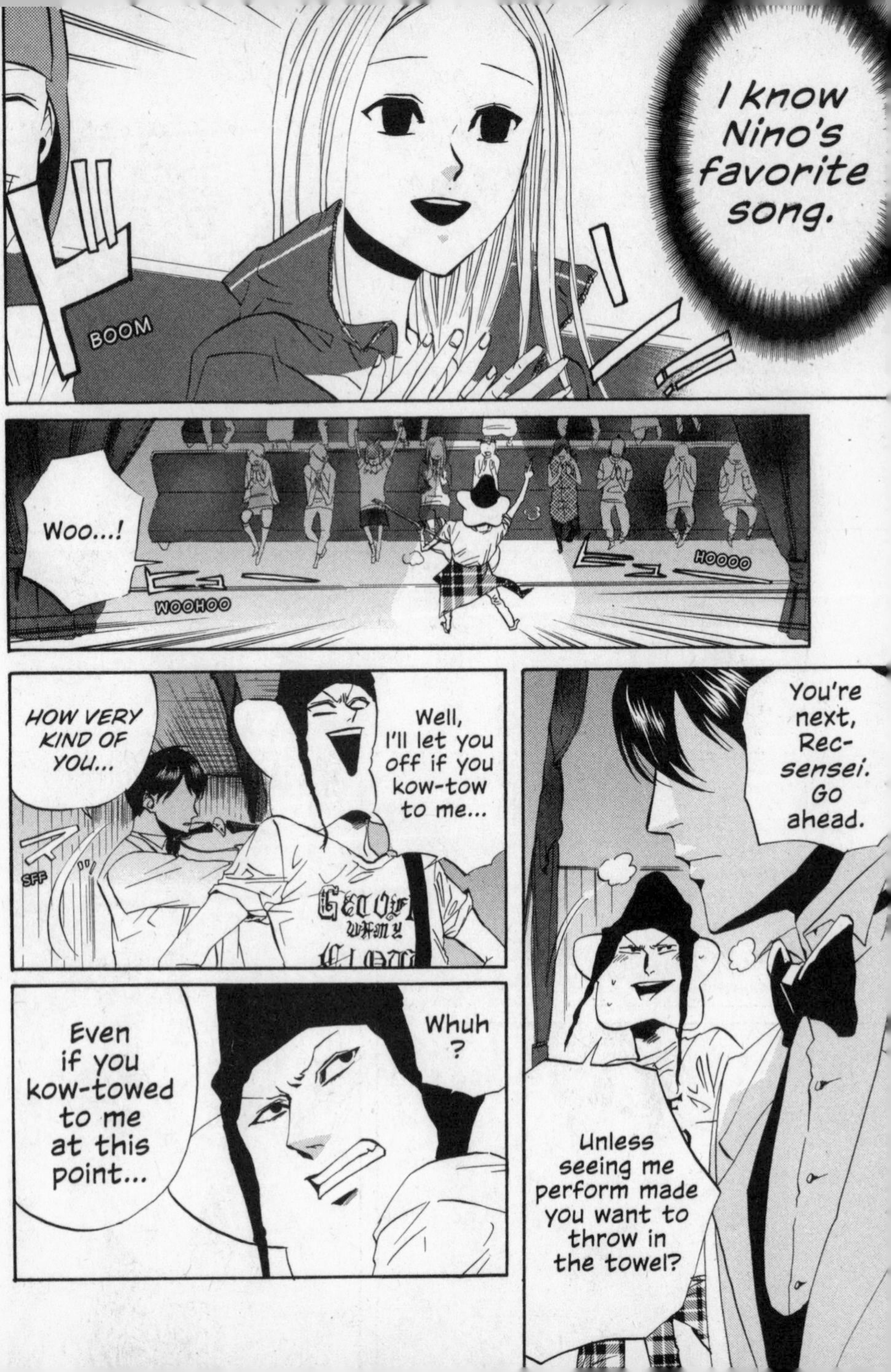
I know Nino's favorite song.
BOOM
Woo...!
HOOOO
WOOHOO
You're next, Rec-sensei. Go ahead.
Unless seeing me perform made you want to throw in the towel?
Well, I'll let you off if you kow-tow to me...
HOW VERY KIND OF YOU...
SFF
Whuh?
Even if you kow-towed to me at this point...

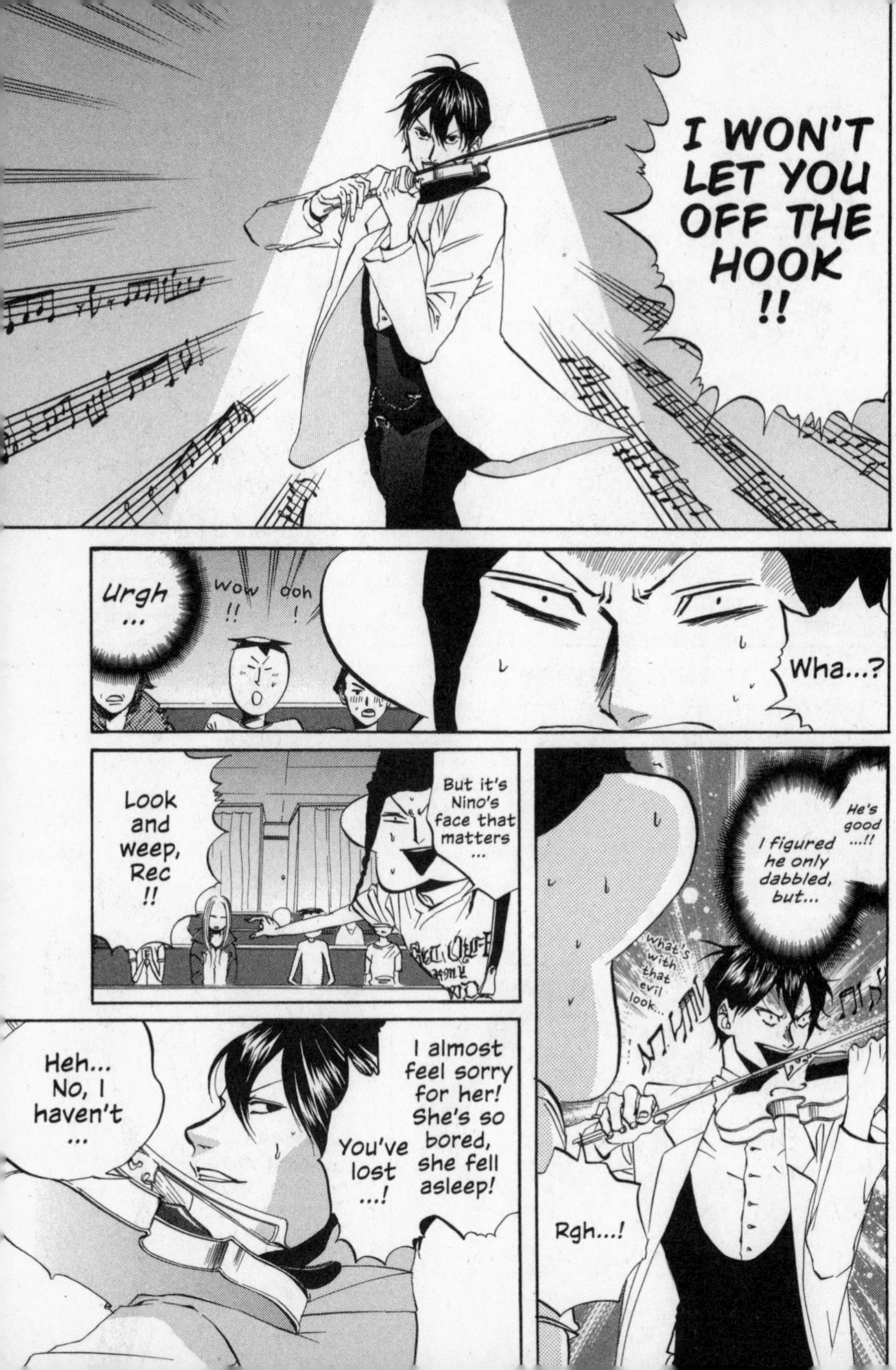
I WON'T LET YOU OFF THE HOOK !!
Wha...?
ooh !
wow !!
Urgh ...
He's good ...!!
I figured he only dabbled, but...
what's with that evil look...
Rgh...!
But it's Nino's face that matters ...
Look and weep, Rec !!
I almost feel sorry for her! She's so bored, she fell asleep!
You've lost ...!
Heh... No, I haven't ...

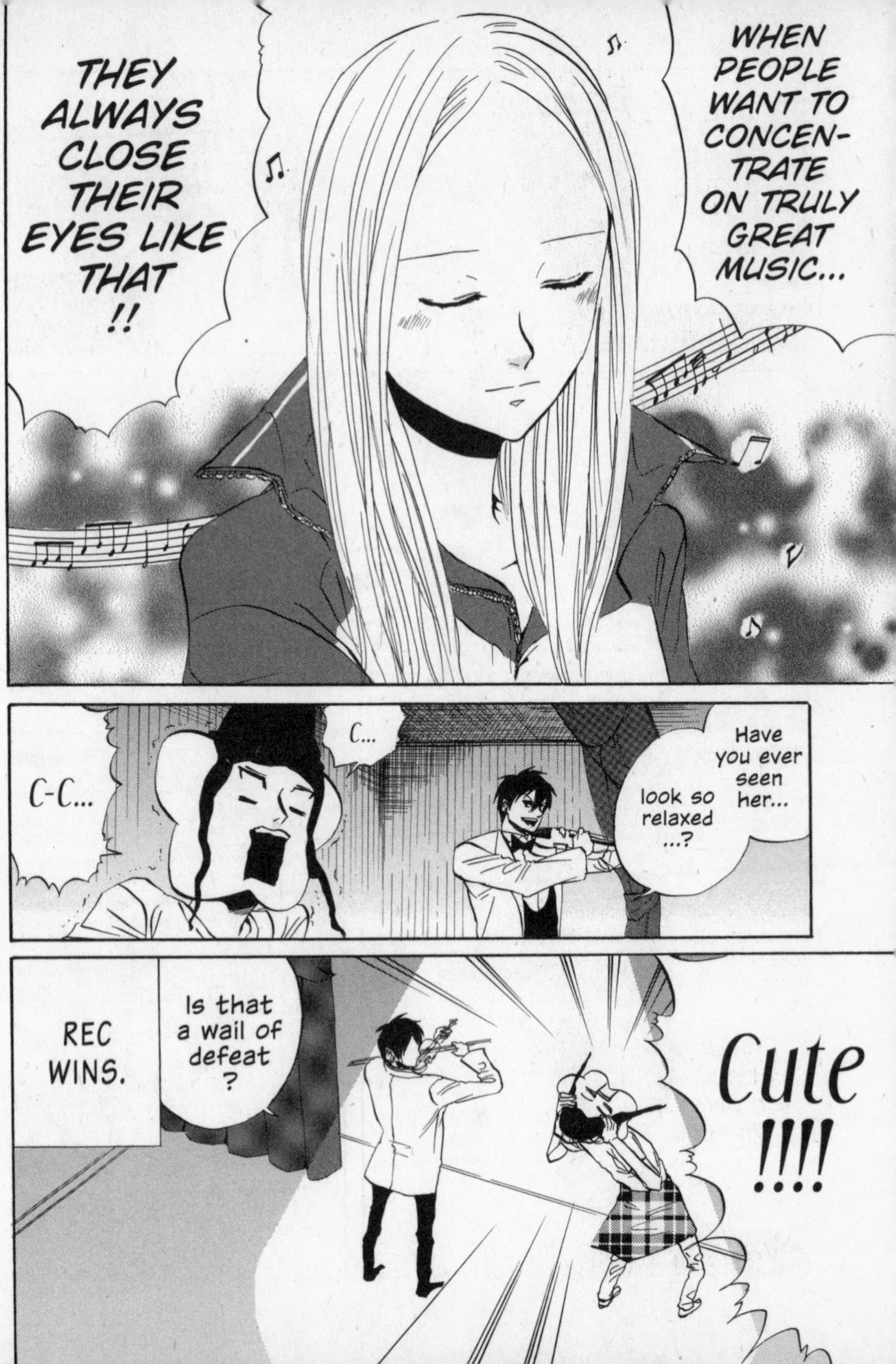
WHEN PEOPLE WANT TO CONCEN-TRATE ON TRULY GREAT MUSIC...
THEY ALWAYS CLOSE THEIR EYES LIKE THAT !!
Have you ever seen her... look so relaxed ...?
C...
C-C...
Cute !!!!
Is that a wail of defeat ?
REC WINS.

Chapter 53: Last Song

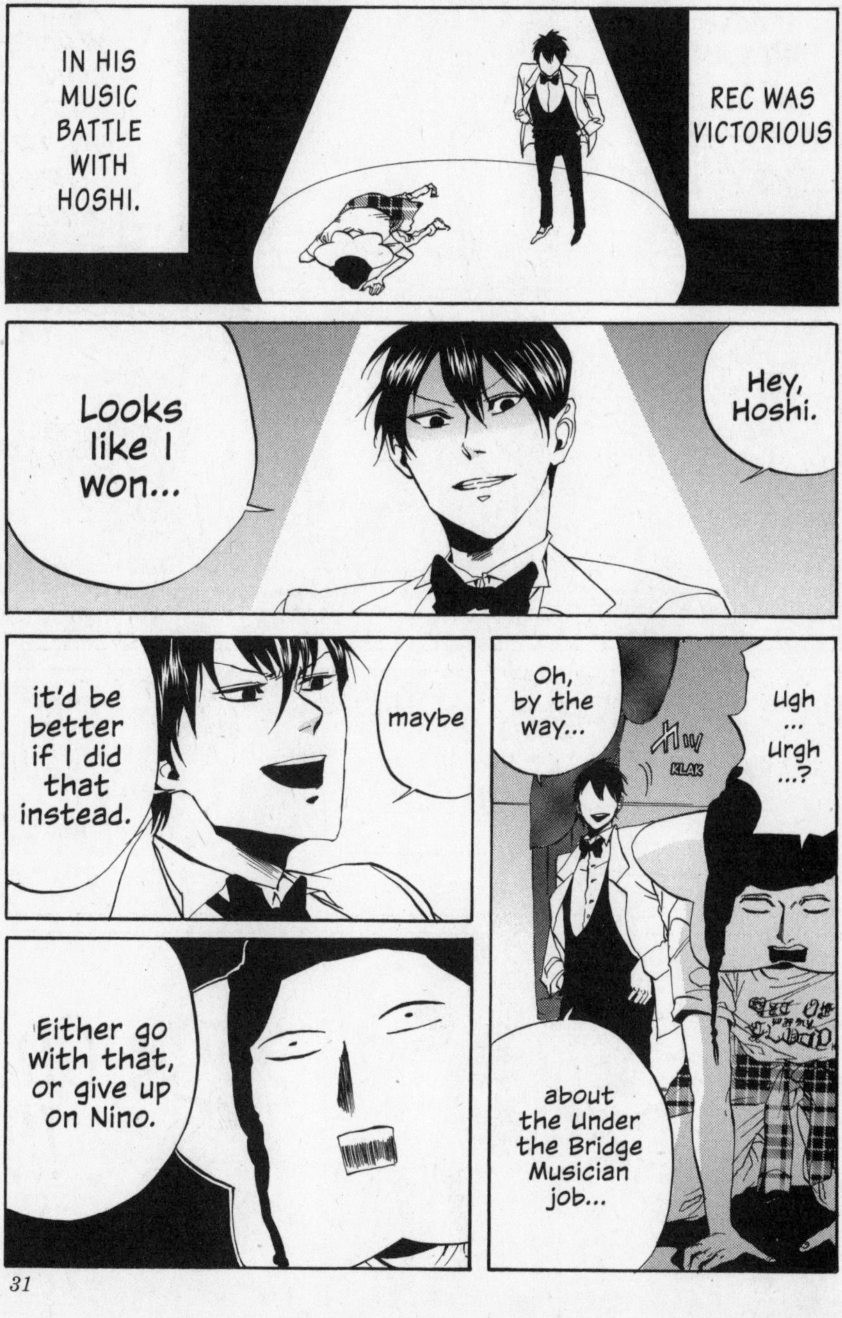
REC WAS VICTORIOUS
IN HIS MUSIC BATTLE WITH HOSHI.
Hey, Hoshi.
Looks like I won...
Ugh ... Urgh ...?
Oh, by the way...
KLAK
about the Under the Bridge Musician job...
maybe
it'd be better if I did that instead.
Either go with that, or give up on Nino.

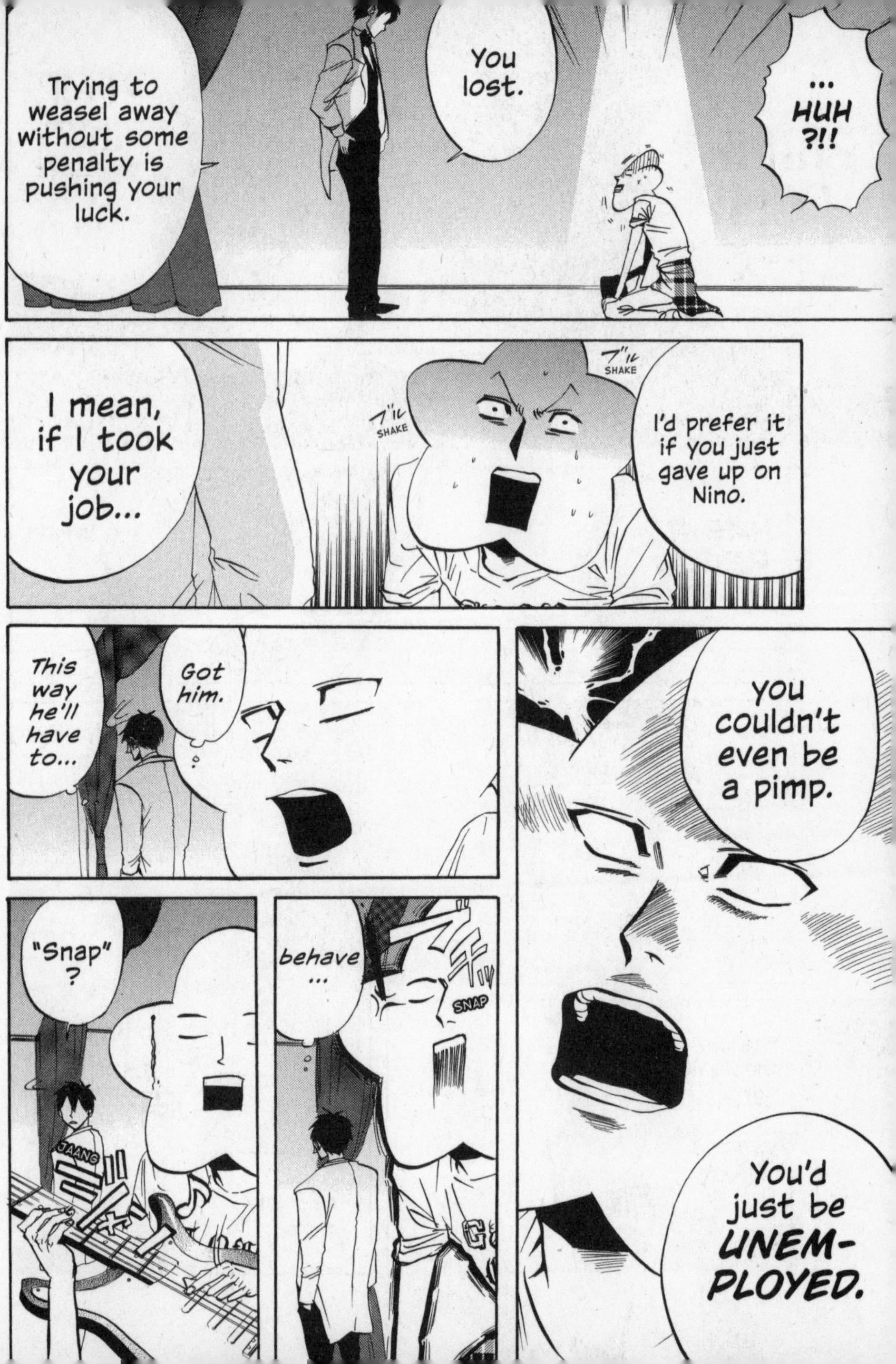
... HUH ?!!
You lost.
Trying to weasel away without some penalty is pushing your luck.
I'd prefer it if you just gave up on Nino.
SHAKE
SHAKE
I mean, if I took your job...
you couldn't even be a pimp.
You'd just be UNEMPLOYED.
Got him.
This way he'll have to...
behave ...
SNAP
"Snap" ?
JAANG

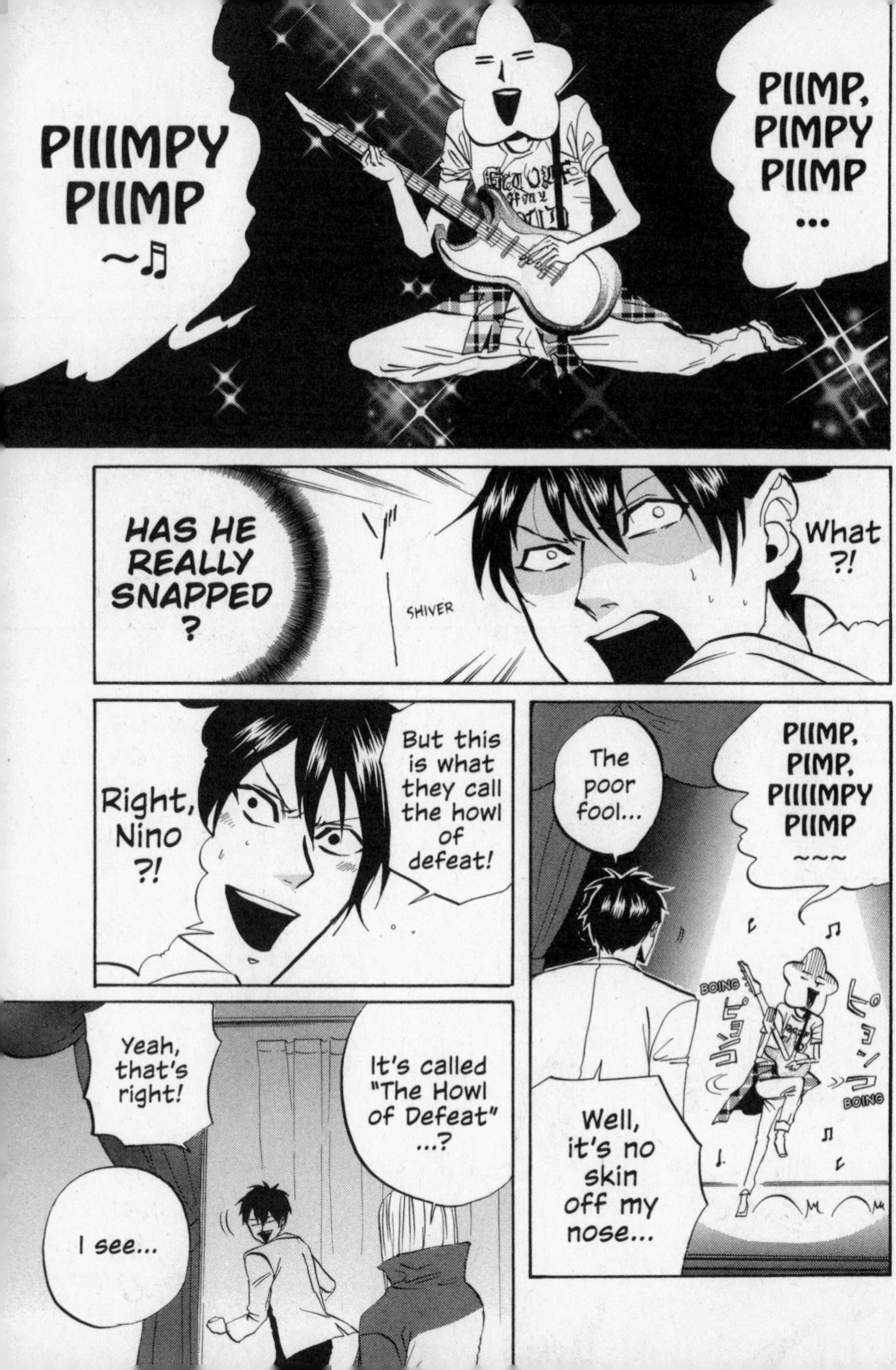
PIIMP, PIMPY PIIMP ...
PIIIMPY PIIMP ~♫
What ?!
HAS HE REALLY SNAPPED ?
SHIVER
PIIMP, PIMP, PIIIIMPY PIIMP ~~~
The poor fool...
BOING
BOING
Well, it's no skin off my nose...
But this is what they call the howl of defeat!
Right, Nino ?!
It's called "The Howl of Defeat" ...?
Yeah, that's right!
I see...

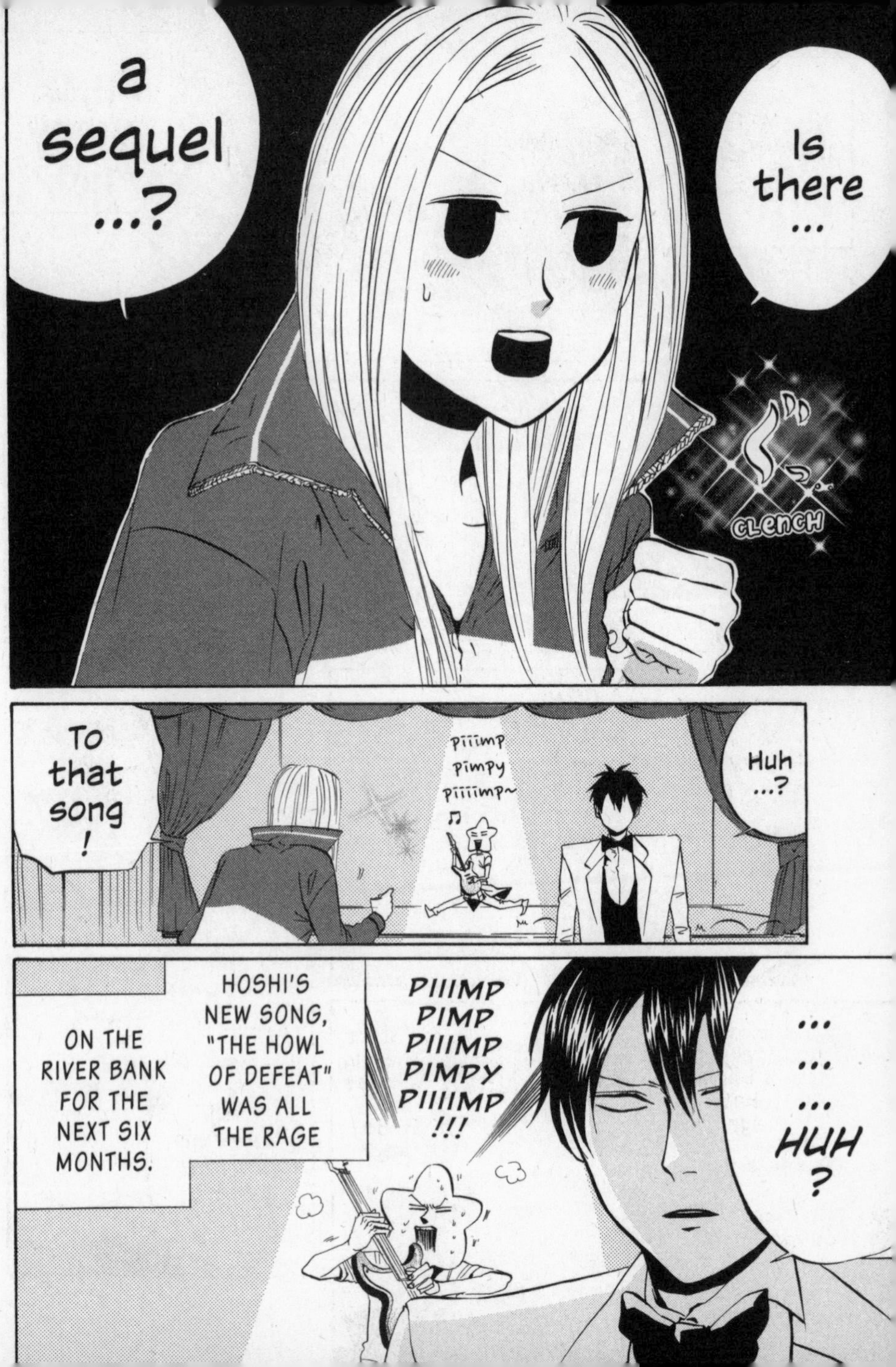
Is there ...
a sequel ...?
CLENCH
Huh ...?
Piiimp Pimpy Piiiimp~
To that song!
... ... HUH ?
PIIIMP PIMP PIIIMP PIMPY PIIIIMP !!!
HOSHI'S NEW SONG, "THE HOWL OF DEFEAT" WAS ALL THE RAGE
ON THE RIVER BANK FOR THE NEXT SIX MONTHS.

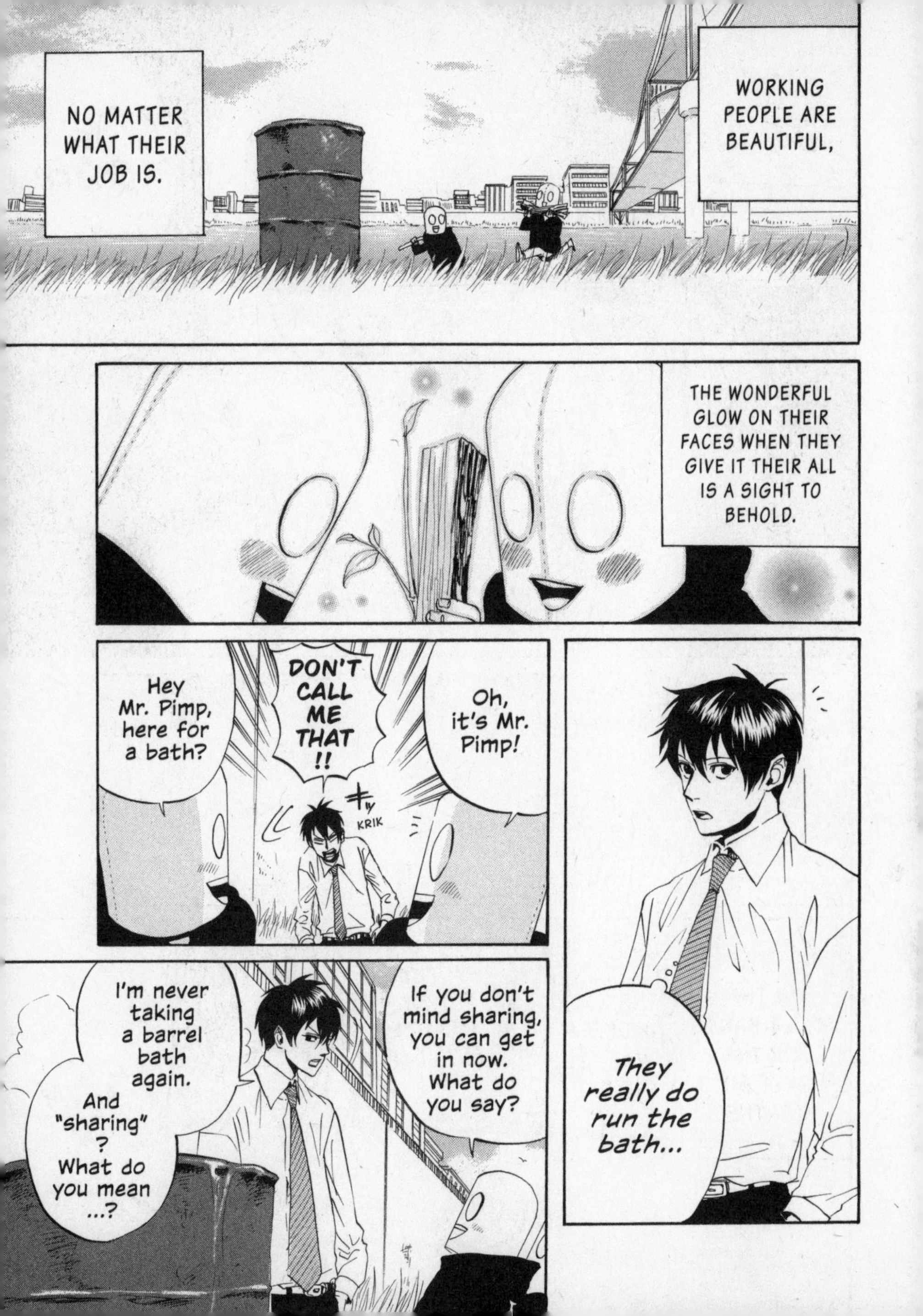
WORKING PEOPLE ARE BEAUTIFUL,
NO MATTER WHAT THEIR JOB IS.
THE WONDERFUL GLOW ON THEIR FACES WHEN THEY GIVE IT THEIR ALL IS A SIGHT TO BEHOLD.
They really do run the bath...
Oh, it's Mr. Pimp!
Hey Mr. Pimp, here for a bath?
DON'T CALL ME THAT!!
KRIK
If you don't mind sharing, you can get in now. What do you say?
I'm never taking a barrel bath again.
And "sharing"? What do you mean ...?

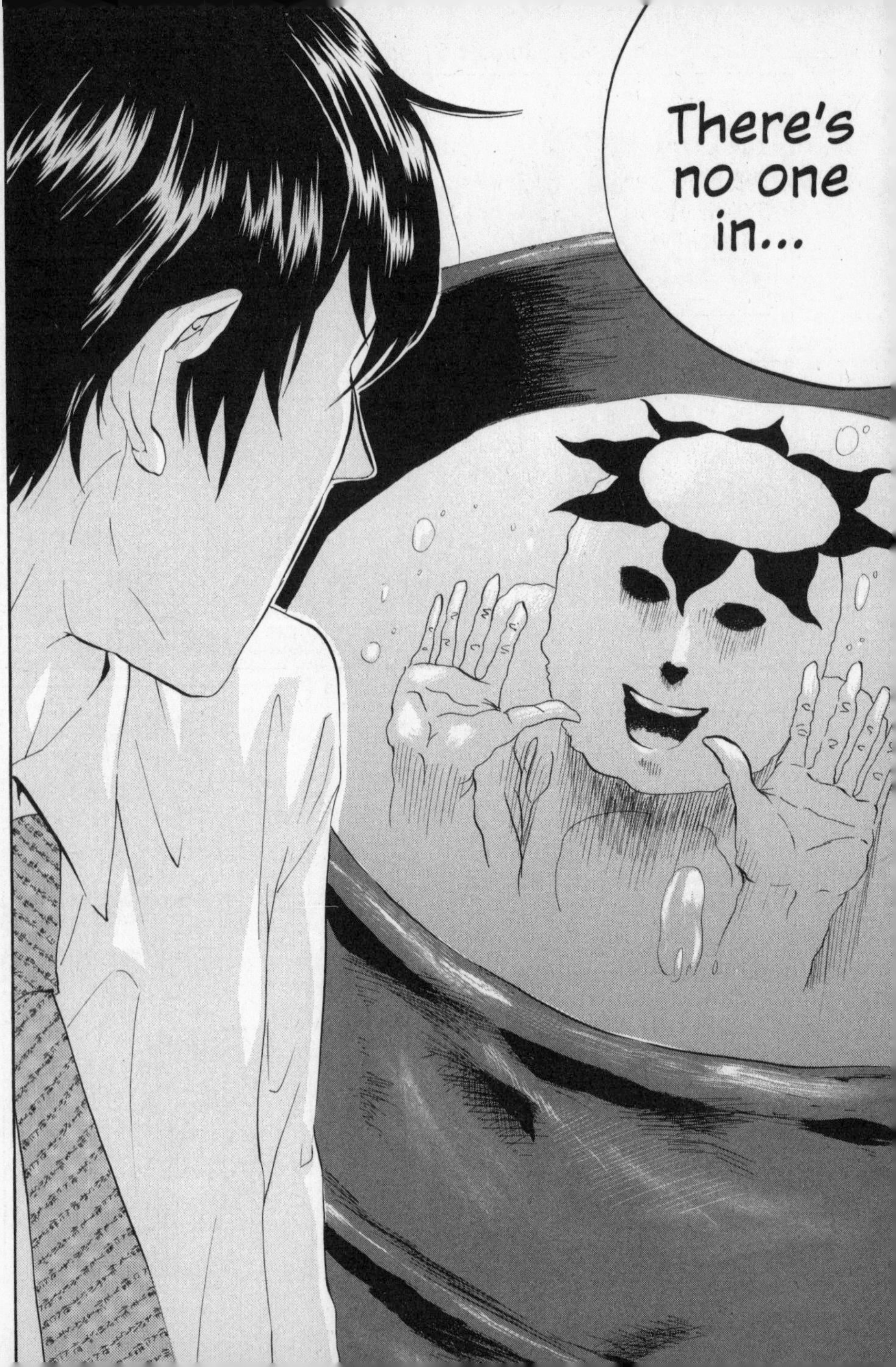
There's no one in...

Chapter 54: Polypropylene

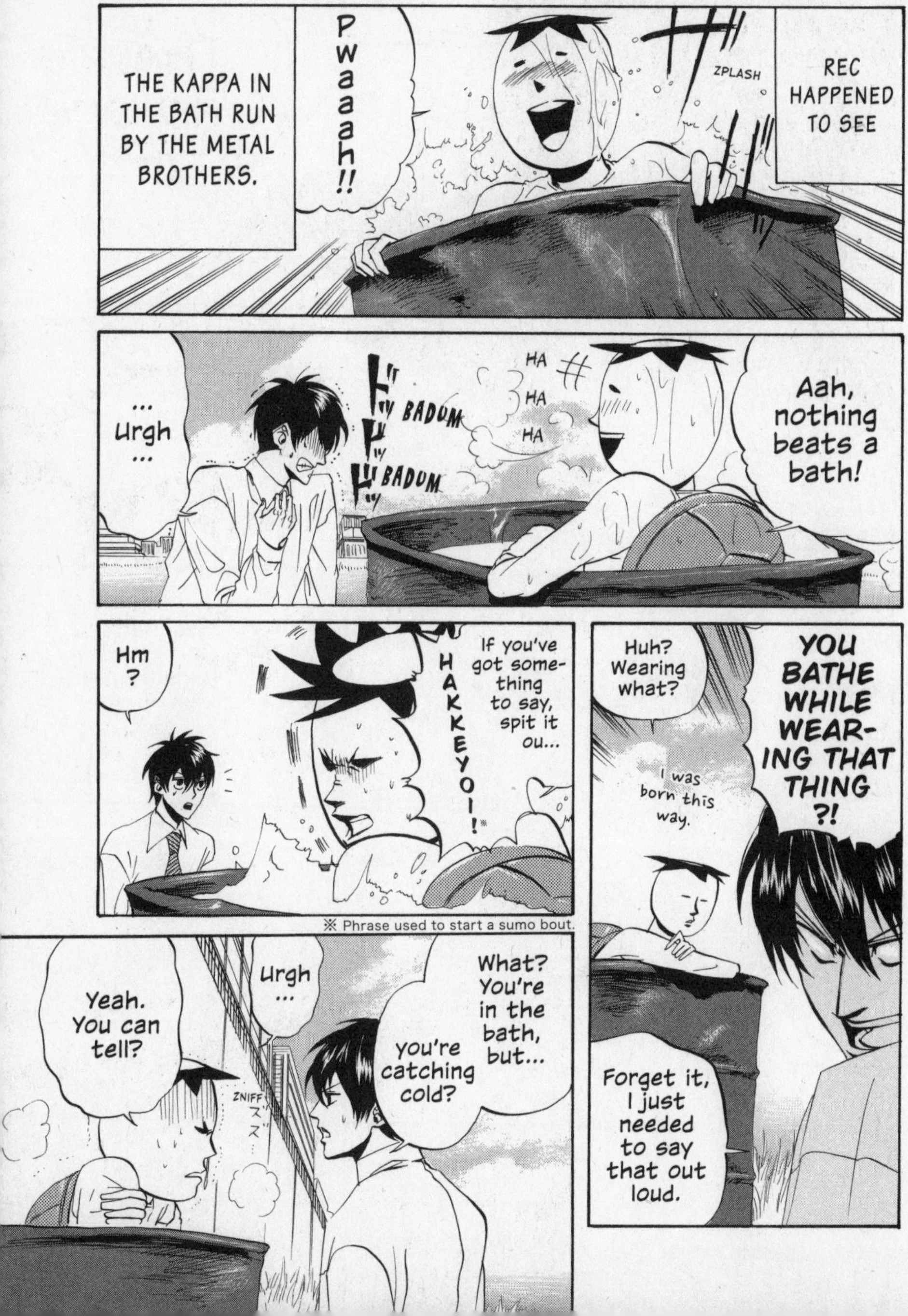
REC HAPPENED TO SEE
ZPLASH
Pwaaah!!
THE KAPPA IN THE BATH RUN BY THE METAL BROTHERS.
Aah, nothing beats a bath!
HA HA HA
BADUM BADUM
... Urgh ...
YOU BATHE WHILE WEARING THAT THING?!
Huh? Wearing what?
I was born this way.
Forget it, I just needed to say that out loud.
If you've got something to say, spit it ou...
HAKKEYOI!※
Hm?
What? You're in the bath, but...
you're catching cold?
Urgh ...
ZNIFF
Yeah. You can tell?
※ Phrase used to start a sumo bout.

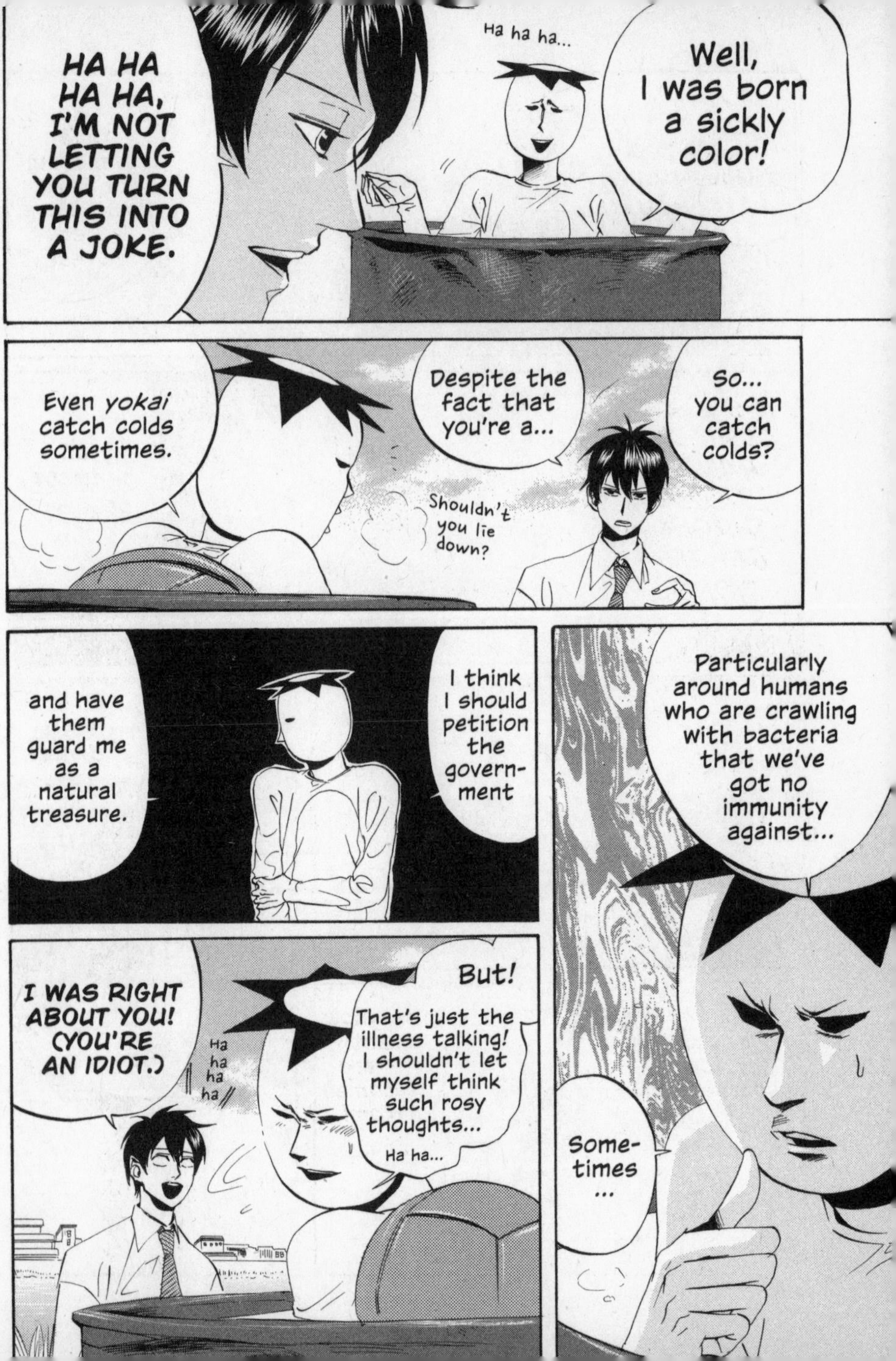
Well, I was born a sickly color!
Ha ha ha...
HA HA HA HA, I'M NOT LETTING YOU TURN THIS INTO A JOKE.
So... you can catch colds?
Despite the fact that you're a...
Shouldn't you lie down?
Even *yokai* catch colds sometimes.
Particularly around humans who are crawling with bacteria that we've got no immunity against...
Some- times ...
I think I should petition the govern- ment
and have them guard me as a natural treasure.
But!
That's just the illness talking! I shouldn't let myself think such rosy thoughts...
Ha ha...
Ha ha ha ha
I WAS RIGHT ABOUT YOU! (YOU'RE AN IDIOT.)

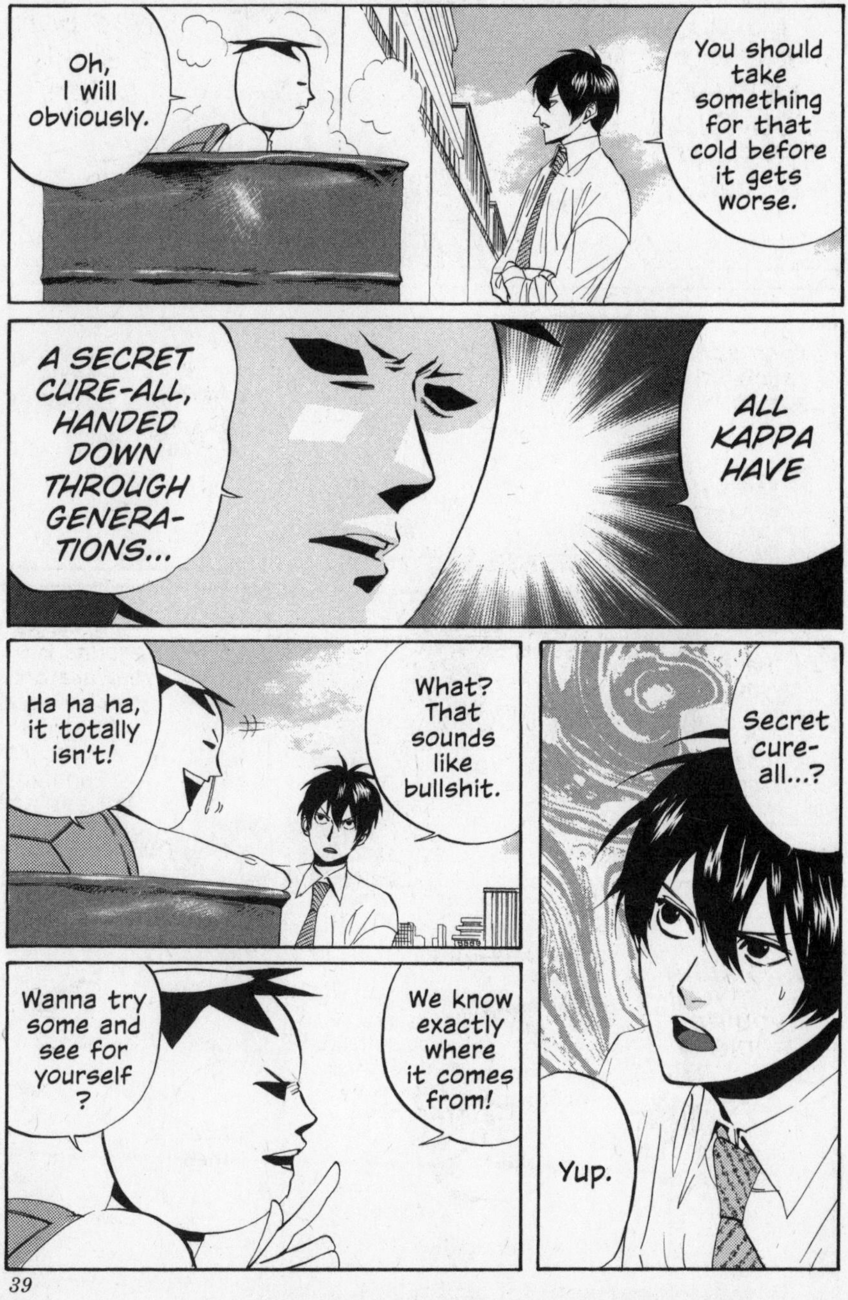
You should take something for that cold before it gets worse.
Oh, I will obviously.
ALL KAPPA HAVE
A SECRET CURE-ALL, HANDED DOWN THROUGH GENERA-TIONS...
Secret cure-all...?
Yup.
What? That sounds like bullshit.
Ha ha ha, it totally isn't!
We know exactly where it comes from!
Wanna try some and see for yourself?

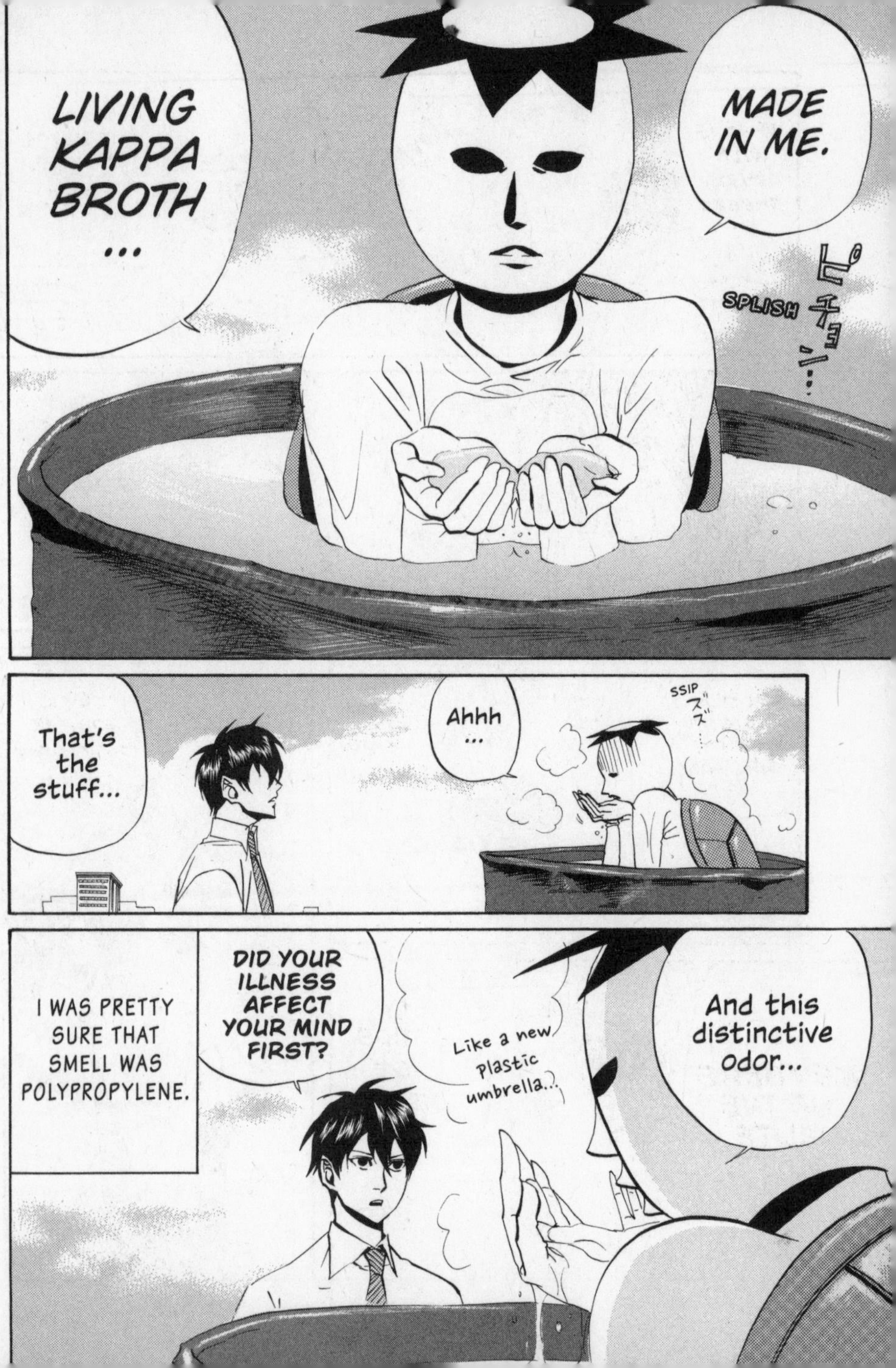
MADE IN ME.
SPLISH
ピチョン…
LIVING KAPPA BROTH ...
SSIP
ズズ…
Ahhh ...
That's the stuff...
And this distinctive odor...
Like a new plastic umbrella...
DID YOUR ILLNESS AFFECT YOUR MIND FIRST?
I WAS PRETTY SURE THAT SMELL WAS POLYPROPYLENE.

Chapter 55: Hint

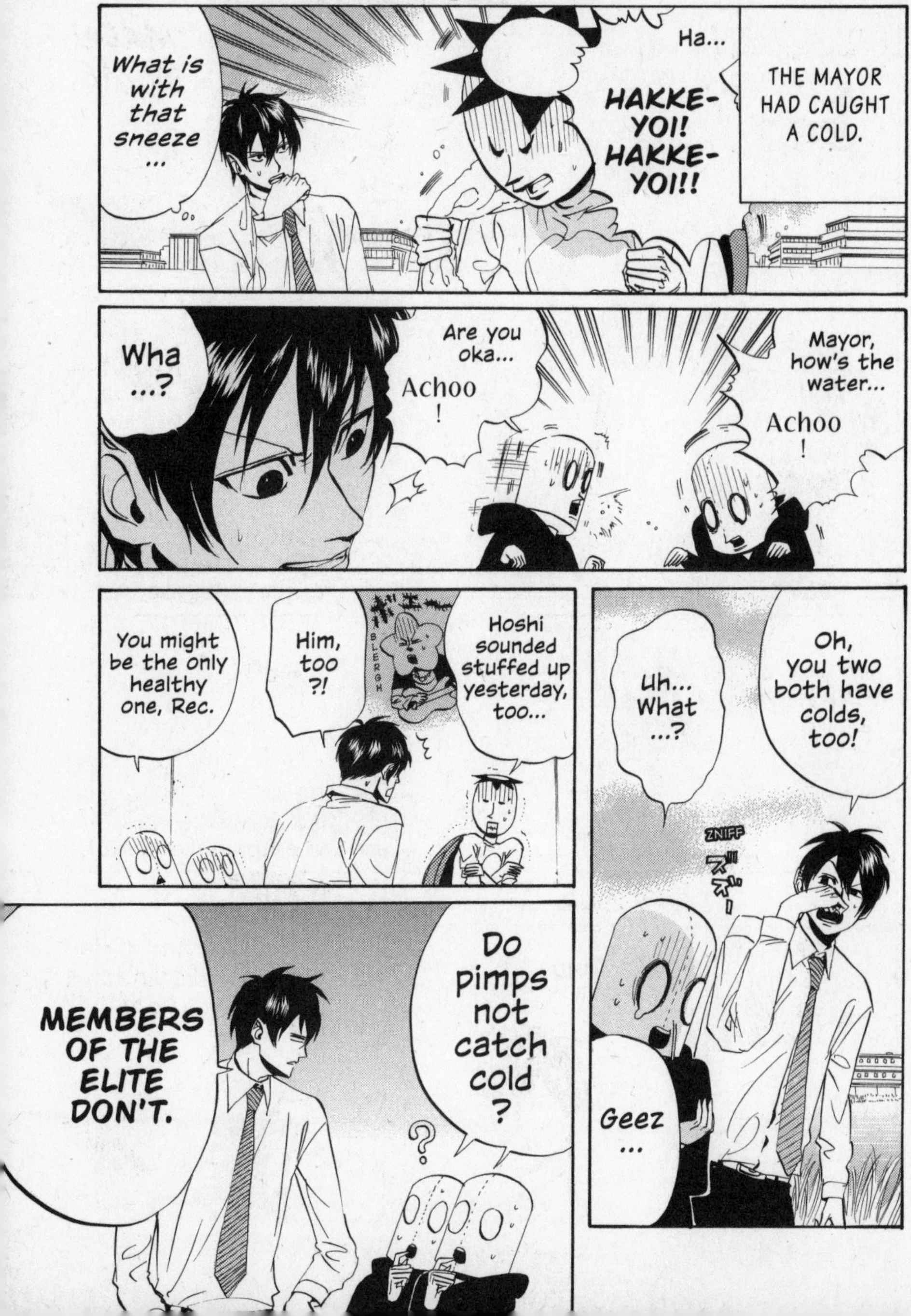
THE MAYOR HAD CAUGHT A COLD.
Ha...
HAKKE-YOI! HAKKE-YOI!!
What is with that sneeze...
Mayor, how's the water...
Achoo!
Are you oka...
Achoo!
Wha...?
Oh, you two both have colds, too!
Uh... What...?
ZNIFF
Geez...
Hoshi sounded stuffed up yesterday, too...
BLERGH
Him, too?!
You might be the only healthy one, Rec.
Do pimps not catch cold?
MEMBERS OF THE ELITE DON'T.

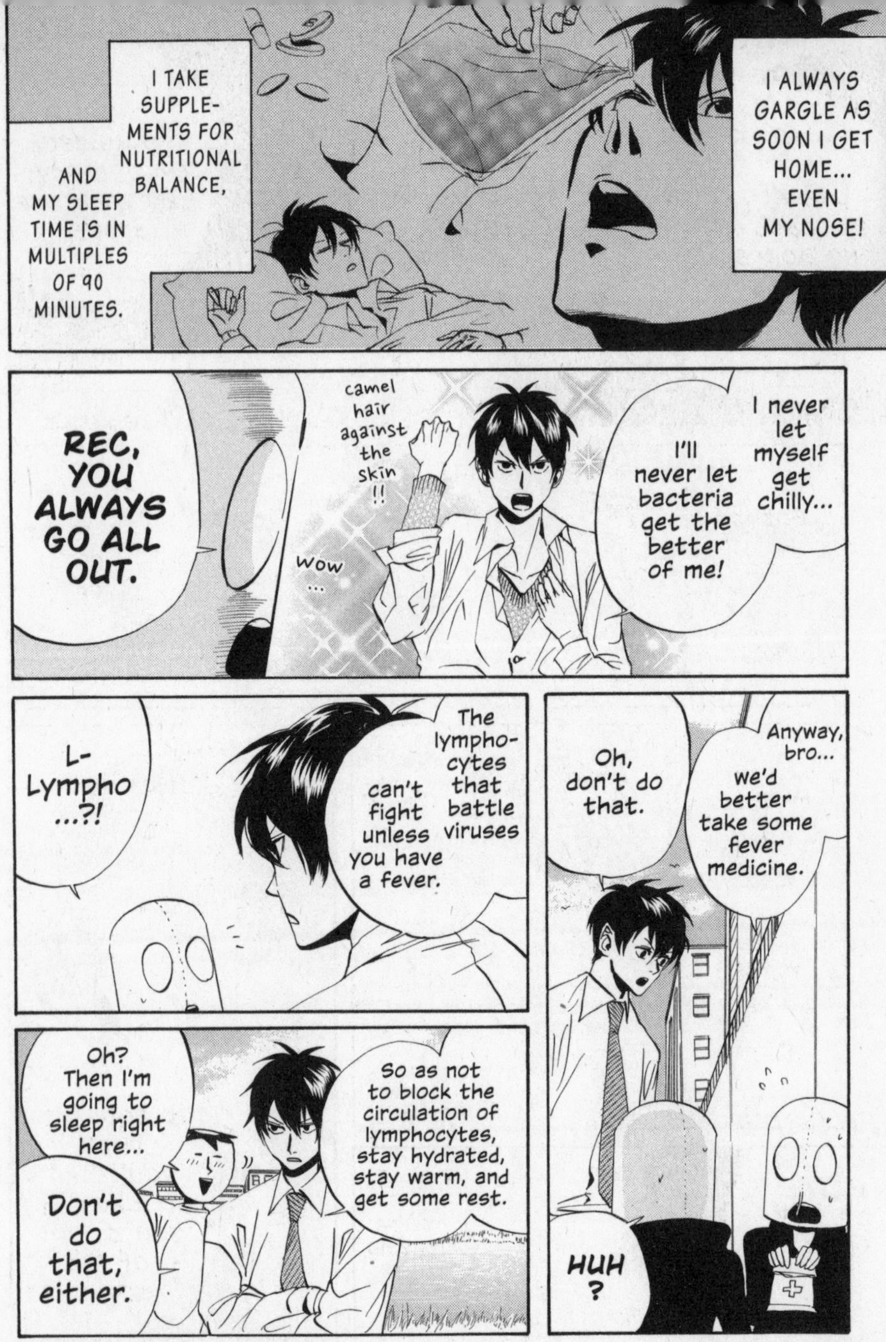
I ALWAYS GARGLE AS SOON I GET HOME... EVEN MY NOSE!
I TAKE SUPPLEMENTS FOR NUTRITIONAL BALANCE,
AND MY SLEEP TIME IS IN MULTIPLES OF 90 MINUTES.
I never let myself get chilly...
I'll never let bacteria get the better of me!
camel hair against the skin!!
wow...
REC, YOU ALWAYS GO ALL OUT.
Anyway, bro... we'd better take some fever medicine.
Oh, don't do that.
HUH?
The lymphocytes that battle viruses can't fight unless you have a fever.
L-Lympho...?!
So as not to block the circulation of lymphocytes, stay hydrated, stay warm, and get some rest.
Oh? Then I'm going to sleep right here...
Don't do that, either.

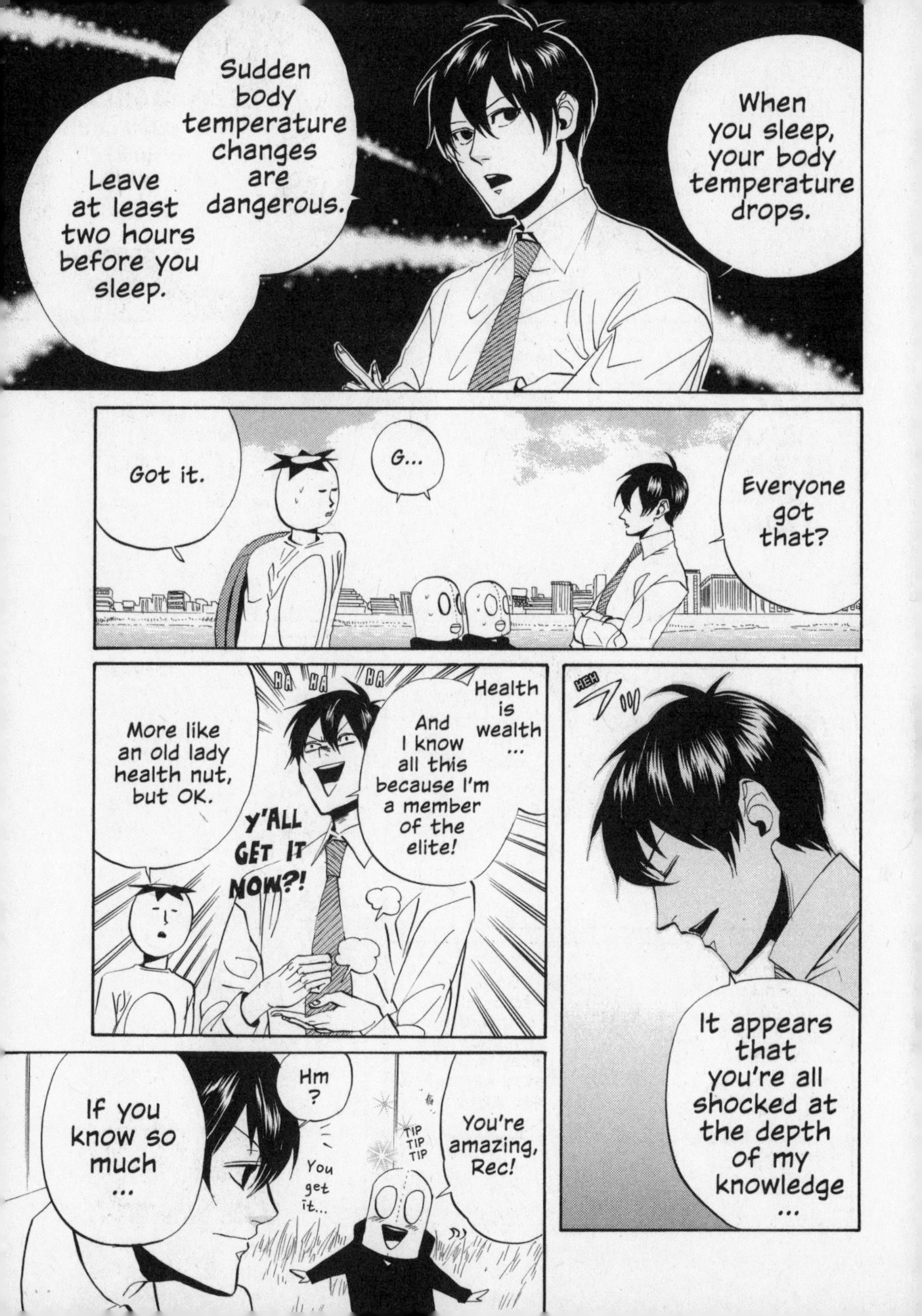
When you sleep, your body temperature drops.
Sudden body temperature changes are dangerous.
Leave at least two hours before you sleep.
Everyone got that?
G...
Got it.
HEH
It appears that you're all shocked at the depth of my knowledge ...
HA HA HA
Health is wealth ...
And I know all this because I'm a member of the elite!
Y'ALL GET IT NOW?!
More like an old lady health nut, but OK.
You're amazing, Rec!
TIP TIP TIP
Hm?
You get it...
If you know so much ...

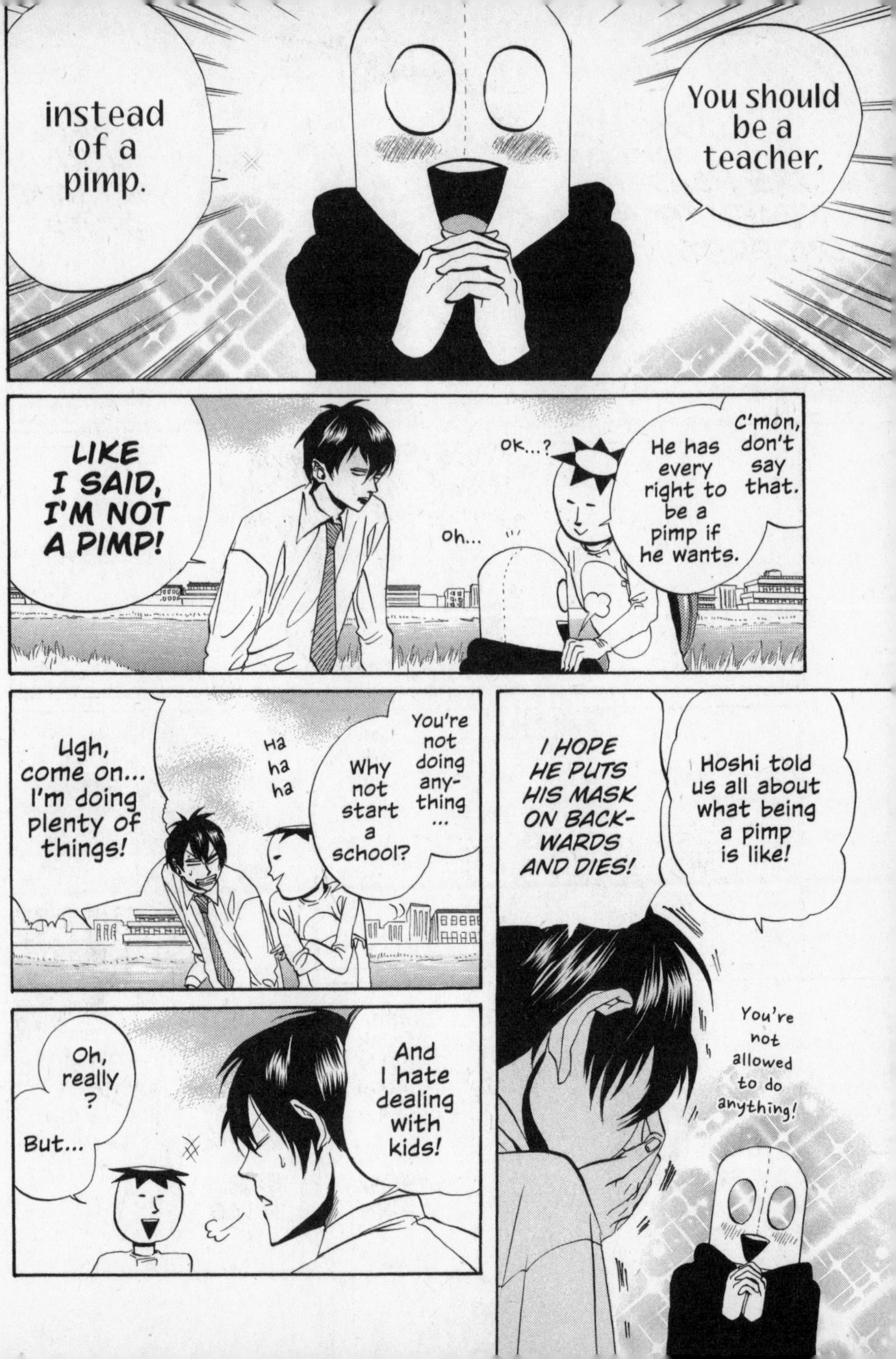
You should be a teacher,
instead of a pimp.
C'mon, don't say that.
He has every right to be a pimp if he wants.
OK...?
Oh...
LIKE I SAID, I'M NOT A PIMP!
Hoshi told us all about what being a pimp is like!
I HOPE HE PUTS HIS MASK ON BACK-WARDS AND DIES!
You're not allowed to do anything!
You're not doing any-thing...
Why not start a school?
Ha ha ha
Ugh, come on... I'm doing plenty of things!
And I hate dealing with kids!
Oh, really?
But...

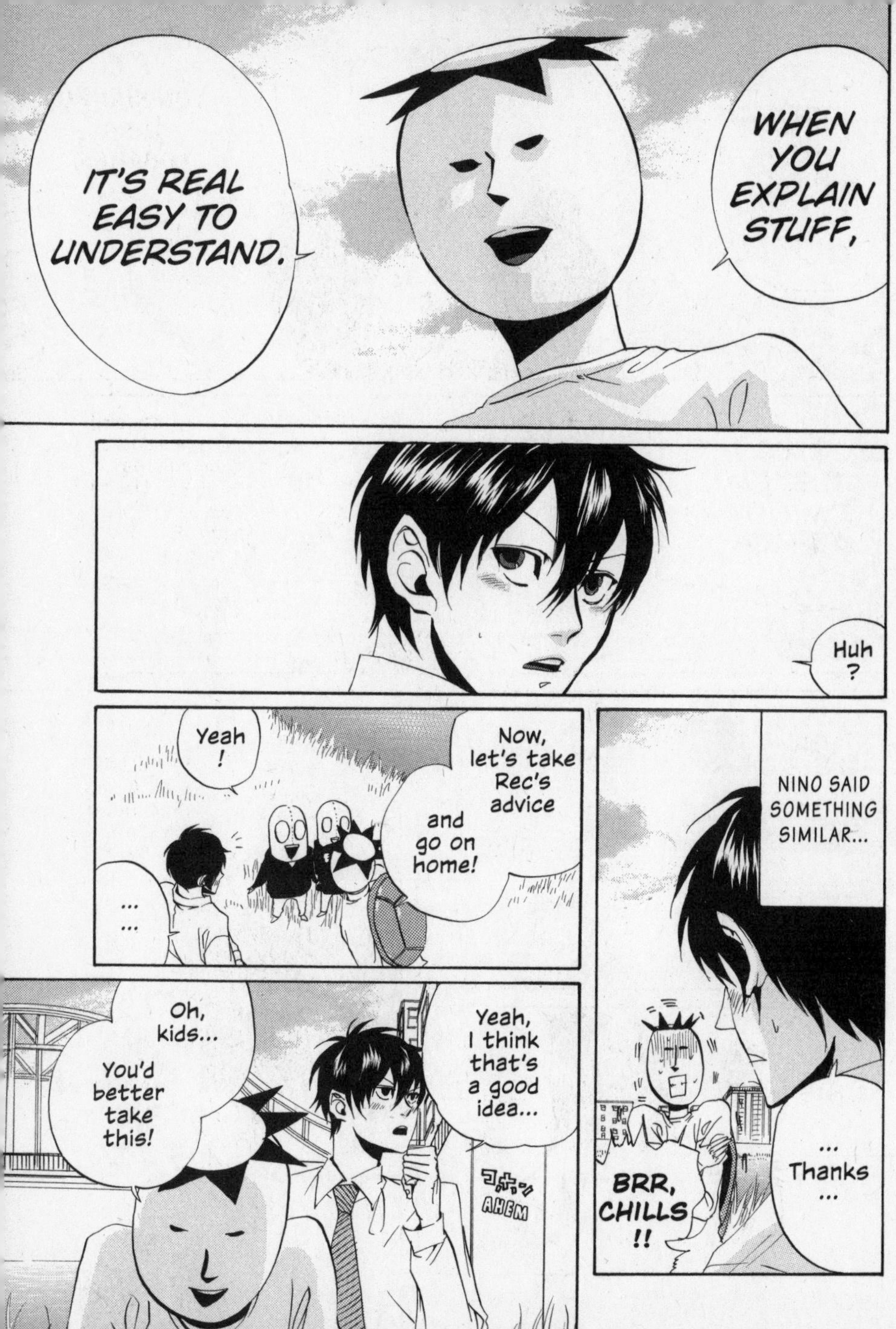
WHEN YOU EXPLAIN STUFF,
IT'S REAL EASY TO UNDERSTAND.
Huh?
NINO SAID SOMETHING SIMILAR...
... Thanks ...
BRR, CHILLS !!
Now, let's take Rec's advice and go on home!
Yeah!
... ...
Yeah, I think that's a good idea...
AHEM
Oh, kids... You'd better take this!

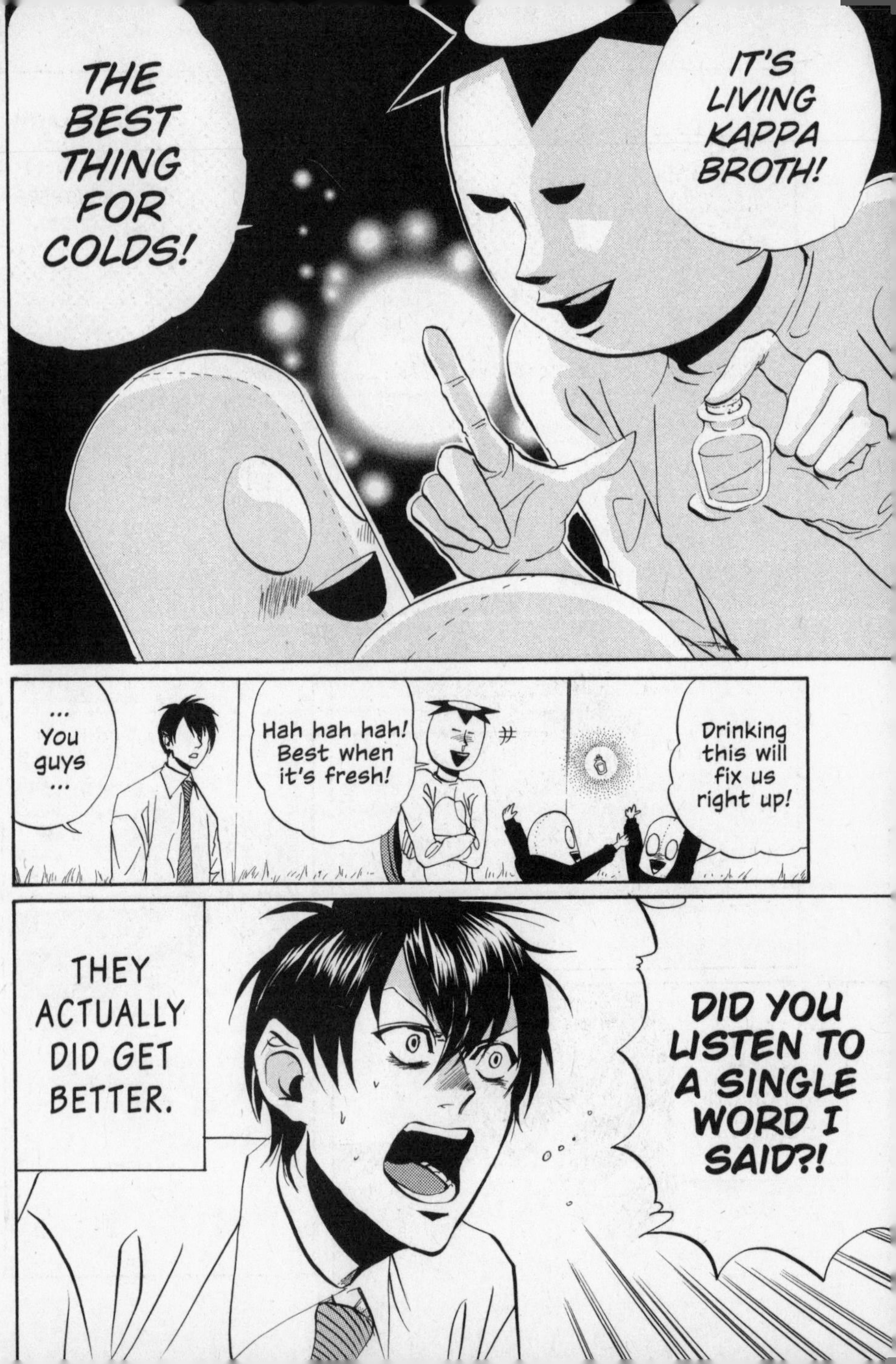
IT'S LIVING KAPPA BROTH!
THE BEST THING FOR COLDS!
Drinking this will fix us right up!
Hah hah hah! Best when it's fresh!
... You guys ...
DID YOU LISTEN TO A SINGLE WORD I SAID?!
THEY ACTUALLY DID GET BETTER.

Chapter 56: Job Chosen

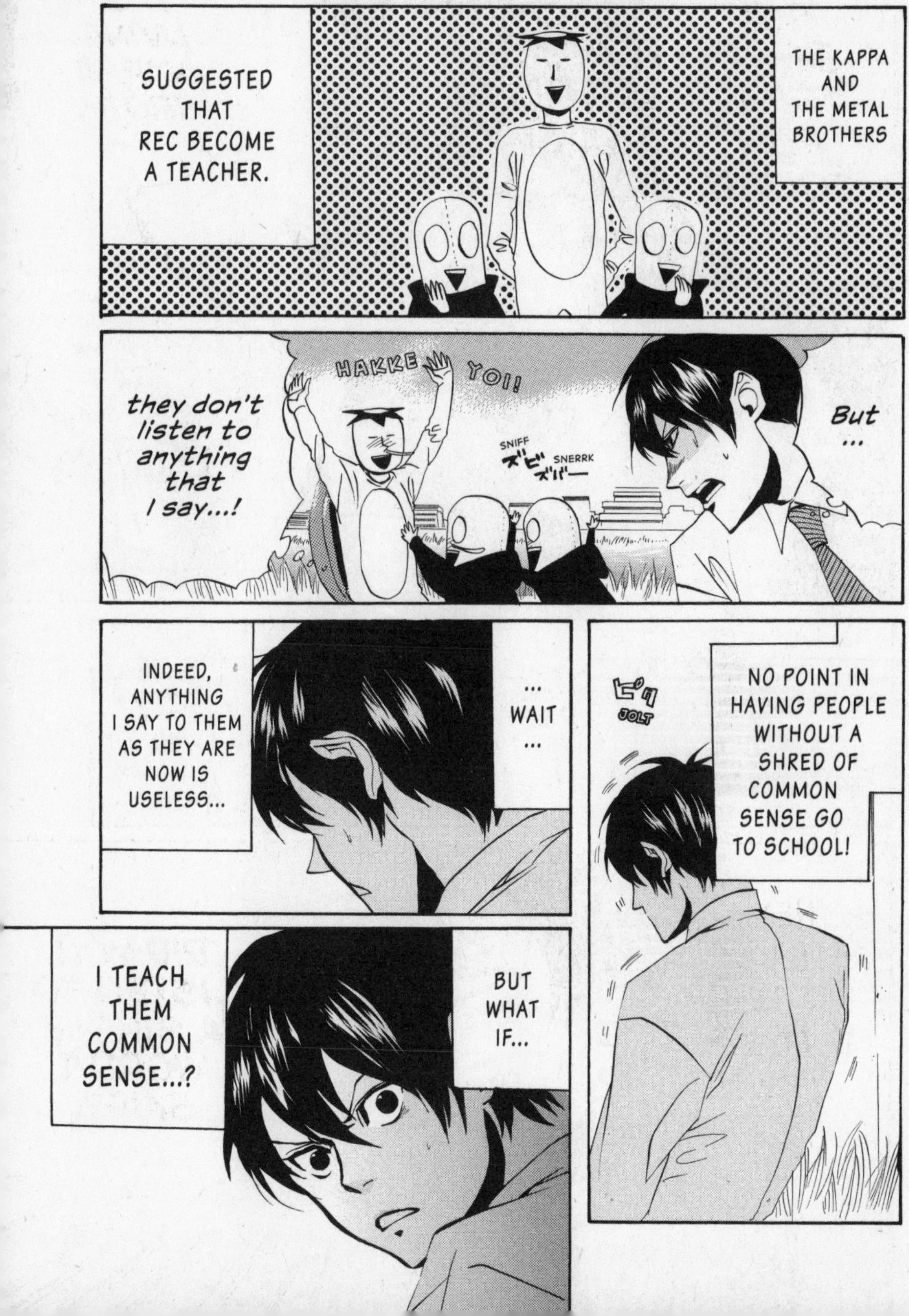
THE KAPPA AND THE METAL BROTHERS
SUGGESTED THAT REC BECOME A TEACHER.
But ...
HAKKE YOI!
SNIFF ズビ
SNERRK ズバー
they don't listen to anything that I say...!
ピク
JOLT
NO POINT IN HAVING PEOPLE WITHOUT A SHRED OF COMMON SENSE GO TO SCHOOL!
... WAIT ...
INDEED, ANYTHING I SAY TO THEM AS THEY ARE NOW IS USELESS...
BUT WHAT IF...
I TEACH THEM COMMON SENSE...?

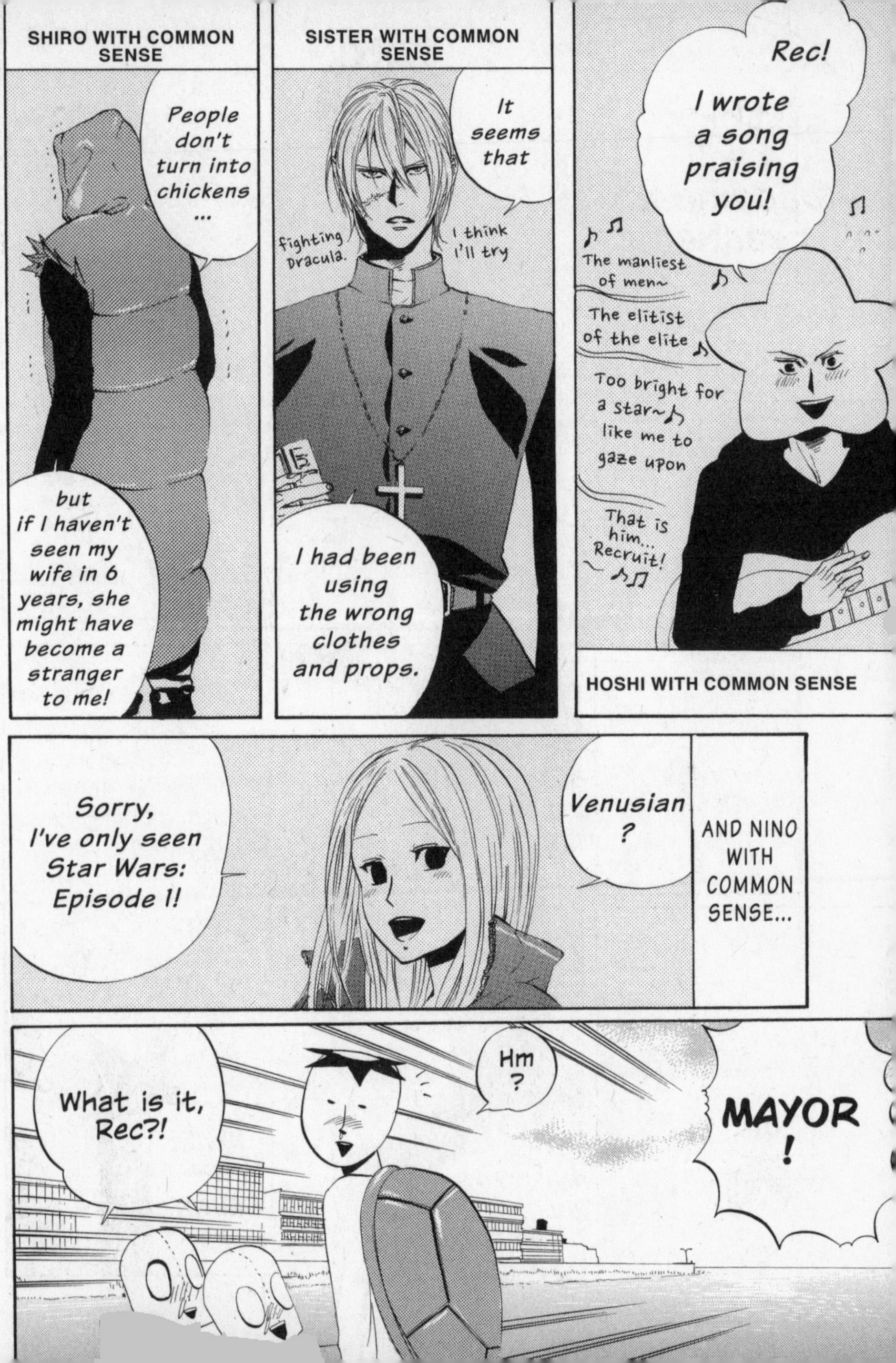
Rec! I wrote a song praising you!
The manliest of men~
The elitist of the elite
Too bright for a star~ like me to gaze upon
That is him... Recruit!
HOSHI WITH COMMON SENSE
SISTER WITH COMMON SENSE
It seems that
I think I'll try
fighting Dracula.
I had been using the wrong clothes and props.
SHIRO WITH COMMON SENSE
People don't turn into chickens ...
but if I haven't seen my wife in 6 years, she might have become a stranger to me!
AND NINO WITH COMMON SENSE...
Venusian?
Sorry, I've only seen Star Wars: Episode 1!
MAYOR!
Hm?
What is it, Rec?!

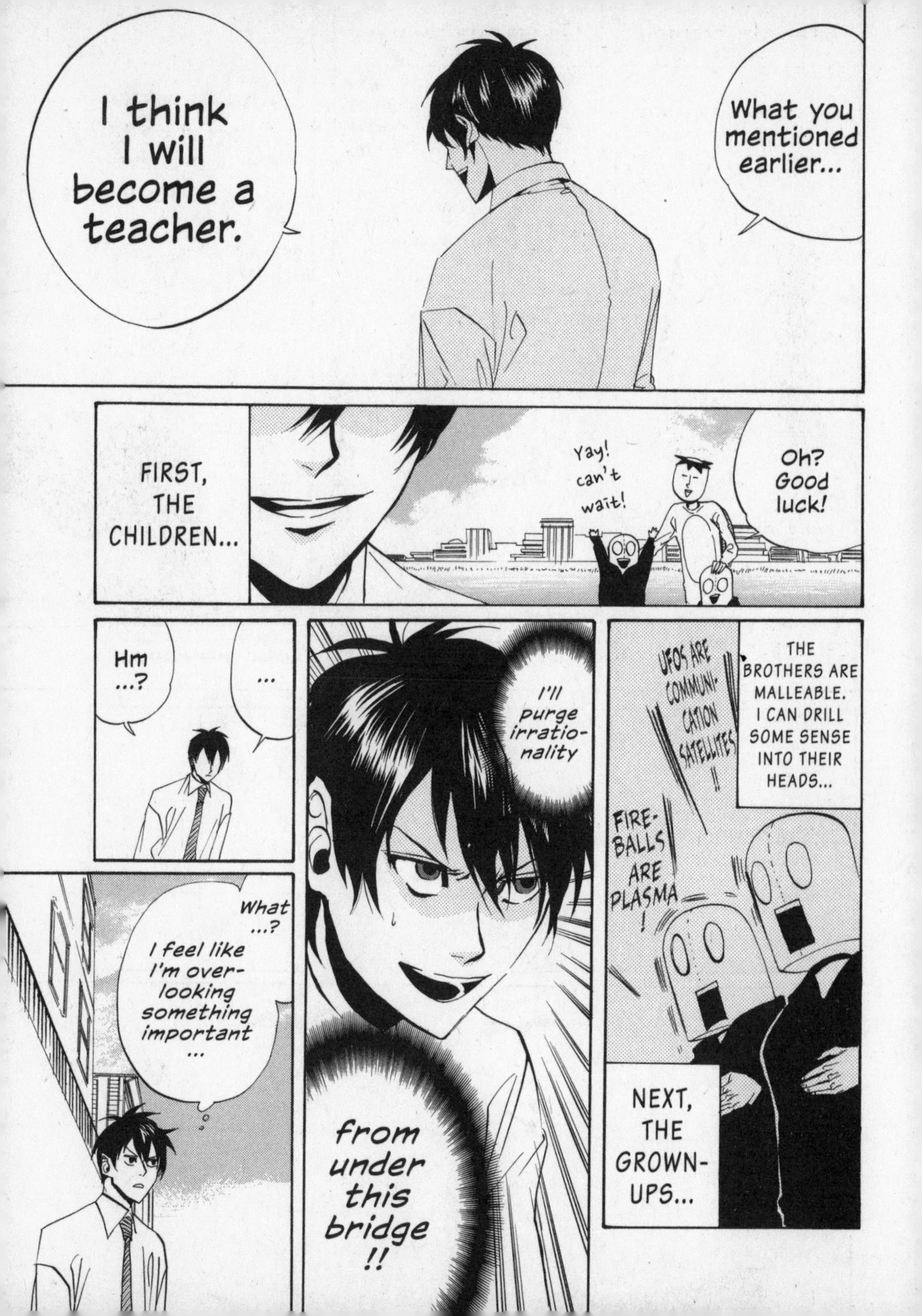
What you mentioned earlier...
I think I will become a teacher.
Oh? Good luck!
Yay! can't wait!
FIRST, THE CHILDREN...
THE BROTHERS ARE MALLEABLE. I CAN DRILL SOME SENSE INTO THEIR HEADS...
UFOS ARE COMMUNICATION SATELLITES!!
FIRE-BALLS ARE PLASMA!
NEXT, THE GROWN-UPS...
I'll purge irrationality
from under this bridge!!
...
Hm...?
What...? I feel like I'm over-looking something important...

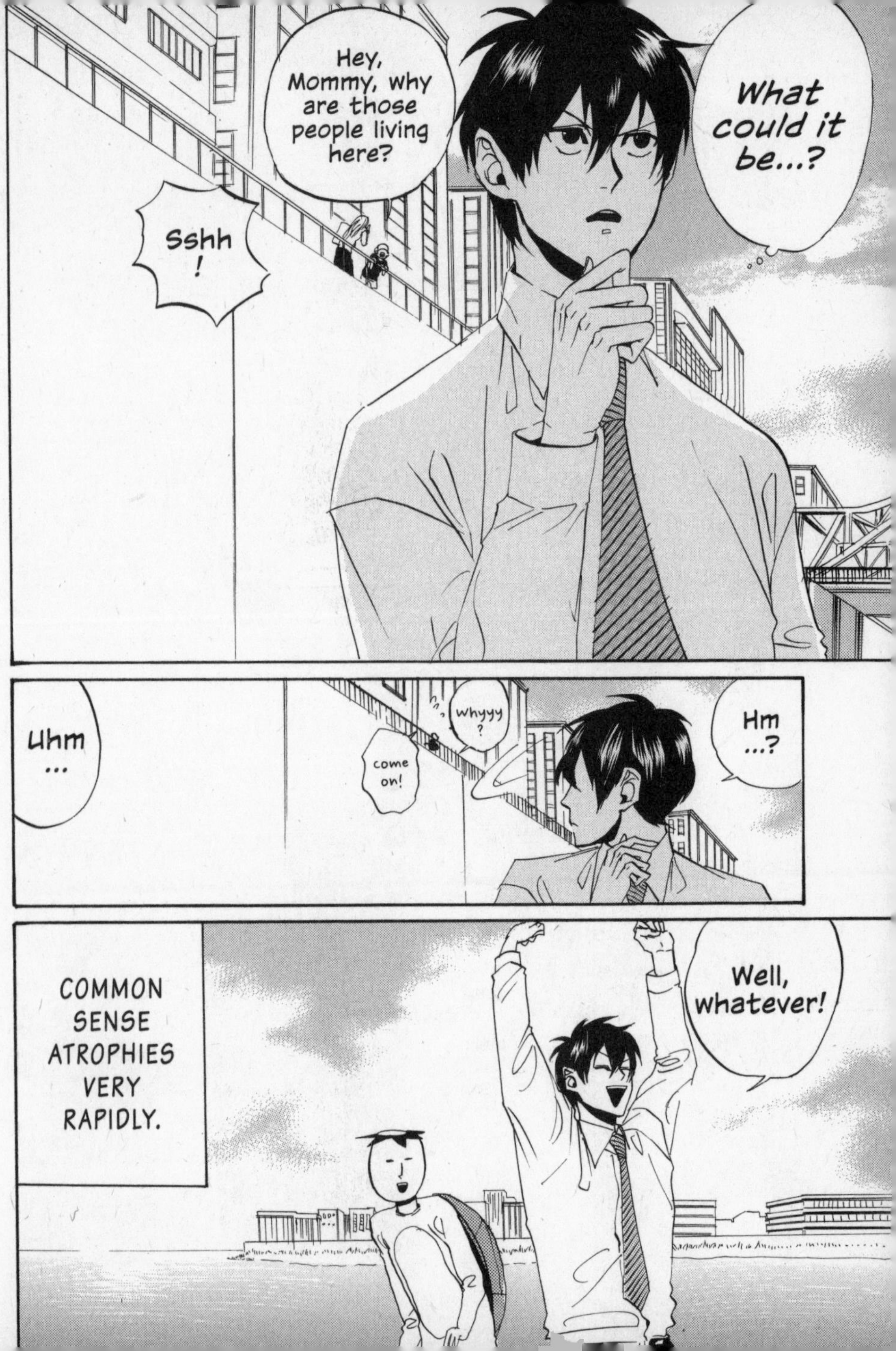
What could it be...?
Hey, Mommy, why are those people living here?
Sshh!
Hm...?
whyyy?
come on!
Uhm...
Well, whatever!
COMMON SENSE ATROPHIES VERY RAPIDLY.

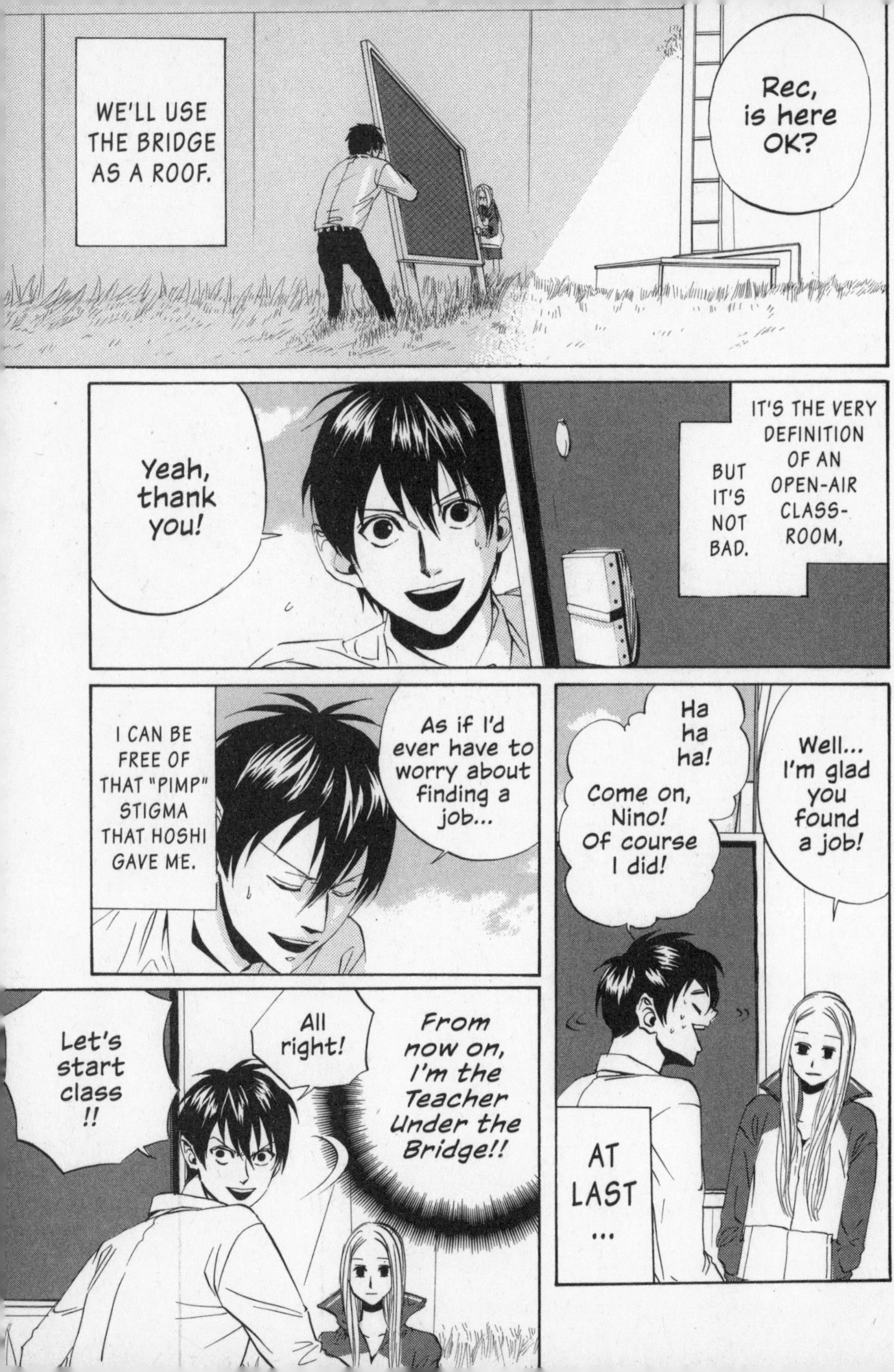
Rec, is here OK?
WE'LL USE THE BRIDGE AS A ROOF.
IT'S THE VERY DEFINITION OF AN OPEN-AIR CLASS-ROOM,
BUT IT'S NOT BAD.
Yeah, thank you!
Well... I'm glad you found a job!
Ha ha ha!
Come on, Nino! Of course I did!
AT LAST ...
As if I'd ever have to worry about finding a job...
I CAN BE FREE OF THAT "PIMP" STIGMA THAT HOSHI GAVE ME.
From now on, I'm the Teacher Under the Bridge!!
All right!
Let's start class !!

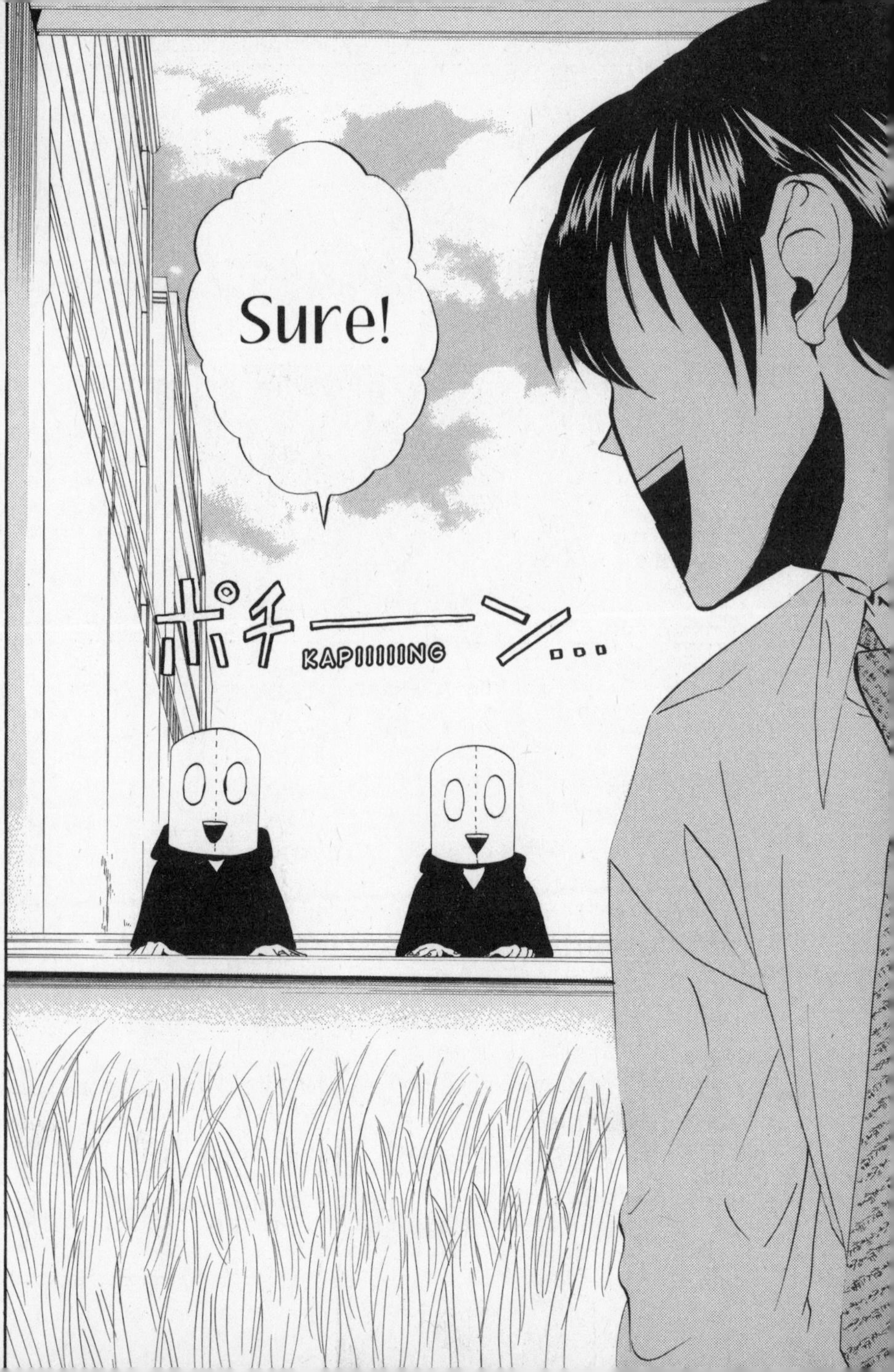
Sure!
ポチーーーン…
KAPIIIIIING

Chapter 57: Teacher Under the Bridge

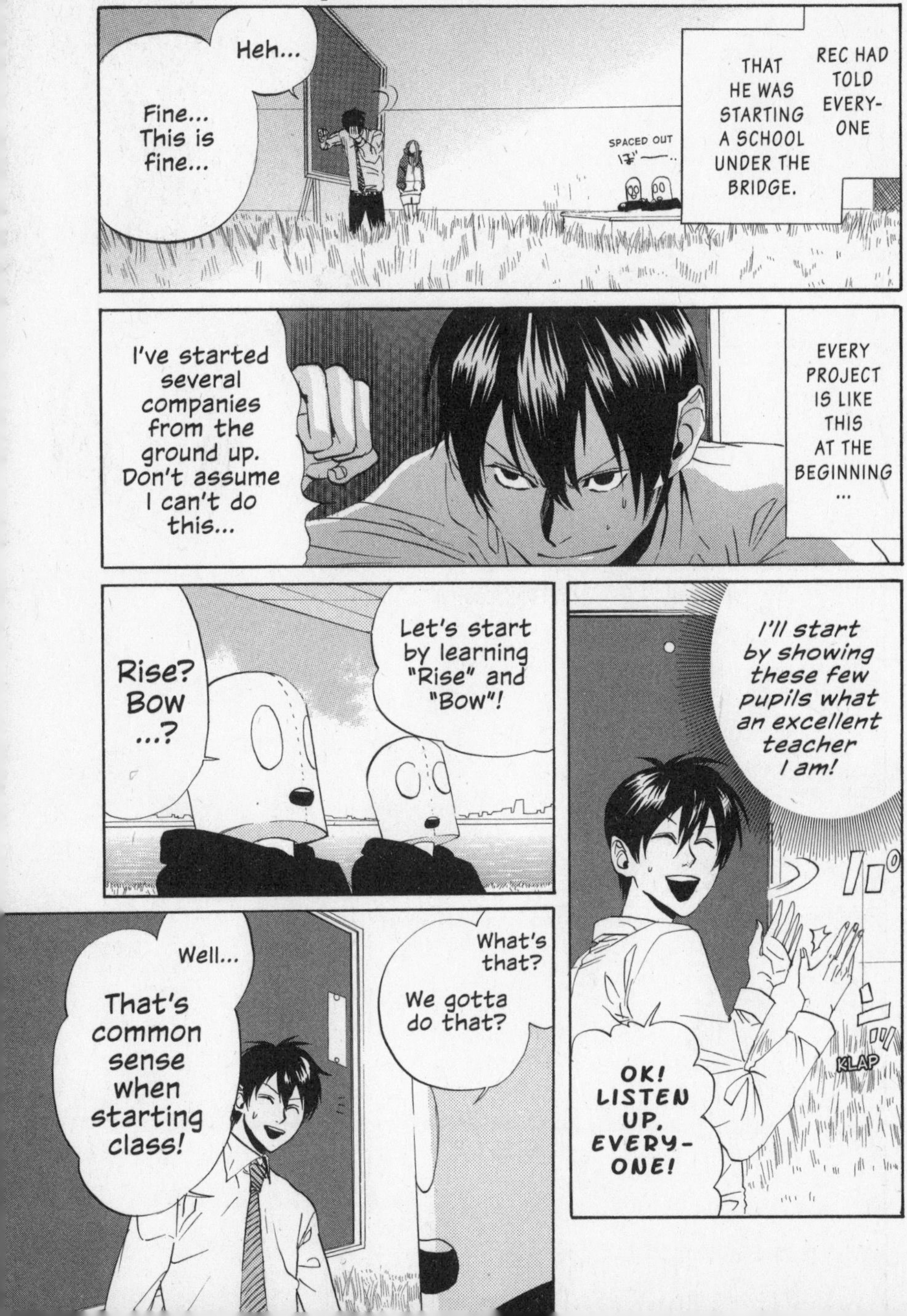
REC HAD TOLD EVERY-ONE
THAT HE WAS STARTING A SCHOOL UNDER THE BRIDGE.
SPACED OUT
Heh...
Fine... This is fine...
EVERY PROJECT IS LIKE THIS AT THE BEGINNING ...
I've started several companies from the ground up. Don't assume I can't do this...
I'll start by showing these few pupils what an excellent teacher I am!
KLAP
OK! LISTEN UP, EVERY-ONE!
Let's start by learning "Rise" and "Bow"!
Rise? Bow ...?
What's that?
We gotta do that?
Well...
That's common sense when starting class!

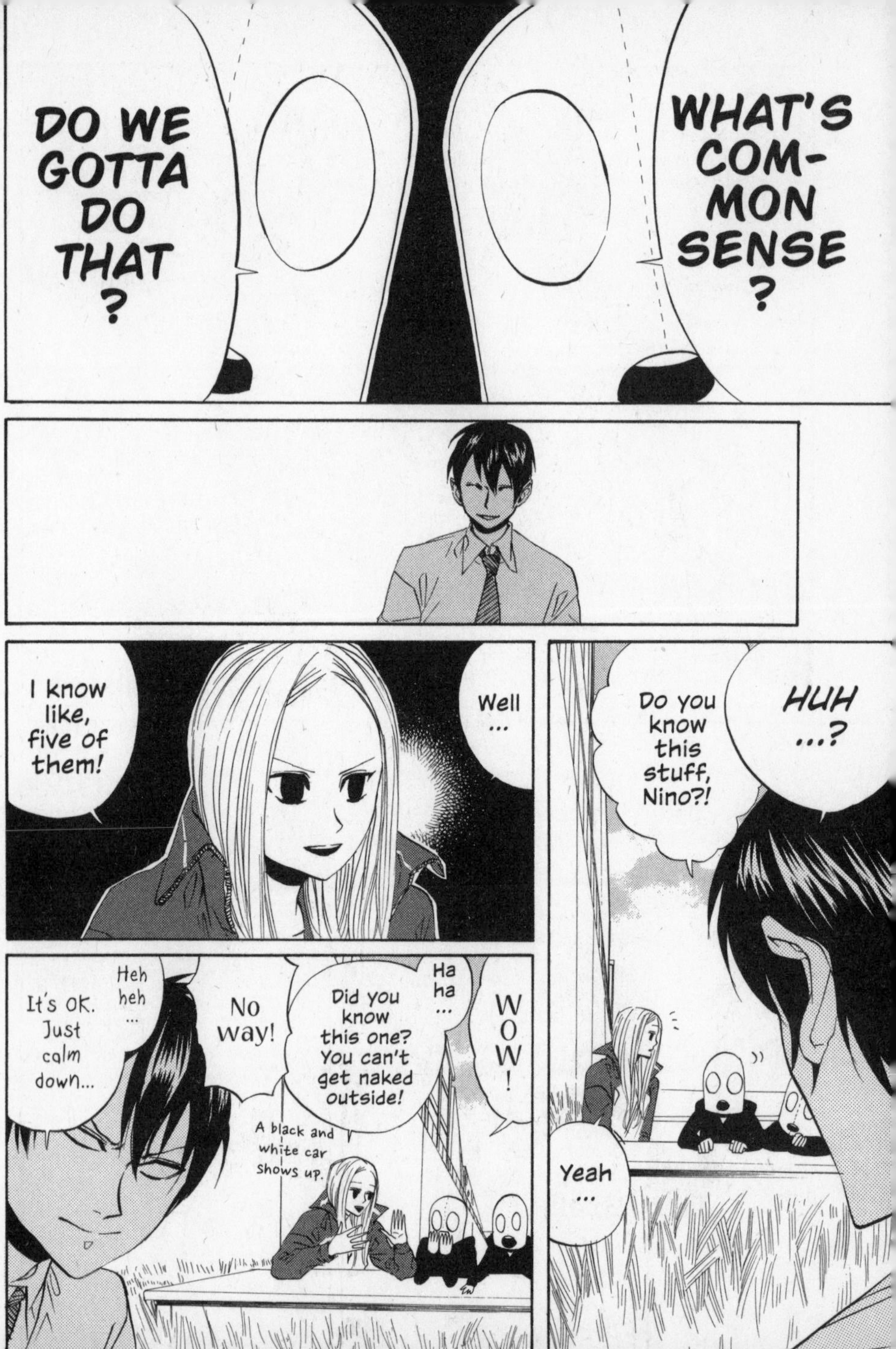
WHAT'S COM-MON SENSE ?
DO WE GOTTA DO THAT ?
HUH ...?
Do you know this stuff, Nino?!
Yeah ...
Well ...
I know like, five of them!
WOW!
Ha ha ...
Did you know this one? You can't get naked outside!
A black and white car shows up.
No way!
Heh heh ...
It's OK. Just calm down...

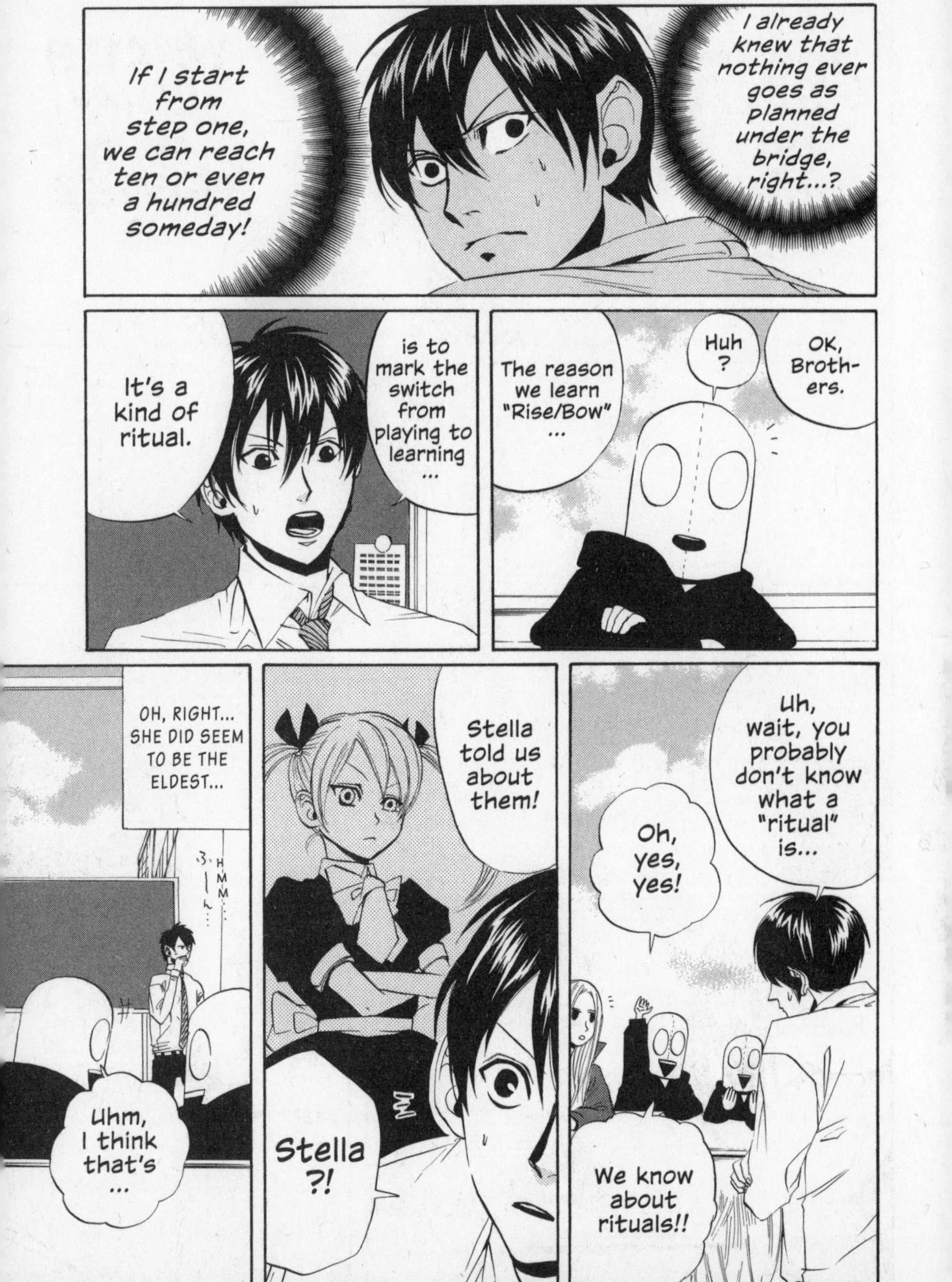

I already knew that nothing ever goes as planned under the bridge, right...?
If I start from step one, we can reach ten or even a hundred someday!
OK, Broth-ers.
Huh ?
The reason we learn "Rise/Bow" ...
is to mark the switch from playing to learning ...
It's a kind of ritual.
Uh, wait, you probably don't know what a "ritual" is...
Oh, yes, yes!
We know about rituals!!
Stella told us about them!
Stella ?!
OH, RIGHT... SHE DID SEEM TO BE THE ELDEST...
HMM...
Uhm, I think that's ...

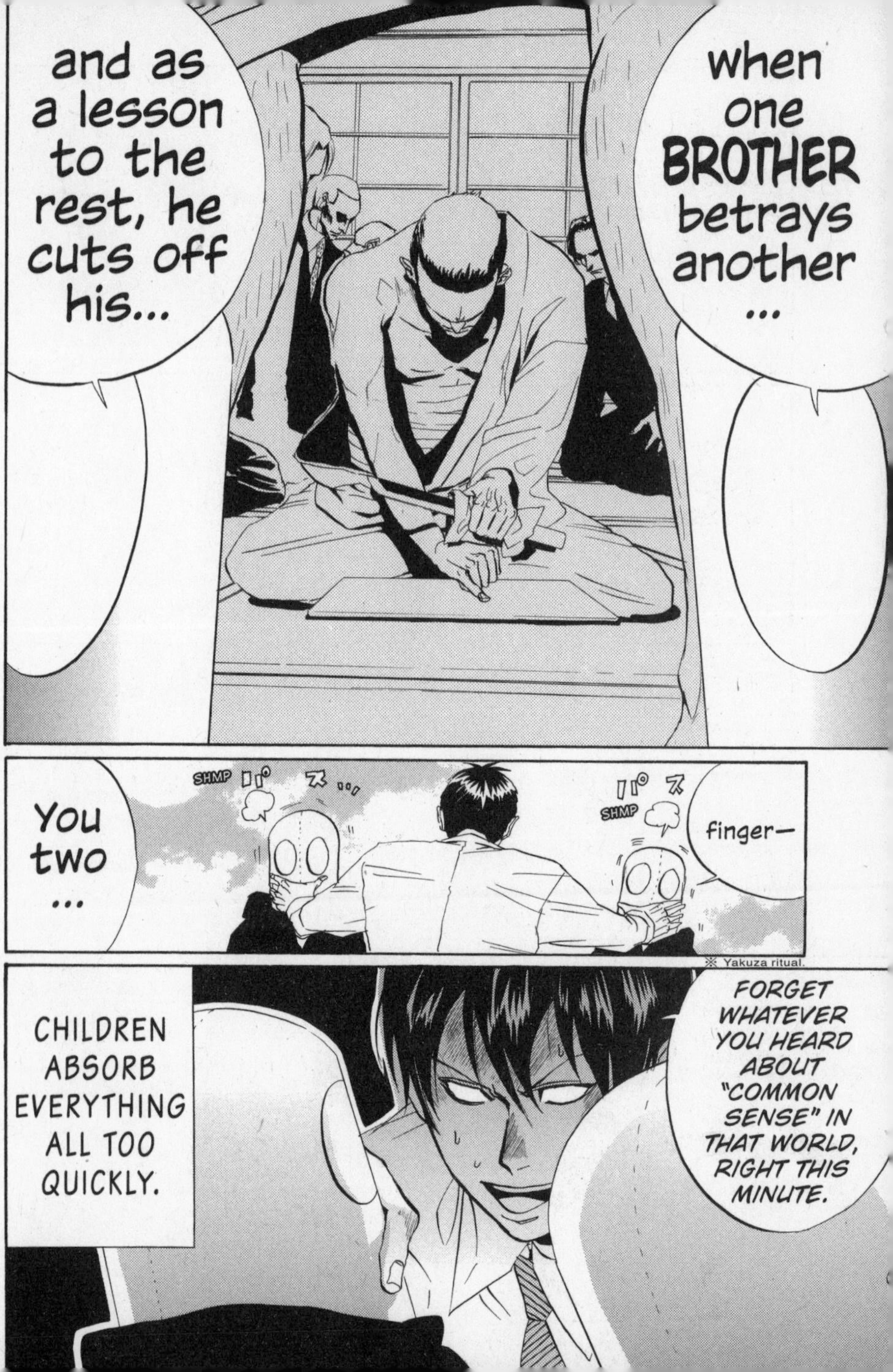
when one BROTHER betrays another ...
and as a lesson to the rest, he cuts off his...
finger—
SHMP
SHMP
You two ...
FORGET WHATEVER YOU HEARD ABOUT "COMMON SENSE" IN THAT WORLD, RIGHT THIS MINUTE.
CHILDREN ABSORB EVERYTHING ALL TOO QUICKLY.

※ Yakuza ritual.

Chapter 58: Interest

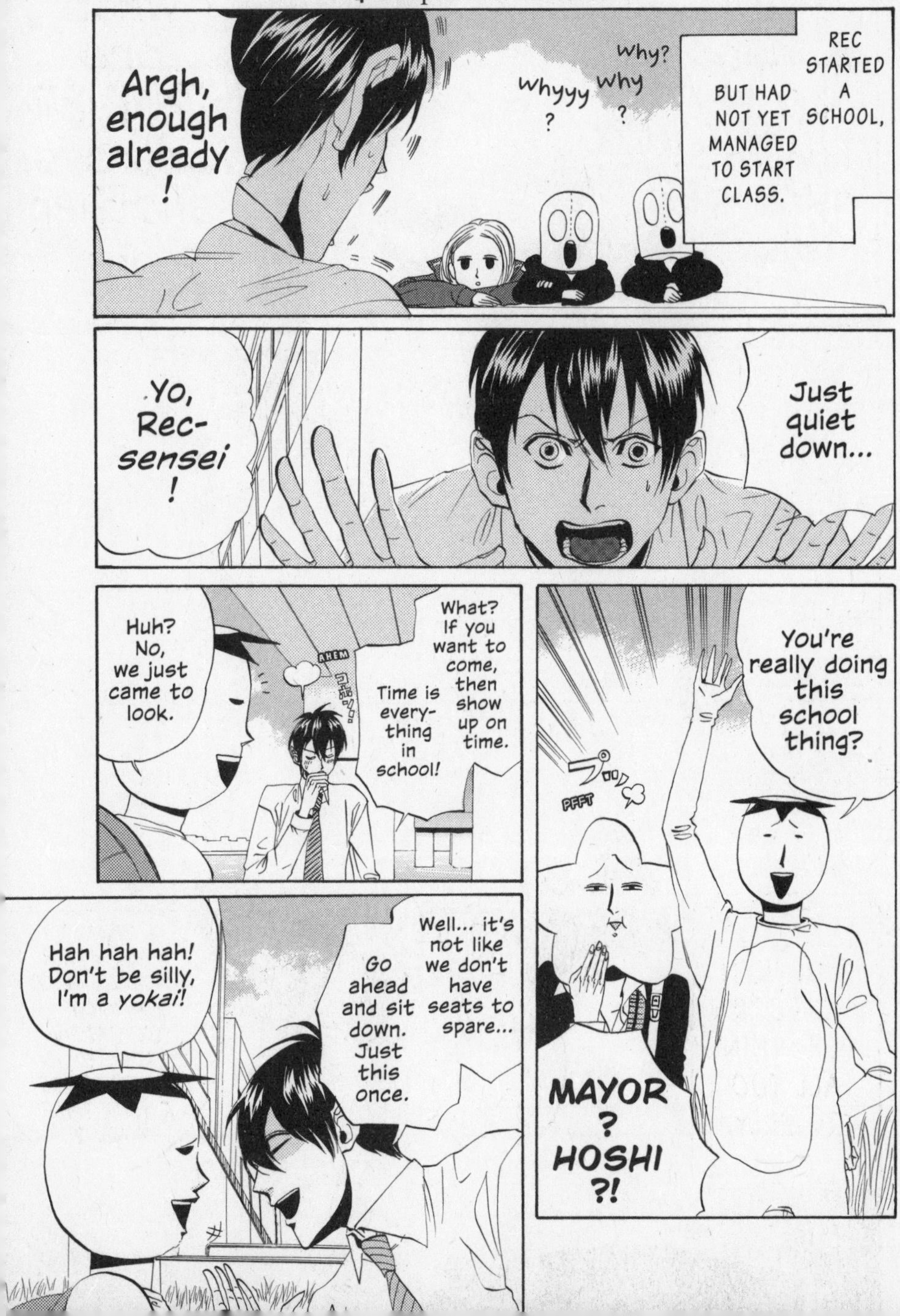
REC STARTED A SCHOOL, BUT HAD NOT YET MANAGED TO START CLASS.
Why? Why?
Whyyy?
Argh, enough already!
Just quiet down...
Yo, Rec-sensei!
You're really doing this school thing?
PFFT
MAYOR? HOSHI?!
What? If you want to come, then show up on time.
Time is everything in school!
AHEM
Huh? No, we just came to look.
Well... it's not like we don't have seats to spare...
Go ahead and sit down. Just this once.
Hah hah hah! Don't be silly, I'm a *yokai*!

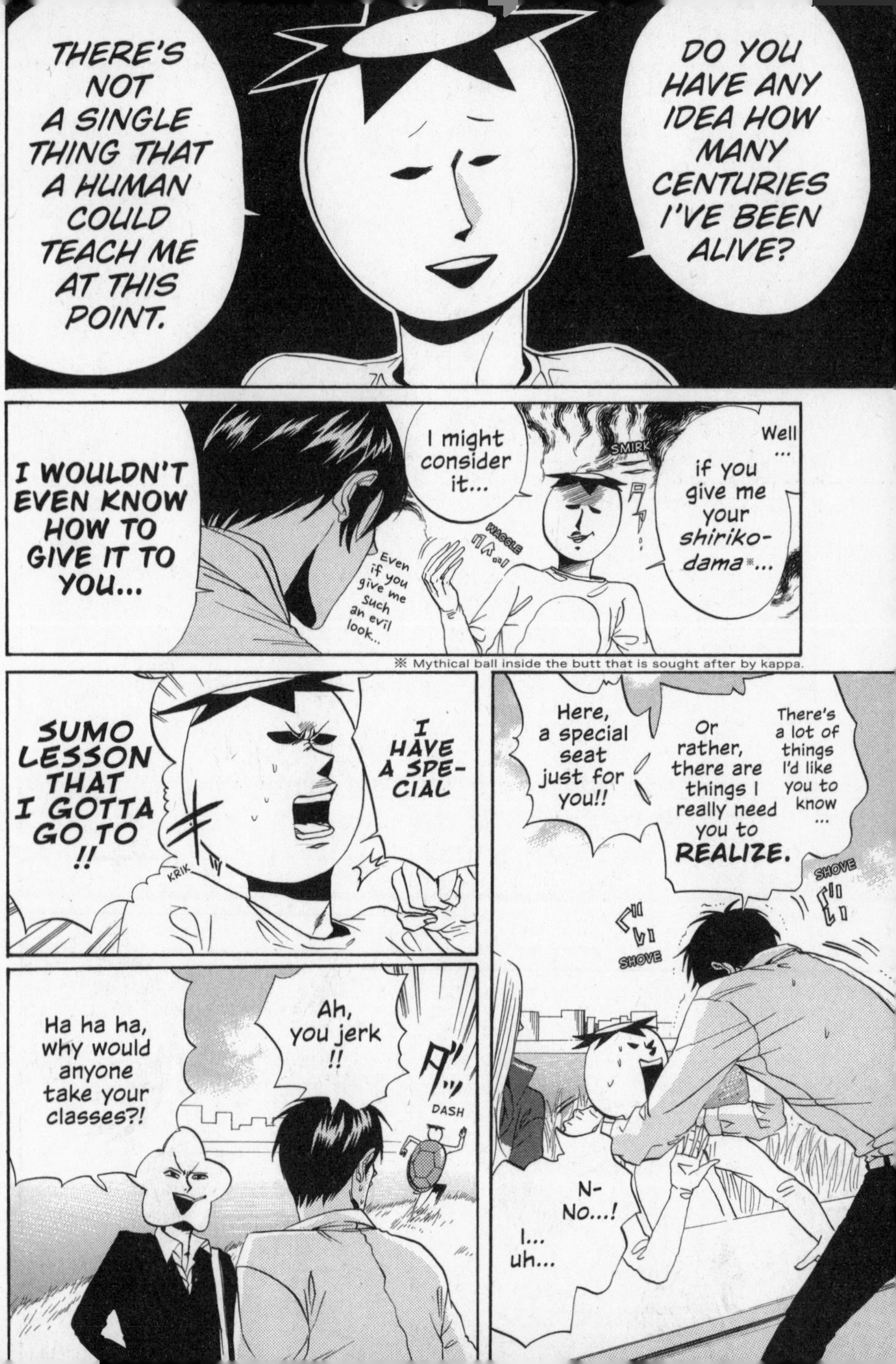
DO YOU HAVE ANY IDEA HOW MANY CENTURIES I'VE BEEN ALIVE?
THERE'S NOT A SINGLE THING THAT A HUMAN COULD TEACH ME AT THIS POINT.
Well ... if you give me your shiriko-dama※...
SMIRK
I might consider it...
WAGGLE
Even if you give me such an evil look...
I WOULDN'T EVEN KNOW HOW TO GIVE IT TO YOU...
There's a lot of things I'd like you to know ...
Or rather, there are things I really need you to **REALIZE.**
Here, a special seat just for you!!
SHOVE
SHOVE
N- No...!
I... uh...
I HAVE A SPECIAL
SUMO LESSON THAT I GOTTA GO TO !!
KRIK
Ah, you jerk !!
DASH
Ha ha ha, why would anyone take your classes?!

※ Mythical ball inside the butt that is sought after by kappa.

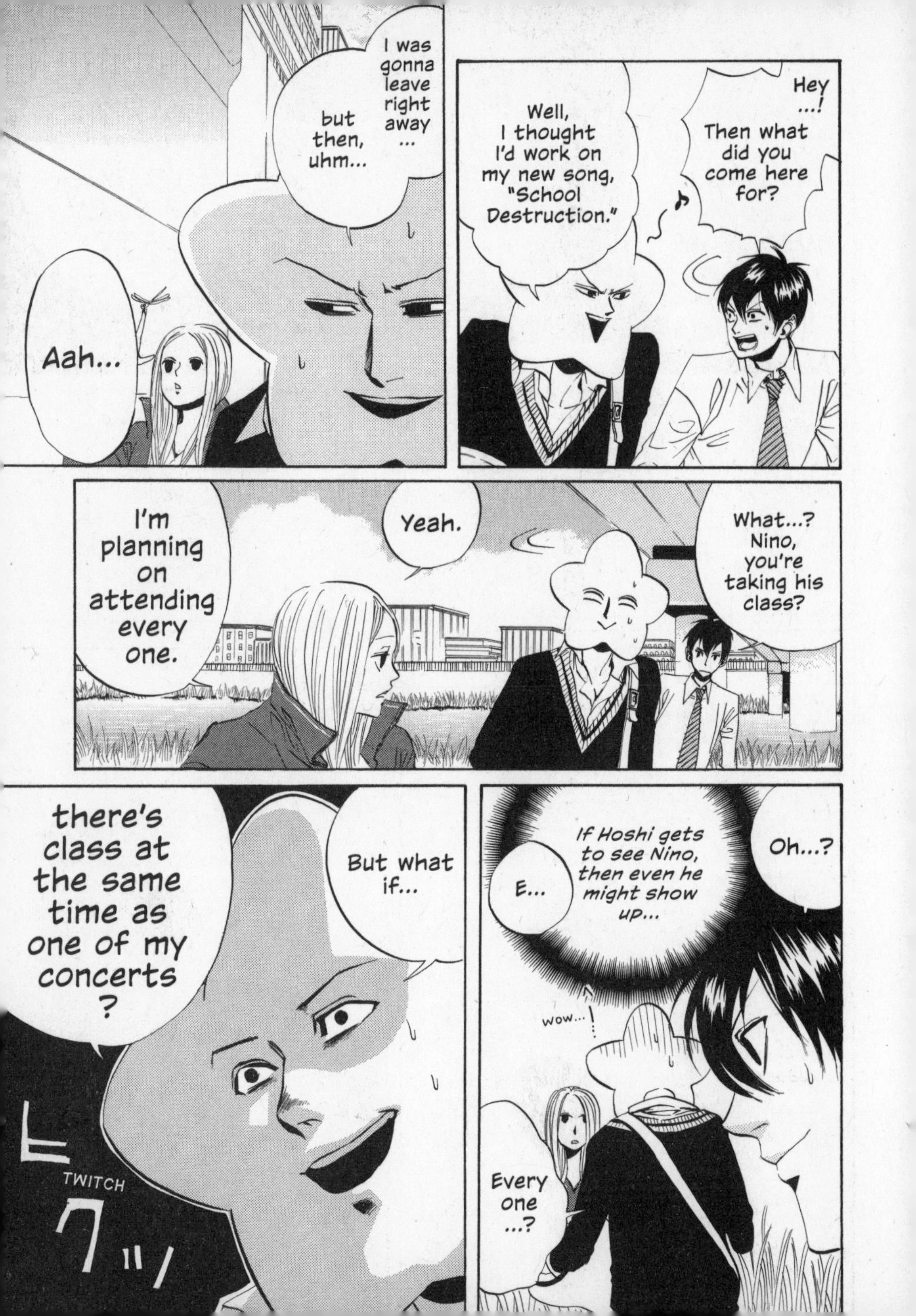
Hey ...! Then what did you come here for?
Well, I thought I'd work on my new song, "School Destruction."
I was gonna leave right away ... but then, uhm...
Aah...
What...? Nino, you're taking his class?
Yeah.
I'm planning on attending every one.
Oh...?
If Hoshi gets to see Nino, then even he might show up...
E...
wow...!
Every one ...?
But what if...
there's class at the same time as one of my concerts ?
TWITCH

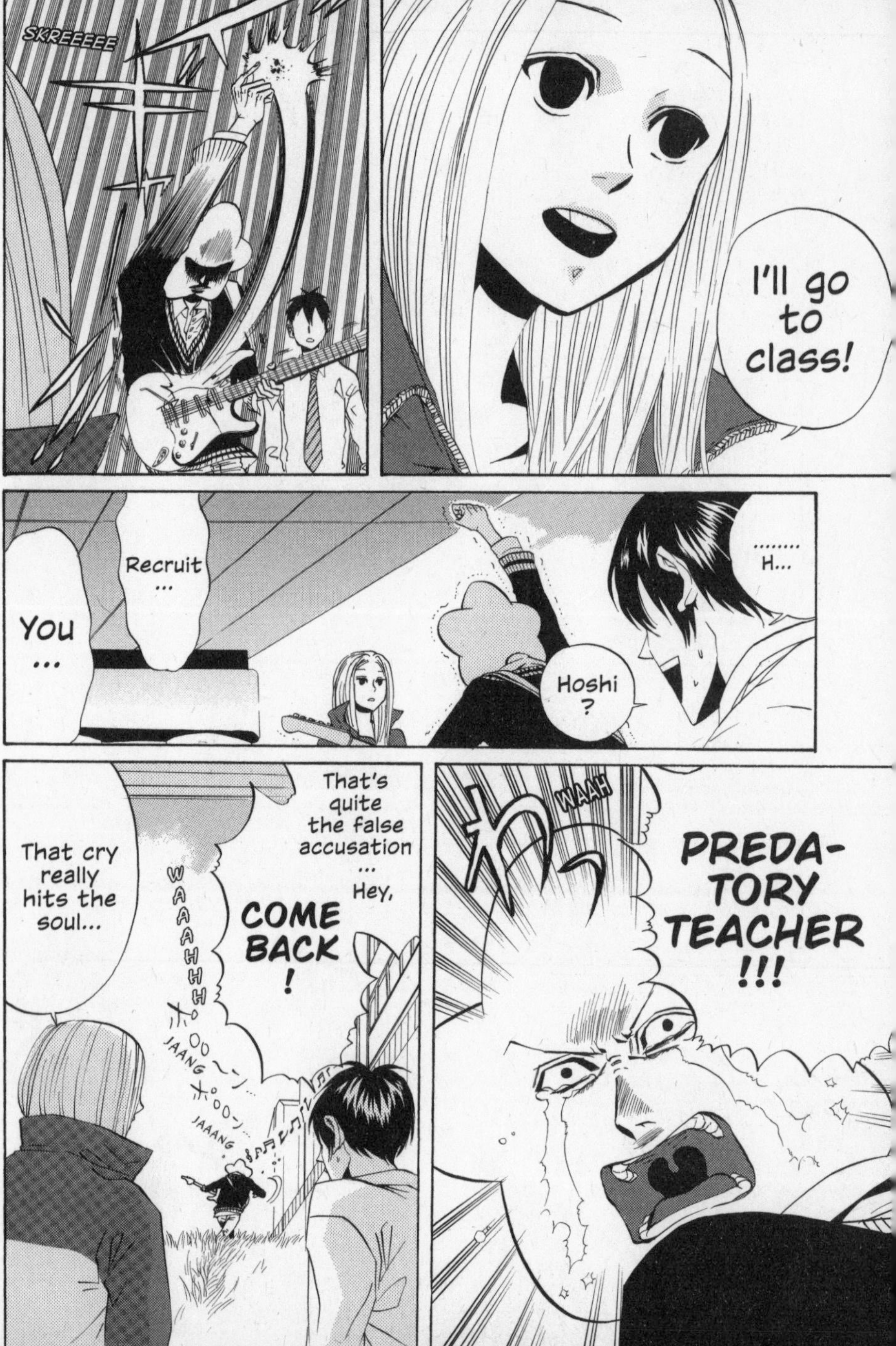
I'll go to class!
SKREEEEE
.... H...
Hoshi ?
Recruit ...
You ...
WAAH
PREDA-TORY TEACHER !!!
That's quite the false accusation ... Hey,
COME BACK !
WAAAAHHH
JAAANG
JAAANG
That cry really hits the soul...

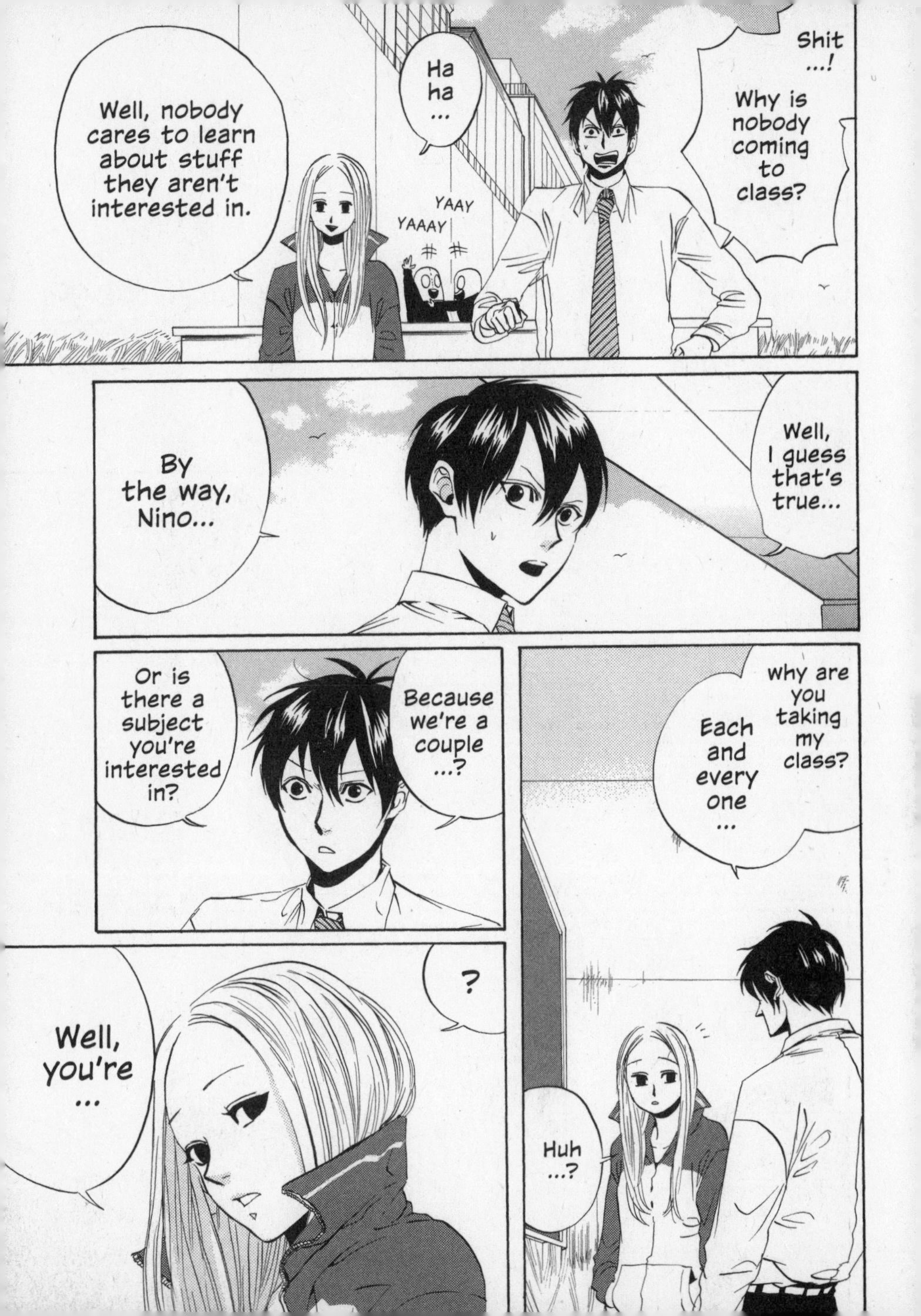
Shit ...!
Why is nobody coming to class?
Ha ha ...
YAAY
YAAAY
Well, nobody cares to learn about stuff they aren't interested in.
Well, I guess that's true...
By the way, Nino...
why are you taking my class?
Each and every one ...
Huh ...?
Because we're a couple ...?
Or is there a subject you're interested in?
?
Well, you're ...

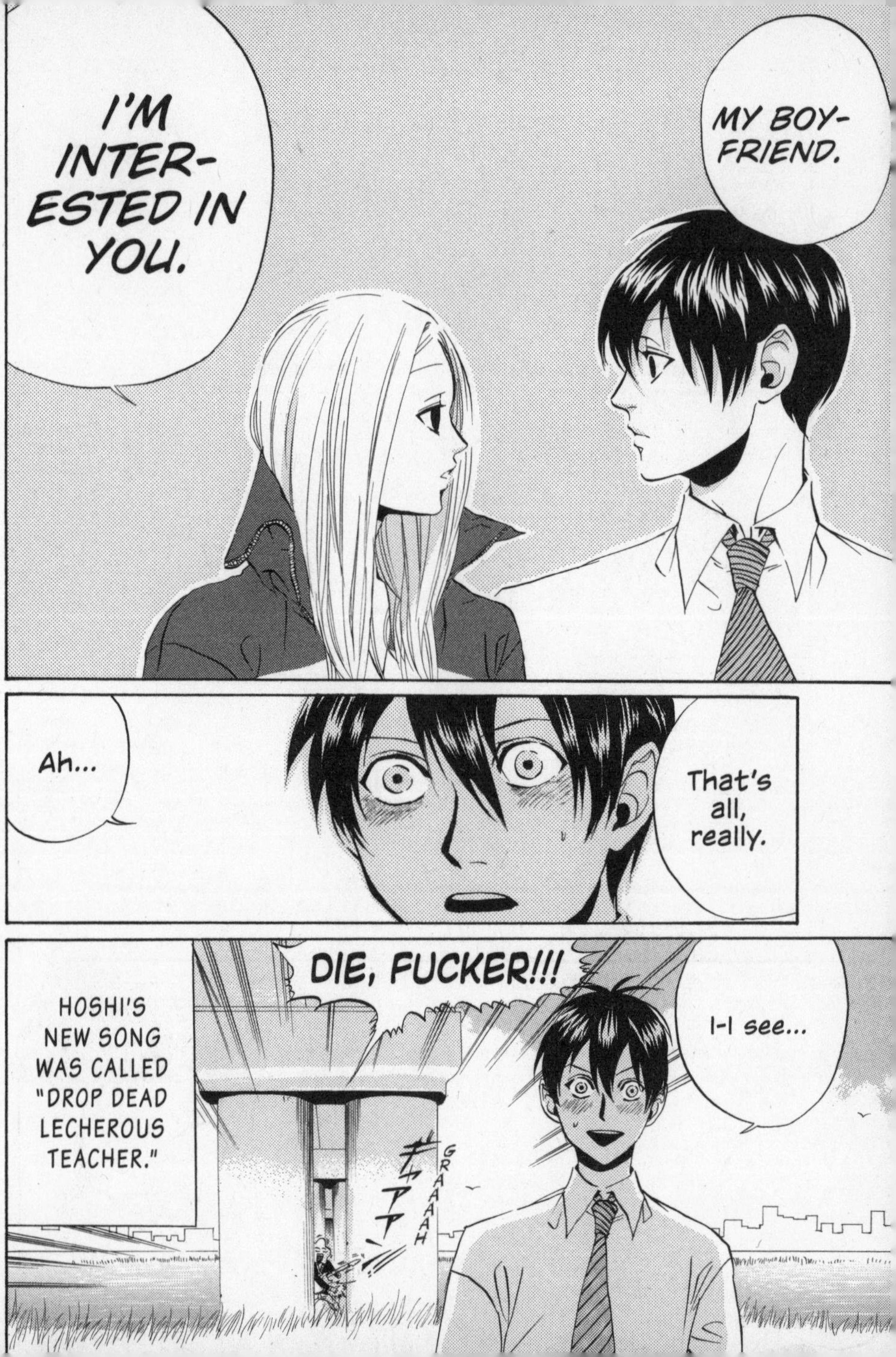
MY BOY-FRIEND.
I'M INTER-ESTED IN YOU.
That's all, really.
Ah...
I-I see...
DIE, FUCKER!!!
HOSHI'S NEW SONG WAS CALLED "DROP DEAD LECHEROUS TEACHER."
GRAAAAH

Chapter 59: Class Begins

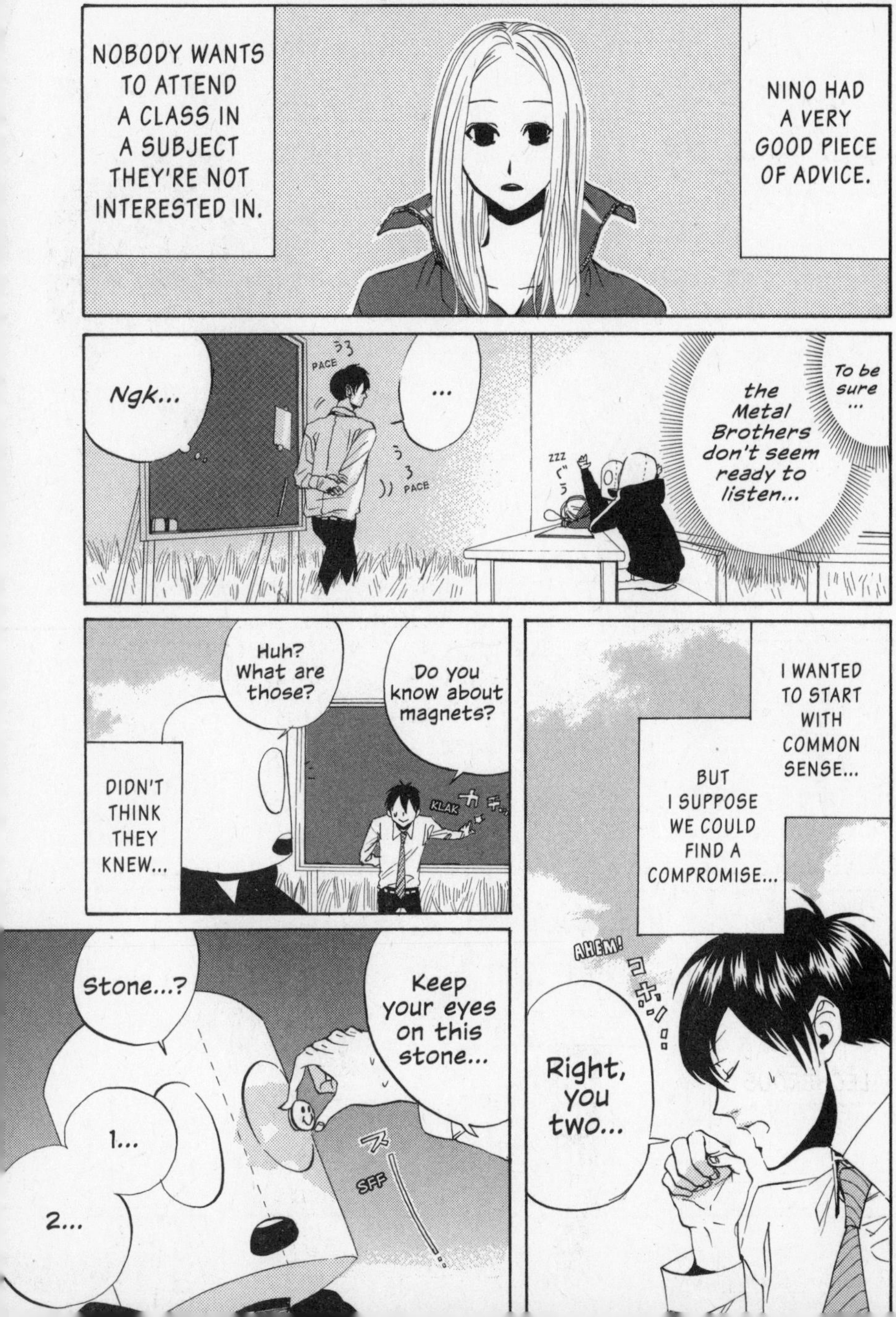

NINO HAD A VERY GOOD PIECE OF ADVICE.
NOBODY WANTS TO ATTEND A CLASS IN A SUBJECT THEY'RE NOT INTERESTED IN.
To be sure...
the Metal Brothers don't seem ready to listen...
ZZZ
...
PACE
Ngk...
PACE
I WANTED TO START WITH COMMON SENSE...
BUT I SUPPOSE WE COULD FIND A COMPROMISE...
Do you know about magnets?
Huh? What are those?
KLAK
DIDN'T THINK THEY KNEW...
AHEM!
Right, you two...
Keep your eyes on this stone...
Stone...?
SFF
1...
2...

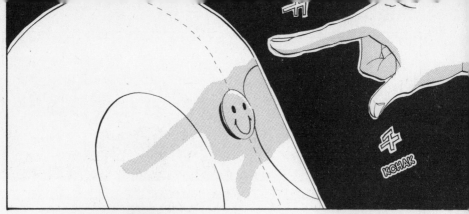

KCHAK

HOW MYSTE- RIOUS !

OH!

WOOOO OOOOW... !!!

...

THANK GOOD- NESS !!!

...

...W ...

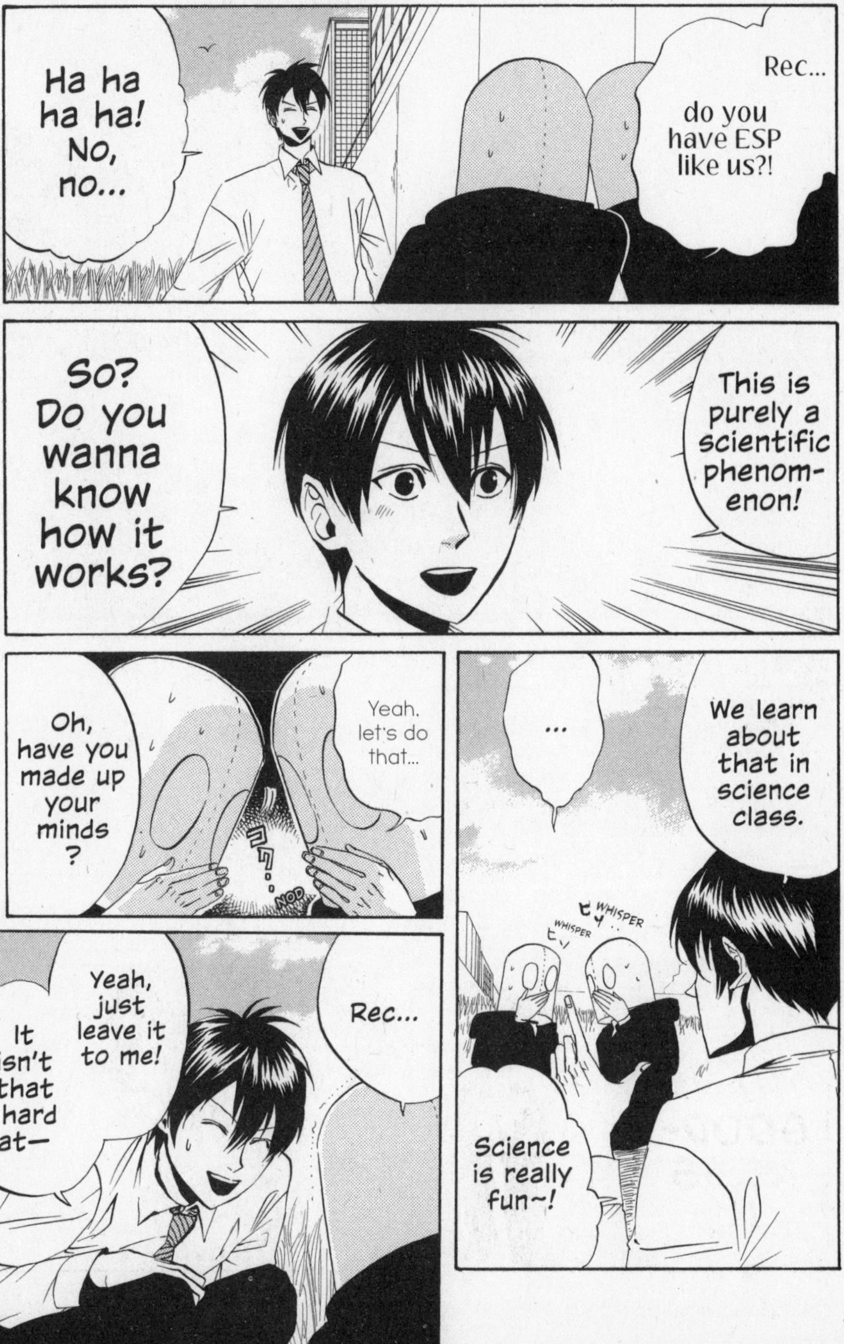
Rec...
do you have ESP like us?!
Ha ha ha ha! No, no...
This is purely a scientific phenom-enon!
So? Do you wanna know how it works?
We learn about that in science class.
...
ヒソ WHISPER
ヒソ WHISPER
Science is really fun~!
Yeah, let's do that...
Oh, have you made up your minds?
コク NOD
Rec...
Yeah, just leave it to me!
It isn't that hard at—

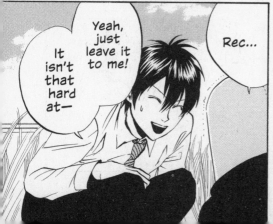

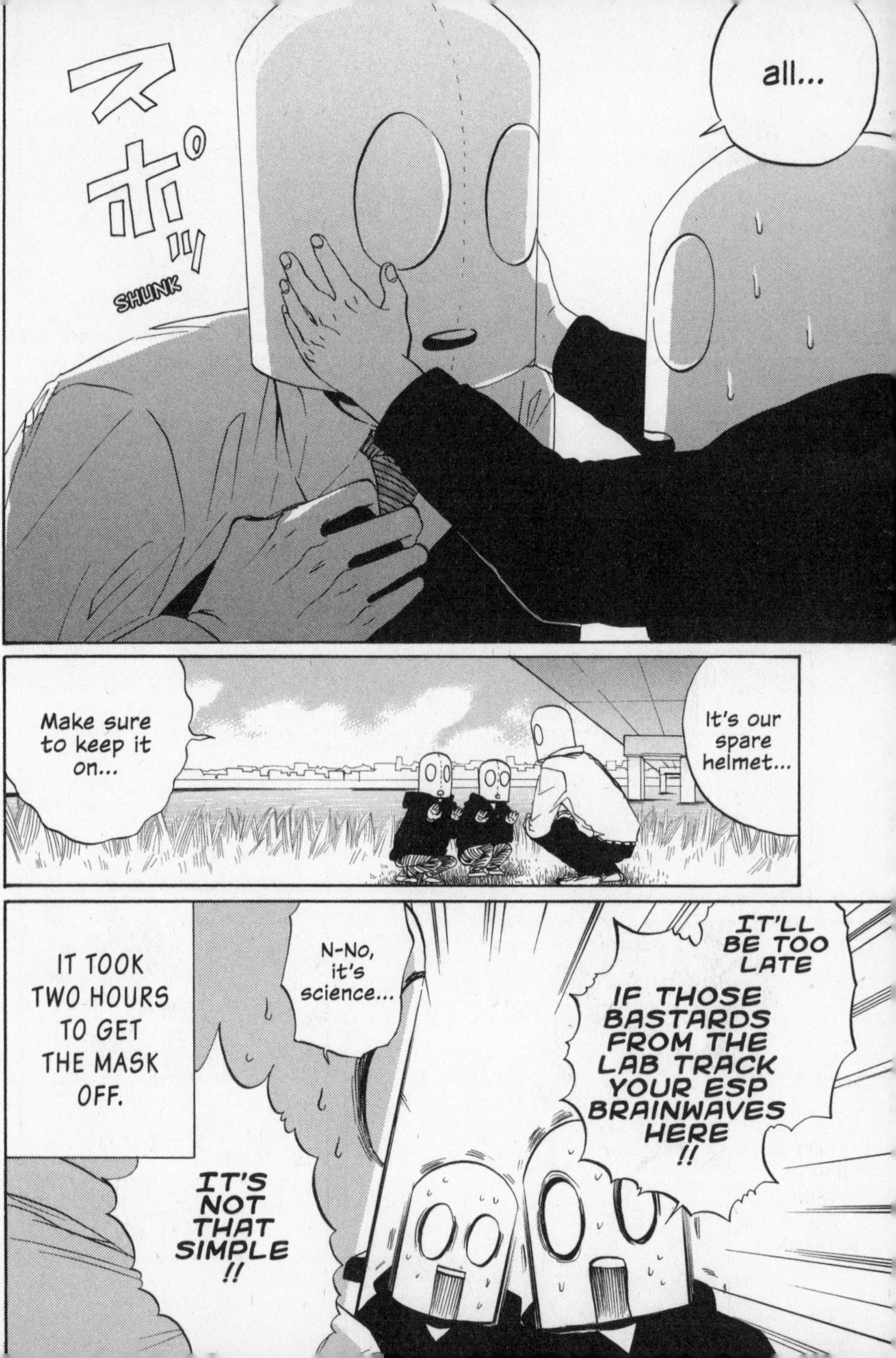
all...
スポッ
SHUNK
It's our spare helmet...
Make sure to keep it on...
IT'LL BE TOO LATE IF THOSE BASTARDS FROM THE LAB TRACK YOUR ESP BRAINWAVES HERE !!
N-No, it's science...
IT TOOK TWO HOURS TO GET THE MASK OFF.
IT'S NOT THAT SIMPLE !!

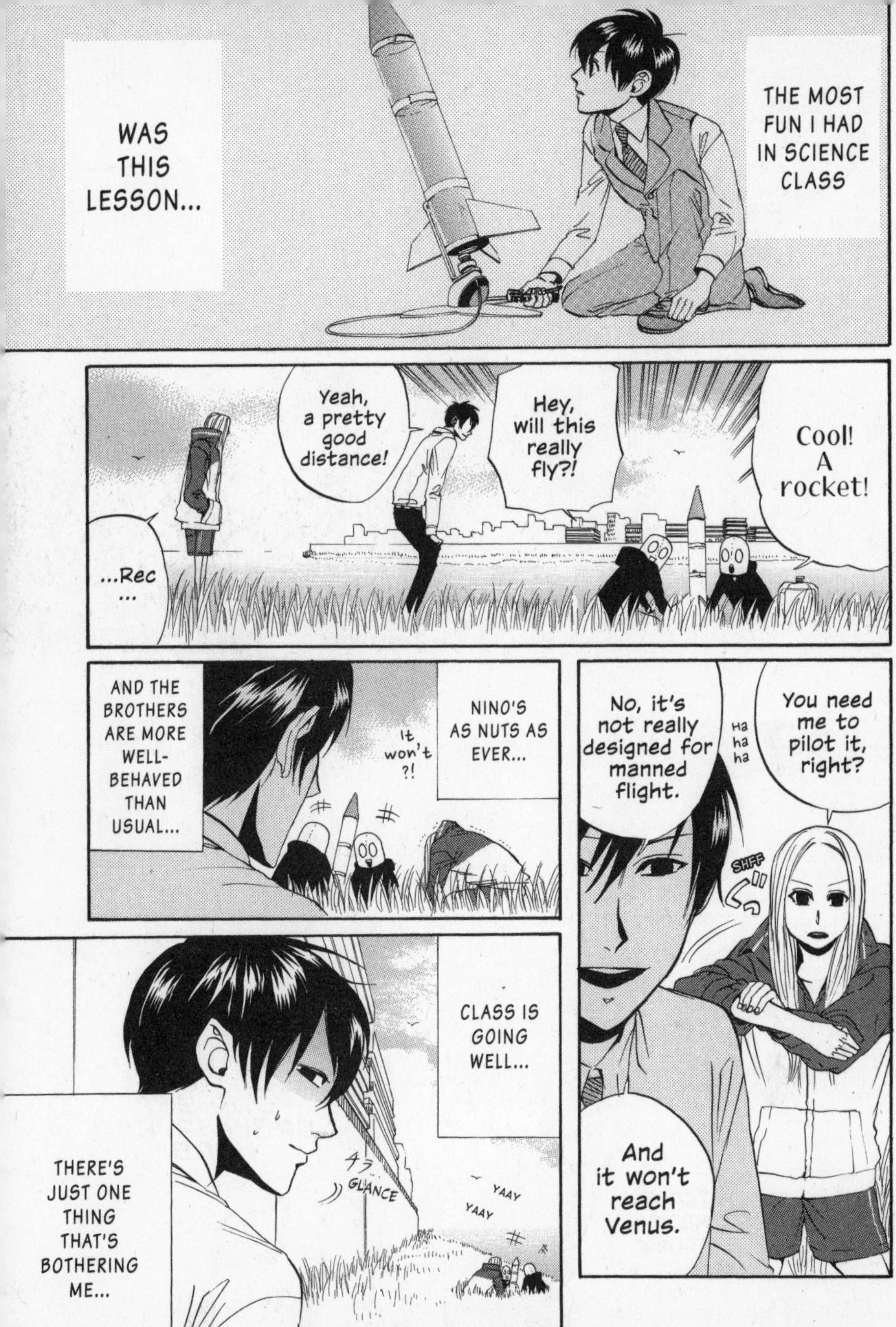
THE MOST FUN I HAD IN SCIENCE CLASS
WAS THIS LESSON...
Cool! A rocket!
Hey, will this really fly?!
Yeah, a pretty good distance!
...Rec ...
You need me to pilot it, right?
Ha ha ha
No, it's not really designed for manned flight.
SHFF
And it won't reach Venus.
NINO'S AS NUTS AS EVER...
It won't?!
AND THE BROTHERS ARE MORE WELL-BEHAVED THAN USUAL...
CLASS IS GOING WELL...
YAAY
YAAY
GLANCE
THERE'S JUST ONE THING THAT'S BOTHERING ME...

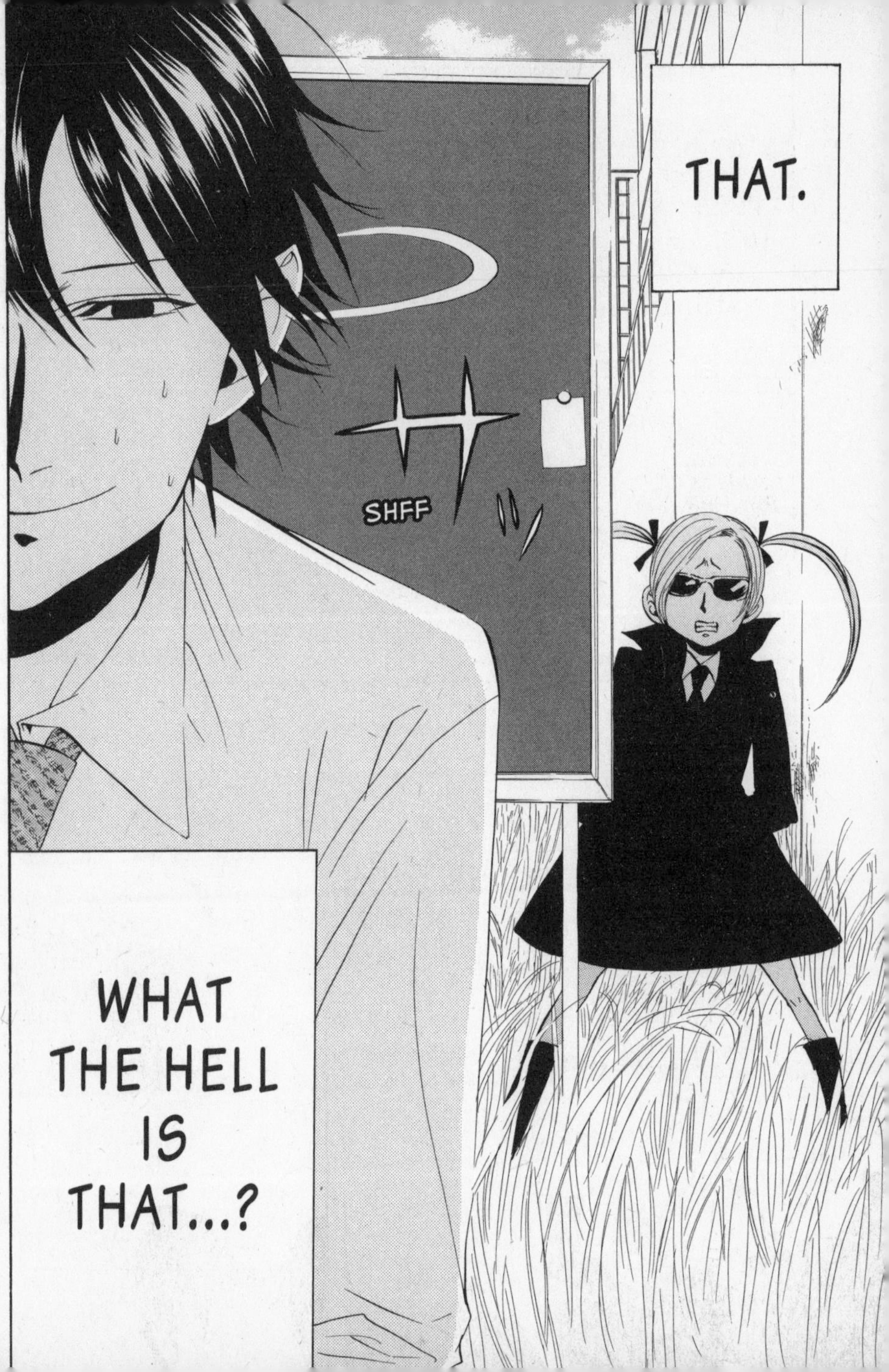
THAT.
SHFF
WHAT THE HELL IS THAT...?

Chapter 60: Territory

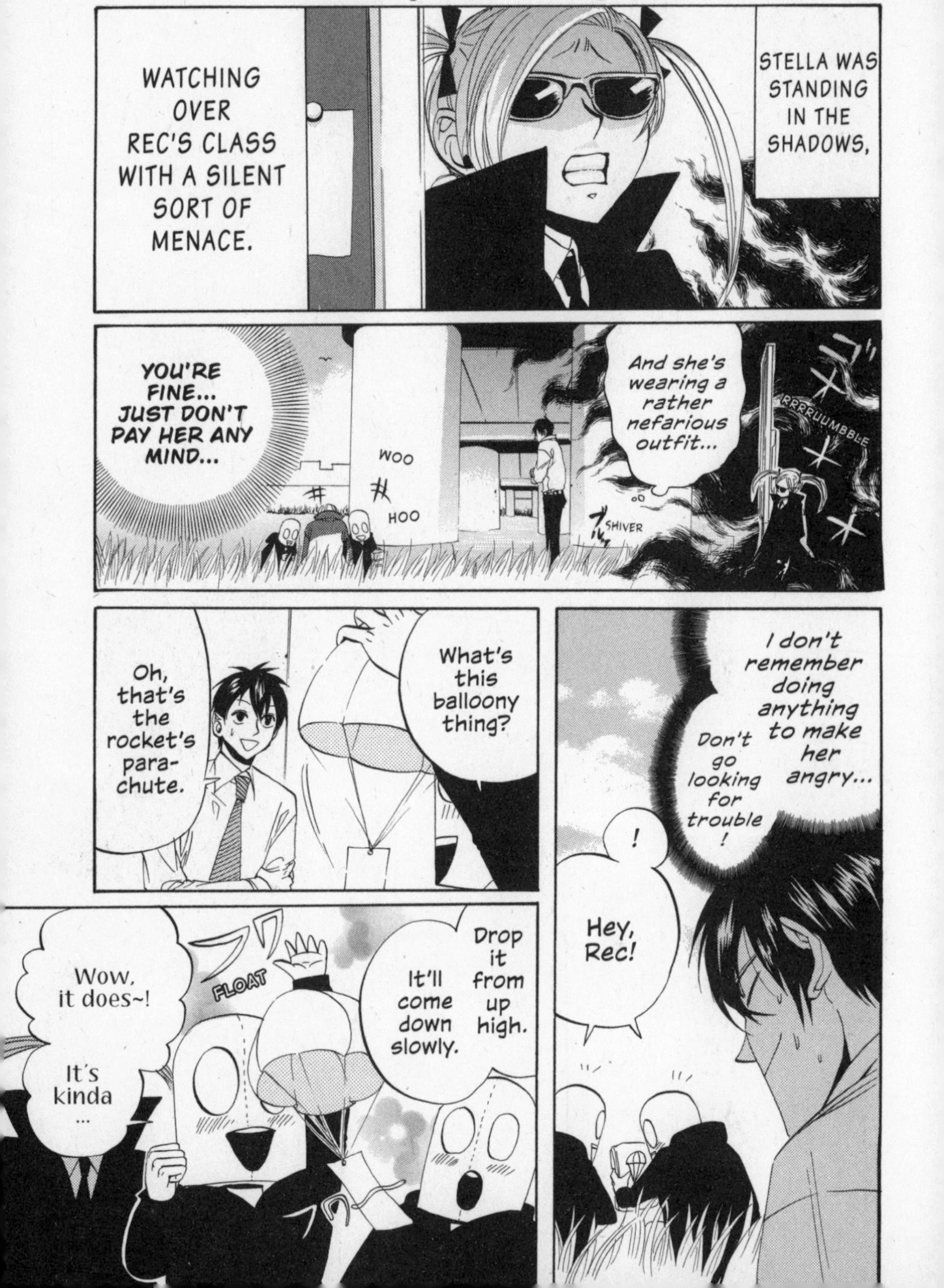
STELLA WAS STANDING IN THE SHADOWS,
WATCHING OVER REC'S CLASS WITH A SILENT SORT OF MENACE.
RRRRUUMBBLE
And she's wearing a rather nefarious outfit...
SHIVER
WOO
HOO
YOU'RE FINE... JUST DON'T PAY HER ANY MIND...
I don't remember doing anything to make her angry...
Don't go looking for trouble!
!
Hey, Rec!
What's this balloony thing?
Oh, that's the rocket's parachute.
Drop it from up high.
It'll come down slowly.
FLOAT
Wow, it does~!
It's kinda ...

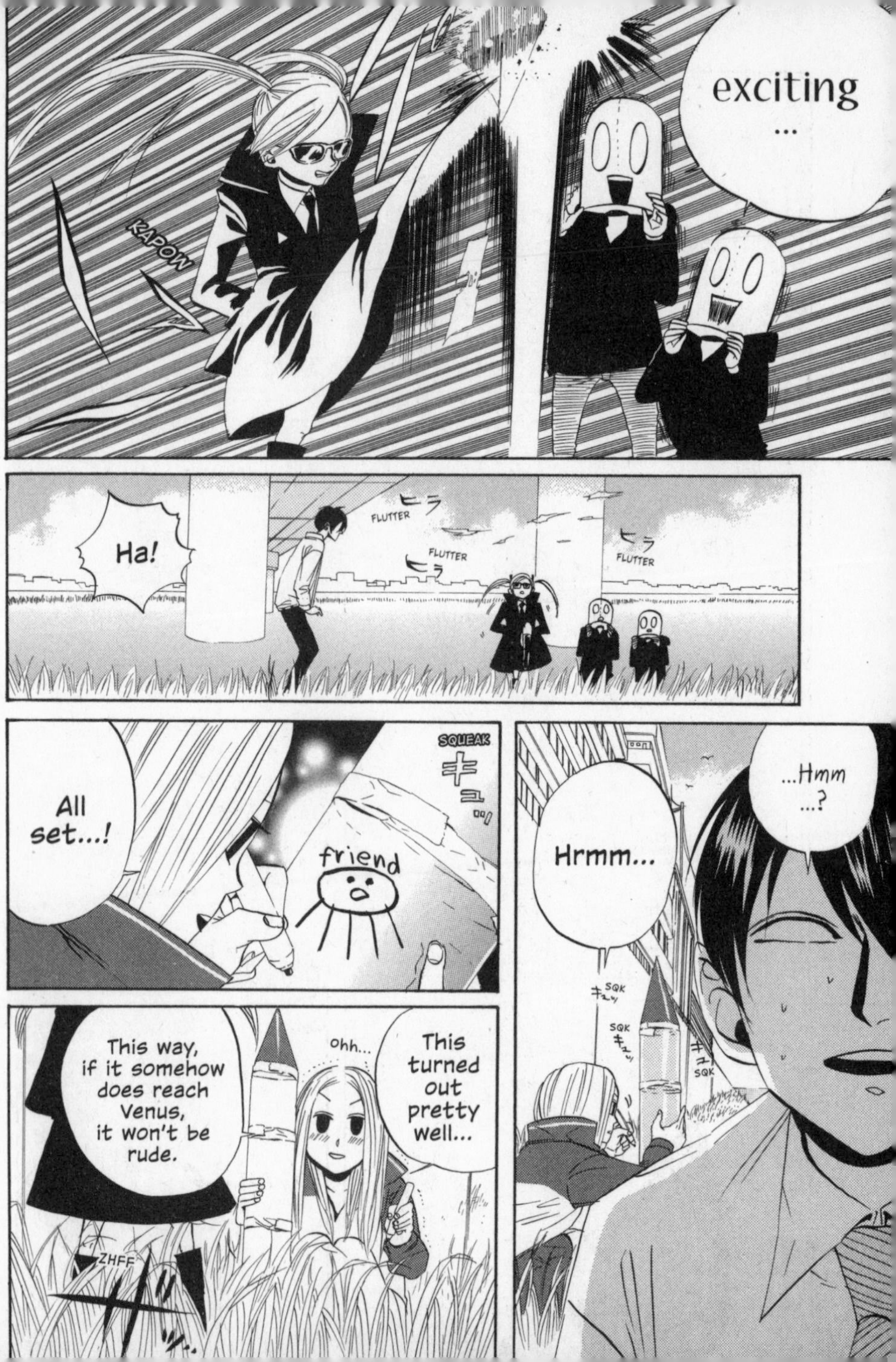
exciting ...
KAPOW
FLUTTER
FLUTTER
FLUTTER
Ha!
...Hmm ...?
Hrmm...
SQK
SQK
SQK
SQUEAK
friend
All set...!
This turned out pretty well...
Ohh...
This way, if it somehow does reach Venus, it won't be rude.
ZHFF

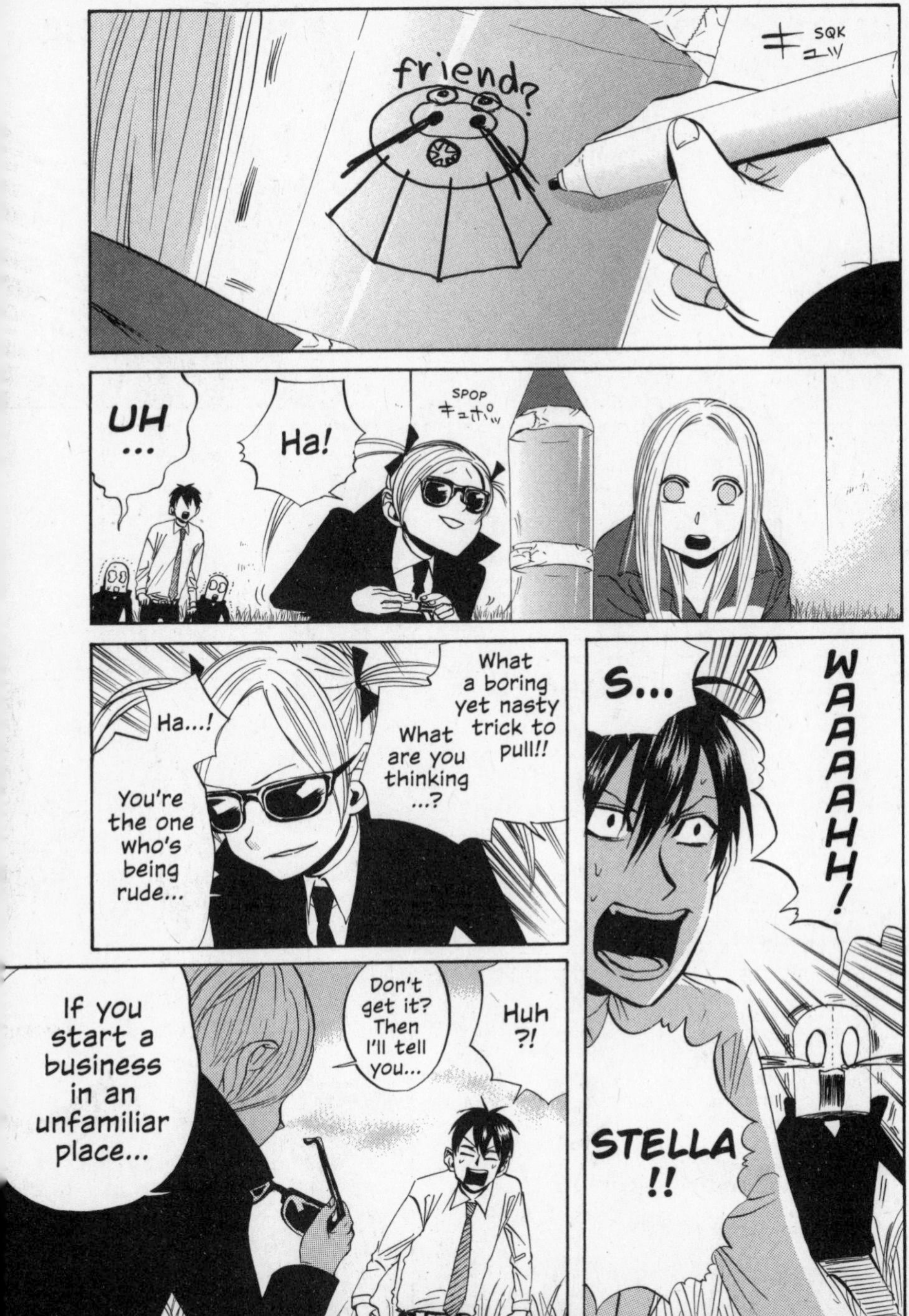
SQK
キュッ
friend?
SPOP
キュポッ
Ha!
UH ...
S...
WAAAAAHH!
STELLA !!
What a boring yet nasty trick to pull!!
What are you thinking ...?
Ha...!
You're the one who's being rude...
Huh ?!
Don't get it? Then I'll tell you...
If you start a business in an unfamiliar place...

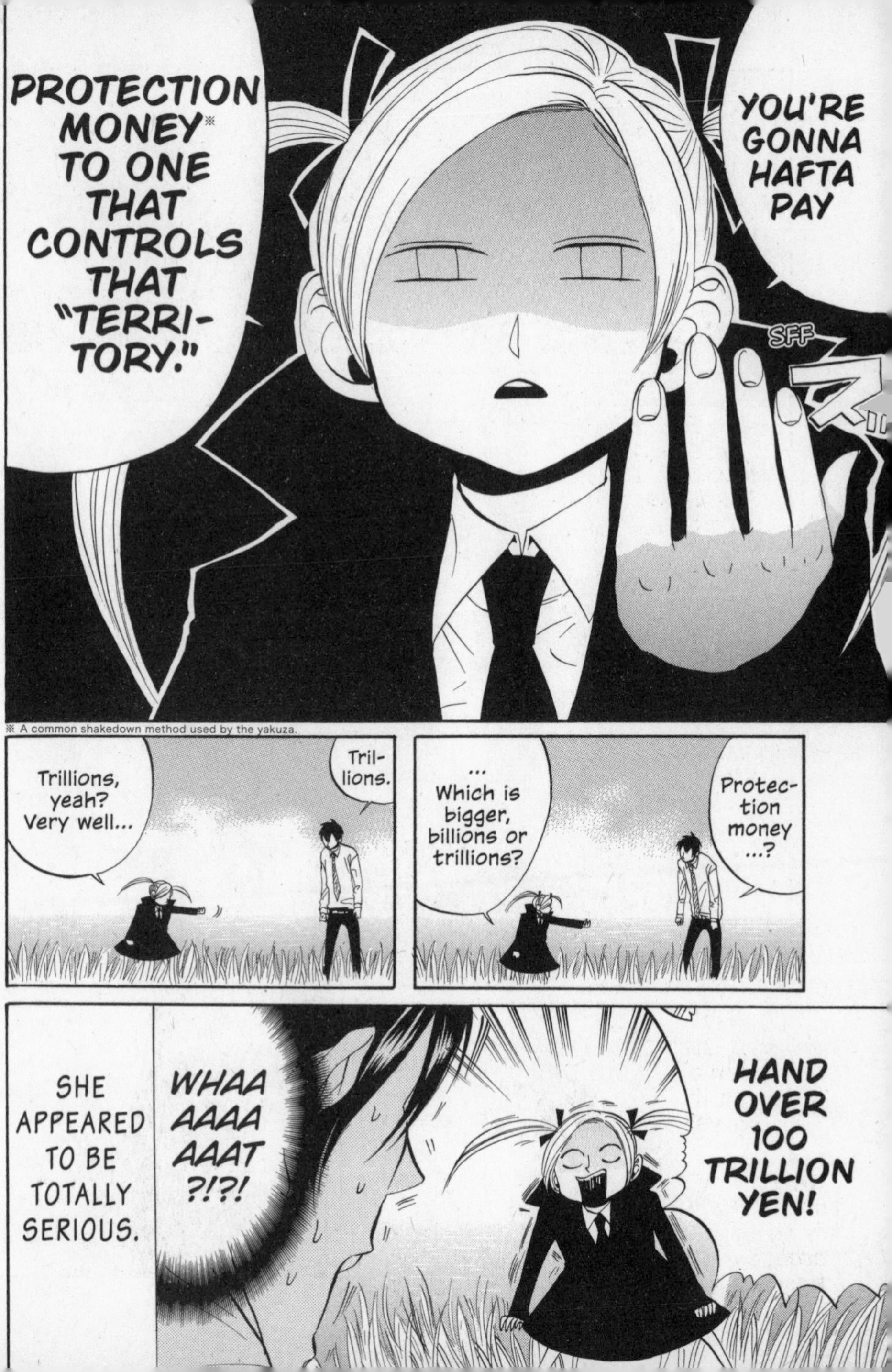
YOU'RE GONNA HAFTA PAY
PROTECTION MONEY※ TO ONE THAT CONTROLS THAT "TERRI-TORY."
SFF
Protec-tion money ...?
... Which is bigger, billions or trillions?
Tril-lions.
Trillions, yeah? Very well...
HAND OVER 100 TRILLION YEN!
WHAA AAAA AAAT ?!?!
SHE APPEARED TO BE TOTALLY SERIOUS.

※ A common shakedown method used by the yakuza.

Chapter 61: Can't Give In

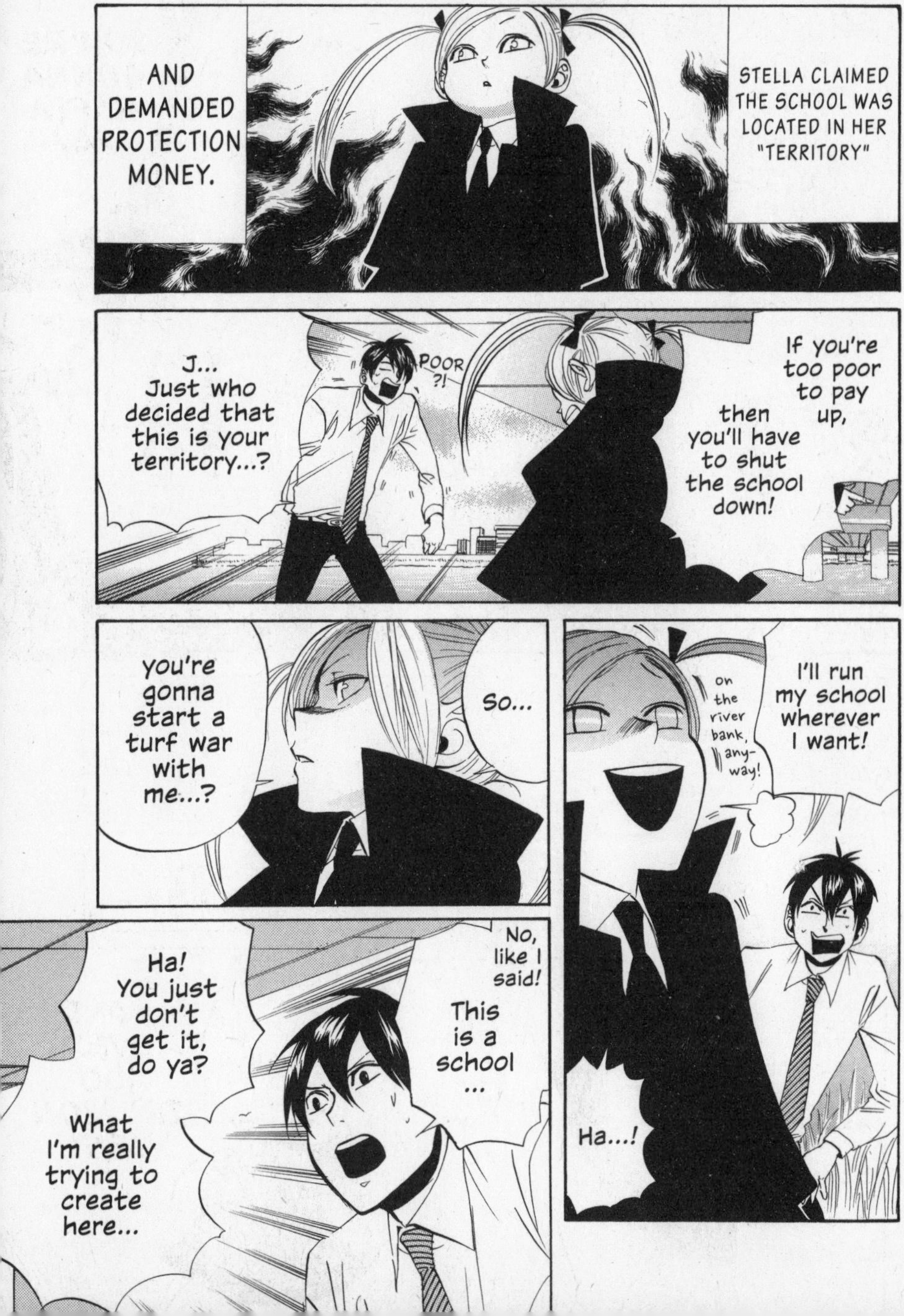
STELLA CLAIMED THE SCHOOL WAS LOCATED IN HER "TERRITORY"
AND DEMANDED PROTECTION MONEY.
If you're too poor to pay up, then you'll have to shut the school down!
POOR ?!
J... Just who decided that this is your territory...?
I'll run my school wherever I want!
On the river bank, anyway!
Ha...!
So...
you're gonna start a turf war with me...?
No, like I said!
This is a school ...
Ha! You just don't get it, do ya?
What I'm really trying to create here...

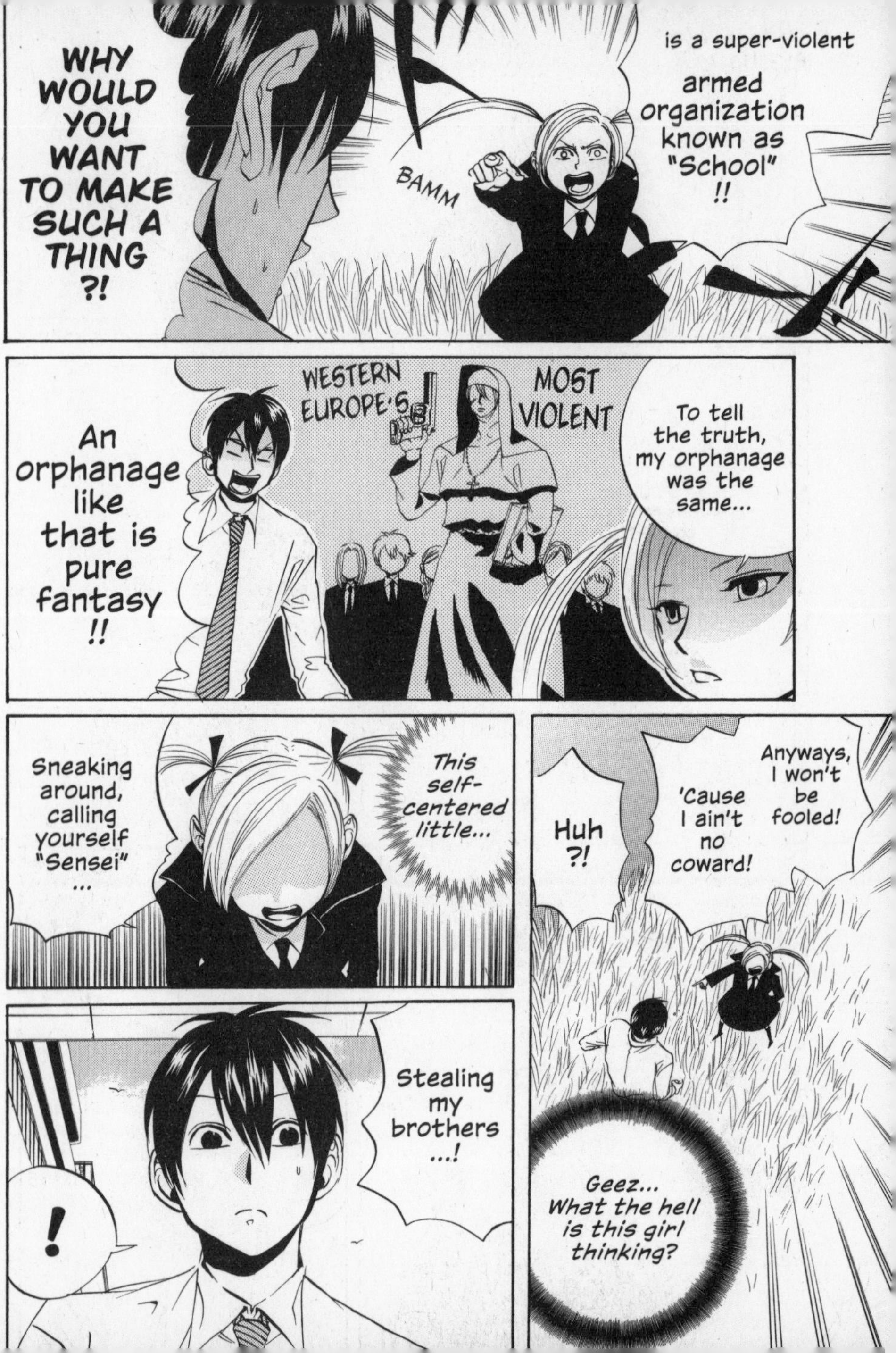
is a super-violent
armed organization known as "School" !!
BAMM
WHY WOULD YOU WANT TO MAKE SUCH A THING ?!
To tell the truth, my orphanage was the same...
WESTERN EUROPE'S MOST VIOLENT
An orphanage like that is pure fantasy !!
Anyways, I won't be fooled!
'Cause I ain't no coward!
Huh ?!
Geez... What the hell is this girl thinking?
This self-centered little...
Sneaking around, calling yourself "Sensei" ...
Stealing my brothers ...!
!

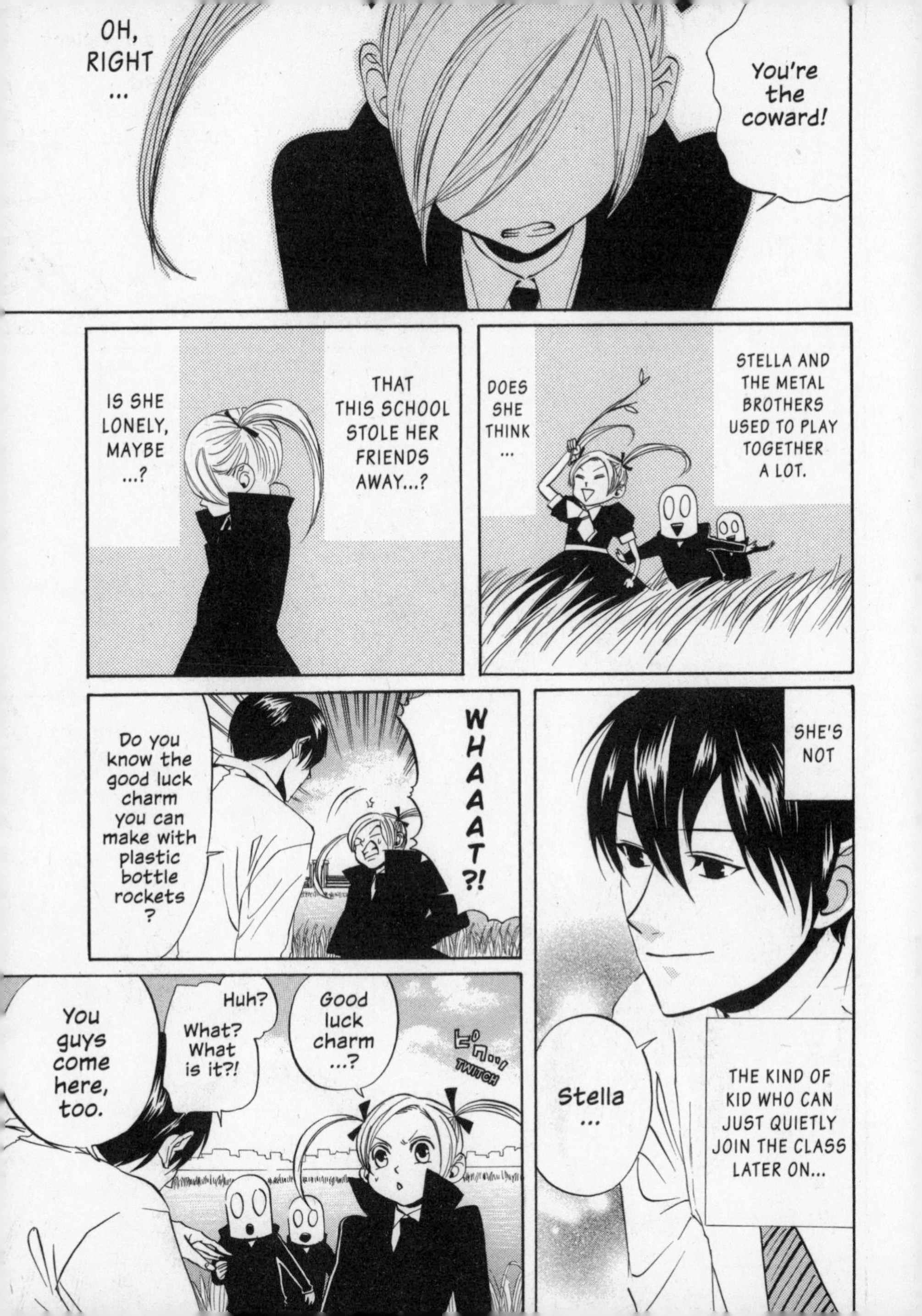
You're the coward!
OH, RIGHT ...
STELLA AND THE METAL BROTHERS USED TO PLAY TOGETHER A LOT.
DOES SHE THINK ...
THAT THIS SCHOOL STOLE HER FRIENDS AWAY...?
IS SHE LONELY, MAYBE ...?
SHE'S NOT
THE KIND OF KID WHO CAN JUST QUIETLY JOIN THE CLASS LATER ON...
Stella ...
WHAAAAT?!
Do you know the good luck charm you can make with plastic bottle rockets ?
TWITCH
Good luck charm ...?
Huh? What? What is it?!
You guys come here, too.

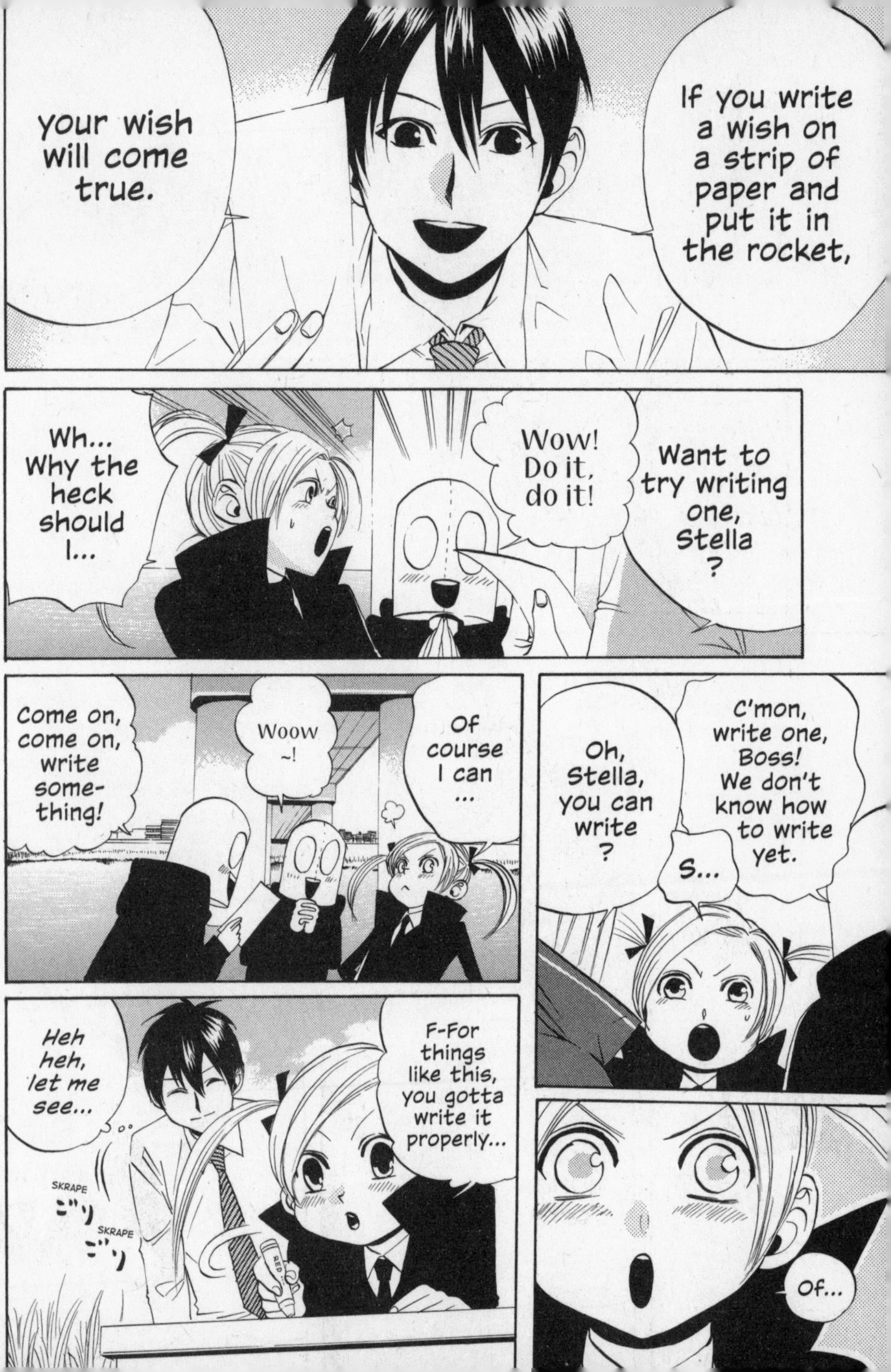

If you write a wish on a strip of paper and put it in the rocket,
your wish will come true.
Want to try writing one, Stella?
Wow! Do it, do it!
Wh... Why the heck should I...
C'mon, write one, Boss! We don't know how to write yet.
Oh, Stella, you can write?
S...
Of...
Of course I can...
Woow~!
Come on, come on, write some-thing!
F-For things like this, you gotta write it properly...
Heh heh, let me see...
SKRAPE
ゴリ
SKRAPE
ゴリ
RED

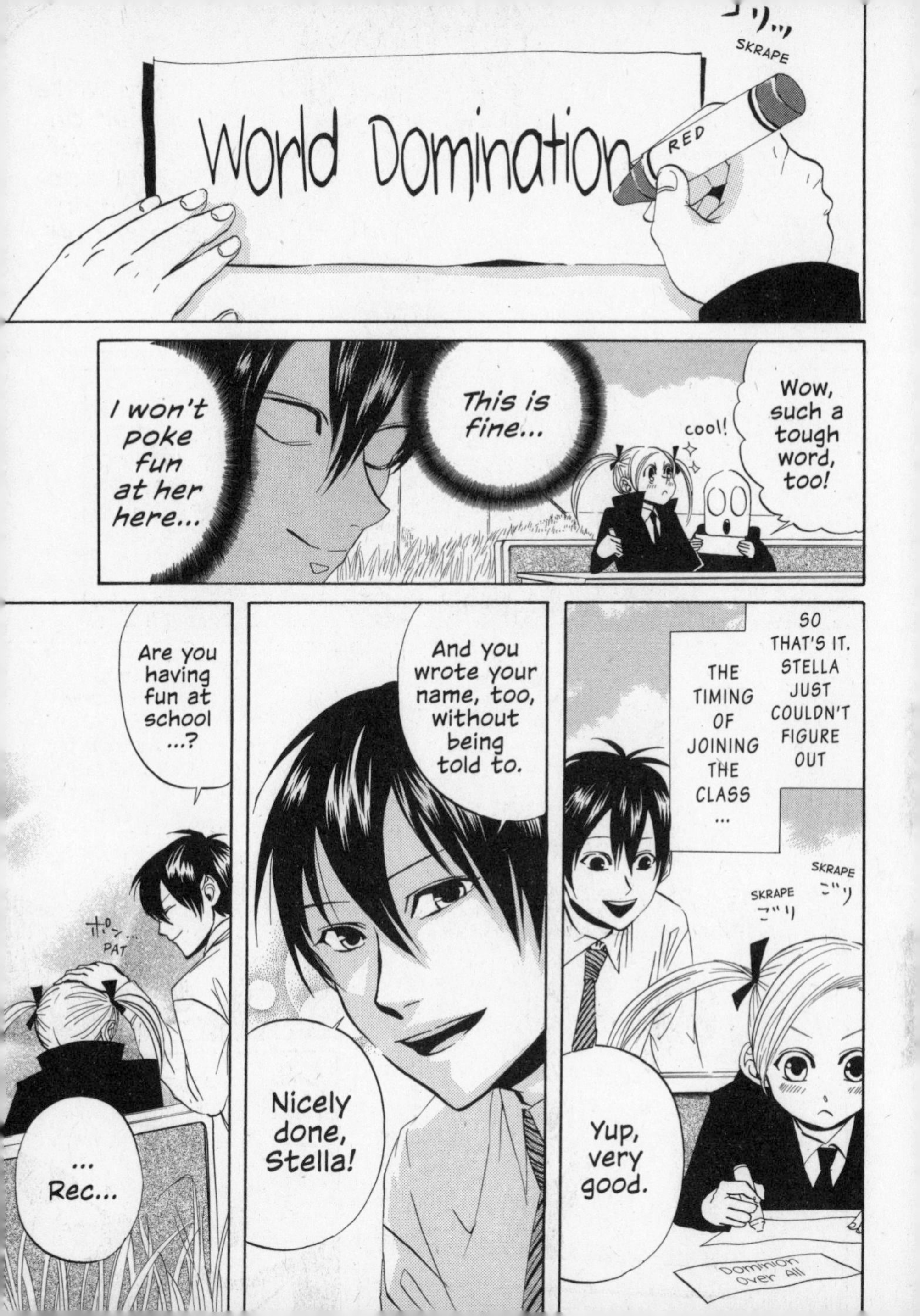
ゴリッ
SKRAPE
World Domination
RED
cool!
Wow, such a tough word, too!
This is fine...
I won't poke fun at her here...
SO THAT'S IT. STELLA JUST COULDN'T FIGURE OUT
THE TIMING OF JOINING THE CLASS ...
SKRAPE
ごリ
SKRAPE
ごリ
Yup, very good.
Dominion Over All
And you wrote your name, too, without being told to.
Nicely done, Stella!
Are you having fun at school ...?
ポン...
PAT
... Rec...

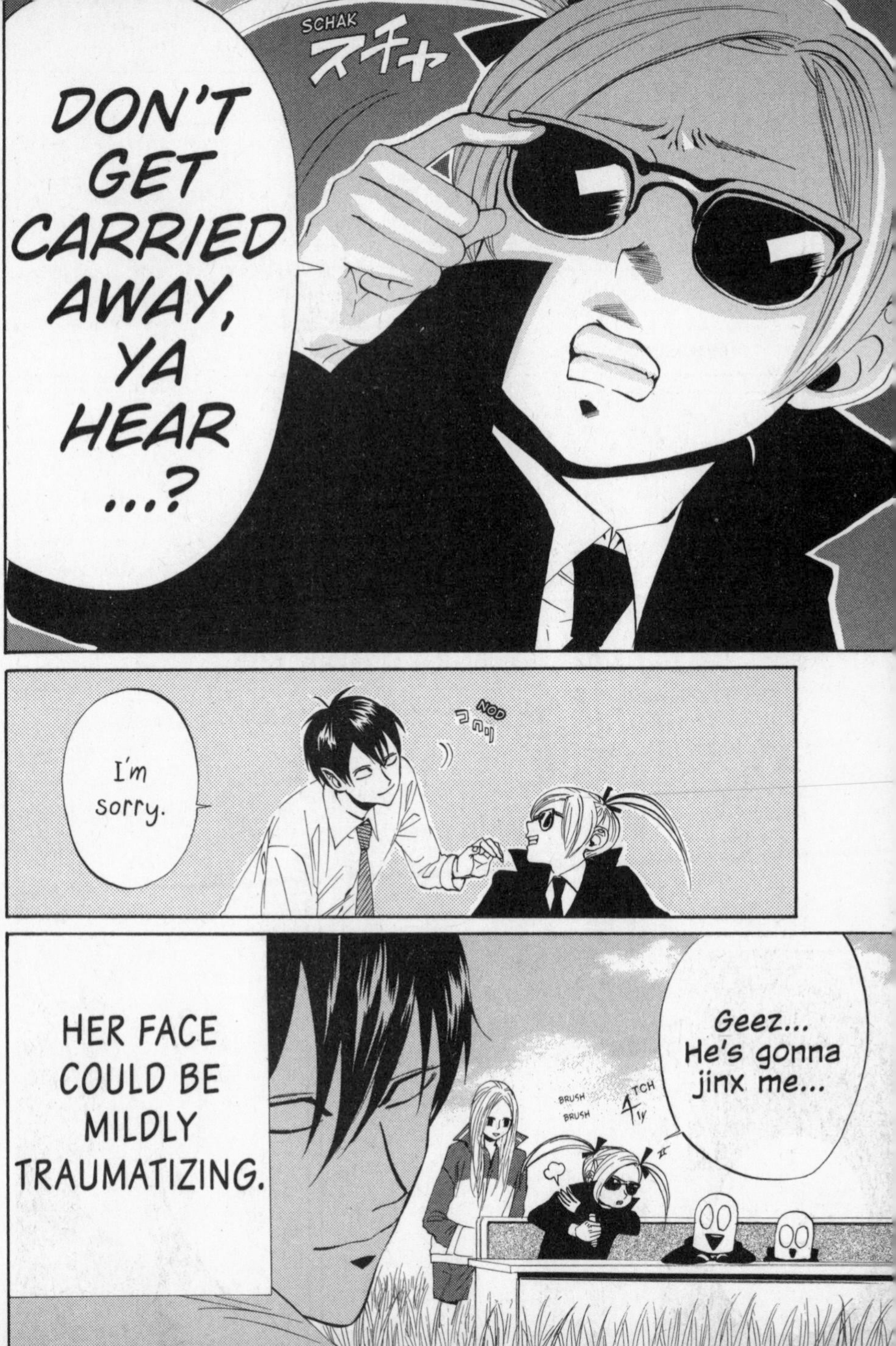
SCHAK
DON'T GET CARRIED AWAY, YA HEAR ...?
NOD
I'm sorry.
Geez... He's gonna jinx me...
TCH
BRUSH BRUSH
HER FACE COULD BE MILDLY TRAUMATIZING.

Chapter 62: People Change Depending On Who They Talk To

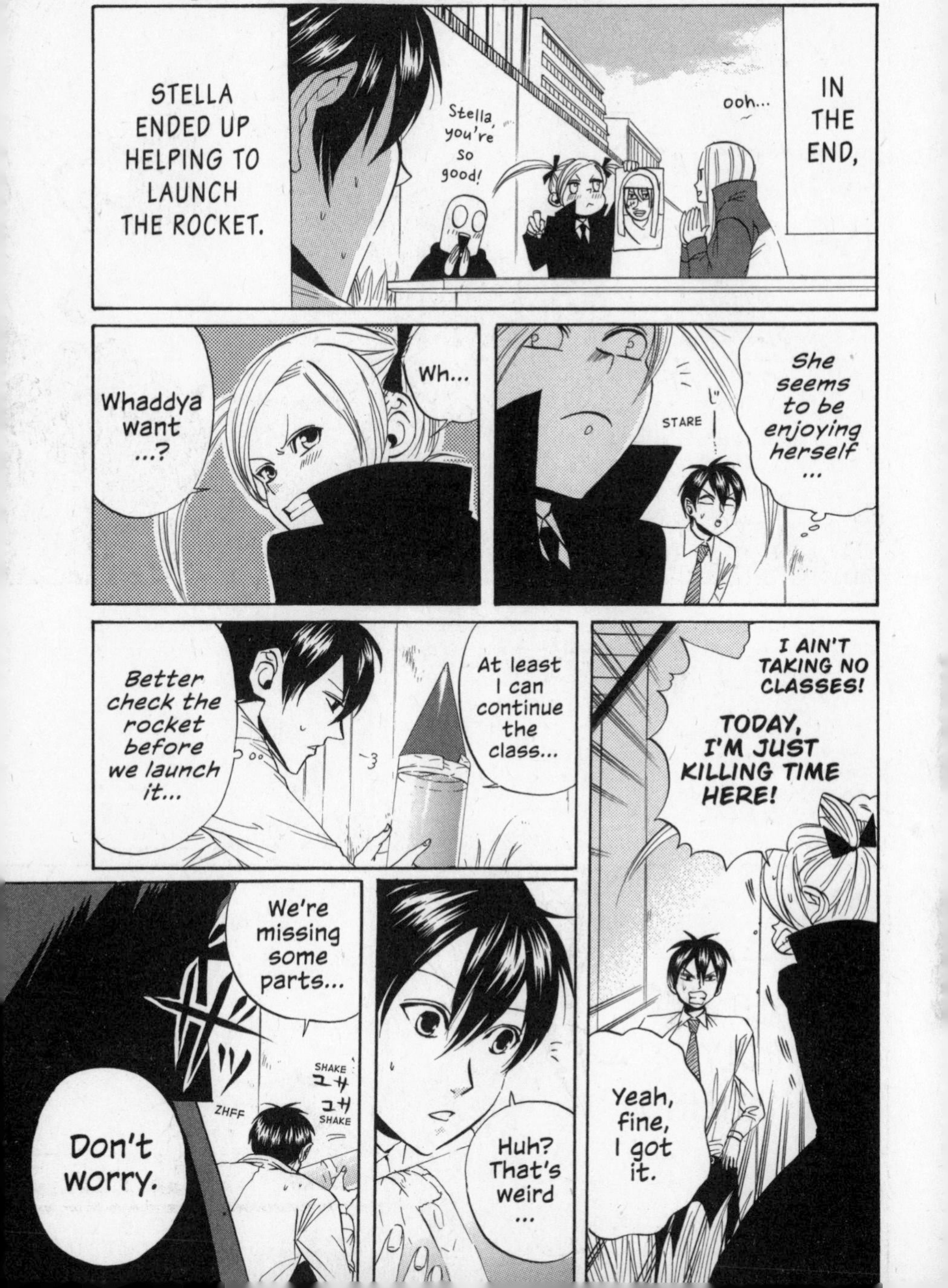
IN THE END,
ooh...
Stella, you're so good!
STELLA ENDED UP HELPING TO LAUNCH THE ROCKET.
She seems to be enjoying herself ...
STARE
Wh...
Whaddya want ...?
I AIN'T TAKING NO CLASSES!
TODAY, I'M JUST KILLING TIME HERE!
Yeah, fine, I got it.
At least I can continue the class...
Better check the rocket before we launch it...
Huh? That's weird ...
We're missing some parts...
SHAKE
SHAKE
ZHFF
Don't worry.

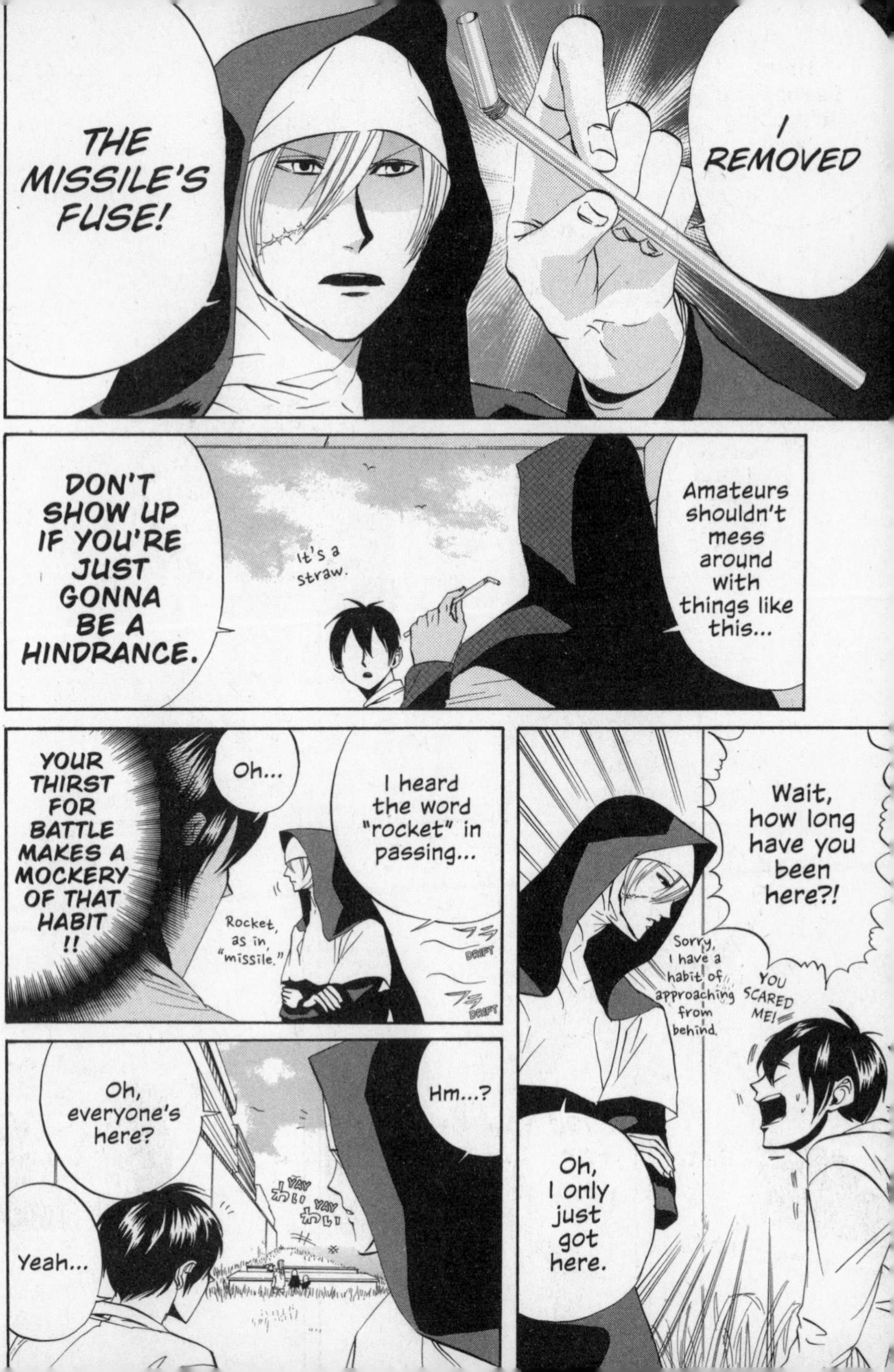
I REMOVED
THE MISSILE'S FUSE!
Amateurs shouldn't mess around with things like this...
It's a straw.
DON'T SHOW UP IF YOU'RE JUST GONNA BE A HINDRANCE.
Wait, how long have you been here?!
YOU SCARED ME!
Sorry, I have a habit of approaching from behind.
Oh, I only just got here.
I heard the word "rocket" in passing...
Oh...
Rocket, as in "missile."
DRIFT
DRIFT
YOUR THIRST FOR BATTLE MAKES A MOCKERY OF THAT HABIT !!
Hm...?
Oh, everyone's here?
YAY
YAY
Yeah...

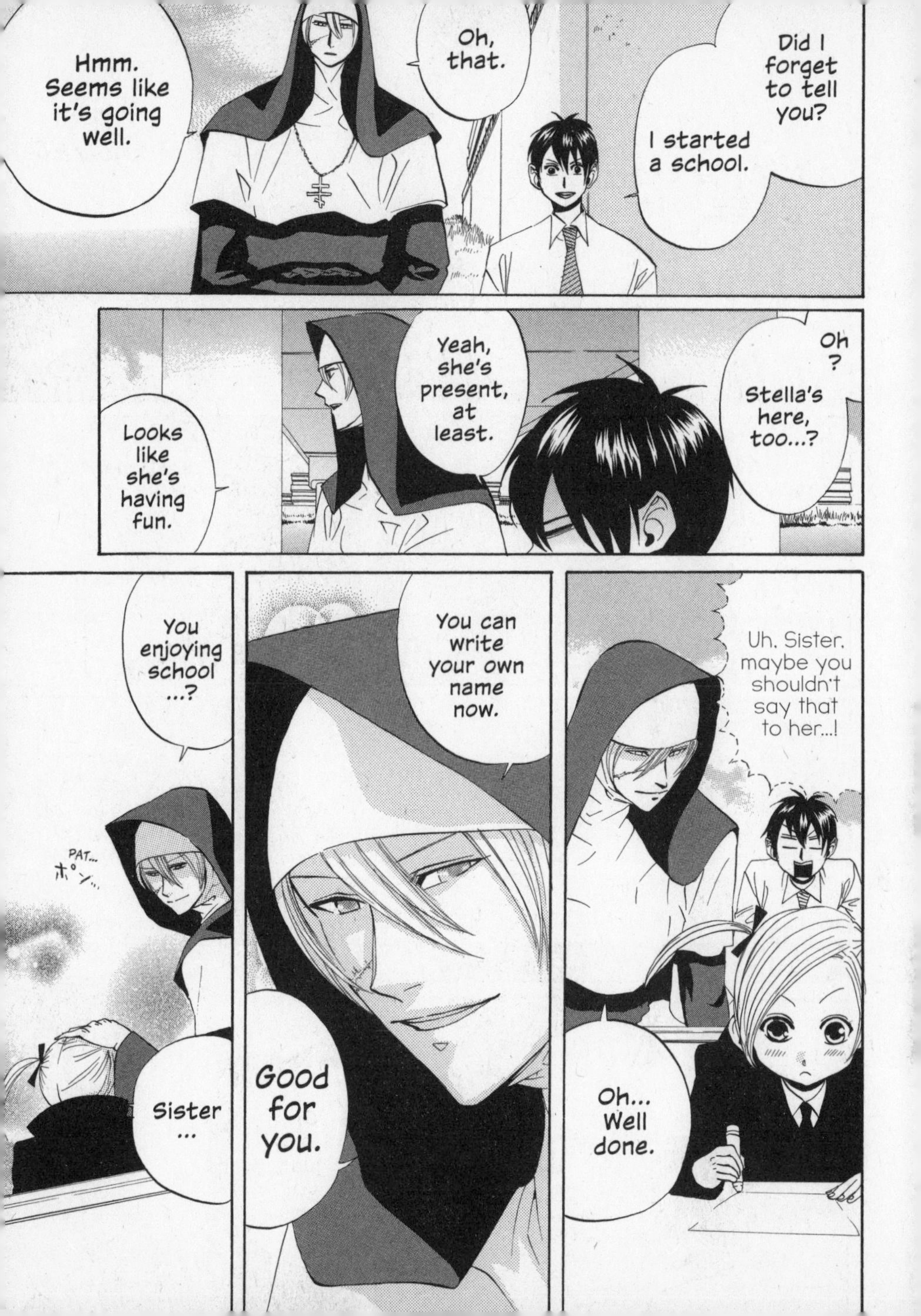
Did I forget to tell you?
I started a school.
Oh, that.
Hmm. Seems like it's going well.
Oh? Stella's here, too...?
Yeah, she's present, at least.
Looks like she's having fun.
Uh, Sister, maybe you shouldn't say that to her...!
Oh... Well done.
You can write your own name now.
Good for you.
You enjoying school ...?
PAT...
ポン…
Sister ...

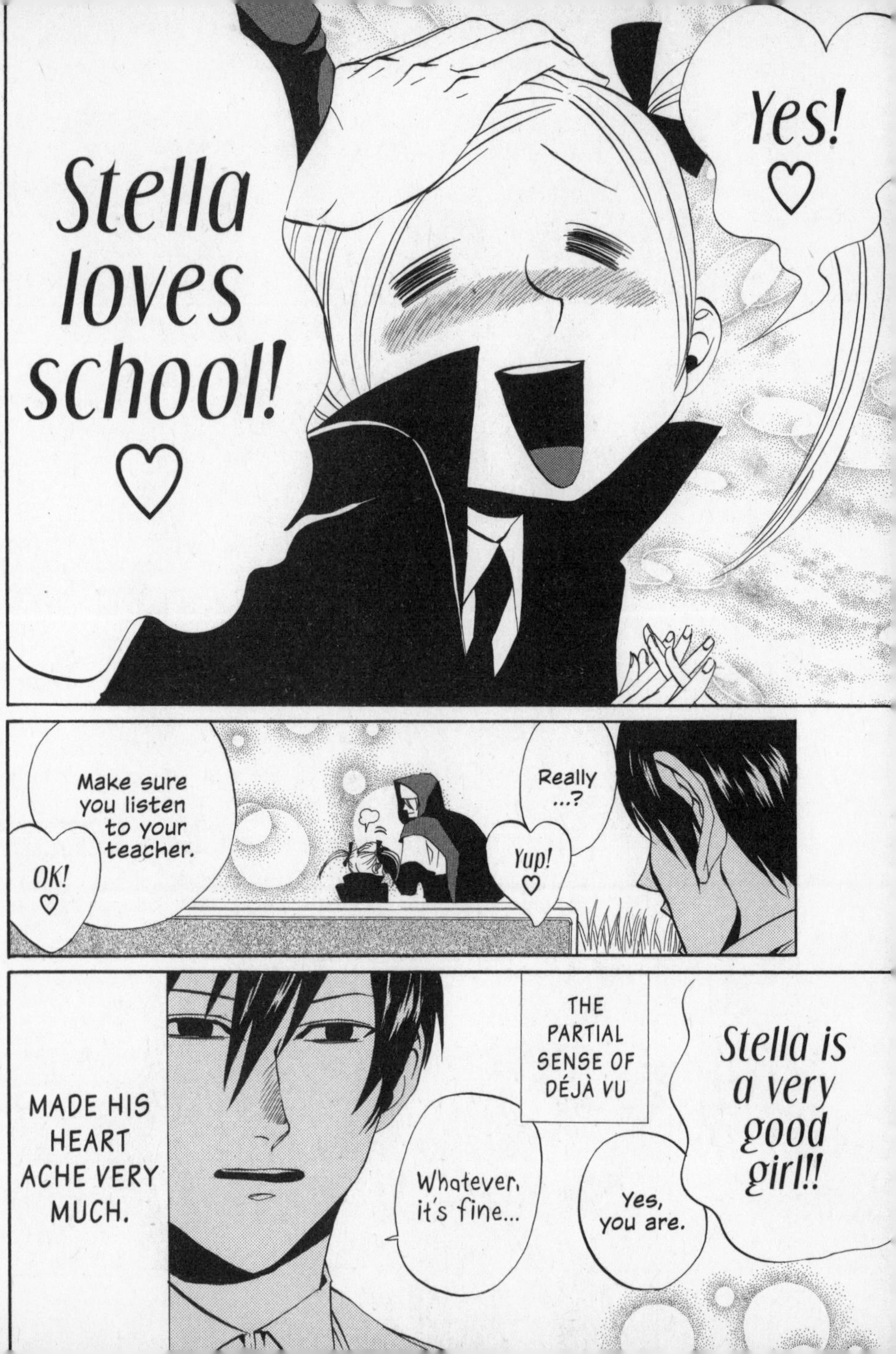
Yes! ♡
Stella loves school! ♡
Really ...?
Yup! ♡
Make sure you listen to your teacher.
OK! ♡
Stella is a very good girl!!
Yes, you are.
THE PARTIAL SENSE OF DÉJÀ VU
Whatever, it's fine...
MADE HIS HEART ACHE VERY MUCH.

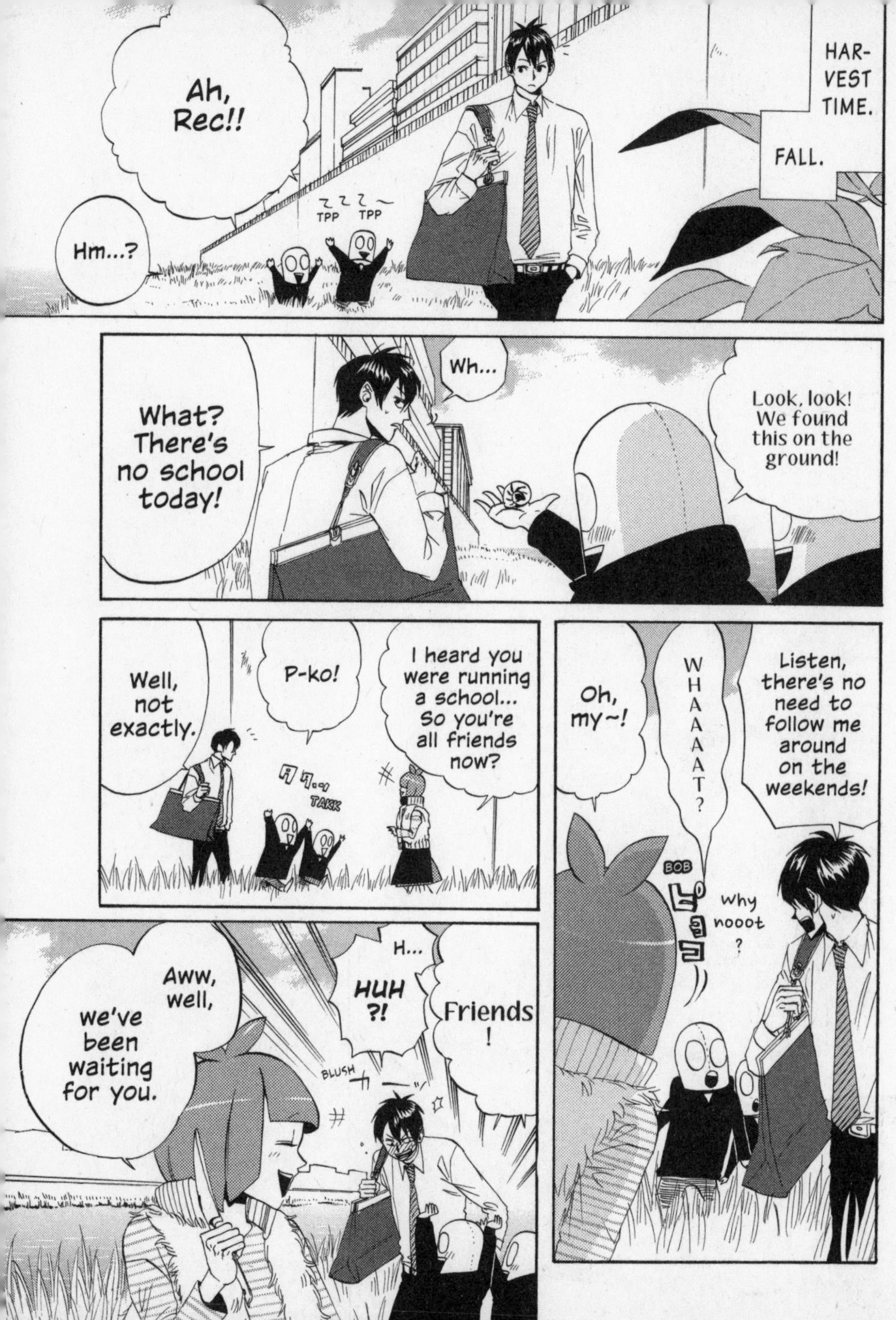
HARVEST TIME.
FALL.
Ah, Rec!!
TPP TPP
Hm...?
Look, look! We found this on the ground!
Wh...
What? There's no school today!
Listen, there's no need to follow me around on the weekends!
Oh, my~!
WHAAAAT?
BOB
Why nooot?
I heard you were running a school... So you're all friends now?
P-ko!
TAKK
Well, not exactly.
Friends!
H...
HUH?!
BLUSH
Aww, well, we've been waiting for you.

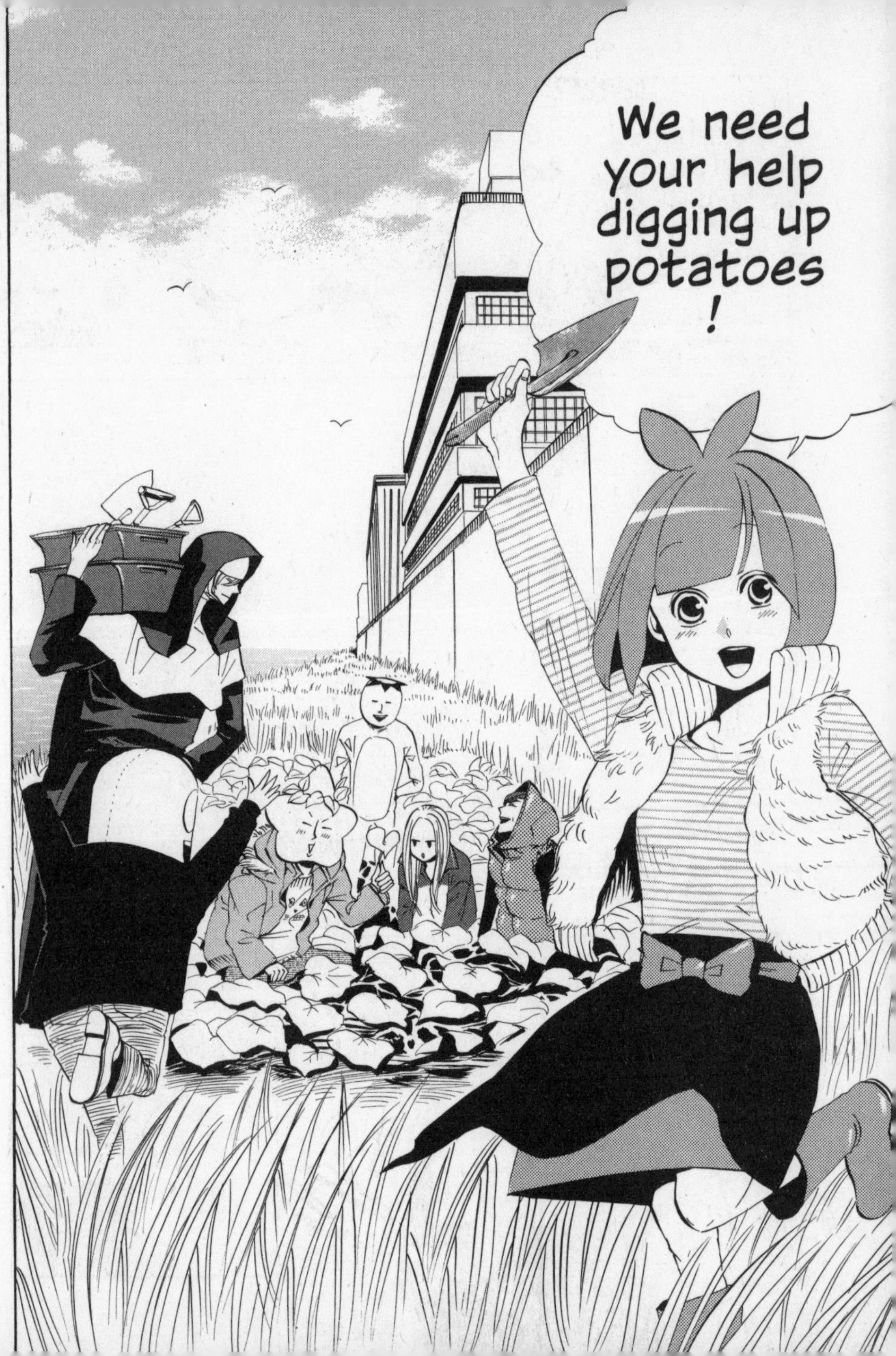
We need your help digging up potatoes!

Chapter 63: Potato Digging

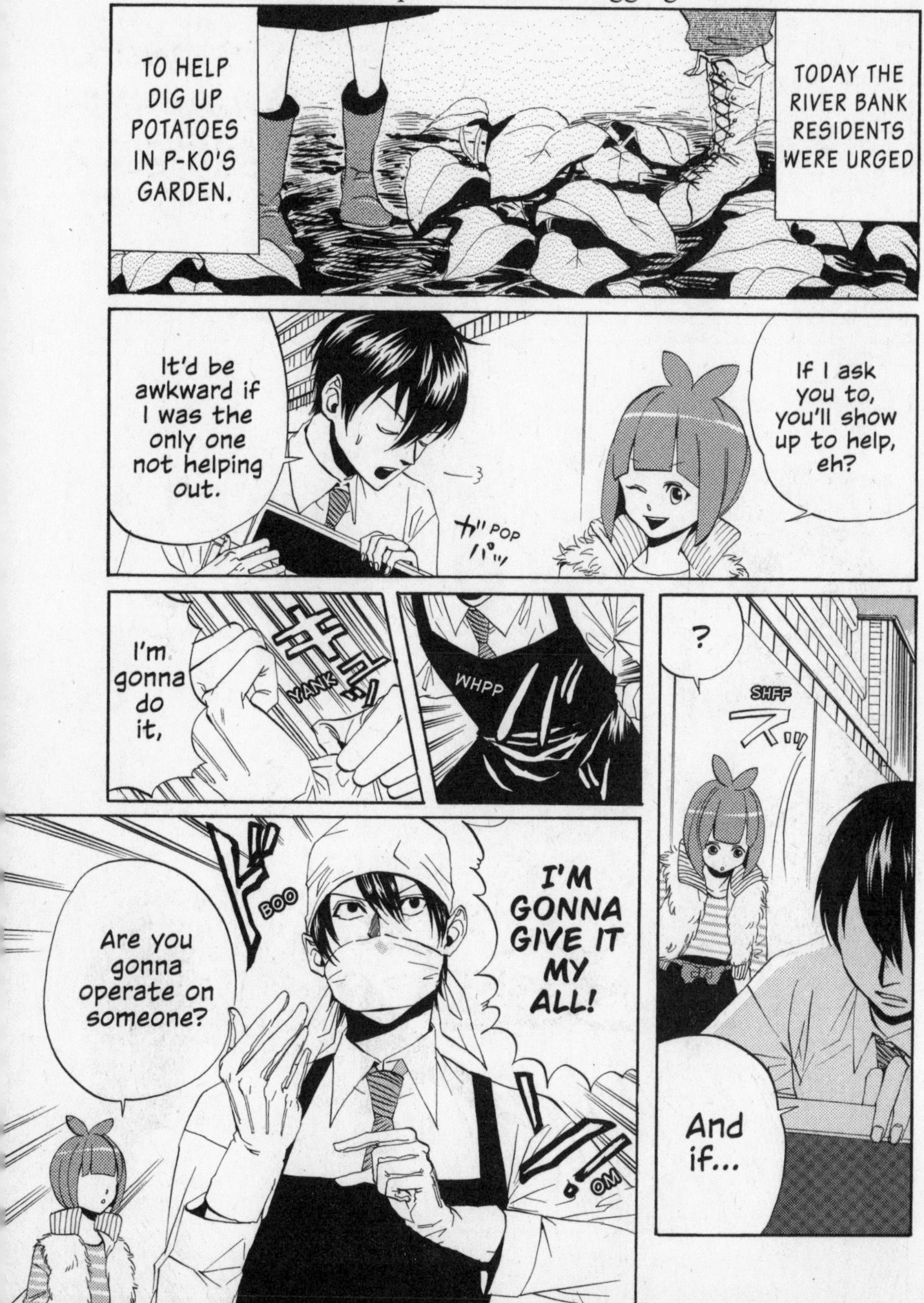
TODAY THE RIVER BANK RESIDENTS WERE URGED
TO HELP DIG UP POTATOES IN P-KO'S GARDEN.
If I ask you to, you'll show up to help, eh?
POP
It'd be awkward if I was the only one not helping out.
?
SHFF
And if...
WHPP
I'm gonna do it,
YANK
I'M GONNA GIVE IT MY ALL!
BOO
OM
Are you gonna operate on someone?

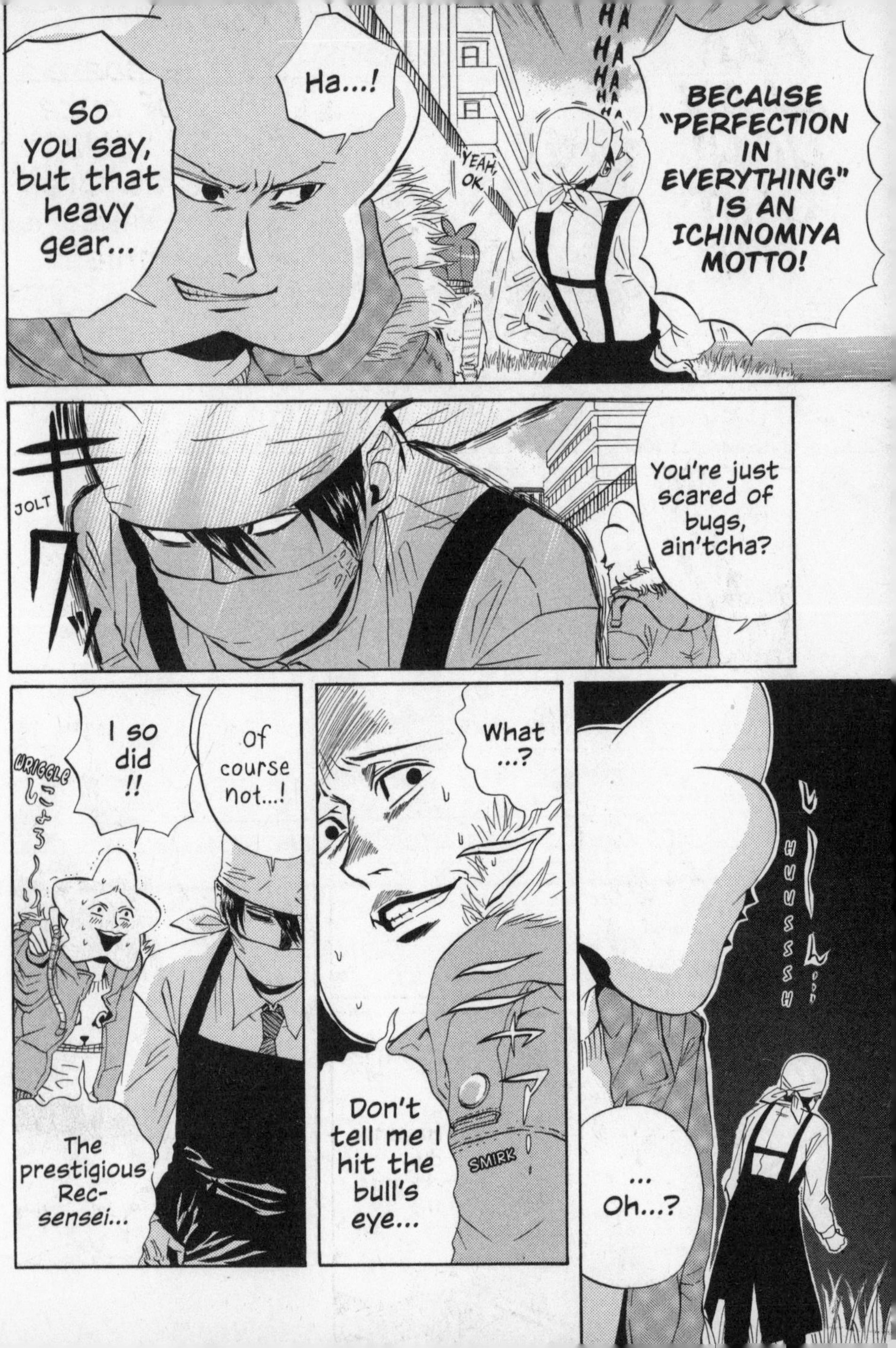
HA HA HA HA HA
BECAUSE "PERFECTION IN EVERYTHING" IS AN ICHINOMIYA MOTTO!
YEAH, OK
Ha...!
So you say, but that heavy gear...
You're just scared of bugs, ain'tcha?
JOLT
HUUSSSH
... Oh...?
What ...?
Don't tell me I hit the bull's eye...
SMIRK
Of course not...!
I so did !!
WRIGGLE
The prestigious Rec-sensei...

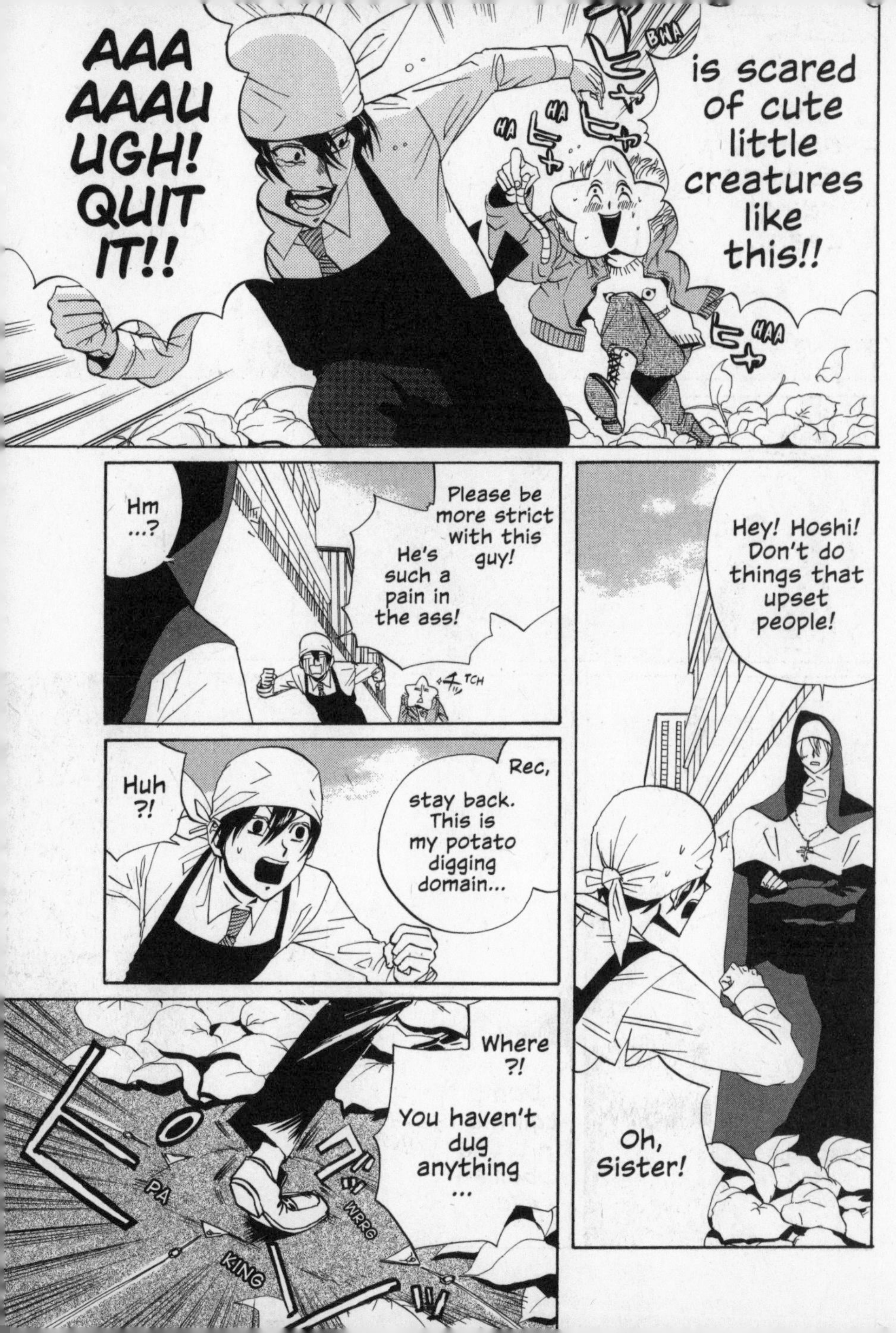
is scared of cute little creatures like this!!
BWA
HA
HA
AAA AAAU UGH! QUIT IT!!
HAA
Hey! Hoshi! Don't do things that upset people!
Oh, Sister!
Please be more strict with this guy!
He's such a pain in the ass!
Hm ...?
TCH
Rec, stay back. This is my potato digging domain...
Huh ?!
Where ?!
You haven't dug anything ...
PA
KING

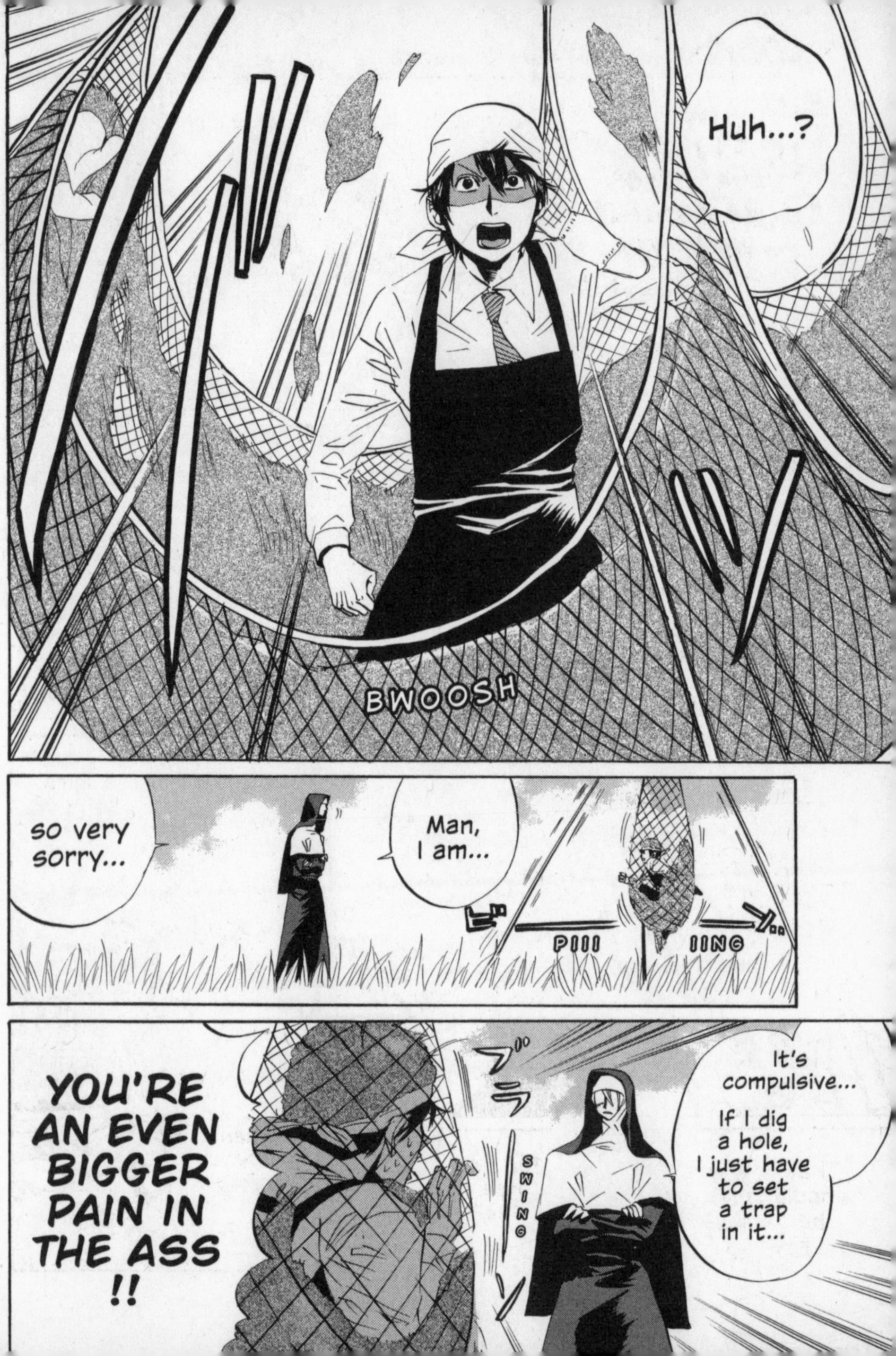
Huh...?
BWOOSH
Man, I am...
so very sorry...
PIII IING
It's compulsive...
If I dig a hole, I just have to set a trap in it...
SWING
YOU'RE AN EVEN BIGGER PAIN IN THE ASS !!

Chapter 64: P-ko and Kappa

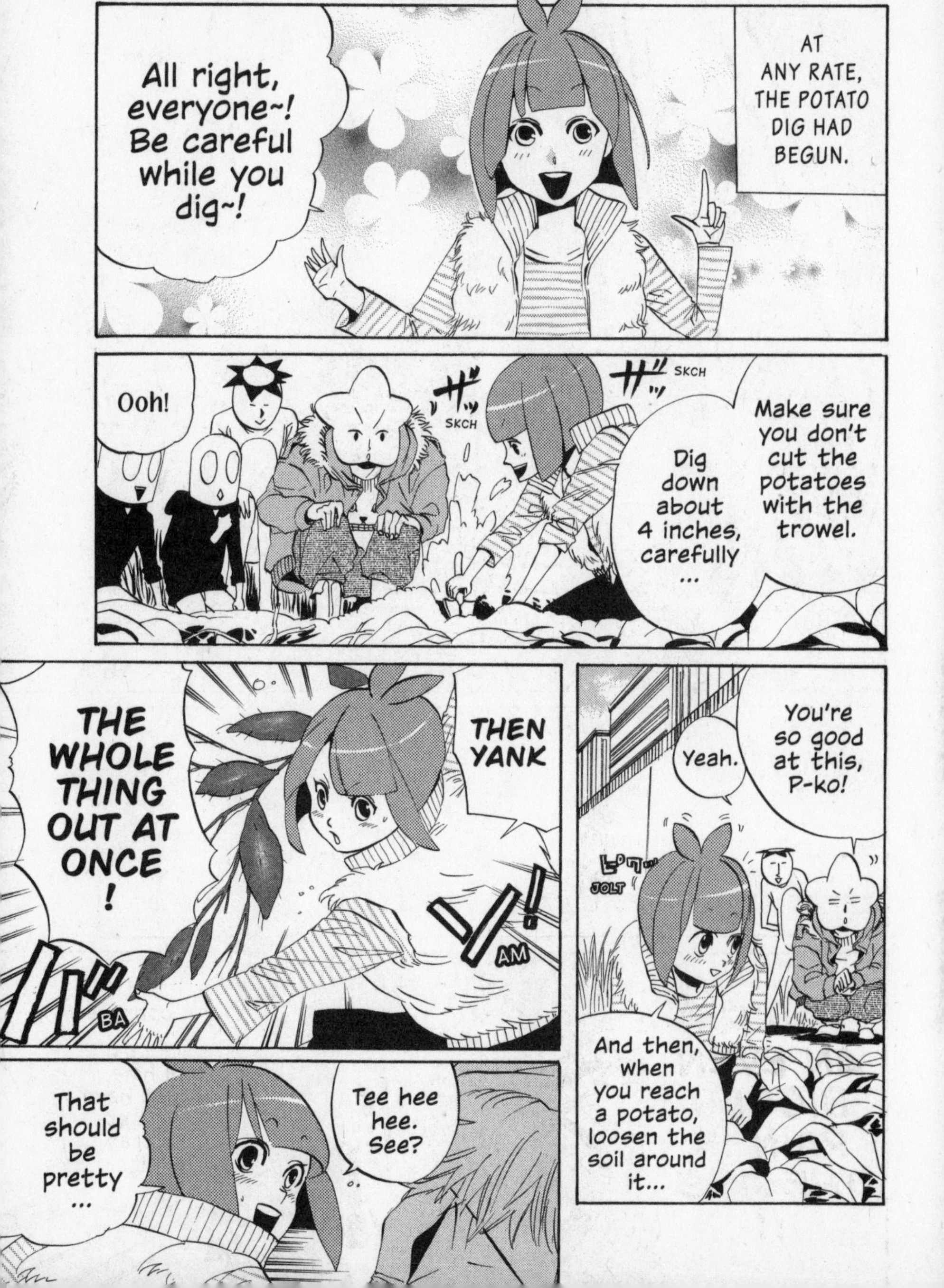

AT ANY RATE, THE POTATO DIG HAD BEGUN.
All right, everyone~! Be careful while you dig~!
Make sure you don't cut the potatoes with the trowel.
Dig down about 4 inches, carefully...
SKCH
SKCH
Ooh!
You're so good at this, P-ko!
Yeah.
JOLT
And then, when you reach a potato, loosen the soil around it...
THEN YANK
THE WHOLE THING OUT AT ONCE!
AM
BA
Tee hee hee. See?
That should be pretty...

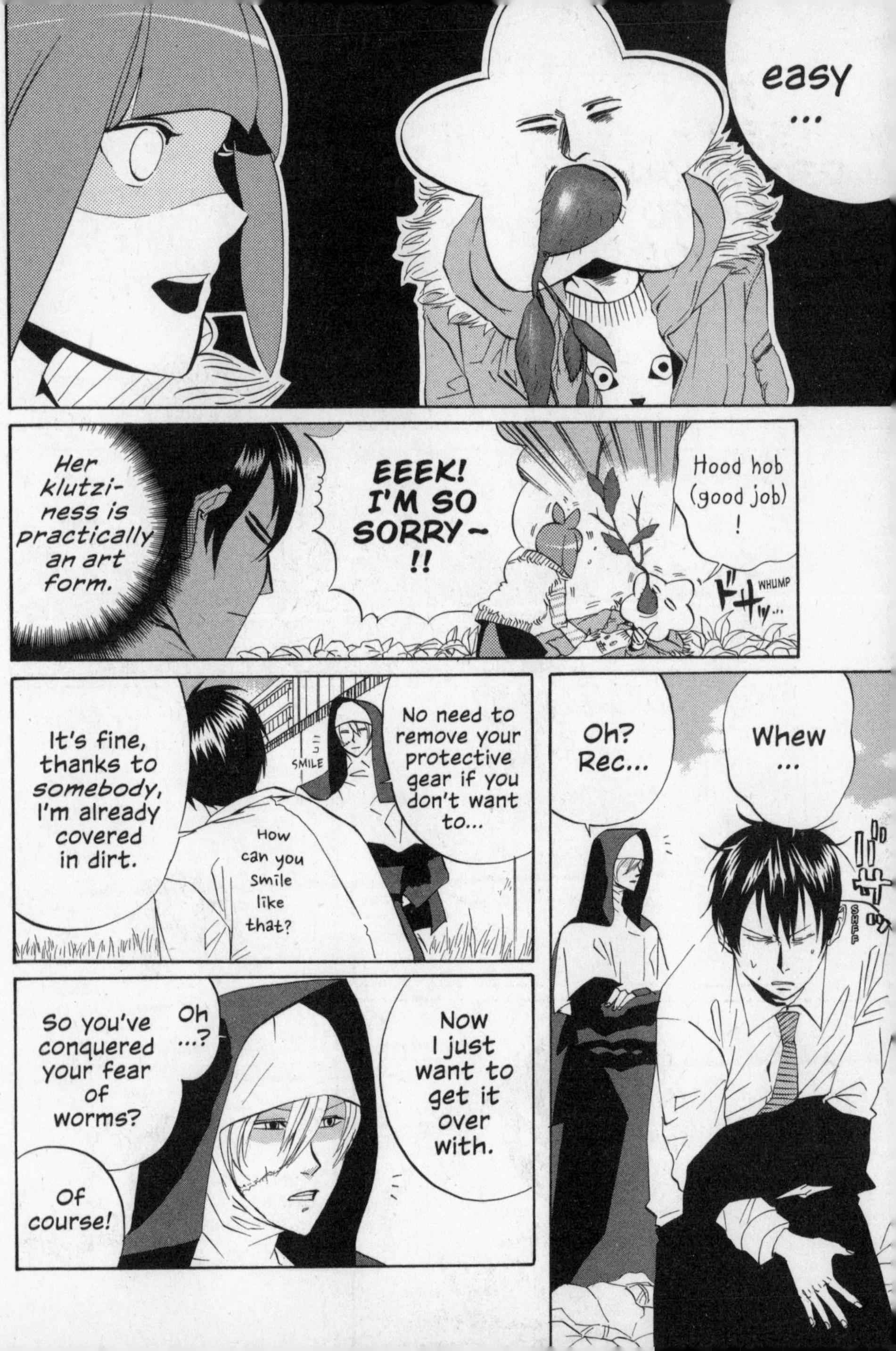
easy ...
Hood hob (good job) !
WHUMP
ドサッ...
EEEK! I'M SO SORRY~ !!
Her klutziness is practically an art form.
Whew ...
Oh? Rec...
SHFF
No need to remove your protective gear if you don't want to...
SMILE
It's fine, thanks to somebody, I'm already covered in dirt.
How can you smile like that?
Now I just want to get it over with.
Oh ...?
So you've conquered your fear of worms?
Of course!

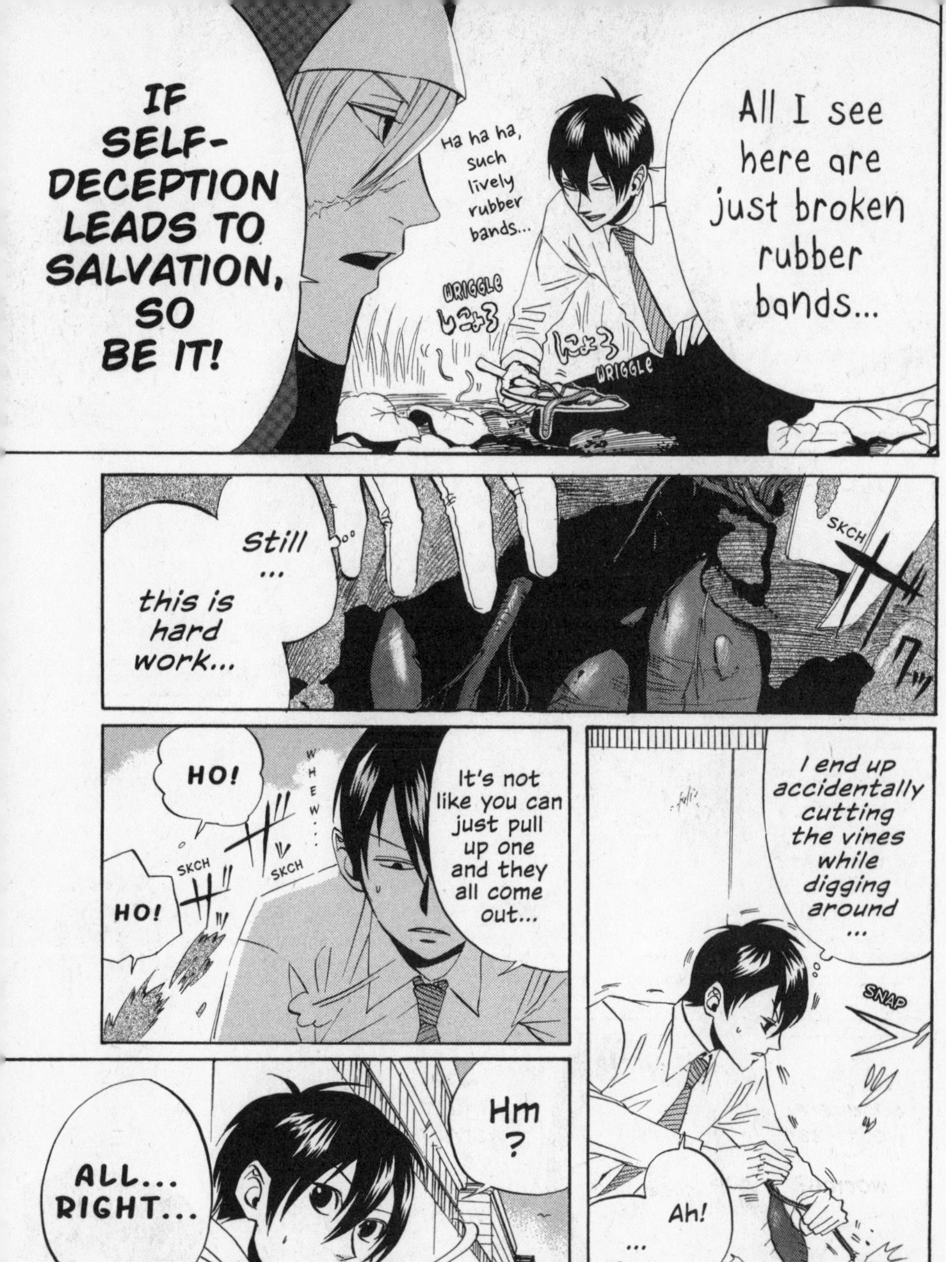

All I see here are just broken rubber bands...
Ha ha ha, such lively rubber bands...
WRIGGLE
にょろ
にょろ
WRIGGLE
IF SELF-DECEPTION LEADS TO SALVATION, SO BE IT!
SKCH
Still ... this is hard work...
I end up accidentally cutting the vines while digging around ...
SNAP
Ah! ... Crap ...
It's not like you can just pull up one and they all come out...
WHEW...
HO!
SKCH
SKCH
HO!
Hm ?
ALL... RIGHT...

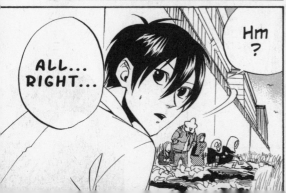

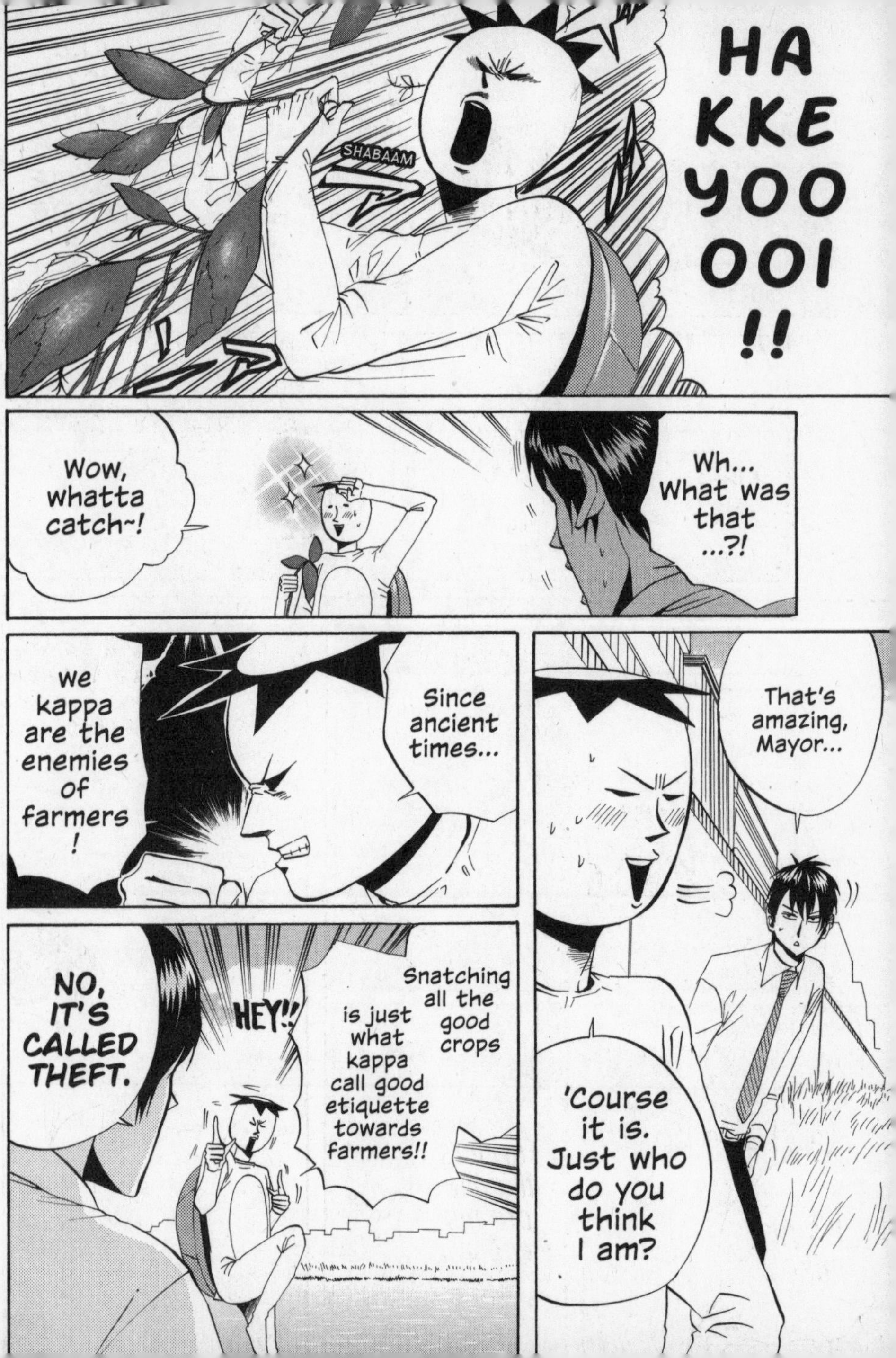
HA KKE YOO OOI !!
SHABAAM
Wh... What was that ...?!
Wow, whatta catch~!
That's amazing, Mayor...
'Course it is. Just who do you think I am?
Since ancient times...
we kappa are the enemies of farmers!
Snatching all the good crops is just what kappa call good etiquette towards farmers!!
HEY!!
NO, IT'S CALLED THEFT.

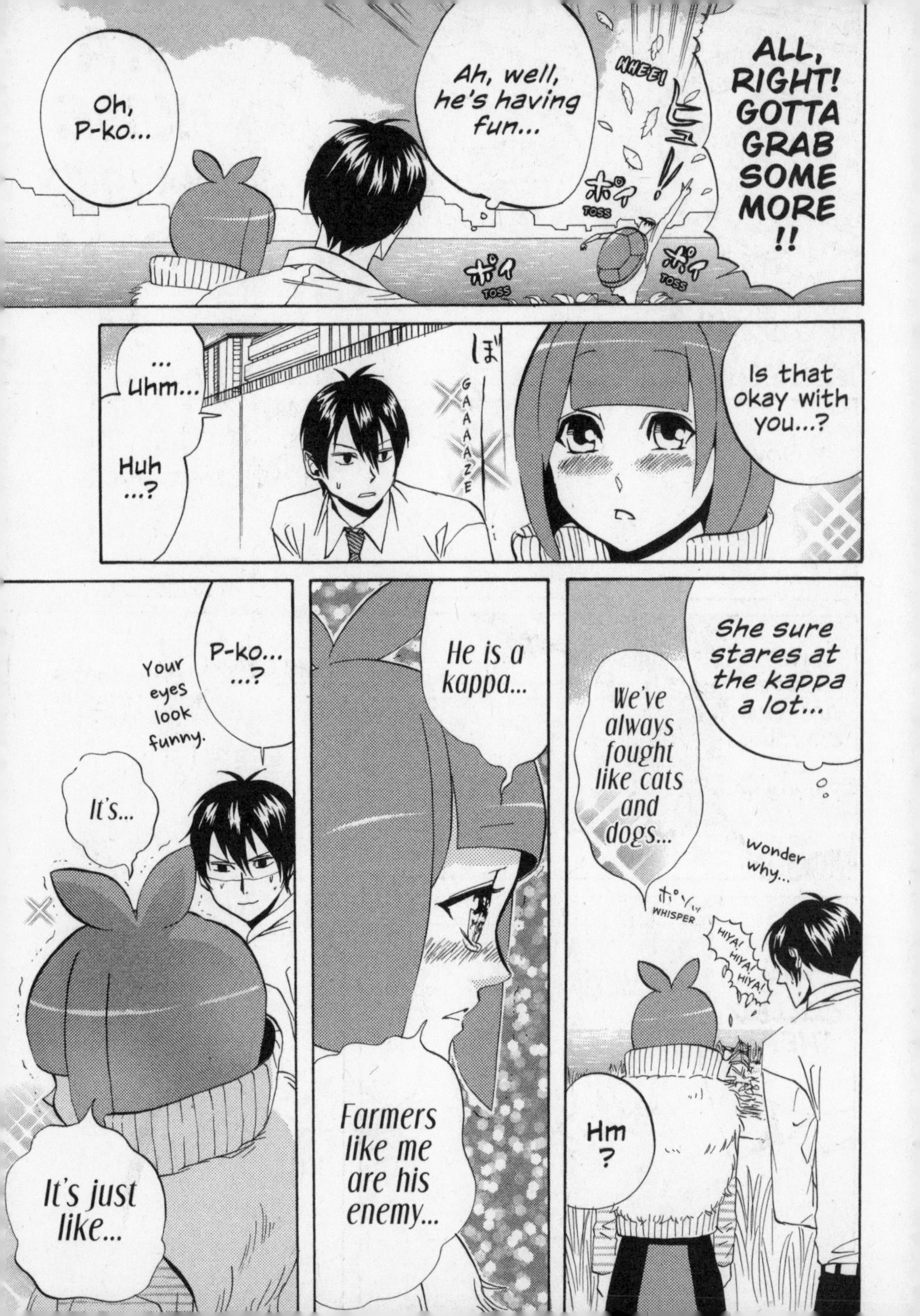
ALL, RIGHT! GOTTA GRAB SOME MORE!!
WHEE!
ヒュ!
ポイ TOSS
ポイ TOSS
ポイ TOSS
Ah, well, he's having fun...
Oh, P-ko...
Is that okay with you...?
ぼ GAAAAAZE
... Uhm...
Huh ...?
She sure stares at the kappa a lot...
We've always fought like cats and dogs...
ポソッ WHISPER
Wonder why...
HIYA! HIYA! HIYA!
Hm ?
He is a kappa...
Farmers like me are his enemy...
P-ko... ...?
Your eyes look funny.
It's...
It's just like...

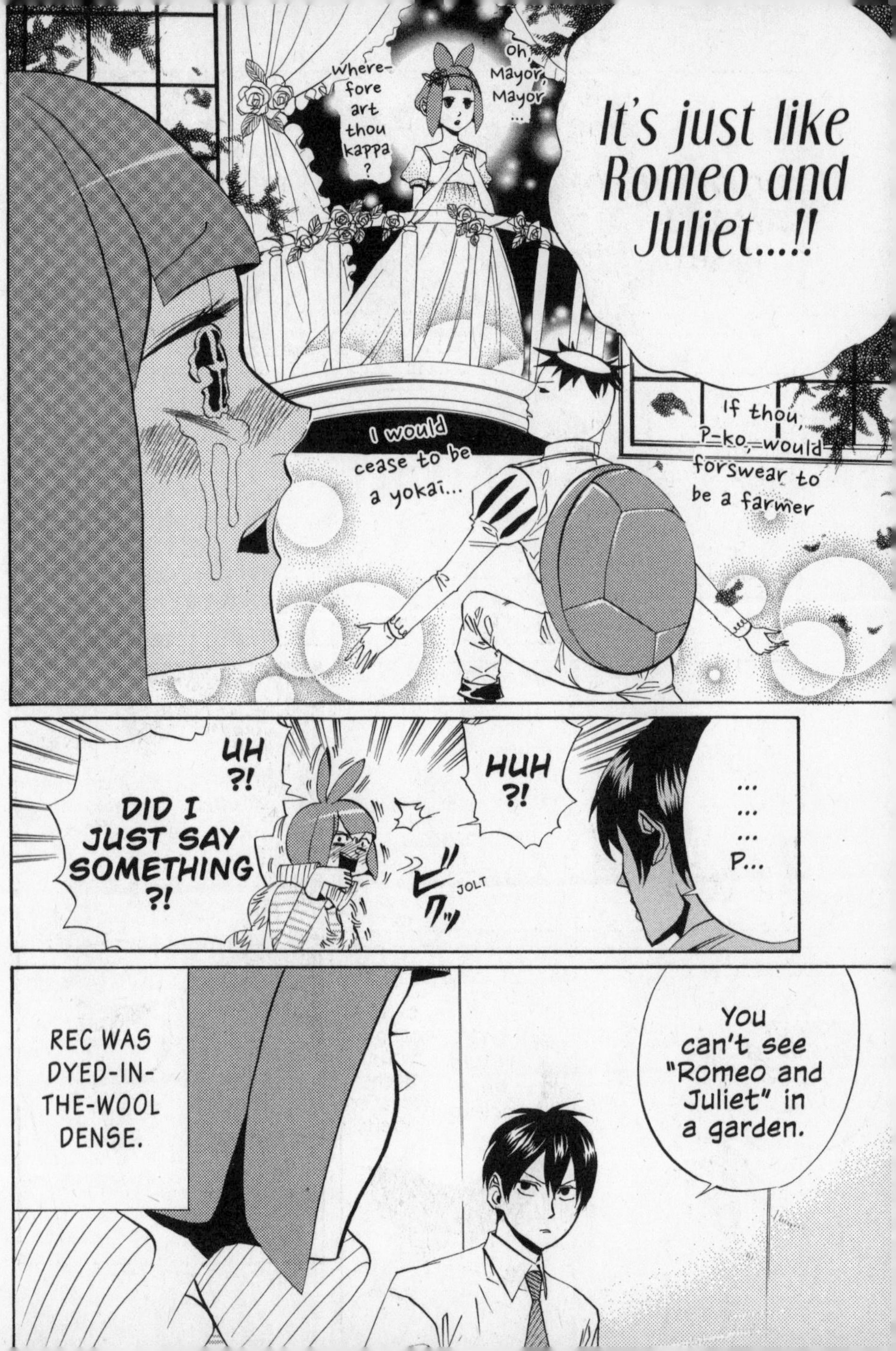
It's just like Romeo and Juliet...!!
Oh, Mayor, Mayor...
Wherefore art thou kappa?
If thou, P-ko, would forswear to be a farmer
I would cease to be a yokai...
... ... P...
HUH ?!
UH ?!
DID I JUST SAY SOMETHING ?!
JOLT
You can't see "Romeo and Juliet" in a garden.
REC WAS DYED-IN-THE-WOOL DENSE.

Chapter 65: We're All...

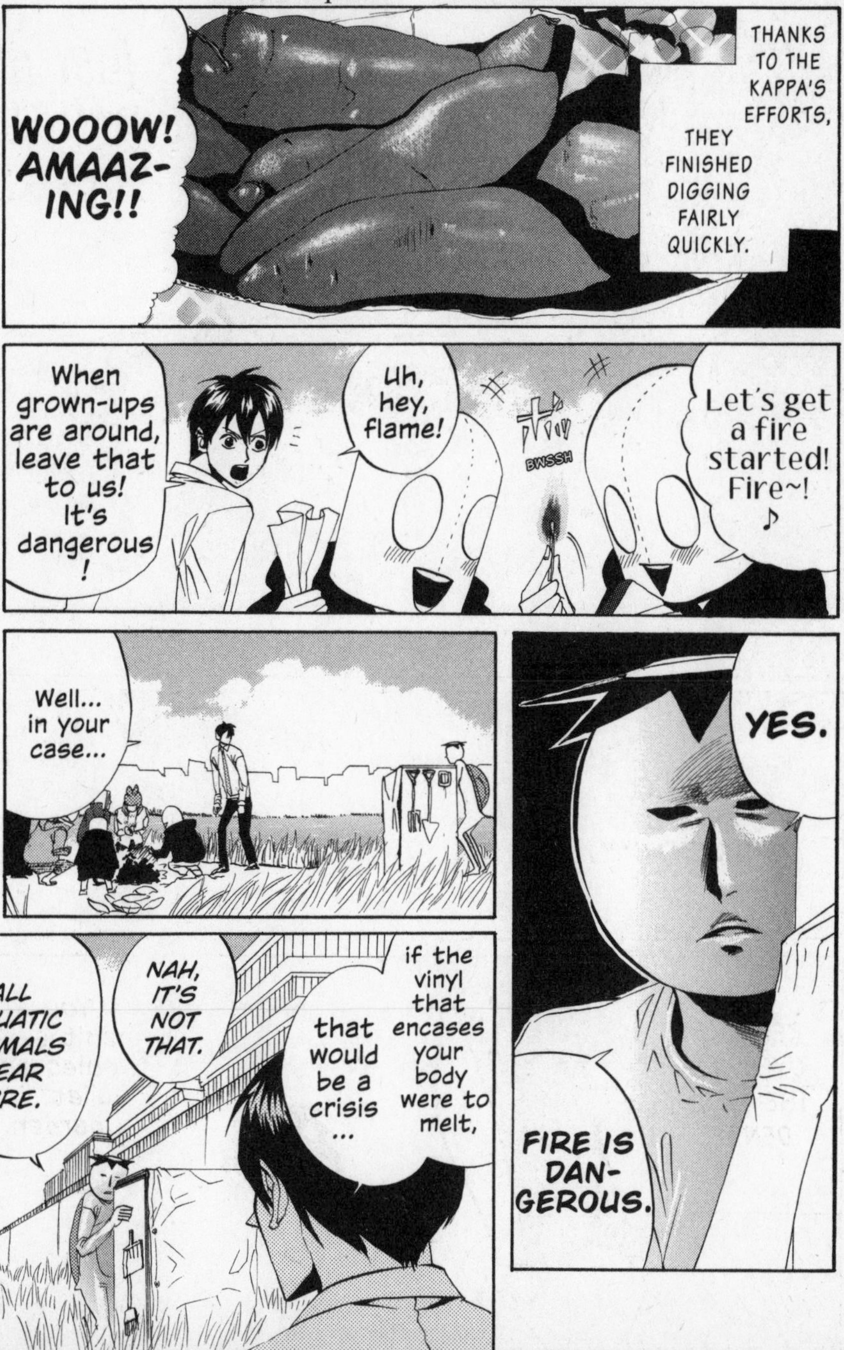
THANKS TO THE KAPPA'S EFFORTS, THEY FINISHED DIGGING FAIRLY QUICKLY.
WOOOW! AMAAZ-ING!!
Let's get a fire started! Fire~! ♪
BWSSH
Uh, hey, flame!
When grown-ups are around, leave that to us! It's dangerous!
YES.
FIRE IS DAN-GEROUS.
Well... in your case...
if the vinyl that encases your body were to melt,
that would be a crisis...
NAH, IT'S NOT THAT.
ALL AQUATIC ANIMALS FEAR FIRE.

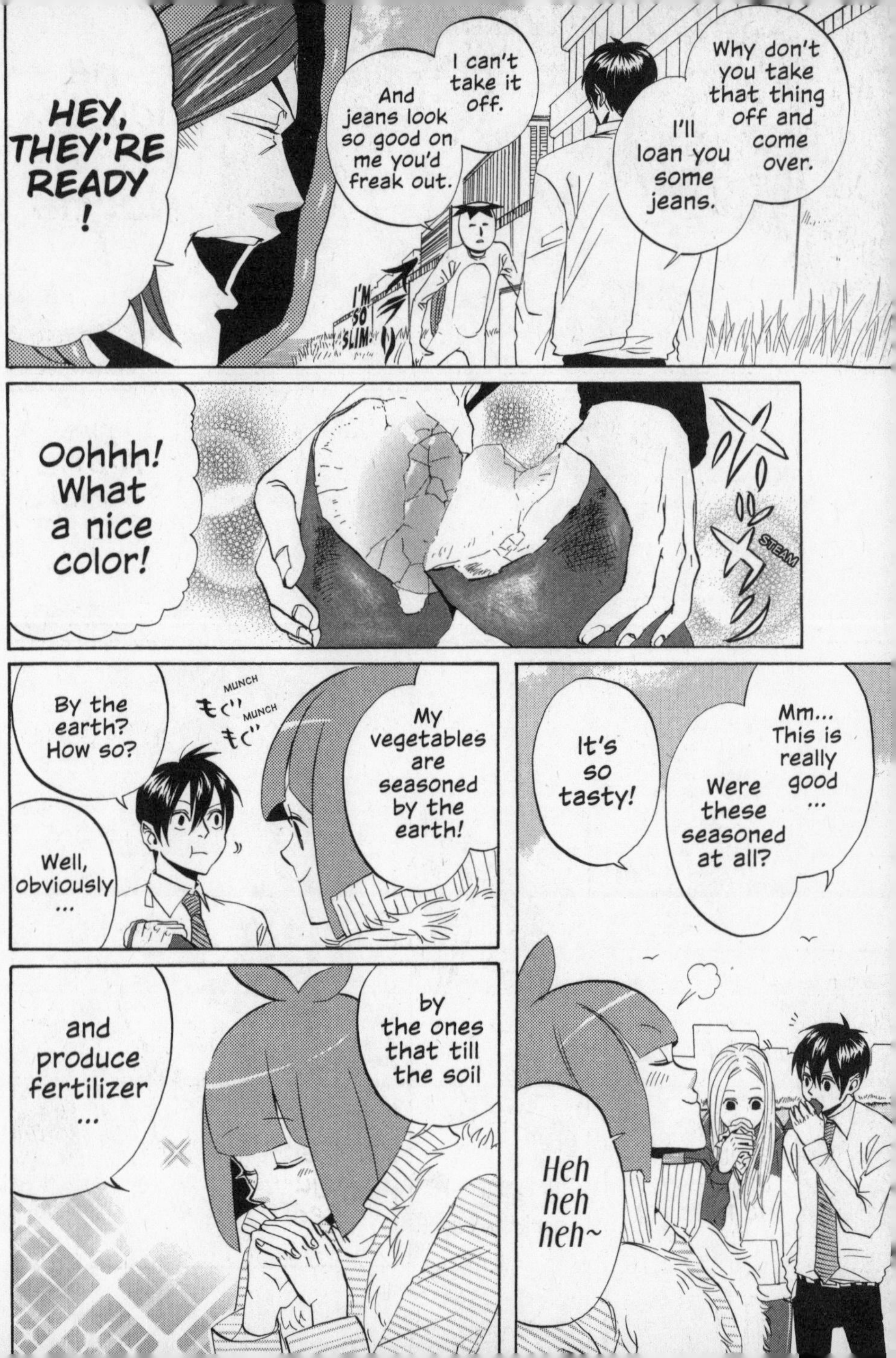
Why don't you take that thing off and come over.
I'll loan you some jeans.
I can't take it off.
And jeans look so good on me you'd freak out.
I'M SO SLIM.
HEY, THEY'RE READY!
STEAM
Oohhh! What a nice color!
Mm... This is really good...
Were these seasoned at all?
It's so tasty!
My vegetables are seasoned by the earth!
MUNCH
もぐ
MUNCH
もぐ
By the earth? How so?
Well, obviously...
Heh heh heh~
by the ones that till the soil
and produce fertilizer...

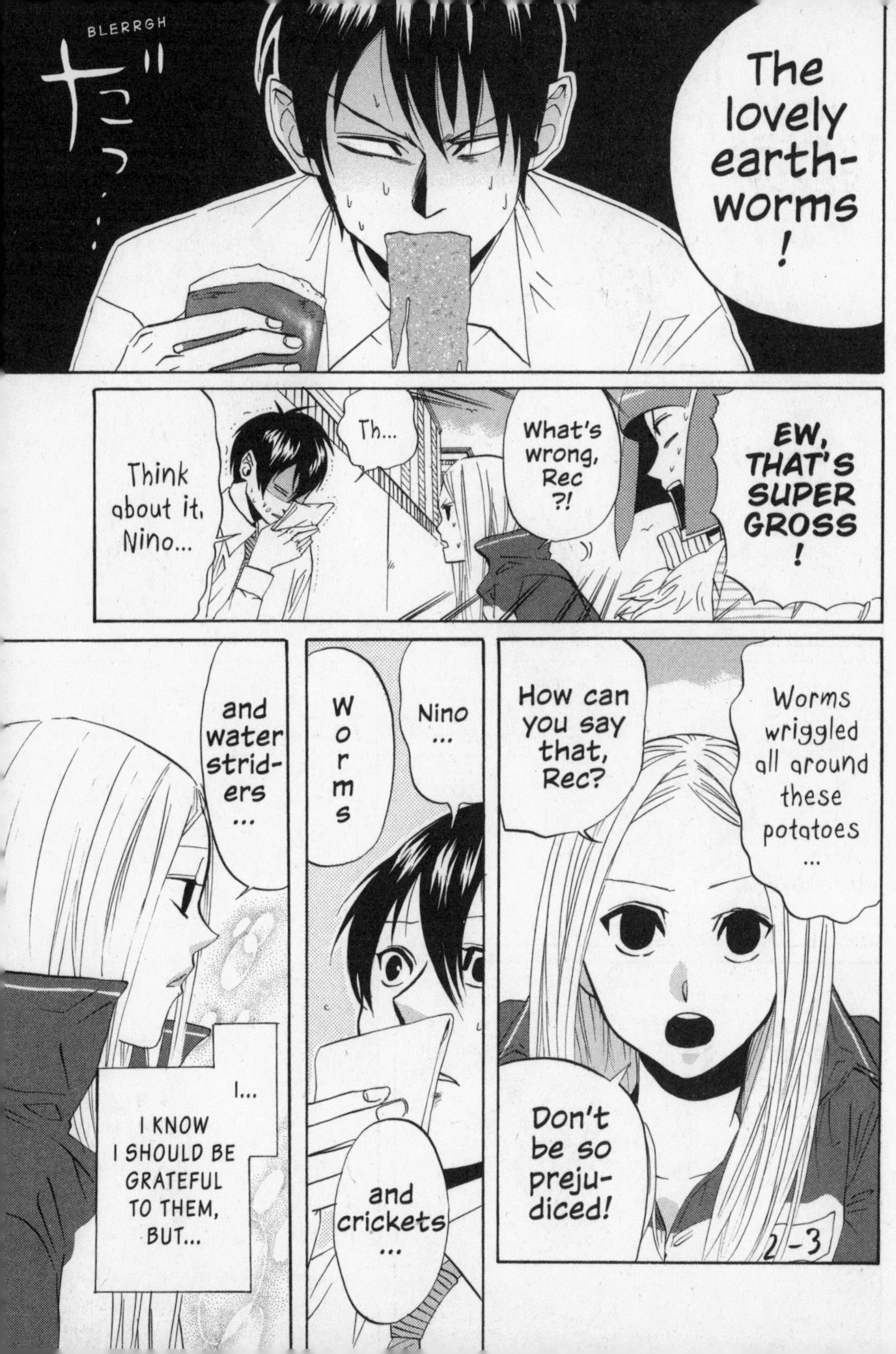
BLERRGH
The lovely earth-worms!
EW, THAT'S SUPER GROSS!
What's wrong, Rec?!
Th...
Think about it, Nino...
Worms wriggled all around these potatoes...
How can you say that, Rec?
Don't be so preju-diced!
2-3
Nino...
Worms
and crickets...
and water strid-ers...
I...
I KNOW I SHOULD BE GRATEFUL TO THEM, BUT...

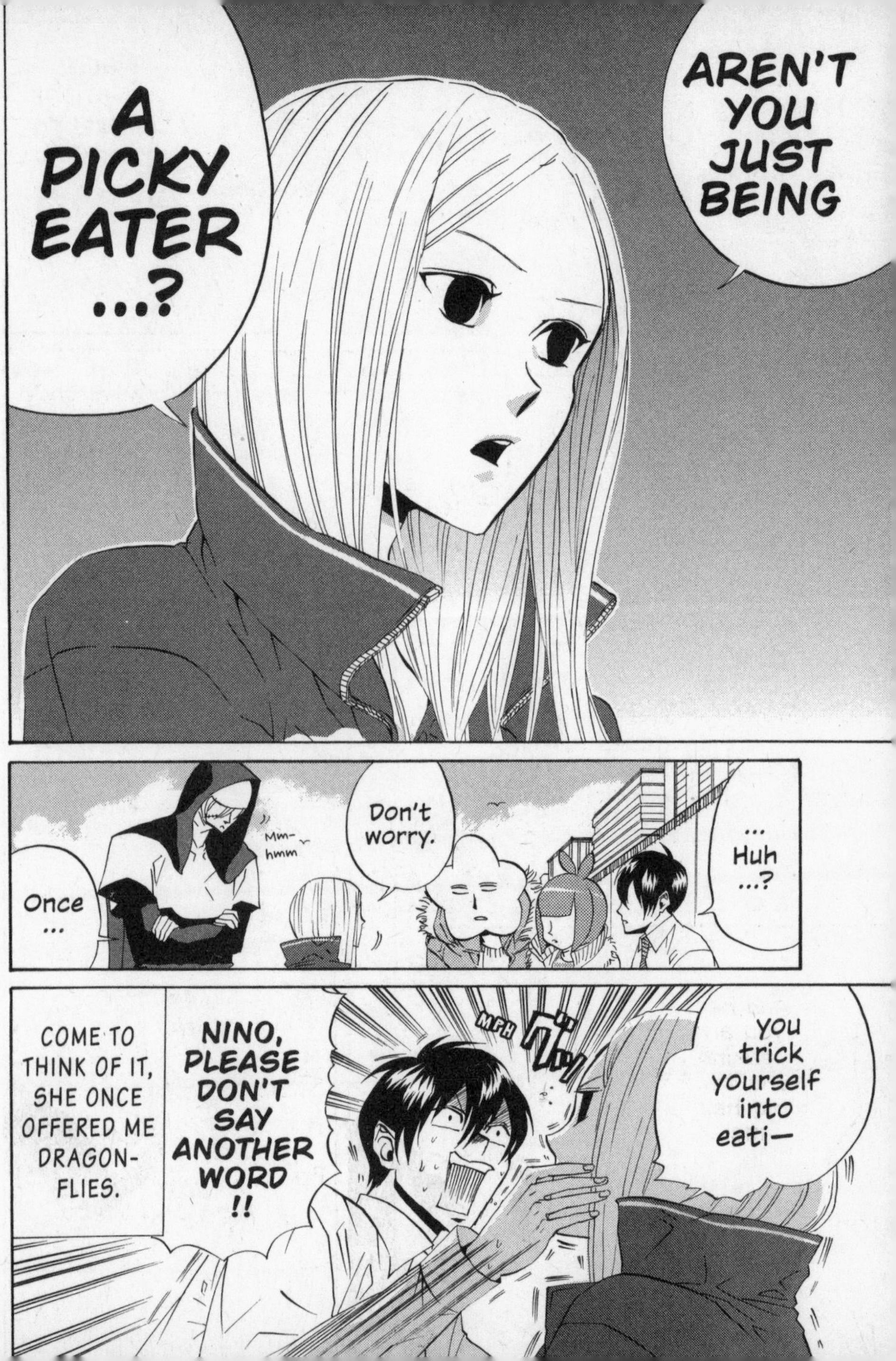
AREN'T YOU JUST BEING
A PICKY EATER ...?
... Huh ...?
Don't worry.
Mm-hmm
Once ...
you trick yourself into eati—
MPH
NINO, PLEASE DON'T SAY ANOTHER WORD !!
COME TO THINK OF IT, SHE ONCE OFFERED ME DRAGON-FLIES.

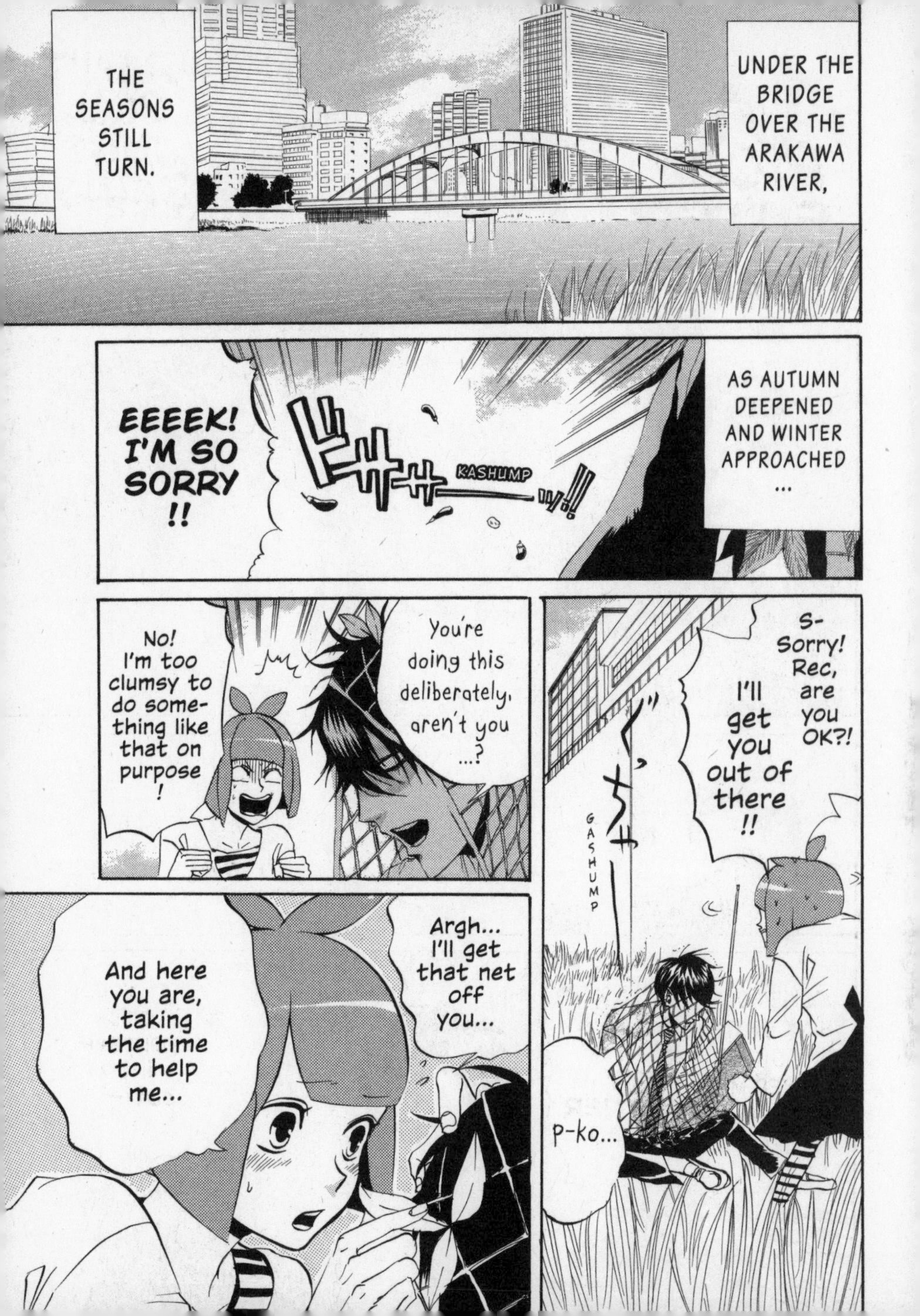
UNDER THE BRIDGE OVER THE ARAKAWA RIVER,
THE SEASONS STILL TURN.
AS AUTUMN DEEPENED AND WINTER APPROACHED ...
KASHUMP
EEEEK! I'M SO SORRY !!
S-Sorry! Rec, are you OK?!
I'll get you out of there !!
GASHUMP
P-ko...
You're doing this deliberately, aren't you ...?
No! I'm too clumsy to do something like that on purpose !
Argh... I'll get that net off you...
And here you are, taking the time to help me...

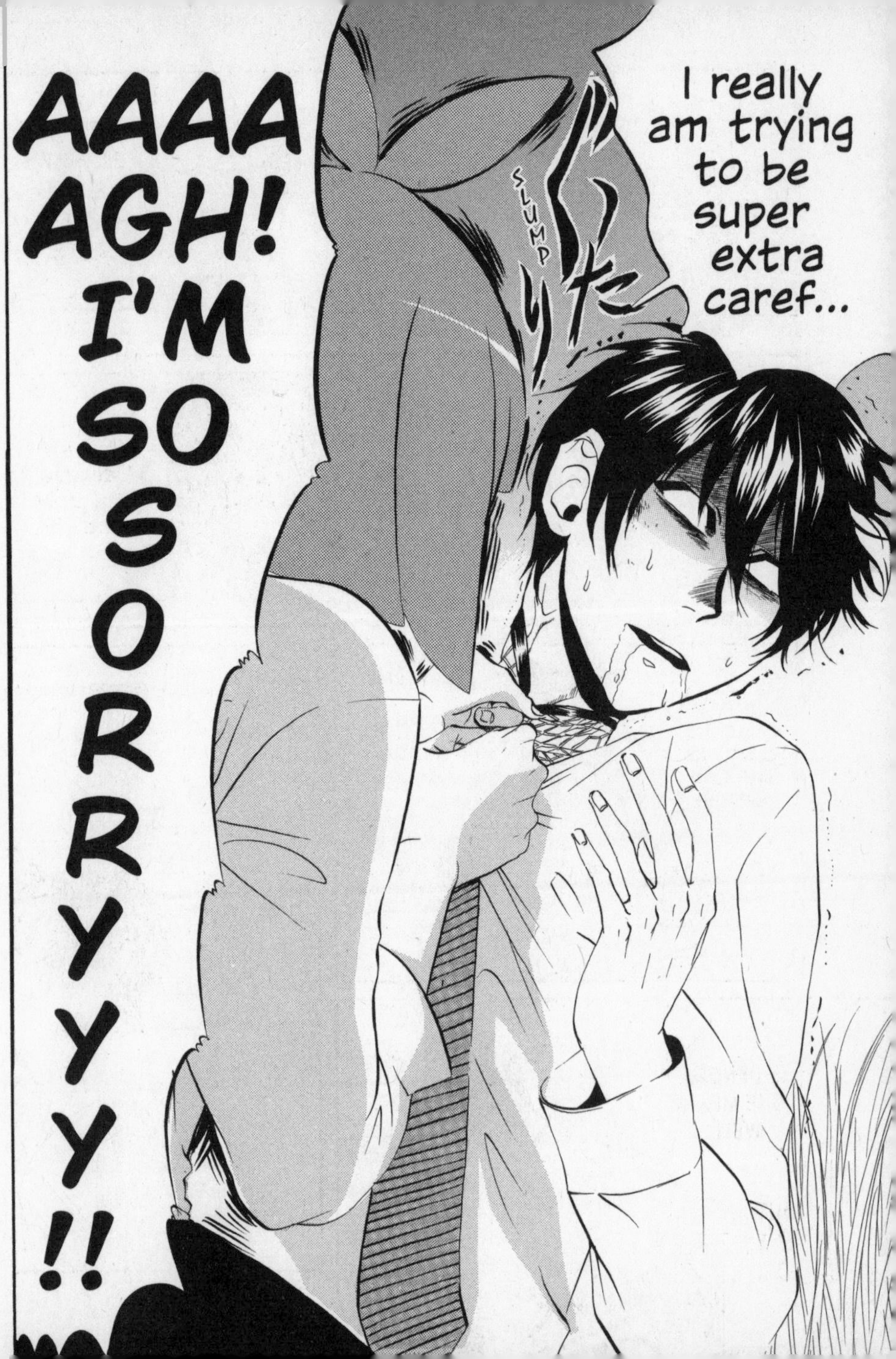
I really am trying to be super extra caref...
SLUMP
AAAAAGH! I'M SO SORRYYY!!

Chapter 66: Winter

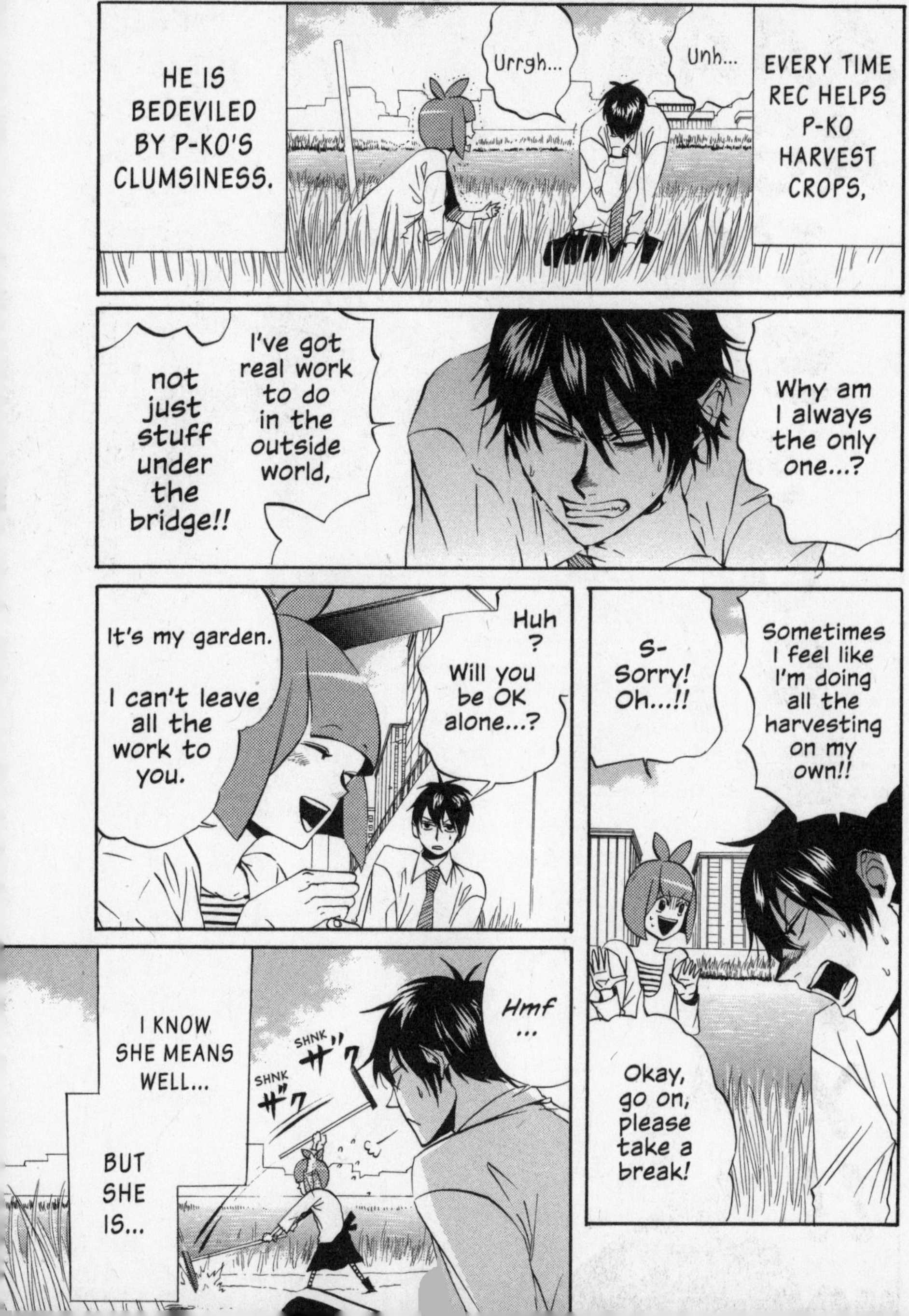
EVERY TIME REC HELPS P-KO HARVEST CROPS,
Unh...
Urrgh...
HE IS BEDEVILED BY P-KO'S CLUMSINESS.
Why am I always the only one...?
I've got real work to do in the outside world,
not just stuff under the bridge!!
Sometimes I feel like I'm doing all the harvesting on my own!!
S- Sorry! Oh...!!
Okay, go on, please take a break!
Huh?
Will you be OK alone...?
It's my garden.
I can't leave all the work to you.
Hmf...
SHNK ザク
SHNK ザク
I KNOW SHE MEANS WELL...
BUT SHE IS...

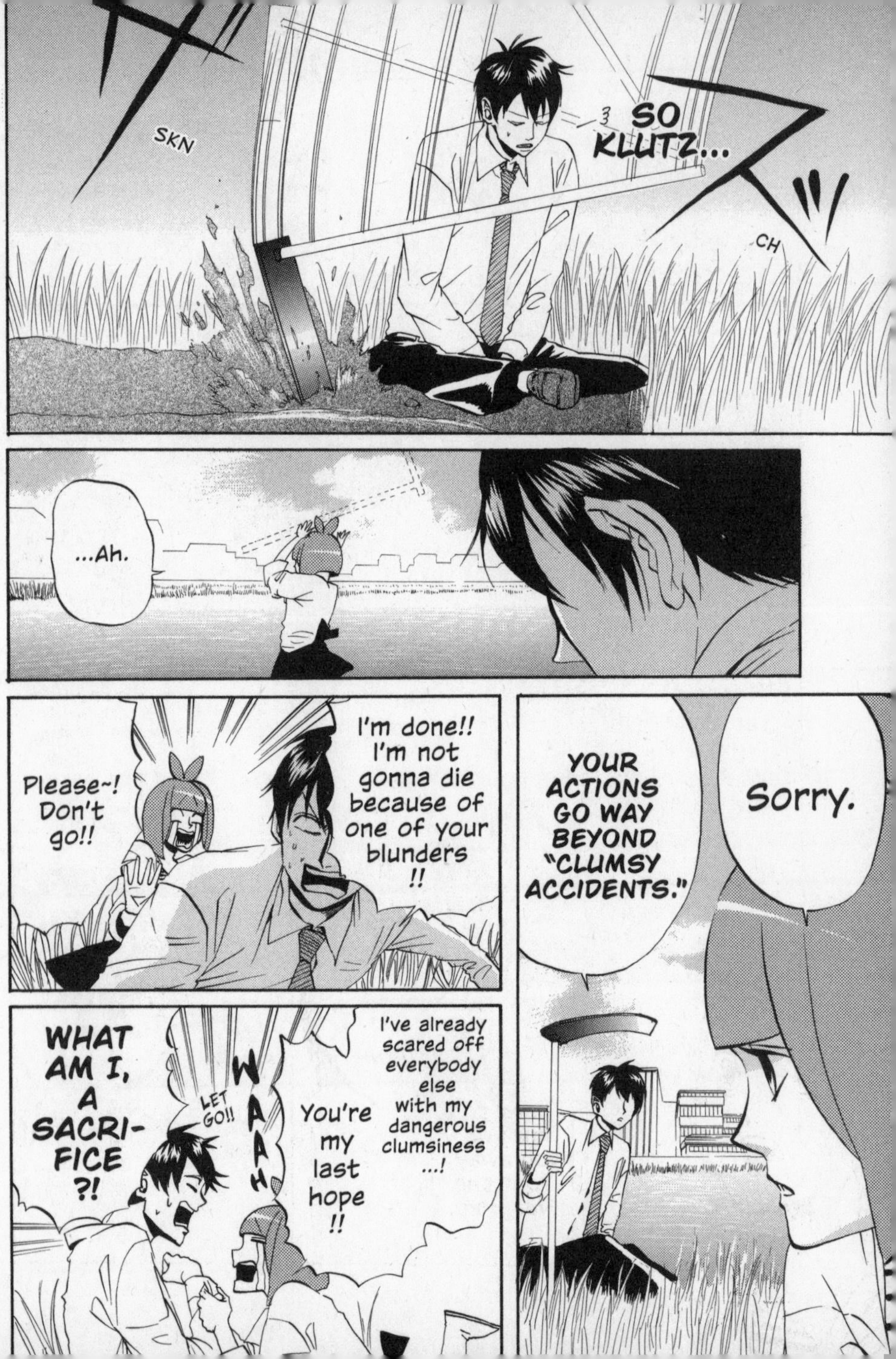
SO KLUTZ...
SKN
CH
...Ah.
Sorry.
YOUR ACTIONS GO WAY BEYOND "CLUMSY ACCIDENTS."
I'm done!! I'm not gonna die because of one of your blunders !!
Please~! Don't go!!
I've already scared off everybody else with my dangerous clumsiness ...!
You're my last hope !!
WAAH
LET GO!!
WHAT AM I, A SACRIFICE ?!

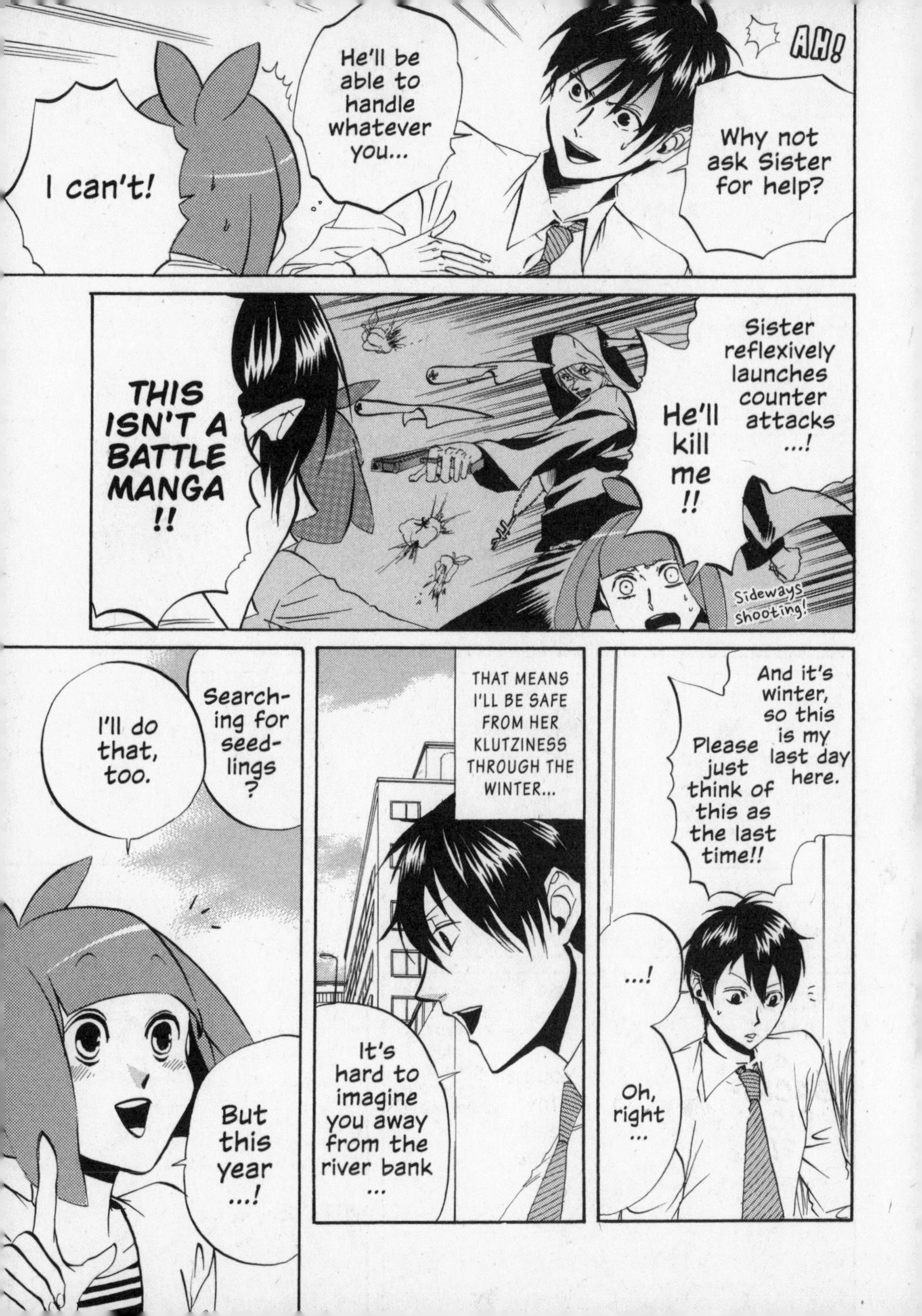
AH!
Why not ask Sister for help?
He'll be able to handle whatever you...
I can't!
Sister reflexively launches counter attacks ...!
He'll kill me !!
THIS ISN'T A BATTLE MANGA !!
Sideways shooting!
And it's winter, so this is my last day here.
Please just think of this as the last time!!
...!
Oh, right ...
THAT MEANS I'LL BE SAFE FROM HER KLUTZINESS THROUGH THE WINTER...
It's hard to imagine you away from the river bank ...
Searching for seedlings?
I'll do that, too.
But this year ...!

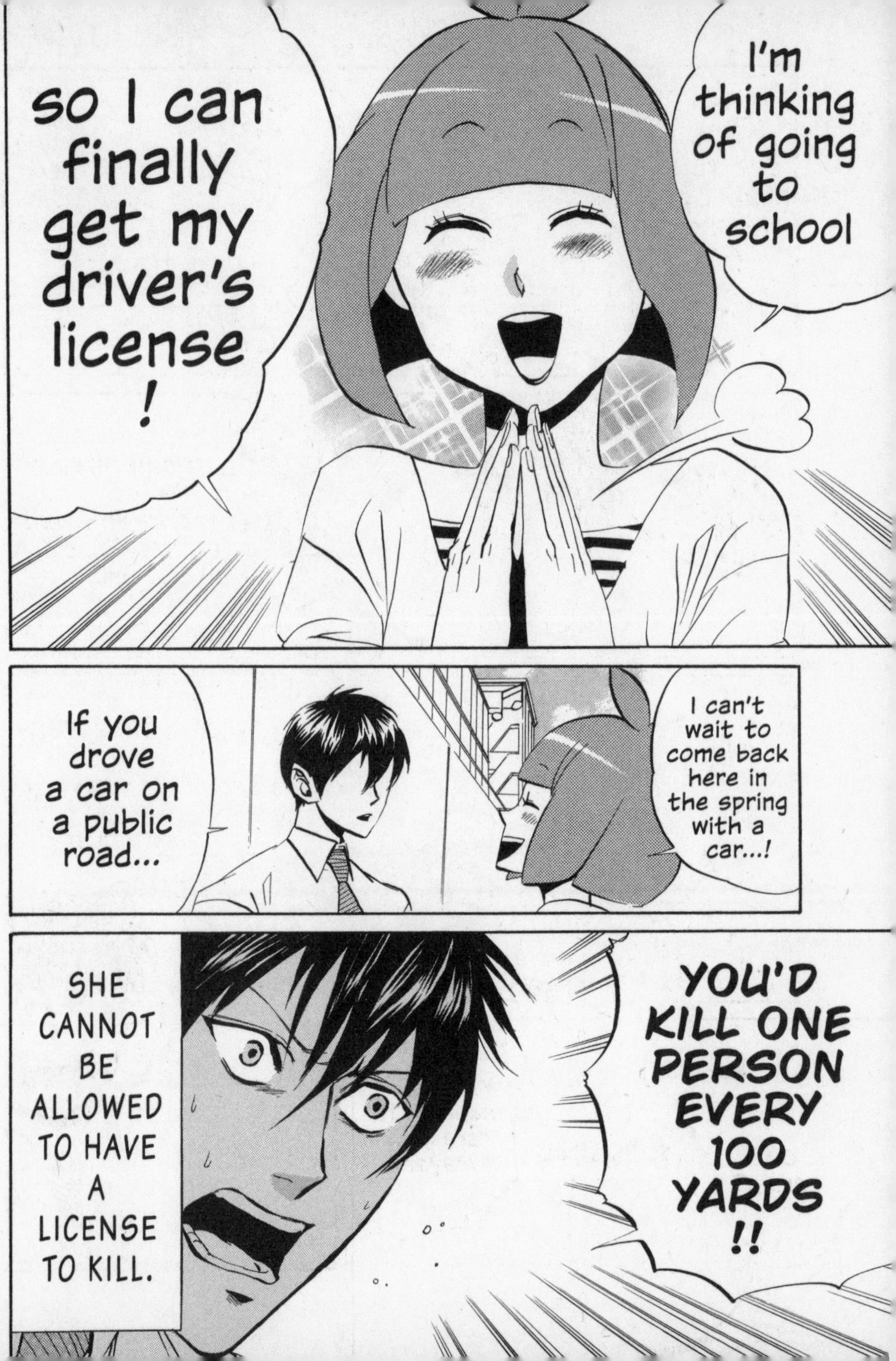
I'm thinking of going to school
so I can finally get my driver's license !
I can't wait to come back here in the spring with a car...!
If you drove a car on a public road...
YOU'D KILL ONE PERSON EVERY 100 YARDS !!
SHE CANNOT BE ALLOWED TO HAVE A LICENSE TO KILL.

Chapter 67: Change

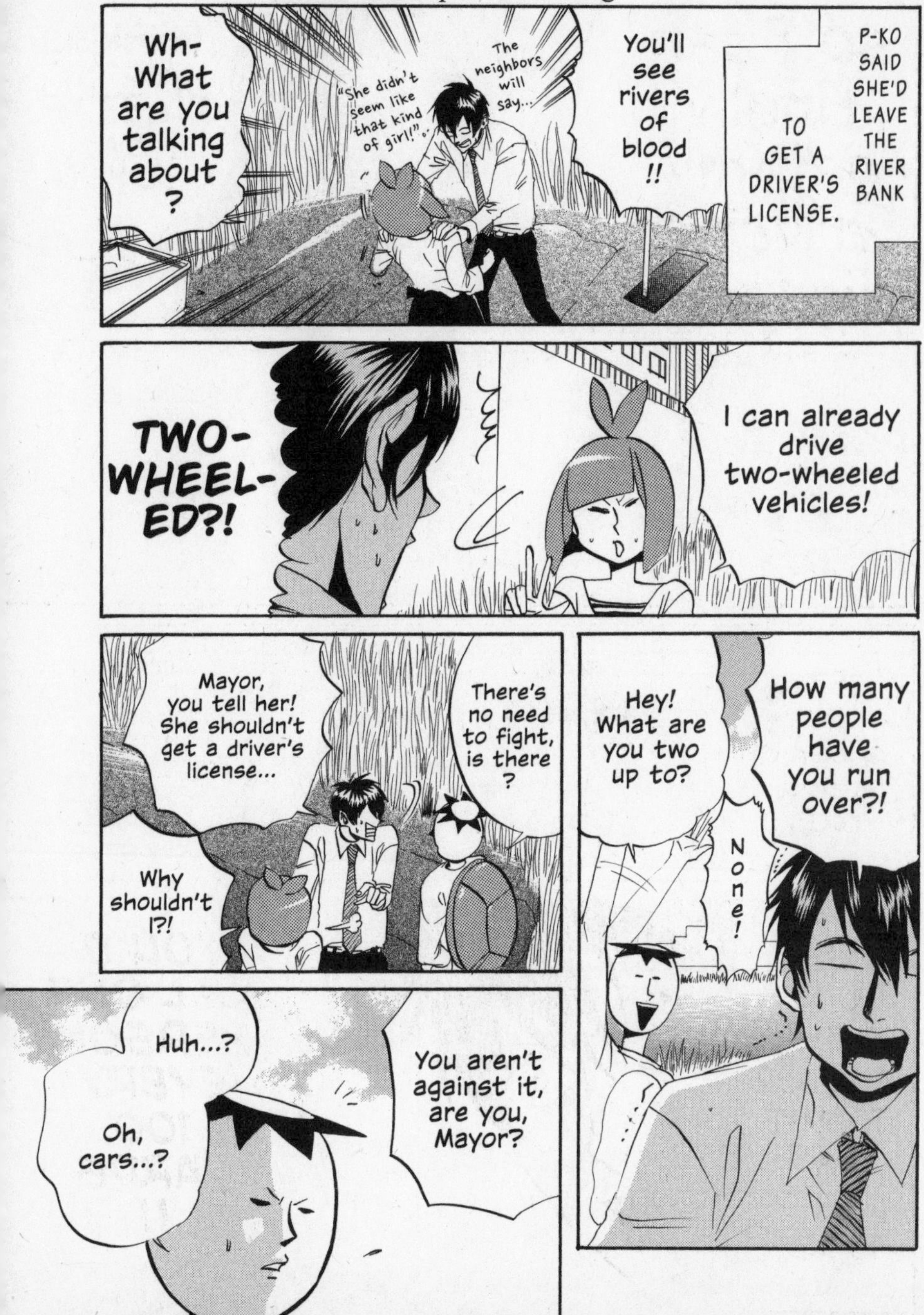
P-KO SAID SHE'D LEAVE THE RIVER BANK
TO GET A DRIVER'S LICENSE.
You'll see rivers of blood !!
The neighbors will say...
"She didn't seem like that kind of girl!"
Wh- What are you talking about ?
I can already drive two-wheeled vehicles!
TWO-WHEELED?!
How many people have you run over?!
Hey! What are you two up to?
None!
There's no need to fight, is there ?
Mayor, you tell her! She shouldn't get a driver's license...
Why shouldn't I?!
You aren't against it, are you, Mayor?
Huh...?
Oh, cars...?

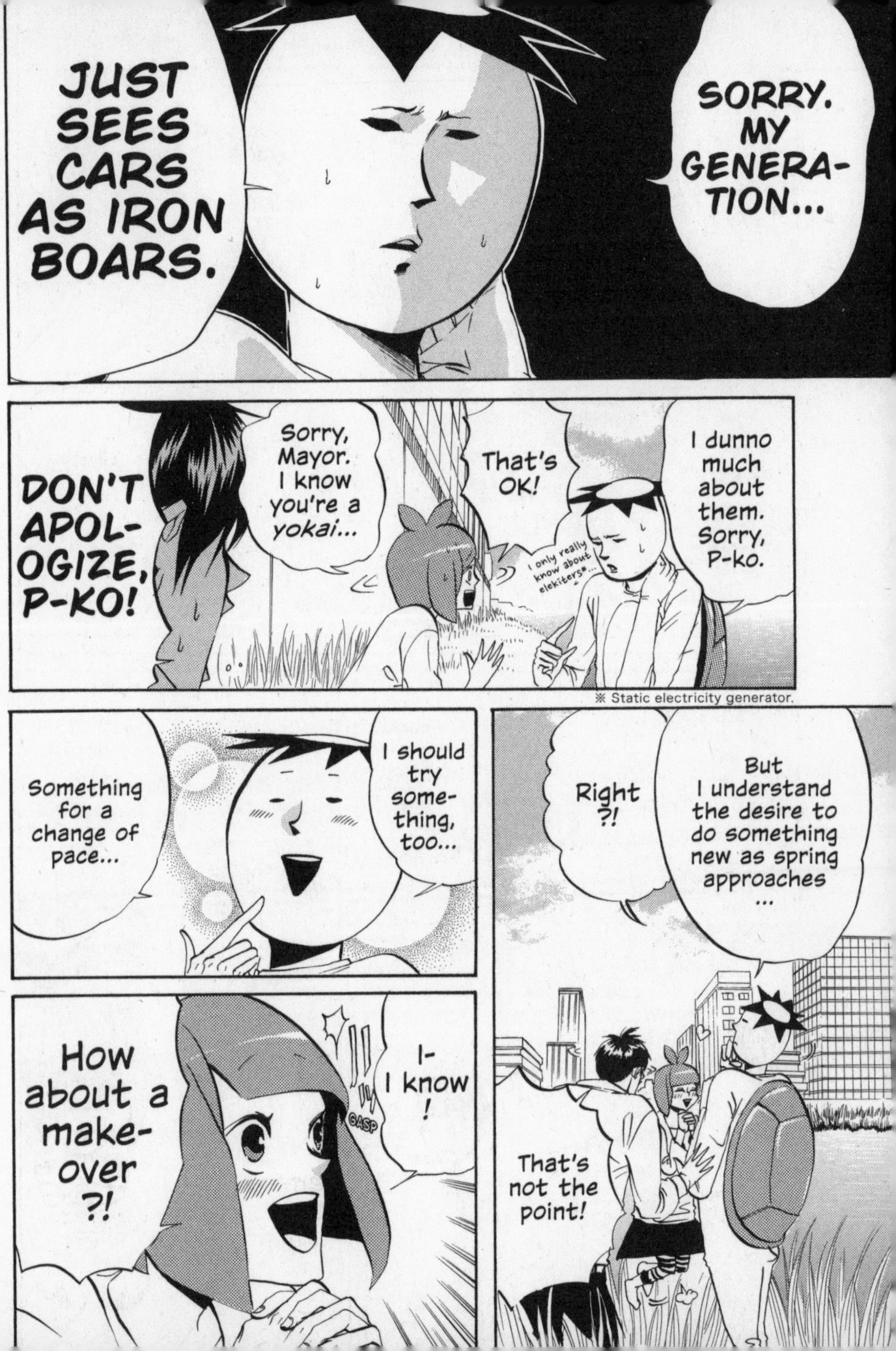
SORRY. MY GENERA-TION...
JUST SEES CARS AS IRON BOARS.
I dunno much about them. Sorry, P-ko.
I only really know about elekiters*...
That's OK!
Sorry, Mayor. I know you're a yokai...
DON'T APOL-OGIZE, P-KO!
※ Static electricity generator.
But I understand the desire to do something new as spring approaches ...
Right ?!
I should try some-thing, too...
Something for a change of pace...
That's not the point!
I- I know !
GASP
How about a make-over ?!

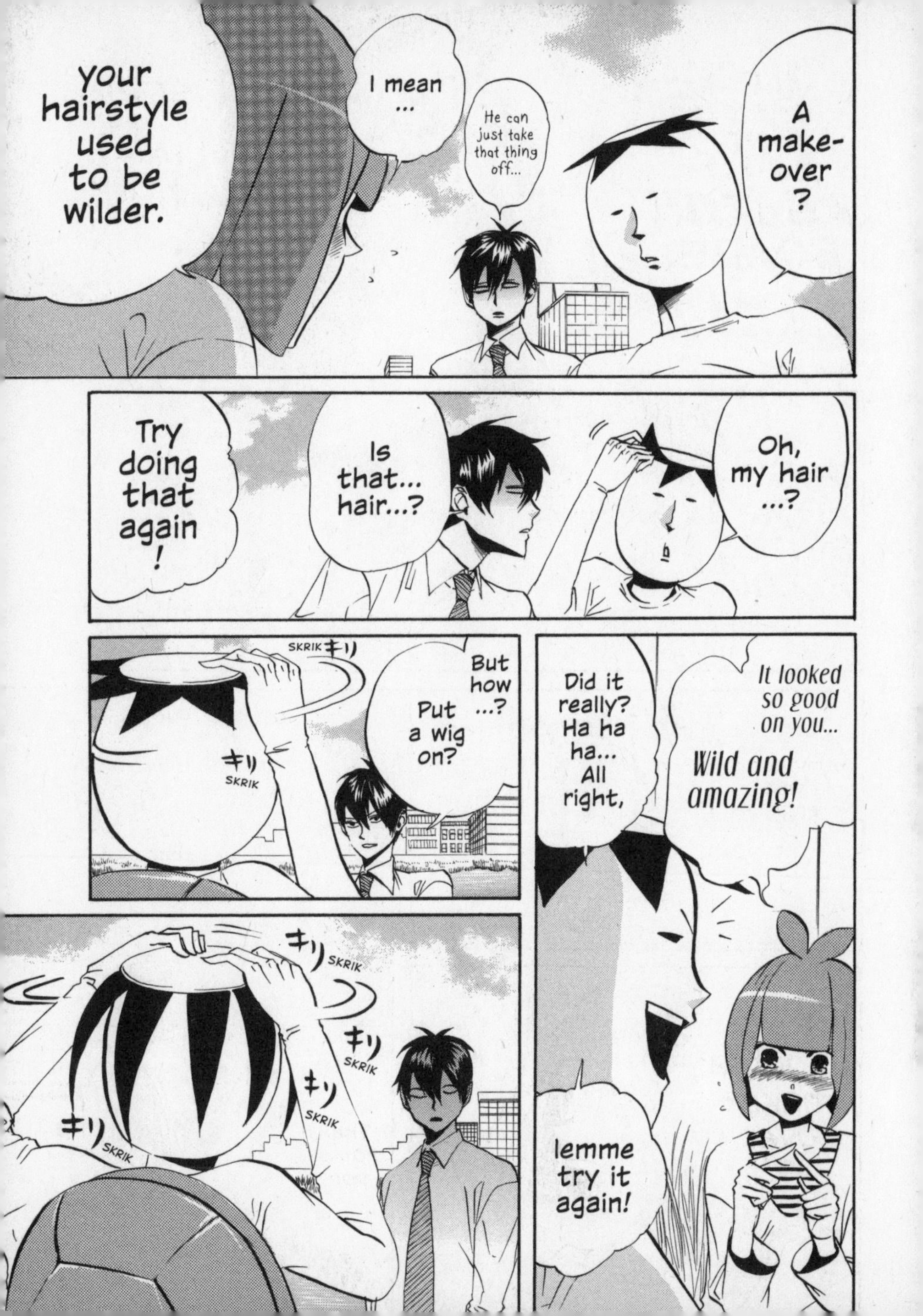
A make-over?
He can just take that thing off...
I mean ...
your hairstyle used to be wilder.
Oh, my hair ...?
Is that... hair...?
Try doing that again!
It looked so good on you...
Wild and amazing!
Did it really? Ha ha ha... All right,
lemme try it again!
キリ SKRIK
But how ...?
Put a wig on?
キリ SKRIK
キリ SKRIK
キリ SKRIK
キリ SKRIK
キリ SKRIK

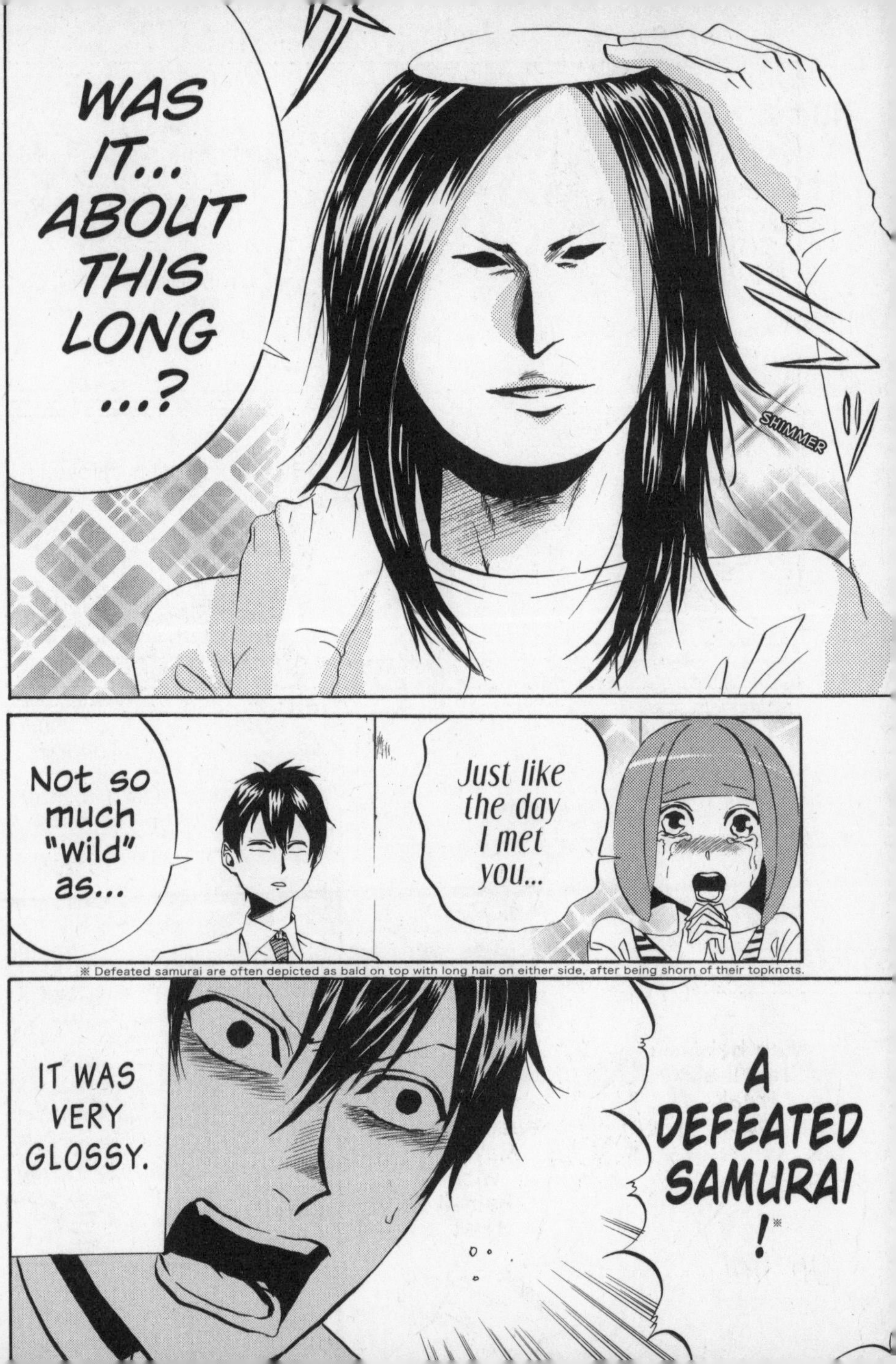
WAS IT... ABOUT THIS LONG ...?
SHIMMER
Just like the day I met you...
Not so much "wild" as...
A DEFEATED SAMURAI!※
IT WAS VERY GLOSSY.
※ Defeated samurai are often depicted as bald on top with long hair on either side, after being shorn of their topknots.

Chapter 68: What is Common Sense?

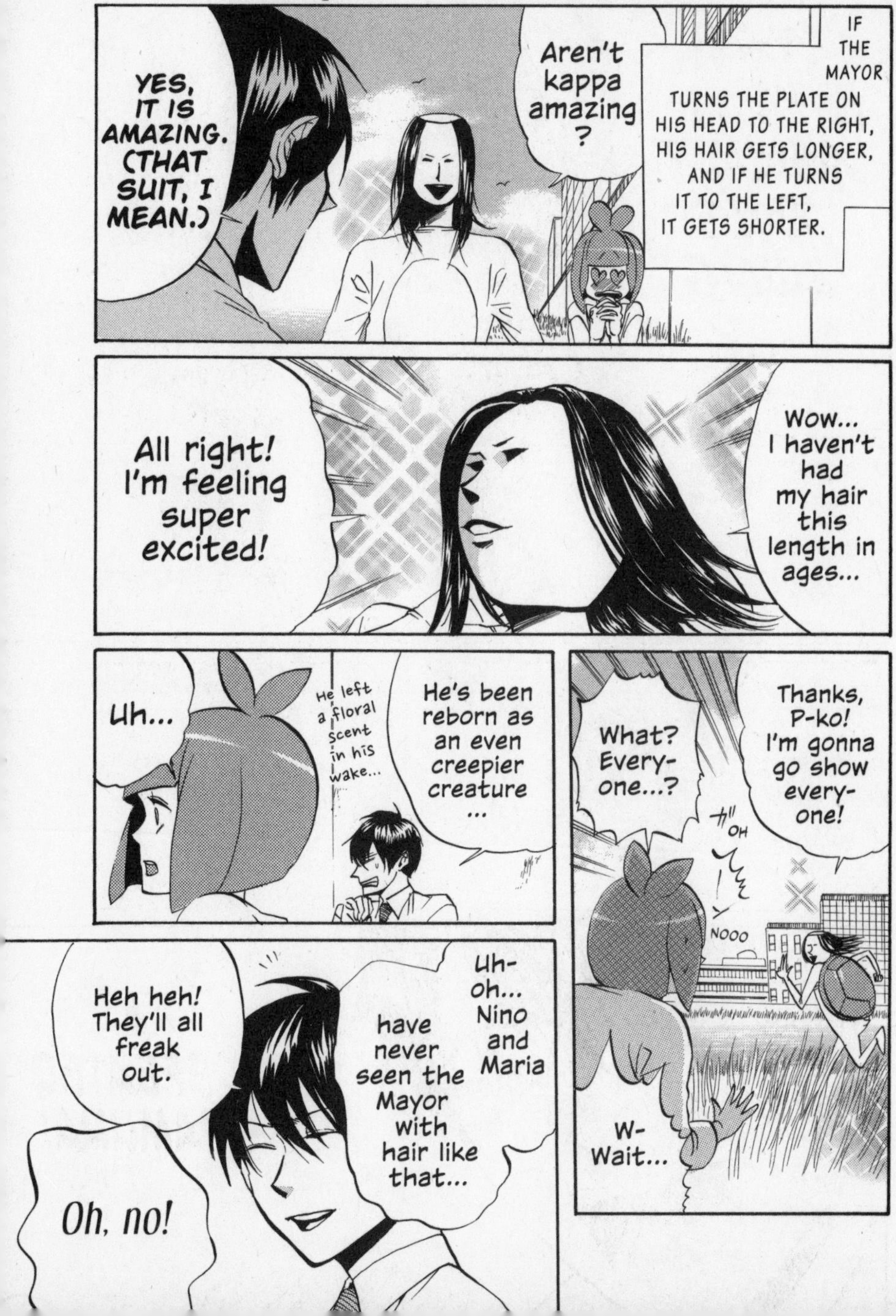
IF THE MAYOR TURNS THE PLATE ON HIS HEAD TO THE RIGHT, HIS HAIR GETS LONGER, AND IF HE TURNS IT TO THE LEFT, IT GETS SHORTER.
Aren't kappa amazing?
YES, IT IS AMAZING. (THAT SUIT, I MEAN.)
Wow... I haven't had my hair this length in ages...
All right! I'm feeling super excited!
Thanks, P-ko! I'm gonna go show every-one!
What? Every-one...?
OH
NOOO
W-Wait...
He's been reborn as an even creepier creature ...
He left a floral scent in his wake...
Uh...
Uh-oh... Nino and Maria have never seen the Mayor with hair like that...
Heh heh! They'll all freak out.
Oh, no!

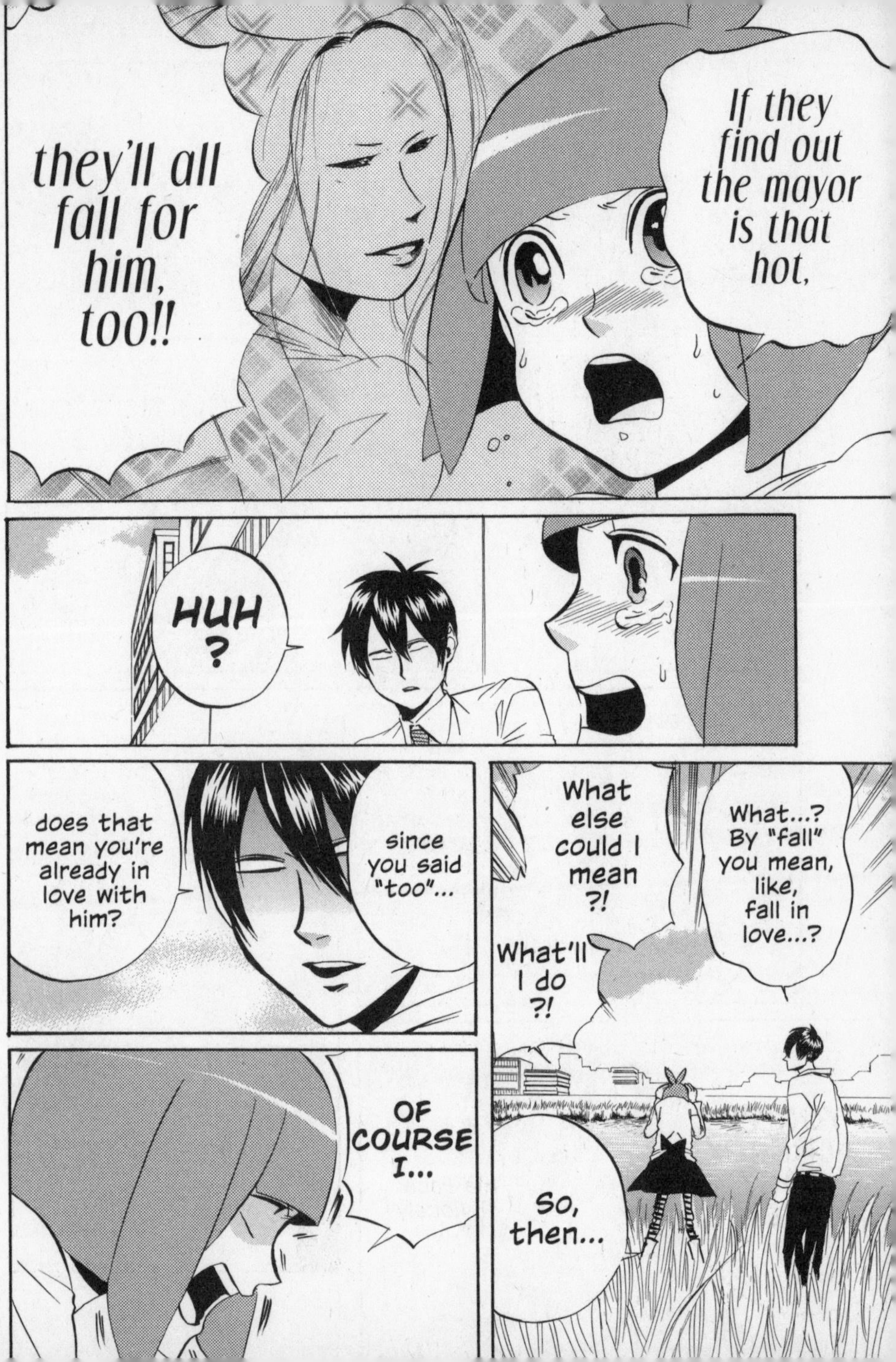
If they find out the mayor is that hot,
they'll all fall for him, too!!
HUH?
What...? By "fall" you mean, like, fall in love...?
What else could I mean?!
What'll I do?!
So, then...
since you said "too"...
does that mean you're already in love with him?
OF COURSE I...

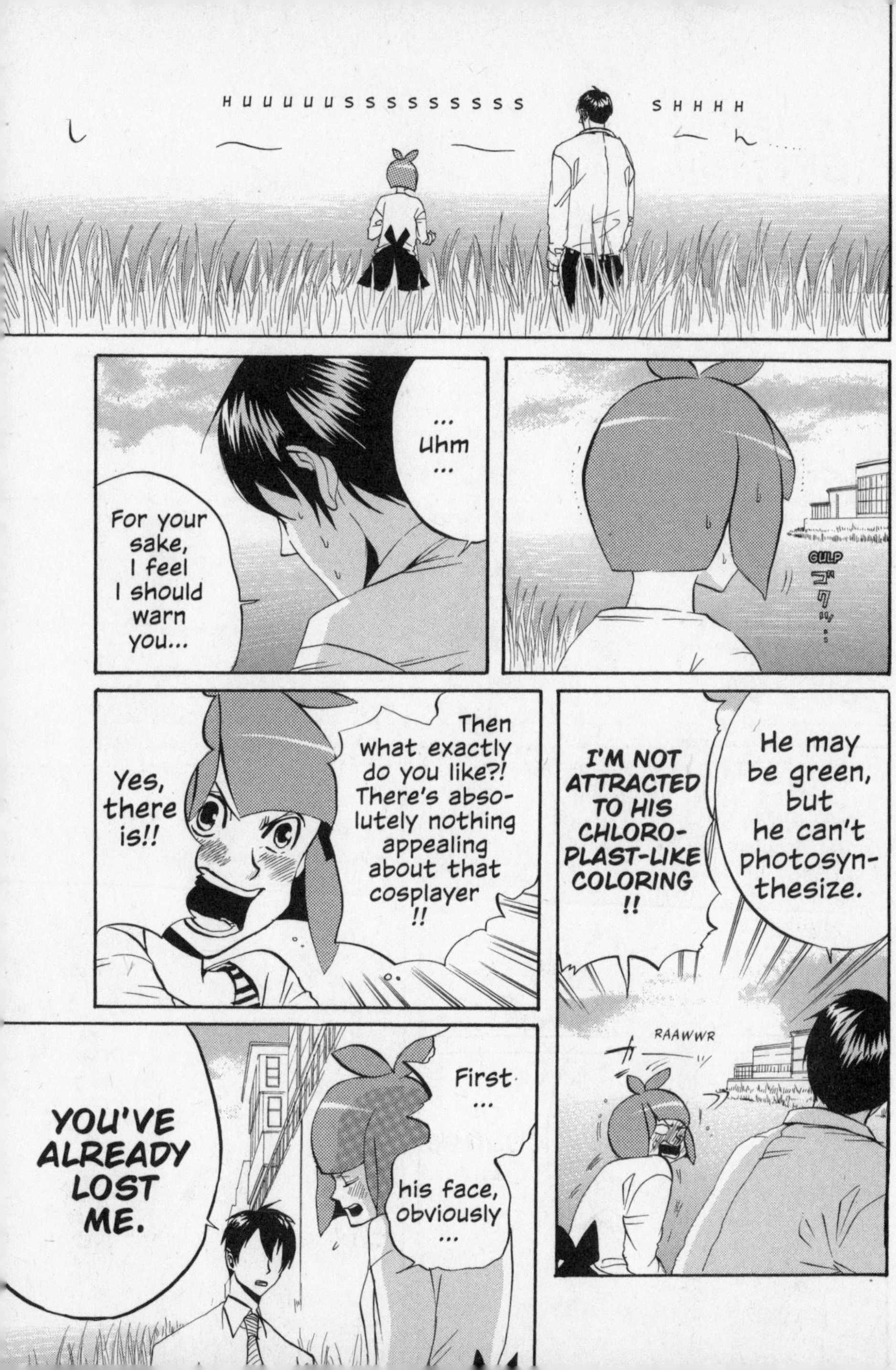
HUUUUUUSSSSSSSSS
SHHHH
GULP
... Uhm ...
For your sake, I feel I should warn you...
He may be green, but he can't photosynthesize.
I'M NOT ATTRACTED TO HIS CHLORO-PLAST-LIKE COLORING !!
Then what exactly do you like?! There's abso-lutely nothing appealing about that cosplayer !!
Yes, there is!!
RAAWWR
First ...
his face, obviously ...
YOU'VE ALREADY LOST ME.

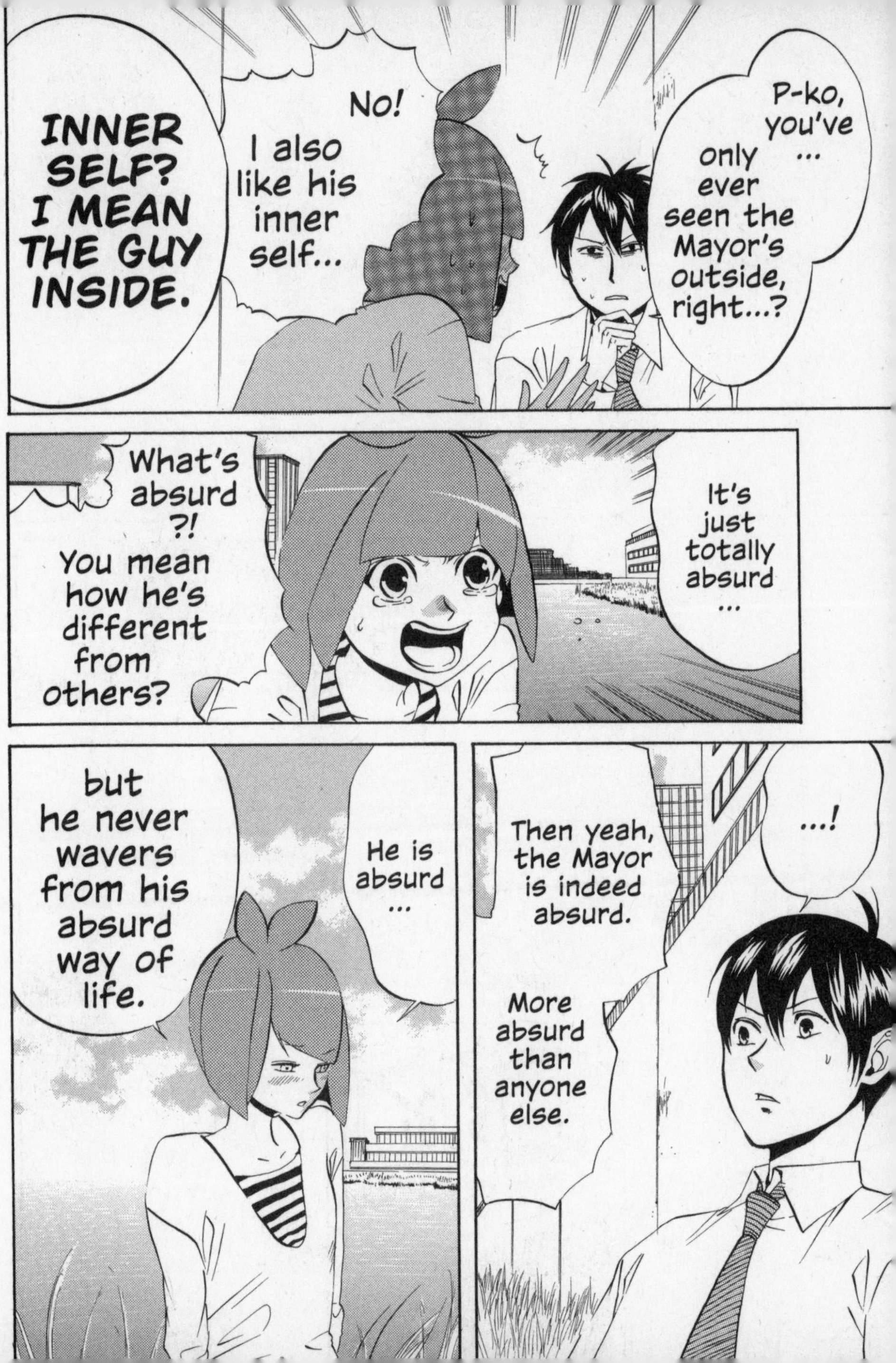
P-ko, you've... only ever seen the Mayor's outside, right...?
No!
I also like his inner self...
INNER SELF? I MEAN THE GUY INSIDE.
It's just totally absurd...
What's absurd?!
You mean how he's different from others?
...!
Then yeah, the Mayor is indeed absurd.
More absurd than anyone else.
He is absurd...
but he never wavers from his absurd way of life.

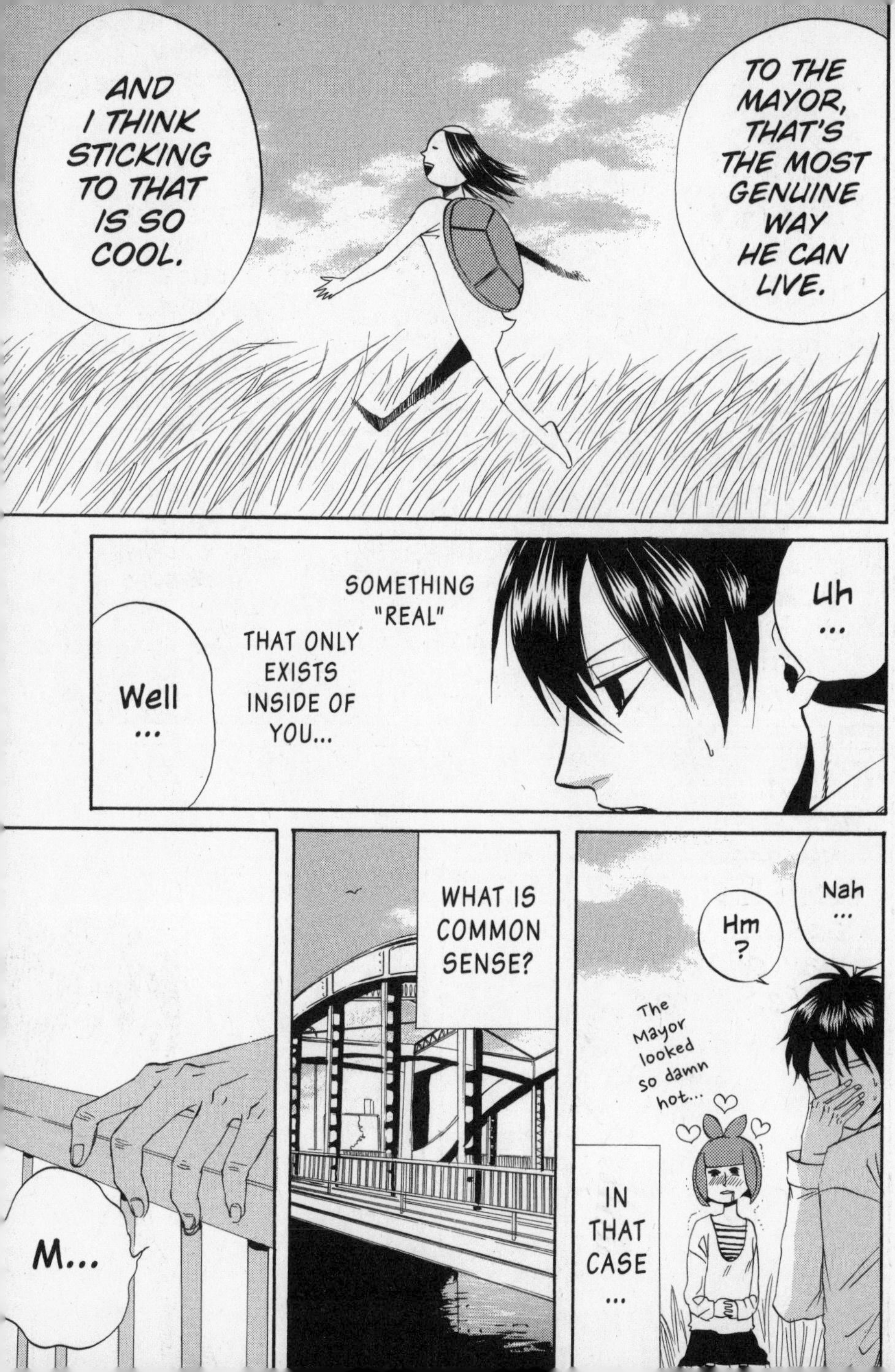
TO THE MAYOR, THAT'S THE MOST GENUINE WAY HE CAN LIVE.
AND I THINK STICKING TO THAT IS SO COOL.
Uh ...
SOMETHING "REAL" THAT ONLY EXISTS INSIDE OF YOU...
Well ...
Nah ...
Hm ?
The Mayor looked so damn hot...
IN THAT CASE ...
WHAT IS COMMON SENSE?
M...

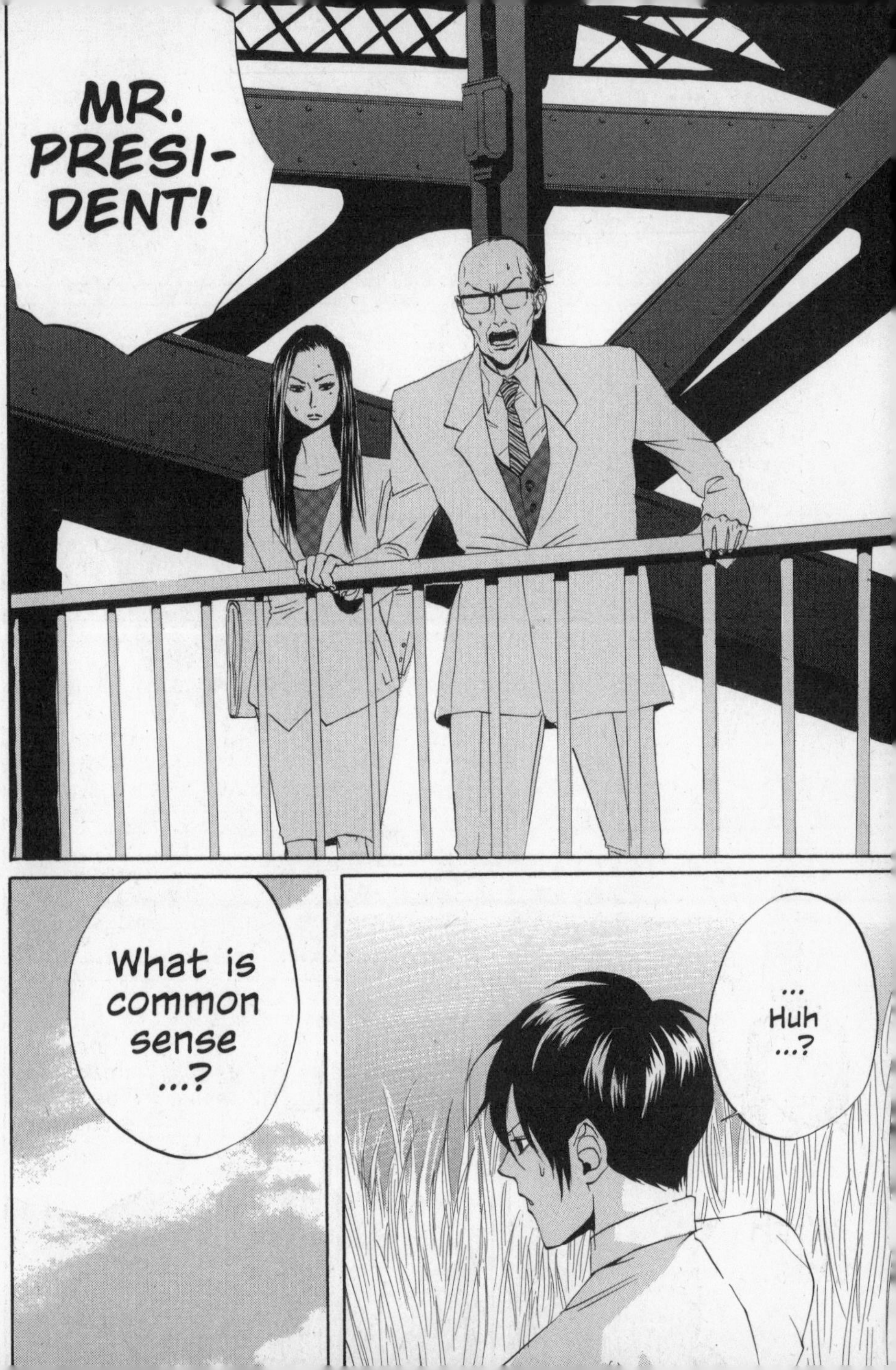
MR. PRESI-DENT!
... Huh ...?
What is common sense ...?

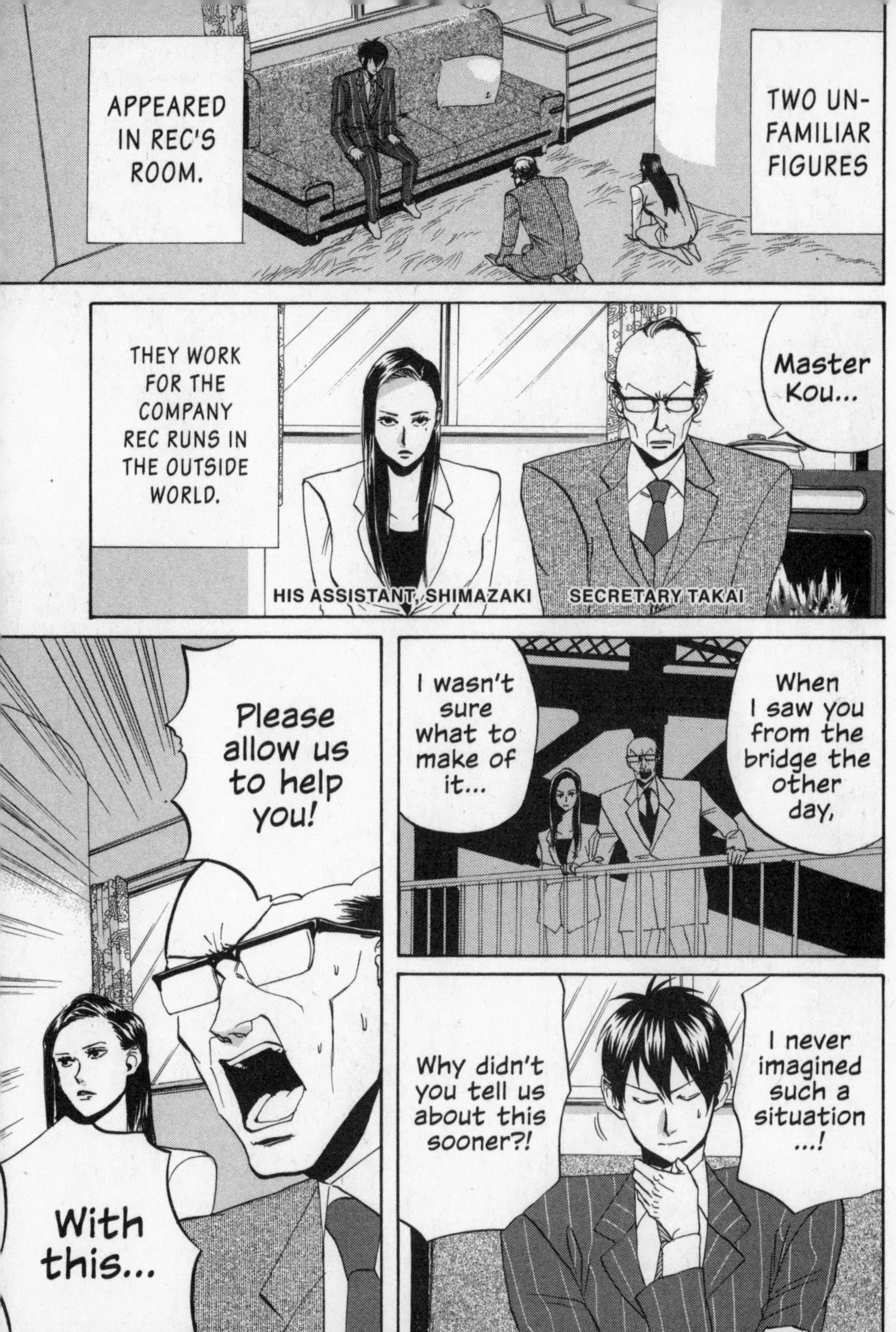
TWO UN-FAMILIAR FIGURES
APPEARED IN REC'S ROOM.
Master Kou...
THEY WORK FOR THE COMPANY REC RUNS IN THE OUTSIDE WORLD.
SECRETARY TAKAI
HIS ASSISTANT, SHIMAZAKI
When I saw you from the bridge the other day,
I wasn't sure what to make of it...
I never imagined such a situation ...!
Why didn't you tell us about this sooner?!
Please allow us to help you!
With this...

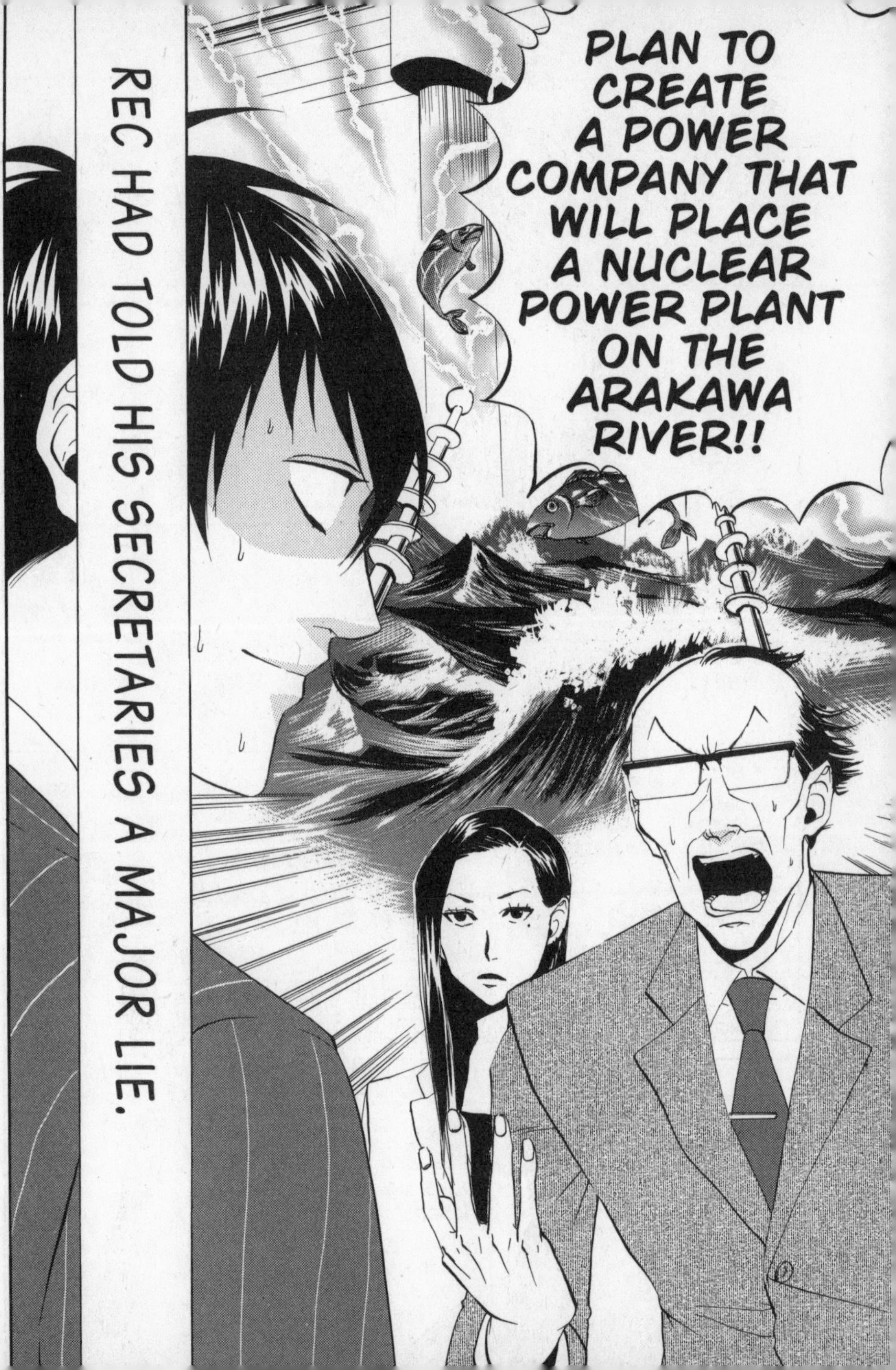
PLAN TO CREATE A POWER COMPANY THAT WILL PLACE A NUCLEAR POWER PLANT ON THE ARAKAWA RIVER!!
REC HAD TOLD HIS SECRETARIES A MAJOR LIE.

Chapter 69: Lie

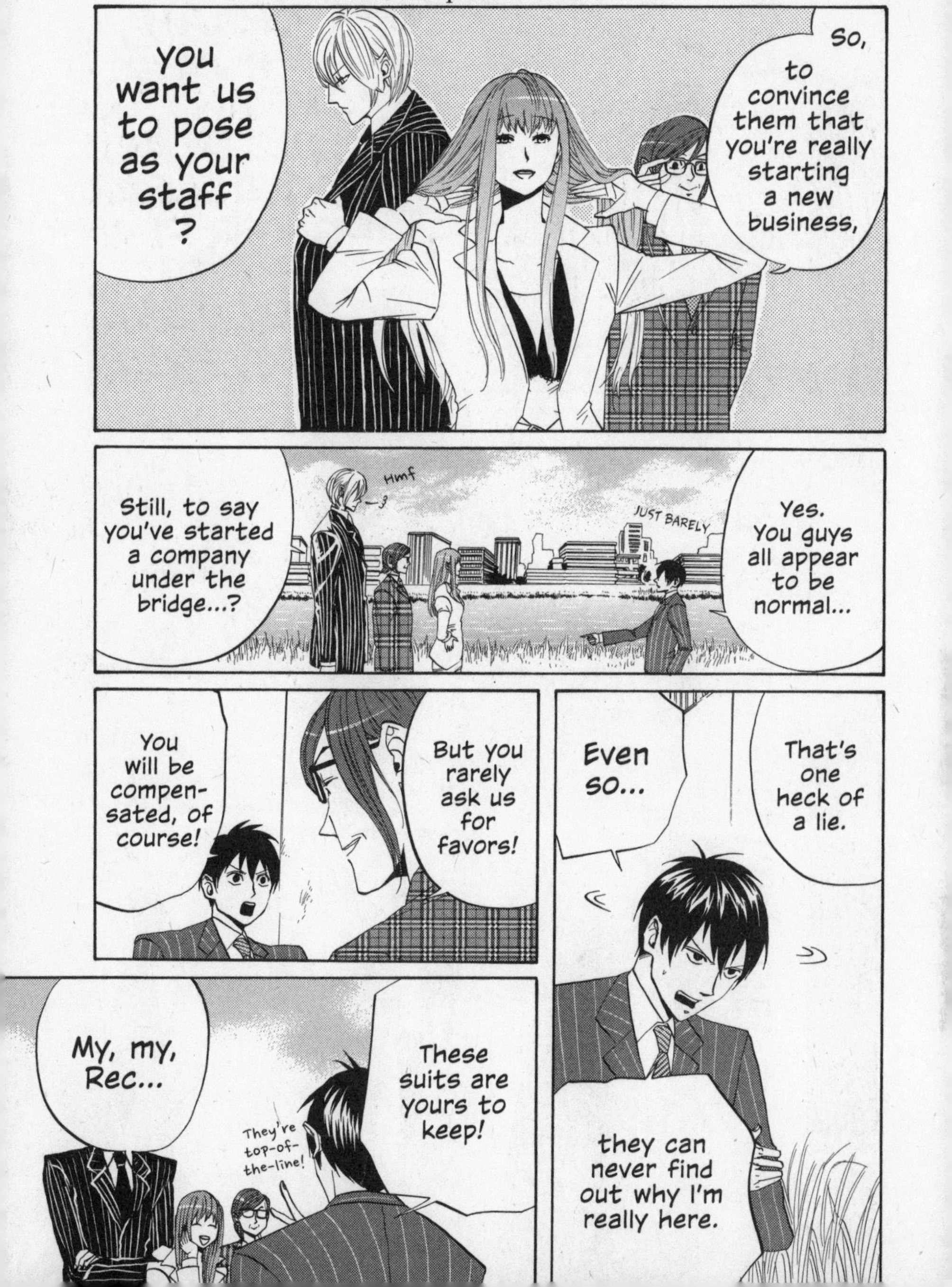
So, to convince them that you're really starting a new business,
you want us to pose as your staff?
Yes. You guys all appear to be normal...
JUST BARELY
Hmf
Still, to say you've started a company under the bridge...?
That's one heck of a lie.
Even so...
they can never find out why I'm really here.
But you rarely ask us for favors!
You will be compensated, of course!
These suits are yours to keep!
They're top-of-the-line!
My, my, Rec...

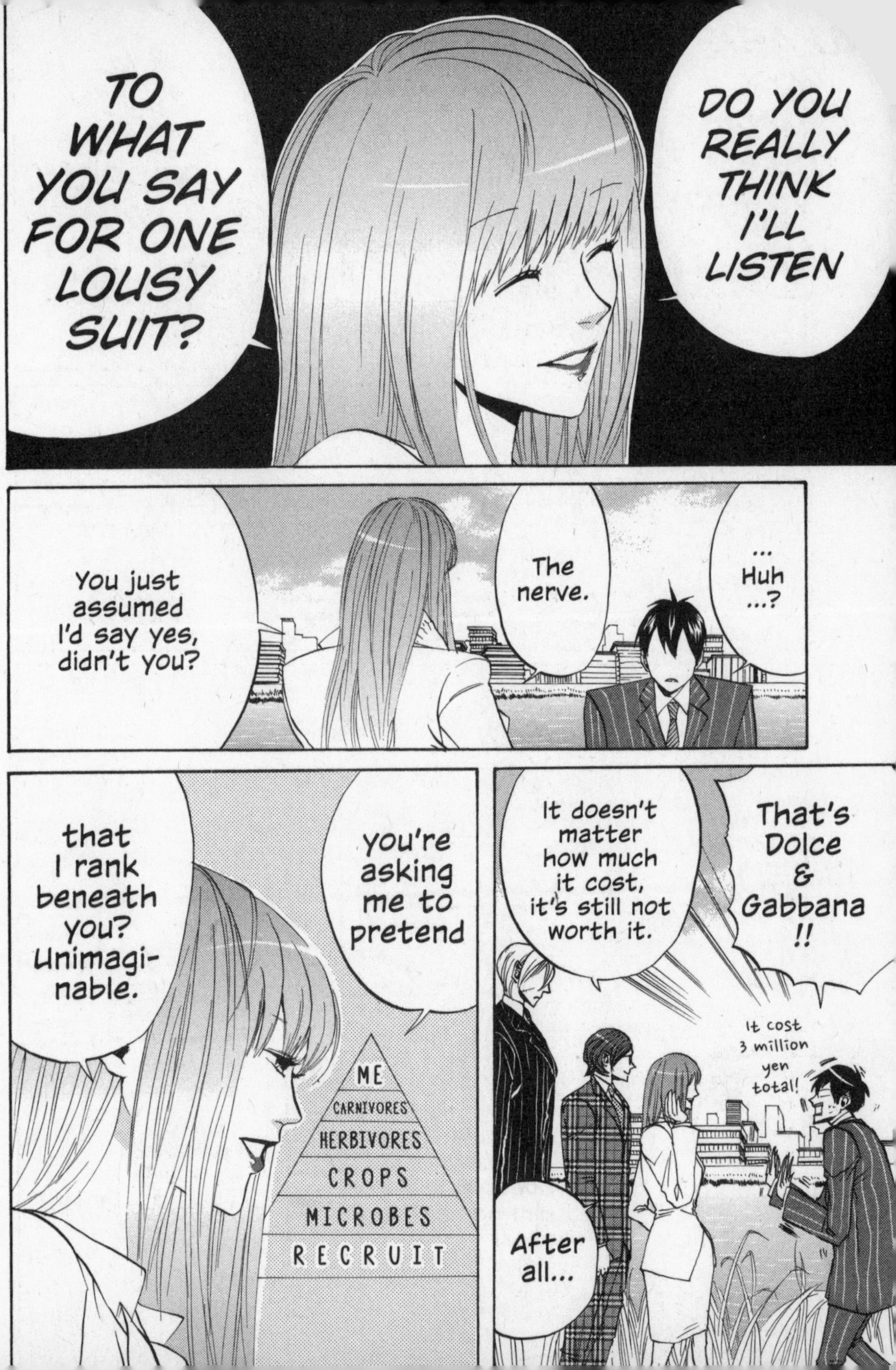
DO YOU REALLY THINK I'LL LISTEN
TO WHAT YOU SAY FOR ONE LOUSY SUIT?
... Huh ...?
The nerve.
You just assumed I'd say yes, didn't you?
That's Dolce & Gabbana !!
It doesn't matter how much it cost, it's still not worth it.
It cost 3 million yen total!
After all...
you're asking me to pretend
that I rank beneath you? Unimagi-nable.
ME
CARNIVORES
HERBIVORES
CROPS
MICROBES
RECRUIT

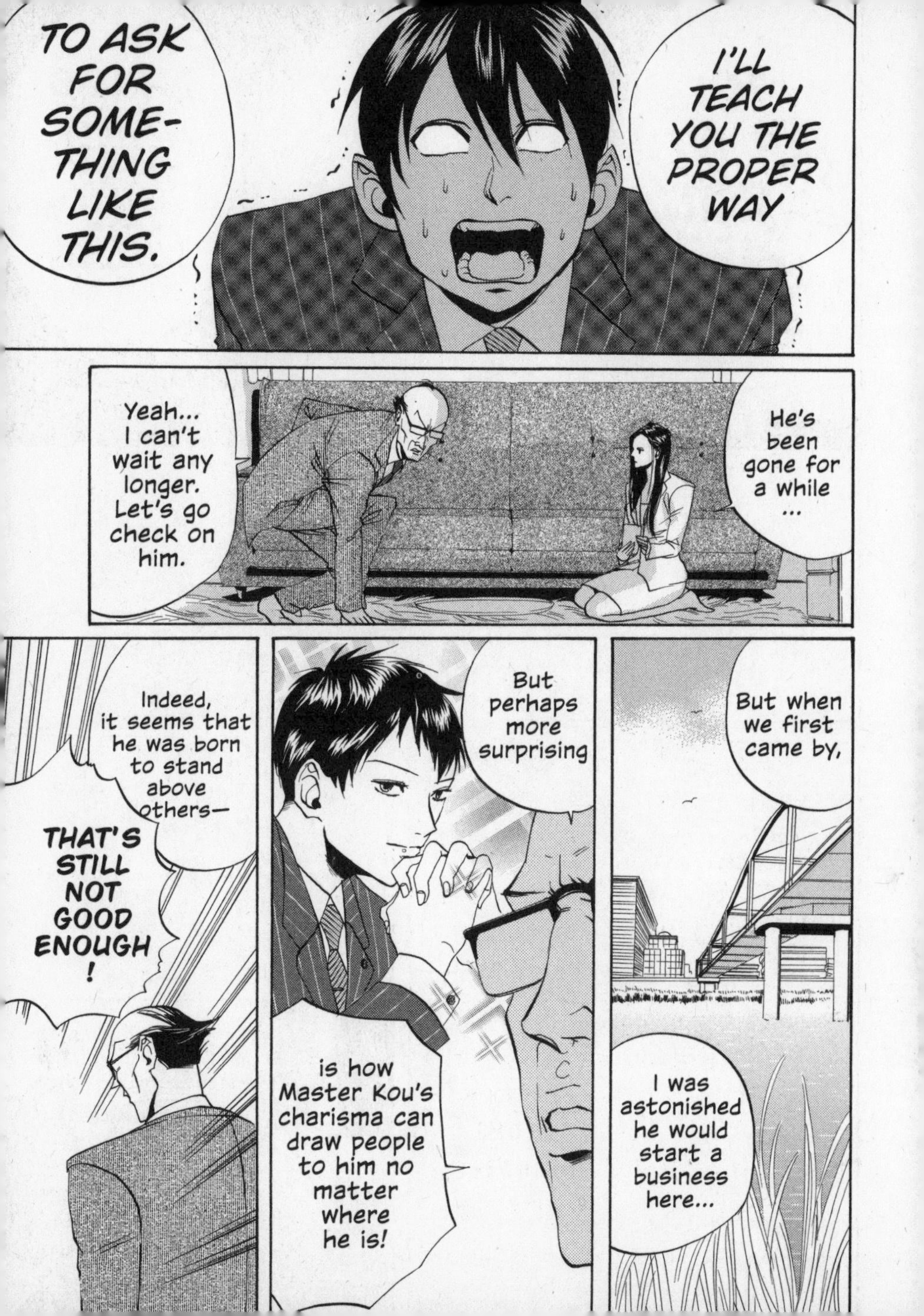
I'LL TEACH YOU THE PROPER WAY
TO ASK FOR SOMETHING LIKE THIS.
He's been gone for a while ...
Yeah... I can't wait any longer. Let's go check on him.
But when we first came by,
I was astonished he would start a business here...
But perhaps more surprising
is how Master Kou's charisma can draw people to him no matter where he is!
Indeed, it seems that he was born to stand above others—
THAT'S STILL NOT GOOD ENOUGH!

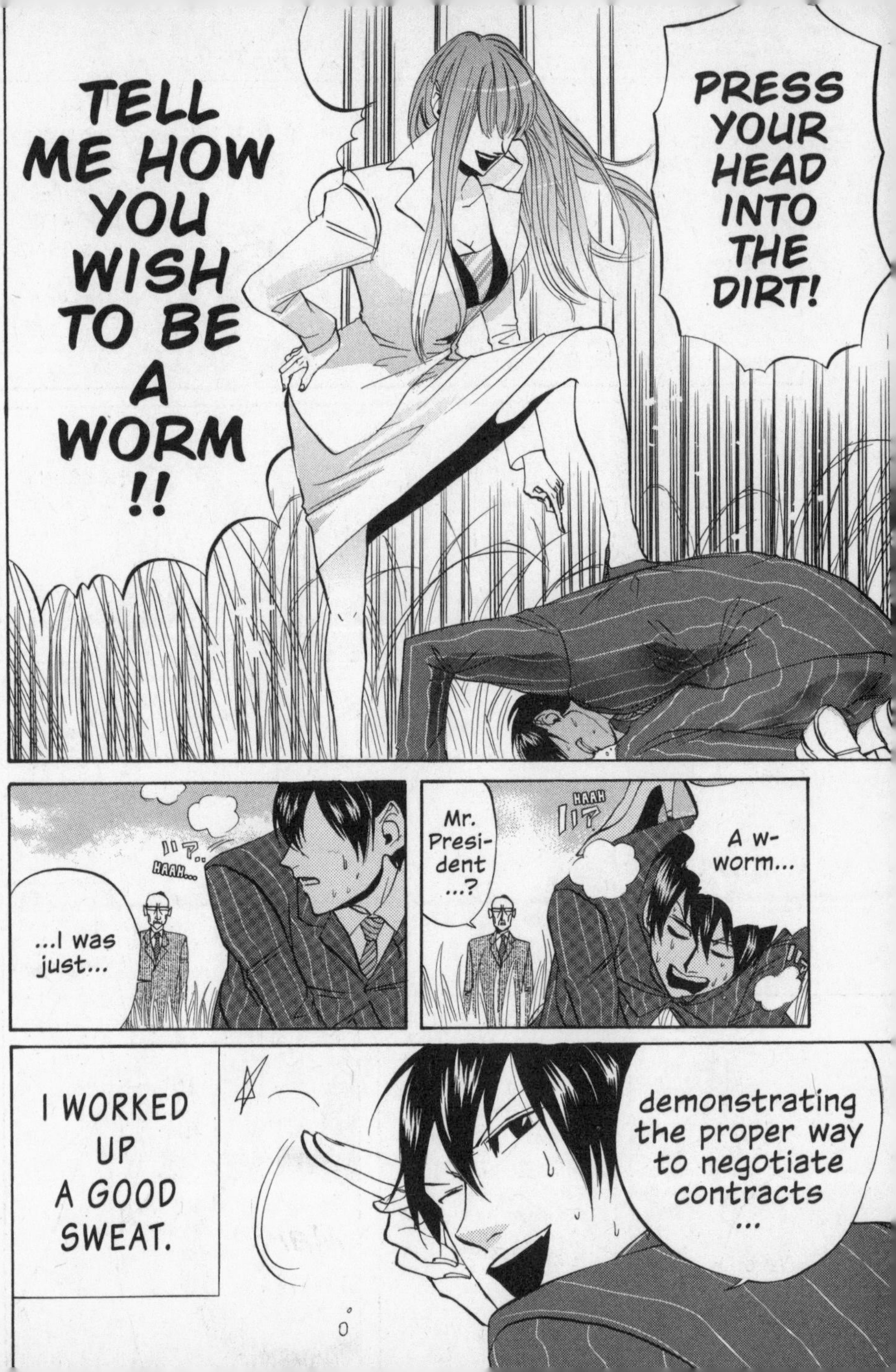
PRESS YOUR HEAD INTO THE DIRT!
TELL ME HOW YOU WISH TO BE A WORM !!
HAAH ハァ
A w-worm...
Mr. Presi-dent ...?
ハァ.. HAAH...
...I was just...
demonstrating the proper way to negotiate contracts ...
I WORKED UP A GOOD SWEAT.

Chapter 70: The Staff Under the Bridge

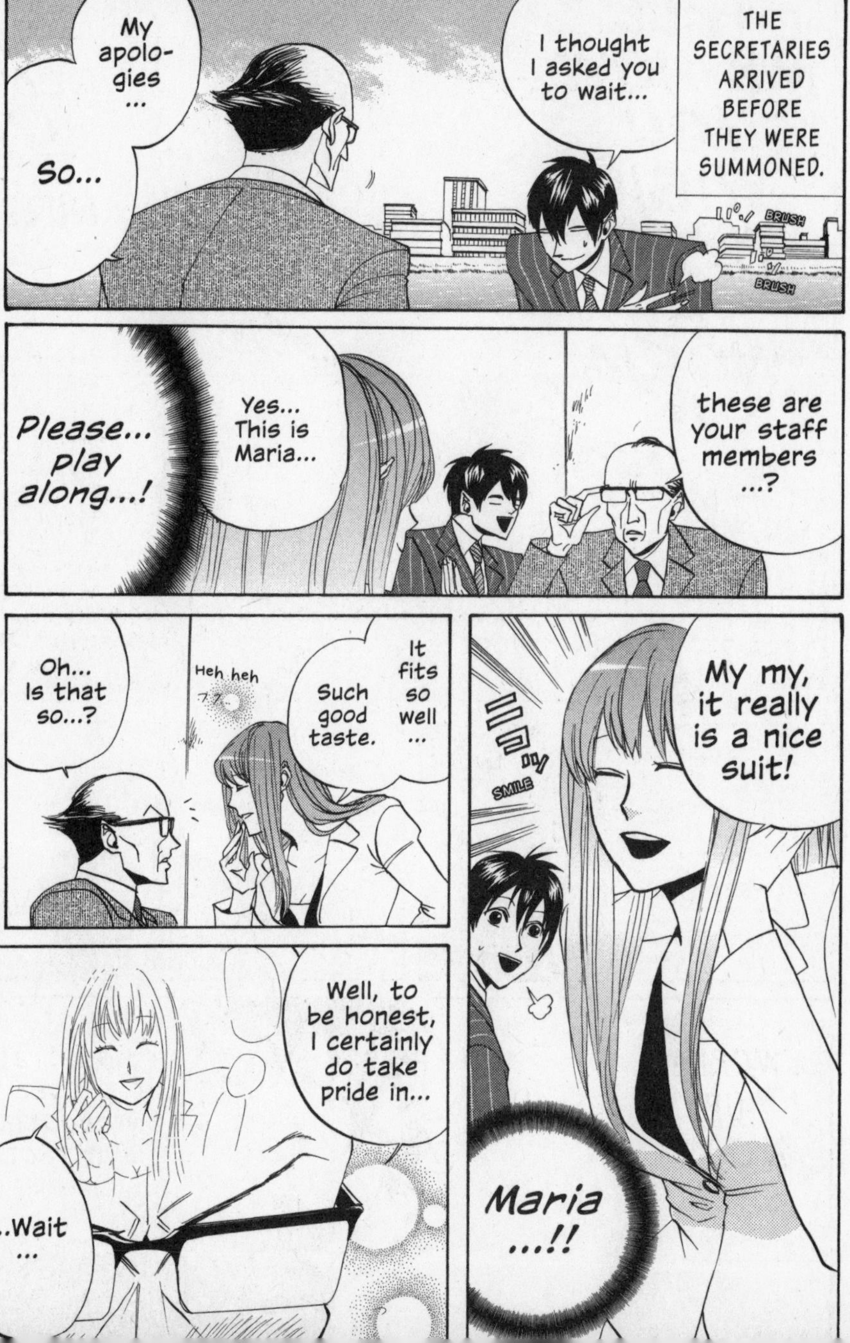
THE SECRETARIES ARRIVED BEFORE THEY WERE SUMMONED.
I thought I asked you to wait...
BRUSH
BRUSH
My apologies...
So...
these are your staff members...?
Yes... This is Maria...
Please... play along...!
My my, it really is a nice suit!
SMILE
Maria...!!
It fits so well...
Such good taste.
Heh heh
Oh... Is that so...?
Well, to be honest, I certainly do take pride in...
...Wait...

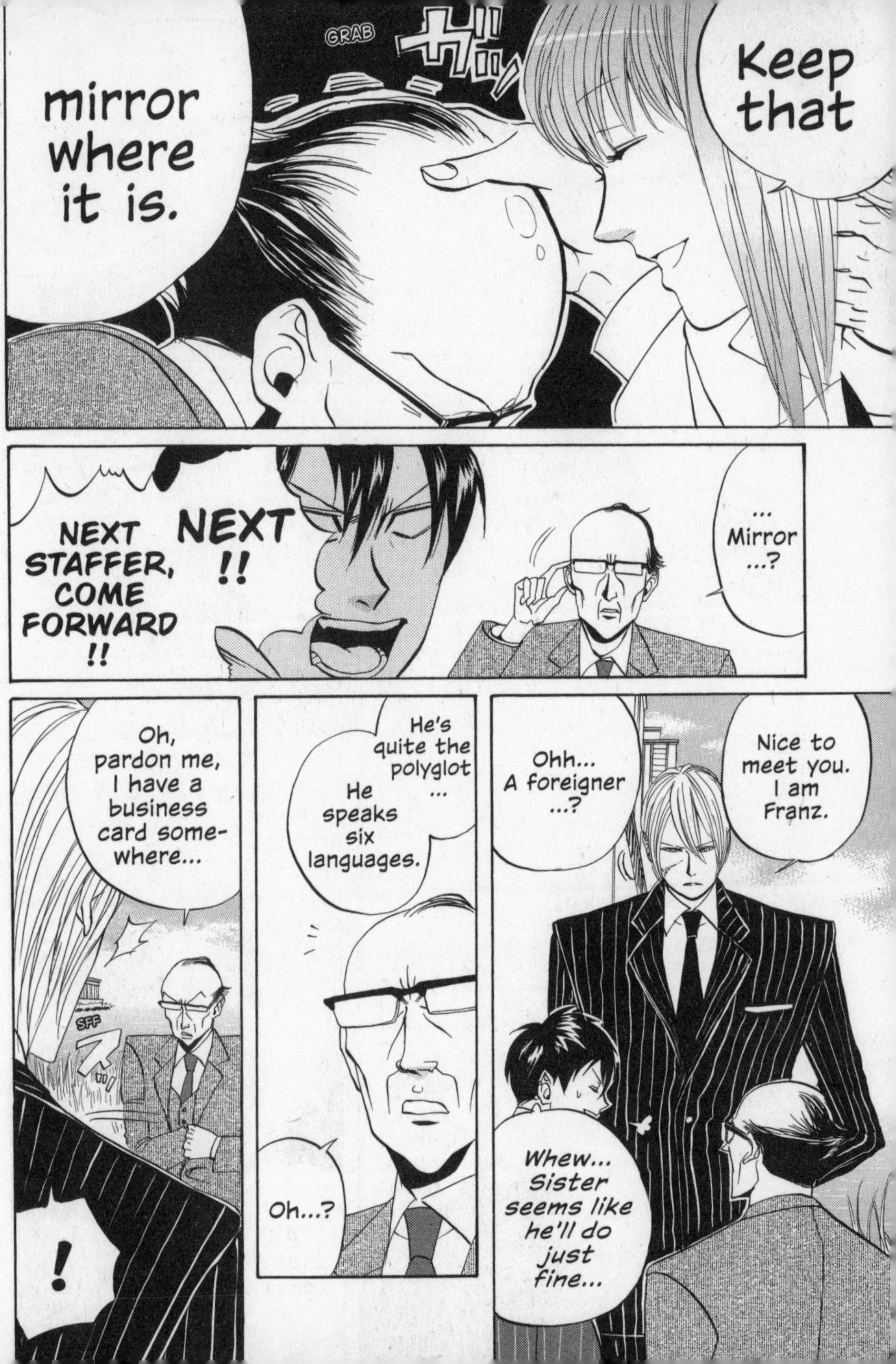
Keep that
GRAB
mirror where it is.
... Mirror ...?
NEXT !!
NEXT STAFFER, COME FORWARD !!
Nice to meet you. I am Franz.
Ohh... A foreigner ...?
Whew... Sister seems like he'll do just fine...
He's quite the polyglot ...
He speaks six languages.
Oh...?
Oh, pardon me, I have a business card somewhere...
SFF
!

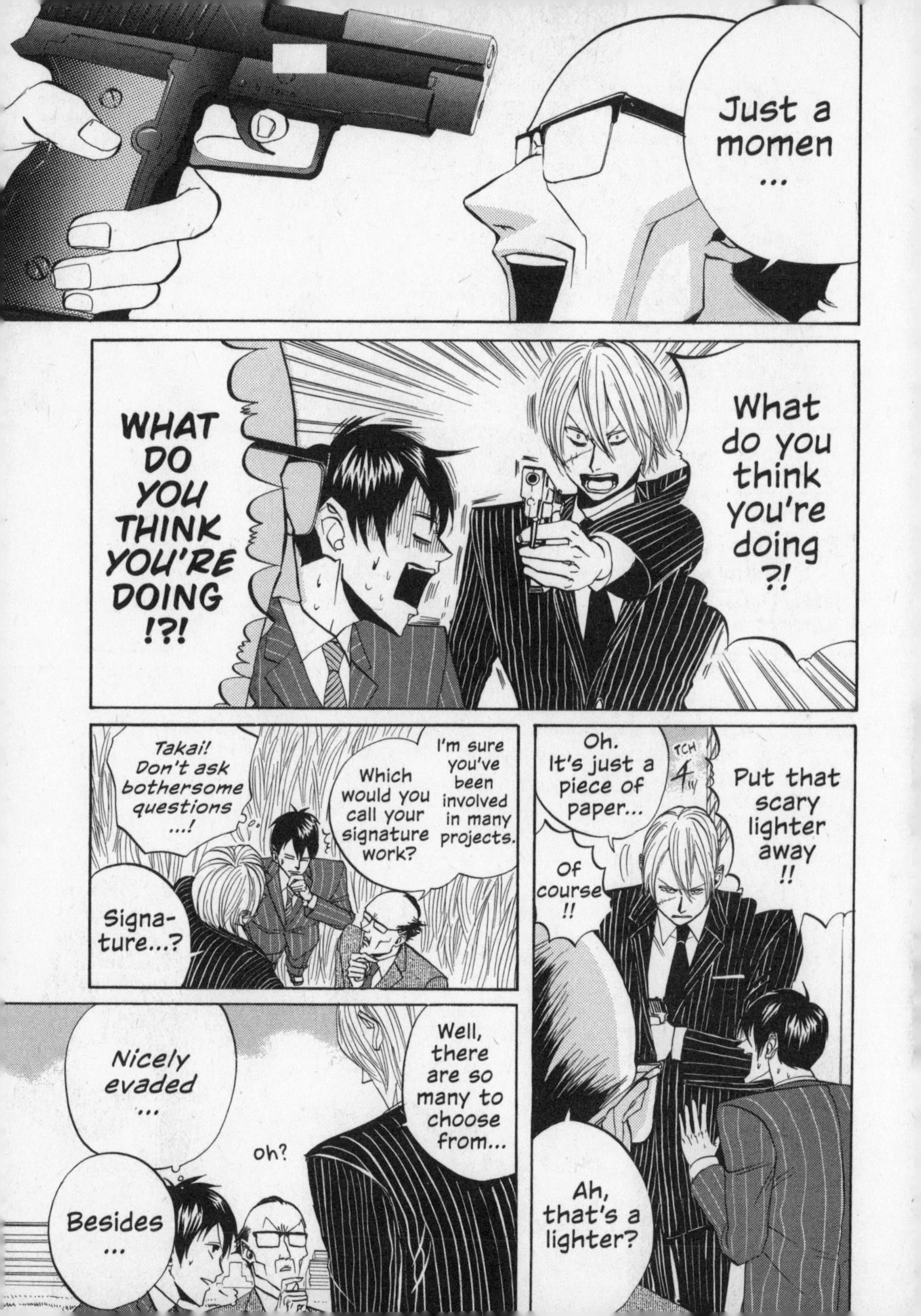
Just a momen ...
What do you think you're doing ?!
WHAT DO YOU THINK YOU'RE DOING !?!
Put that scary lighter away !!
Oh. It's just a piece of paper...
TCH
Of course !!
Ah, that's a lighter?
I'm sure you've been involved in many projects.
Which would you call your signature work?
Takai! Don't ask bothersome questions ...!
Signa- ture...?
Well, there are so many to choose from...
Nicely evaded ...
oh?
Besides ...

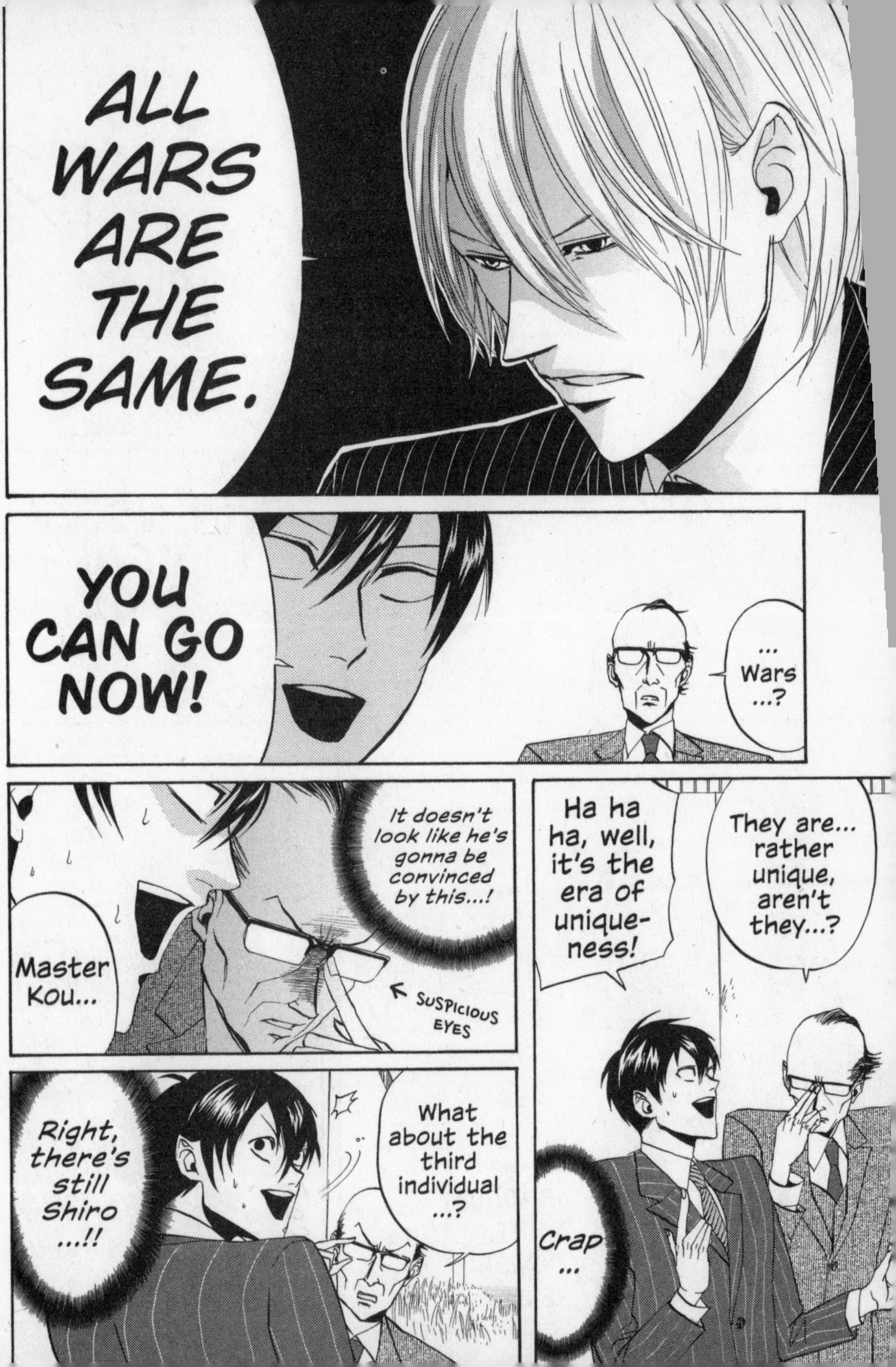
ALL WARS ARE THE SAME.
... Wars ...?
YOU CAN GO NOW!
They are... rather unique, aren't they...?
Ha ha ha, well, it's the era of unique-ness!
Crap ...
It doesn't look like he's gonna be convinced by this...!
Master Kou...
SUSPICIOUS EYES
What about the third individual ...?
Right, there's still Shiro ...!!

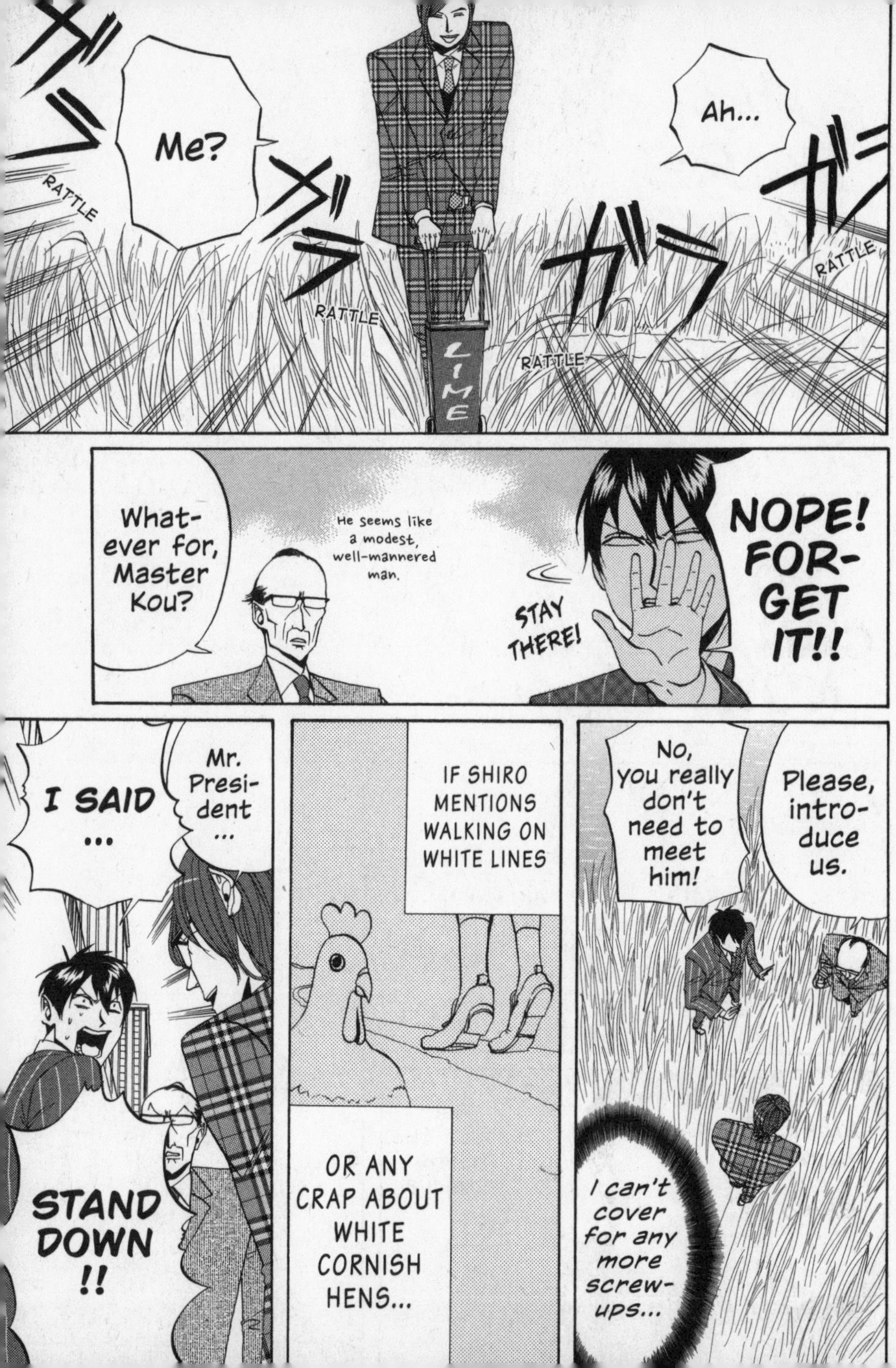
Ah...
RATTLE
RATTLE
RATTLE
Me?
RATTLE
NOPE! FOR-GET IT!!
STAY THERE!
He seems like a modest, well-mannered man.
What-ever for, Master Kou?
Please, intro-duce us.
No, you really don't need to meet him!
I can't cover for any more screw-ups...
IF SHIRO MENTIONS WALKING ON WHITE LINES
OR ANY CRAP ABOUT WHITE CORNISH HENS...
Mr. Presi-dent ...
I SAID ...
STAND DOWN !!

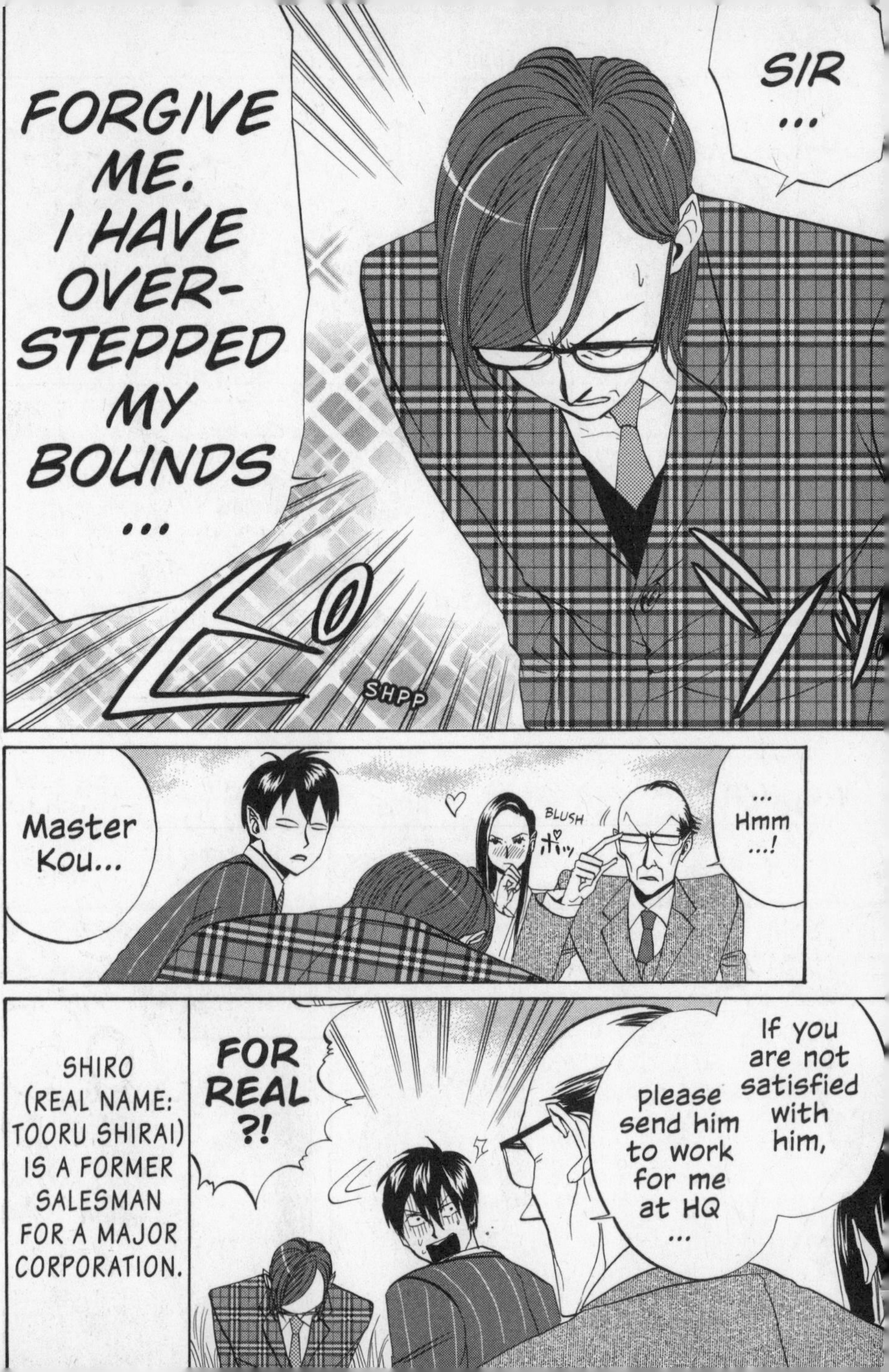
SIR ...
FORGIVE ME. I HAVE OVER-STEPPED MY BOUNDS ...
SHPP
... Hmm ...!
BLUSH
ポッ
Master Kou...
If you are not satisfied with him,
please send him to work for me at HQ ...
FOR REAL?!
SHIRO (REAL NAME: TOORU SHIRAI) IS A FORMER SALESMAN FOR A MAJOR CORPORATION.

Chapter 71: Secretary

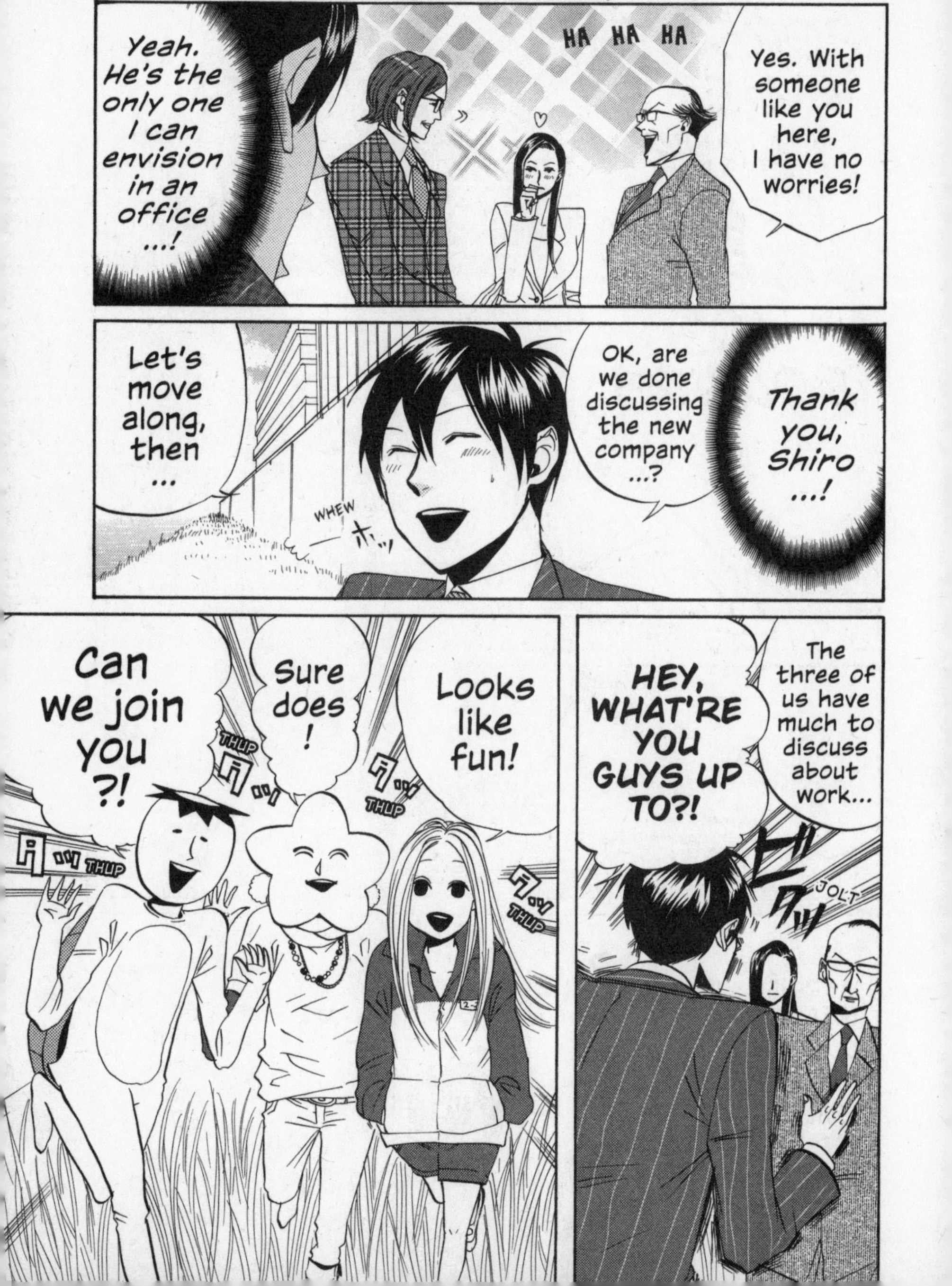
Yes. With someone like you here, I have no worries!
HA HA HA
Yeah. He's the only one I can envision in an office ...!
Thank you, Shiro ...!
OK, are we done discussing the new company ...?
WHEW
Let's move along, then ...
The three of us have much to discuss about work...
HEY, WHAT'RE YOU GUYS UP TO?!
JOLT
Looks like fun!
THUP
Sure does!
THUP
Can we join you?!
THUP
THUP

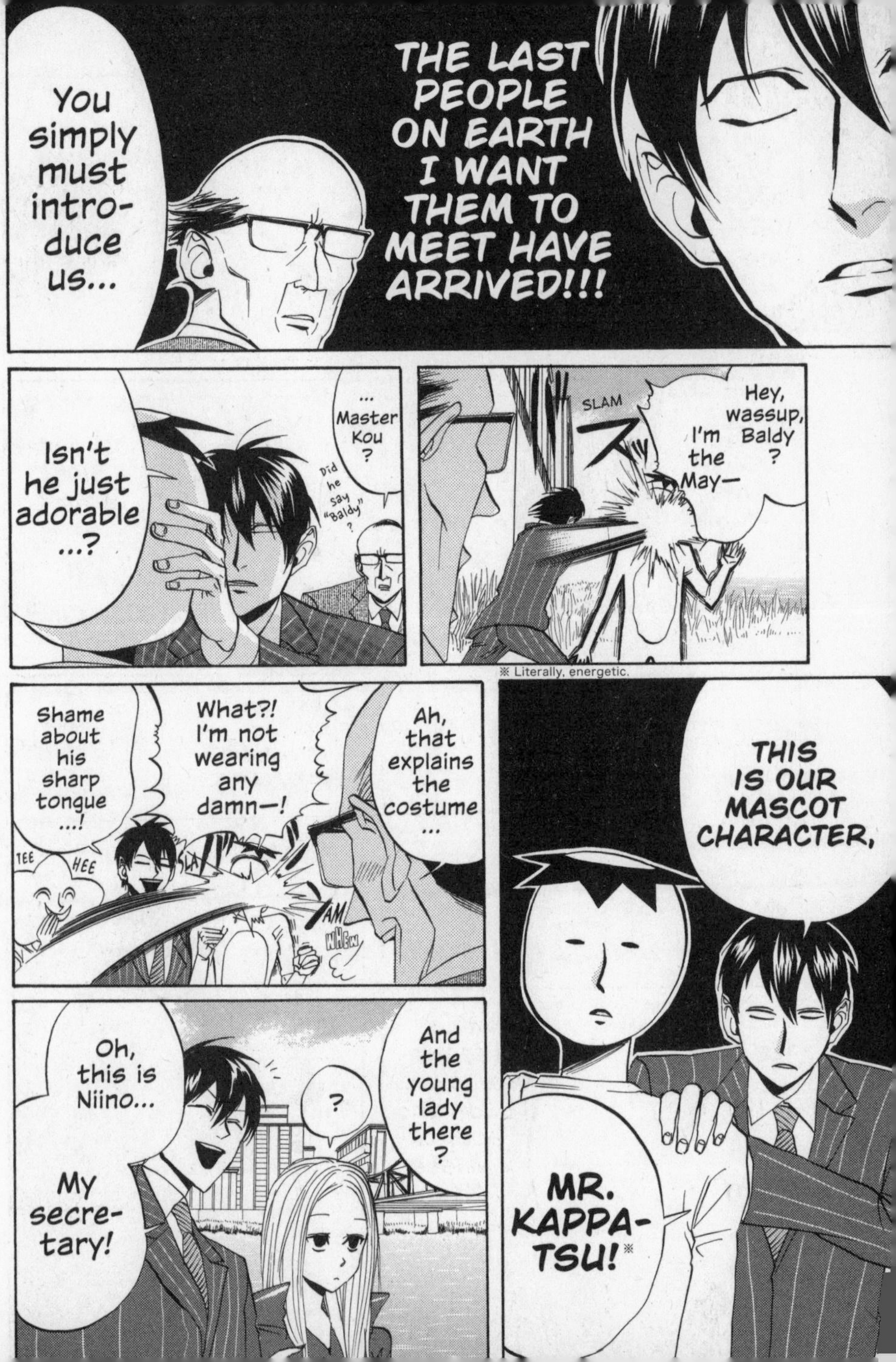
THE LAST PEOPLE ON EARTH I WANT THEM TO MEET HAVE ARRIVED!!!
You simply must introduce us...
Hey, wassup, Baldy?
I'm the May—
SLAM
... Master Kou?
Did he say "Baldy"?
Isn't he just adorable ...?
THIS IS OUR MASCOT CHARACTER,
MR. KAPPATSU!※
Ah, that explains the costume ...
What?! I'm not wearing any damn—!
Shame about his sharp tongue ...!
TEE HEE
WHEW
And the young lady there?
?
Oh, this is Niino...
My secretary!

※ Literally, energetic.

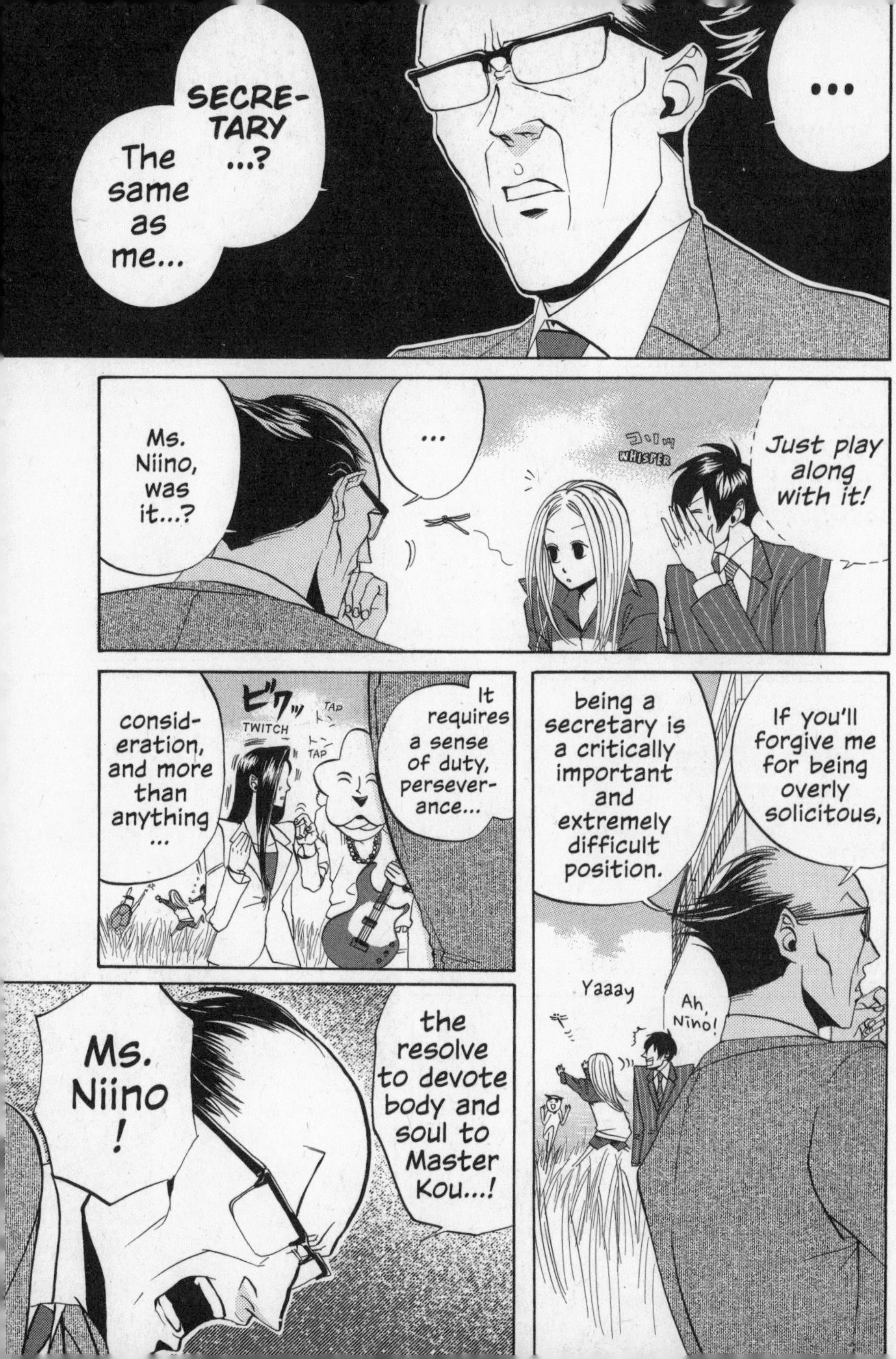
...
SECRETARY ...?
The same as me...
Just play along with it!
コソッ
WHISPER
...
Ms. Niino, was it...?
If you'll forgive me for being overly solicitous,
being a secretary is a critically important and extremely difficult position.
Ah, Nino!
Yaaay
It requires a sense of duty, perseverance...
ビクッ
TWITCH
TAP
TAP
consideration, and more than anything ...
the resolve to devote body and soul to Master Kou...!
Ms. Niino !

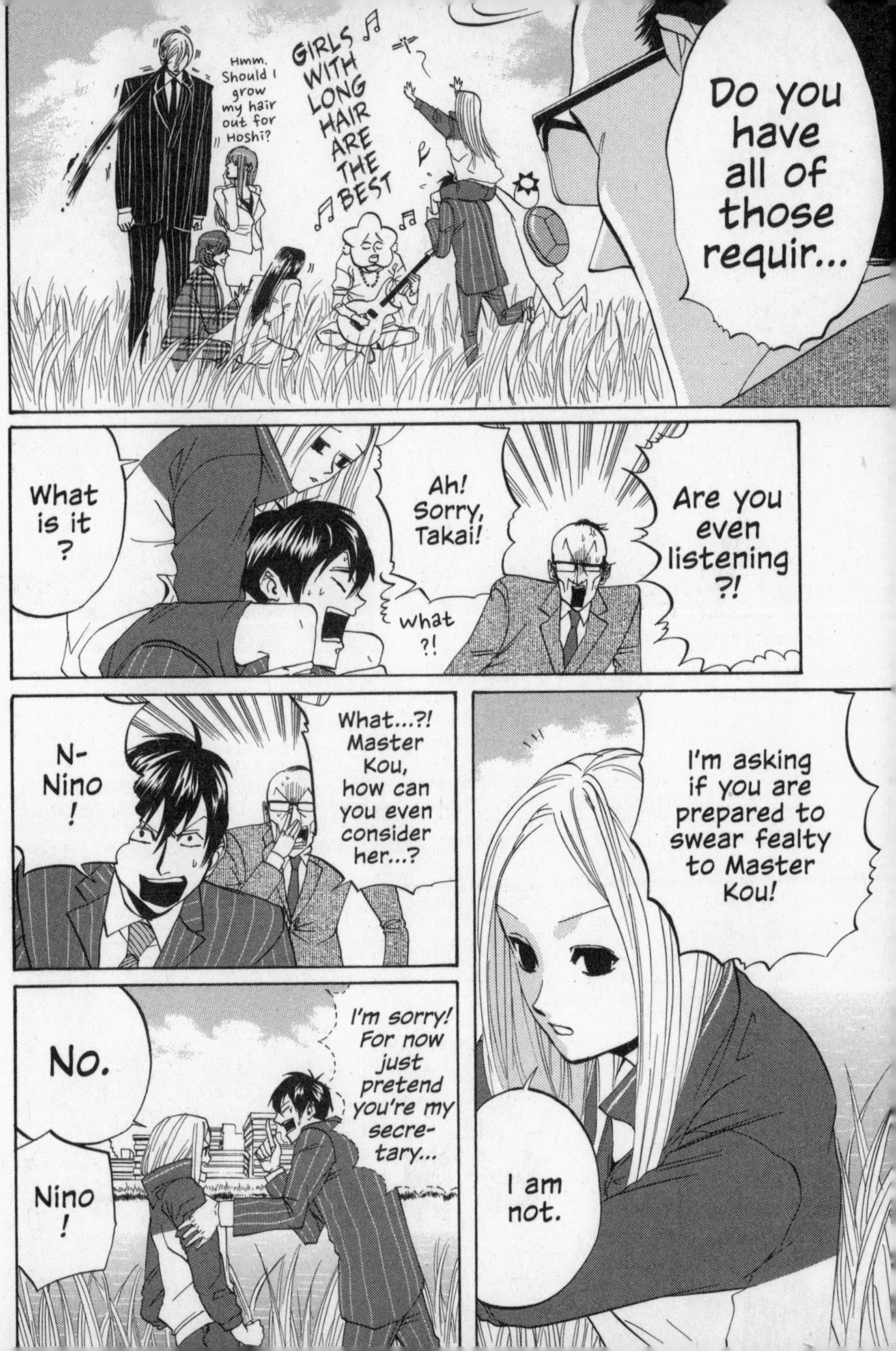
Do you have all of those requir...
GIRLS WITH LONG HAIR ARE THE BEST
Hmm. Should I grow my hair out for Hoshi?
Are you even listening ?!
Ah! Sorry, Takai!
what ?!
What is it ?
I'm asking if you are prepared to swear fealty to Master Kou!
I am not.
What...?! Master Kou, how can you even consider her...?
N-Nino !
I'm sorry! For now just pretend you're my secre-tary...
No.
Nino !

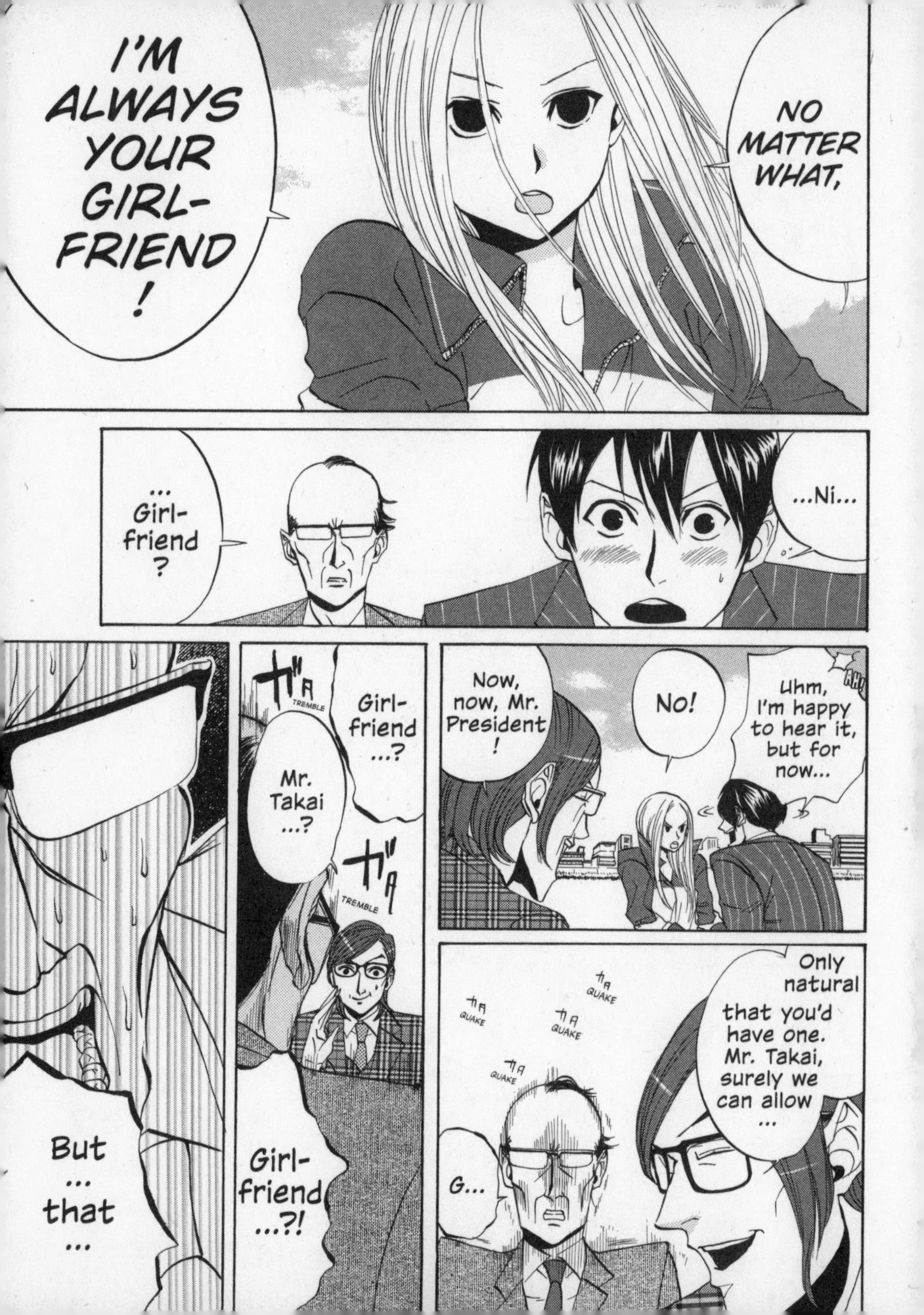
NO MATTER WHAT,
I'M ALWAYS YOUR GIRL-FRIEND!
...Ni...
...Girl-friend?
AH!
Uhm, I'm happy to hear it, but for now...
No!
Now, now, Mr. President!
Only natural that you'd have one. Mr. Takai, surely we can allow...
QUAKE
QUAKE
QUAKE
QUAKE
G...
TREMBLE
Girl-friend...?
Mr. Takai...?
TREMBLE
Girl-friend...?!
But... that...

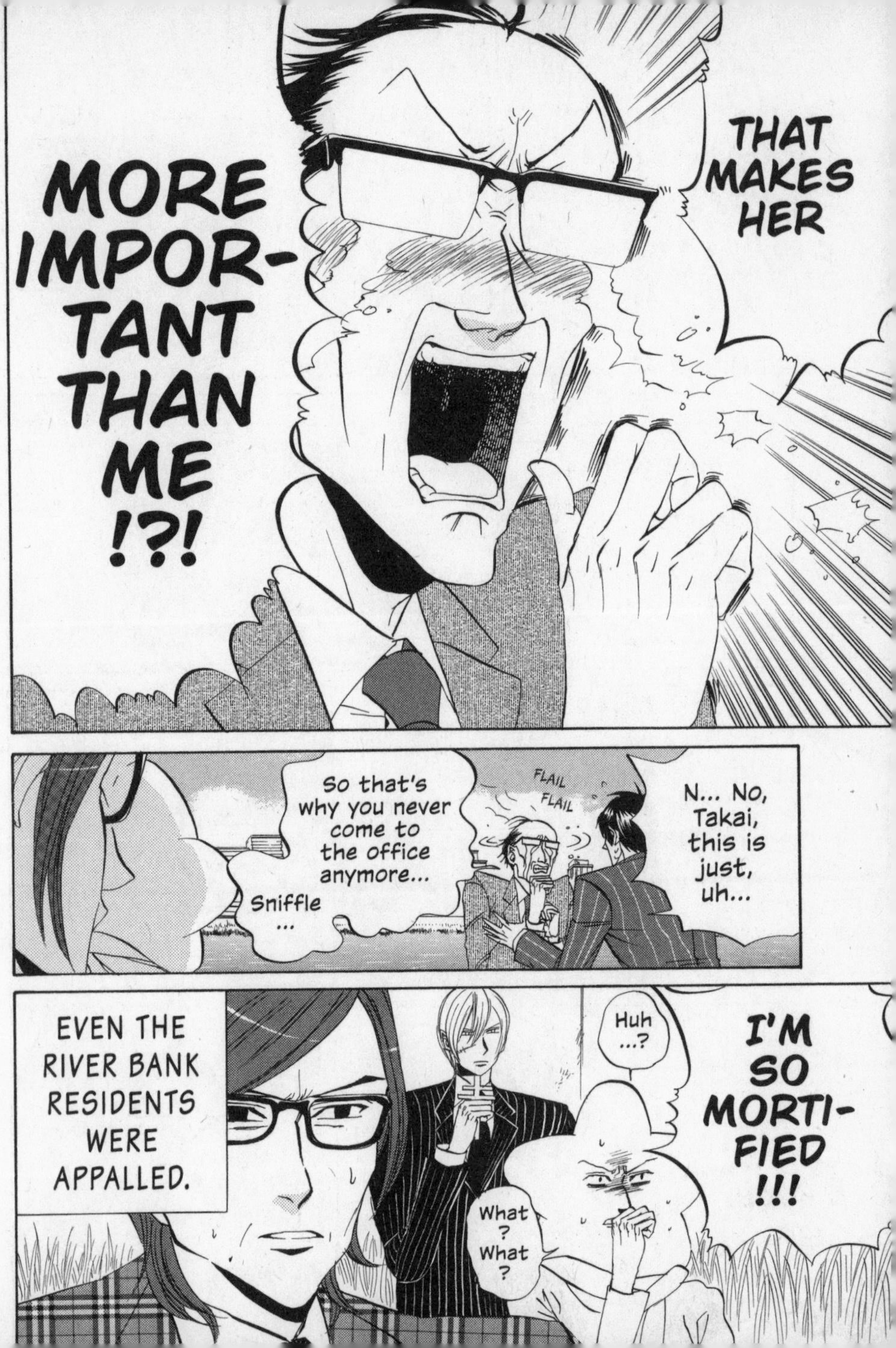
THAT MAKES HER
MORE IMPOR-TANT THAN ME !?!
N... No, Takai, this is just, uh...
FLAIL FLAIL
So that's why you never come to the office anymore...
Sniffle ...
I'M SO MORTI-FIED !!!
Huh ...?
What ? What ?
EVEN THE RIVER BANK RESIDENTS WERE APPALLED.

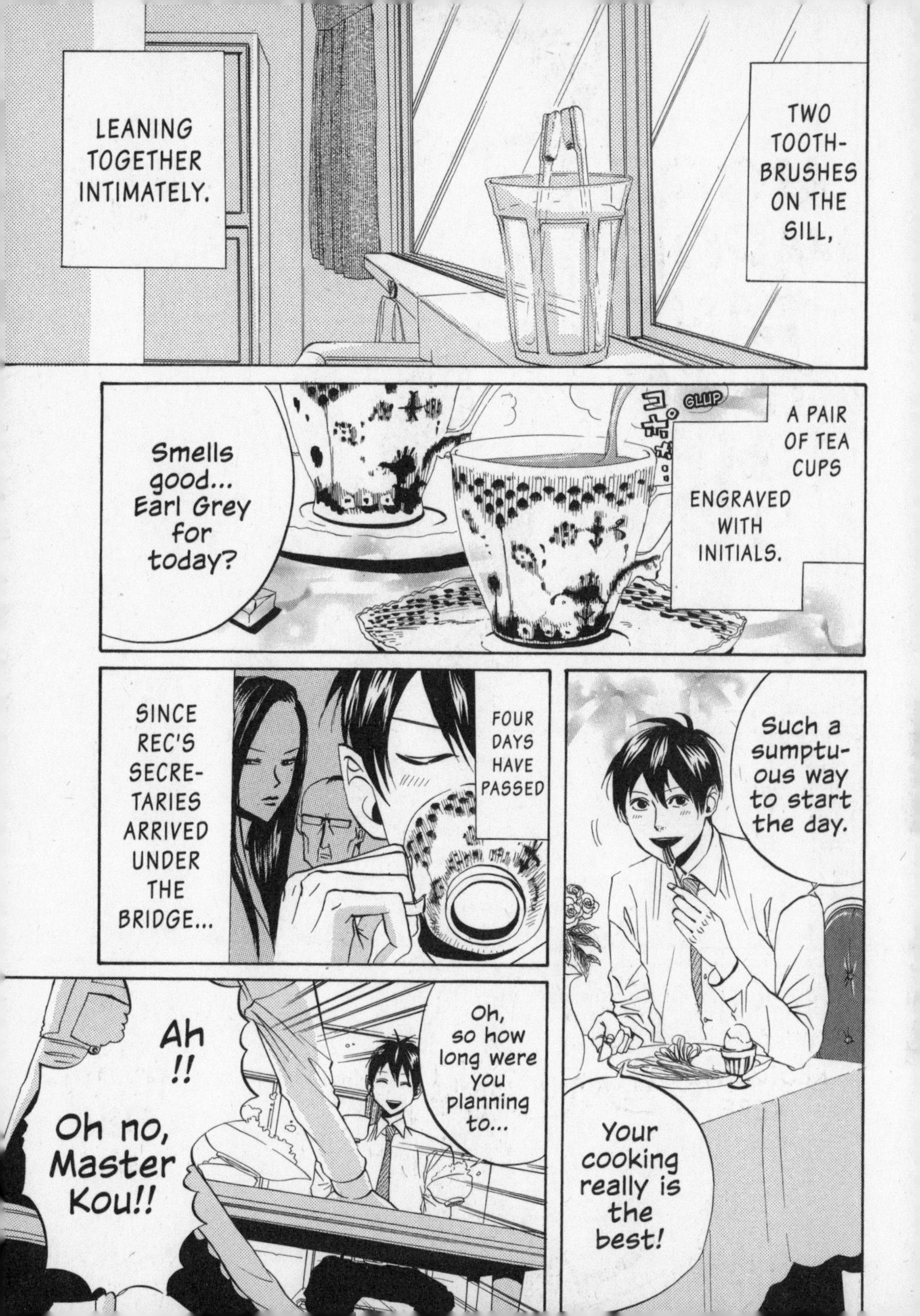

TWO TOOTH-BRUSHES ON THE SILL,
LEANING TOGETHER INTIMATELY.
GLUP
A PAIR OF TEA CUPS
ENGRAVED WITH INITIALS.
Smells good... Earl Grey for today?
Such a sumptuous way to start the day.
Your cooking really is the best!
FOUR DAYS HAVE PASSED
SINCE REC'S SECRETARIES ARRIVED UNDER THE BRIDGE...
Oh, so how long were you planning to...
Ah !!
Oh no, Master Kou!!

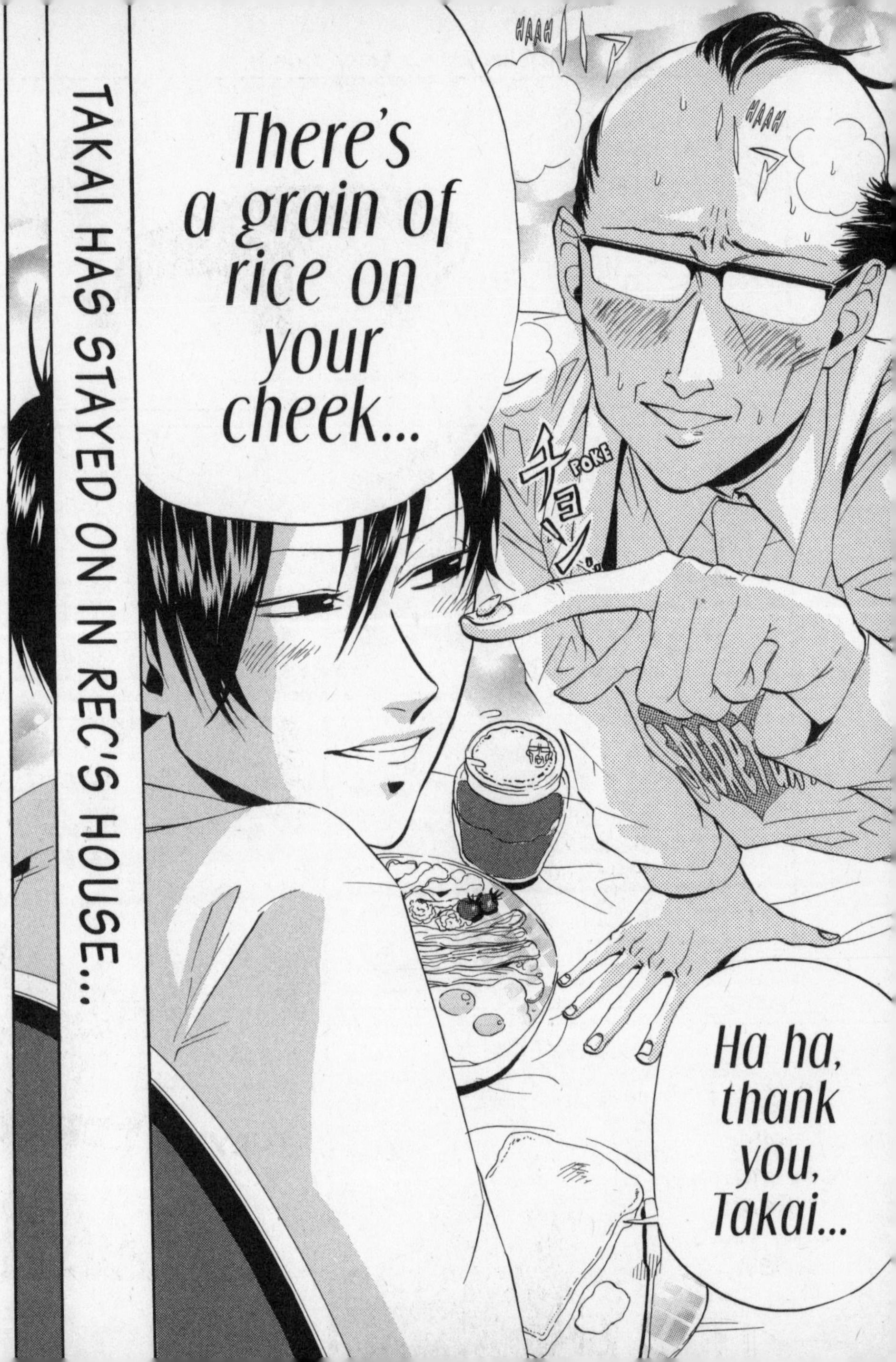
HAAH
HAAH
There's a grain of rice on your cheek...
POKE
Ha ha, thank you, Takai...
TAKAI HAS STAYED ON IN REC'S HOUSE...

Chapter 72: Deep Bonds

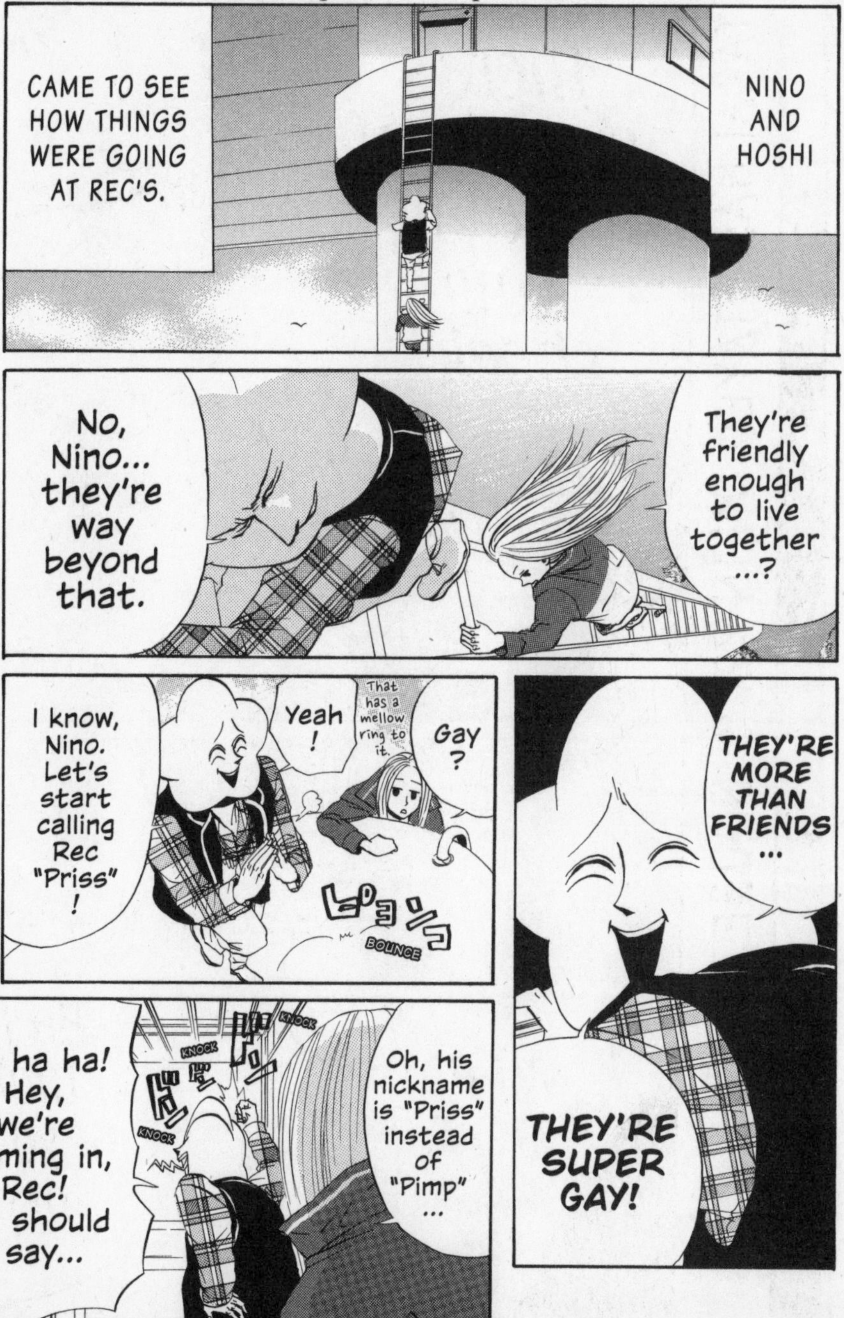
NINO AND HOSHI
CAME TO SEE HOW THINGS WERE GOING AT REC'S.
They're friendly enough to live together ...?
No, Nino... they're way beyond that.
THEY'RE MORE THAN FRIENDS ...
THEY'RE SUPER GAY!
Gay ?
That has a mellow ring to it.
Yeah !
I know, Nino. Let's start calling Rec "Priss" !
BOUNCE
KNOCK
KNOCK
KNOCK
Oh, his nickname is "Priss" instead of "Pimp" ...
Ha ha ha! Hey, we're coming in, Rec! Or should I say...

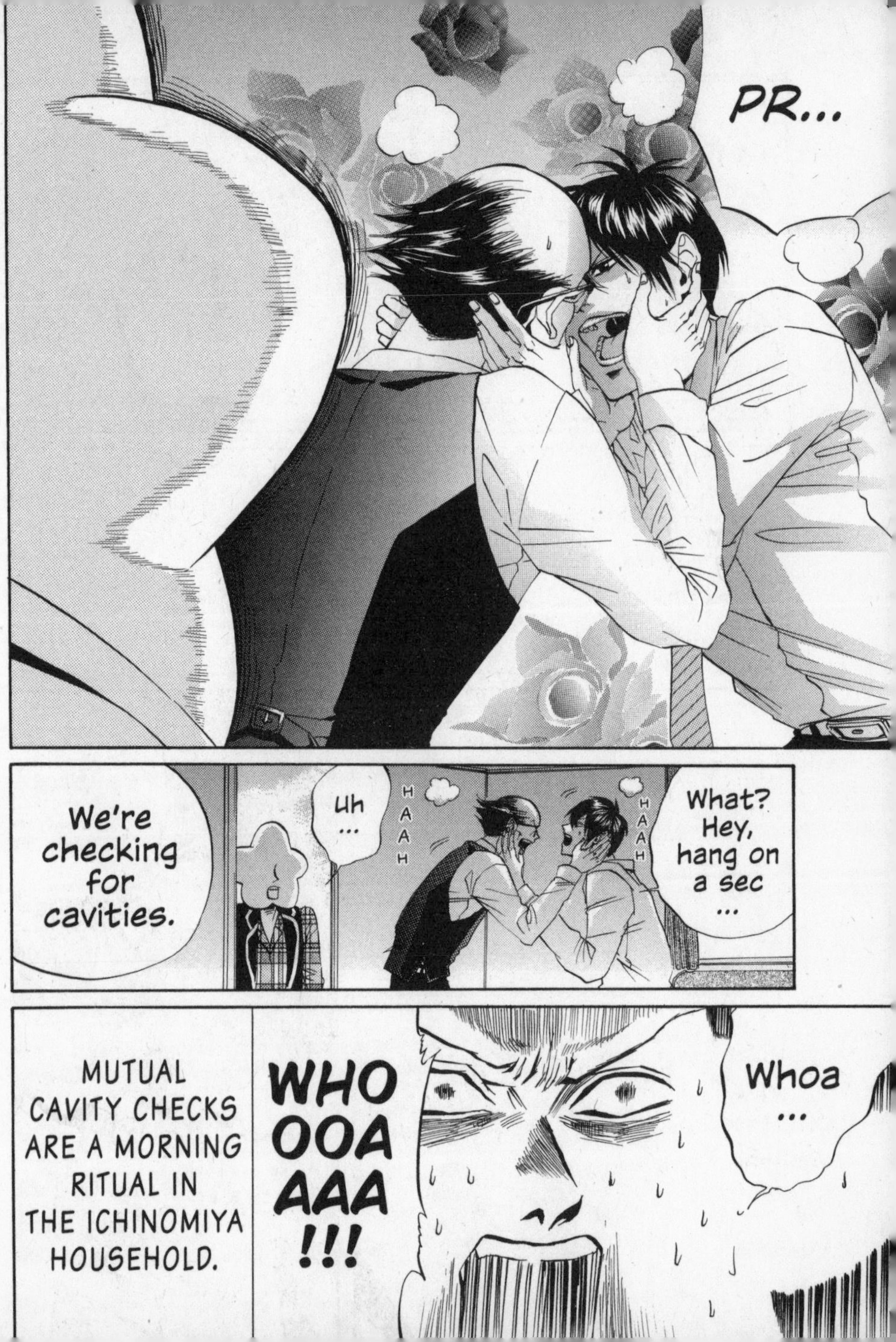
PR...
What? Hey, hang on a sec ...
HAAAH
HAAAH
Uh ...
We're checking for cavities.
Whoa ...
WHOOOAAAA !!!
MUTUAL CAVITY CHECKS ARE A MORNING RITUAL IN THE ICHINOMIYA HOUSEHOLD.

Chapter 73: First...

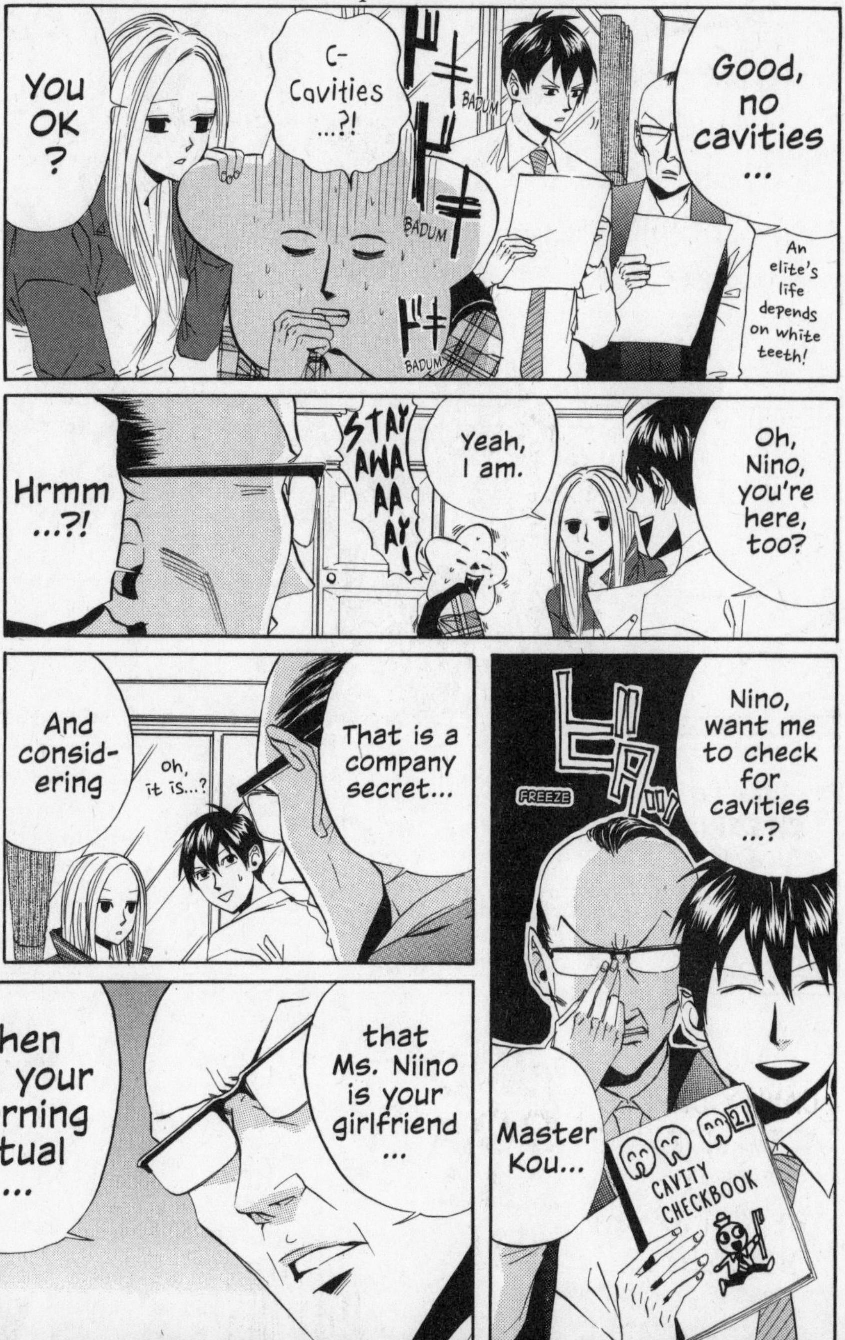
Good, no cavities ...
An elite's life depends on white teeth!
BADUM
BADUM
BADUM
C-Cavities ...?!
You OK ?
Oh, Nino, you're here, too?
Yeah, I am.
STAY AWAAAAAY!
Hrmm ...?!
Nino, want me to check for cavities ...?
FREEZE
Master Kou...
CAVITY CHECKBOOK
That is a company secret...
Oh, it is...?
And consid-ering
that Ms. Niino is your girlfriend ...
then for your morning ritual ...

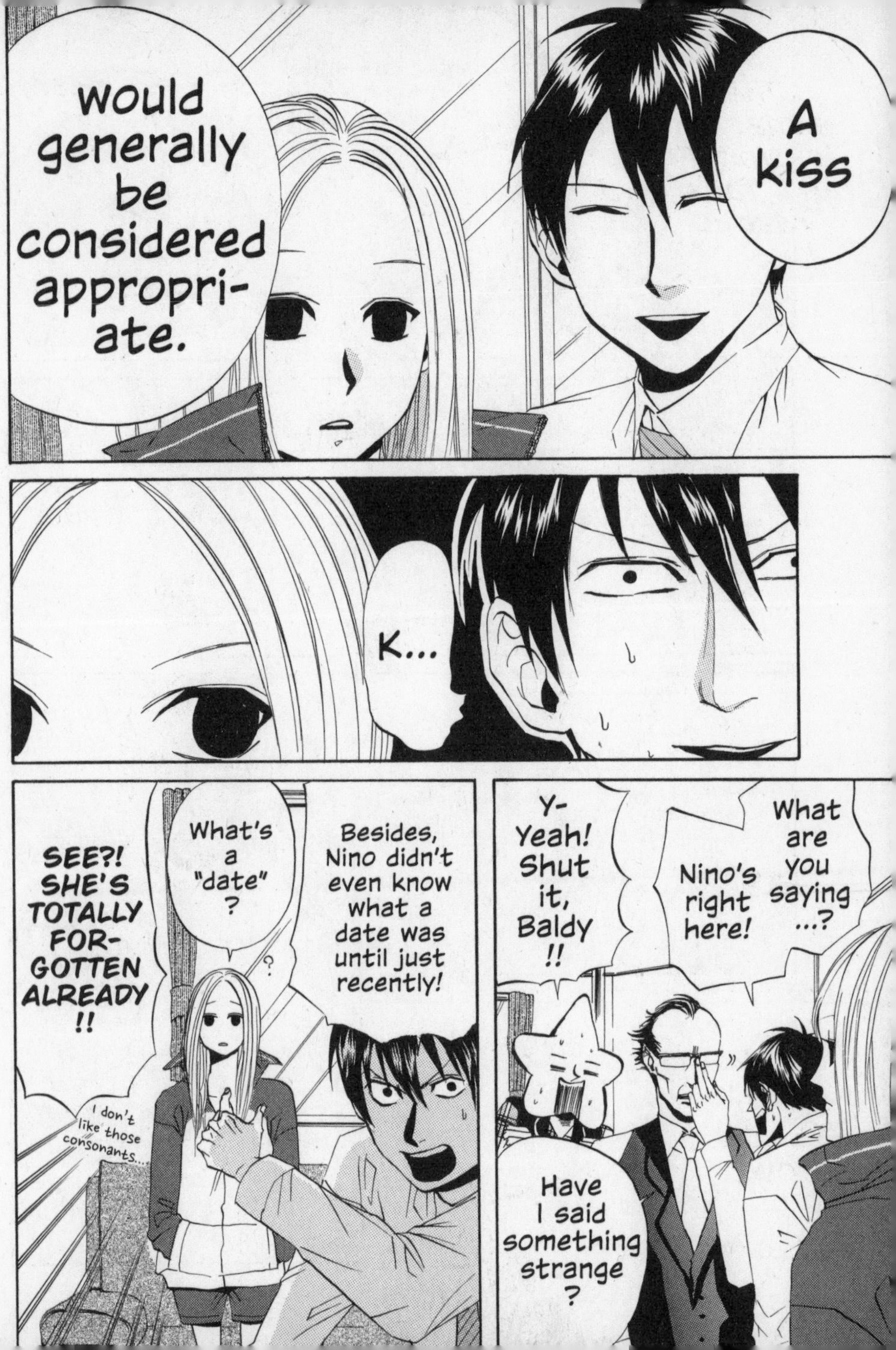
A kiss
would generally be considered appropri-ate.
K...
What are you saying ...?
Nino's right here!
Y-Yeah! Shut it, Baldy !!
Have I said something strange ?
Besides, Nino didn't even know what a date was until just recently!
What's a "date" ?
?
SEE?! SHE'S TOTALLY FOR-GOTTEN ALREADY !!
I don't like those consonants....

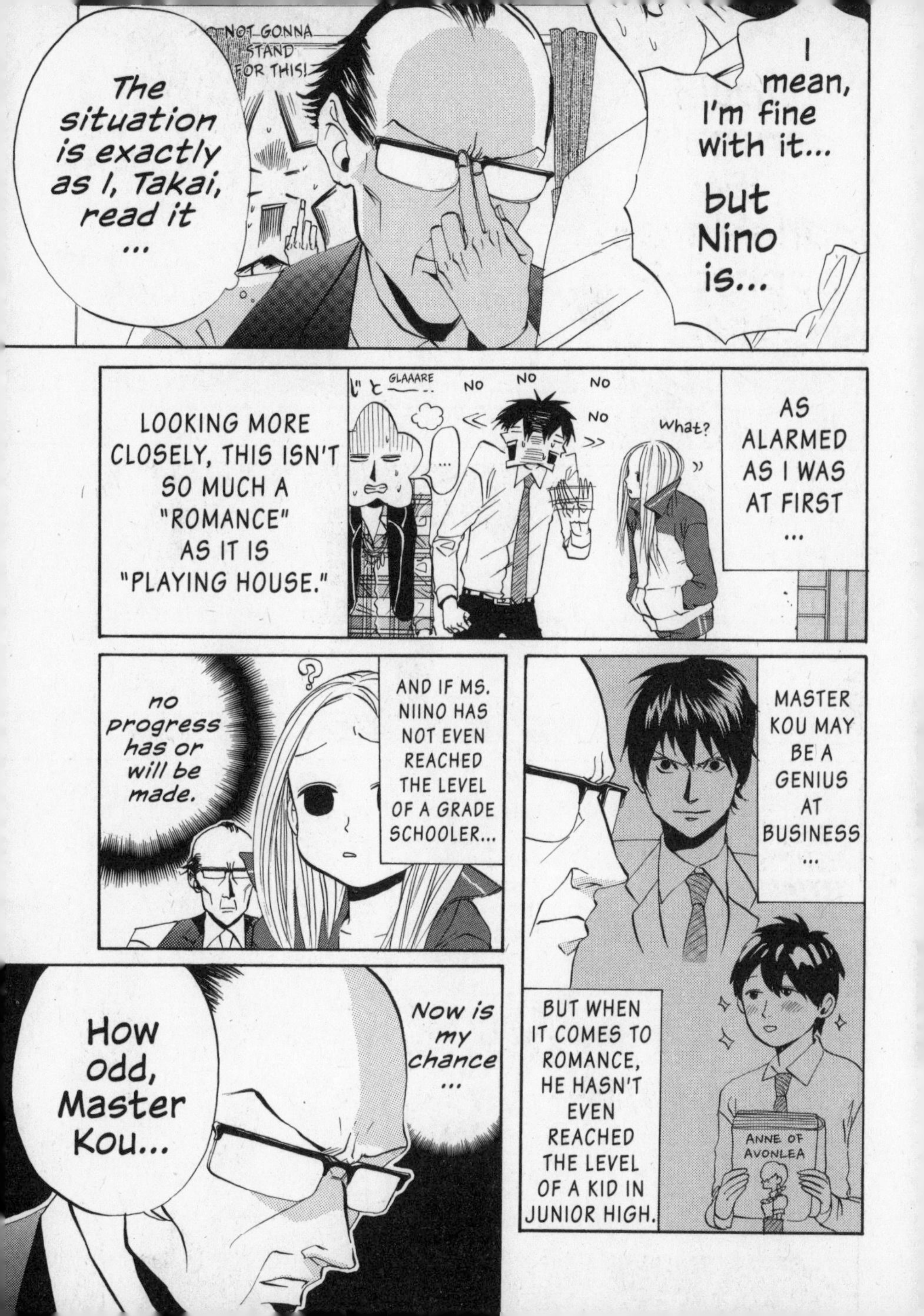
I mean, I'm fine with it... but Nino is...
NOT GONNA STAND FOR THIS!
The situation is exactly as I, Takai, read it ...
AS ALARMED AS I WAS AT FIRST ...
What?
NO
NO
NO
NO
...
じと GLAAARE
LOOKING MORE CLOSELY, THIS ISN'T SO MUCH A "ROMANCE" AS IT IS "PLAYING HOUSE."
MASTER KOU MAY BE A GENIUS AT BUSINESS ...
BUT WHEN IT COMES TO ROMANCE, HE HASN'T EVEN REACHED THE LEVEL OF A KID IN JUNIOR HIGH.
ANNE OF AVONLEA
AND IF MS. NIINO HAS NOT EVEN REACHED THE LEVEL OF A GRADE SCHOOLER...
?
no progress has or will be made.
Now is my chance ...
How odd, Master Kou...

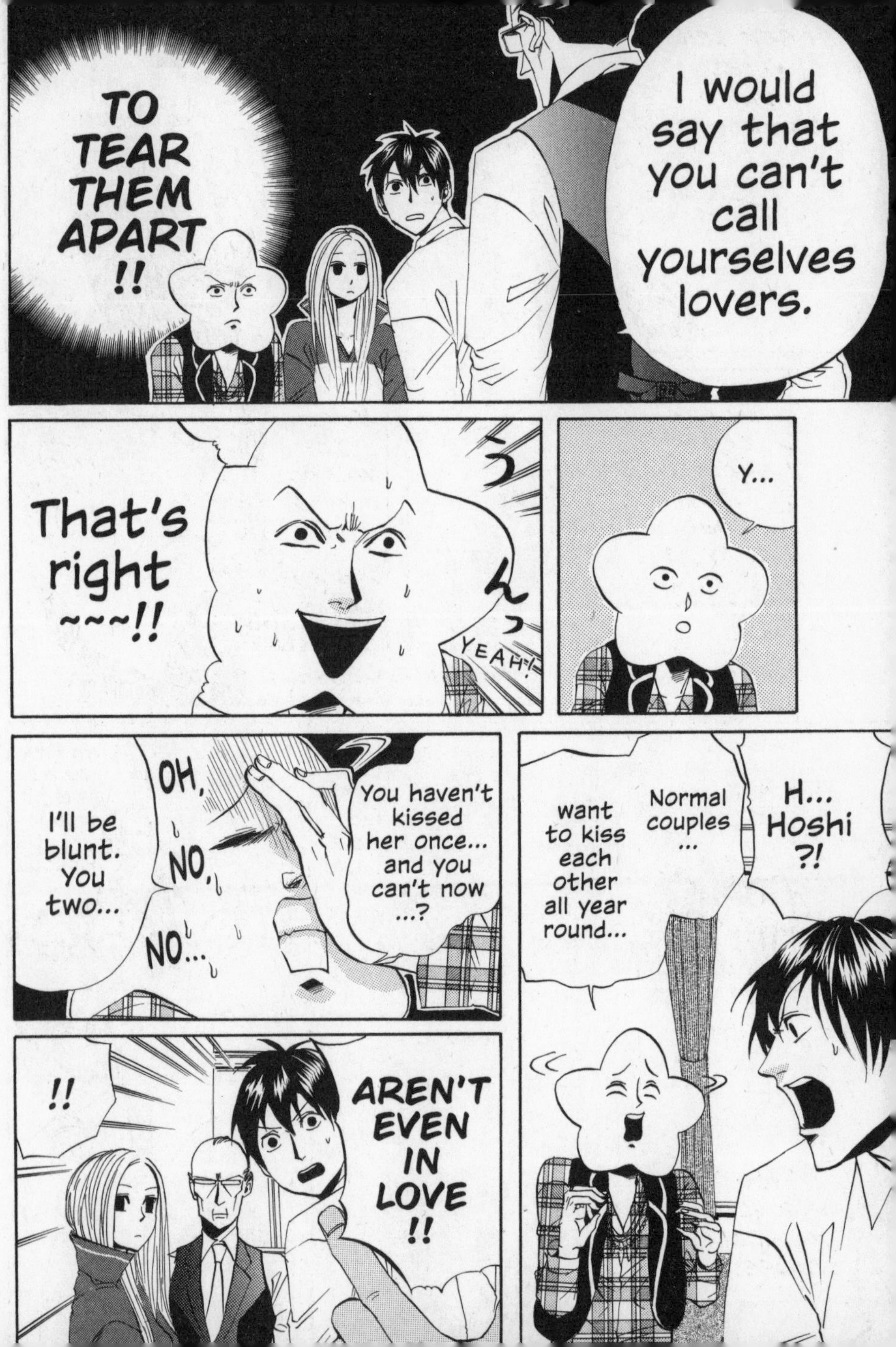
I would say that you can't call yourselves lovers.
TO TEAR THEM APART !!
Y...
That's right ~~~!!
YEAH!
H... Hoshi ?!
Normal couples ...
want to kiss each other all year round...
You haven't kissed her once... and you can't now ...?
OH, NO, NO...
I'll be blunt. You two...
AREN'T EVEN IN LOVE !!
!!

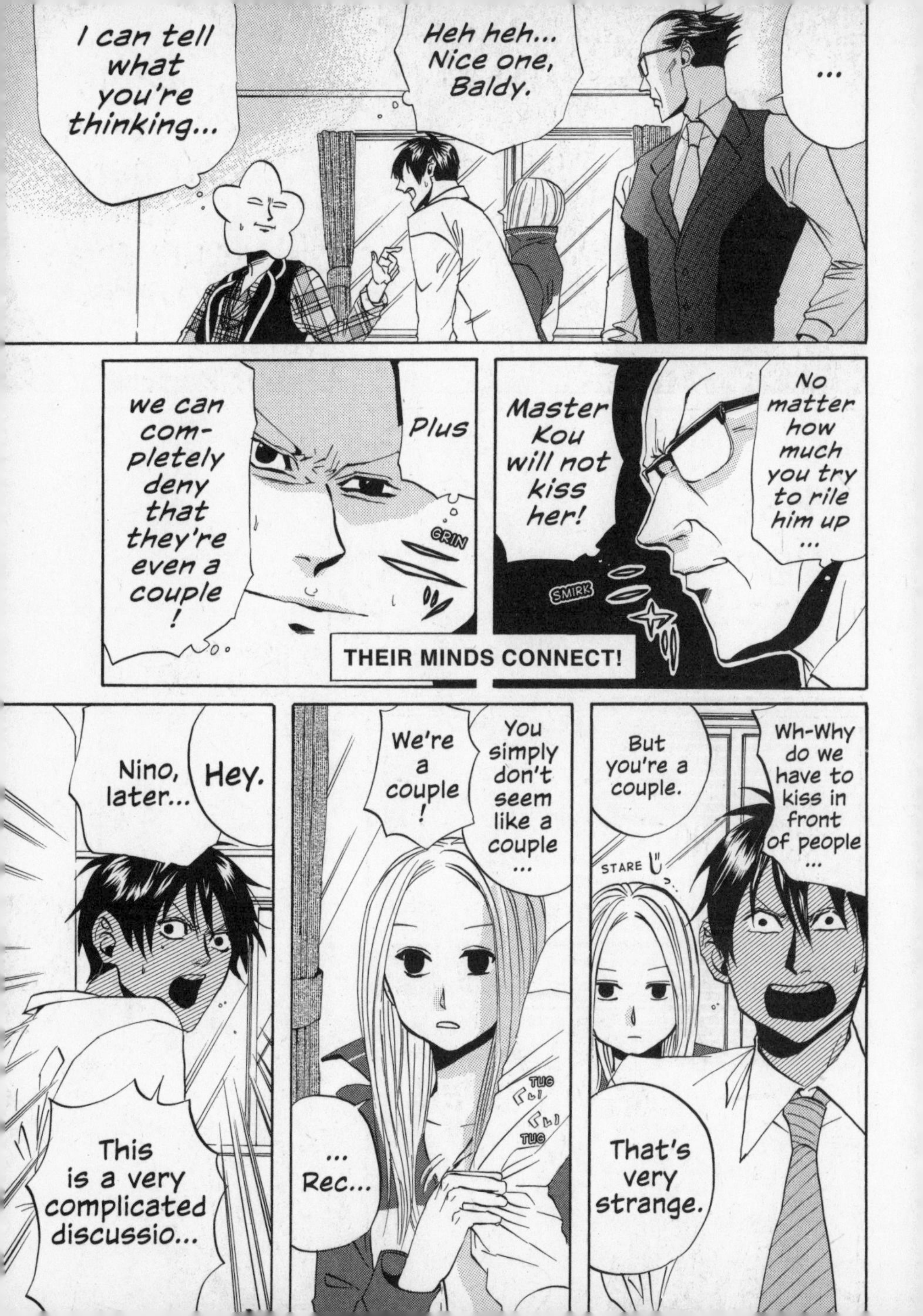
...
Heh heh... Nice one, Baldy.
I can tell what you're thinking...
No matter how much you try to rile him up ...
Master Kou will not kiss her!
SMIRK
Plus
we can completely deny that they're even a couple !
GRIN
THEIR MINDS CONNECT!
Wh-Why do we have to kiss in front of people ...
But you're a couple.
STARE
That's very strange.
You simply don't seem like a couple ...
We're a couple !
TUG
TUG
... Rec...
Hey.
Nino, later...
This is a very complicated discussio...

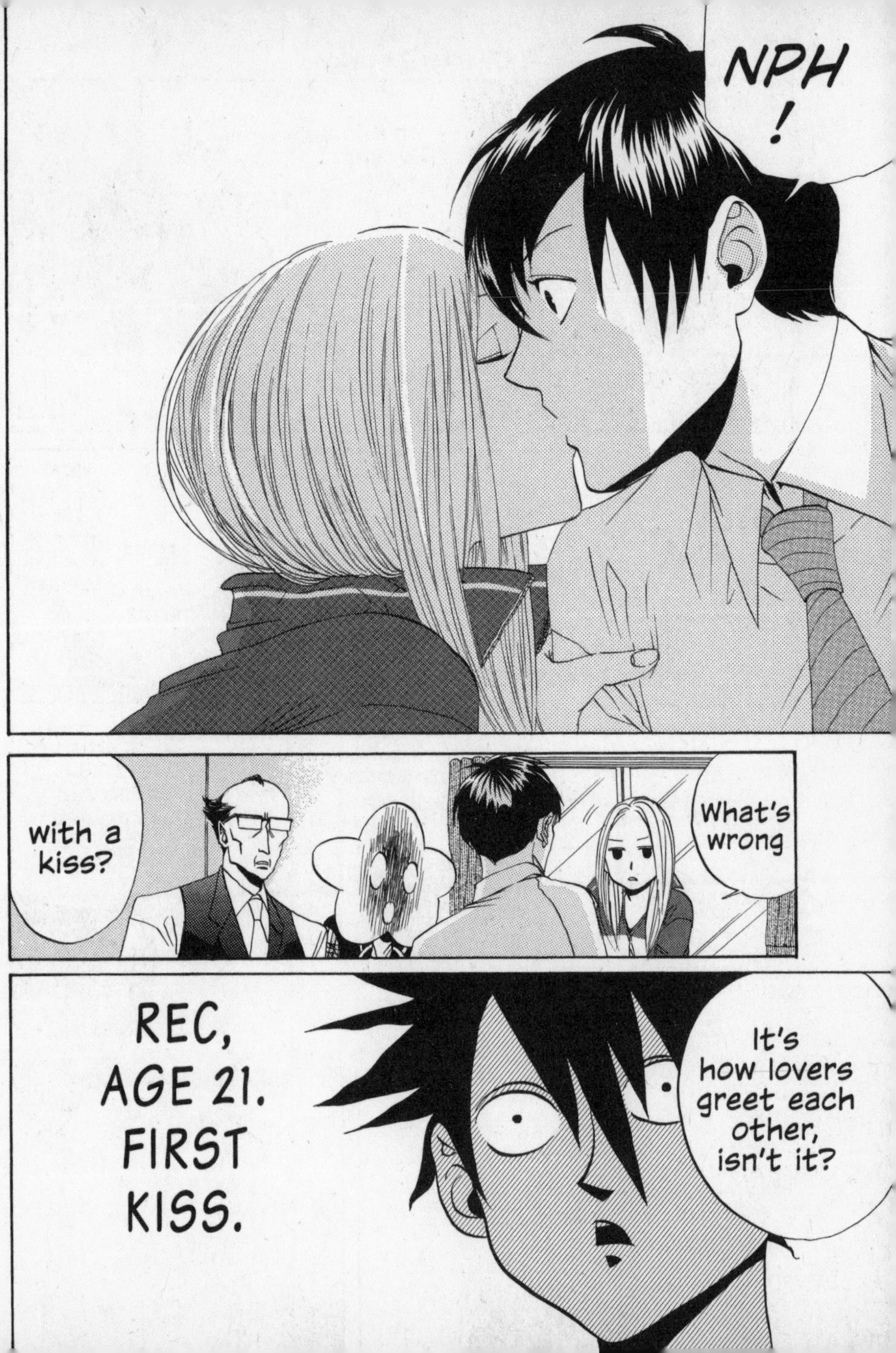
NPH!
What's wrong
with a kiss?
It's how lovers greet each other, isn't it?
REC, AGE 21. FIRST KISS.

Chapter 74: Alone

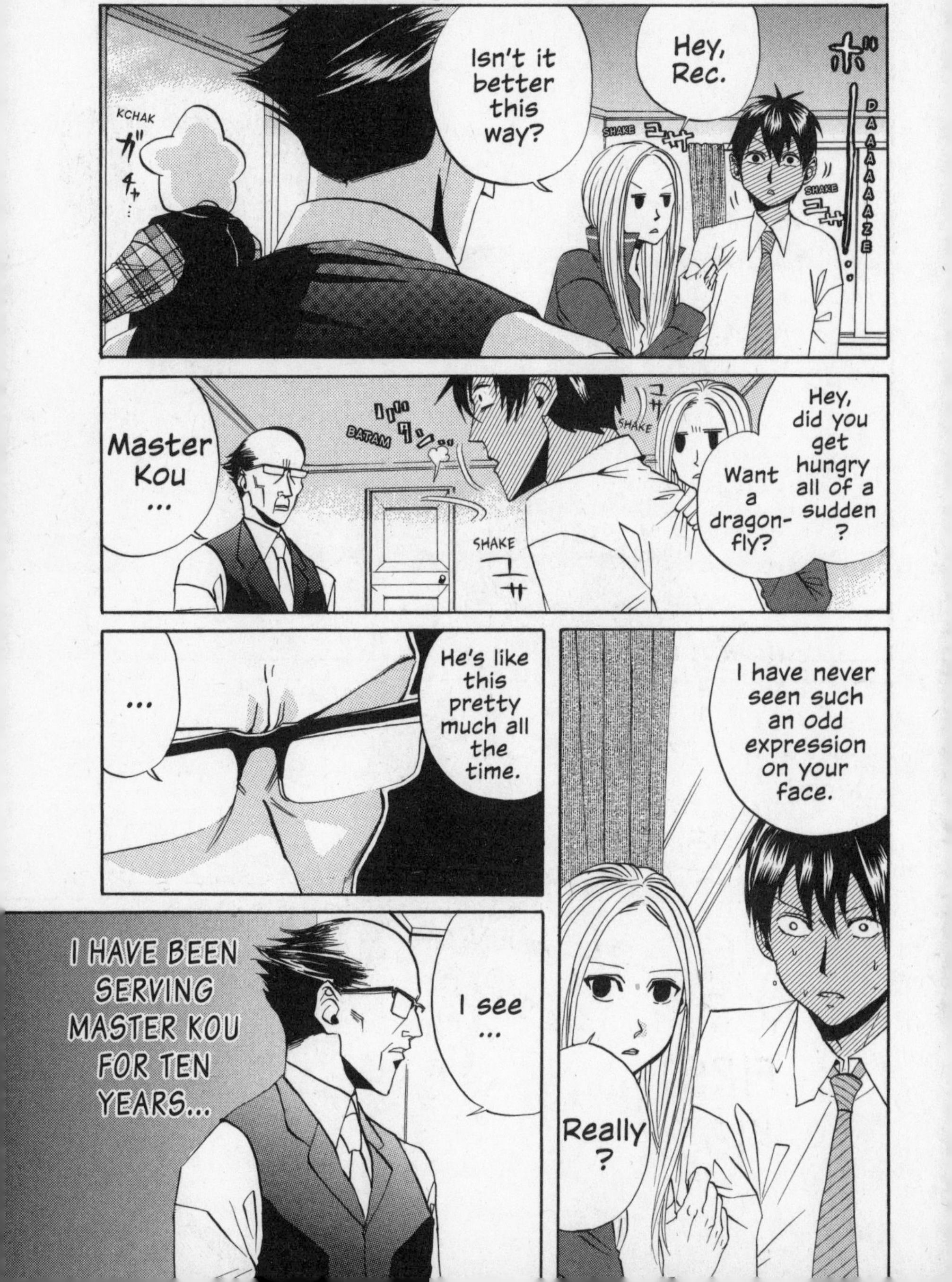
Hey, Rec.
Isn't it better this way?
SHAKE
SHAKE
DAAAAAAAAZE
KCHAK
Hey, did you get hungry all of a sudden?
Want a dragonfly?
SHAKE
SHAKE
BATAM
Master Kou ...
I have never seen such an odd expression on your face.
Really?
He's like this pretty much all the time.
...
I see ...
I HAVE BEEN SERVING MASTER KOU FOR TEN YEARS...

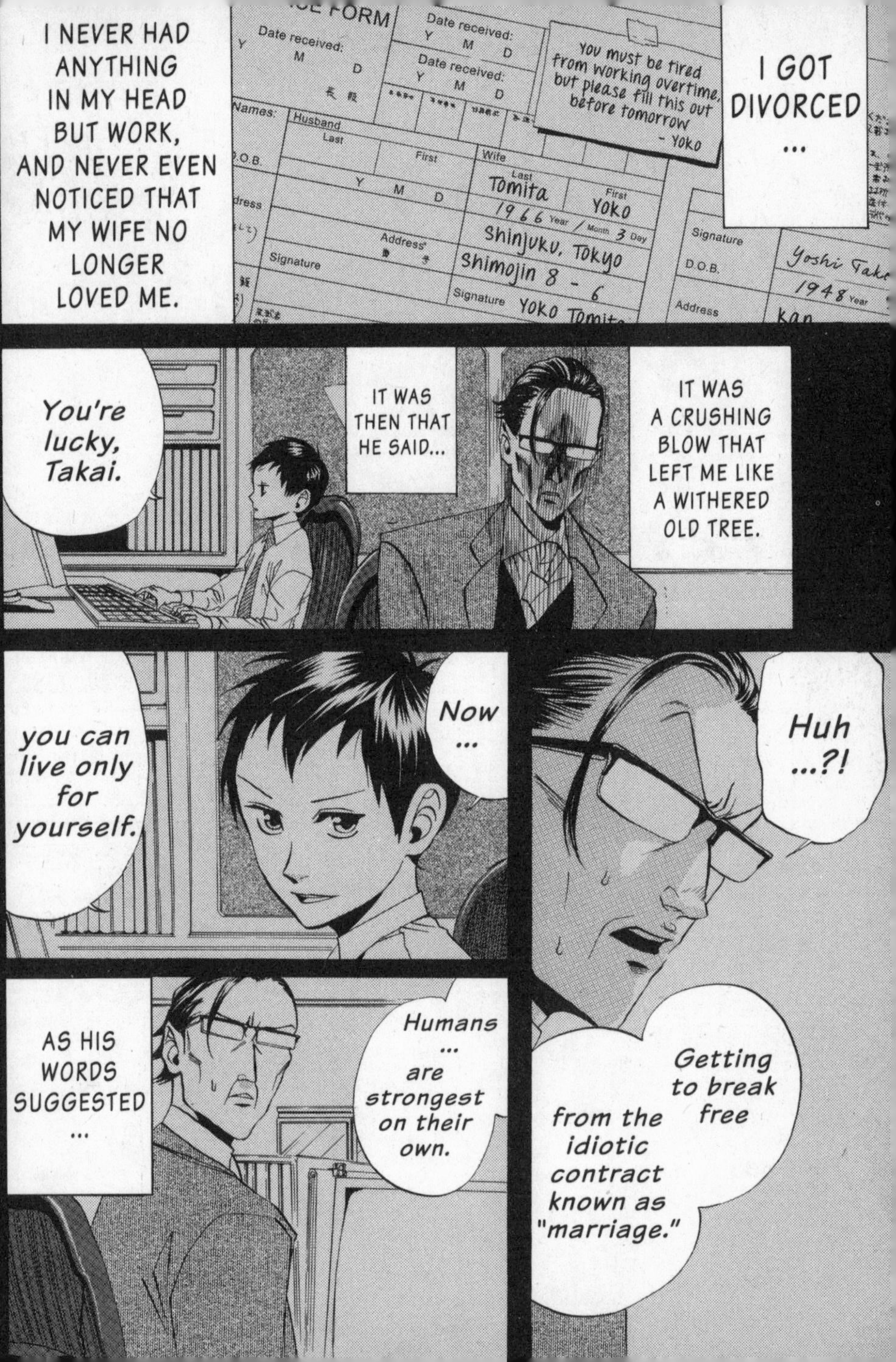
I GOT DIVORCED ...
You must be tired from working overtime, but please fill this out before tomorrow - Yoko
Date received: Y M D
Names: Husband Last First Wife Last Tomita First Yoko
1966 Year / Month 3 Day
Shinjuku, Tokyo Shimojin 8 - 6
Signature Yoko Tomita
I NEVER HAD ANYTHING IN MY HEAD BUT WORK, AND NEVER EVEN NOTICED THAT MY WIFE NO LONGER LOVED ME.
IT WAS A CRUSHING BLOW THAT LEFT ME LIKE A WITHERED OLD TREE.
IT WAS THEN THAT HE SAID...
You're lucky, Takai.
Huh ...?!
Now ...
you can live only for yourself.
Getting to break free from the idiotic contract known as "marriage."
Humans ... are strongest on their own.
AS HIS WORDS SUGGESTED ...

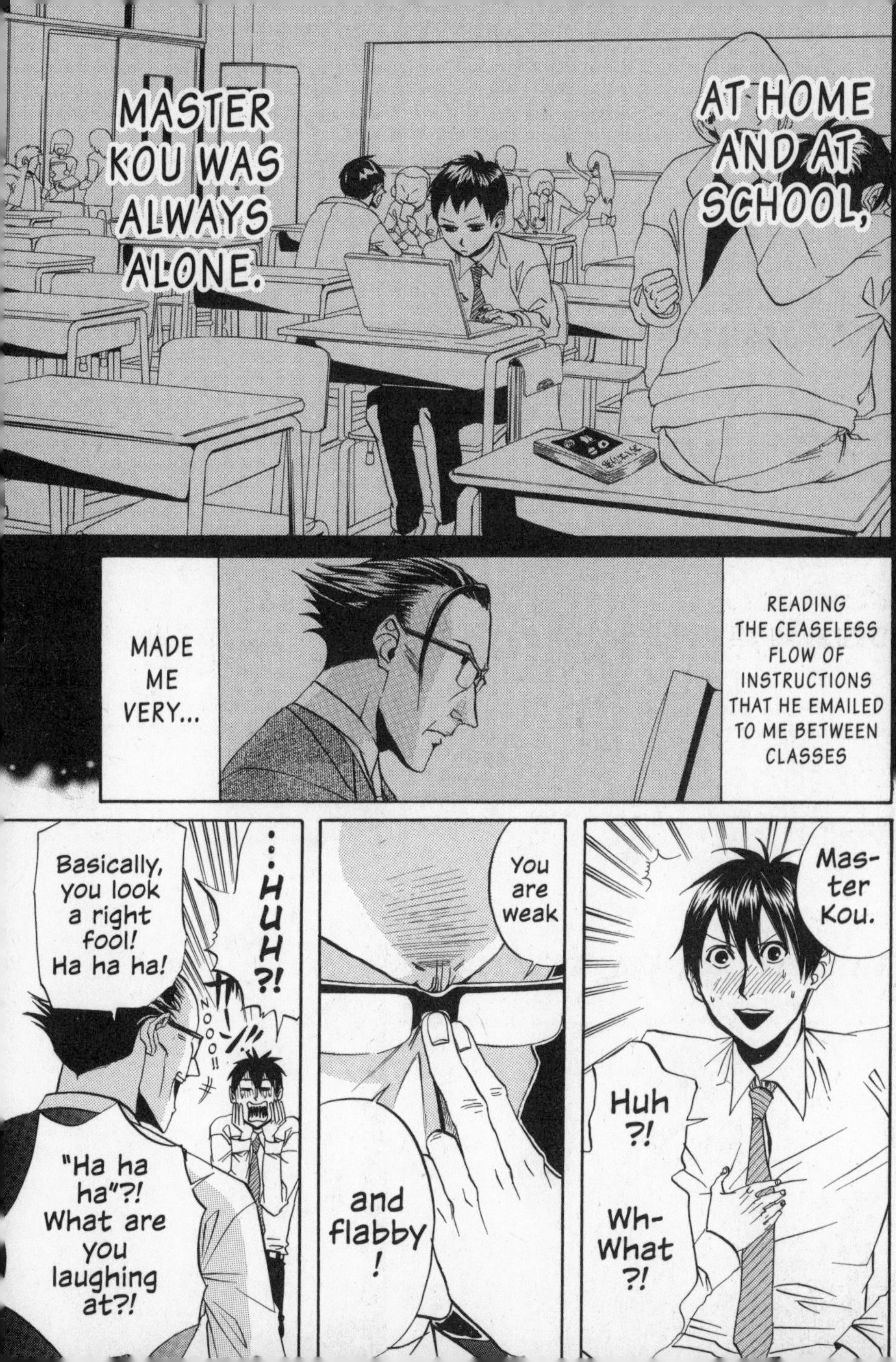
AT HOME AND AT SCHOOL,
MASTER KOU WAS ALWAYS ALONE.
READING THE CEASELESS FLOW OF INSTRUCTIONS THAT HE EMAILED TO ME BETWEEN CLASSES
MADE ME VERY...
Mas-ter Kou.
Huh ?!
Wh- What ?!
You are weak
and flabby !
...HUH?!
Basically, you look a right fool! Ha ha ha!
NOOO!!
"Ha ha ha"?! What are you laughing at?!

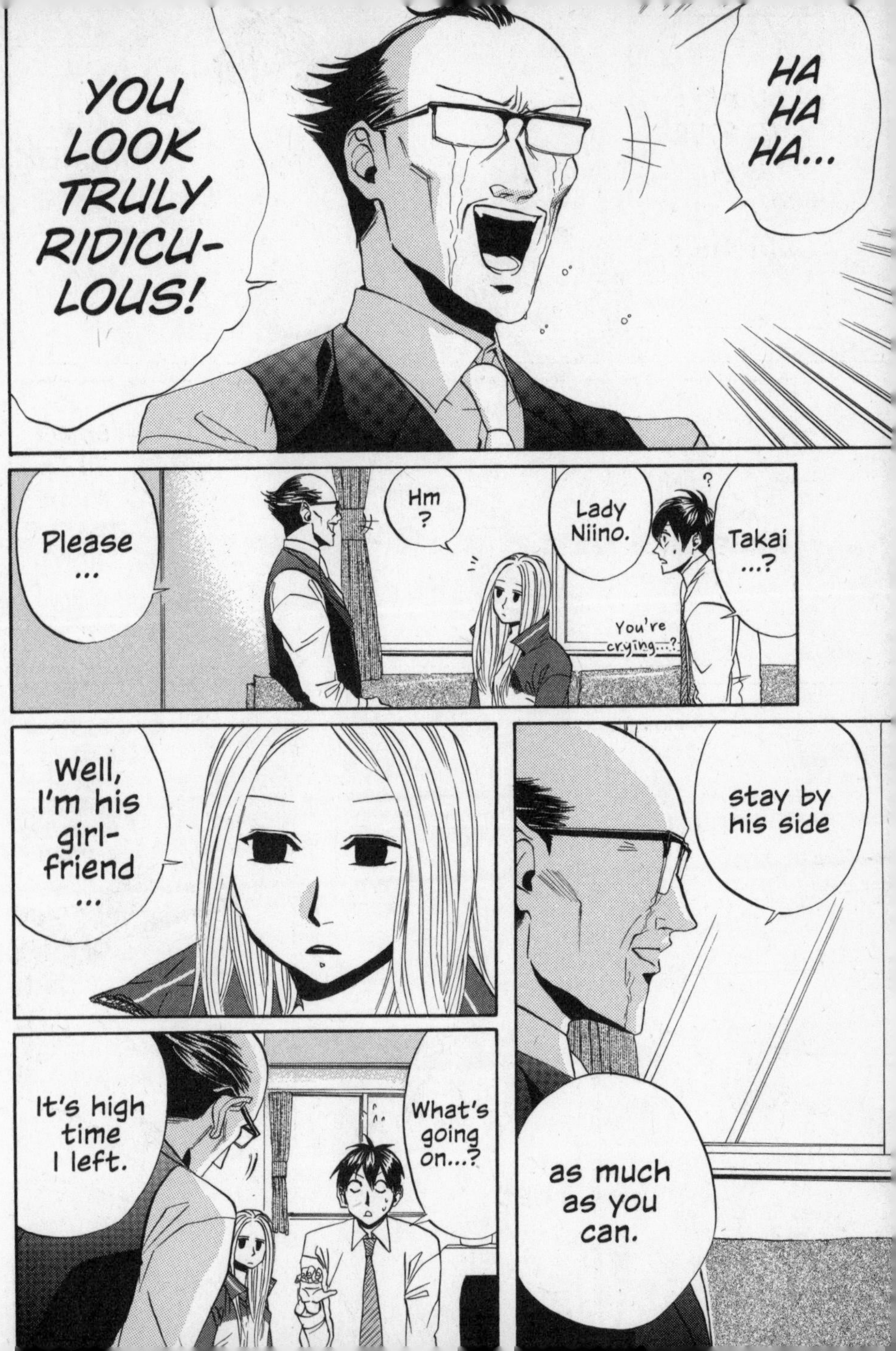
HA HA HA...
YOU LOOK TRULY RIDICU-LOUS!
Takai ...?
You're crying...?
Lady Niino.
Hm ?
Please ...
stay by his side
as much as you can.
Well, I'm his girl-friend ...
What's going on...?
It's high time I left.

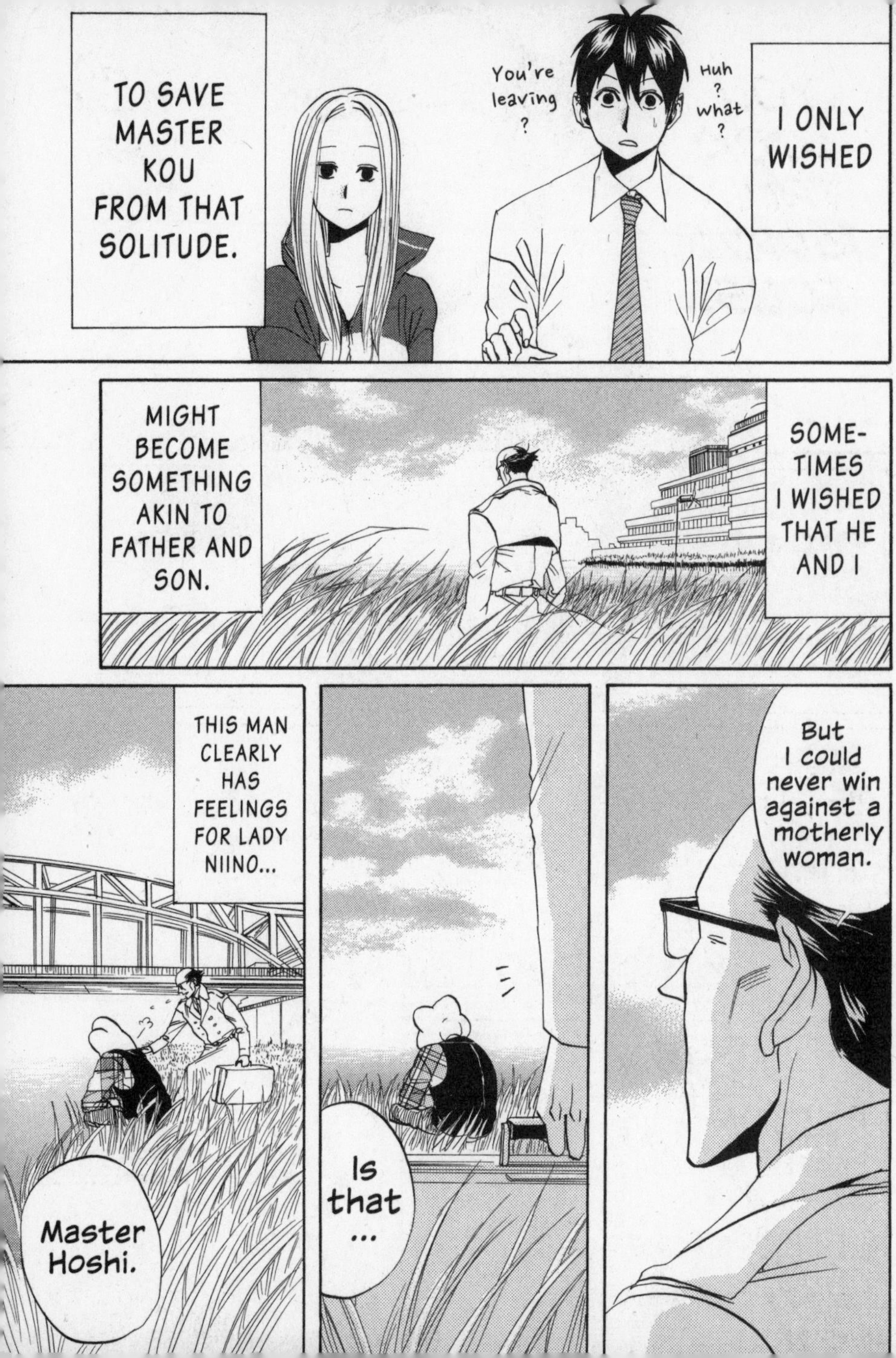
I ONLY WISHED
Huh? what?
You're leaving?
TO SAVE MASTER KOU FROM THAT SOLITUDE.
SOME-TIMES I WISHED THAT HE AND I
MIGHT BECOME SOMETHING AKIN TO FATHER AND SON.
But I could never win against a motherly woman.
Is that ...
THIS MAN CLEARLY HAS FEELINGS FOR LADY NIINO...
Master Hoshi.

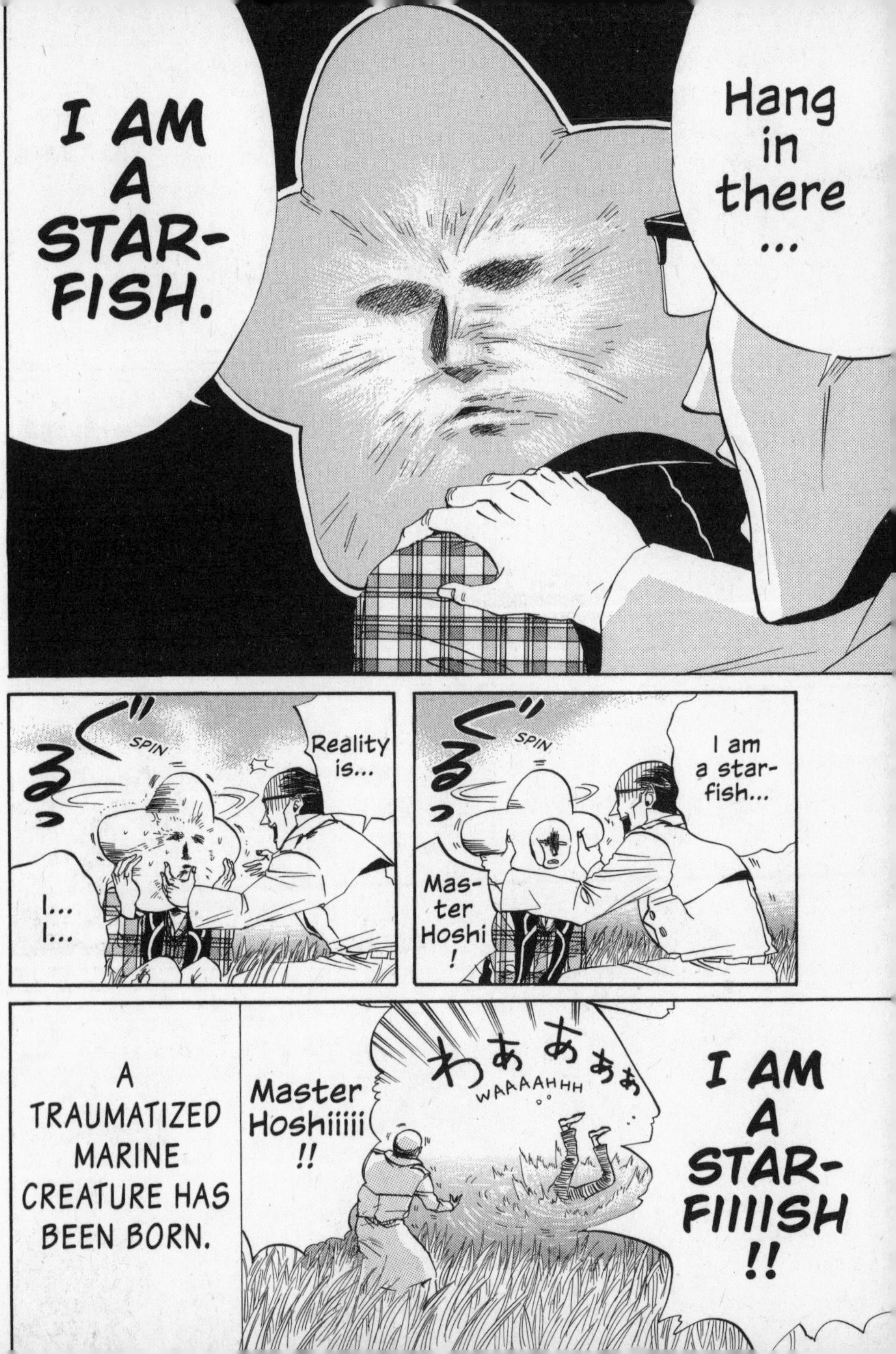
Hang in there ...
I AM A STAR-FISH.
I am a star-fish...
ぐるっ
SPIN
Mas-ter Hoshi!
Reality is...
ぐるっ
SPIN
I... I...
I AM A STAR-FIIIISH!!
わあああぁぁ
WAAAAHHH
Master Hoshiiiiii!!
A TRAUMATIZED MARINE CREATURE HAS BEEN BORN.

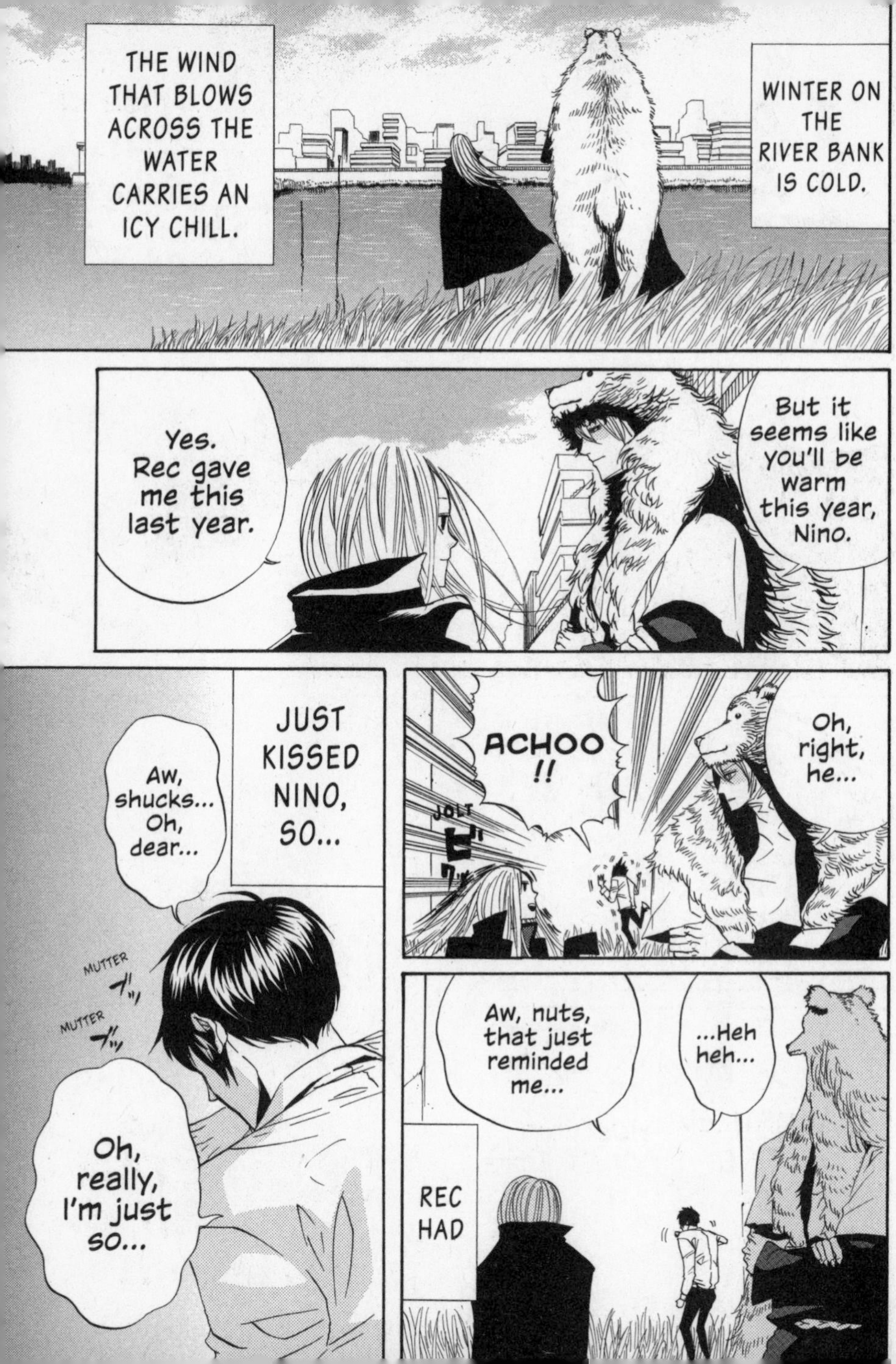
WINTER ON THE RIVER BANK IS COLD.
THE WIND THAT BLOWS ACROSS THE WATER CARRIES AN ICY CHILL.
But it seems like you'll be warm this year, Nino.
Yes. Rec gave me this last year.
Oh, right, he...
ACHOO !!
JOLT
...Heh heh...
Aw, nuts, that just reminded me...
REC HAD
JUST KISSED NINO, SO...
Aw, shucks... Oh, dear...
MUTTER
MUTTER
Oh, really, I'm just so...

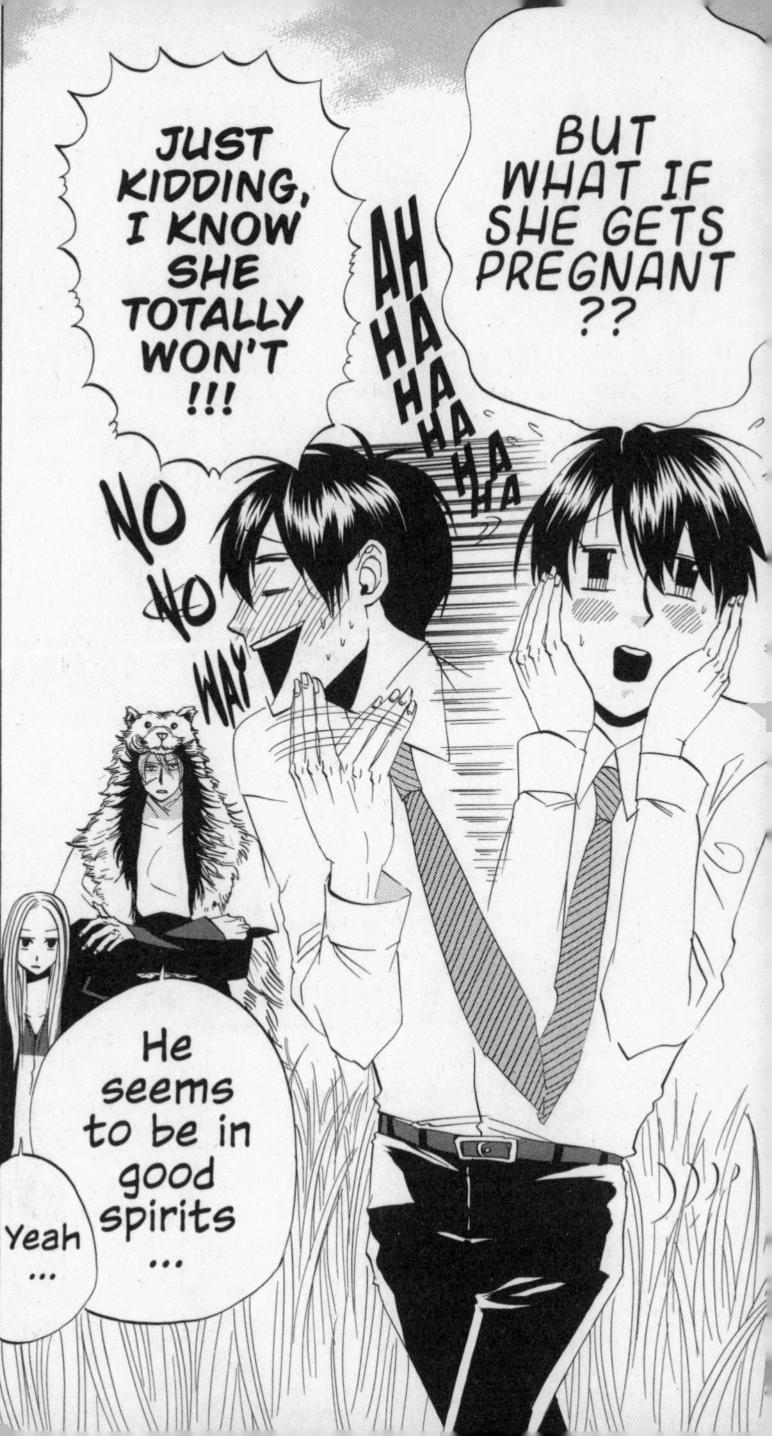

HE IS PRANCING ALONE THROUGH FLOWERING FIELDS IN HIS MIND.

Chapter 75: Blue Bird

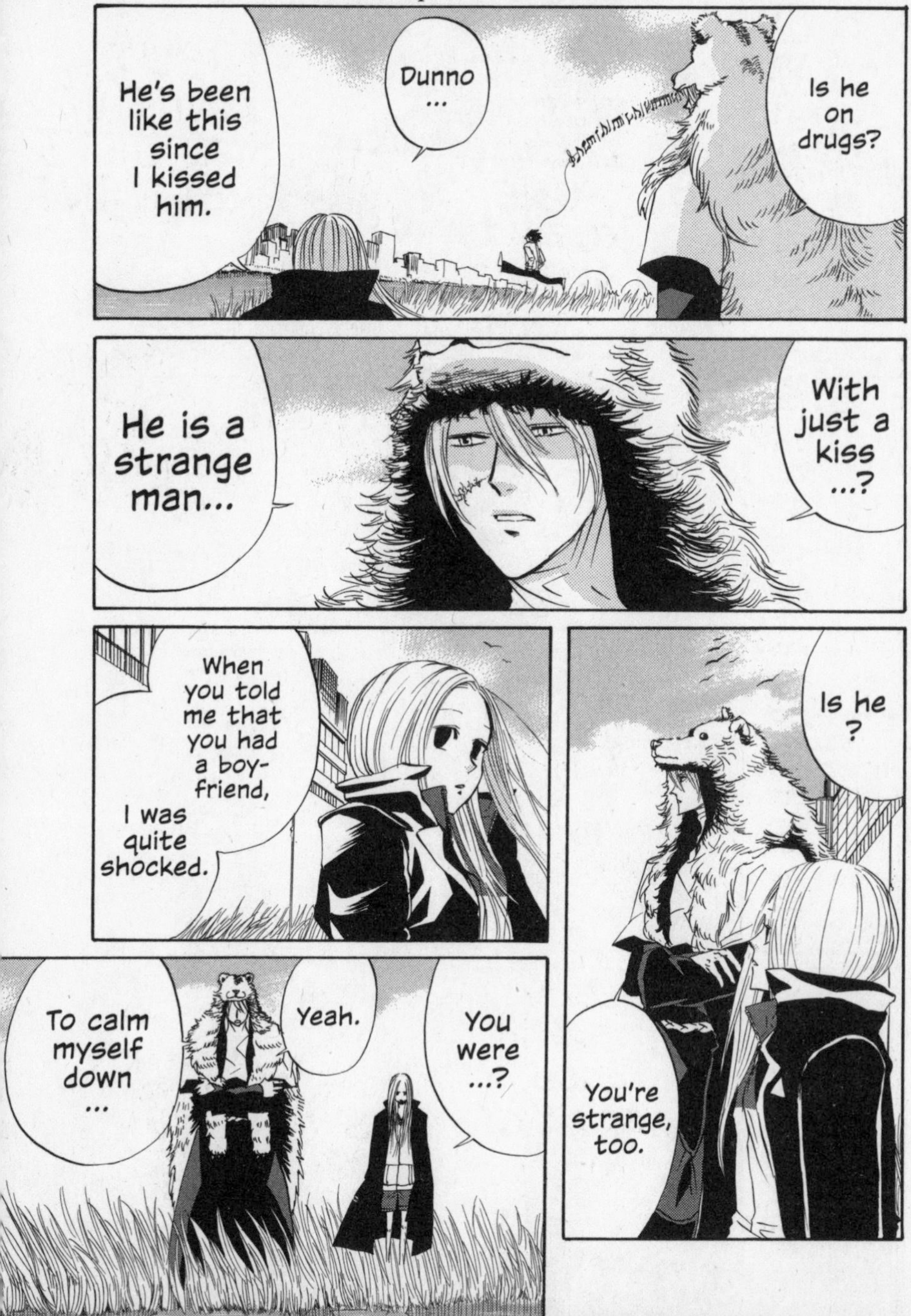

Is he on drugs?
Dunno ...
He's been like this since I kissed him.
With just a kiss ...?
He is a strange man...
Is he ?
You're strange, too.
When you told me that you had a boy-friend, I was quite shocked.
You were ...?
Yeah.
To calm myself down ...

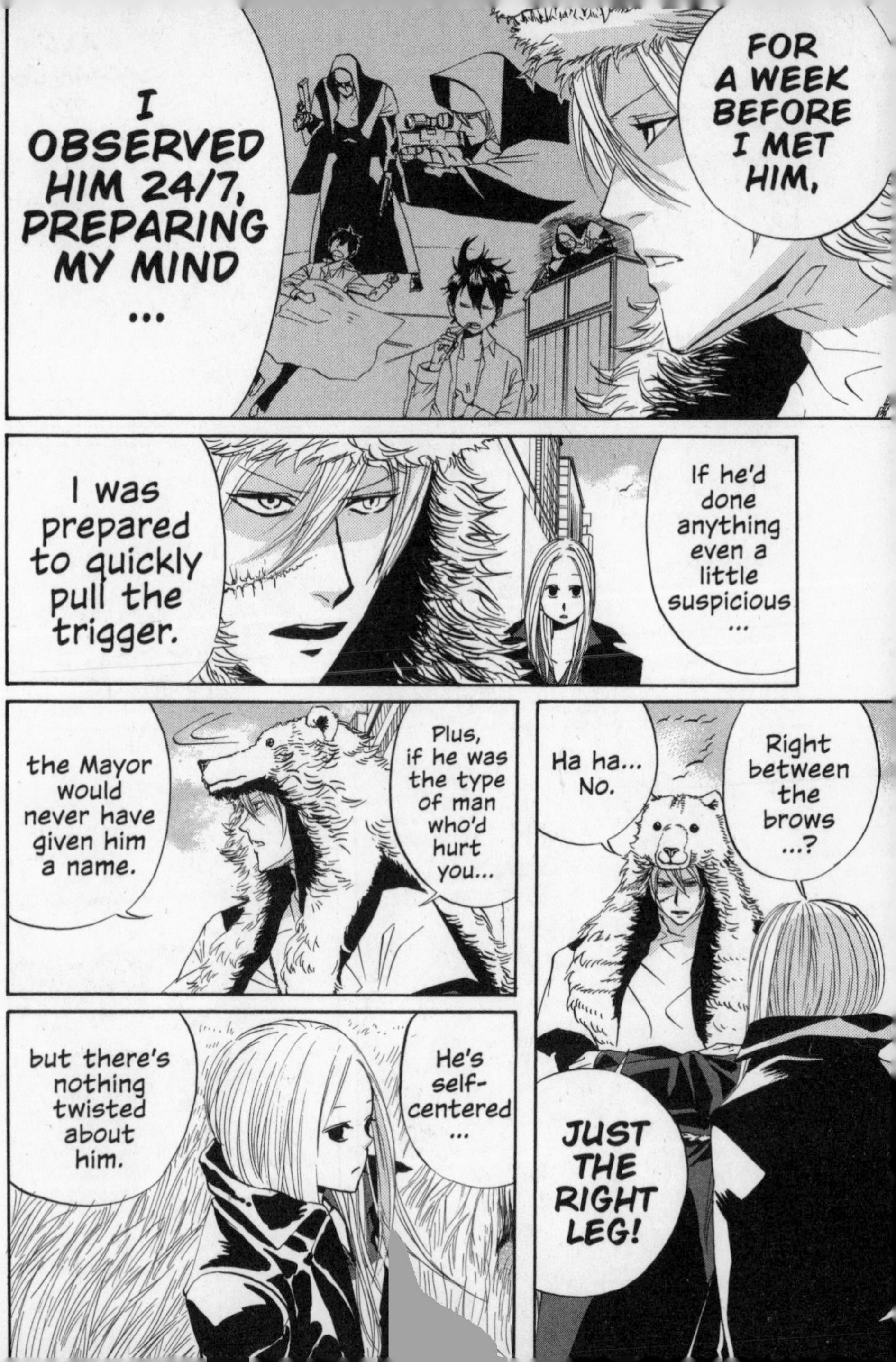
FOR A WEEK BEFORE I MET HIM,
I OBSERVED HIM 24/7, PREPARING MY MIND ...
If he'd done anything even a little suspicious ...
I was prepared to quickly pull the trigger.
Right between the brows ...?
Ha ha... No.
JUST THE RIGHT LEG!
Plus, if he was the type of man who'd hurt you...
the Mayor would never have given him a name.
He's self-centered ...
but there's nothing twisted about him.

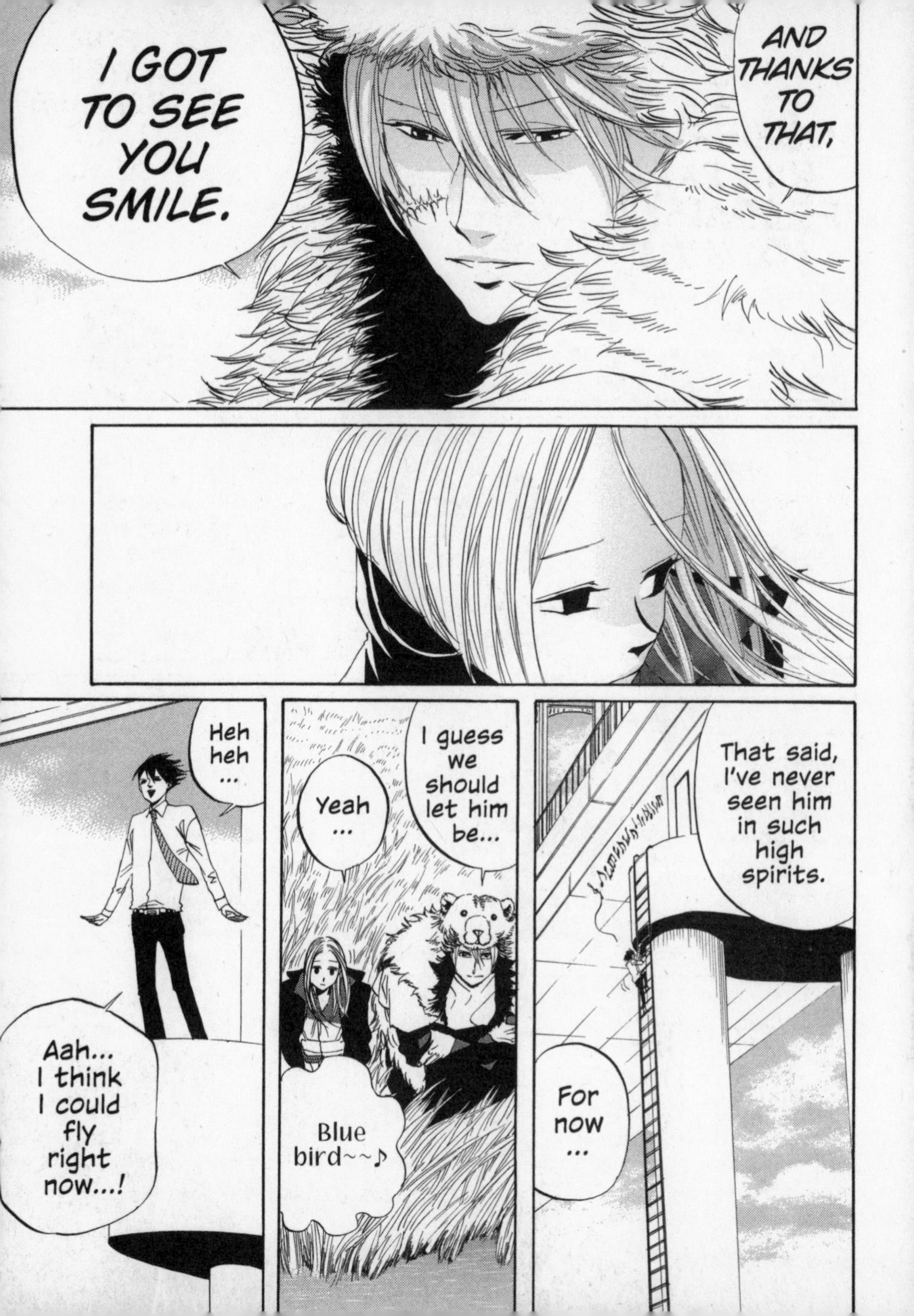
AND THANKS TO THAT,
I GOT TO SEE YOU SMILE.
That said, I've never seen him in such high spirits.
For now...
I guess we should let him be...
Yeah...
Blue bird~~♪
Heh heh...
Aah... I think I could fly right now...!

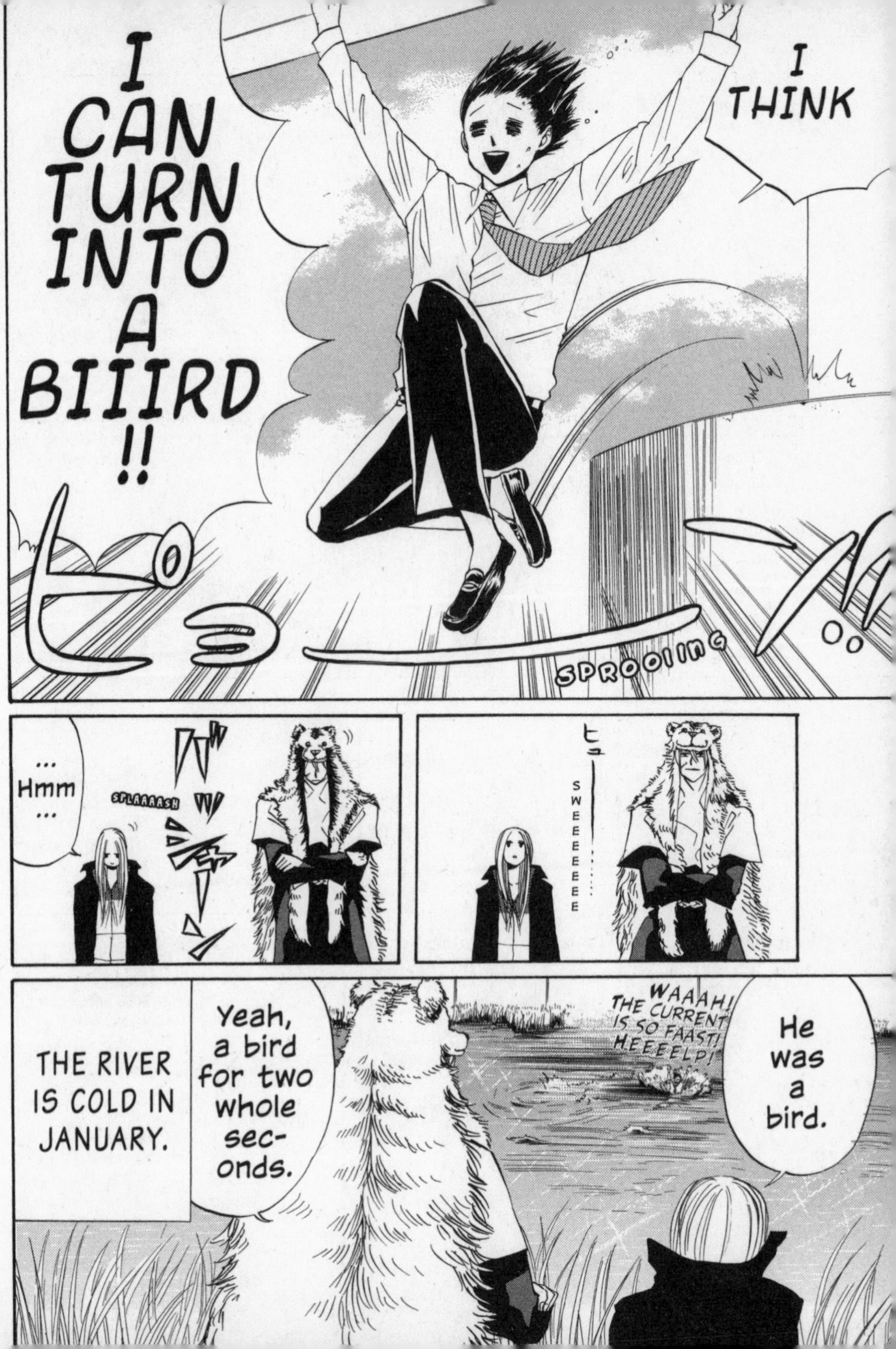
I THINK
I CAN TURN INTO A BIIIRD !!
SPROOIING
SWEEEEEEEE.....
... Hmm ...
SPLAAAASH
He was a bird.
WAAAH! THE CURRENT IS SO FAAST! HEEEELP!
Yeah, a bird for two whole sec-onds.
THE RIVER IS COLD IN JANUARY.

Chapter 76: Present

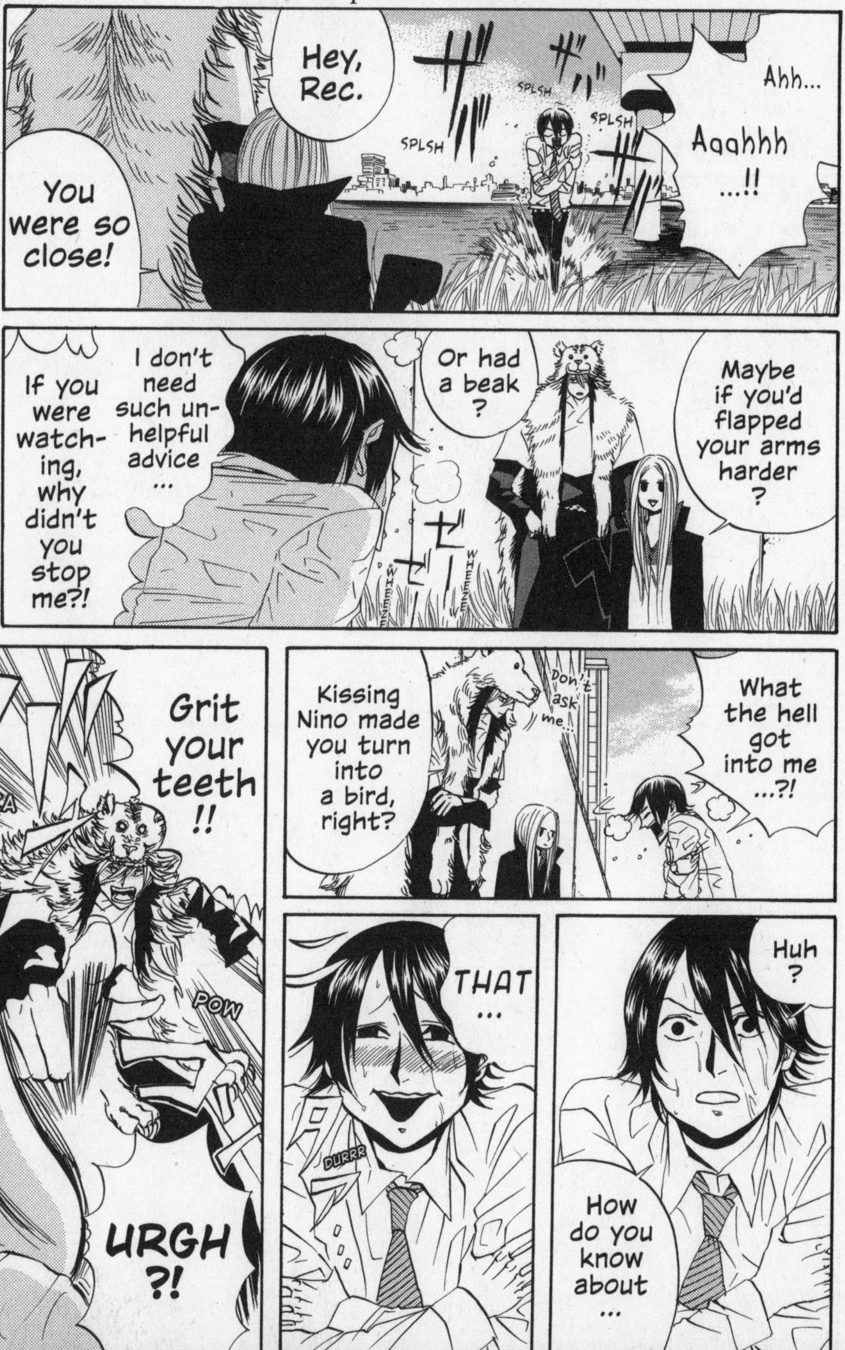
Ahh...
Aaahhh ...!!
SPLSH
SPLSH
SPLSH
Hey, Rec.
You were so close!
Maybe if you'd flapped your arms harder?
Or had a beak?
WHEEZE
WHEEZE
I don't need such un-helpful advice...
If you were watching, why didn't you stop me?!
What the hell got into me ...?!
Don't ask me...
Kissing Nino made you turn into a bird, right?
Huh?
How do you know about...
THAT...
DURRR
Grit your teeth!!
KA
POW
URGH?!

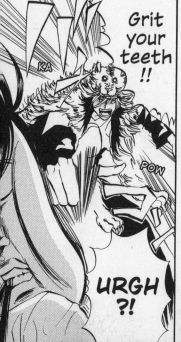

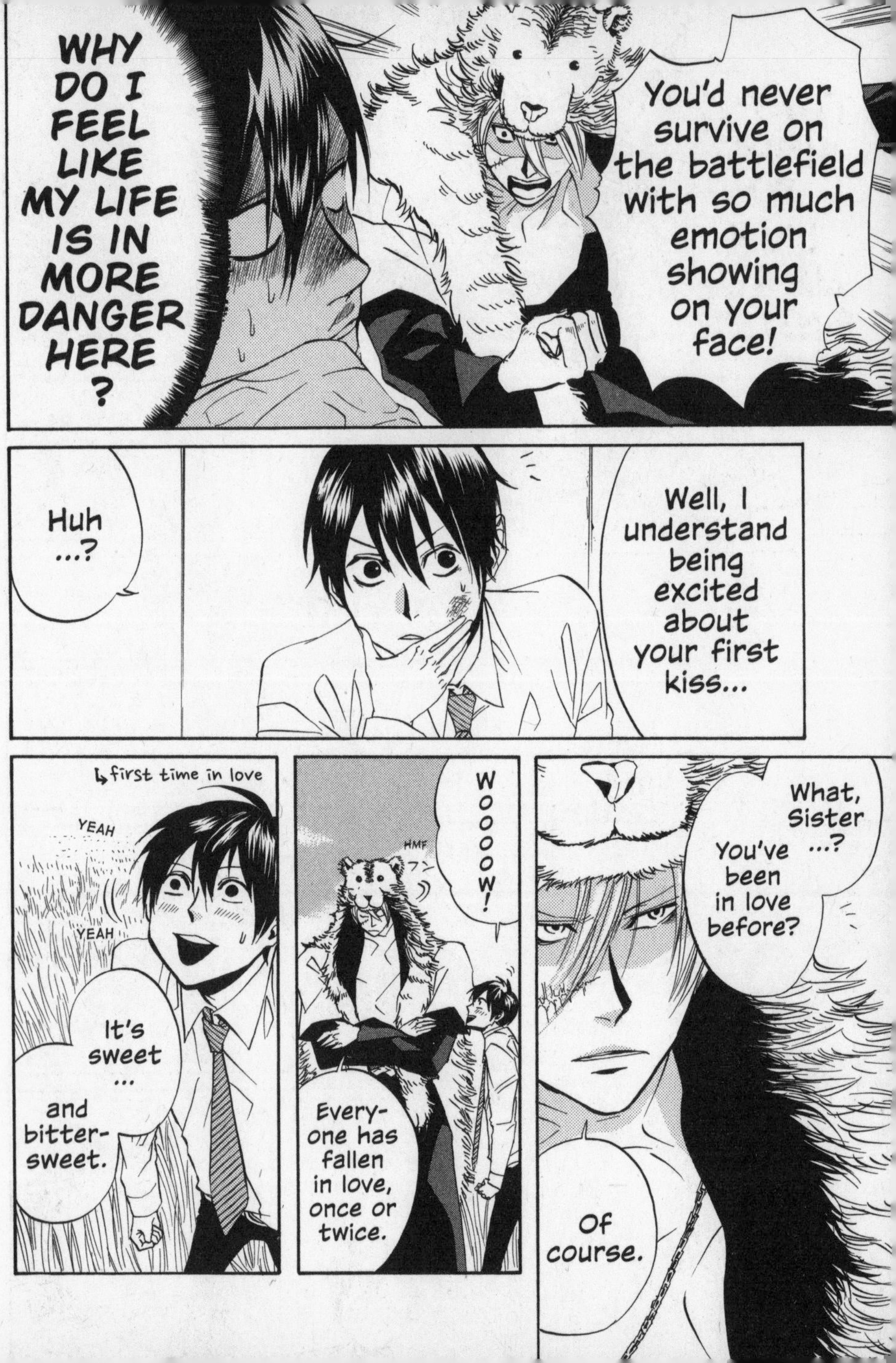
You'd never survive on the battlefield with so much emotion showing on your face!
WHY DO I FEEL LIKE MY LIFE IS IN MORE DANGER HERE ?
Well, I understand being excited about your first kiss...
Huh ...?
What, Sister ...? You've been in love before?
Of course.
WOOOOOW!
HMF
Every-one has fallen in love, once or twice.
first time in love
YEAH
YEAH
It's sweet ...
and bitter-sweet.

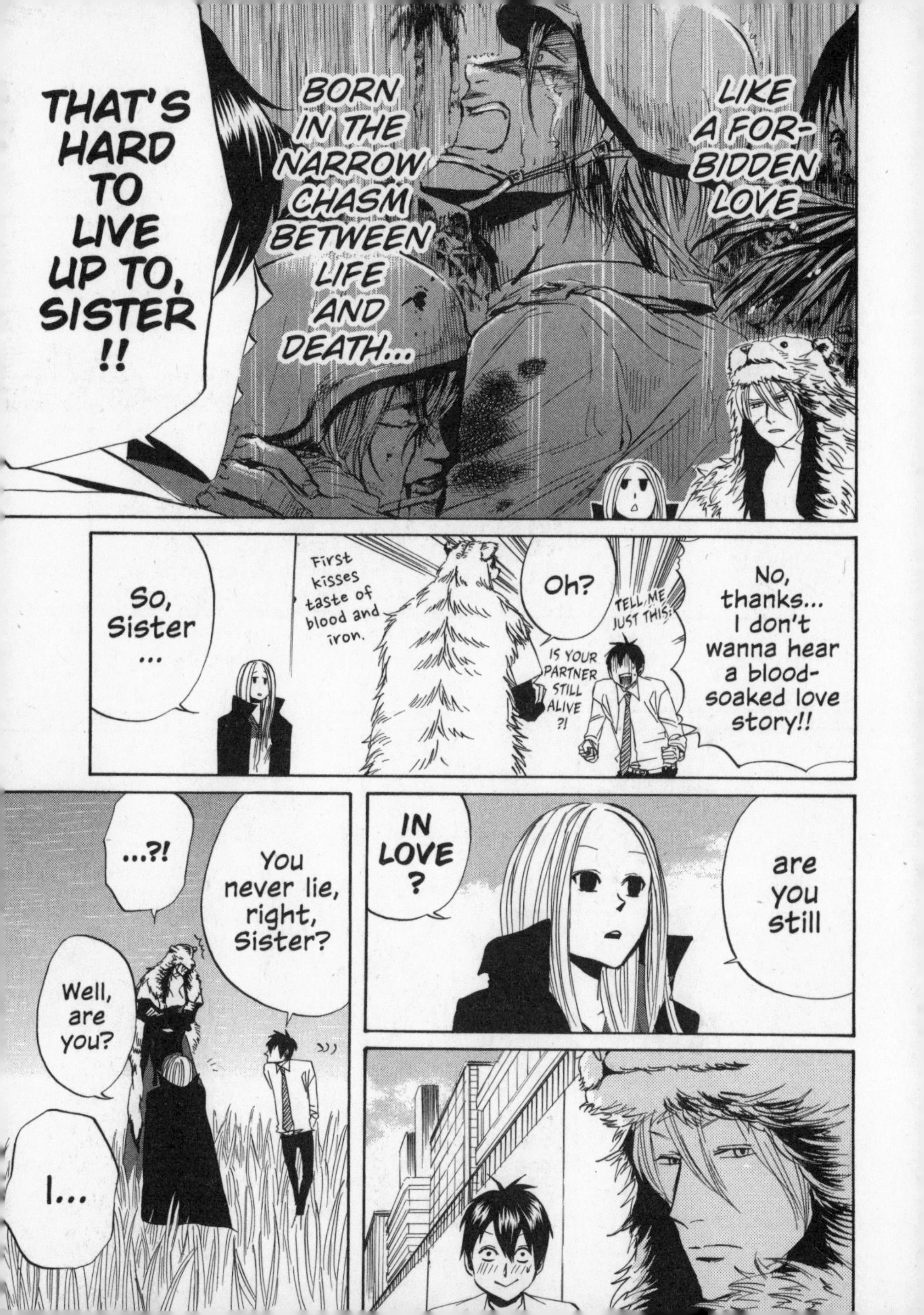
LIKE A FOR-BIDDEN LOVE
BORN IN THE NARROW CHASM BETWEEN LIFE AND DEATH...
THAT'S HARD TO LIVE UP TO, SISTER !!
No, thanks... I don't wanna hear a blood-soaked love story!!
TELL ME JUST THIS:
IS YOUR PARTNER STILL ALIVE ?!
Oh?
First kisses taste of blood and iron.
So, Sister ...
are you still
IN LOVE ?
You never lie, right, Sister?
...?!
Well, are you?
I...

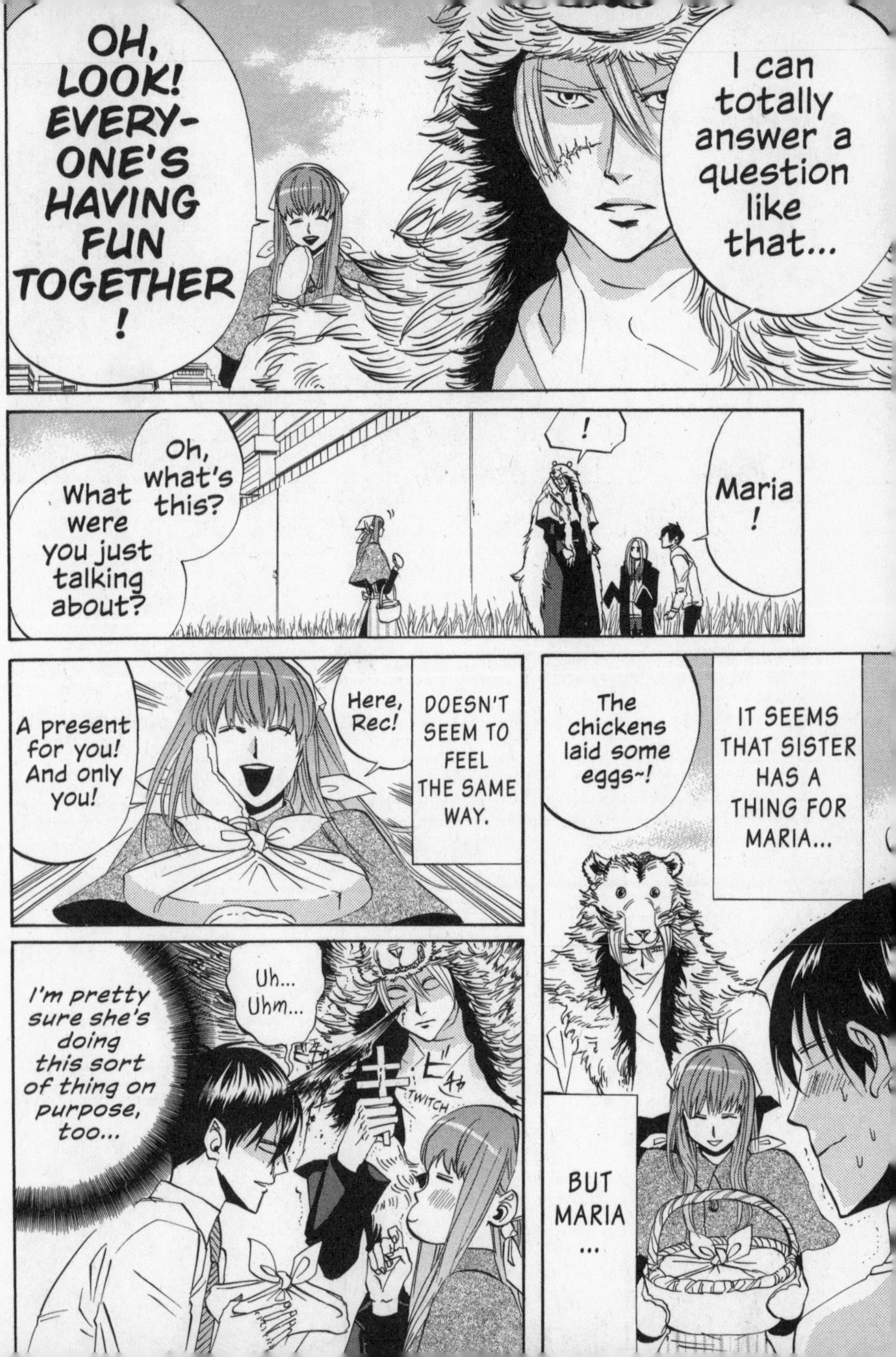
I can totally answer a question like that...
OH, LOOK! EVERY-ONE'S HAVING FUN TOGETHER!
Maria!
!
Oh, what's this?
What were you just talking about?
IT SEEMS THAT SISTER HAS A THING FOR MARIA...
The chickens laid some eggs~!
BUT MARIA...
DOESN'T SEEM TO FEEL THE SAME WAY.
Here, Rec!
A present for you! And only you!
Uh... Uhm...
TWITCH
I'm pretty sure she's doing this sort of thing on purpose, too...

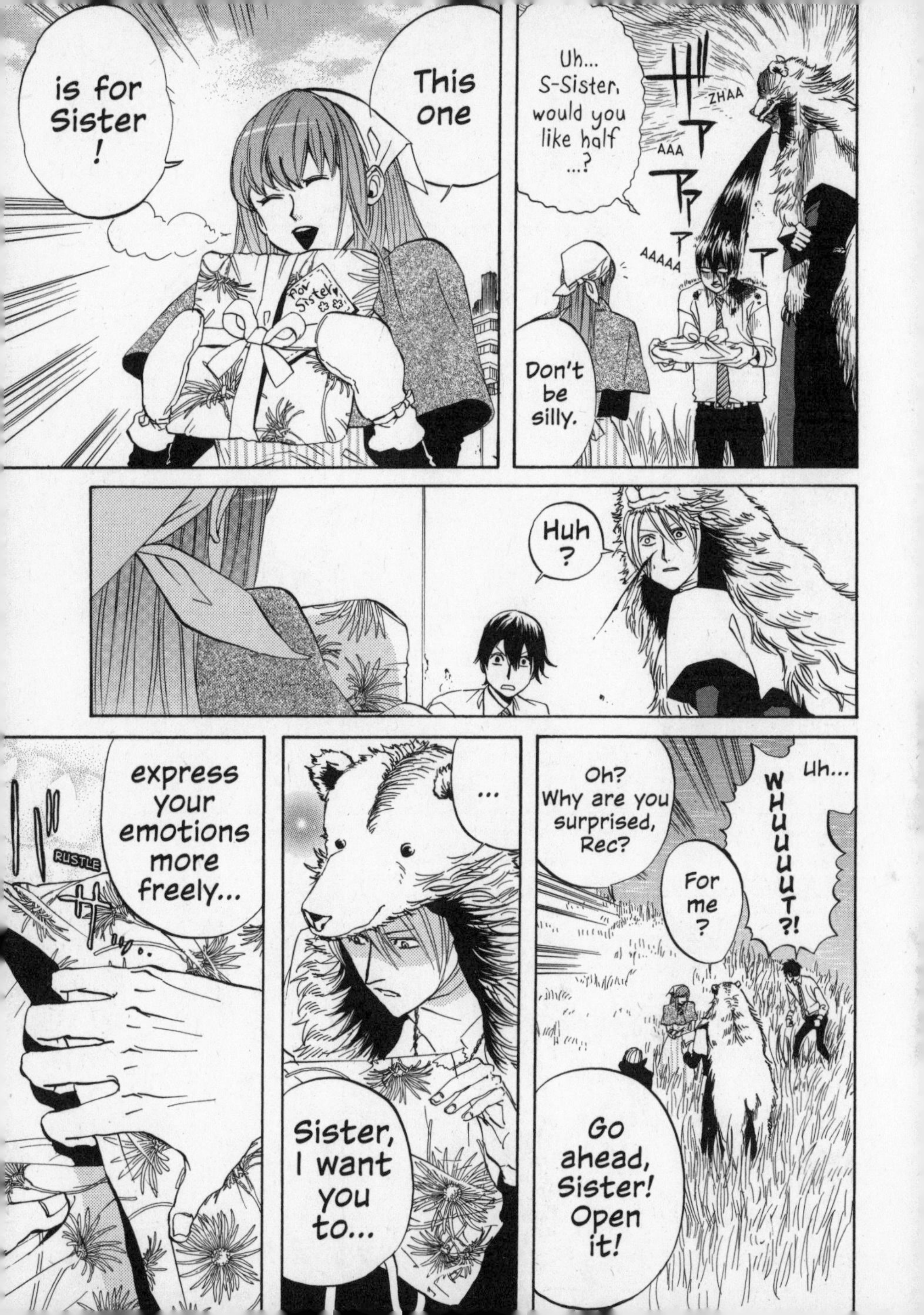
ZHAA
Uh... S-Sister, would you like half ...?
AAA
AAAAA
Don't be silly.
This one
is for Sister!
For Sister
Huh?
Uh... WHUUUUT?!
Oh? Why are you surprised, Rec?
For me?
Go ahead, Sister! Open it!
...
Sister, I want you to...
express your emotions more freely...
RUSTLE

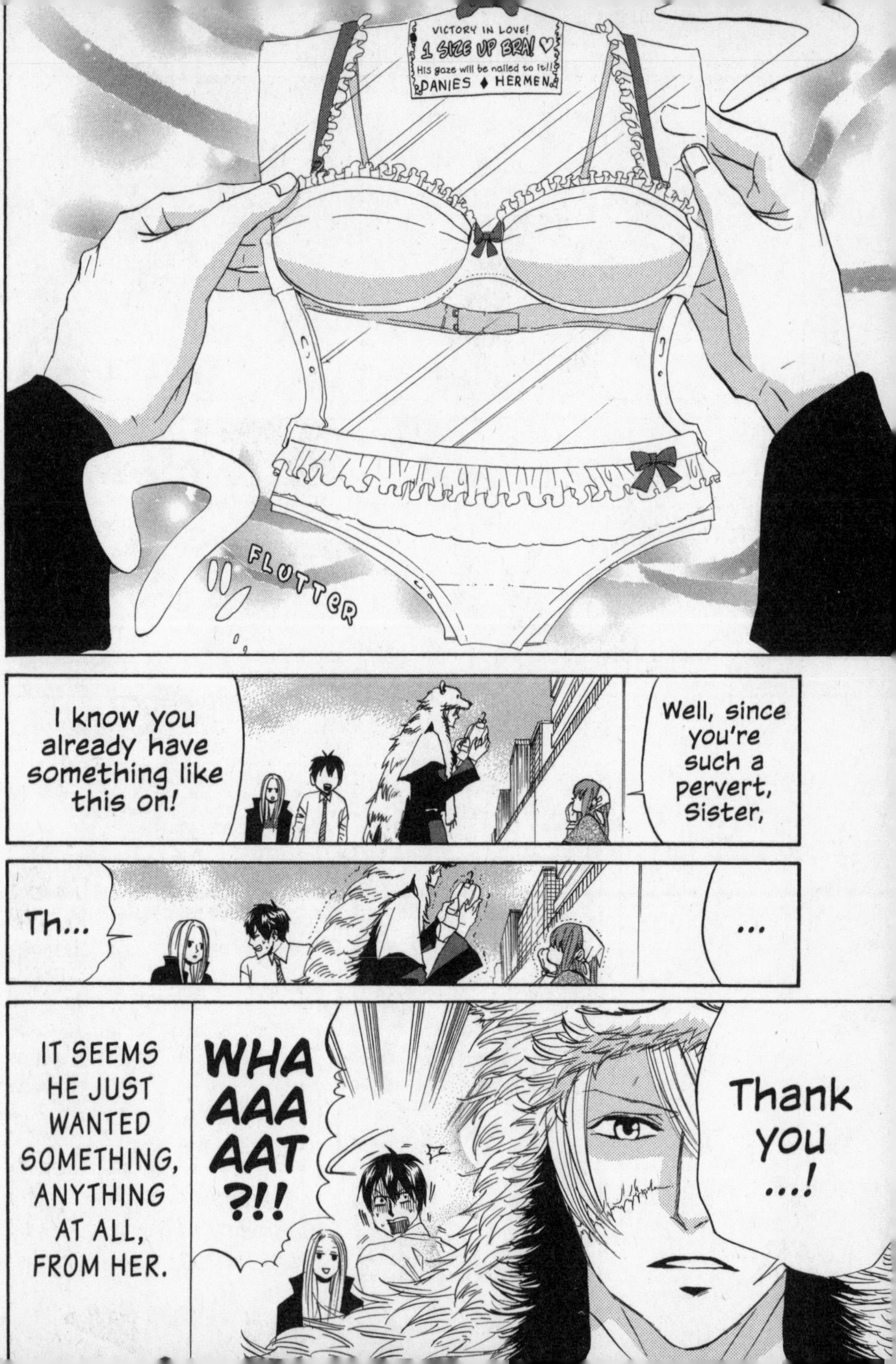

VICTORY IN LOVE!
1 SIZE UP BRA! ♥
His gaze will be nailed to it!!
DANIES ◆ HERMEN
FLUTTER
Well, since you're such a pervert, Sister,
I know you already have something like this on!
...
Th...
Thank you ...!
WHAAAAAAAT?!!
IT SEEMS HE JUST WANTED SOMETHING, ANYTHING AT ALL, FROM HER.

Chapter 77: Parents

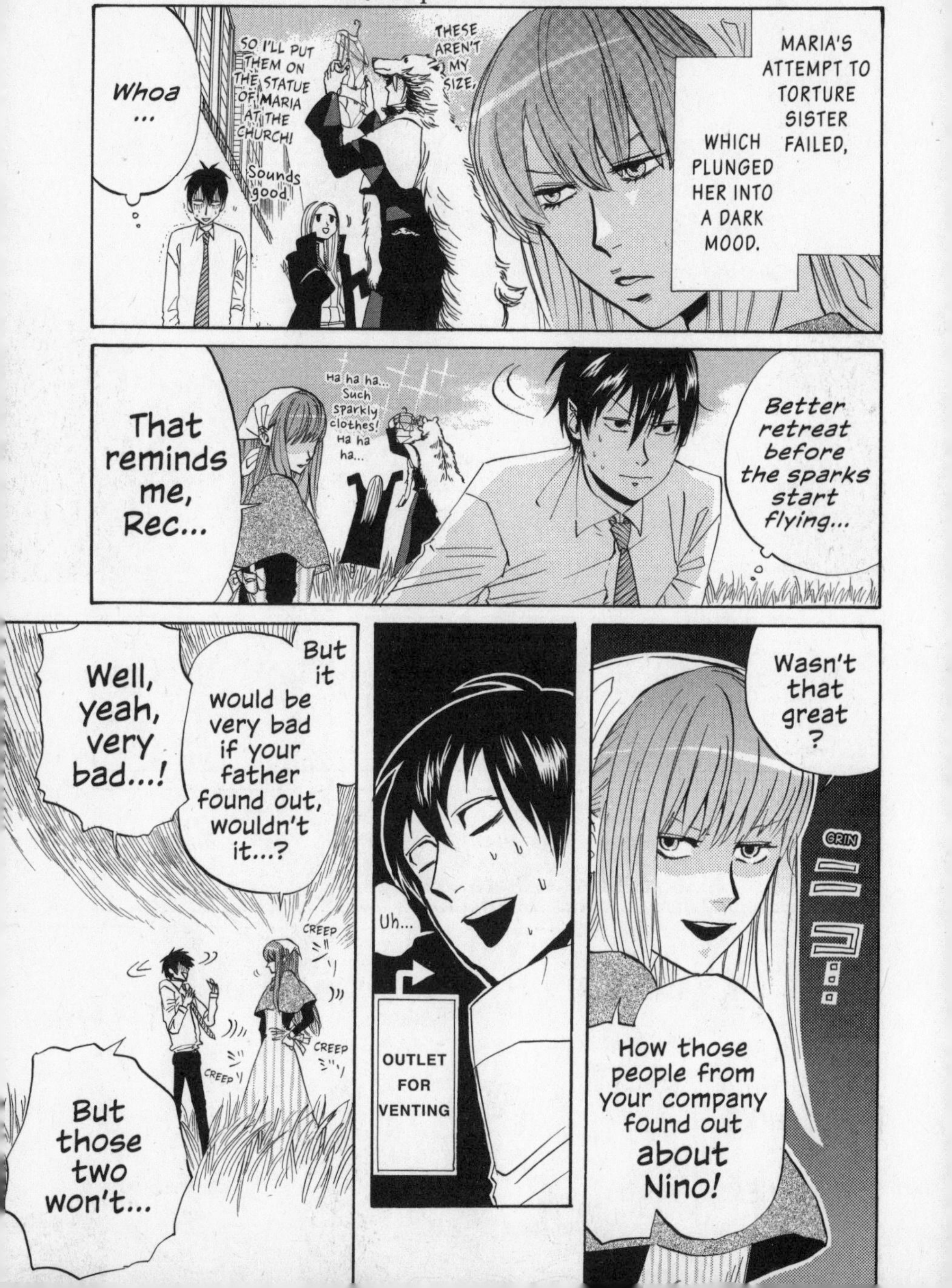
MARIA'S ATTEMPT TO TORTURE SISTER FAILED, WHICH PLUNGED HER INTO A DARK MOOD.
THESE AREN'T MY SIZE,
SO I'LL PUT THEM ON THE STATUE OF MARIA AT THE CHURCH!
Sounds good.
Whoa ...
Better retreat before the sparks start flying...
Ha ha ha... Such sparkly clothes! Ha ha ha...
That reminds me, Rec...
Wasn't that great?
GRIN
How those people from your company found out about Nino!
Uh...
OUTLET FOR VENTING
But it would be very bad if your father found out, wouldn't it...?
Well, yeah, very bad...!
CREEP
CREEP
CREEP
But those two won't...

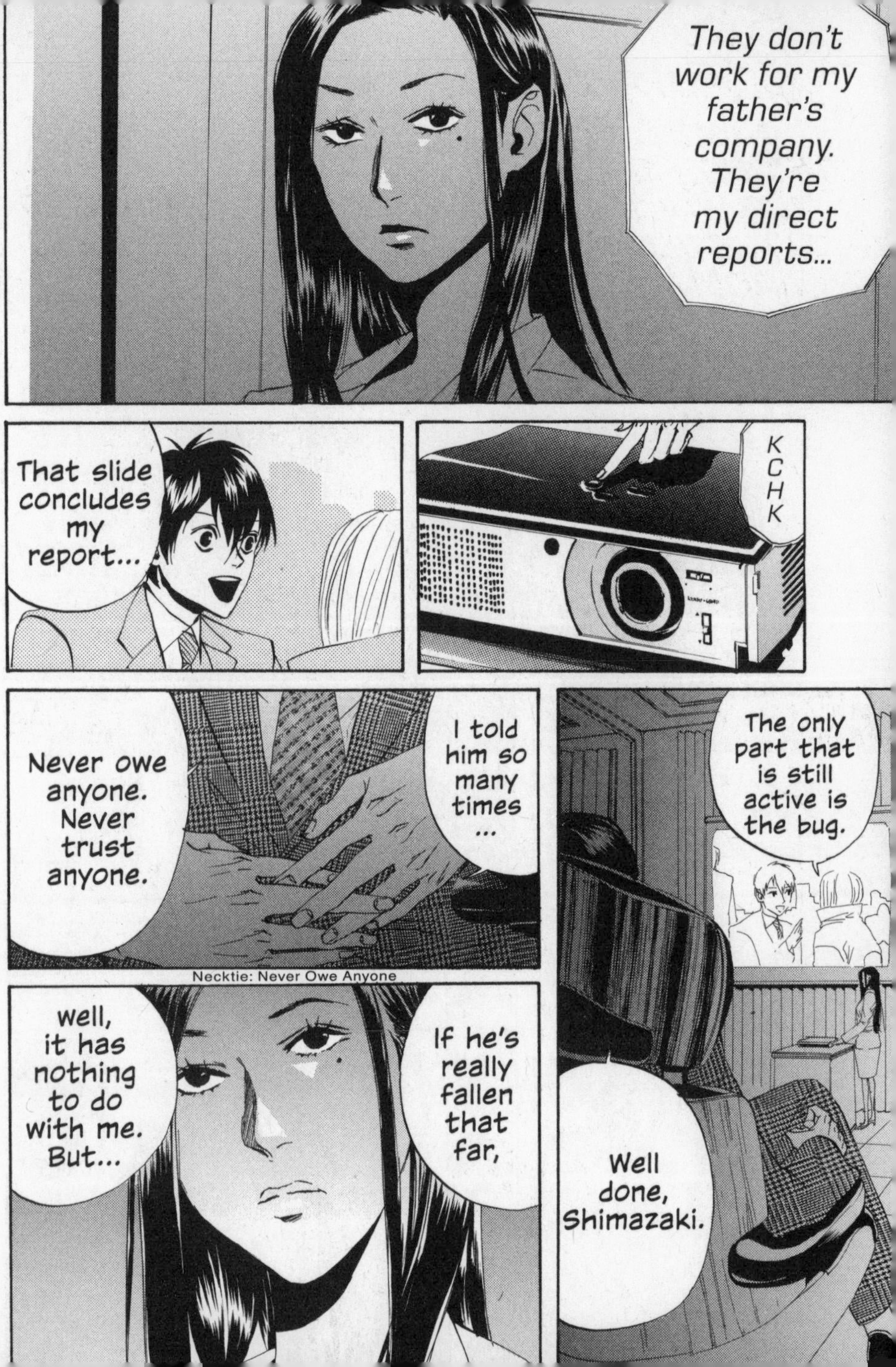
They don't work for my father's company. They're my direct reports...
KCHK
That slide concludes my report...
The only part that is still active is the bug.
Well done, Shimazaki.
I told him so many times ...
Never owe anyone. Never trust anyone.
Necktie: Never Owe Anyone
If he's really fallen that far,
well, it has nothing to do with me. But...

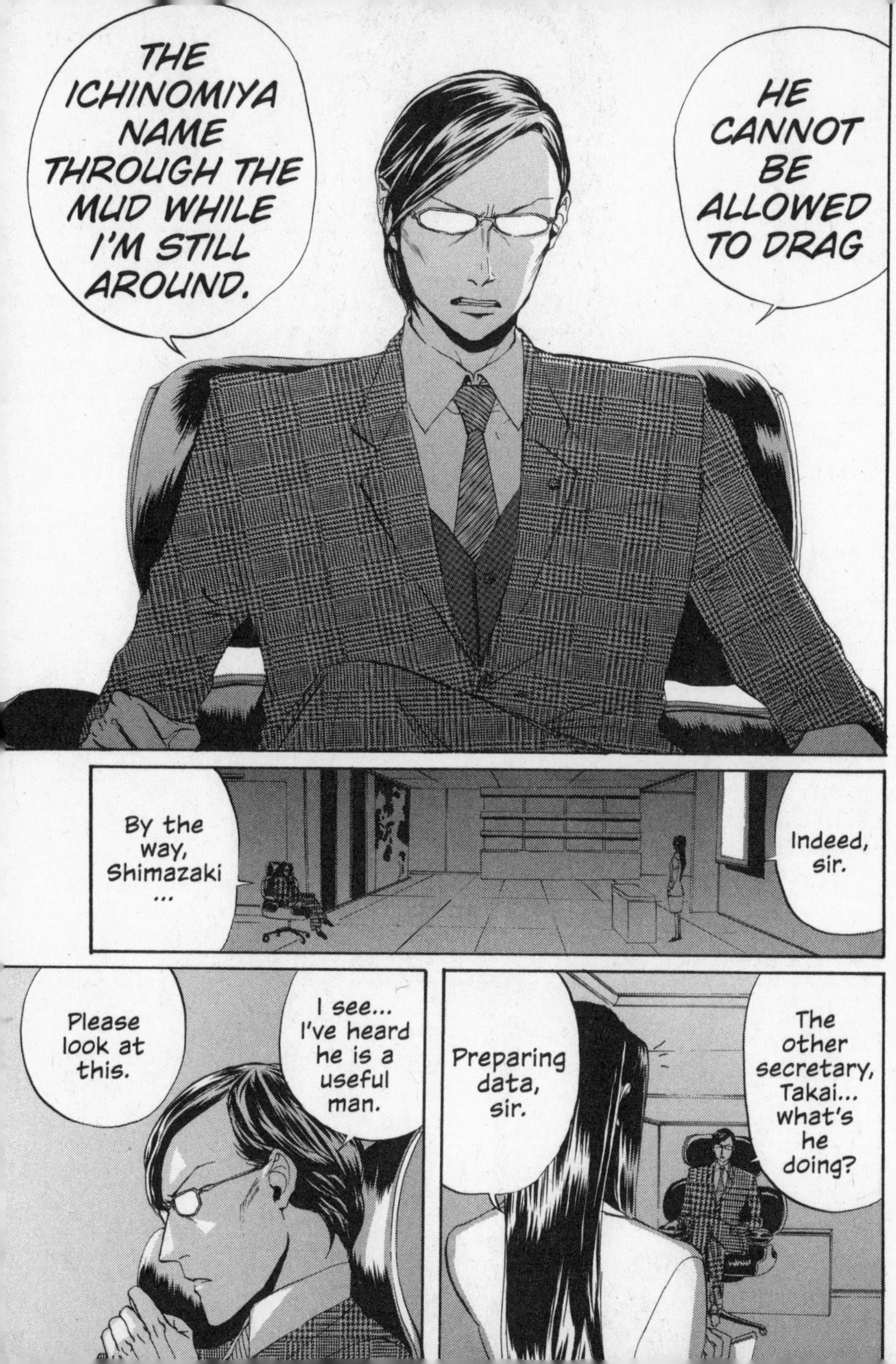
HE CANNOT BE ALLOWED TO DRAG
THE ICHINOMIYA NAME THROUGH THE MUD WHILE I'M STILL AROUND.
Indeed, sir.
By the way, Shimazaki ...
The other secretary, Takai... what's he doing?
Preparing data, sir.
I see... I've heard he is a useful man.
Please look at this.

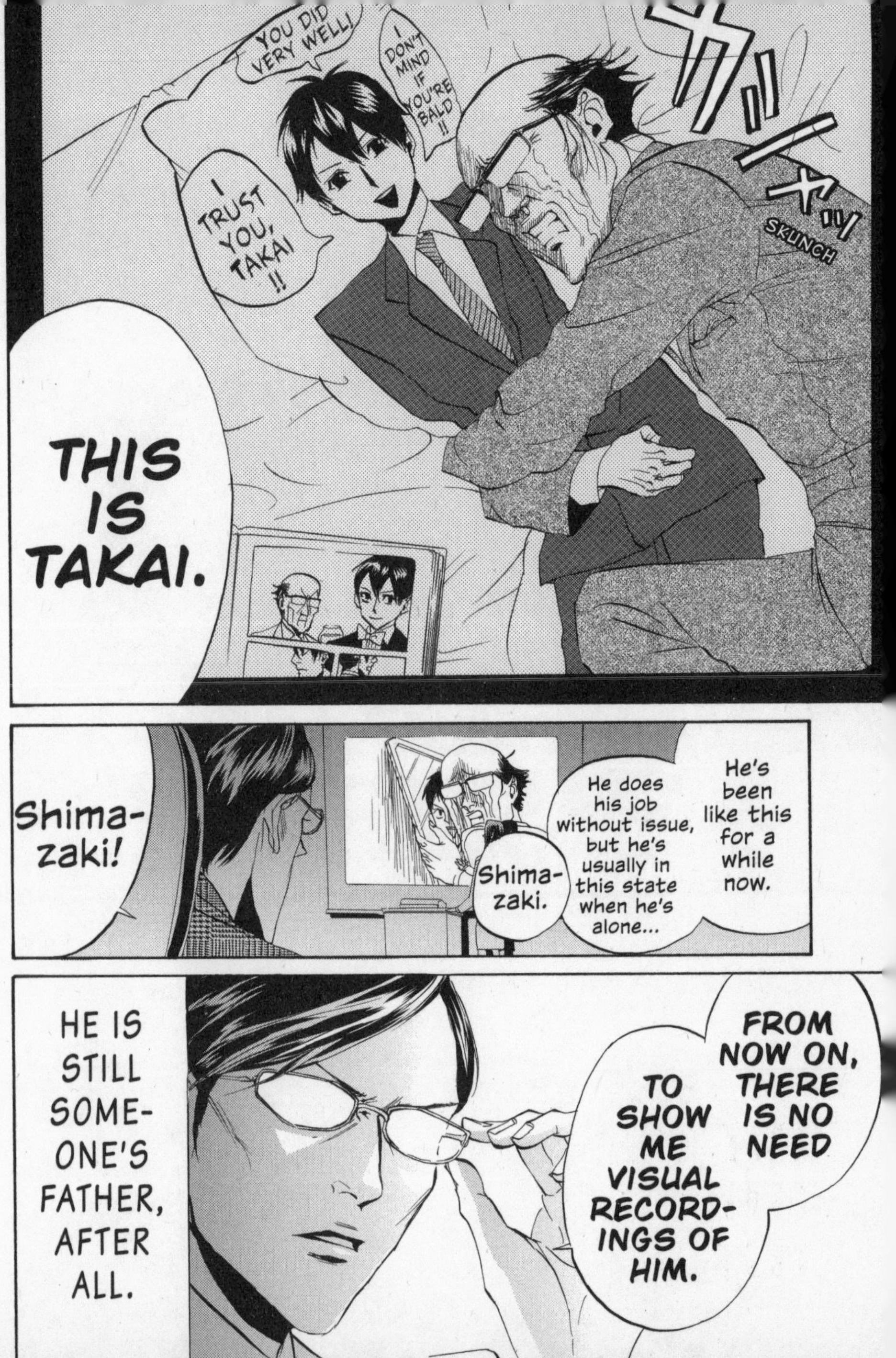
SKUNCH
I DON'T MIND IF YOU'RE BALD!!
YOU DID VERY WELL!
I TRUST YOU, TAKAI!!
THIS IS TAKAI.
He's been like this for a while now.
He does his job without issue, but he's usually in this state when he's alone...
Shimazaki.
Shimazaki!
FROM NOW ON, THERE IS NO NEED TO SHOW ME VISUAL RECORDINGS OF HIM.
HE IS STILL SOMEONE'S FATHER, AFTER ALL.

ARAKAWA
UNDER
THE BRIDGE

AFTERWORD

Arakawa volume 3! My last series ended at three volumes, so it feels like a personal victory! This is entirely because of you, dear reader. Thank you! I'm going to work even harder now, and have fun drawing this series!

With that in mind, here is a bonus manga I didn't work very hard on at all.

↓ ↓ Report Manga

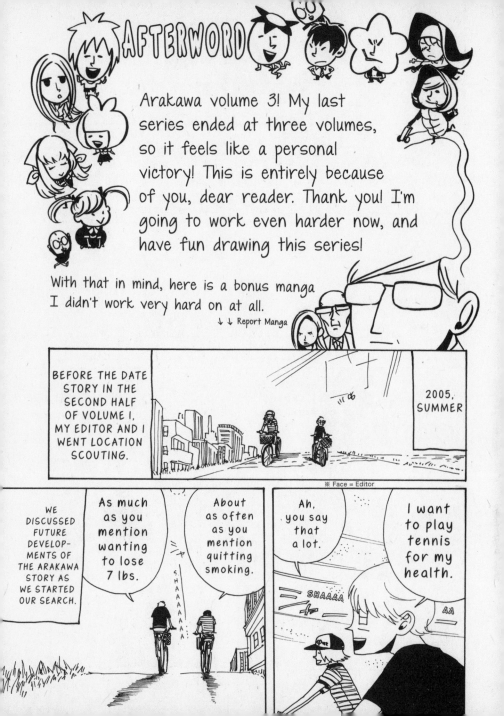

2005, SUMMER
BEFORE THE DATE STORY IN THE SECOND HALF OF VOLUME 1, MY EDITOR AND I WENT LOCATION SCOUTING.
※ Face = Editor
I want to play tennis for my health.
Ah, you say that a lot.
SHAAAAA
AA
About as often as you mention quitting smoking.
SHAAAAAAA
As much as you mention wanting to lose 7 lbs.
WE DISCUSSED FUTURE DEVELOPMENTS OF THE ARAKAWA STORY AS WE STARTED OUR SEARCH.

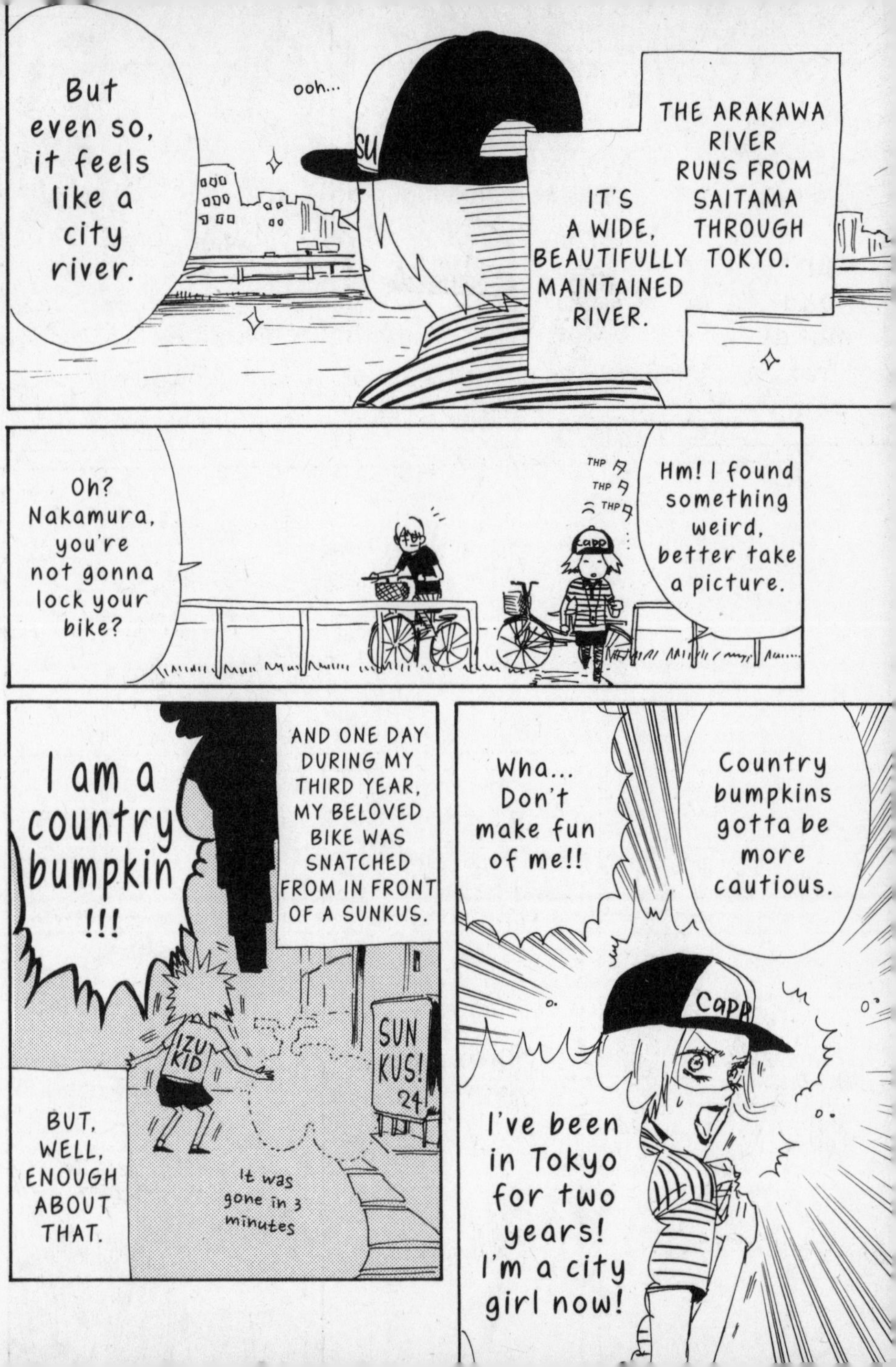
THE ARAKAWA RIVER RUNS FROM SAITAMA THROUGH TOKYO.
IT'S A WIDE, BEAUTIFULLY MAINTAINED RIVER.
ooh...
But even so, it feels like a city river.
Hm! I found something weird, better take a picture.
THP THP THP
Oh? Nakamura, you're not gonna lock your bike?
Country bumpkins gotta be more cautious.
Wha... Don't make fun of me!!
I've been in Tokyo for two years! I'm a city girl now!
AND ONE DAY DURING MY THIRD YEAR, MY BELOVED BIKE WAS SNATCHED FROM IN FRONT OF A SUNKUS.
I am a country bumpkin!!!
SUNKUS! 24
IZU KID
BUT, WELL, ENOUGH ABOUT THAT.
It was gone in 3 minutes

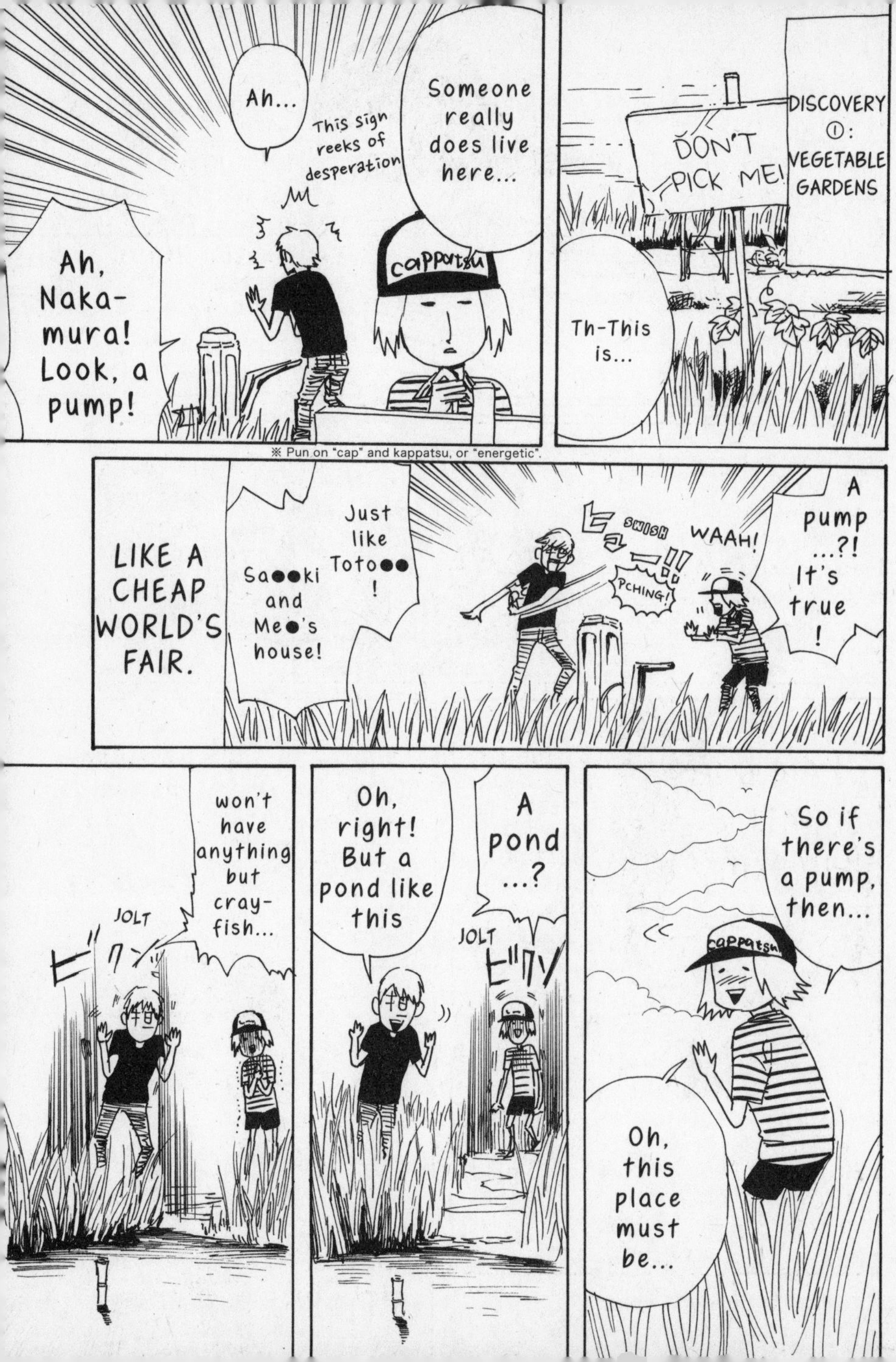
DISCOVERY ①: VEGETABLE GARDENS
DON'T PICK ME!
Th-This is...
Someone really does live here...
Ah...
This sign reeks of desperation
cappatsu
Ah, Naka-mura! Look, a pump!
A pump ...?! It's true!
WAAH!
SWISH
PCHING!
Just like Toto●●!
Sa●●ki and Me●'s house!
LIKE A CHEAP WORLD'S FAIR.
So if there's a pump, then...
cappatsu
Oh, this place must be...
A pond ...?
JOLT
Oh, right! But a pond like this
won't have anything but cray-fish...
JOLT
※ Pun on "cap" and kappatsu, or "energetic".

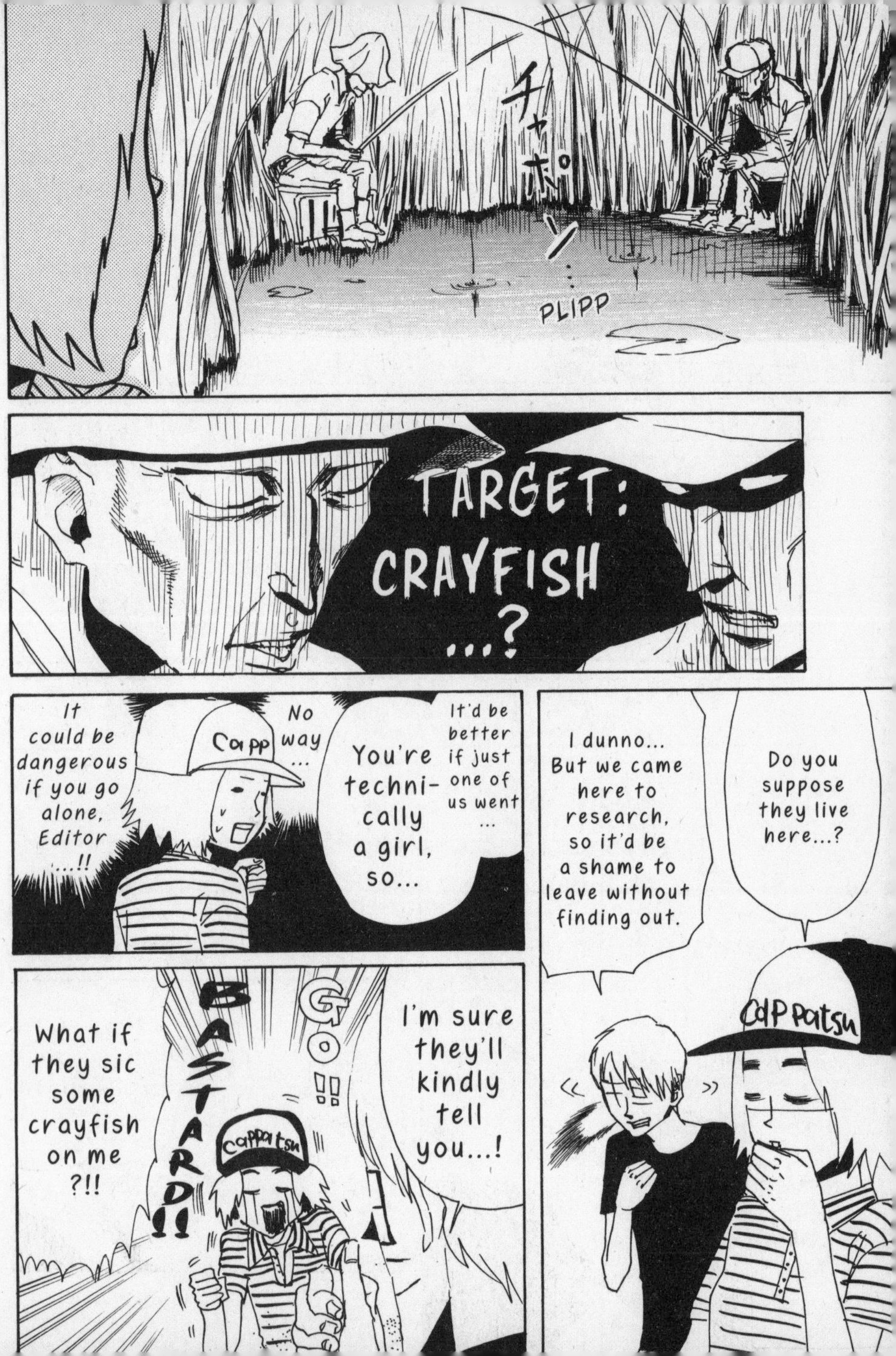
チャポン
PLIPP
TARGET: CRAYFISH ...?
Do you suppose they live here...?
I dunno... But we came here to research, so it'd be a shame to leave without finding out.
Cappatsu
It'd be better if just one of us went ...
You're techni-cally a girl, so...
No way ...
Capp
It could be dangerous if you go alone, Editor ...!!
I'm sure they'll kindly tell you...!
GO!!
BASTARD!!
cappatsu
What if they sic some crayfish on me ?!!

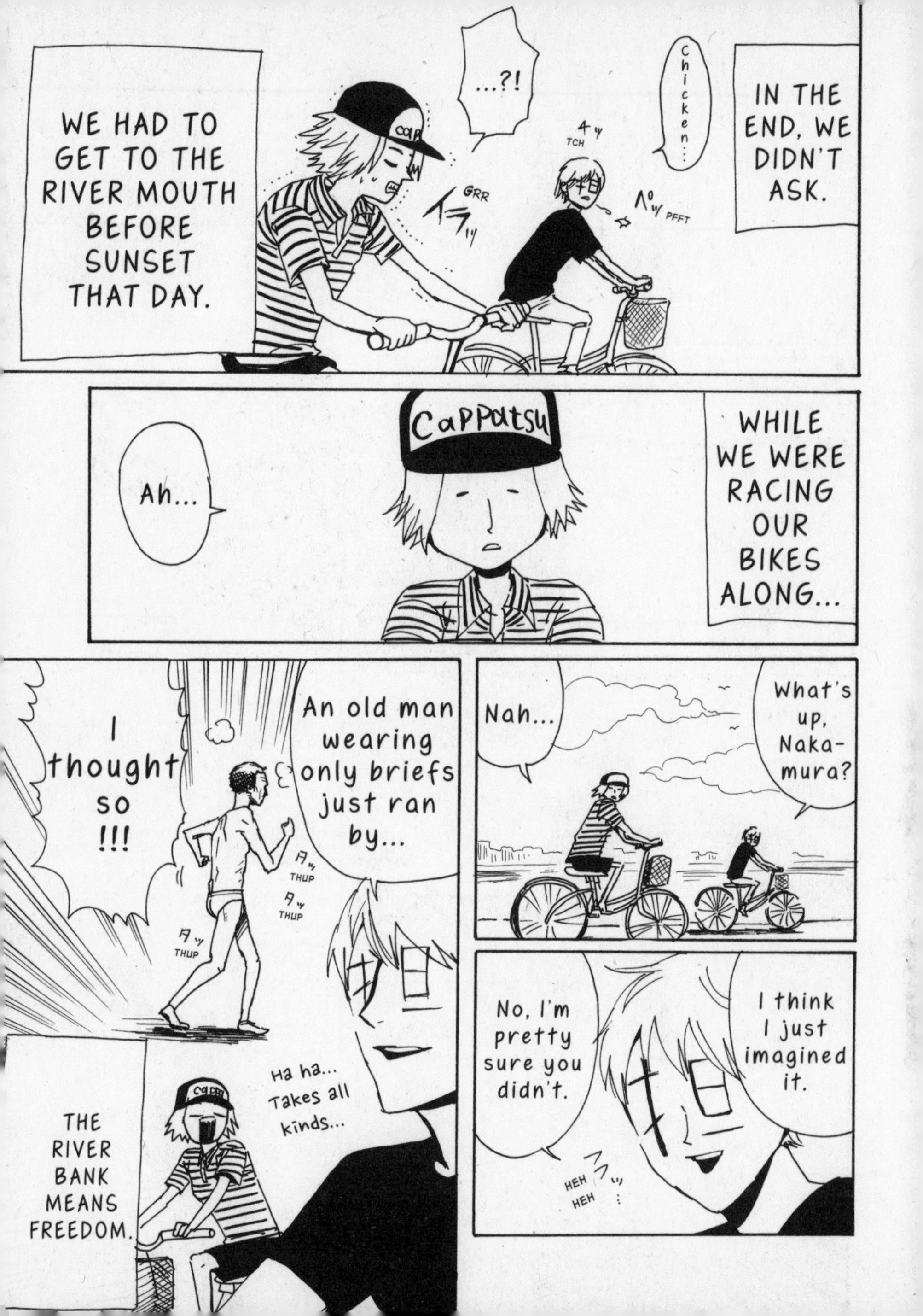
IN THE END, WE DIDN'T ASK.
Chicken...
PFFT
TCH
GRR
...?!
WE HAD TO GET TO THE RIVER MOUTH BEFORE SUNSET THAT DAY.
WHILE WE WERE RACING OUR BIKES ALONG...
CaPPatsu
Ah...
What's up, Naka-mura?
Nah...
An old man wearing only briefs just ran by...
THUP
THUP
THUP
I thought so !!!
I think I just imagined it.
No, I'm pretty sure you didn't.
HEH HEH
Ha ha... Takes all kinds...
THE RIVER BANK MEANS FREEDOM.

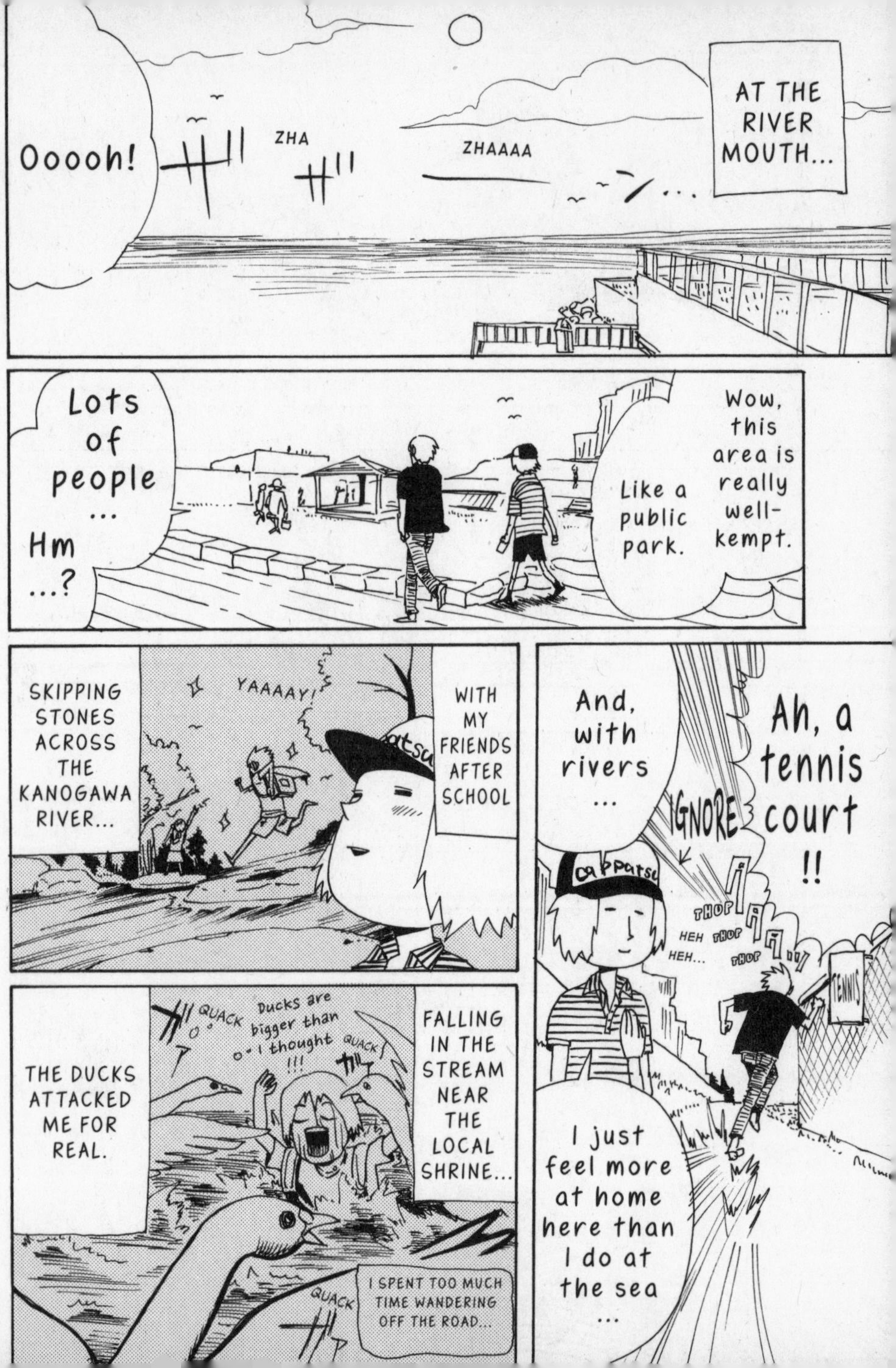
AT THE RIVER MOUTH...
ZHAAAA
ZHA
Ooooh!
Wow, this area is really well-kempt.
Like a public park.
Lots of people ... Hm ...?
Ah, a tennis court !!
And, with rivers ...
IGNORE
THOP
HEH HEH...
THOP
THOP
I just feel more at home here than I do at the sea ...
WITH MY FRIENDS AFTER SCHOOL
YAAAAY!
SKIPPING STONES ACROSS THE KANOGAWA RIVER...
FALLING IN THE STREAM NEAR THE LOCAL SHRINE...
QUACK
Ducks are bigger than I thought !!!
QUACK
THE DUCKS ATTACKED ME FOR REAL.
I SPENT TOO MUCH TIME WANDERING OFF THE ROAD...
QUACK

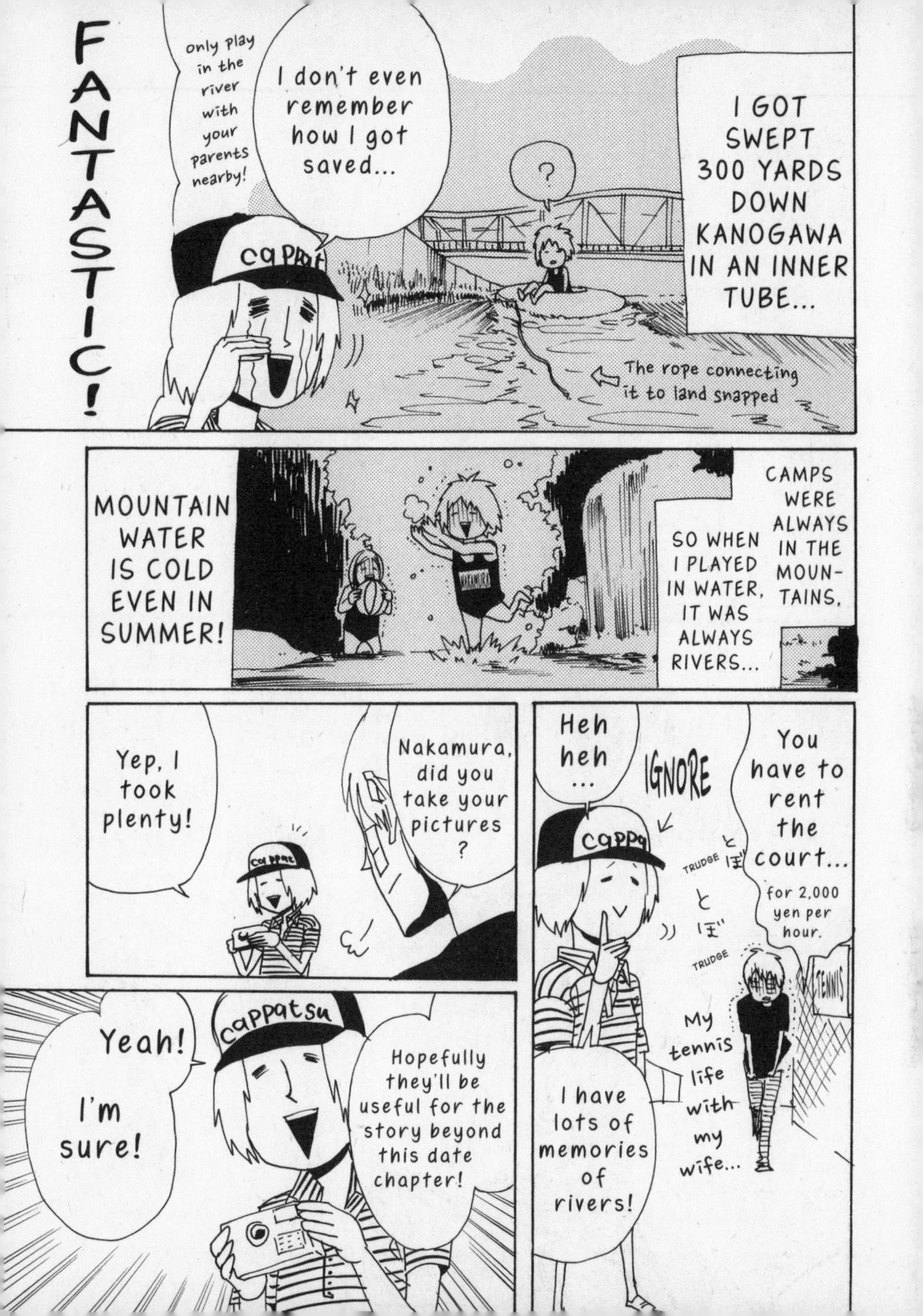
I GOT SWEPT 300 YARDS DOWN KANOGAWA IN AN INNER TUBE...
?
The rope connecting it to land snapped
I don't even remember how I got saved...
only play in the river with your parents nearby!
FANTASTIC!
CAMPS WERE ALWAYS IN THE MOUN-TAINS,
SO WHEN I PLAYED IN WATER, IT WAS ALWAYS RIVERS...
MOUNTAIN WATER IS COLD EVEN IN SUMMER!
NAKAMURA
You have to rent the court...
for 2,000 yen per hour.
IGNORE
Heh heh ...
TRUDGE とぼ
とぼ TRUDGE
TENNIS
My tennis life with my wife...
I have lots of memories of rivers!
Nakamura, did you take your pictures?
Yep, I took plenty!
cappatsu
Hopefully they'll be useful for the story beyond this date chapter!
Yeah!
I'm sure!

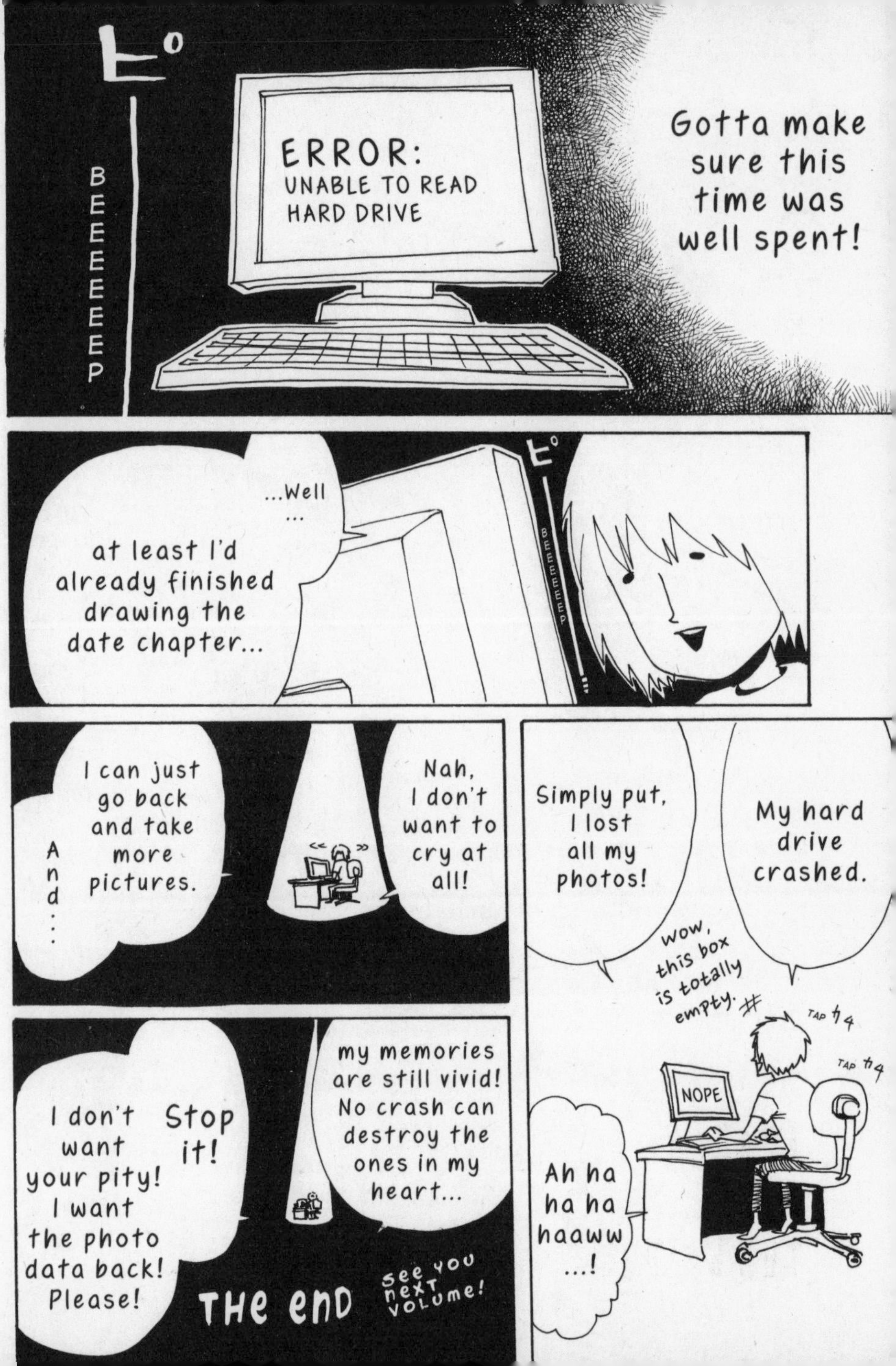

Gotta make sure this time was well spent!
ERROR: UNABLE TO READ HARD DRIVE
ピ
BEEEEEEEP
ピ
BEEEEEEEP
...Well ...
at least I'd already finished drawing the date chapter...
My hard drive crashed.
Simply put, I lost all my photos!
wow, this box is totally empty. #
TAP TAP
TAP TAP
NOPE
Ah ha ha ha haaww ...!
Nah, I don't want to cry at all!
I can just go back and take more pictures.
And...
my memories are still vivid! No crash can destroy the ones in my heart...
Stop it!
I don't want your pity! I want the photo data back! Please!
THE END
see you next volume!

ARAKAWA
UNDER
THE BRIDGE

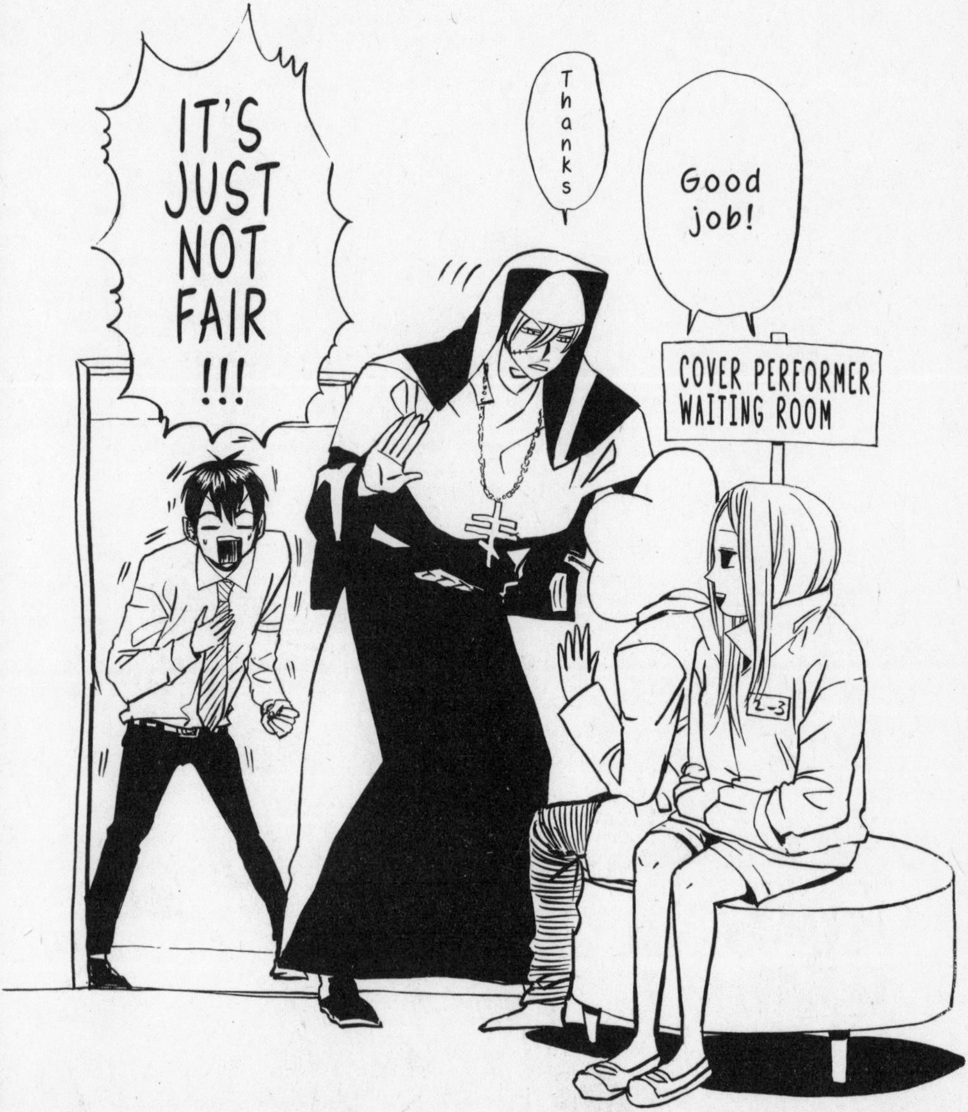
Good job!
Thanks
COVER PERFORMER WAITING ROOM
IT'S JUST NOT FAIR !!!
2-3

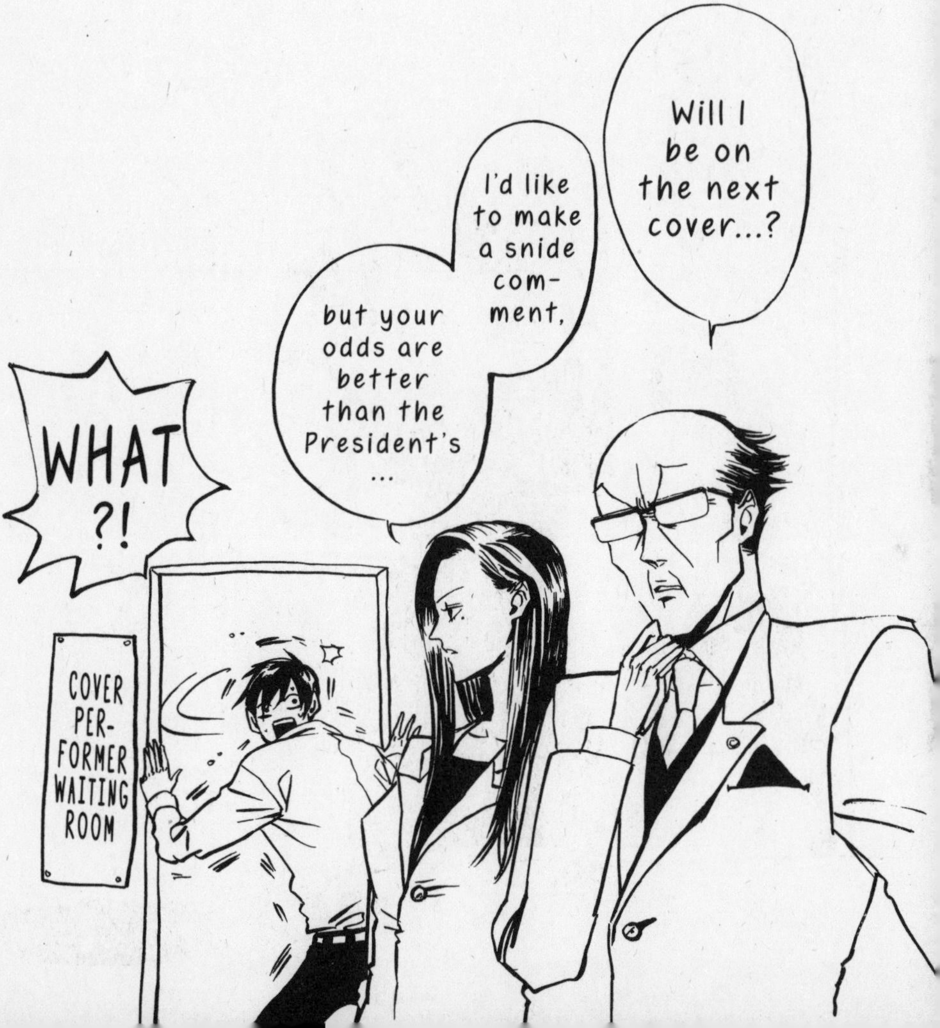
Will I be on the next cover...?
I'd like to make a snide com-ment,
but your odds are better than the President's ...
WHAT ?!
COVER PER-FORMER WAITING ROOM

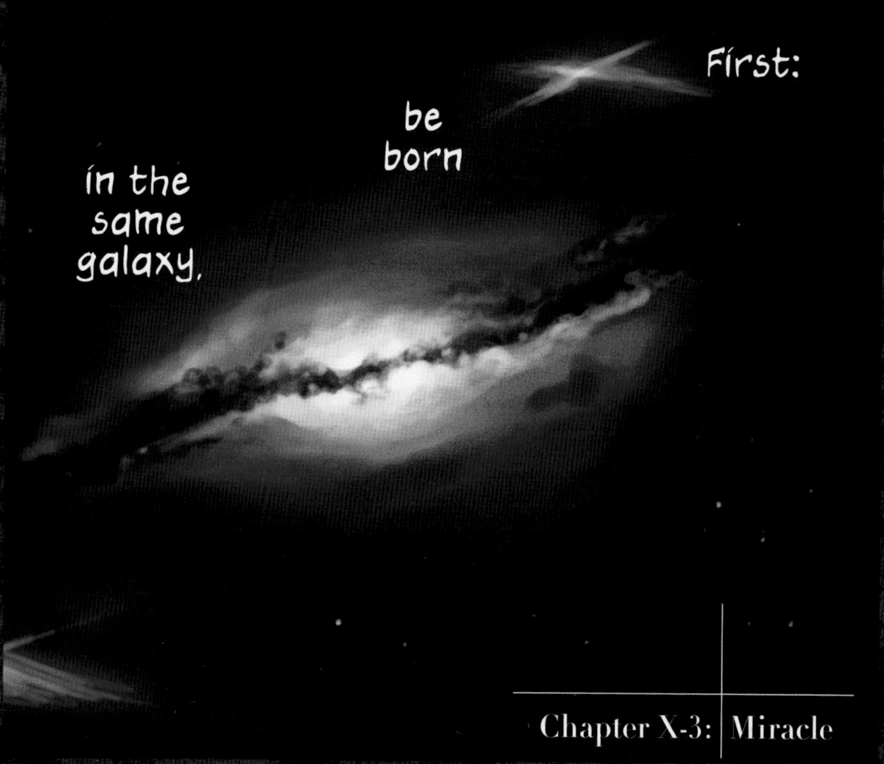
First:
be born
in the same galaxy.
Chapter X-3: Miracle

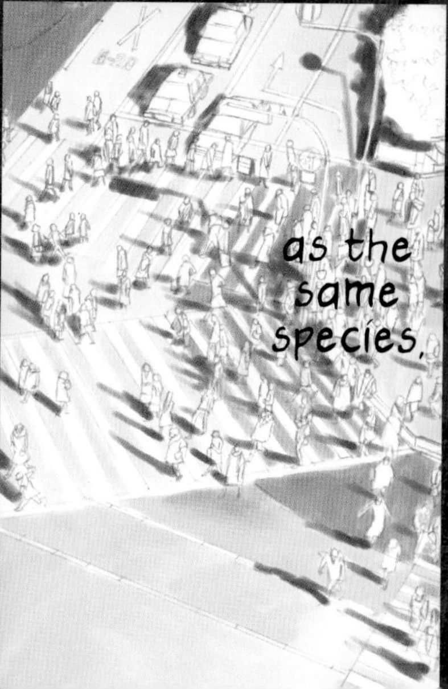
as the same species,

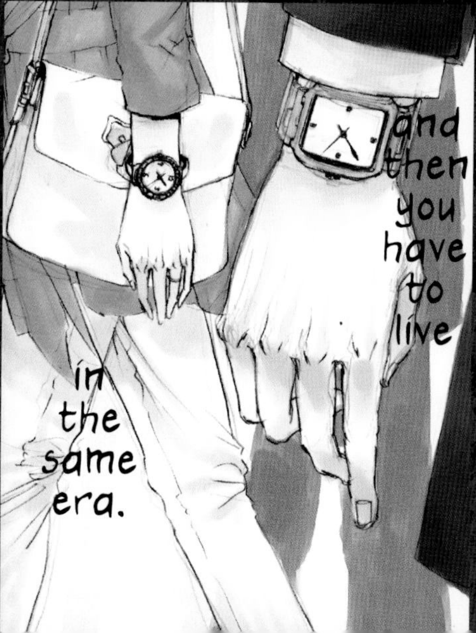
and then you have to live
in the same era.

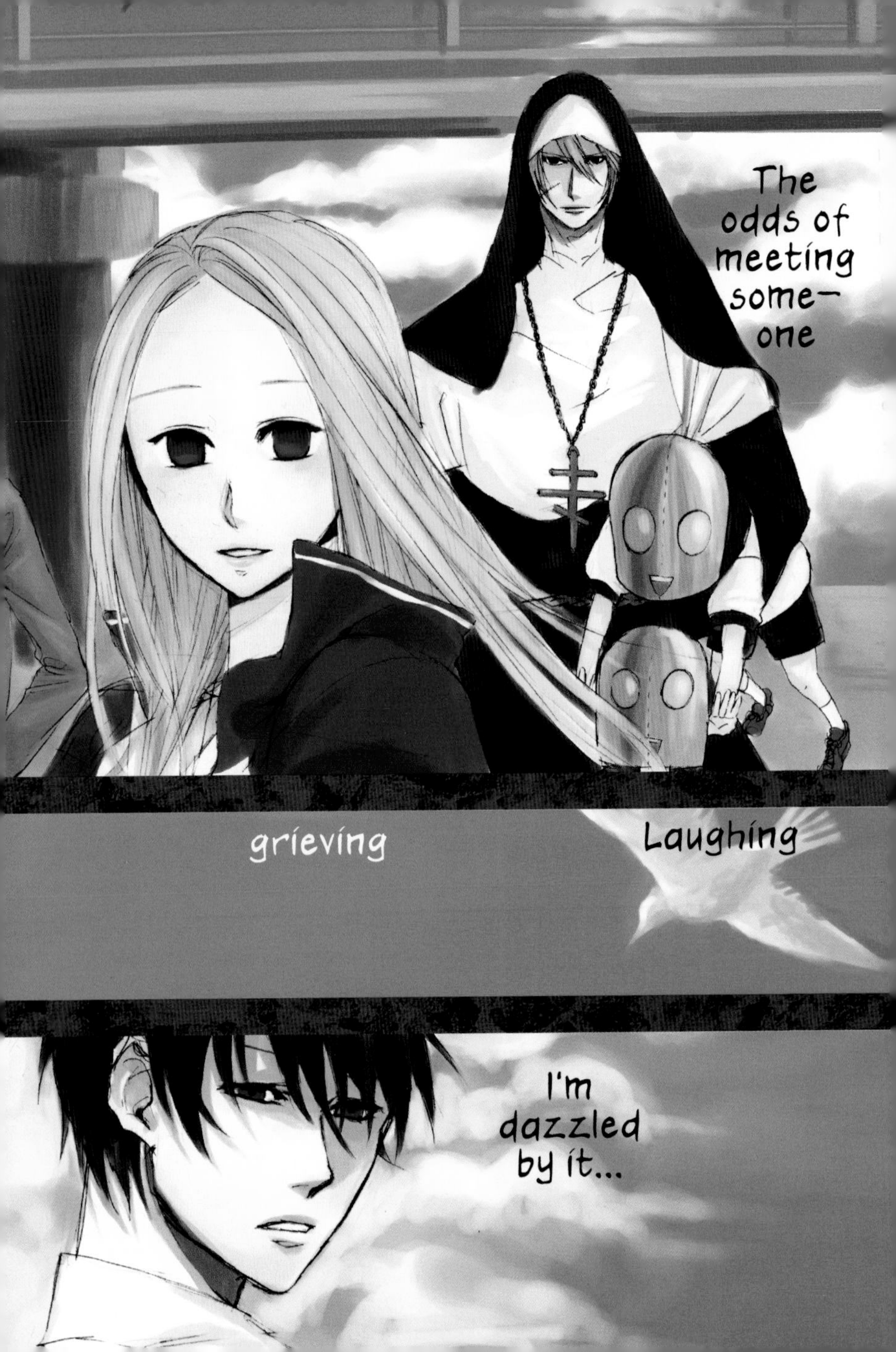
The odds of meeting some-one
Laughing
grieving
I'm dazzled by it...

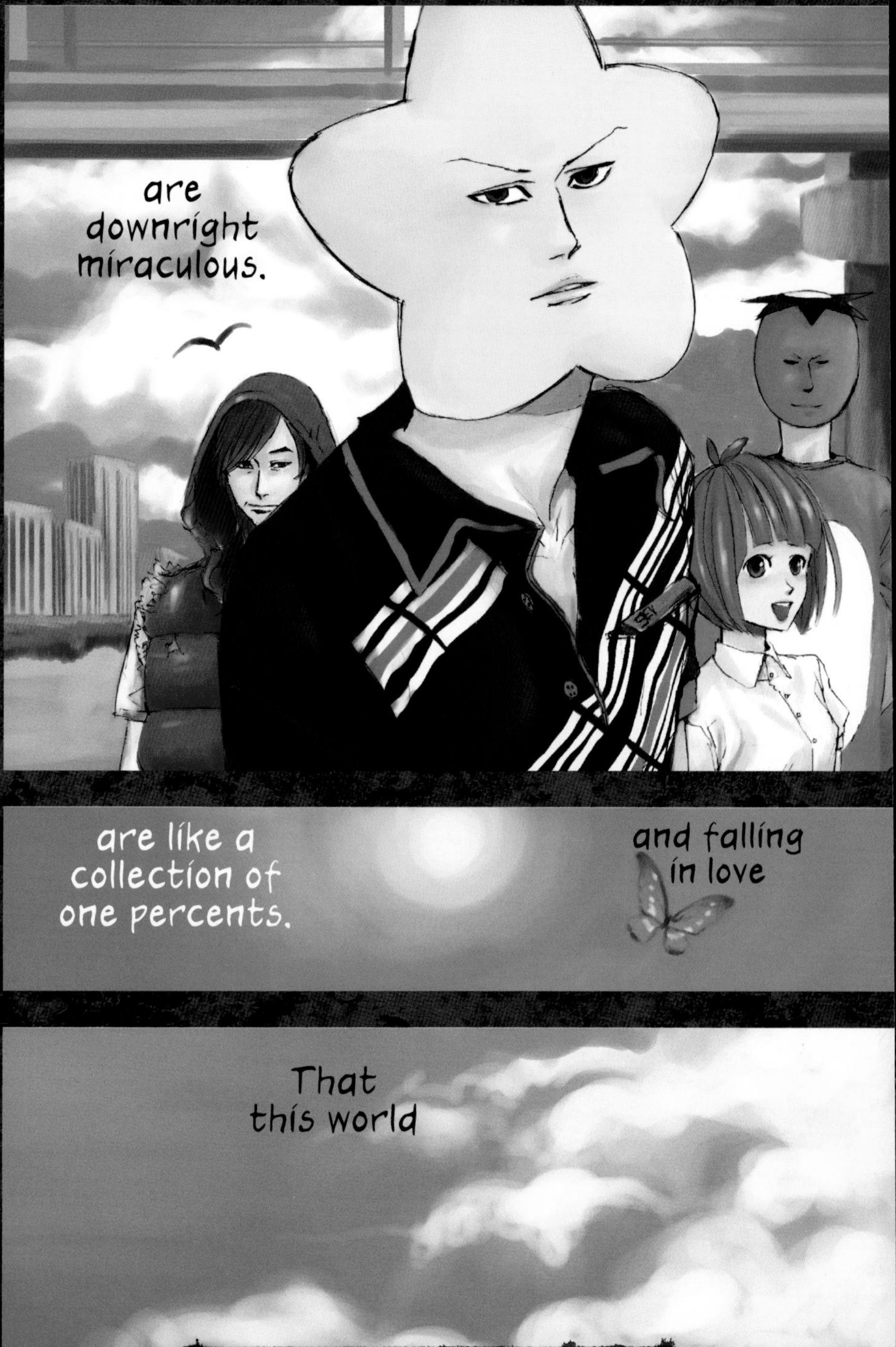
are downright miraculous.
and falling in love
are like a collection of one percents.
That this world

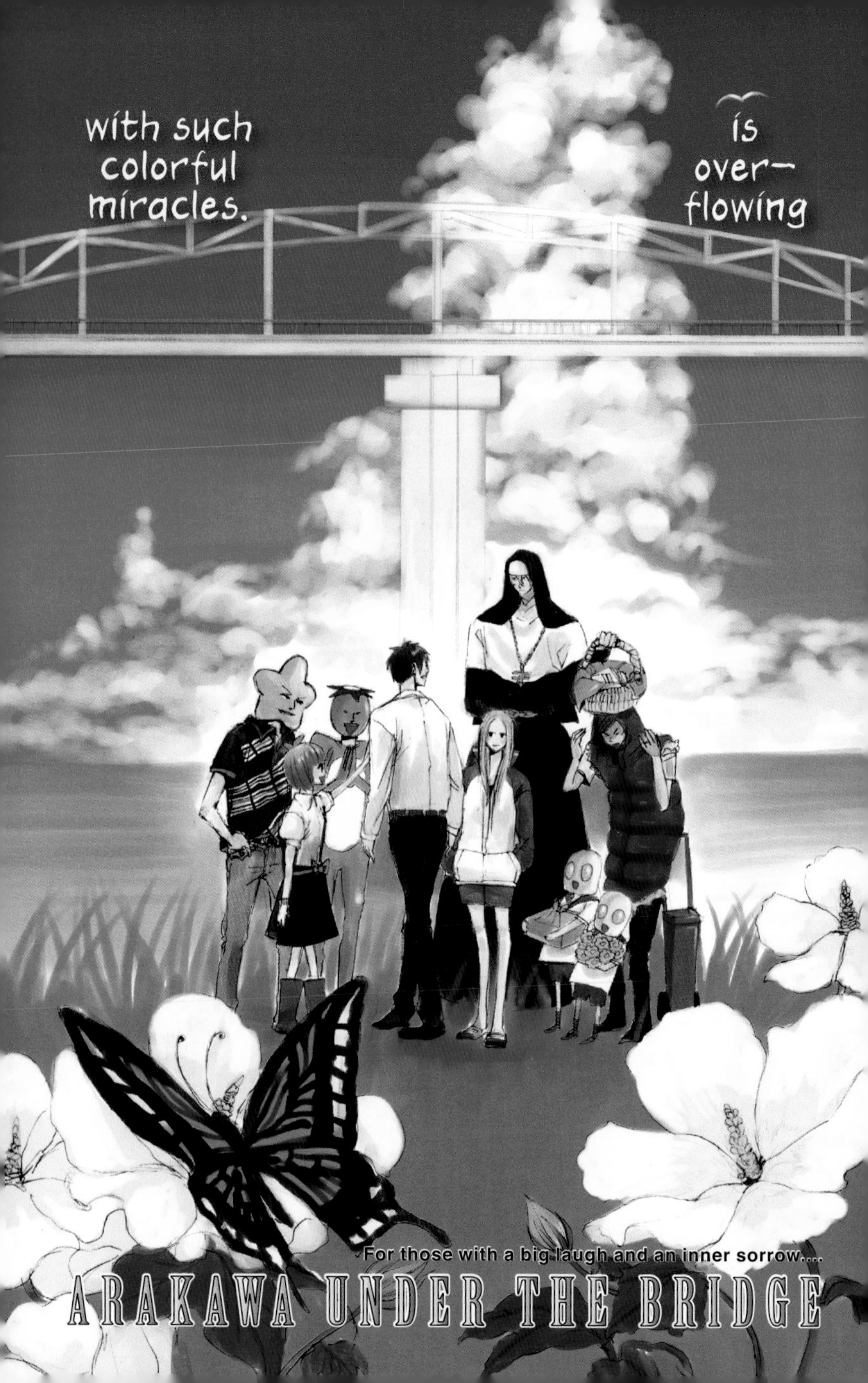
is over-flowing
with such colorful miracles.
For those with a big laugh and an inner sorrow....
ARAKAWA UNDER THE BRIDGE

I found a picture of me from when I was small, when I was a wild child running around the fields and hills. 4.3 miles to school and back, wearing a heavy backpack. Going to school was like undergoing intensive training for something. I managed to get there by walking only on white lines.

—Hikaru Nakamura

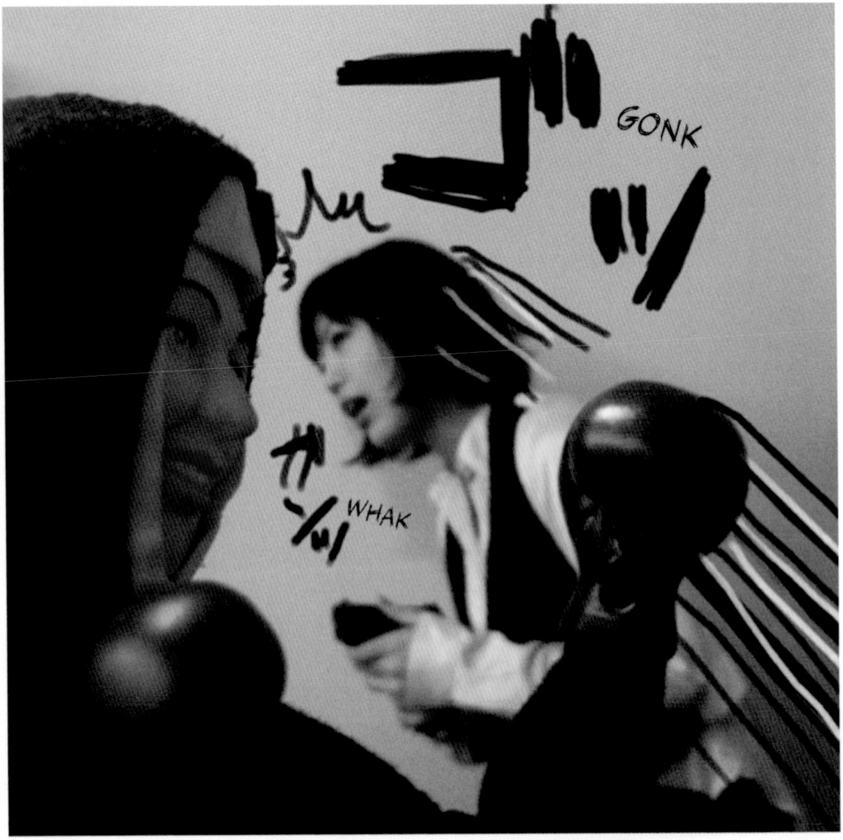
GONK
WHAK

Sister is based on a Punching Nun we bought on a trip to Hawaii when I was a kid. Each of the kids got one, so we had three. Hard to believe, but I used to fall asleep with mine in my arms.

—Hikaru Nakamura

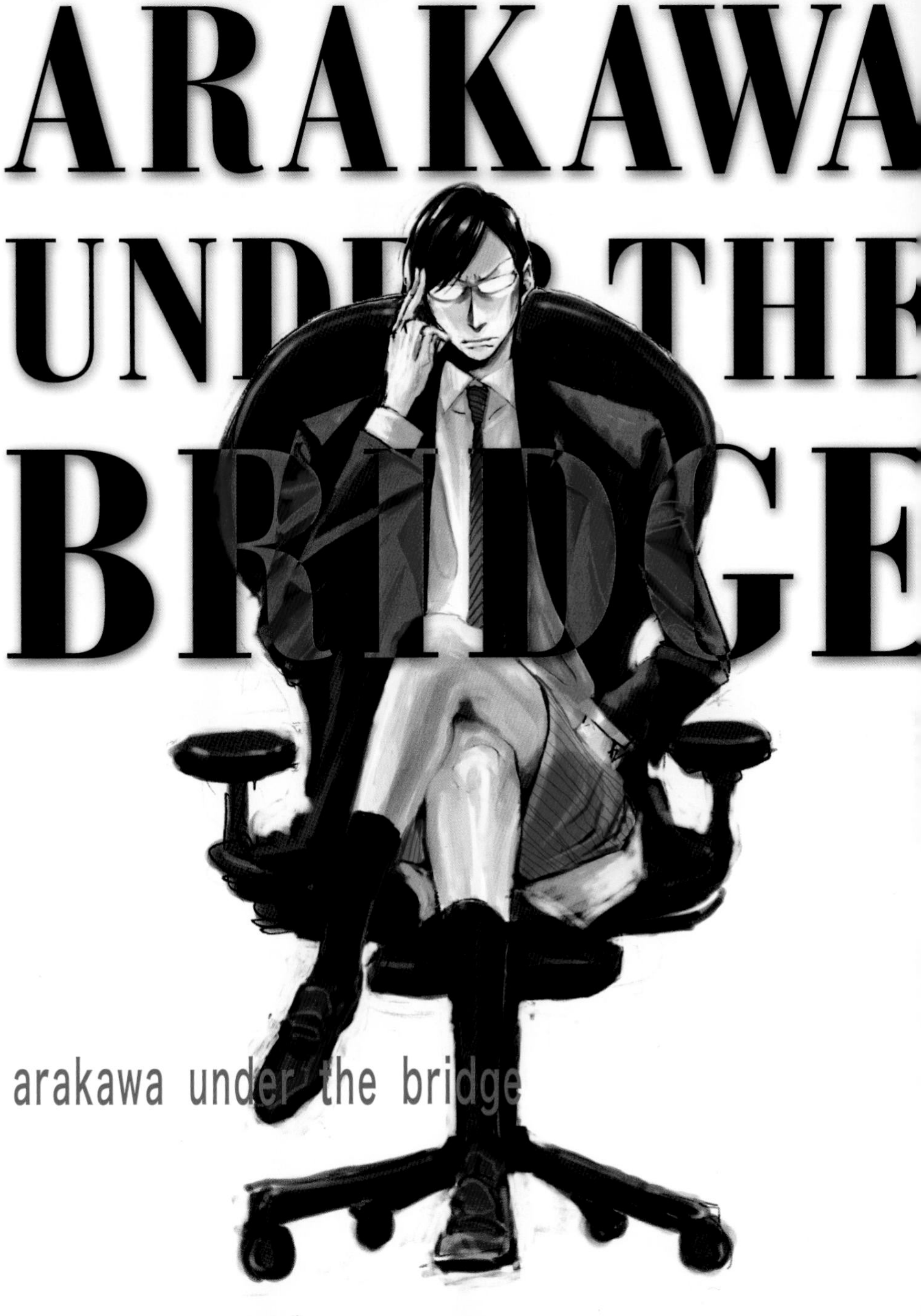
ARAKAWA UNDER THE BRIDGE
arakawa under the bridge

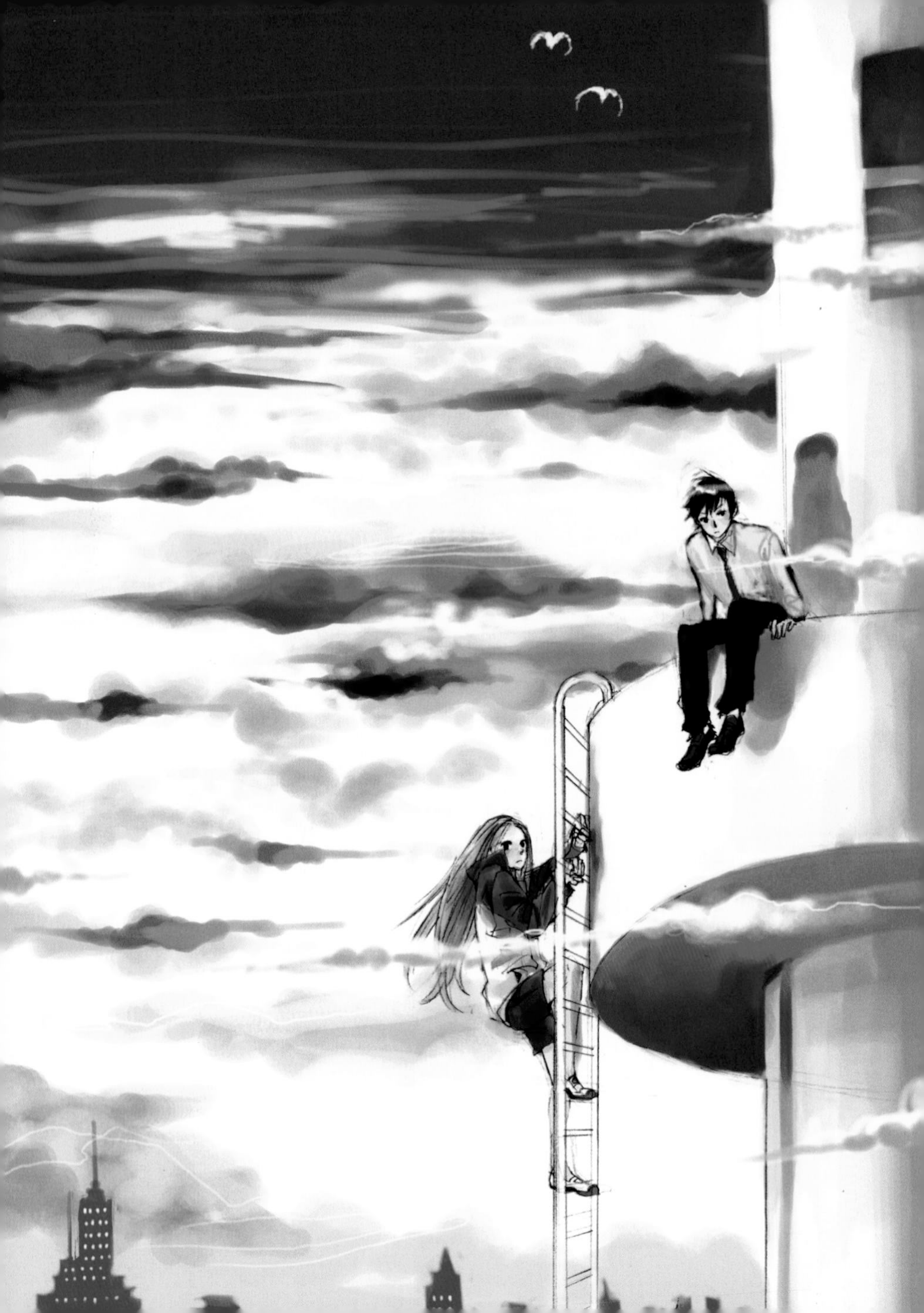

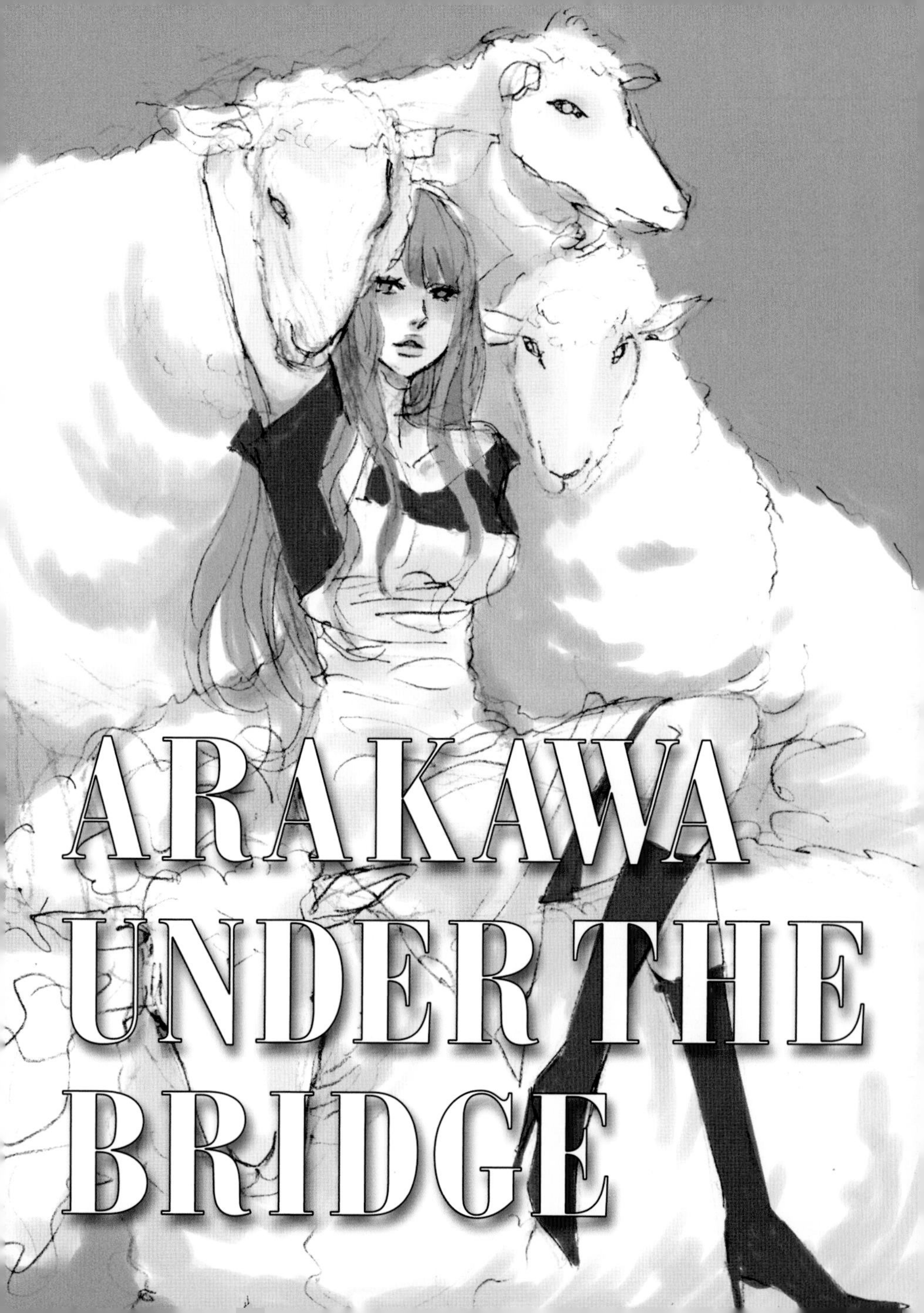
ARAKAWA
UNDER THE
BRIDGE

CONTENTS

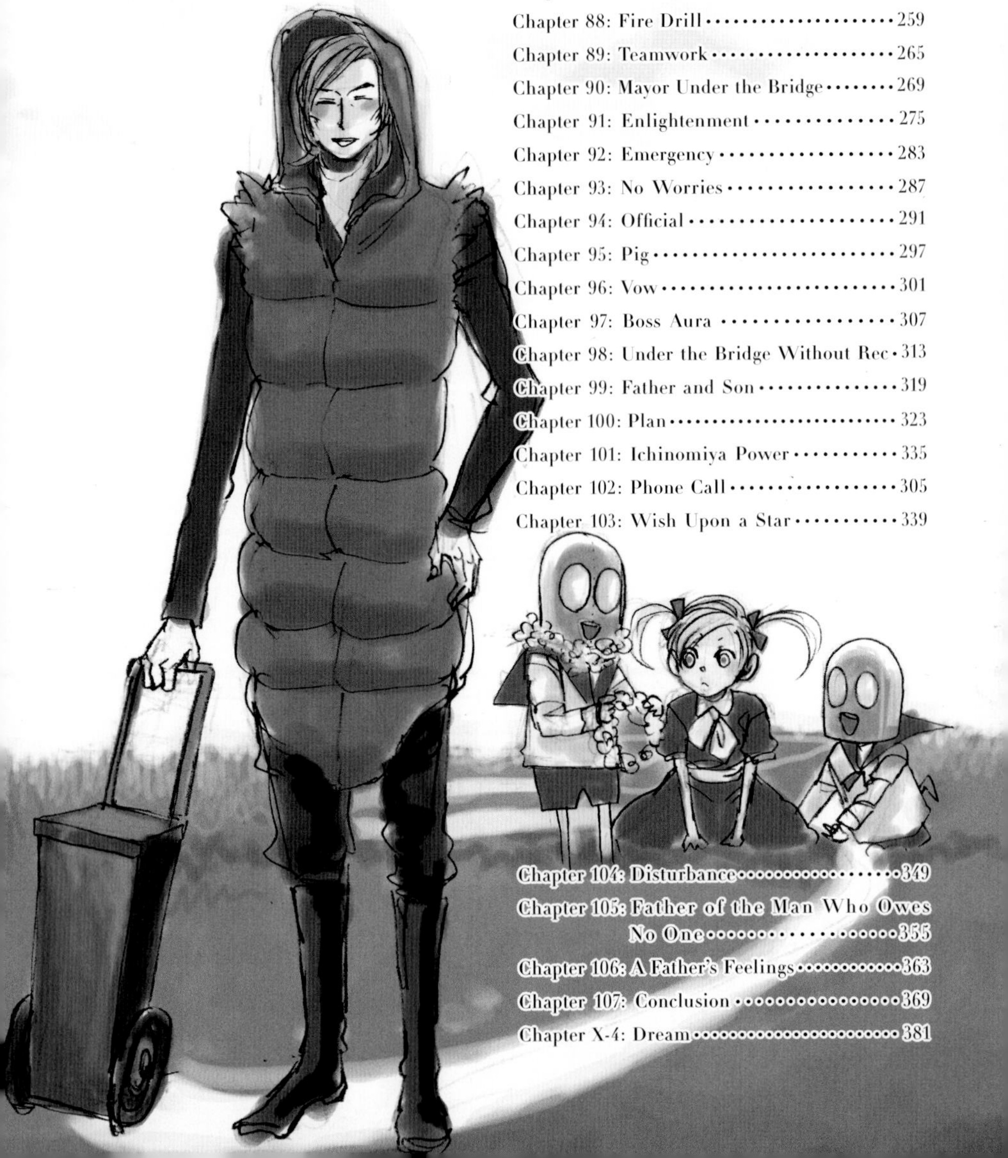

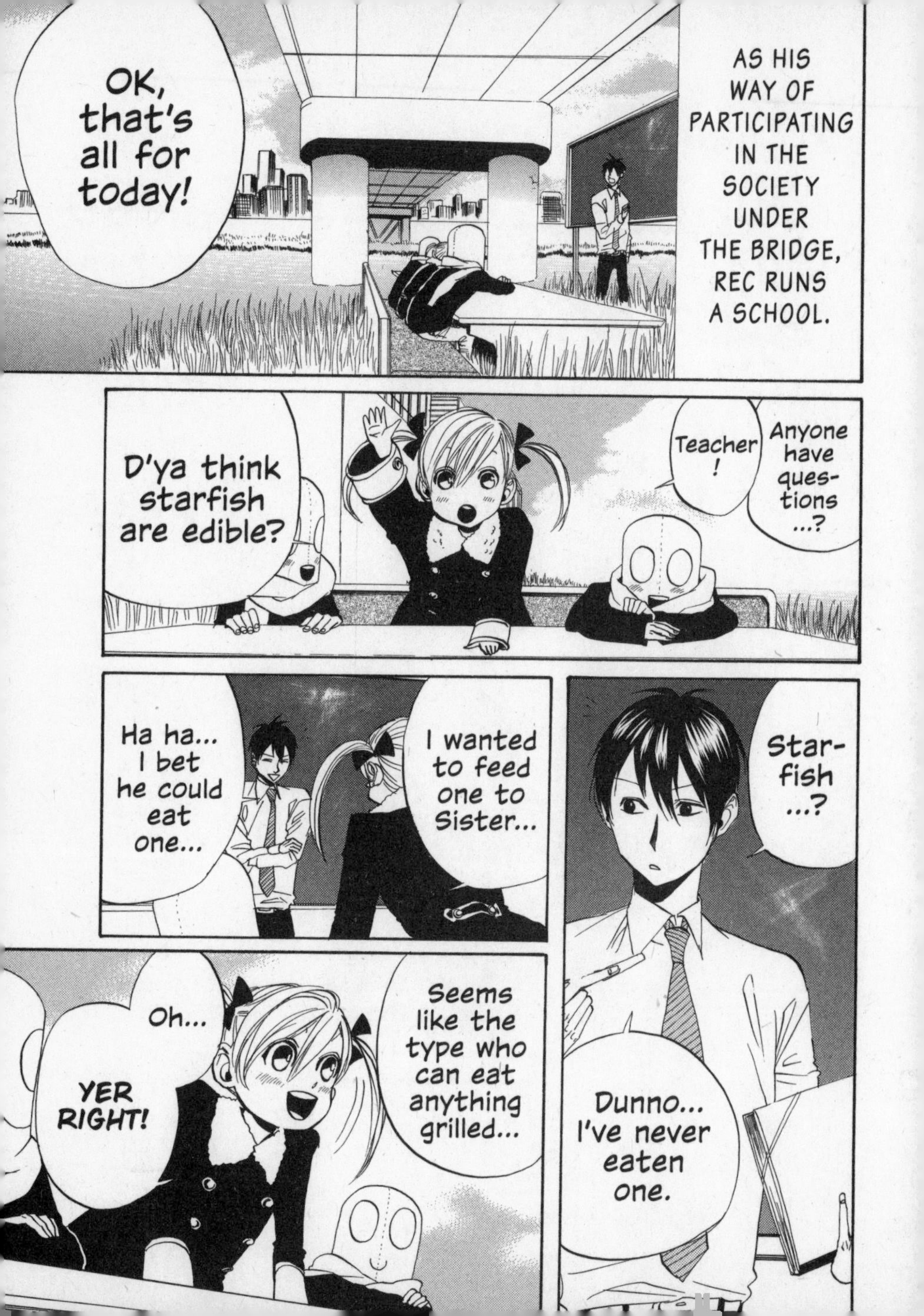
AS HIS WAY OF PARTICIPATING IN THE SOCIETY UNDER THE BRIDGE, REC RUNS A SCHOOL.
OK, that's all for today!
Anyone have ques-tions ...?
Teacher!
D'ya think starfish are edible?
Star-fish ...?
Dunno... I've never eaten one.
I wanted to feed one to Sister...
Ha ha... I bet he could eat one...
Seems like the type who can eat anything grilled...
Oh...
YER RIGHT!

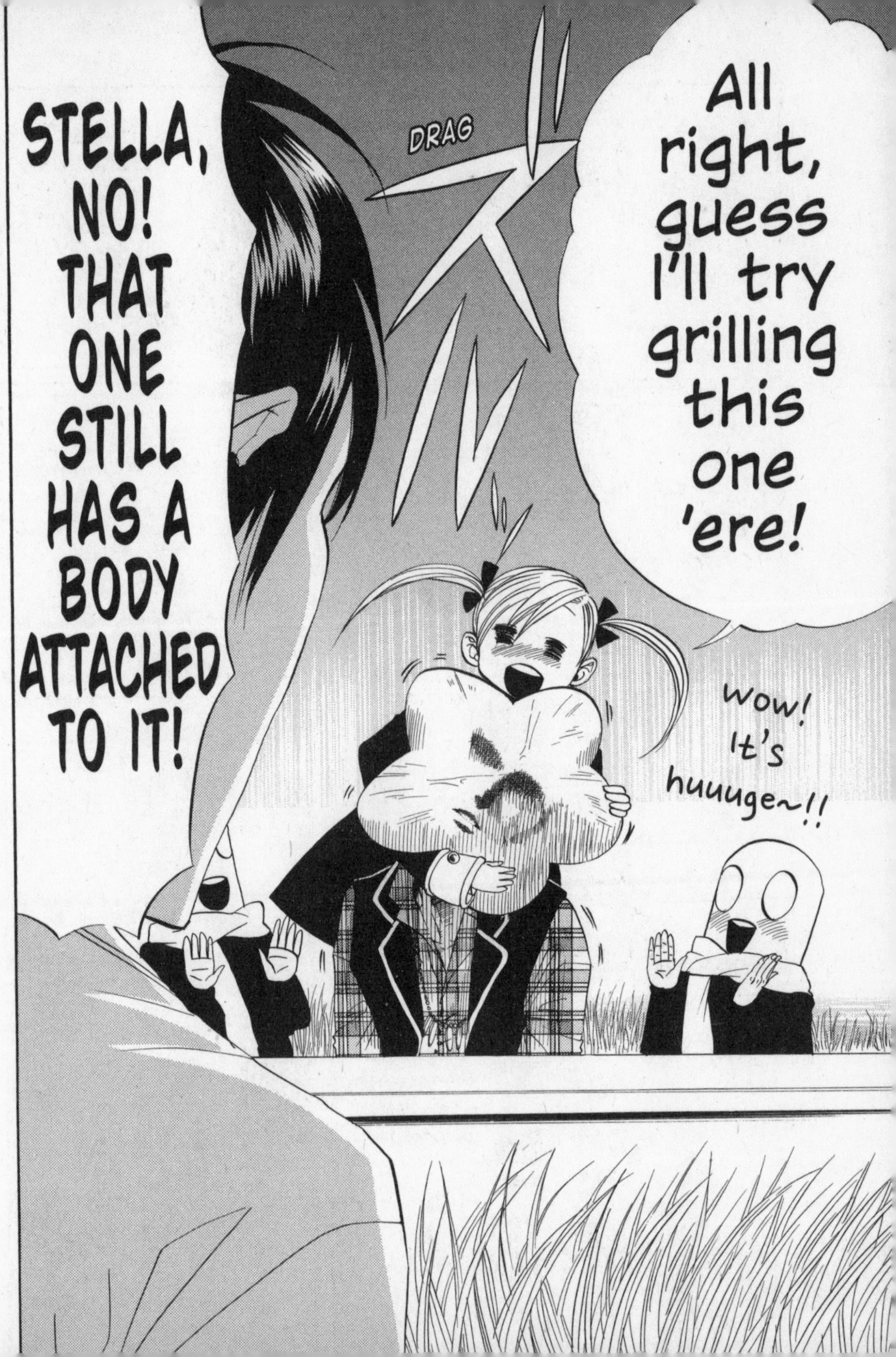
All right, guess I'll try grilling this one 'ere!
DRAG
wow! It's huuuge~!!
STELLA, NO! THAT ONE STILL HAS A BODY ATTACHED TO IT!

Chapter 78: Present

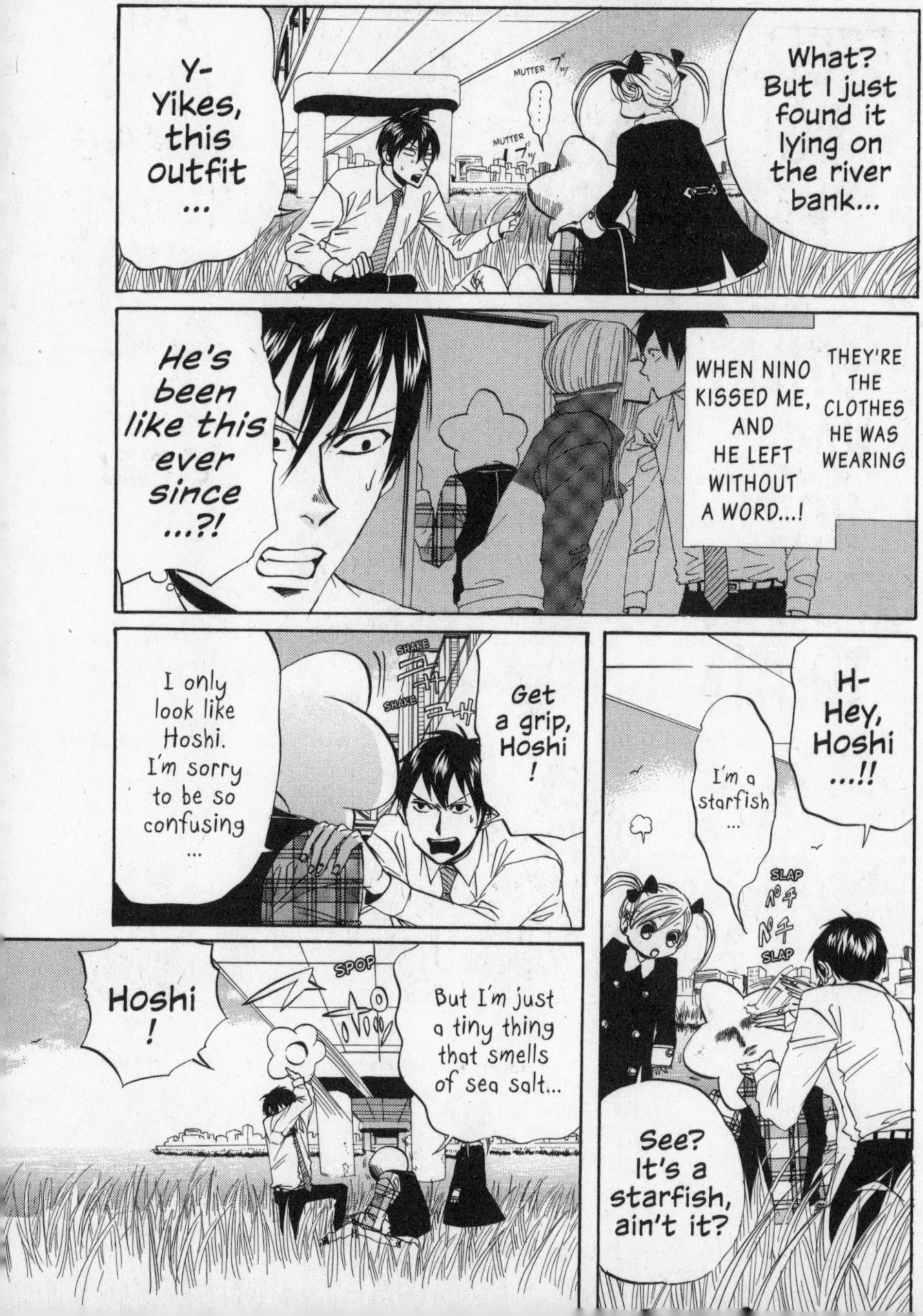
What? But I just found it lying on the river bank...
MUTTER
...
MUTTER
Y-Yikes, this outfit...
THEY'RE THE CLOTHES HE WAS WEARING
WHEN NINO KISSED ME, AND HE LEFT WITHOUT A WORD...!
He's been like this ever since...?!
H-Hey, Hoshi...!!
I'm a starfish...
SLAP
SLAP
See? It's a starfish, ain't it?
Get a grip, Hoshi!
SHAKE
SHAKE
I only look like Hoshi. I'm sorry to be so confusing...
But I'm just a tiny thing that smells of sea salt...
SPOP
Hoshi!

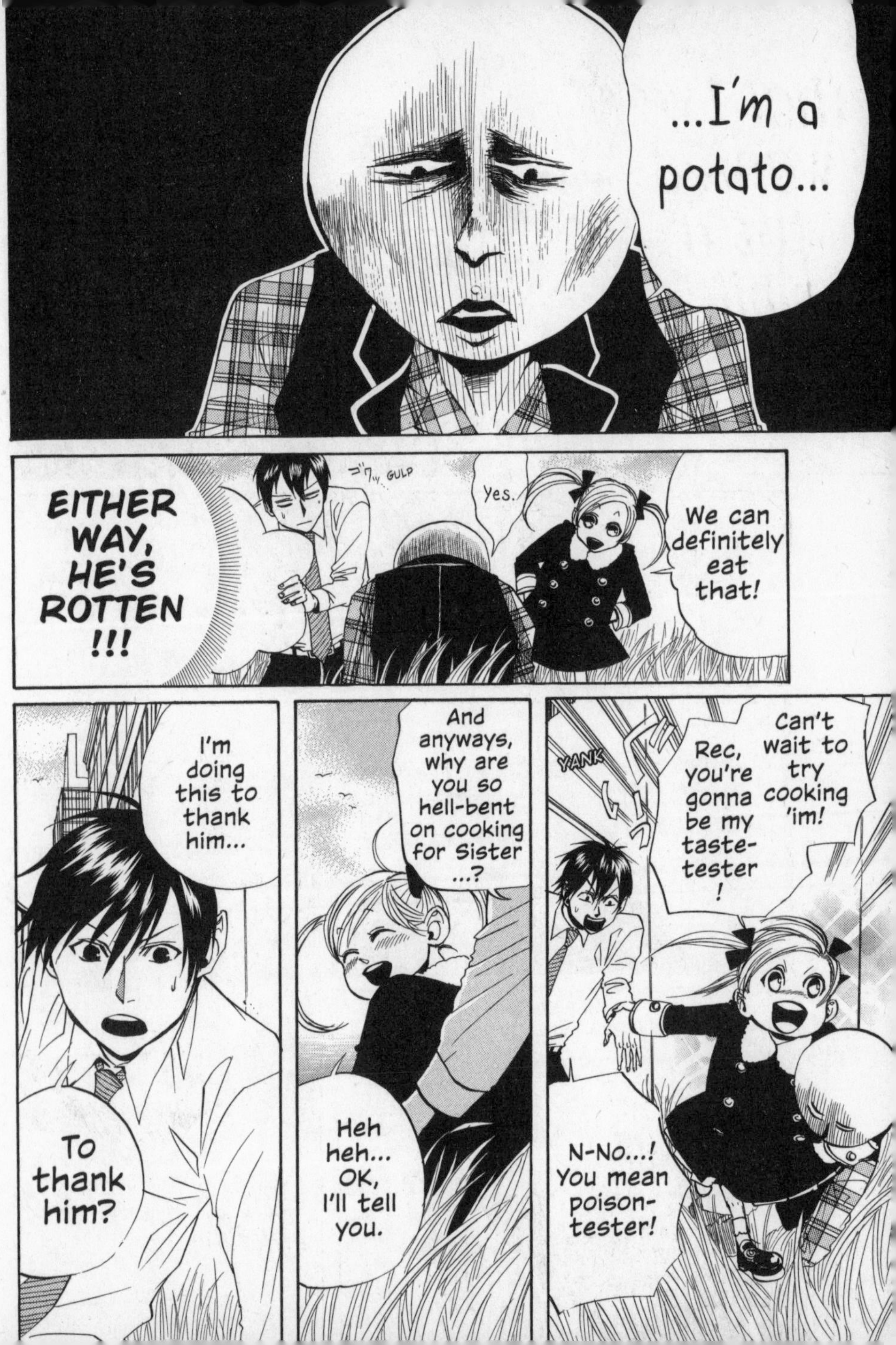
...I'm a potato...
We can definitely eat that!
Yes.
GULP
EITHER WAY, HE'S ROTTEN!!!
Can't wait to try cooking 'im!
Rec, you're gonna be my taste-tester!
YANK
N-No...! You mean poison-tester!
And anyways, why are you so hell-bent on cooking for Sister...?
Heh heh... OK, I'll tell you.
I'm doing this to thank him...
To thank him?

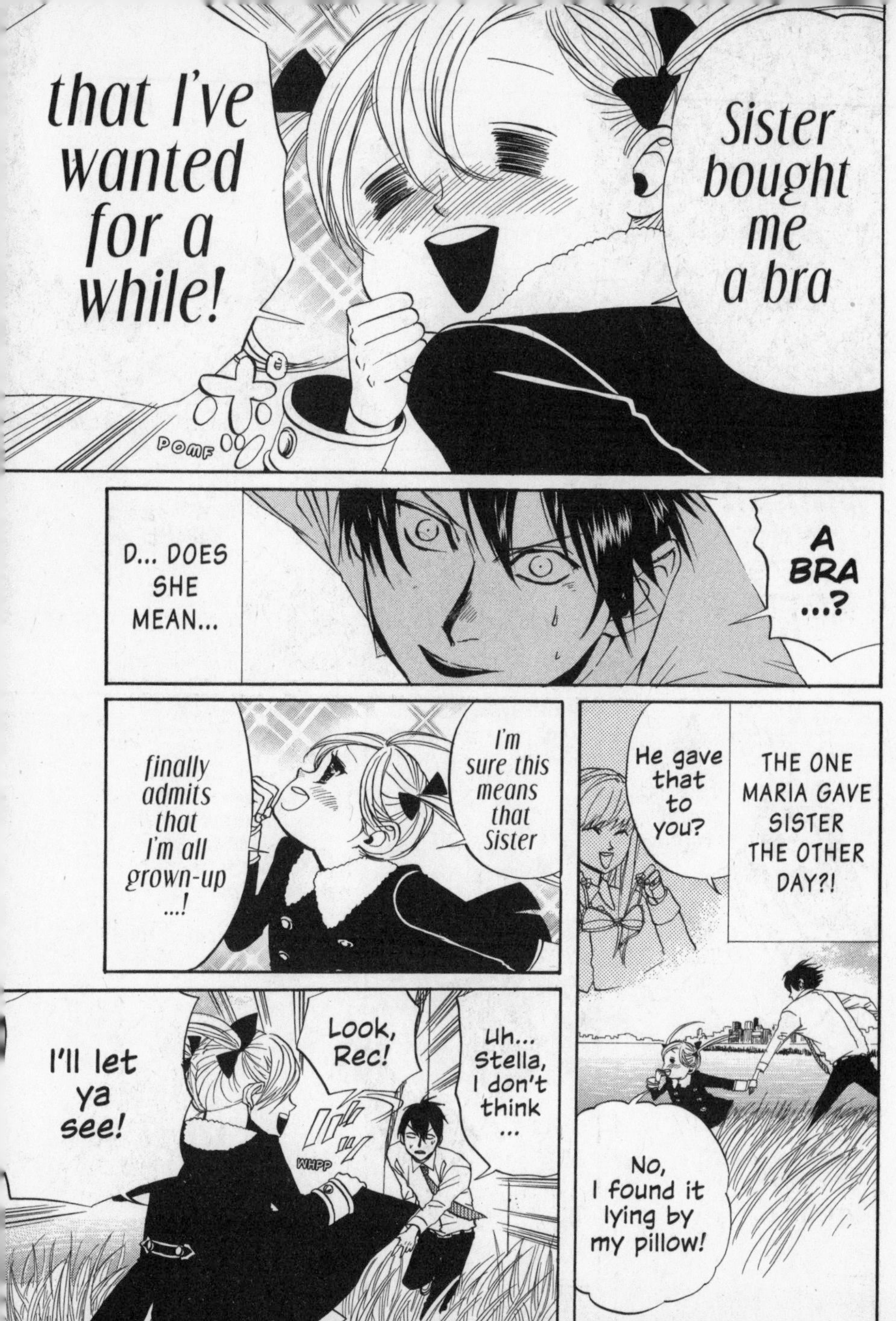

Sister bought me a bra
that I've wanted for a while!
POMF
A BRA ...?
D... DOES SHE MEAN...
THE ONE MARIA GAVE SISTER THE OTHER DAY?!
He gave that to you?
I'm sure this means that Sister
finally admits that I'm all grown-up ...!
No, I found it lying by my pillow!
Uh... Stella, I don't think ...
Look, Rec!
WHPP
I'll let ya see!

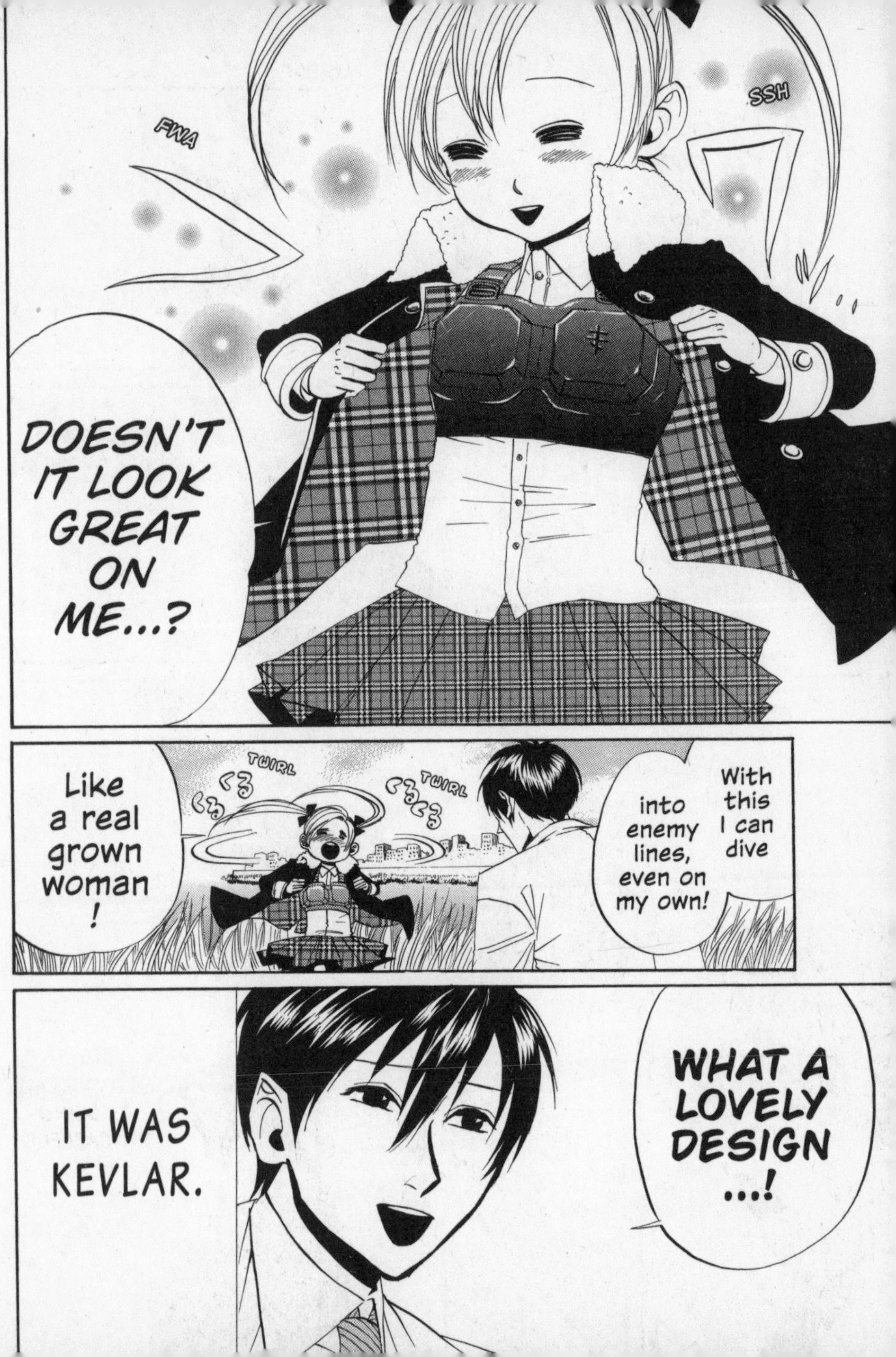
SSH
FWA
DOESN'T IT LOOK GREAT ON ME...?
With this I can dive into enemy lines, even on my own!
TWIRL
くるくる
TWIRL
くるくる
Like a real grown woman!
WHAT A LOVELY DESIGN...!
IT WAS KEVLAR.

Chapter 79: Trigger

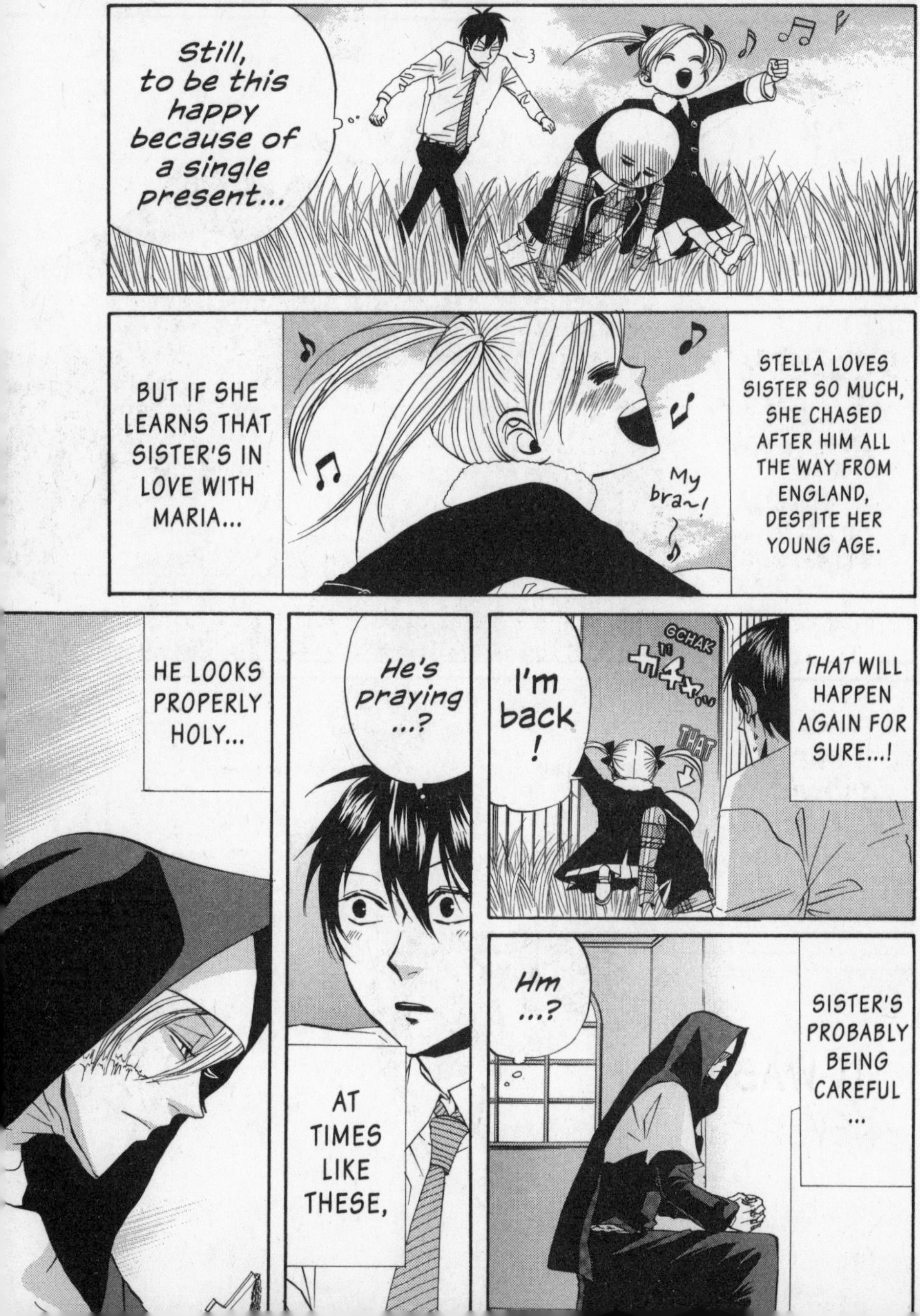
Still, to be this happy because of a single present...
STELLA LOVES SISTER SO MUCH, SHE CHASED AFTER HIM ALL THE WAY FROM ENGLAND, DESPITE HER YOUNG AGE.
My bra~!
BUT IF SHE LEARNS THAT SISTER'S IN LOVE WITH MARIA...
THAT WILL HAPPEN AGAIN FOR SURE...!
GCHAK
THAT
I'm back!
SISTER'S PROBABLY BEING CAREFUL ...
Hm ...?
He's praying ...?
AT TIMES LIKE THESE,
HE LOOKS PROPERLY HOLY...

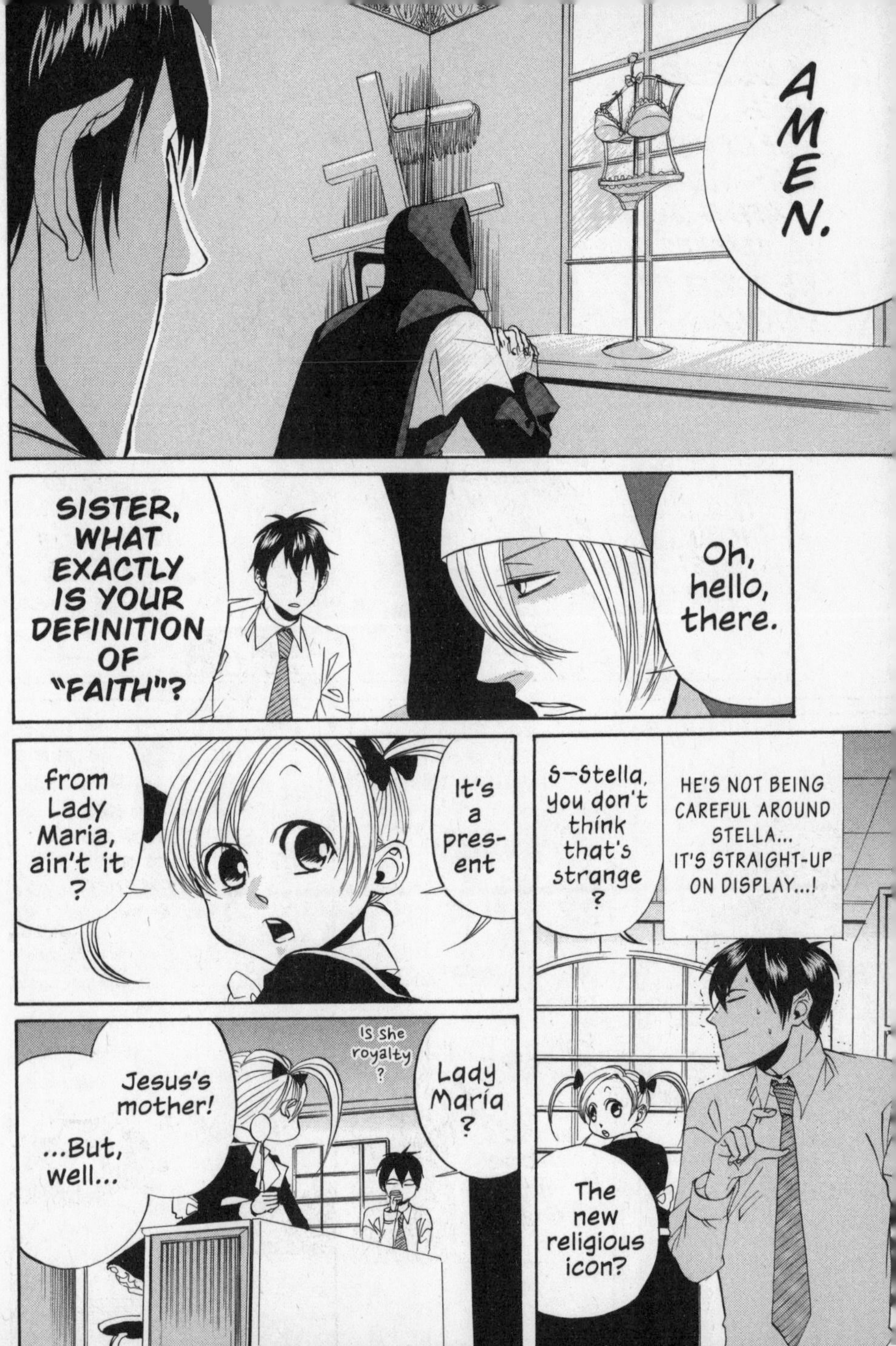
AMEN.
Oh, hello, there.
SISTER, WHAT EXACTLY IS YOUR DEFINITION OF "FAITH"?
HE'S NOT BEING CAREFUL AROUND STELLA... IT'S STRAIGHT-UP ON DISPLAY...!
S-Stella, you don't think that's strange?
The new religious icon?
It's a present
from Lady Maria, ain't it?
Lady Maria?
Is she royalty?
Jesus's mother!
...But, well...

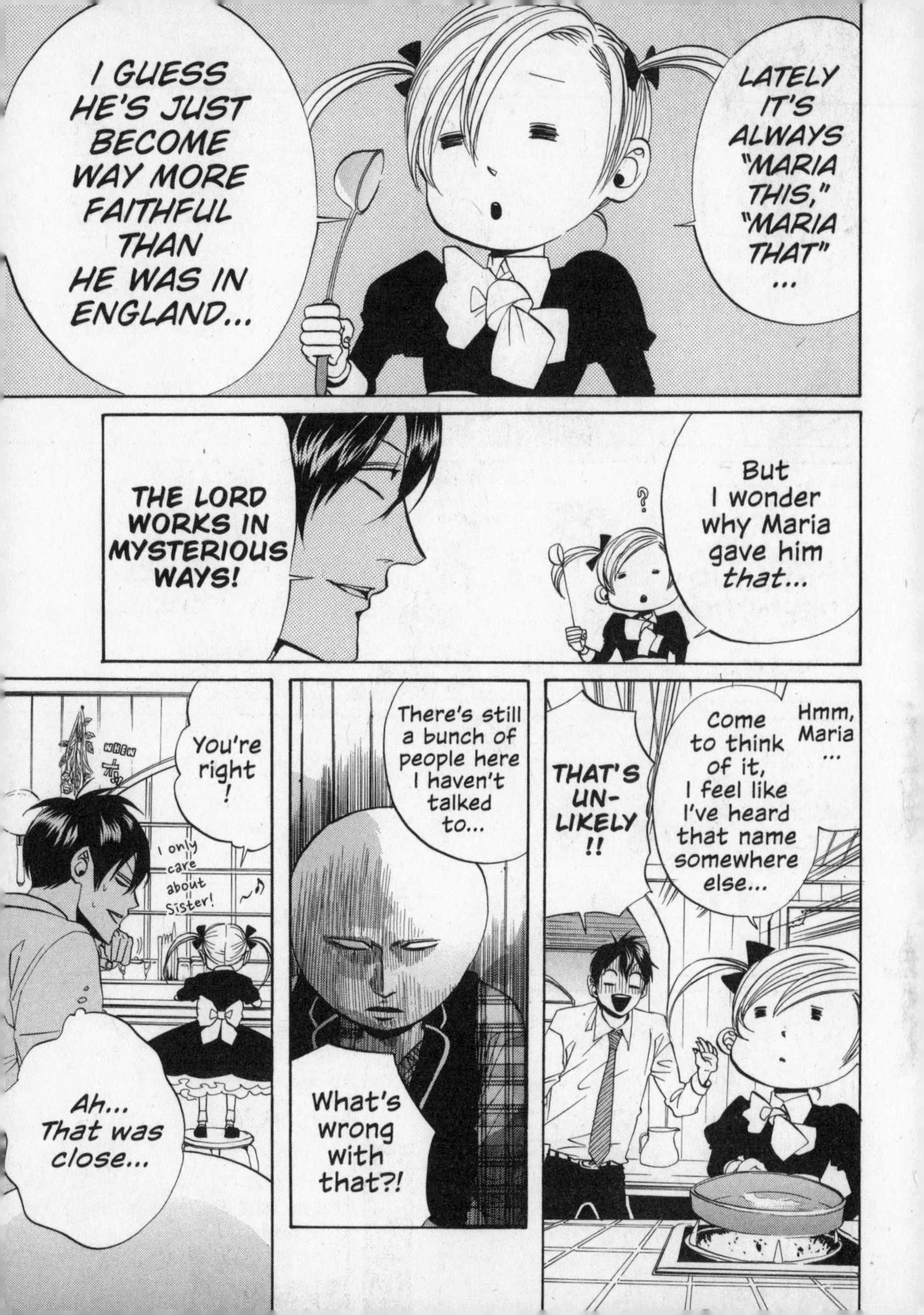
LATELY IT'S ALWAYS "MARIA THIS," "MARIA THAT" ...
I GUESS HE'S JUST BECOME WAY MORE FAITHFUL THAN HE WAS IN ENGLAND...
But I wonder why Maria gave him *that*...
?
THE LORD WORKS IN MYSTERIOUS WAYS!
Hmm, Maria ...
Come to think of it, I feel like I've heard that name somewhere else...
THAT'S UN-LIKELY !!
There's still a bunch of people here I haven't talked to...
What's wrong with that?!
You're right!
I only care about Sister!
~♪
WHEW
Ah... That was close...

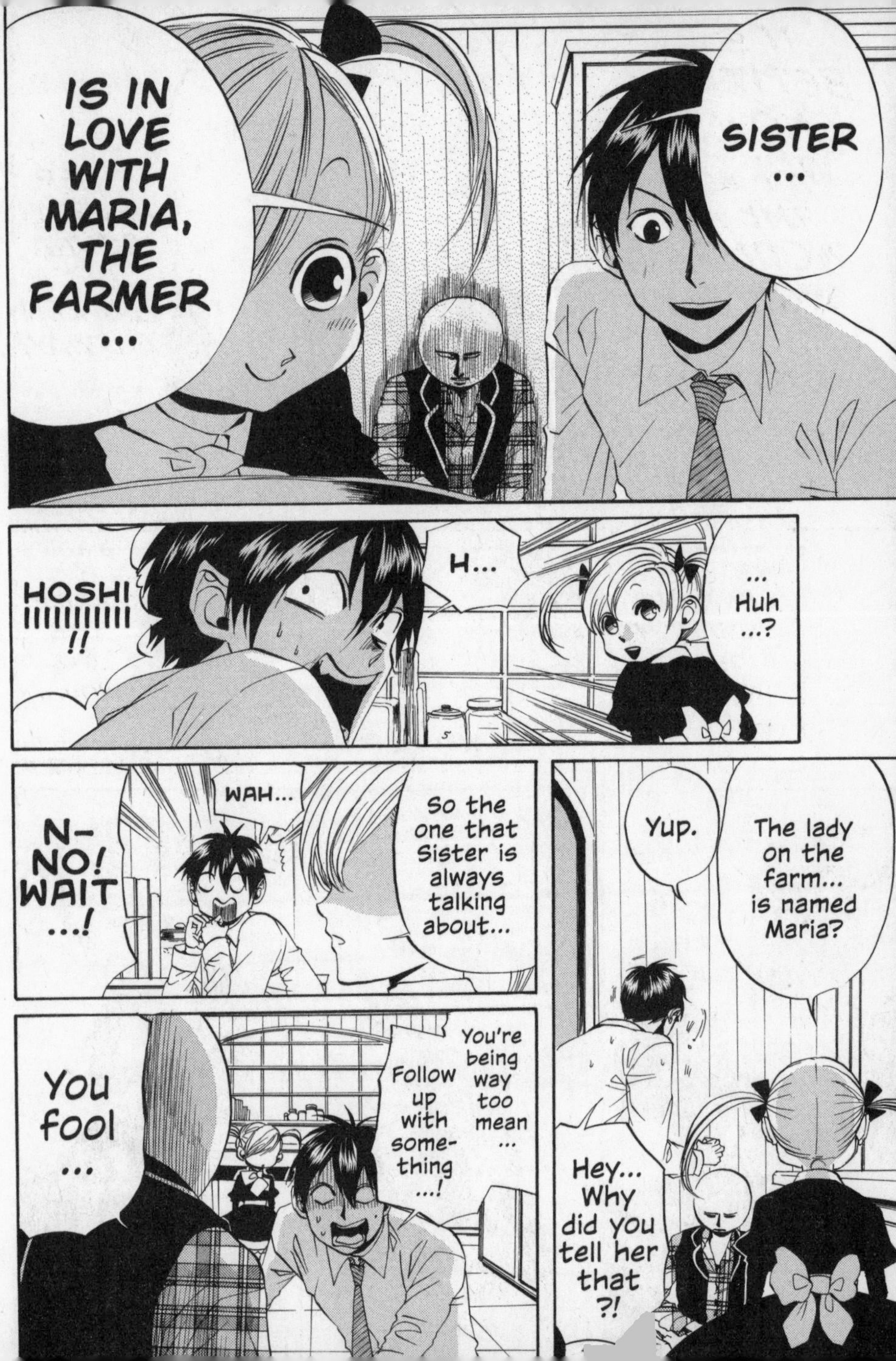
SISTER ...
IS IN LOVE WITH MARIA, THE FARMER ...
... Huh ...?
H...
HOSHIIIIIIIIIIII!!
The lady on the farm... is named Maria?
Yup.
Hey... Why did you tell her that ?!
So the one that Sister is always talking about...
WAH...
N-NO! WAIT ...!
You're being way too mean ...
Follow up with some-thing ...!
You fool ...

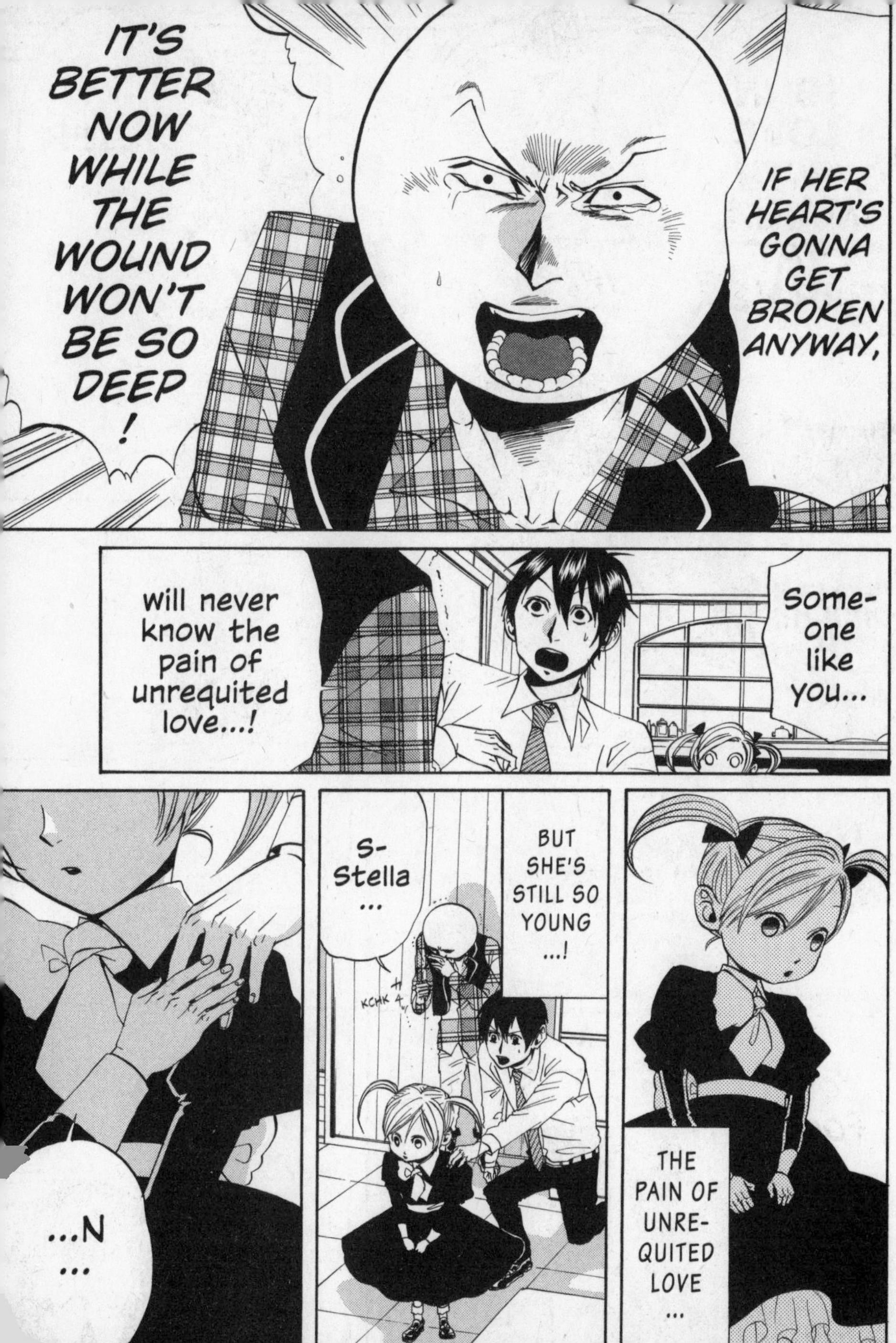
IF HER HEART'S GONNA GET BROKEN ANYWAY,
IT'S BETTER NOW WHILE THE WOUND WON'T BE SO DEEP!
Some-one like you...
will never know the pain of unrequited love...!
THE PAIN OF UNRE-QUITED LOVE ...
BUT SHE'S STILL SO YOUNG ...!
S-Stella ...
KCHK
...N ...

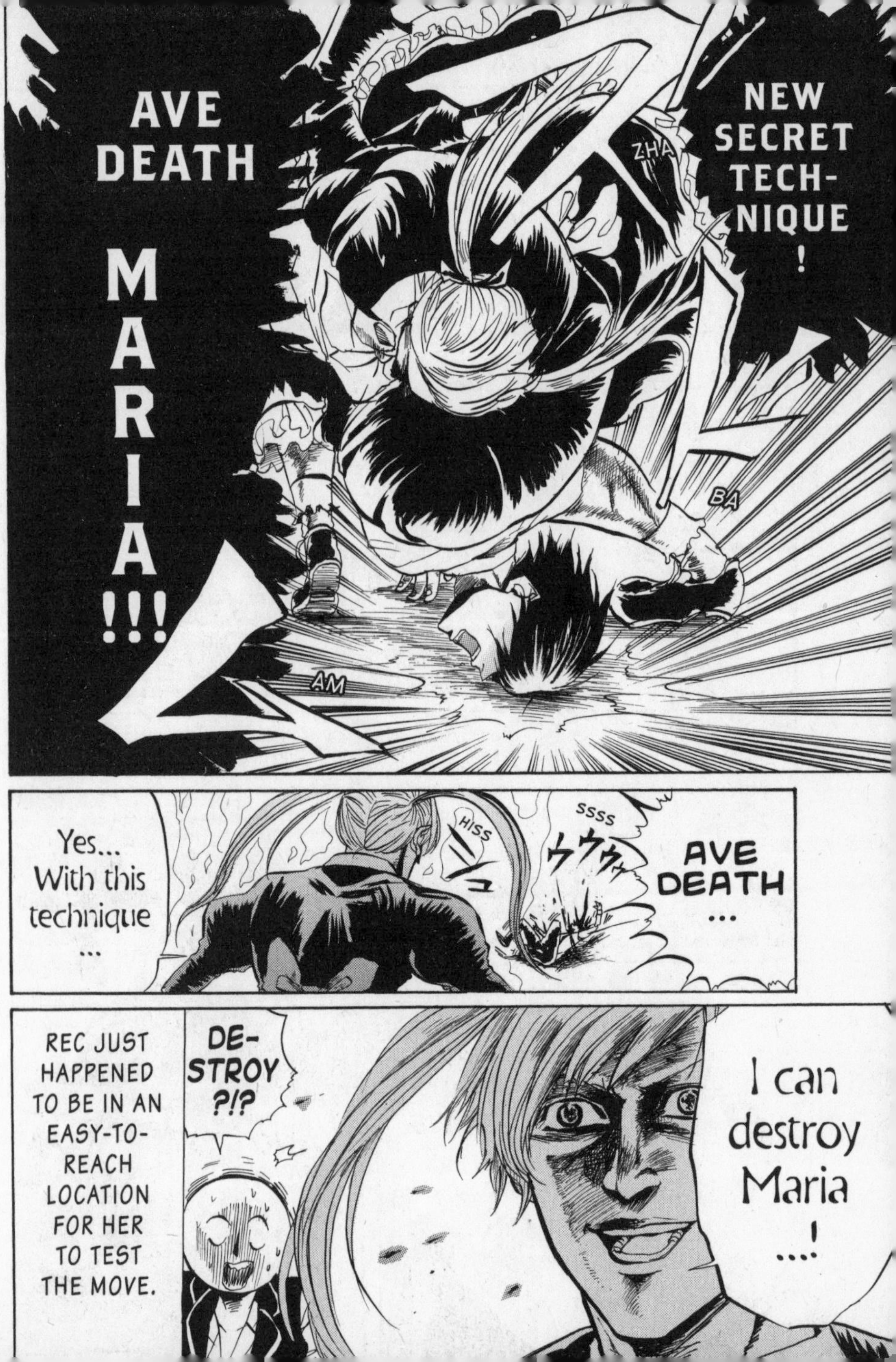
NEW SECRET TECH-NIQUE!
ZHA
AVE DEATH MARIA!!!
BA
AM
AVE DEATH ...
SSSS
HISS
Yes... With this technique ...
I can destroy Maria ...!
DE-STROY ?!?
REC JUST HAPPENED TO BE IN AN EASY-TO-REACH LOCATION FOR HER TO TEST THE MOVE.

Chapter 80: Mad Heartbreak Brothers

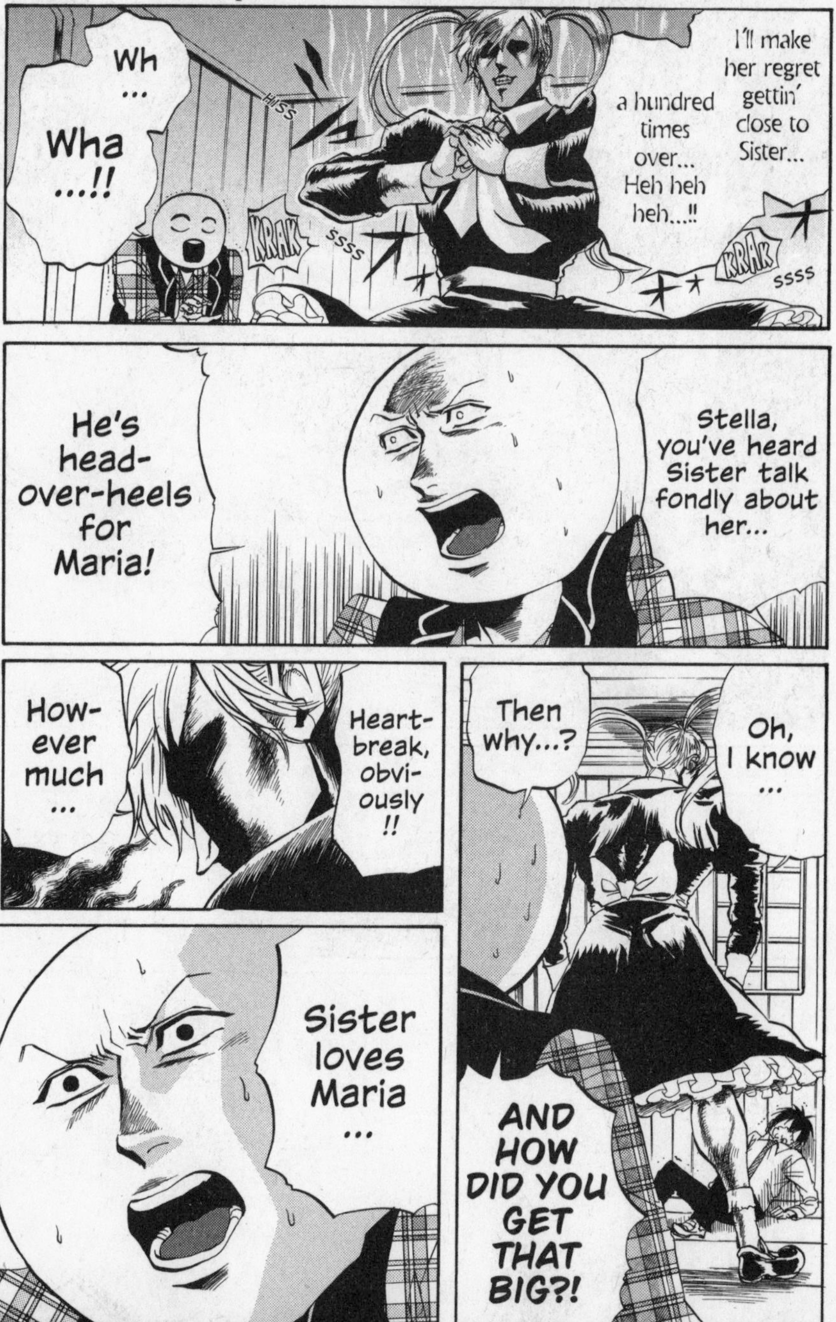
I'll make her regret gettin' close to Sister...
a hundred times over... Heh heh heh...!!
KRAK
ssss
HISS
Wh... Wha...!!
KRAK
ssss
Stella, you've heard Sister talk fondly about her...
He's head-over-heels for Maria!
Oh, I know...
Then why...?
AND HOW DID YOU GET THAT BIG?!
Heart-break, obvi-ously!!
How-ever much...
Sister loves Maria...

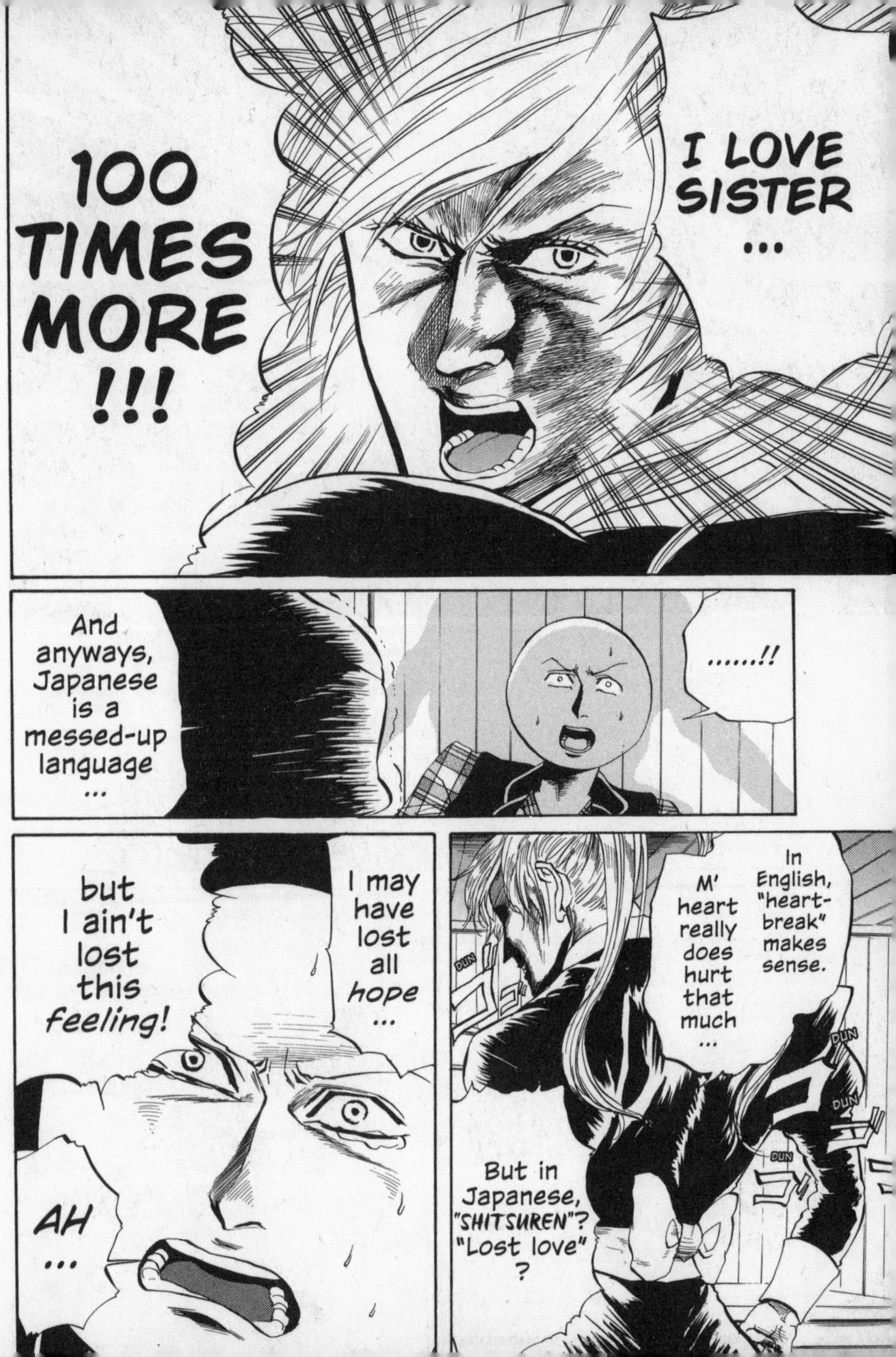
I LOVE SISTER ...
100 TIMES MORE !!!
......!!
And anyways, Japanese is a messed-up language ...
In English, "heart-break" makes sense.
M' heart really does hurt that much ...
DUN
DUN
DUN
DUN
But in Japanese, "SHITSUREN"? "Lost love"?
I may have lost all *hope* ...
but I ain't lost this *feeling!*
AH ...

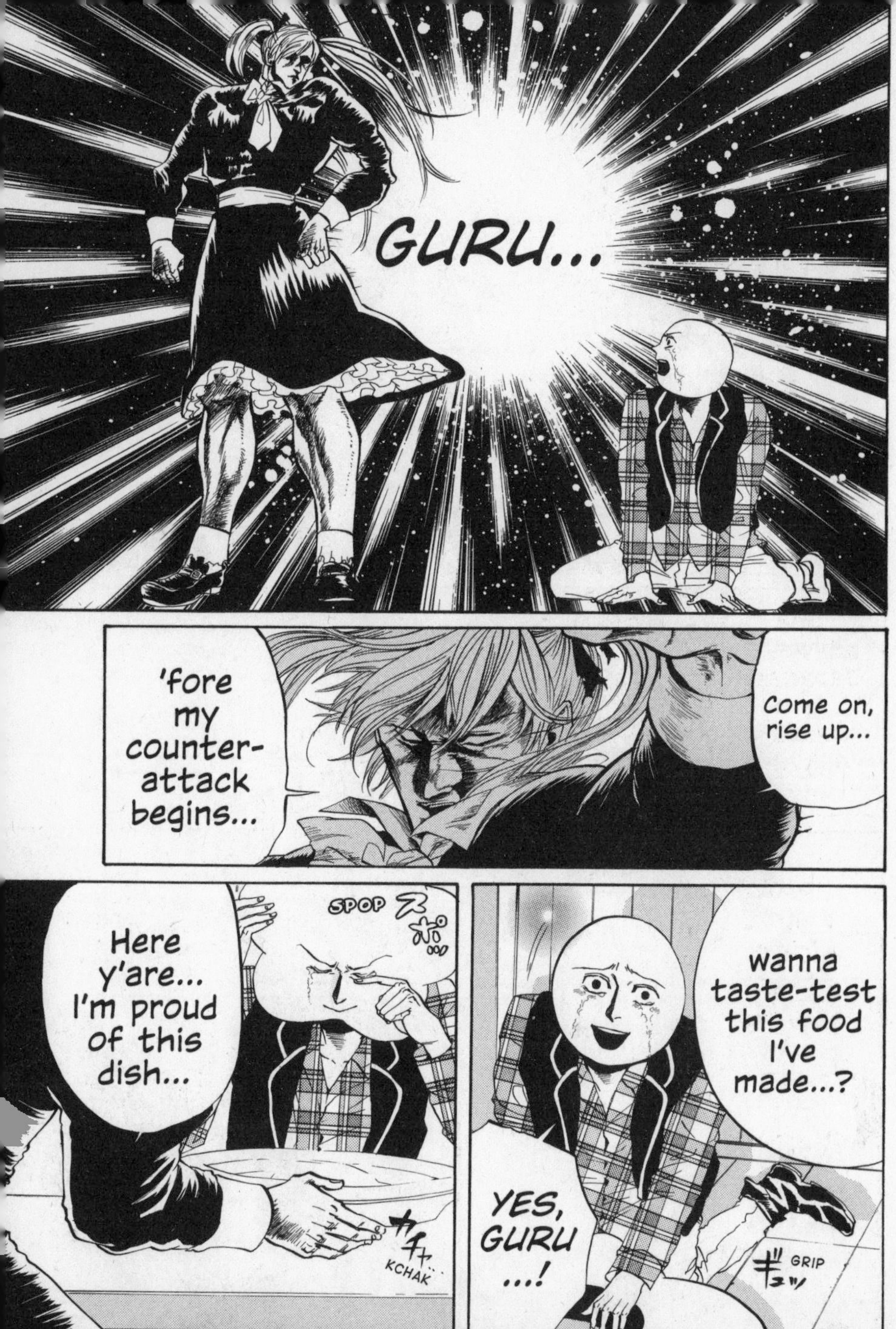
GURU...
Come on, rise up...
'fore my counter-attack begins...
wanna taste-test this food I've made...?
YES, GURU...!
GRIP
SPOP
Here y'are... I'm proud of this dish...
KCHAK

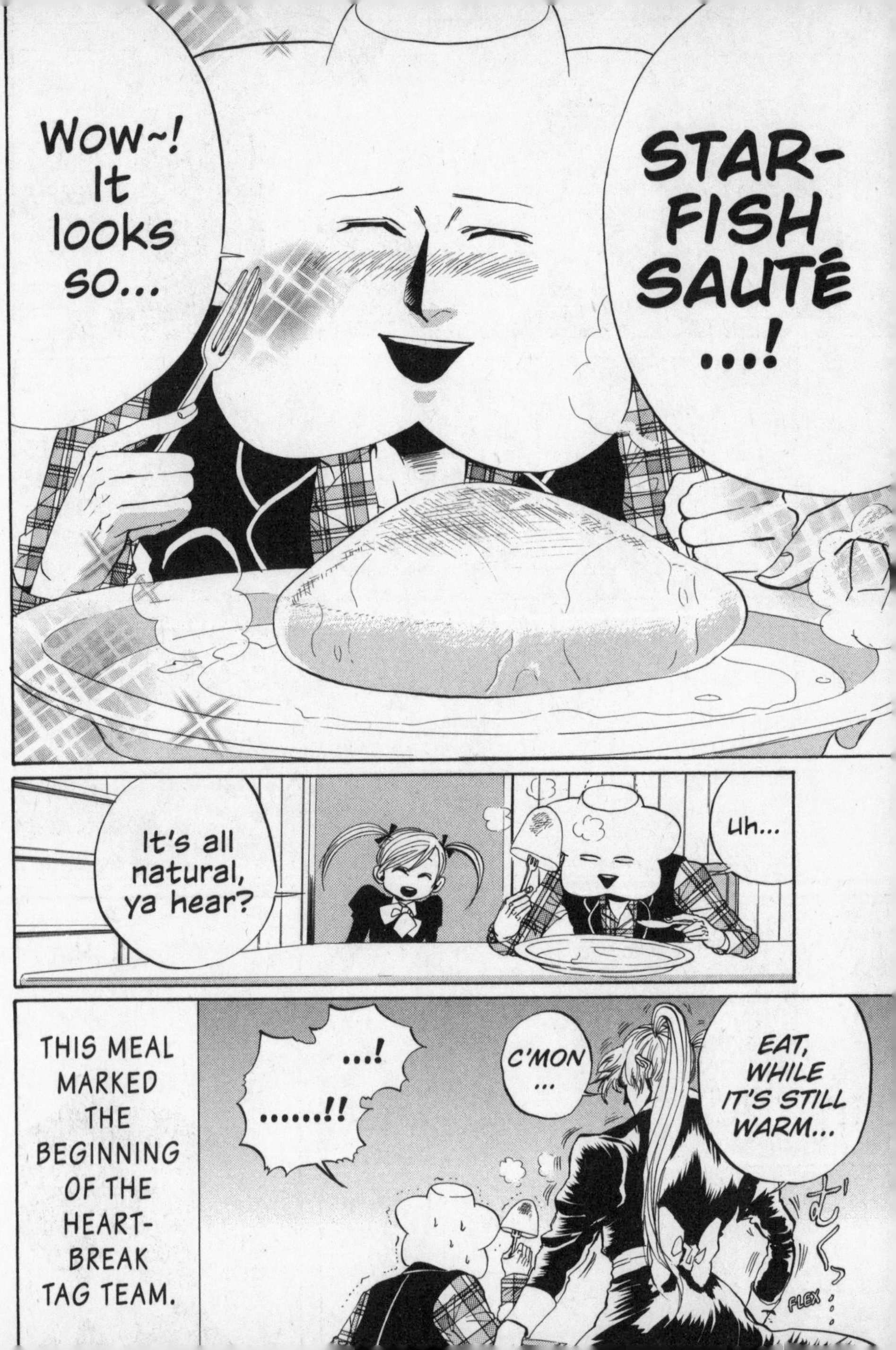
STAR-FISH SAUTÉ ...!
Wow~! It looks so...
Uh...
It's all natural, ya hear?
EAT, WHILE IT'S STILL WARM...
C'MON ...
...!
......!!
FLEX
THIS MEAL MARKED THE BEGINNING OF THE HEART-BREAK TAG TEAM.

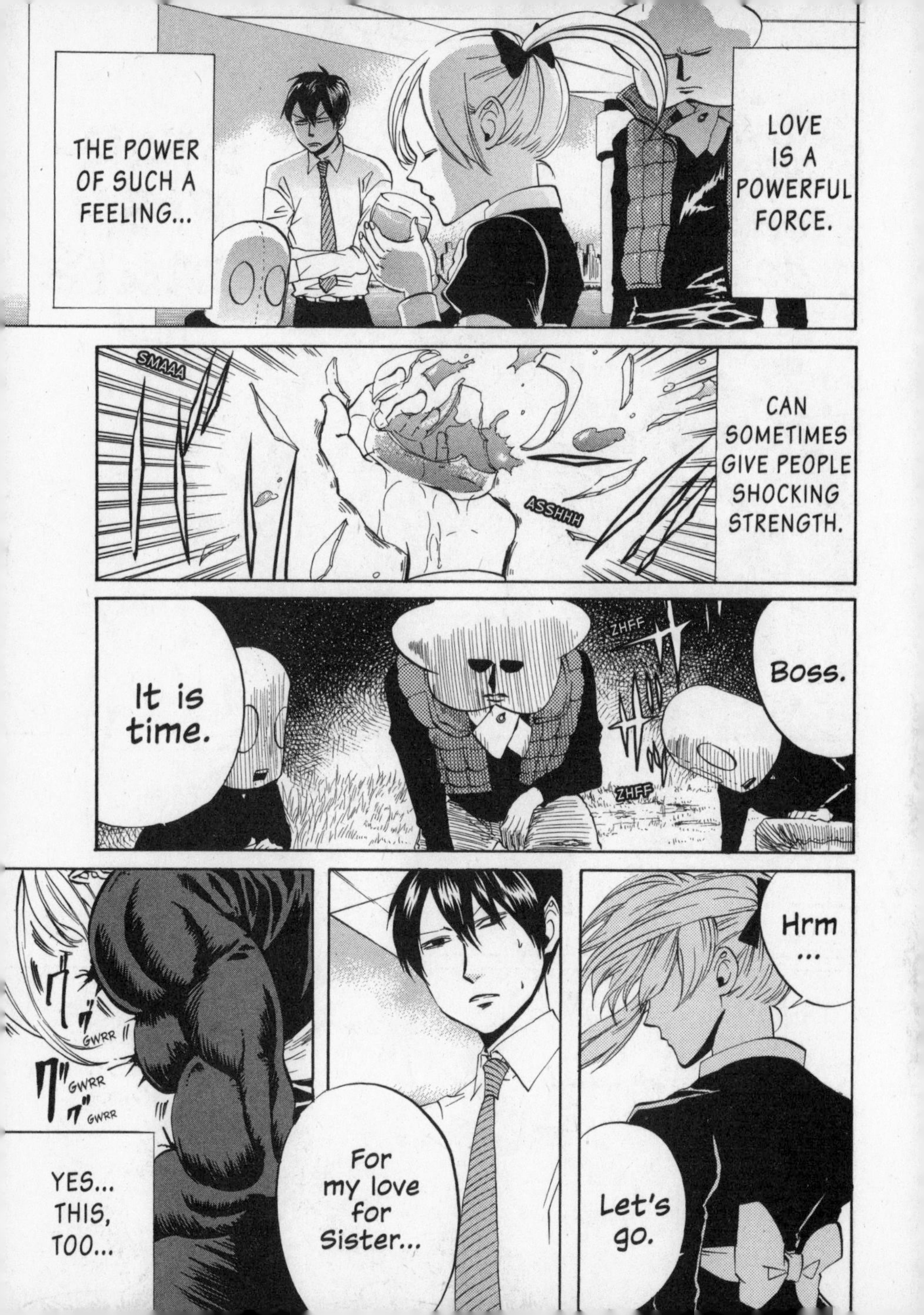

LOVE IS A POWERFUL FORCE.
THE POWER OF SUCH A FEELING...
SMAAA
ASSHHH
CAN SOMETIMES GIVE PEOPLE SHOCKING STRENGTH.
ZHFF
Boss.
ZHFF
It is time.
Hrm ...
Let's go.
For my love for Sister...
GWRR
GWRR
GWRR
YES... THIS, TOO...

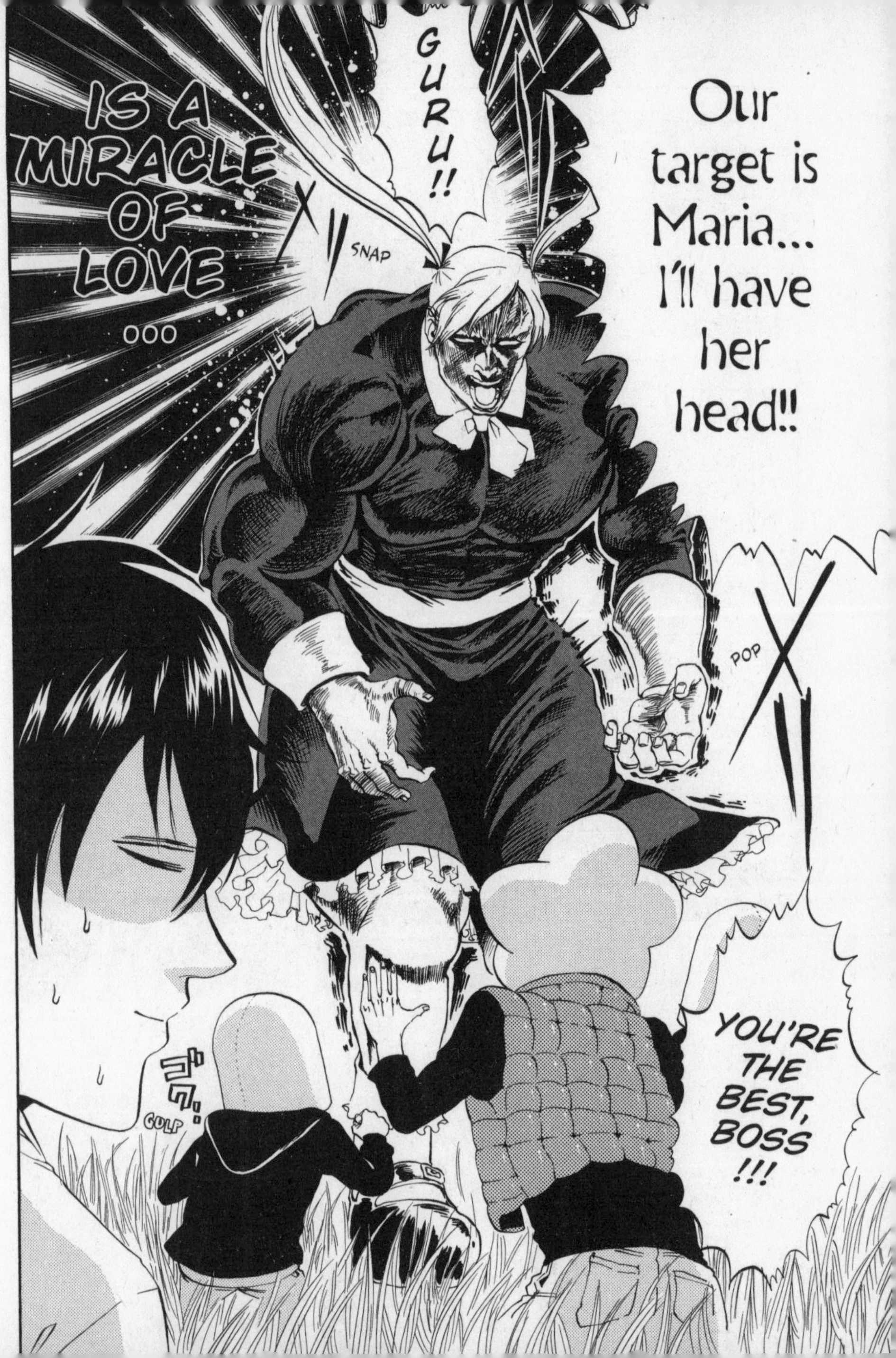
Our target is Maria... I'll have her head!!
GURU!!
SNAP
IS A MIRACLE OF LOVE ...
POP
YOU'RE THE BEST, BOSS!!!
GULP

Chapter 81: Lord of Violence

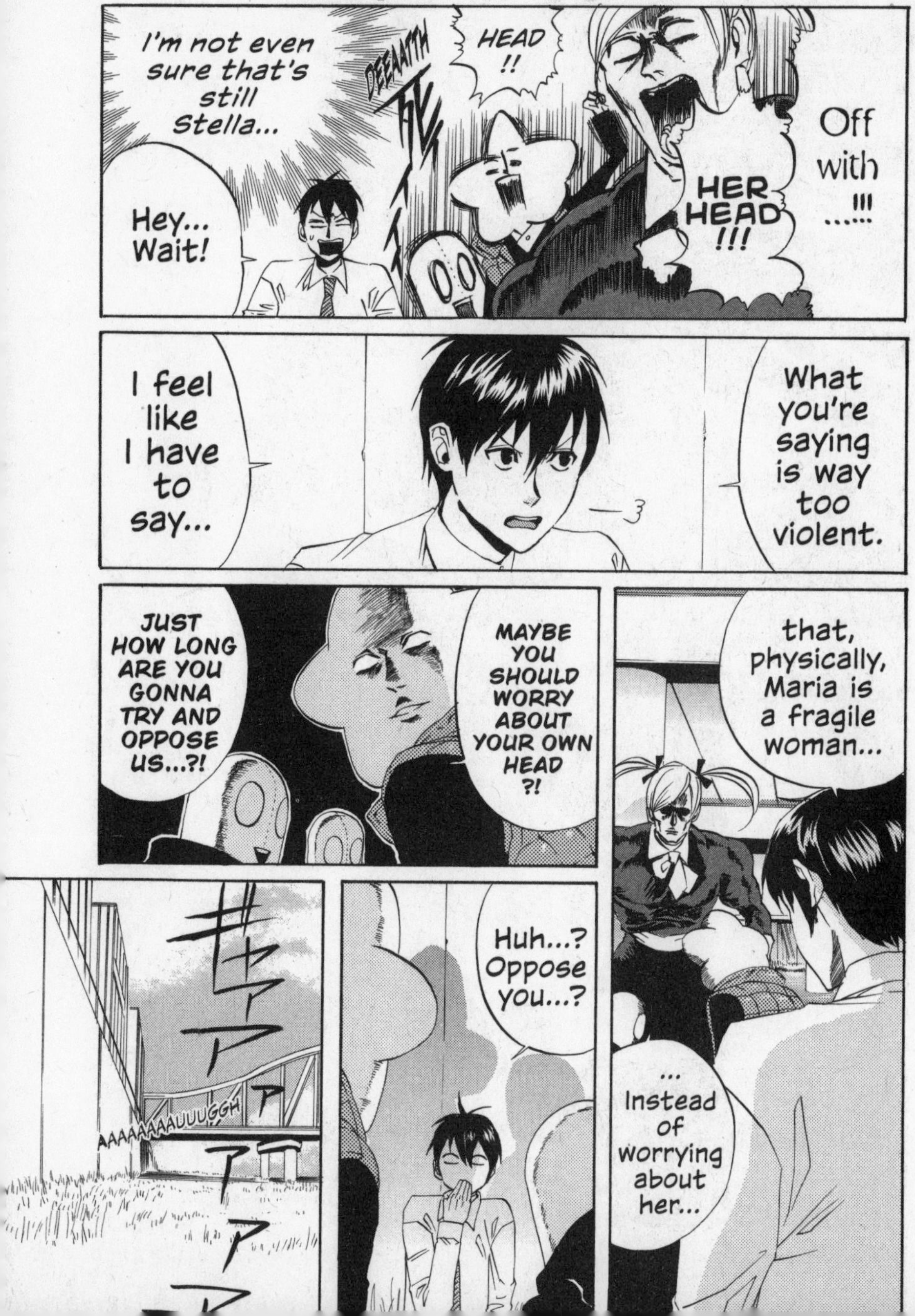
Off with ...!!!
HER HEAD !!!
HEAD !!
DEEAAATH
I'm not even sure that's still Stella...
Hey... Wait!
What you're saying is way too violent.
I feel like I have to say...
that, physically, Maria is a fragile woman...
... Instead of worrying about her...
MAYBE YOU SHOULD WORRY ABOUT YOUR OWN HEAD ?!
JUST HOW LONG ARE YOU GONNA TRY AND OPPOSE US...?!
Huh...? Oppose you...?
AAAAAAAAUUUGGH

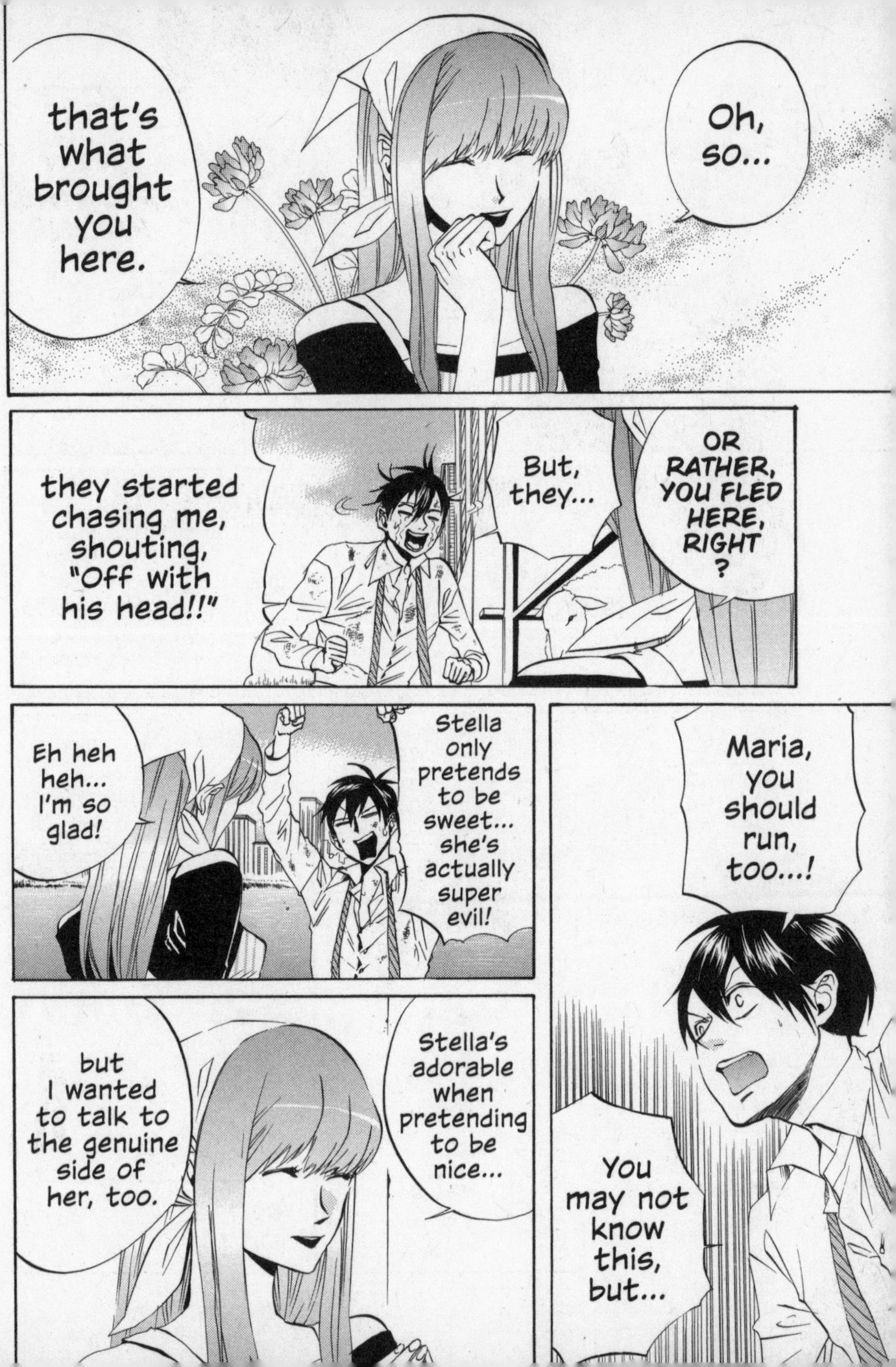
Oh, so...
that's what brought you here.
OR RATHER, YOU FLED HERE, RIGHT?
But, they...
they started chasing me, shouting, "Off with his head!!"
Maria, you should run, too...!
You may not know this, but...
Stella only pretends to be sweet... she's actually super evil!
Eh heh heh... I'm so glad!
Stella's adorable when pretending to be nice...
but I wanted to talk to the genuine side of her, too.

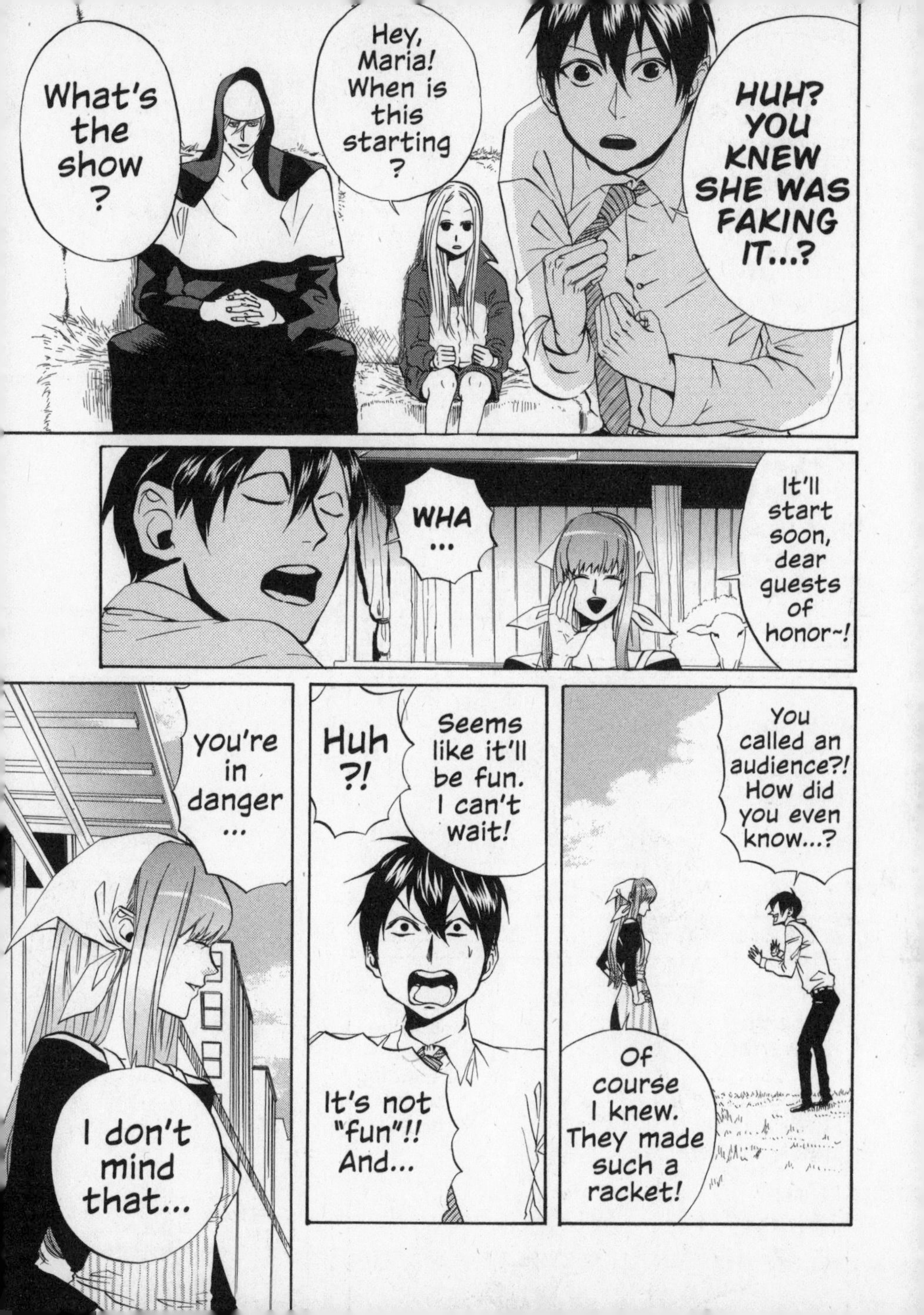
HUH? YOU KNEW SHE WAS FAKING IT...?
Hey, Maria! When is this starting?
What's the show?
It'll start soon, dear guests of honor~!
WHA...
You called an audience?! How did you even know...?
Of course I knew. They made such a racket!
Seems like it'll be fun. I can't wait!
Huh?!
It's not "fun"!! And...
you're in danger...
I don't mind that...

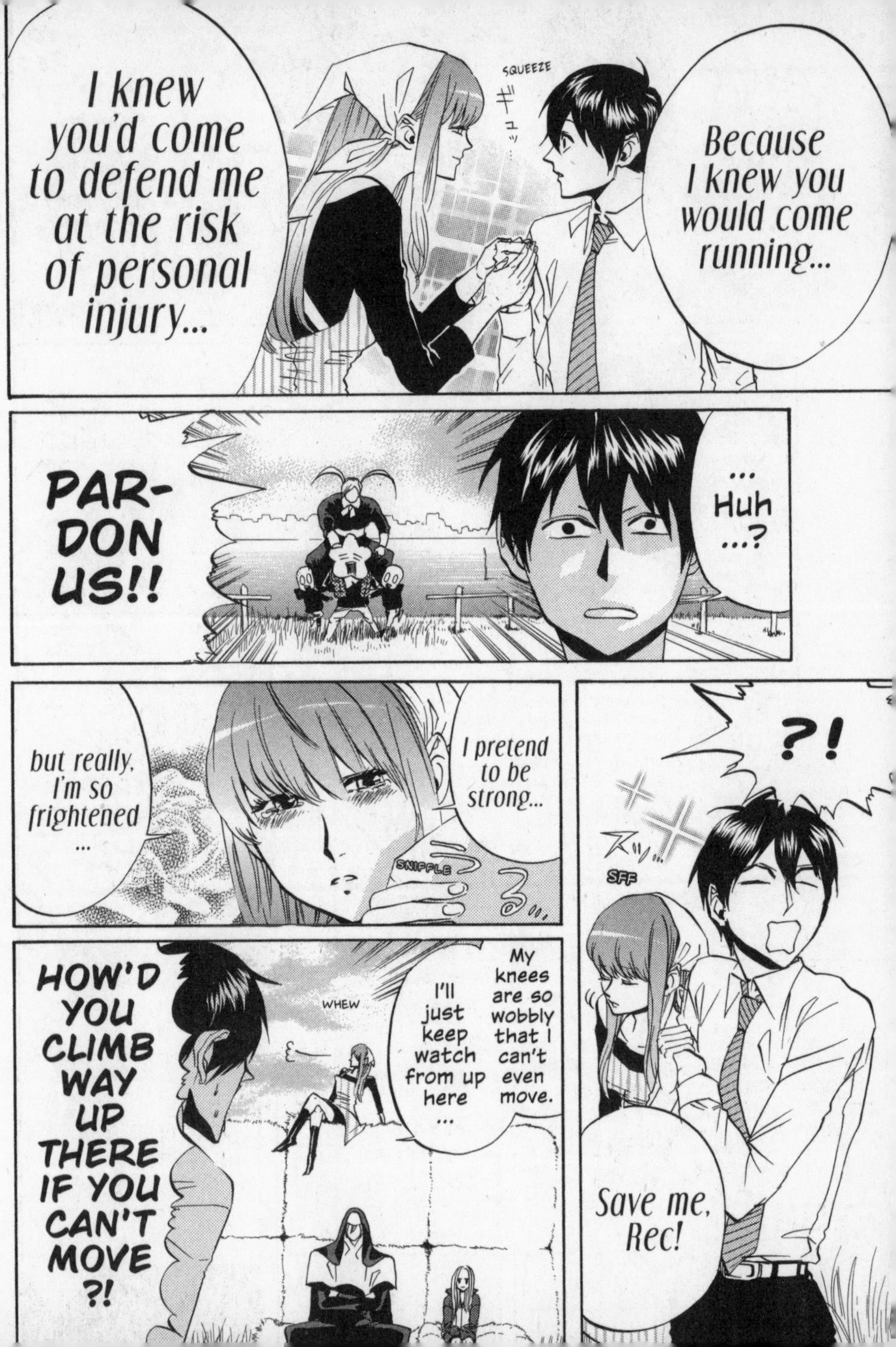
Because I knew you would come running...
SQUEEZE
ギュッ…
I knew you'd come to defend me at the risk of personal injury...
... Huh ...?
PARDON US!!
?!
SFF
Save me, Rec!
I pretend to be strong...
SNIFFLE
but really, I'm so frightened ...
My knees are so wobbly that I can't even move.
I'll just keep watch from up here ...
WHEW
HOW'D YOU CLIMB WAY UP THERE IF YOU CAN'T MOVE?!

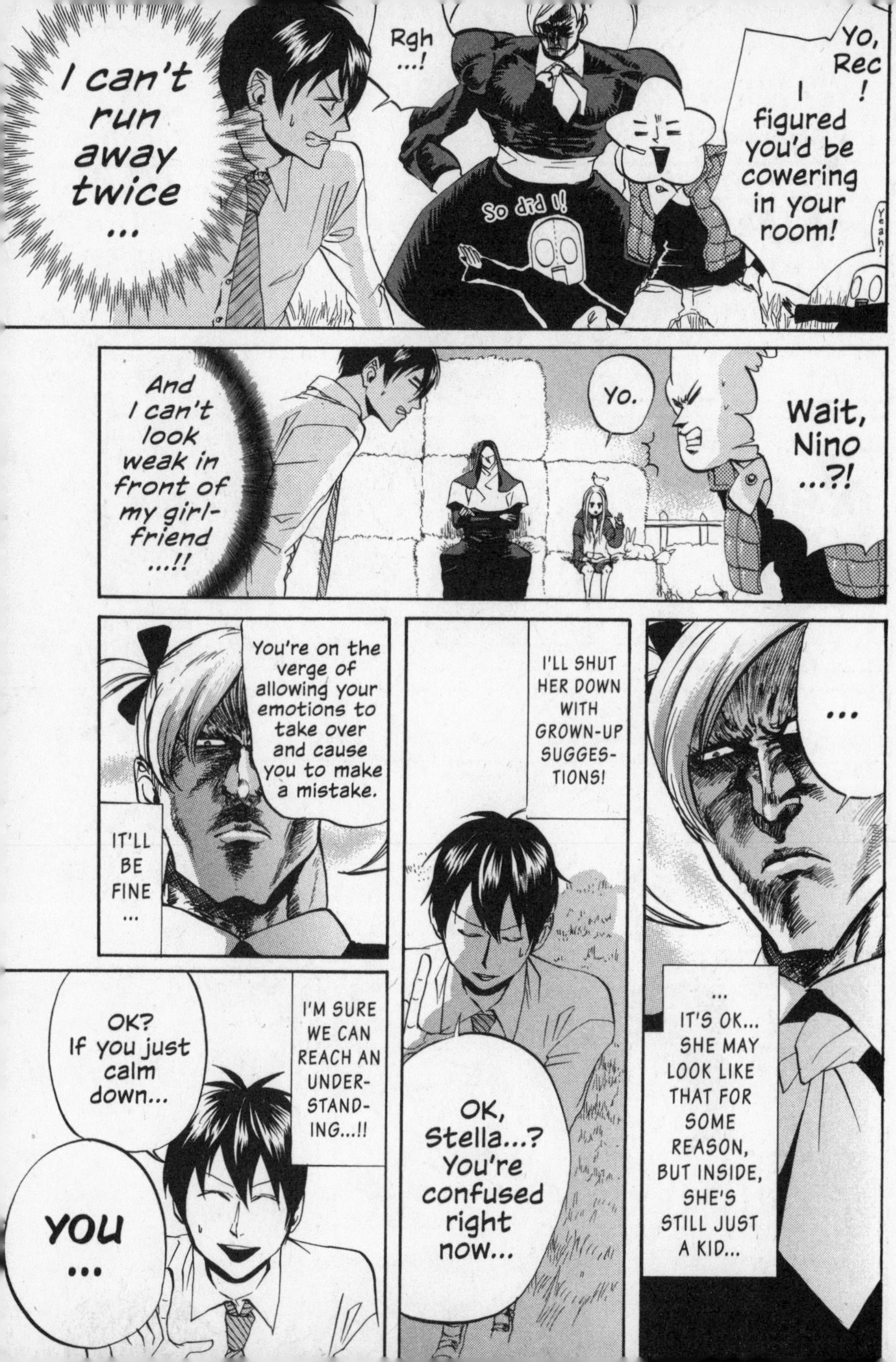
Yo, Rec! I figured you'd be cowering in your room!
Yeah!
Rgh ...!
So did I!
I can't run away twice ...
Wait, Nino ...?!
Yo.
And I can't look weak in front of my girl-friend ...!!
...
... IT'S OK... SHE MAY LOOK LIKE THAT FOR SOME REASON, BUT INSIDE, SHE'S STILL JUST A KID...
I'LL SHUT HER DOWN WITH GROWN-UP SUGGES-TIONS!
OK, Stella...? You're confused right now...
You're on the verge of allowing your emotions to take over and cause you to make a mistake.
IT'LL BE FINE ...
I'M SURE WE CAN REACH AN UNDER-STAND-ING...!!
OK? If you just calm down...
YOU ...

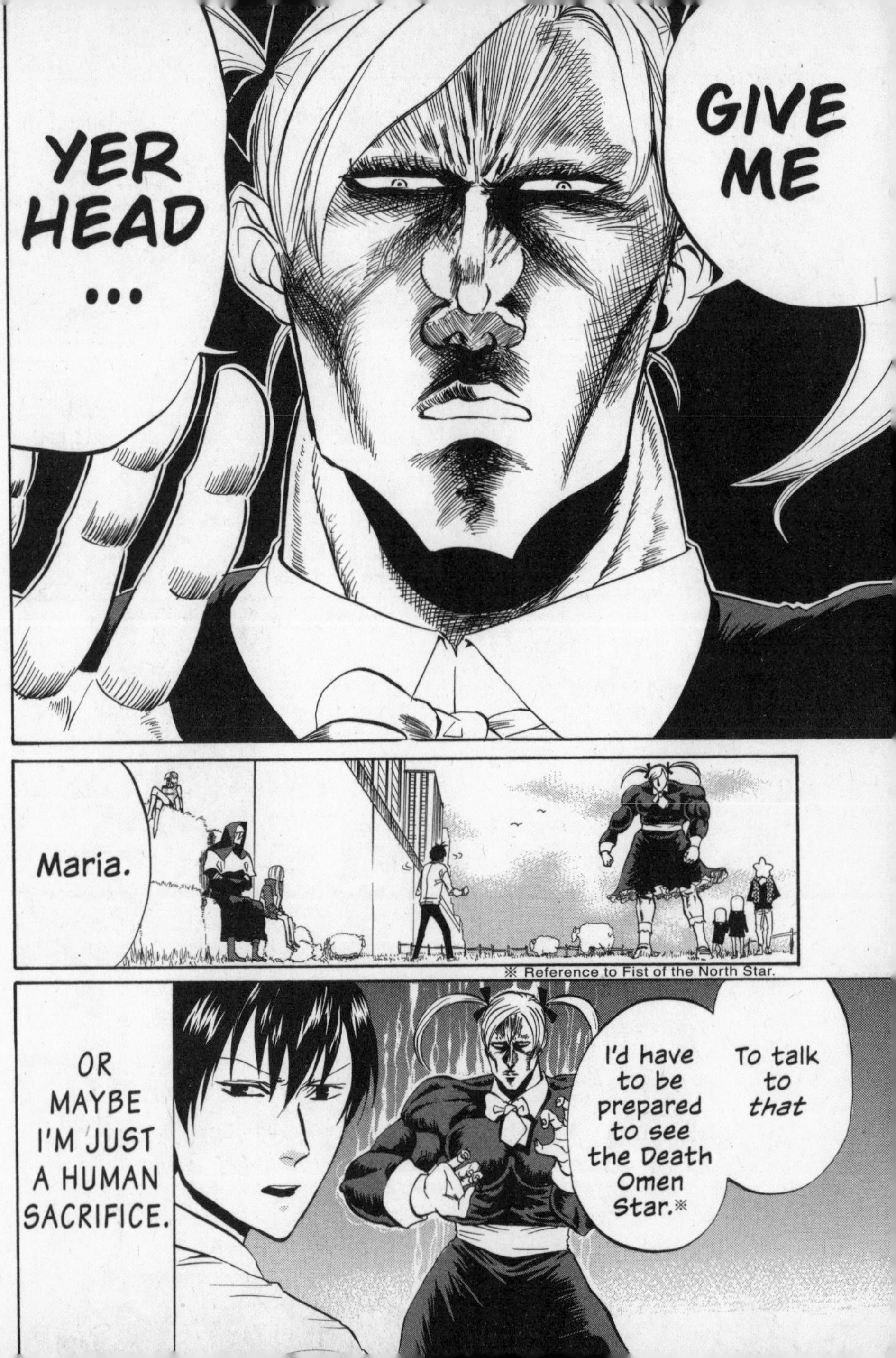
GIVE ME
YER HEAD ...
Maria.
To talk to *that*
I'd have to be prepared to see the Death Omen Star.※
OR MAYBE I'M JUST A HUMAN SACRIFICE.

※ Reference to Fist of the North Star.

Chapter 82: Maria's Secret

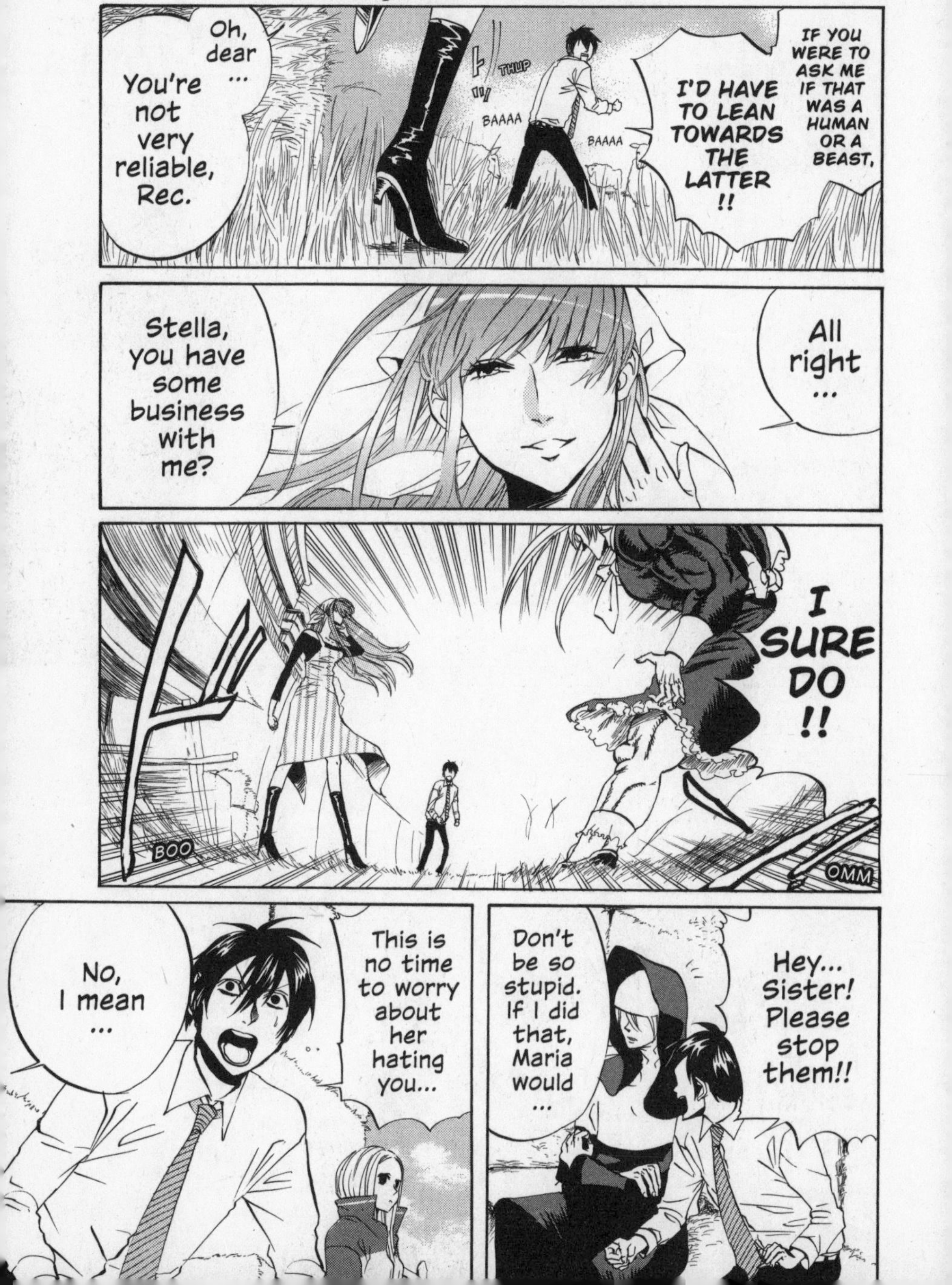
IF YOU WERE TO ASK ME IF THAT WAS A HUMAN OR A BEAST,
I'D HAVE TO LEAN TOWARDS THE LATTER !!
BAAAA
THUP
BAAAA
Oh, dear ... You're not very reliable, Rec.
All right ...
Stella, you have some business with me?
I SURE DO !!
OMM
BOO
Hey... Sister! Please stop them!!
Don't be so stupid. If I did that, Maria would ...
This is no time to worry about her hating you...
No, I mean ...

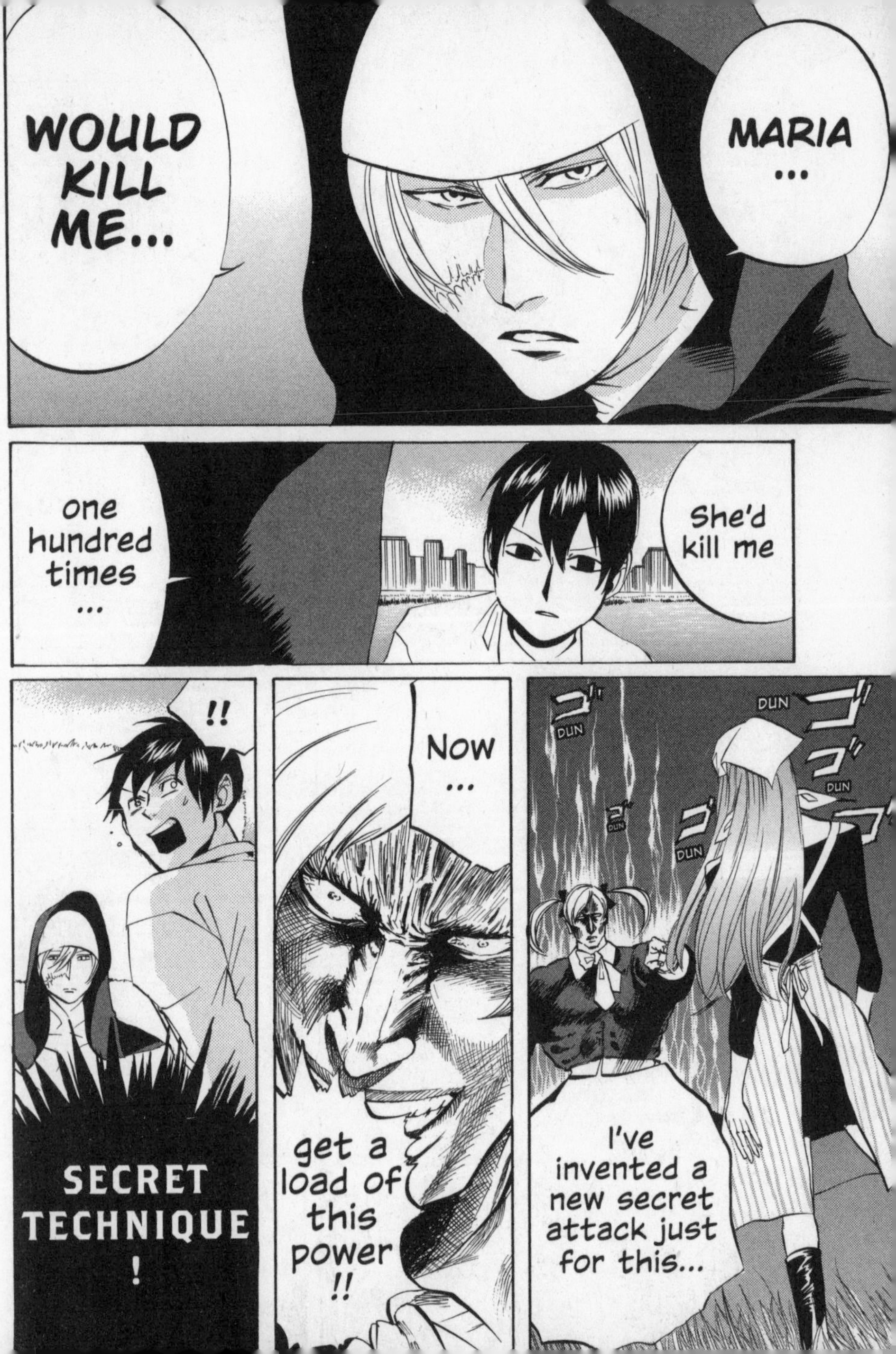
MARIA ...
WOULD KILL ME...
She'd kill me
one hundred times ...
DUN
DUN
DUN
DUN
DUN
I've invented a new secret attack just for this...
Now ...
get a load of this power !!
!!
SECRET TECHNIQUE !

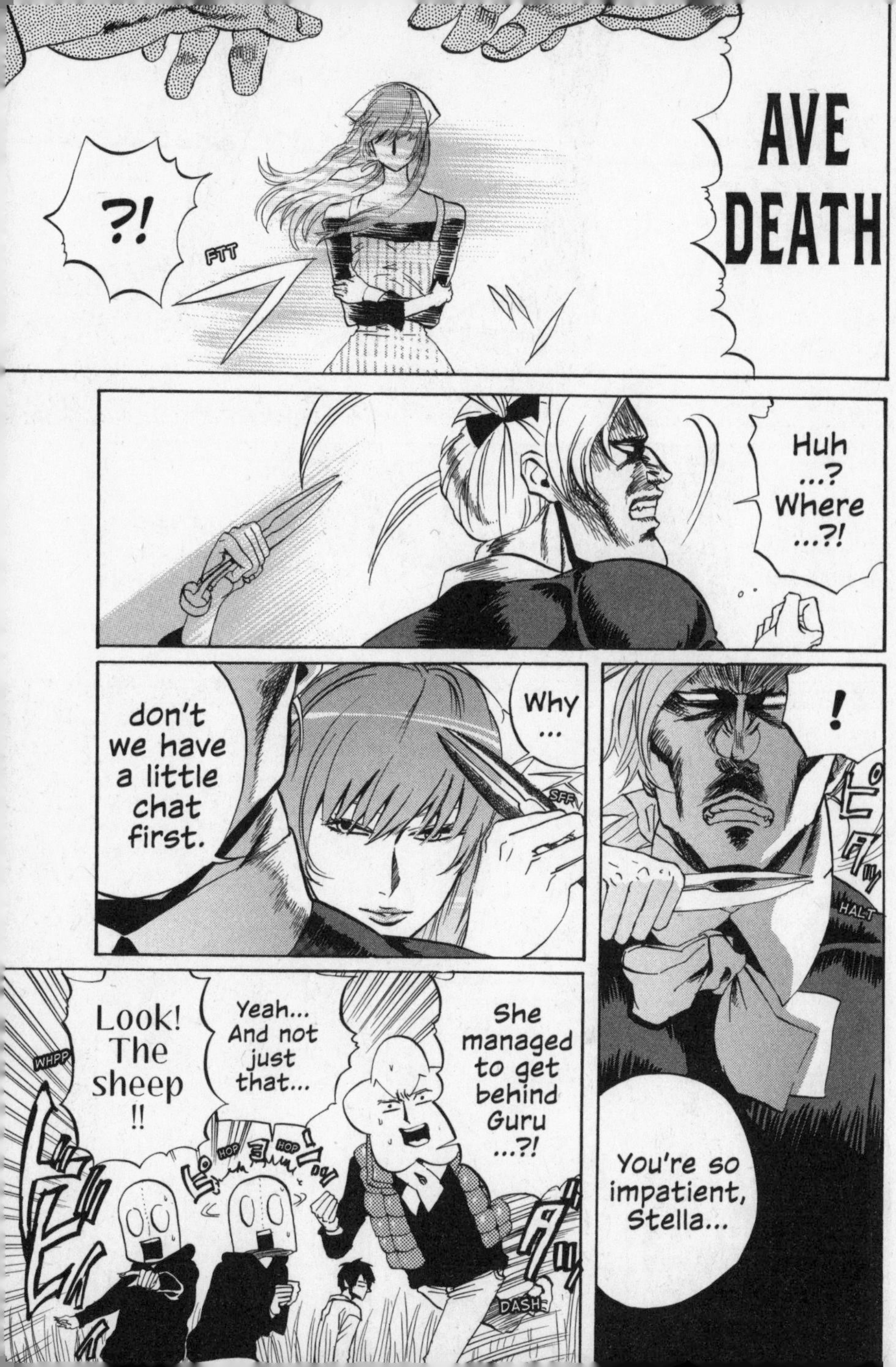
AVE DEATH
?!
FTT
Huh ...? Where ...?!
!
HALT
You're so impatient, Stella...
Why ...
don't we have a little chat first.
SFF
She managed to get behind Guru ...?!
Yeah... And not just that...
Look! The sheep !!
WHPP
HOP
HOP
DASH

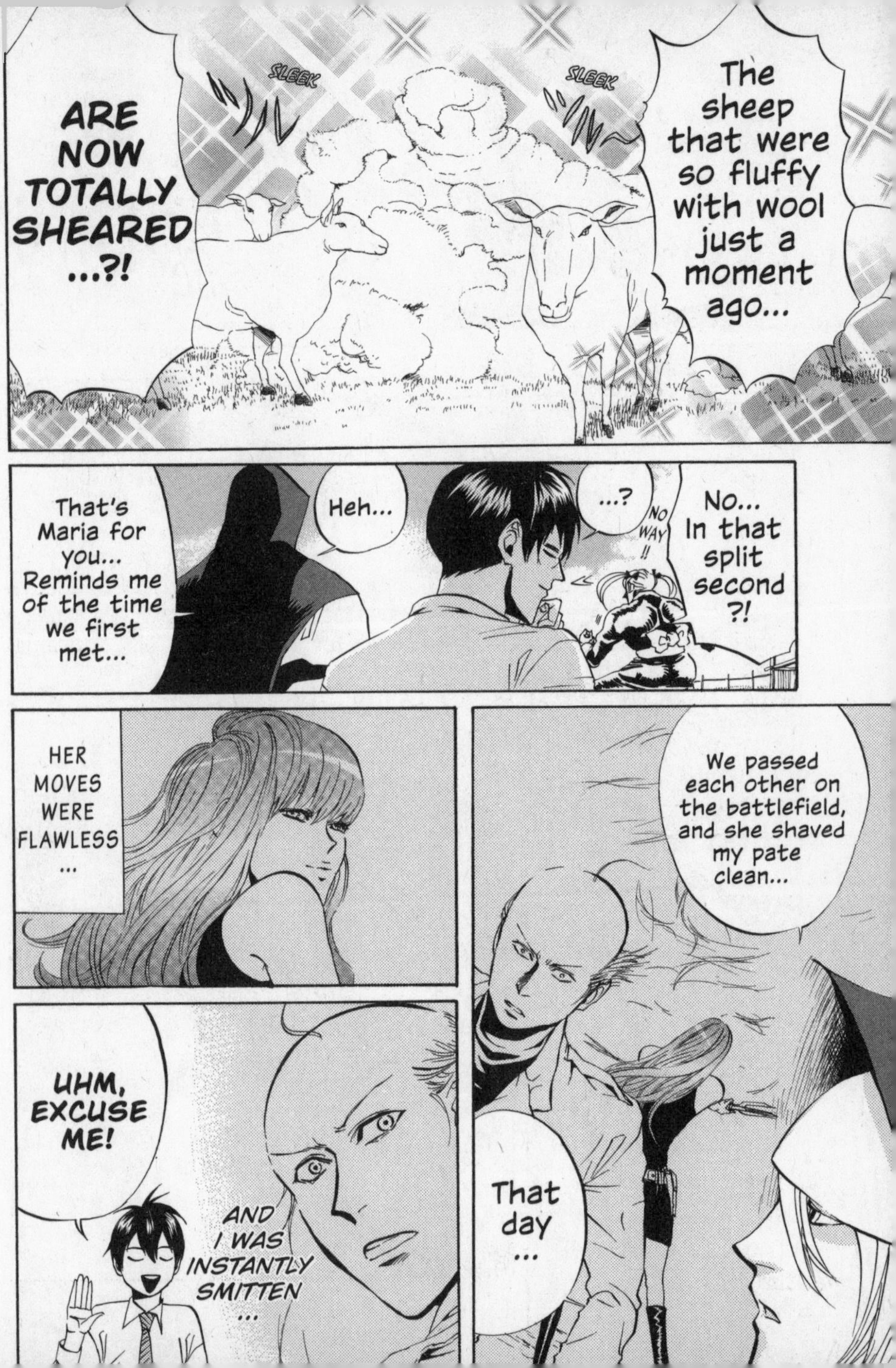
The sheep that were so fluffy with wool just a moment ago...
SLEEK
SLEEK
ARE NOW TOTALLY SHEARED ...?!
No... In that split second ?!
NO WAY !!
...?
Heh...
That's Maria for you... Reminds me of the time we first met...
We passed each other on the battlefield, and she shaved my pate clean...
That day ...
HER MOVES WERE FLAWLESS ...
AND I WAS INSTANTLY SMITTEN ...
UHM, EXCUSE ME!

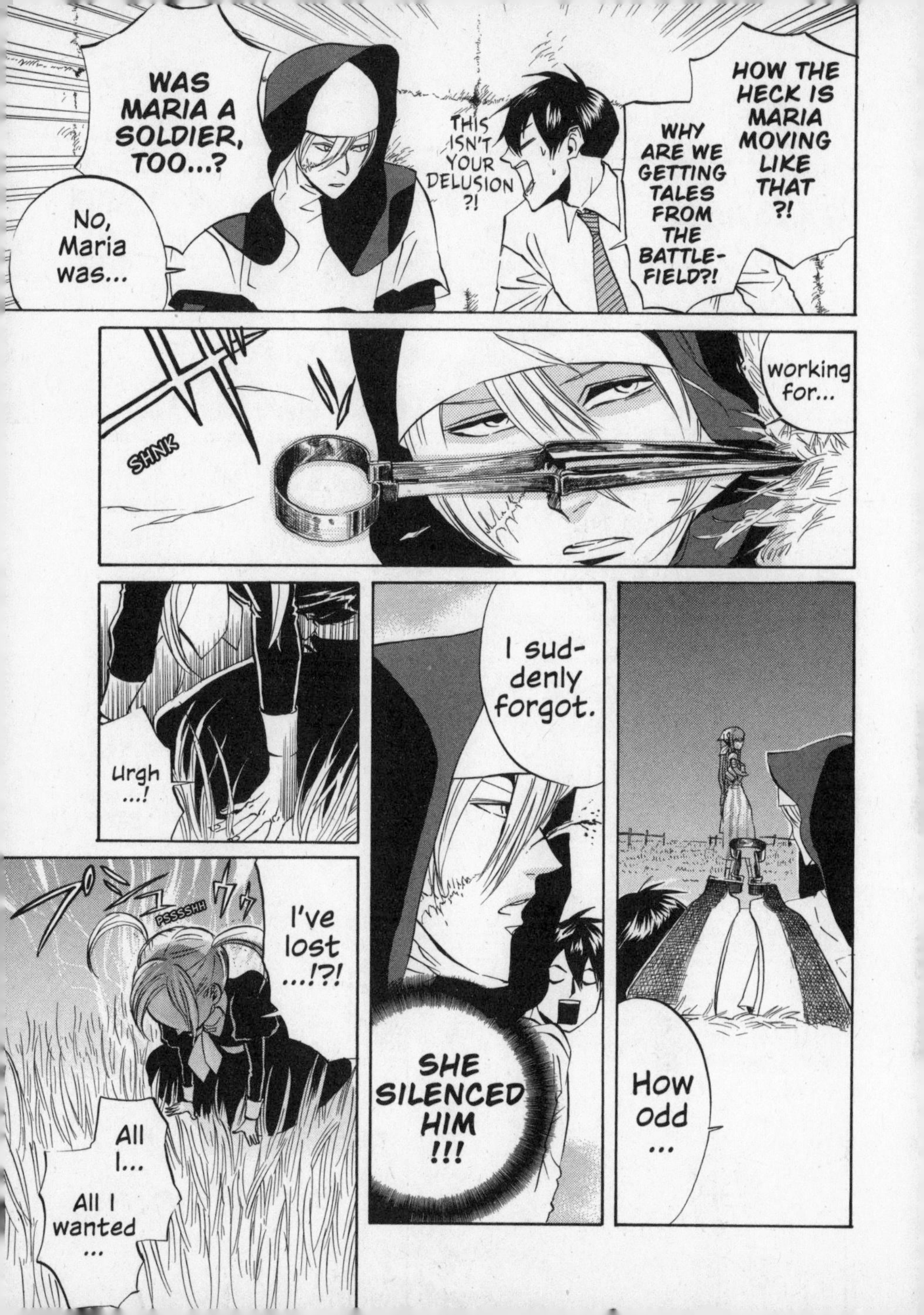
HOW THE HECK IS MARIA MOVING LIKE THAT?!
WHY ARE WE GETTING TALES FROM THE BATTLE-FIELD?!
THIS ISN'T YOUR DELUSION?!
WAS MARIA A SOLDIER, TOO...?
No, Maria was...
working for...
SHNK
How odd...
I sud-denly forgot.
SHE SILENCED HIM!!!
Urgh...!
PSSSSHH
I've lost...!?!
All I...
All I wanted...

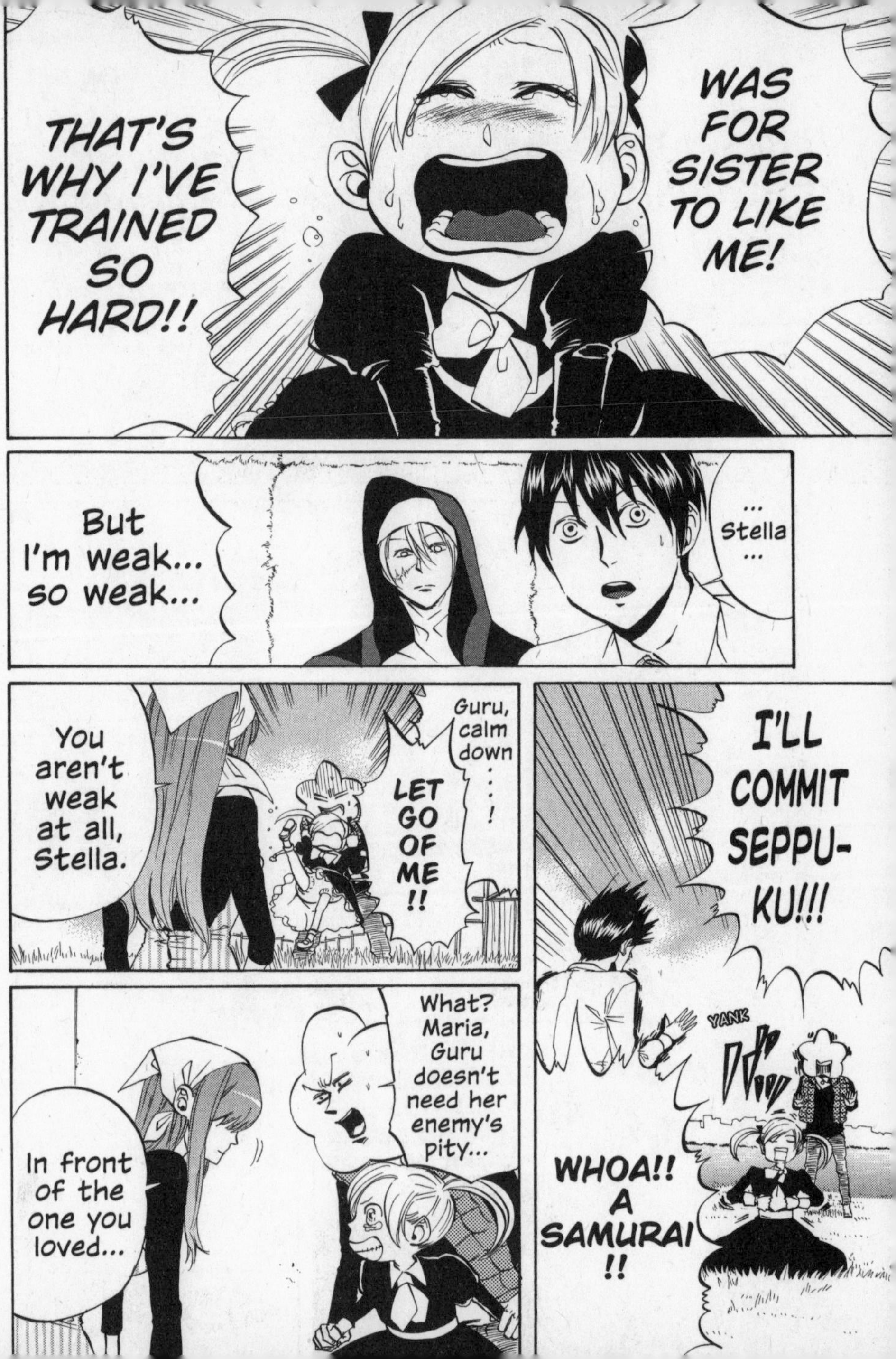
WAS FOR SISTER TO LIKE ME!
THAT'S WHY I'VE TRAINED SO HARD!!
... Stella ...
But I'm weak... so weak...
I'LL COMMIT SEPPUKU!!!
YANK
WHOA!! A SAMURAI!!
Guru, calm down...!
LET GO OF ME!!
You aren't weak at all, Stella.
What? Maria, Guru doesn't need her enemy's pity...
In front of the one you loved...

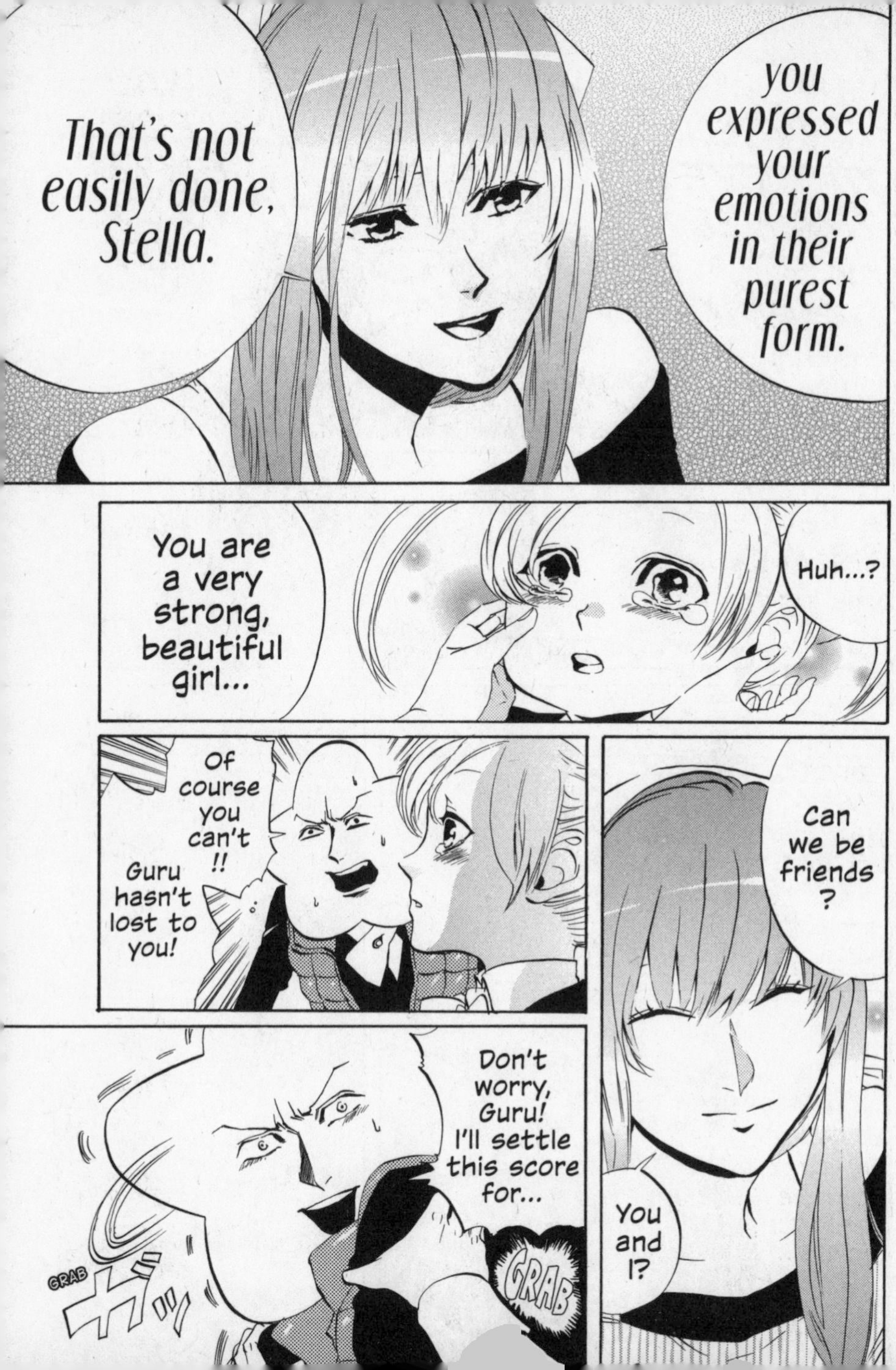
you expressed your emotions in their purest form.
That's not easily done, Stella.
Huh...?
You are a very strong, beautiful girl...
Can we be friends?
You and I?
Of course you can't!!
Guru hasn't lost to you!
Don't worry, Guru! I'll settle this score for...
GRAB
GRAB

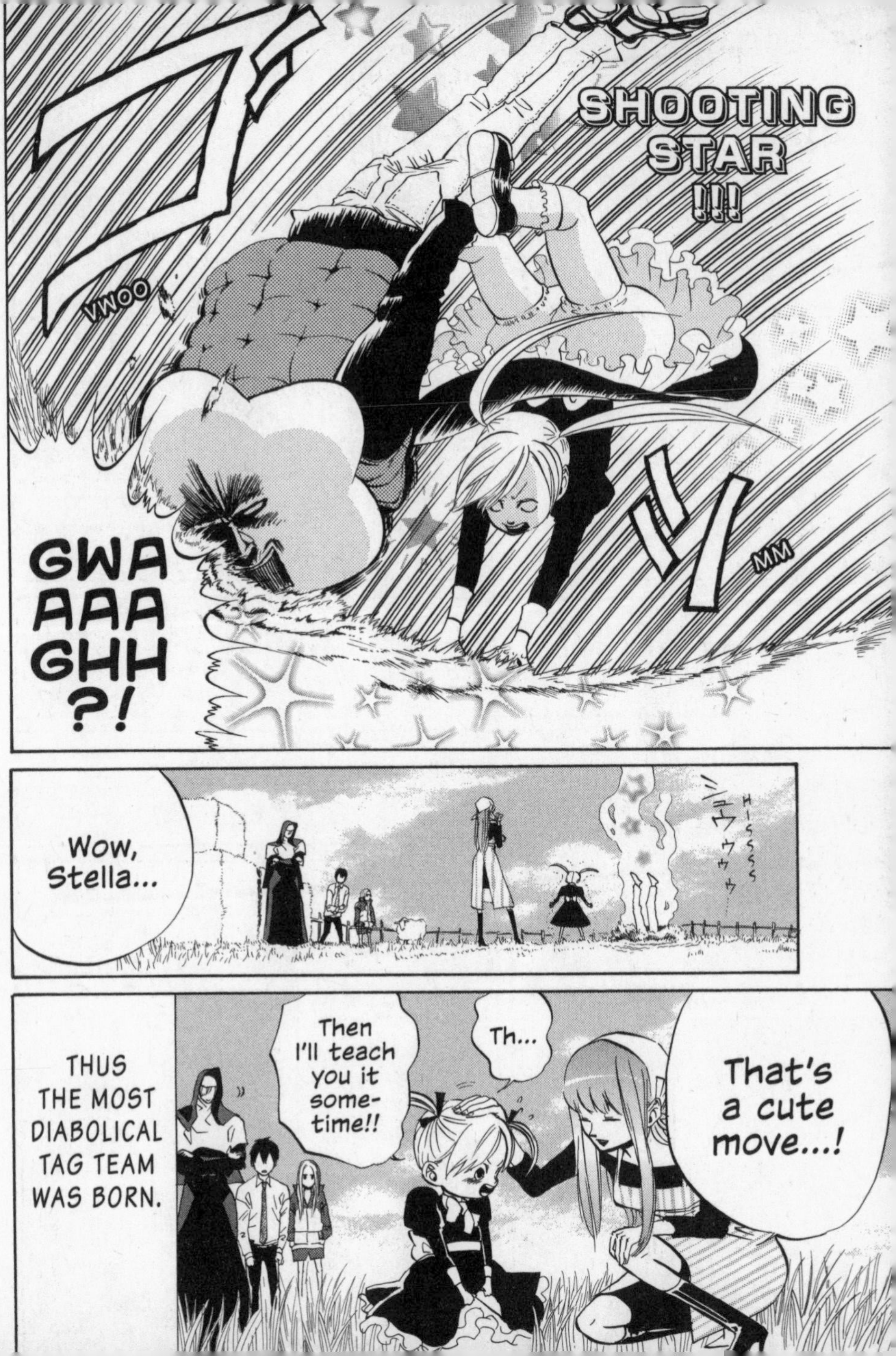
SHOOTING STAR !!!
MM
VWOO
GWAAAAGHH?!
HISSS
Wow, Stella...
That's a cute move...!
Th...
Then I'll teach you it some-time!!
THUS THE MOST DIABOLICAL TAG TEAM WAS BORN.

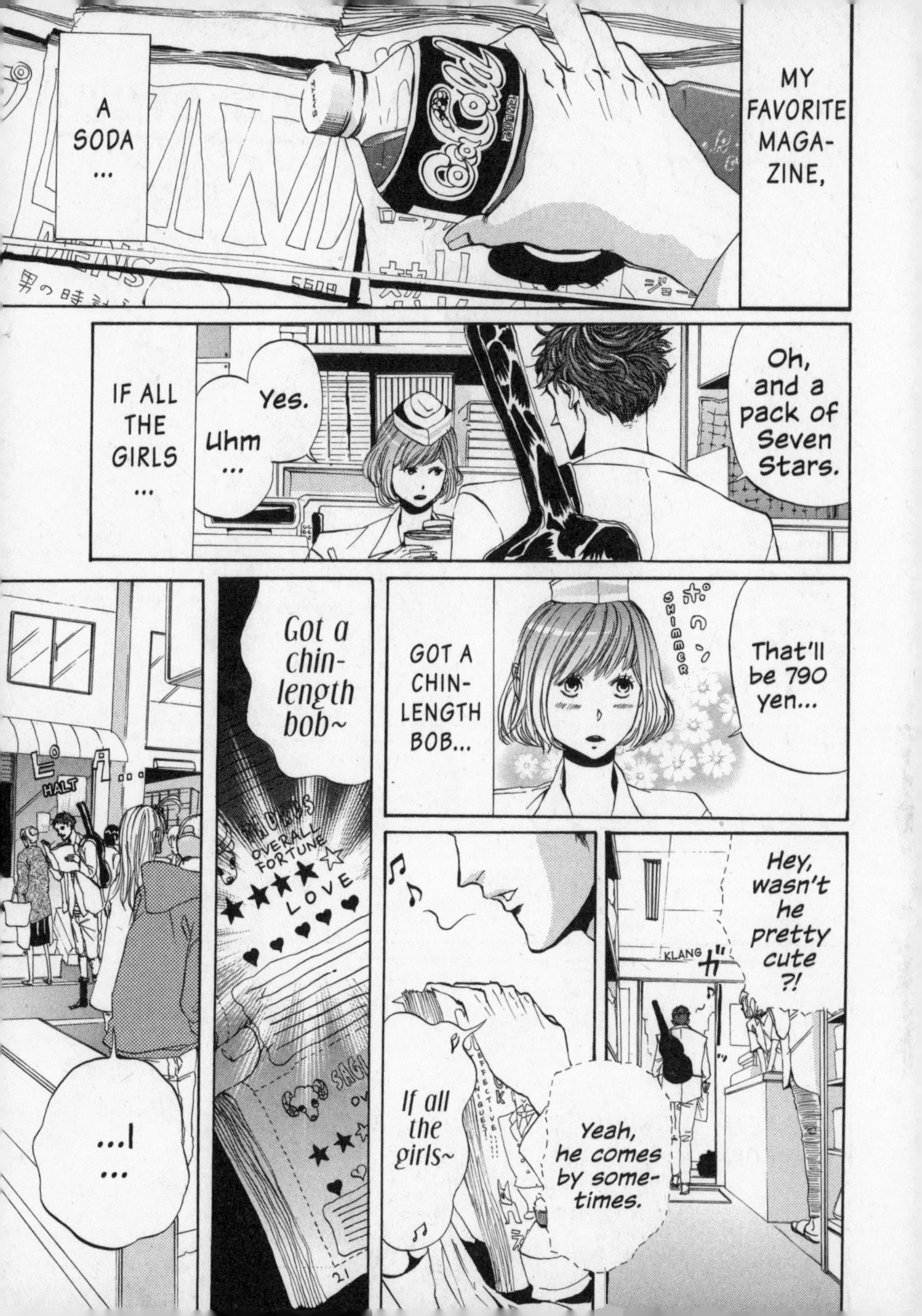
MY FAVORITE MAGA-ZINE,
A SODA ...
Oh, and a pack of Seven Stars.
Yes. Uhm ...
IF ALL THE GIRLS ...
That'll be 790 yen...
SHIMMER
GOT A CHIN-LENGTH BOB...
Hey, wasn't he pretty cute ?!
KLANG
Yeah, he comes by some-times.
If all the girls~
EFFECTIVE
Got a chin-length bob~
OVERALL FORTUNE
LOVE
HALT
...I ...

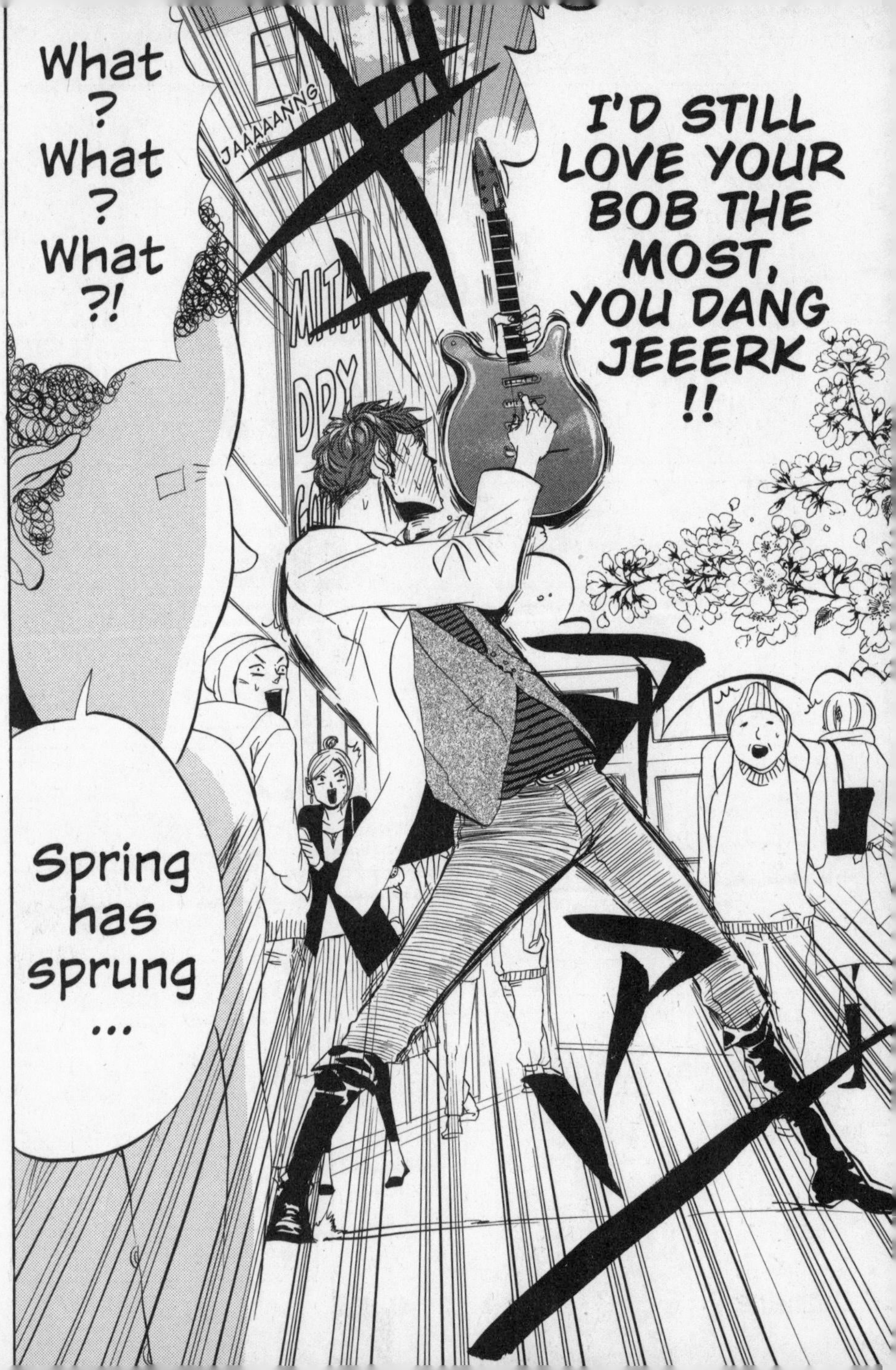
I'D STILL LOVE YOUR BOB THE MOST, YOU DANG JEEERK!!
JAAAAANNG
What? What? What?!
Spring has sprung...

Chapter 83: True Form

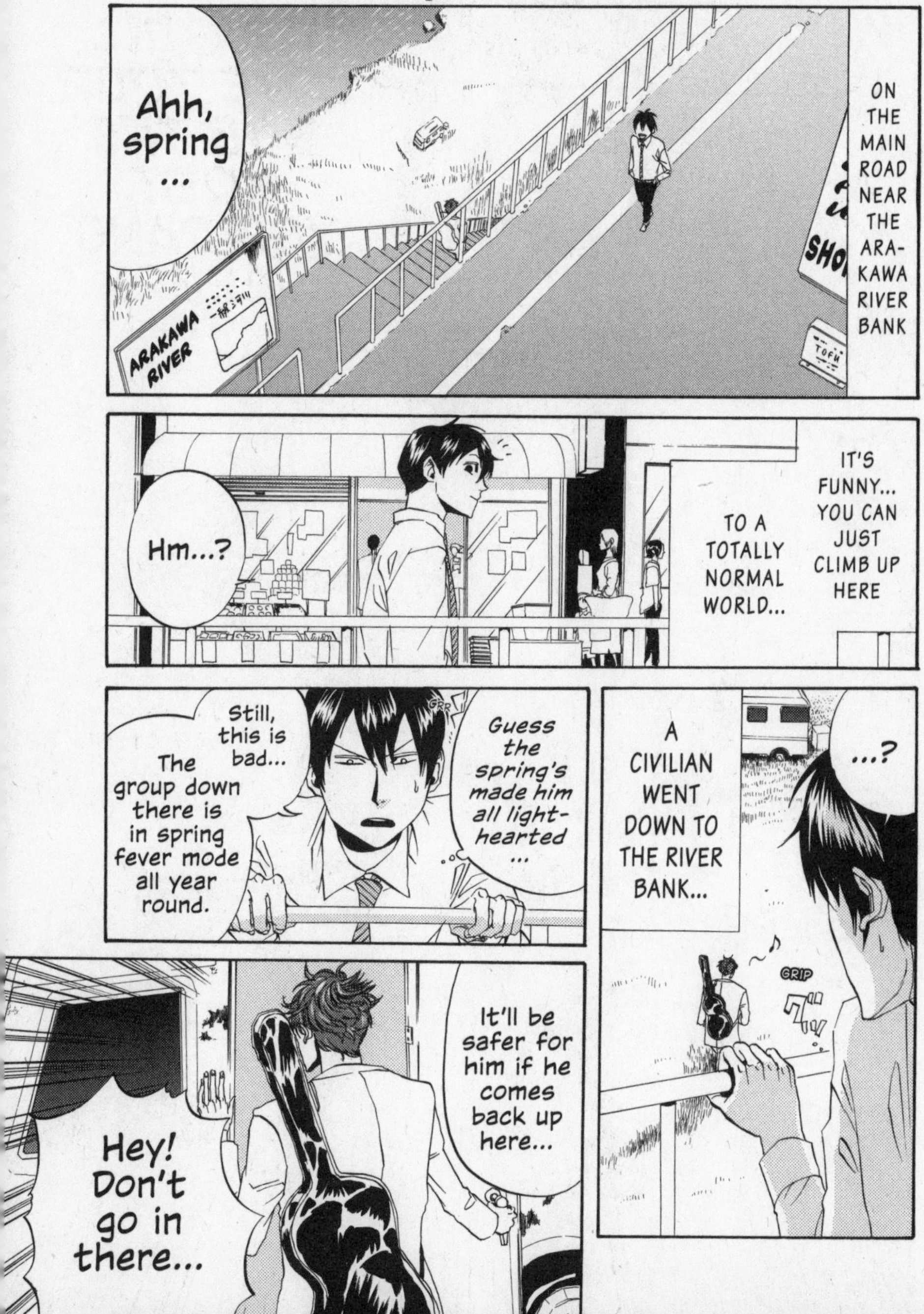
ON THE MAIN ROAD NEAR THE ARAKAWA RIVER BANK
SHO
TOFU
Ahh, spring ...
ARAKAWA RIVER
IT'S FUNNY... YOU CAN JUST CLIMB UP HERE
TO A TOTALLY NORMAL WORLD...
Hm...?
...?
A CIVILIAN WENT DOWN TO THE RIVER BANK...
GRIP
Guess the spring's made him all light-hearted ...
GRR
Still, this is bad...
The group down there is in spring fever mode all year round.
It'll be safer for him if he comes back up here...
Hey! Don't go in there...

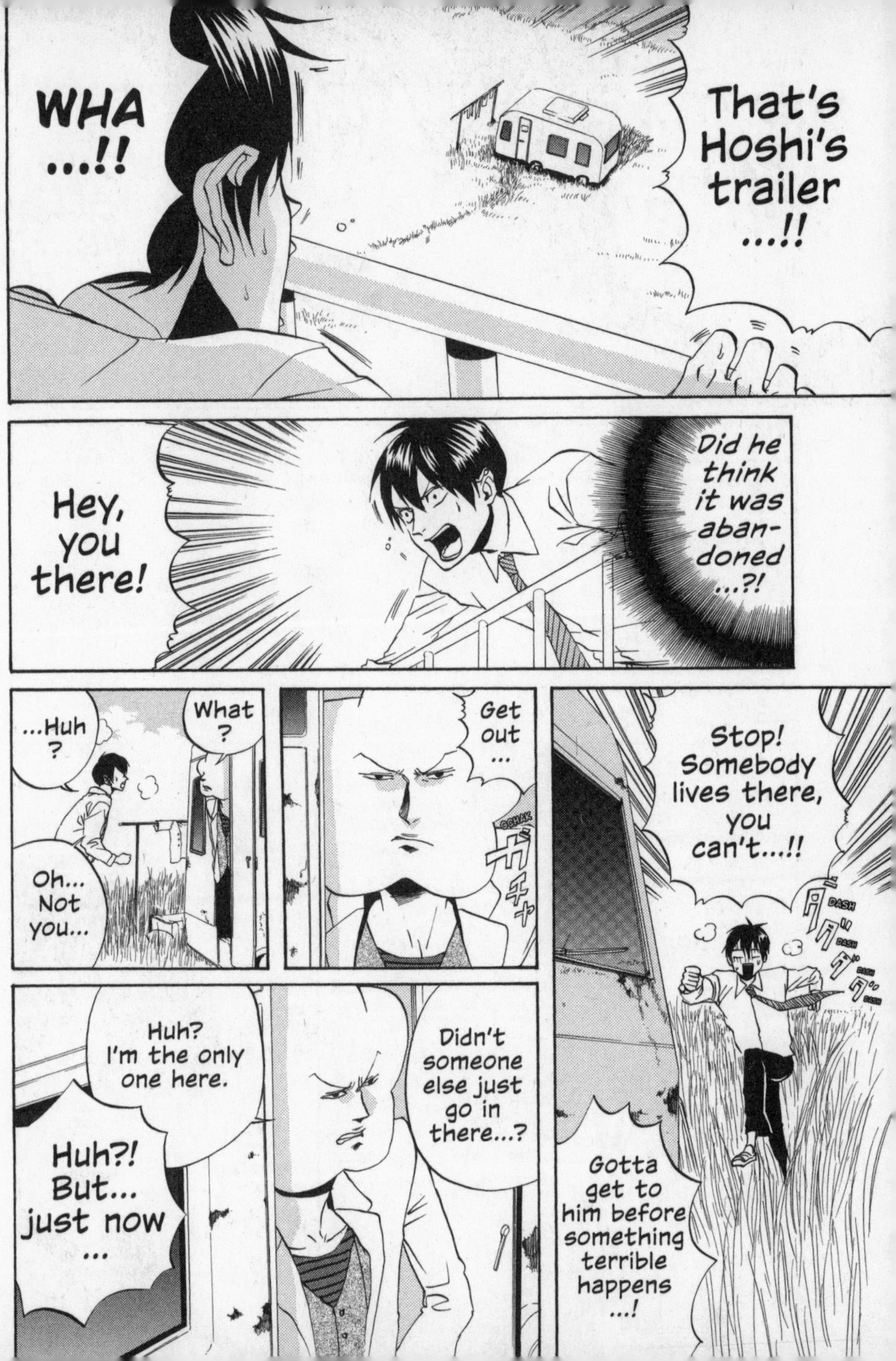
That's Hoshi's trailer ...!!
WHA ...!!
Did he think it was aban-doned ...?!
Hey, you there!
Stop! Somebody lives there, you can't...!!
DASH
DASH
DASH
DASH
Gotta get to him before something terrible happens ...!
Get out ...
GOHAK
What ?
...Huh ?
Oh... Not you...
Didn't someone else just go in there...?
Huh? I'm the only one here.
Huh?! But... just now ...

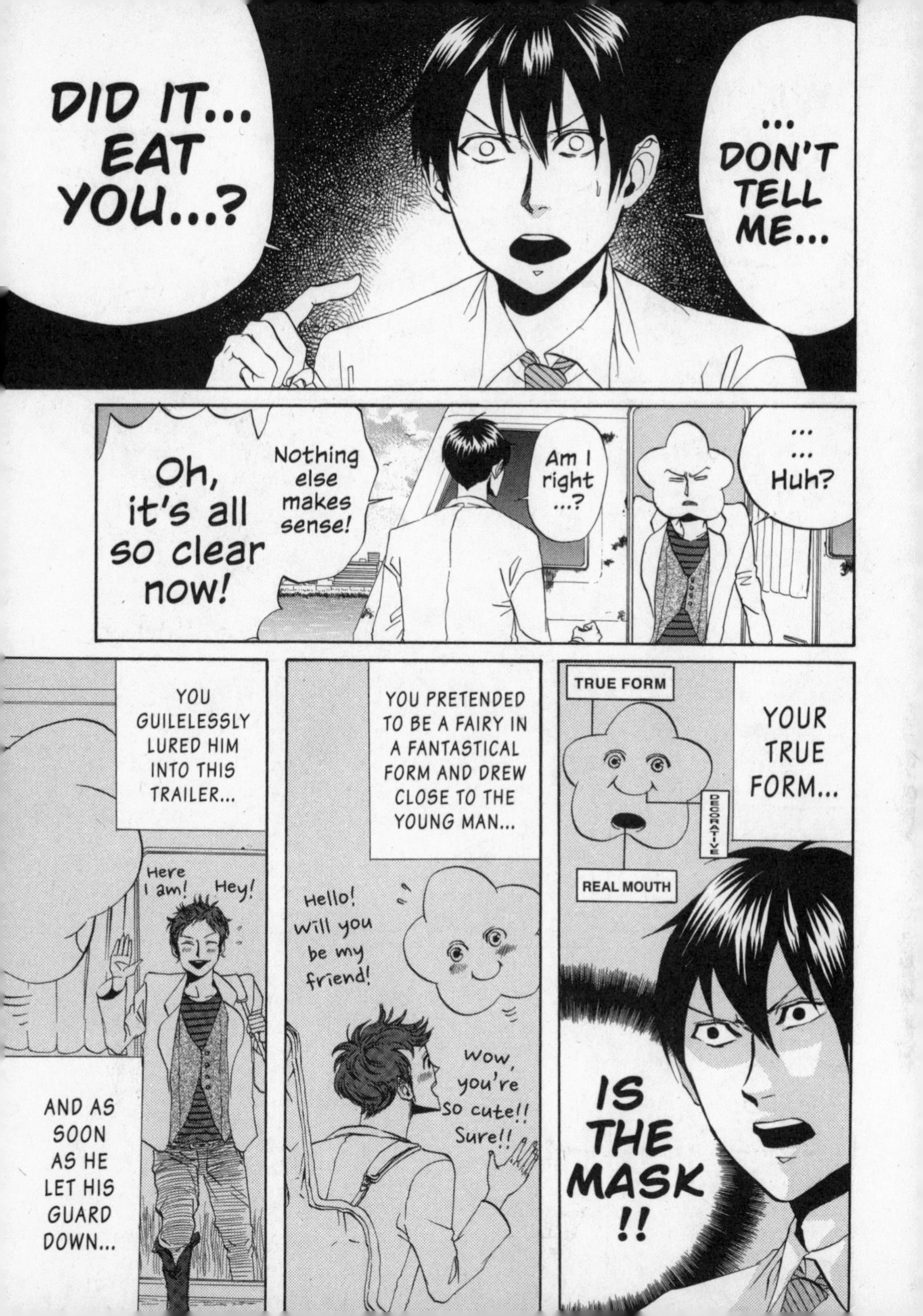

... DON'T TELL ME...
DID IT... EAT YOU...?
...
...
Huh?
Am I right ...?
Nothing else makes sense!
Oh, it's all so clear now!
YOUR TRUE FORM...
TRUE FORM
DECORATIVE
REAL MOUTH
IS THE MASK !!
YOU PRETENDED TO BE A FAIRY IN A FANTASTICAL FORM AND DREW CLOSE TO THE YOUNG MAN...
Hello! Will you be my friend!
Wow, you're so cute!! Sure!!
YOU GUILELESSLY LURED HIM INTO THIS TRAILER...
Hey!
Here I am!
AND AS SOON AS HE LET HIS GUARD DOWN...

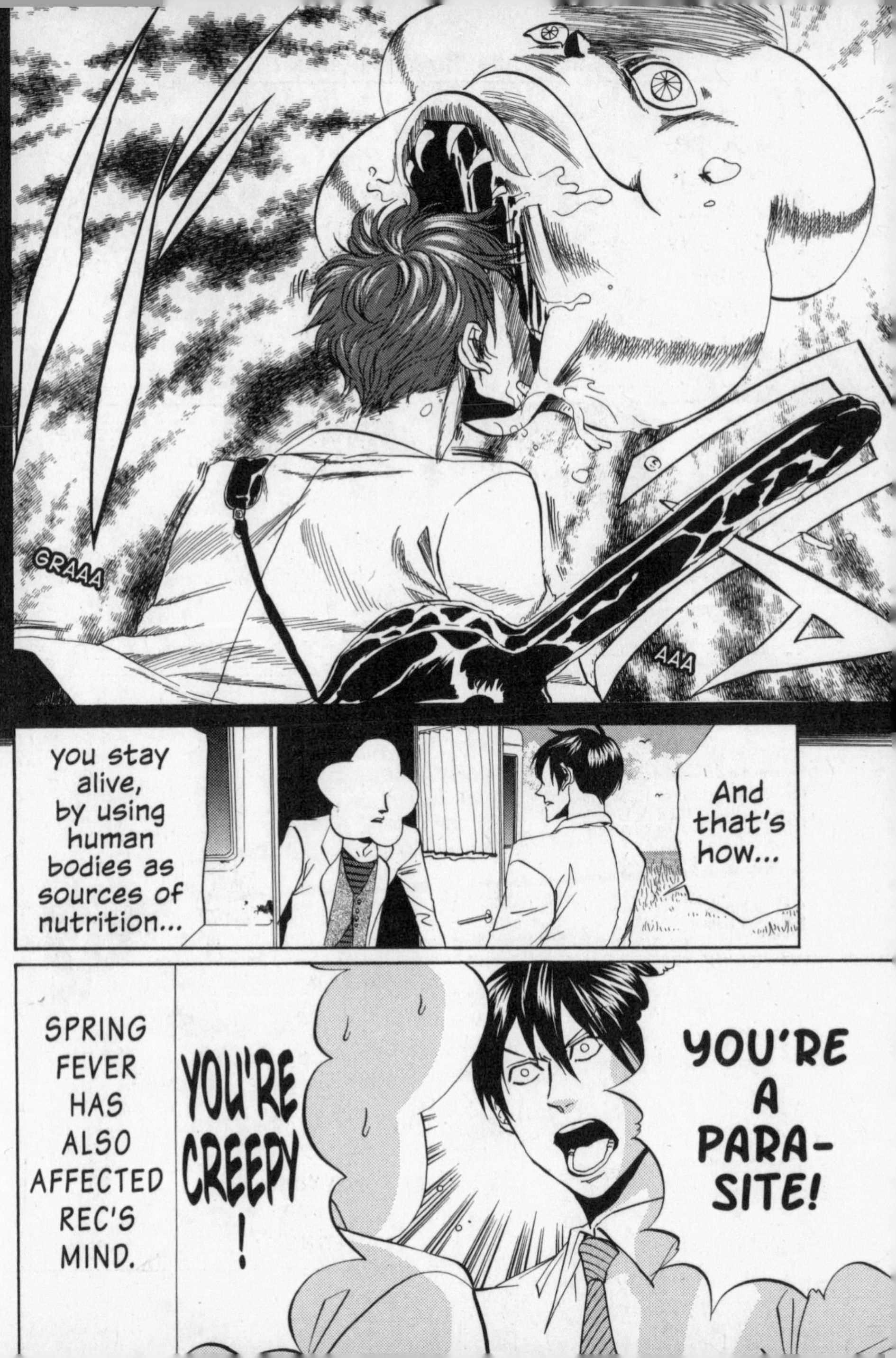
GRAAA
AAA
And that's how...
you stay alive, by using human bodies as sources of nutrition...
YOU'RE A PARA-SITE!
YOU'RE CREEPY!
SPRING FEVER HAS ALSO AFFECTED REC'S MIND.

Chapter 84: First-Magnitude Star

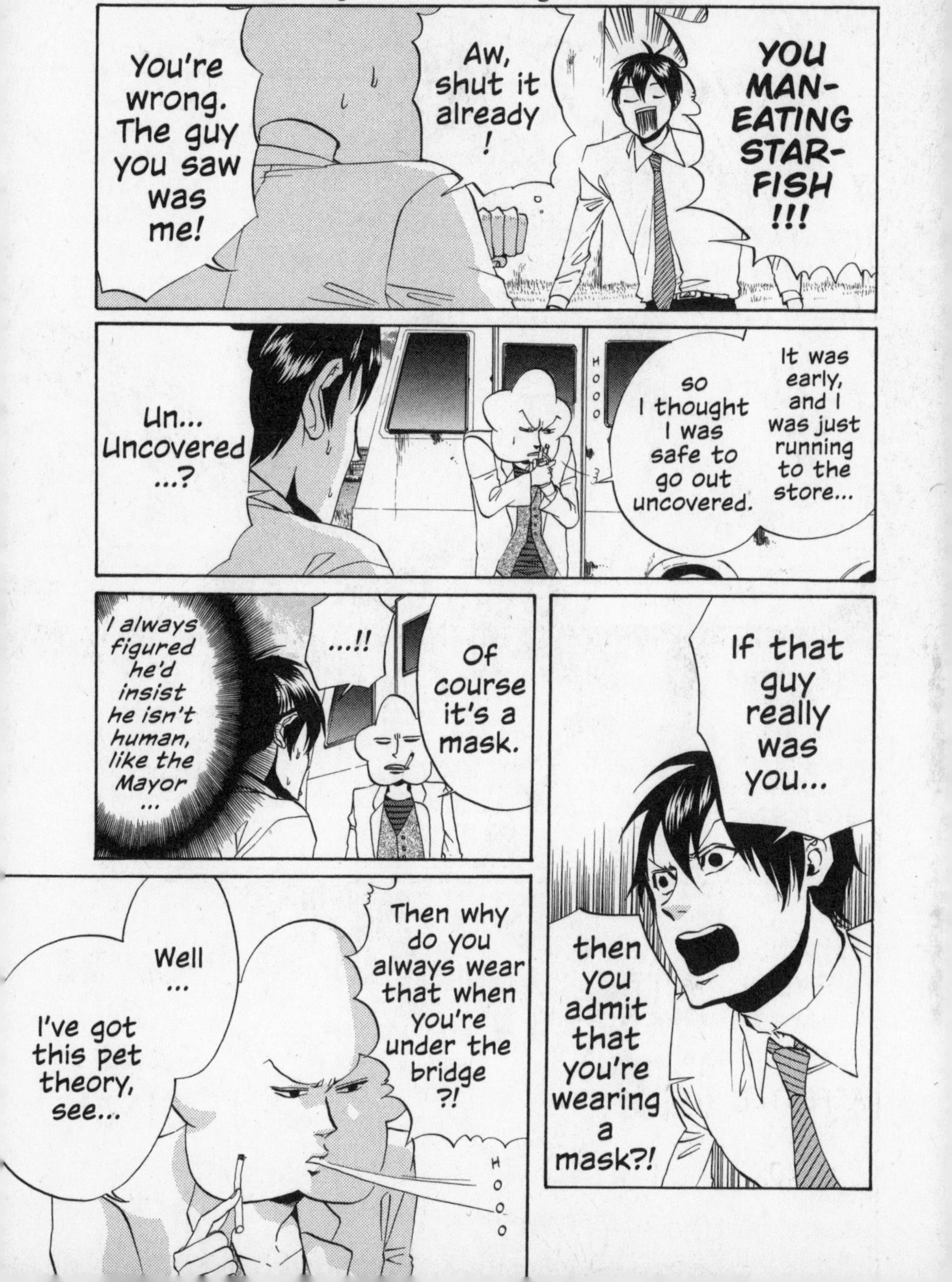
YOU MAN-EATING STAR-FISH!!!
Aw, shut it already!
You're wrong. The guy you saw was me!
It was early, and I was just running to the store...
so I thought I was safe to go out uncovered.
HOOO
Un... Uncovered...?
If that guy really was you...
then you admit that you're wearing a mask?!
Of course it's a mask.
...!!
I always figured he'd insist he isn't human, like the Mayor...
Then why do you always wear that when you're under the bridge?!
Well...
I've got this pet theory, see...
HOOOO

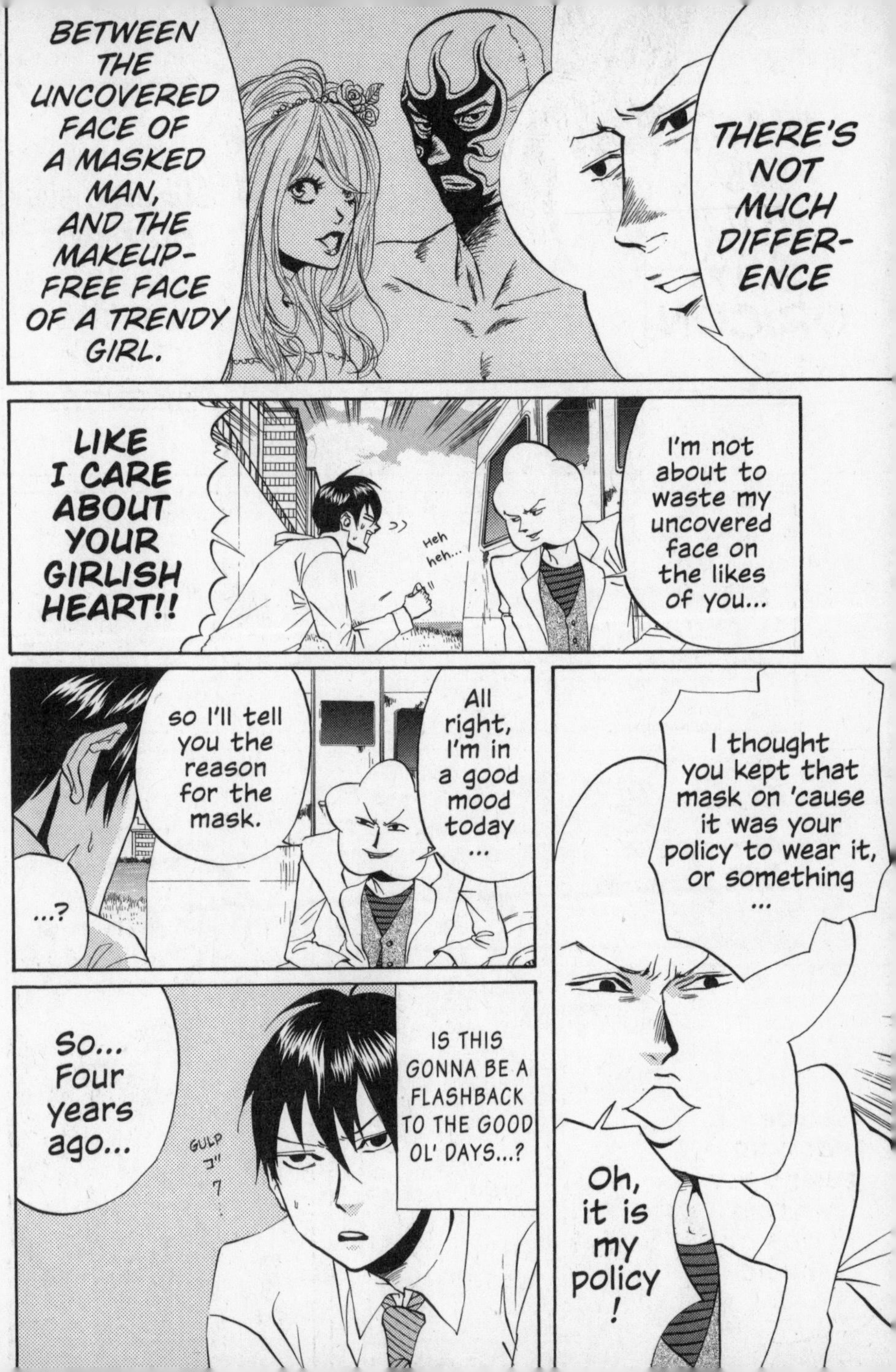
THERE'S NOT MUCH DIFFER-ENCE
BETWEEN THE UNCOVERED FACE OF A MASKED MAN, AND THE MAKEUP-FREE FACE OF A TRENDY GIRL.
I'm not about to waste my uncovered face on the likes of you...
Heh heh...
LIKE I CARE ABOUT YOUR GIRLISH HEART!!
I thought you kept that mask on 'cause it was your policy to wear it, or something ...
Oh, it is my policy!
All right, I'm in a good mood today ...
so I'll tell you the reason for the mask.
...?
IS THIS GONNA BE A FLASHBACK TO THE GOOD OL' DAYS...?
GULP
So... Four years ago...

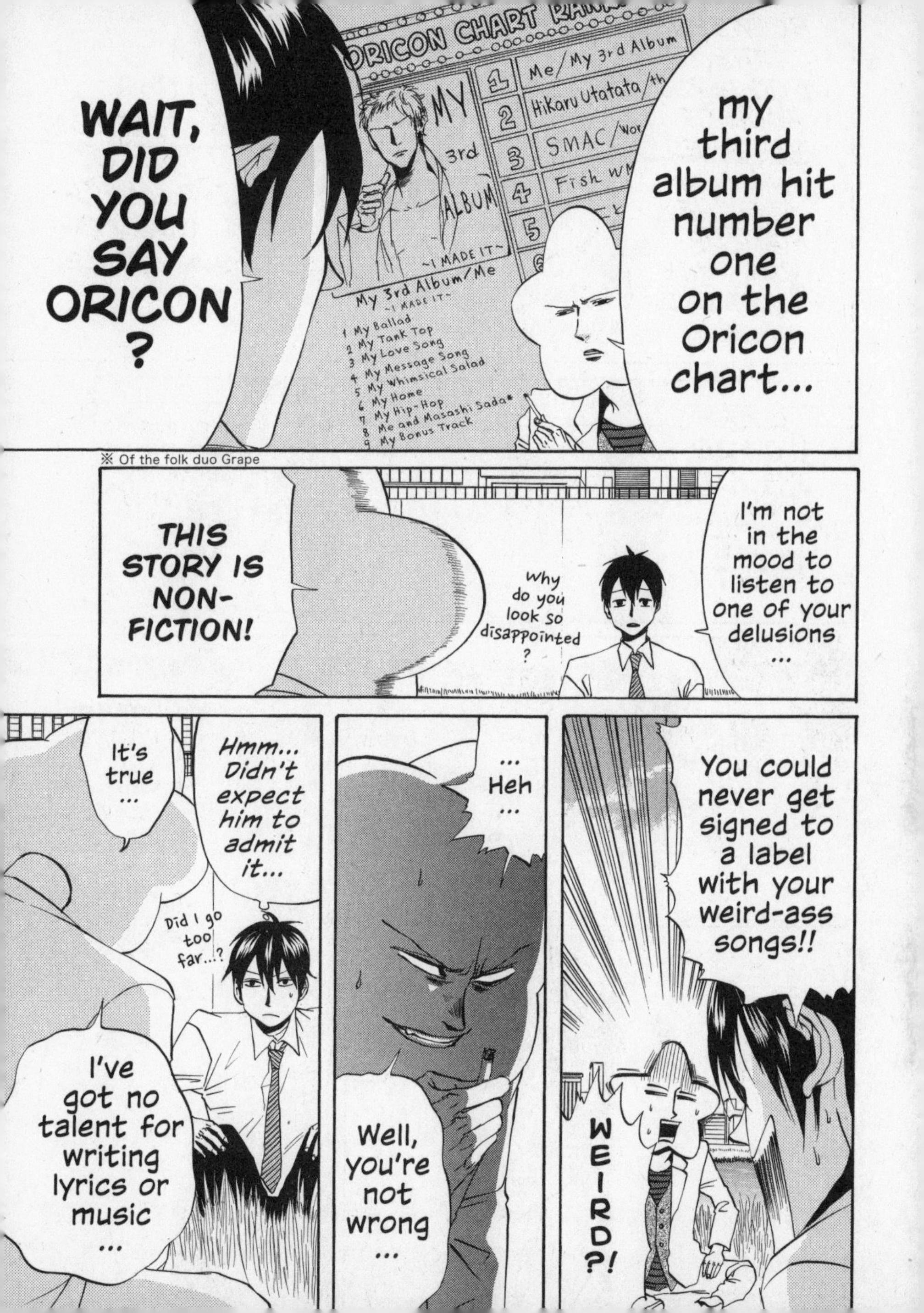
ORICON CHART
Me/My 3rd Album
Hikaru Utatata/th
SMAC/Wor
Fish WM
MY 3rd ALBUM ~I MADE IT~
My 3rd Album/Me
~I MADE IT~
1 My Ballad
2 My Tank Top
3 My Love Song
4 My Message Song
5 My Whimsical Salad
6 My Home
7 My Hip-Hop
8 Me and Masashi Sada※
9 My Bonus Track
my third album hit number one on the Oricon chart...
WAIT, DID YOU SAY ORICON?
I'm not in the mood to listen to one of your delusions ...
Why do you look so disappointed ?
THIS STORY IS NON-FICTION!
You could never get signed to a label with your weird-ass songs!!
WEIRD?!
... Heh ...
Well, you're not wrong ...
Hmm... Didn't expect him to admit it...
It's true ...
Did I go too far...?
I've got no talent for writing lyrics or music ...
※ Of the folk duo Grape

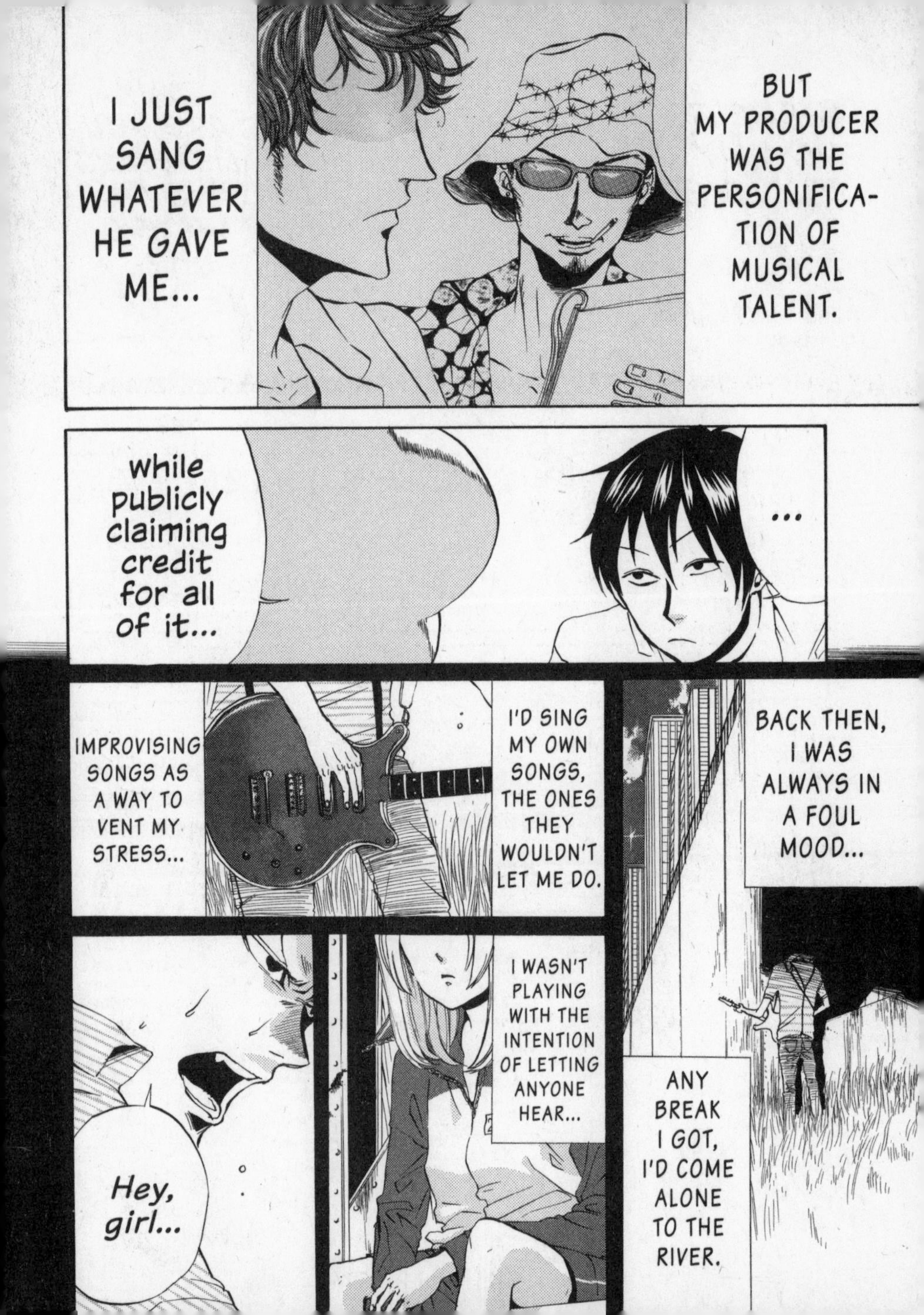
BUT MY PRODUCER WAS THE PERSONIFICA-TION OF MUSICAL TALENT.
I JUST SANG WHATEVER HE GAVE ME...
...
while publicly claiming credit for all of it...
BACK THEN, I WAS ALWAYS IN A FOUL MOOD...
ANY BREAK I GOT, I'D COME ALONE TO THE RIVER.
I'D SING MY OWN SONGS, THE ONES THEY WOULDN'T LET ME DO.
IMPROVISING SONGS AS A WAY TO VENT MY STRESS...
I WASN'T PLAYING WITH THE INTENTION OF LETTING ANYONE HEAR...
Hey, girl...

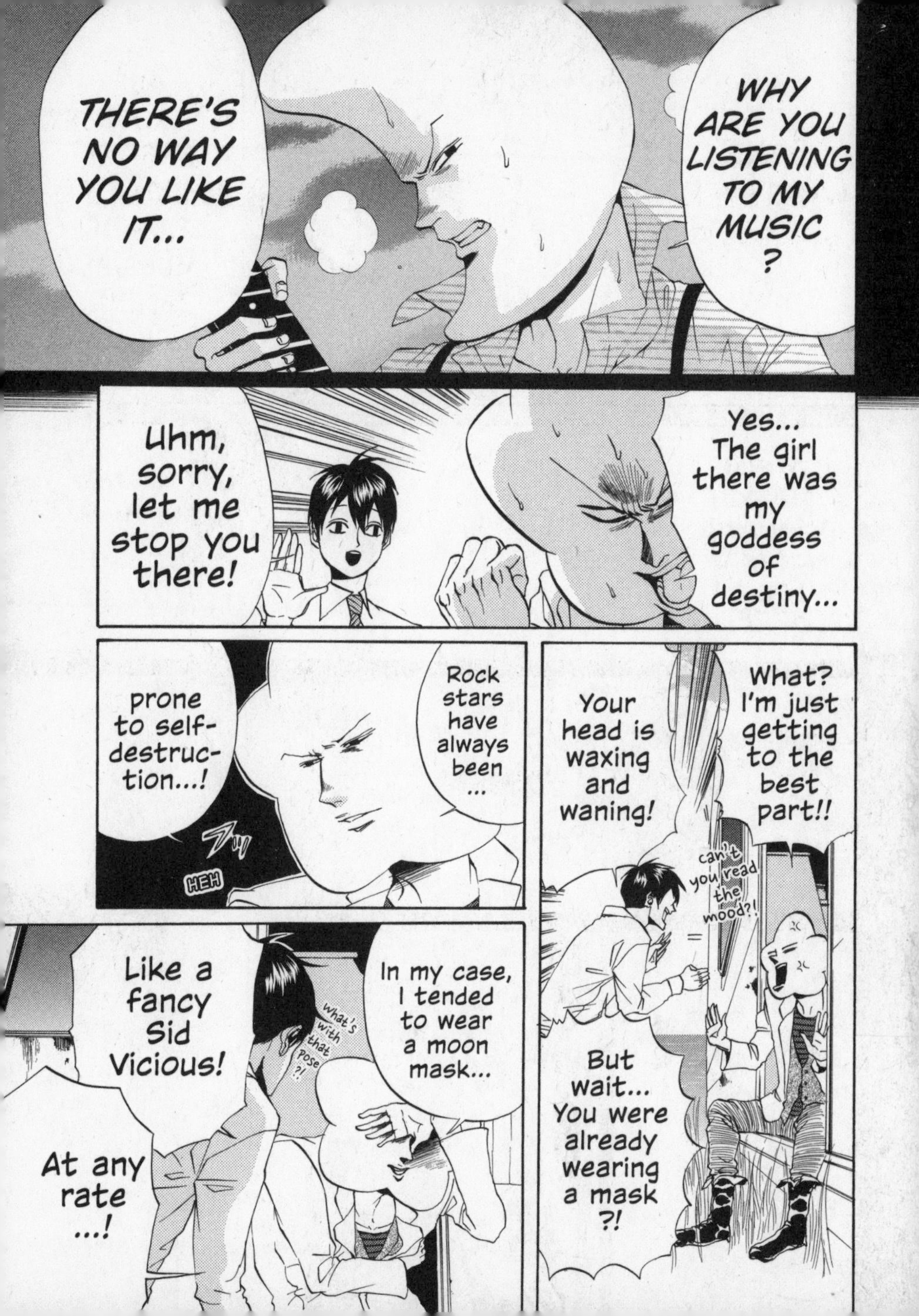
WHY ARE YOU LISTENING TO MY MUSIC ?
THERE'S NO WAY YOU LIKE IT...
Yes... The girl there was my goddess of destiny...
Uhm, sorry, let me stop you there!
What? I'm just getting to the best part!!
Your head is waxing and waning!
can't you read the mood?!
But wait... You were already wearing a mask ?!
Rock stars have always been ...
prone to self-destruction...!
HEH
In my case, I tended to wear a moon mask...
what's with that pose ?!
Like a fancy Sid Vicious!
At any rate ...!

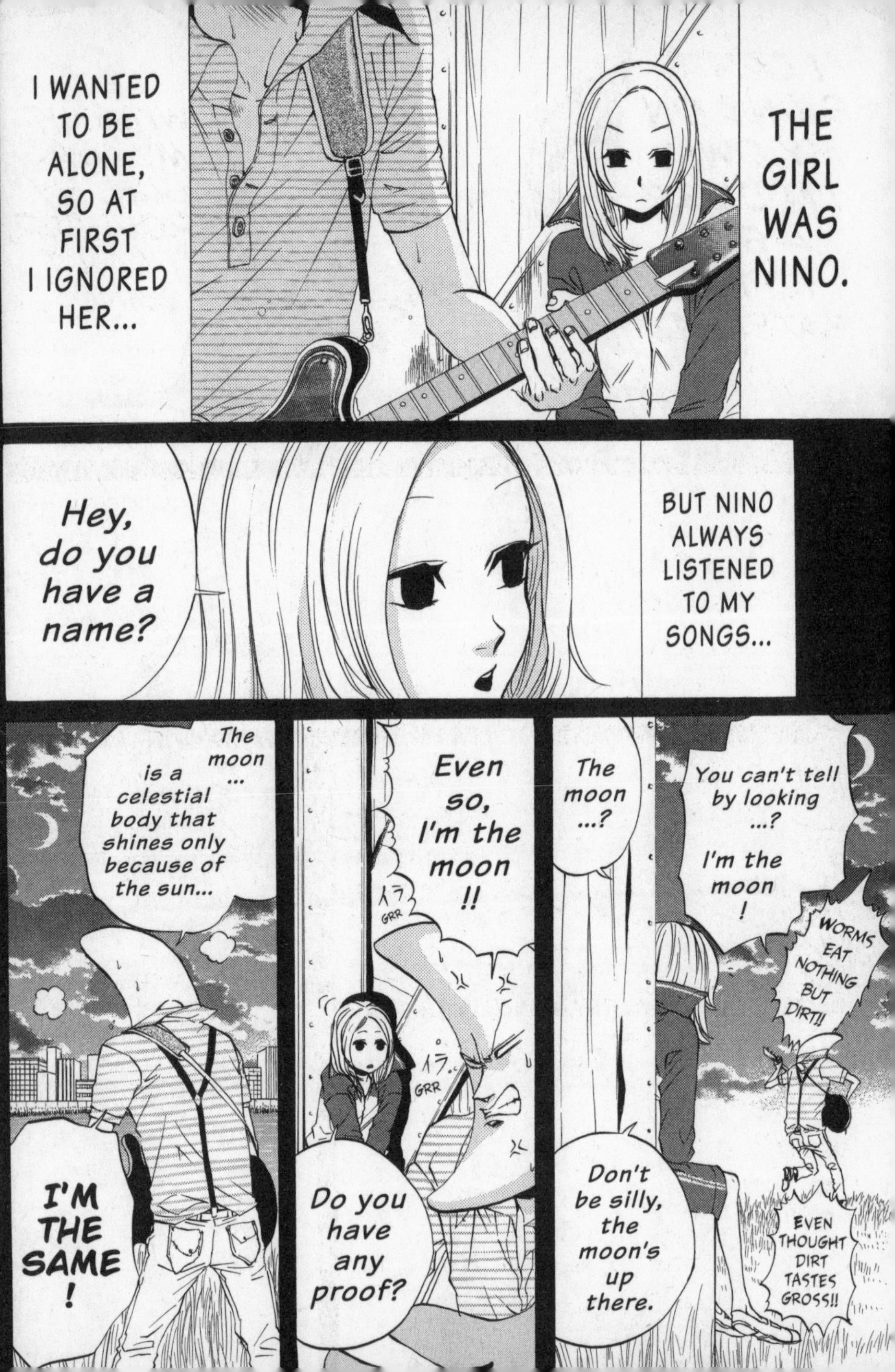
THE GIRL WAS NINO.
I WANTED TO BE ALONE, SO AT FIRST I IGNORED HER...
BUT NINO ALWAYS LISTENED TO MY SONGS...
Hey, do you have a name?
You can't tell by looking ...? I'm the moon !
WORMS EAT NOTHING BUT DIRT!!
EVEN THOUGHT DIRT TASTES GROSS!!
The moon ...?
Don't be silly, the moon's up there.
Even so, I'm the moon !!
イラ GRR
イラ GRR
Do you have any proof?
The moon ... is a celestial body that shines only because of the sun...
I'M THE SAME !

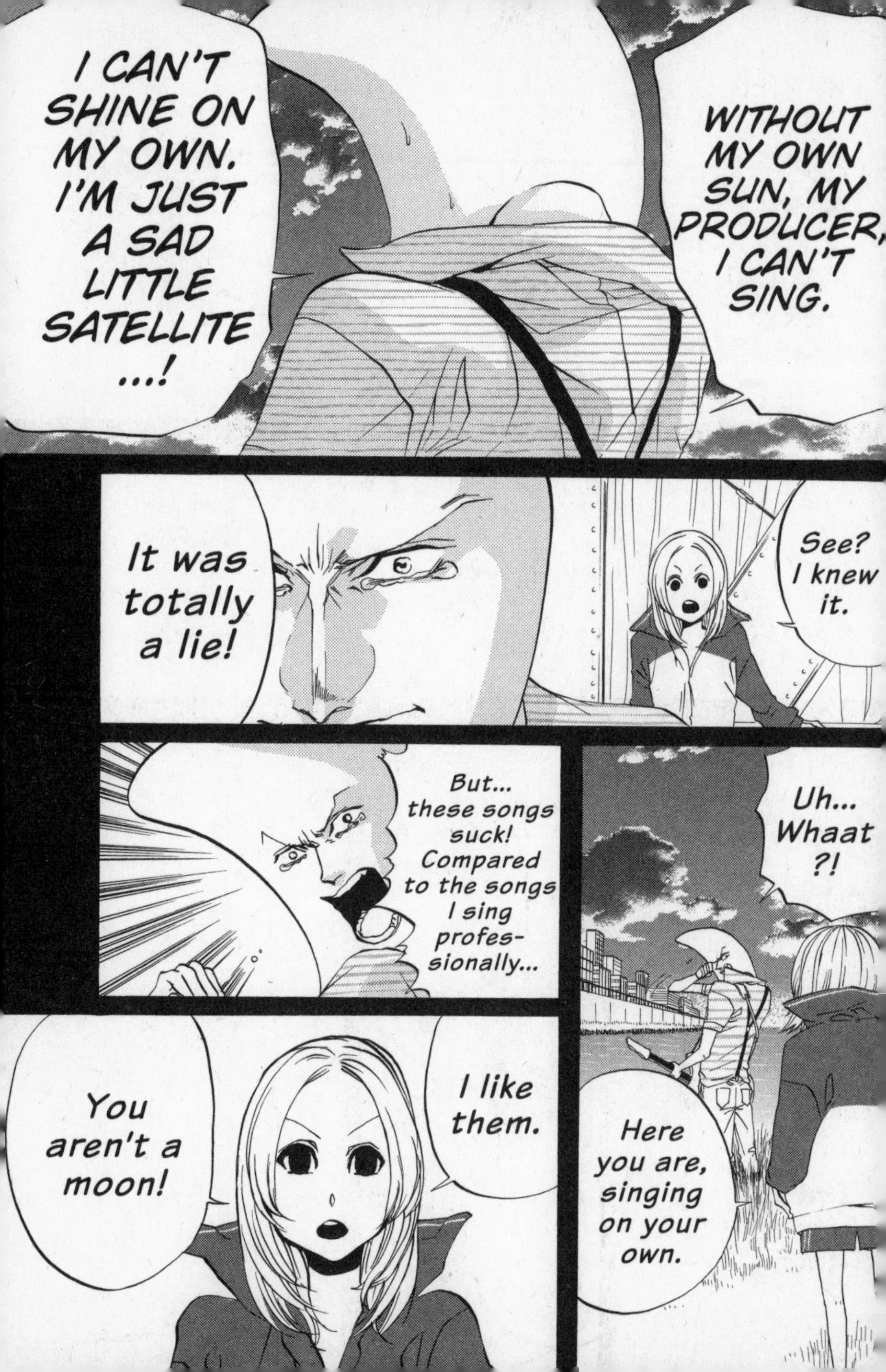
WITHOUT MY OWN SUN, MY PRODUCER, I CAN'T SING.
I CAN'T SHINE ON MY OWN. I'M JUST A SAD LITTLE SATELLITE ...!
See? I knew it.
It was totally a lie!
Uh... Whaat ?!
Here you are, singing on your own.
But... these songs suck! Compared to the songs I sing profes-sionally...
I like them.
You aren't a moon!

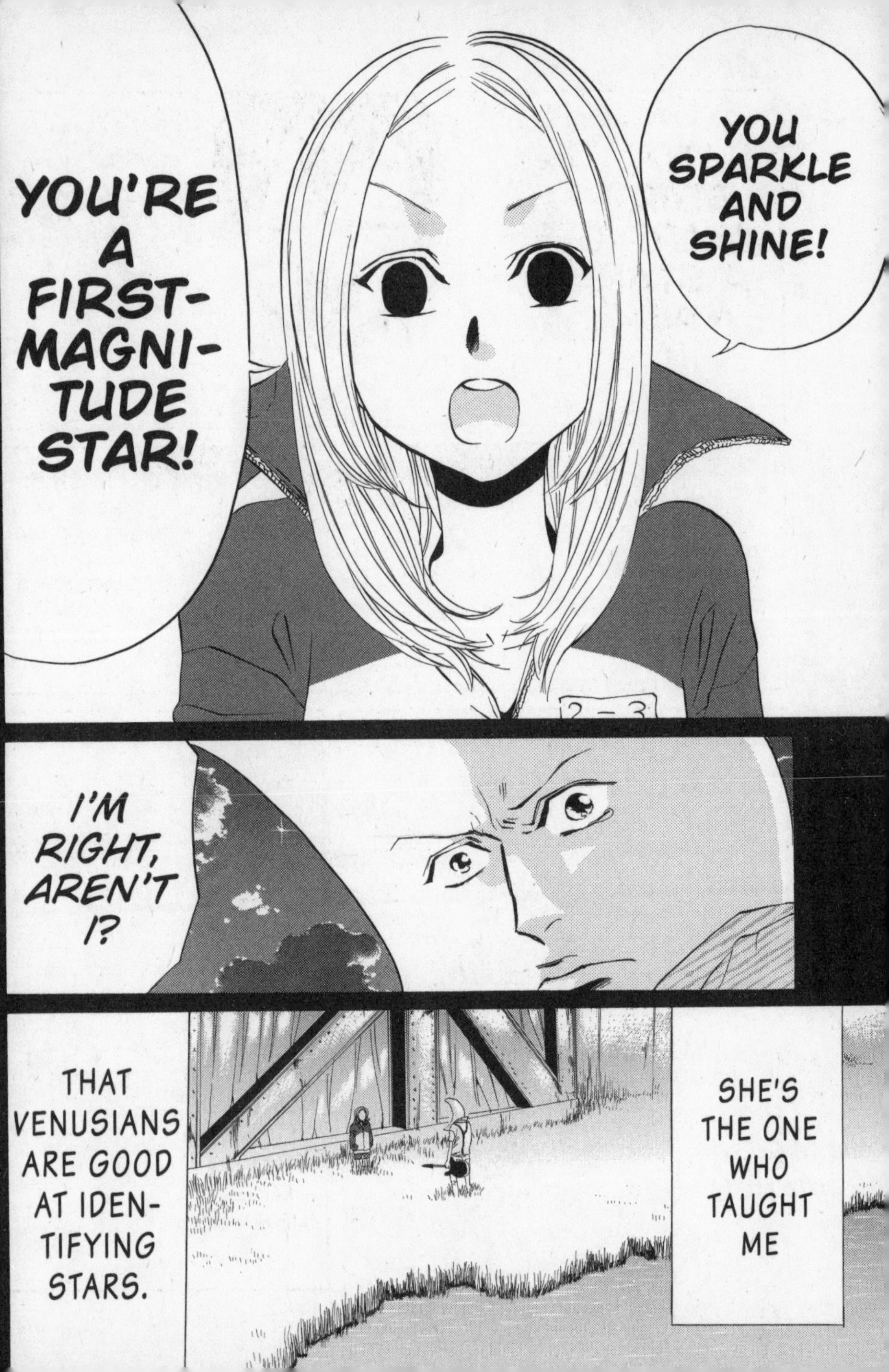
YOU SPARKLE AND SHINE!
YOU'RE A FIRST-MAGNITUDE STAR!
I'M RIGHT, AREN'T I?
SHE'S THE ONE WHO TAUGHT ME
THAT VENUSIANS ARE GOOD AT IDENTIFYING STARS.

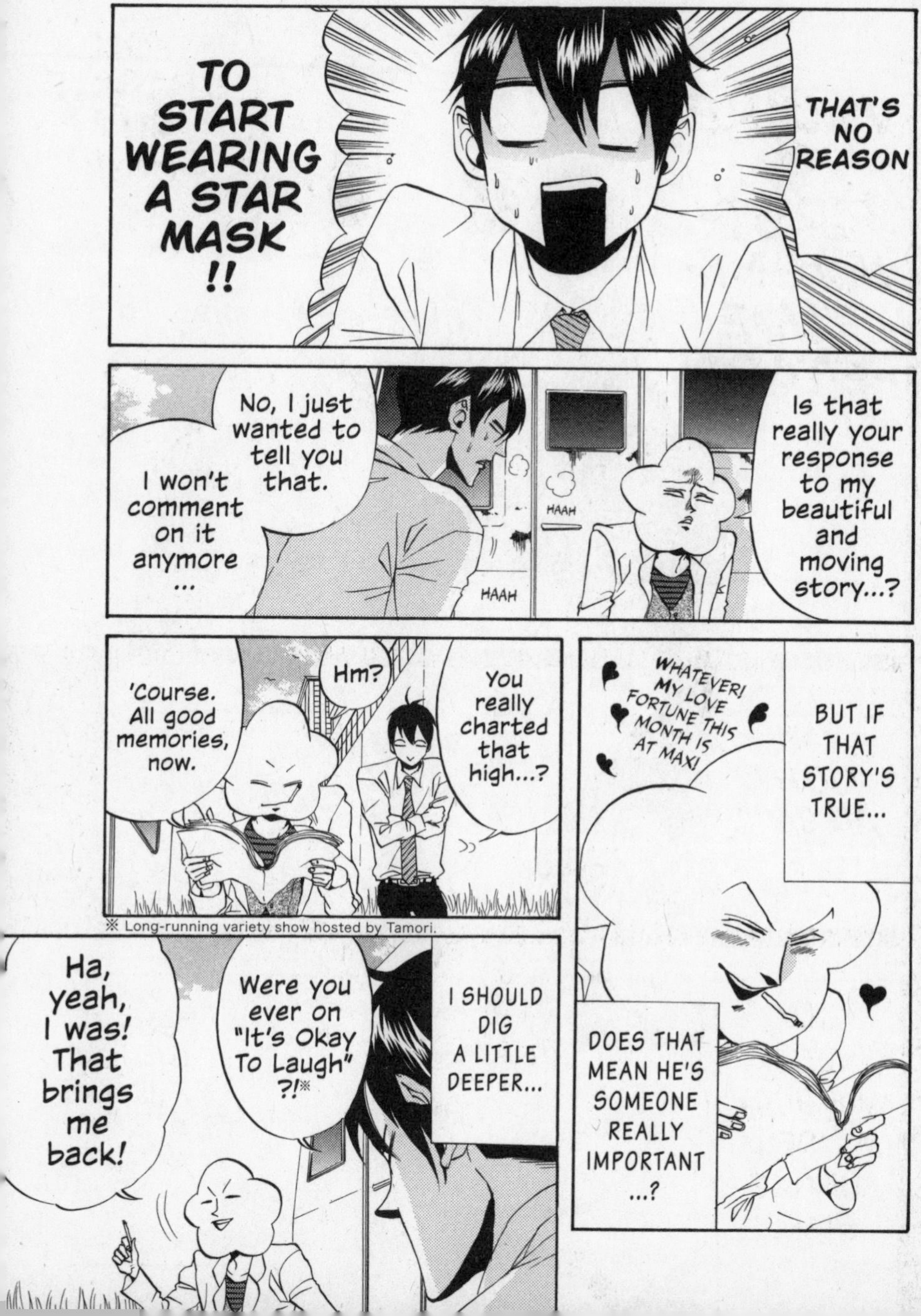

THAT'S NO REASON
TO START WEARING A STAR MASK !!
Is that really your response to my beautiful and moving story...?
HAAH
No, I just wanted to tell you that.
HAAH
I won't comment on it anymore ...
WHATEVER! MY LOVE FORTUNE THIS MONTH IS AT MAX!
BUT IF THAT STORY'S TRUE...
DOES THAT MEAN HE'S SOMEONE REALLY IMPORTANT ...?
You really charted that high...?
Hm?
'Course. All good memories, now.
I SHOULD DIG A LITTLE DEEPER...
Were you ever on "It's Okay To Laugh" ?!※
Ha, yeah, I was! That brings me back!

※ Long-running variety show hosted by Tamori.

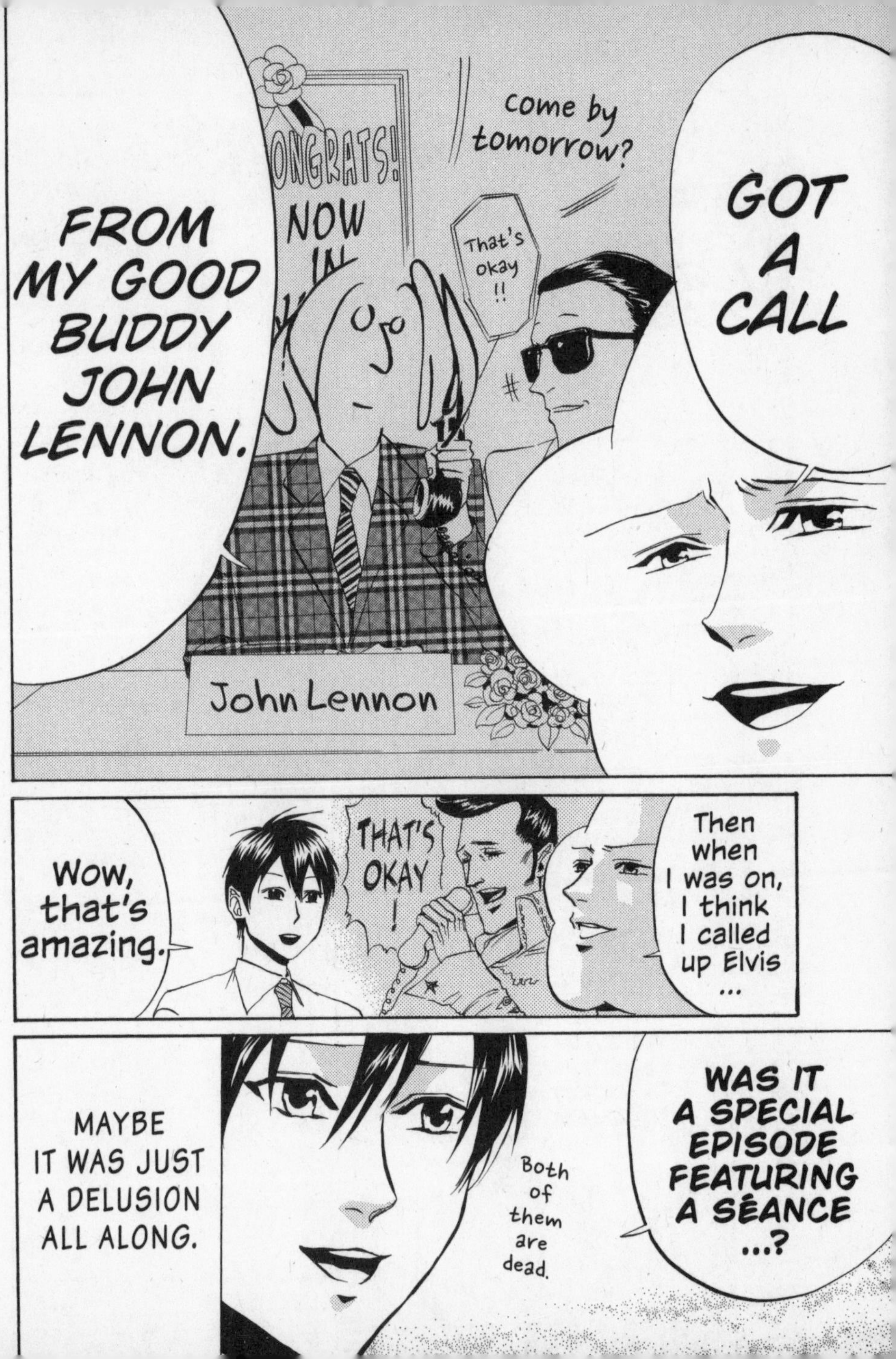
GOT A CALL
come by tomorrow?
That's okay !!
ONGRATS! NOW IN
FROM MY GOOD BUDDY JOHN LENNON.
John Lennon
Then when I was on, I think I called up Elvis ...
THAT'S OKAY !
Wow, that's amazing.
WAS IT A SPECIAL EPISODE FEATURING A SÉANCE ...?
Both of them are dead.
MAYBE IT WAS JUST A DELUSION ALL ALONG.

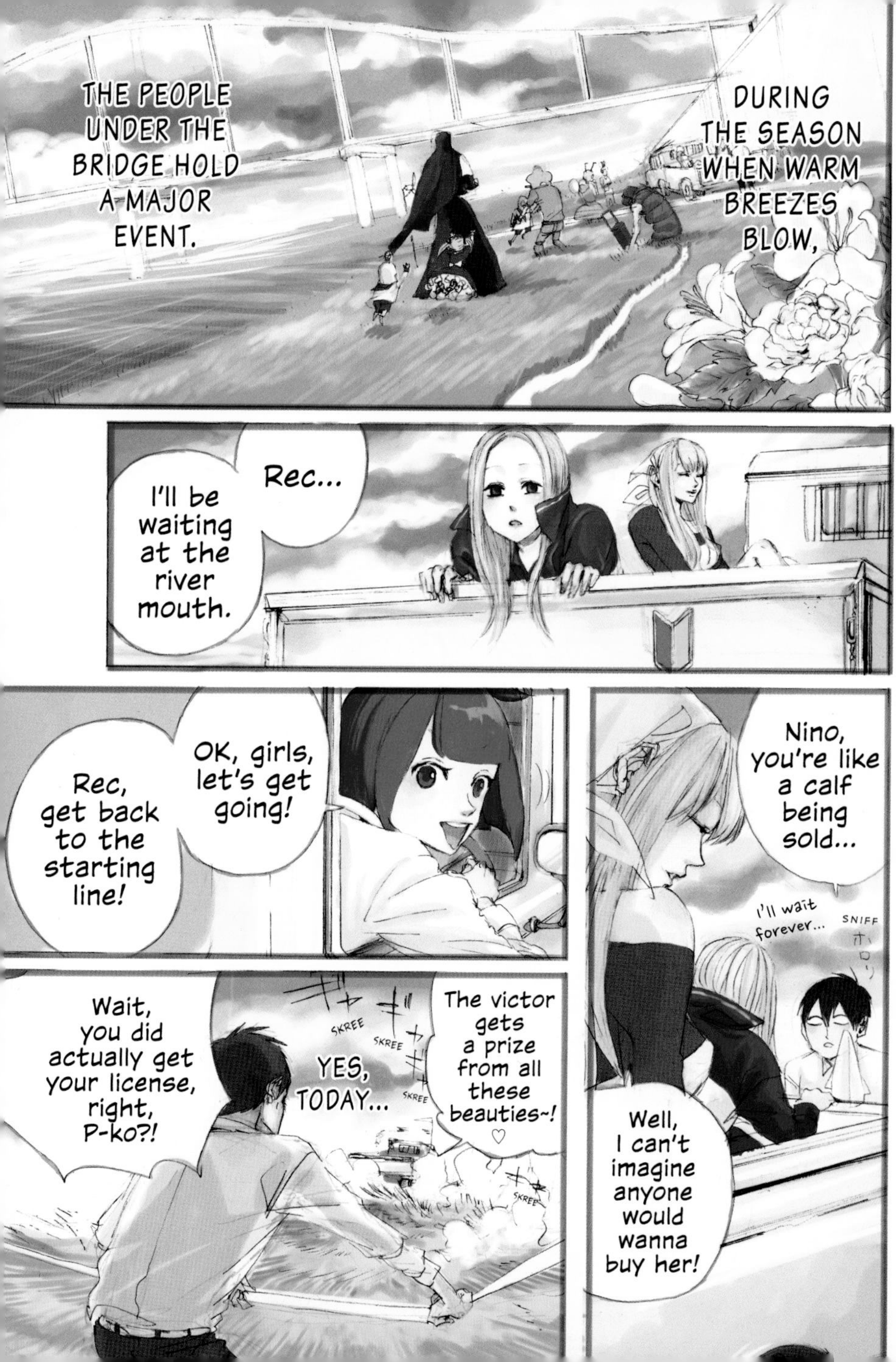
DURING THE SEASON WHEN WARM BREEZES BLOW,
THE PEOPLE UNDER THE BRIDGE HOLD A MAJOR EVENT.
Rec...
I'll be waiting at the river mouth.
Nino, you're like a calf being sold...
I'll wait forever...
SNIFF
Well, I can't imagine anyone would wanna buy her!
OK, girls, let's get going!
Rec, get back to the starting line!
The victor gets a prize from all these beauties~! ♡
SKREE
SKREE
SKREE
SKREE
YES, TODAY...
Wait, you did actually get your license, right, P-ko?!

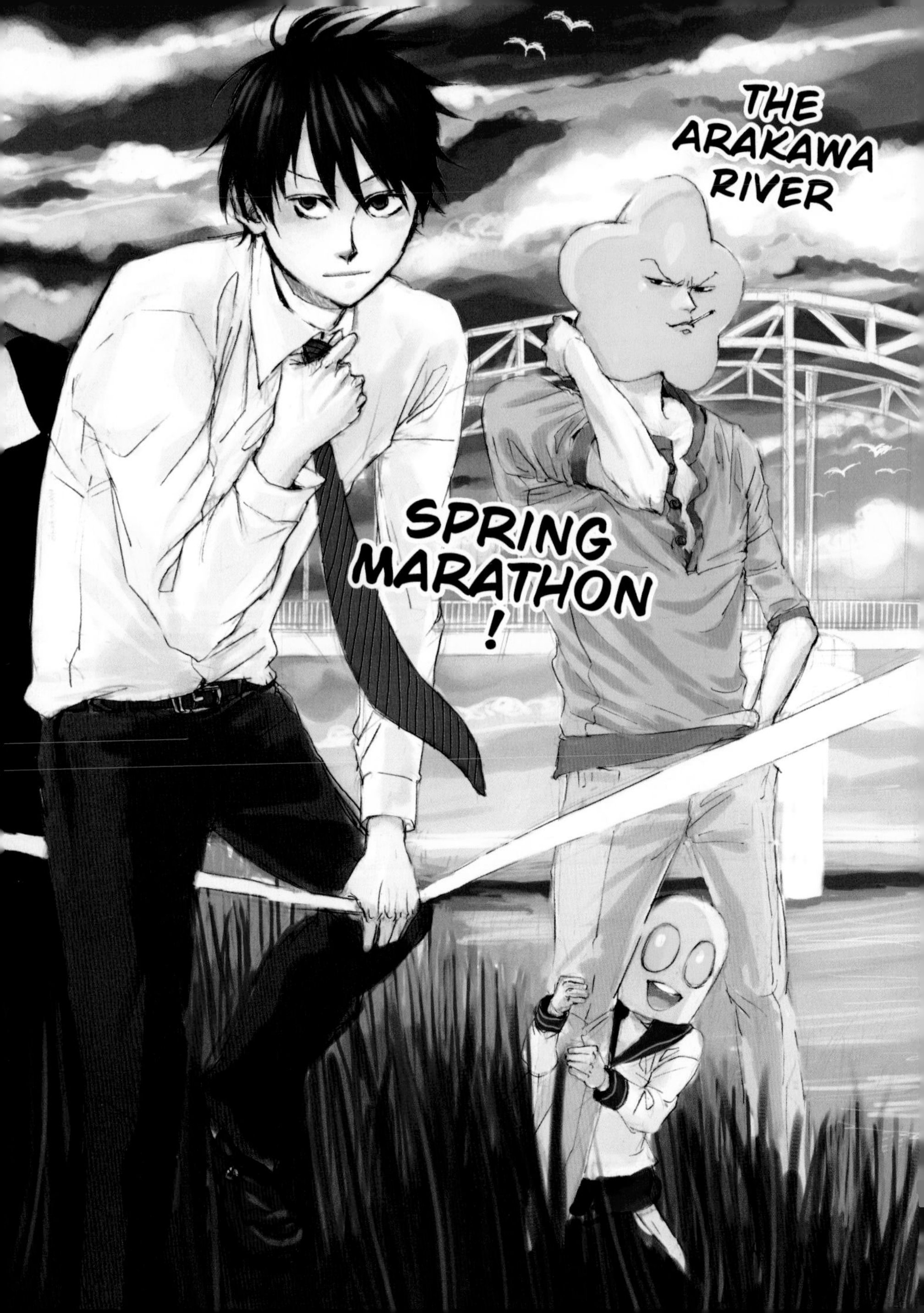
THE ARAKAWA RIVER
SPRING MARATHON!

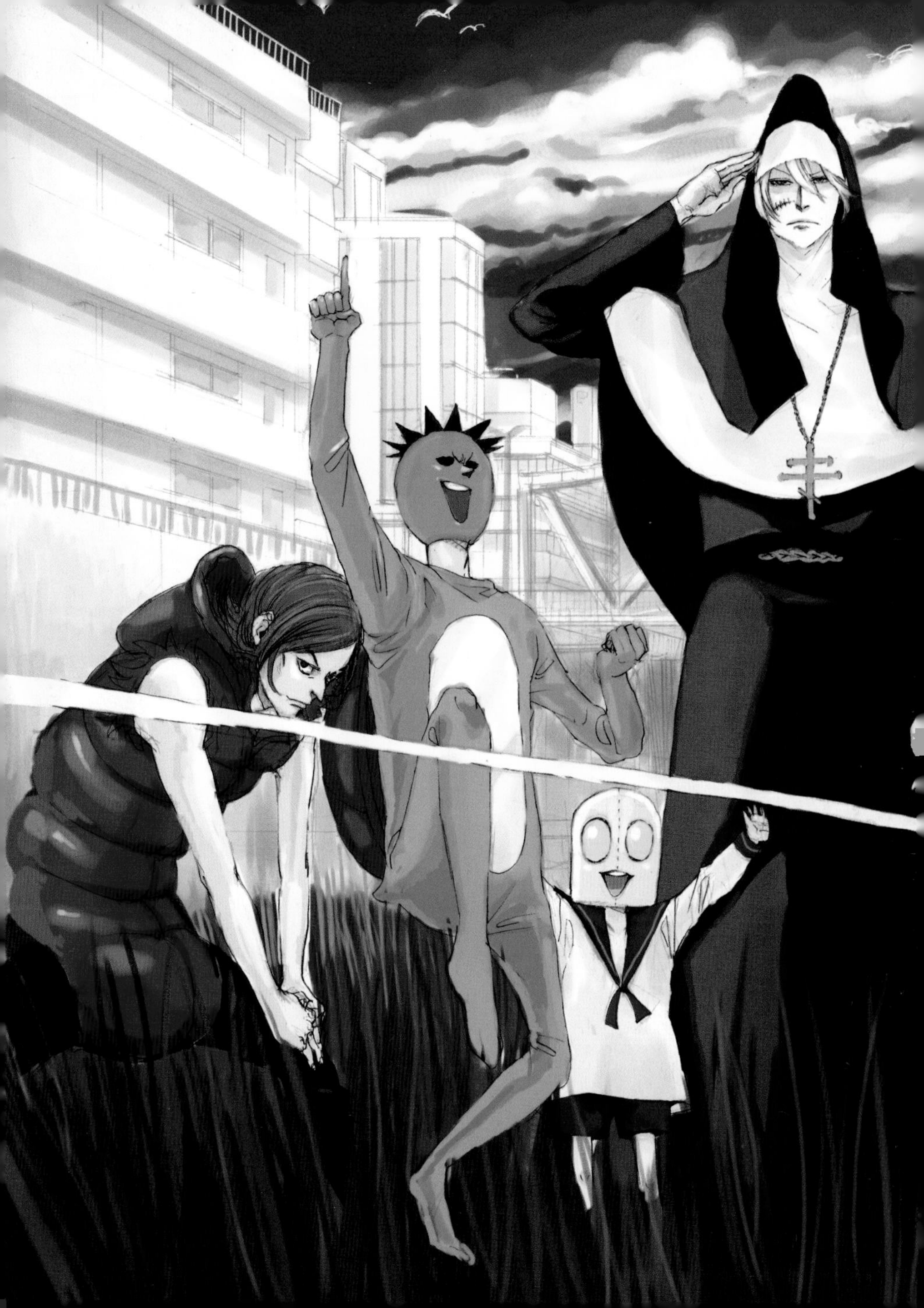

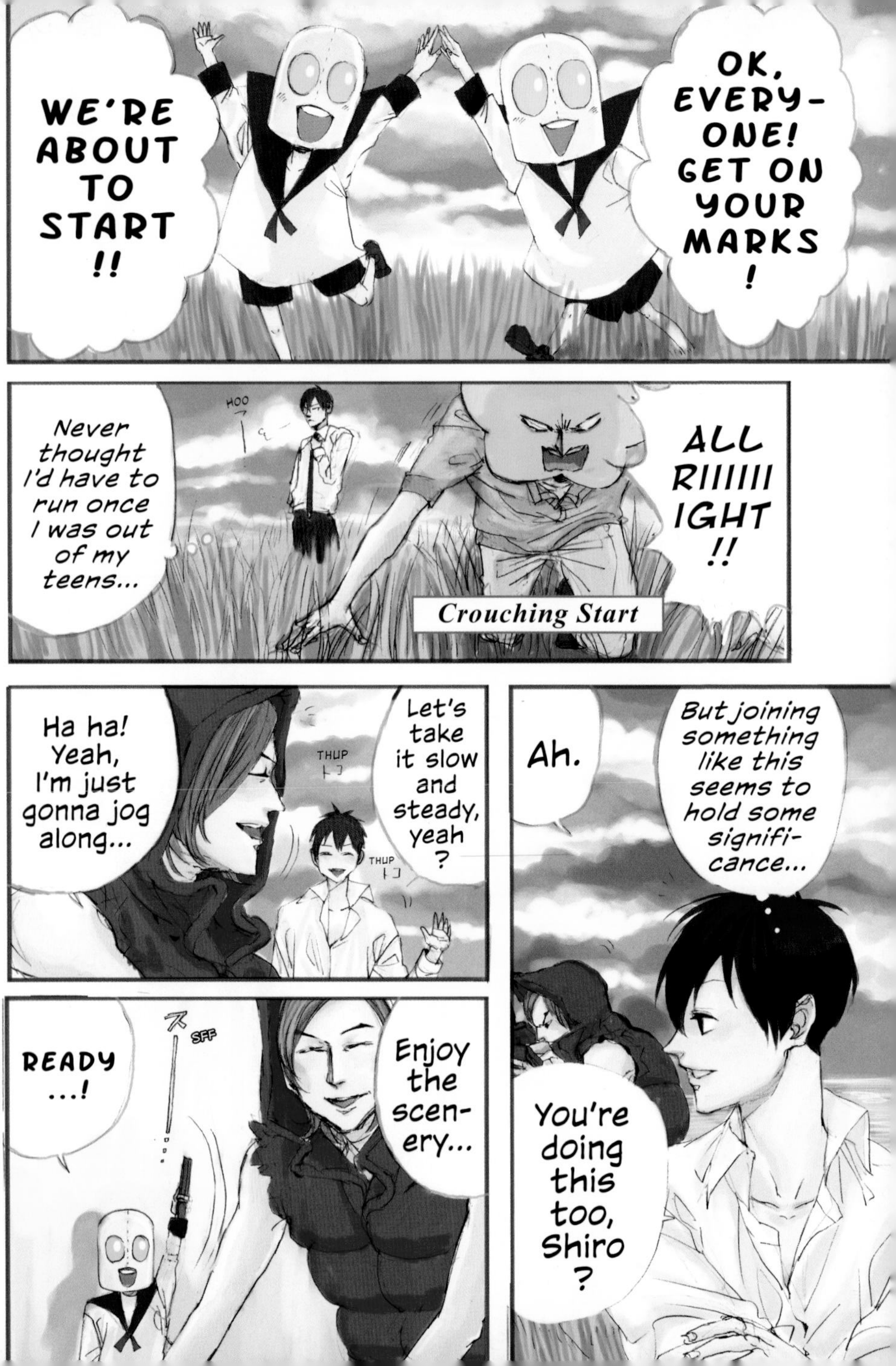
OK, EVERYONE! GET ON YOUR MARKS!
WE'RE ABOUT TO START!!
ALL RIIIIII IGHT!!
Crouching Start
HOO
Never thought I'd have to run once I was out of my teens...
Ah.
But joining something like this seems to hold some significance...
You're doing this too, Shiro?
Let's take it slow and steady, yeah?
THUP
THUP
Ha ha! Yeah, I'm just gonna jog along...
Enjoy the scenery...
SFF
READY...!

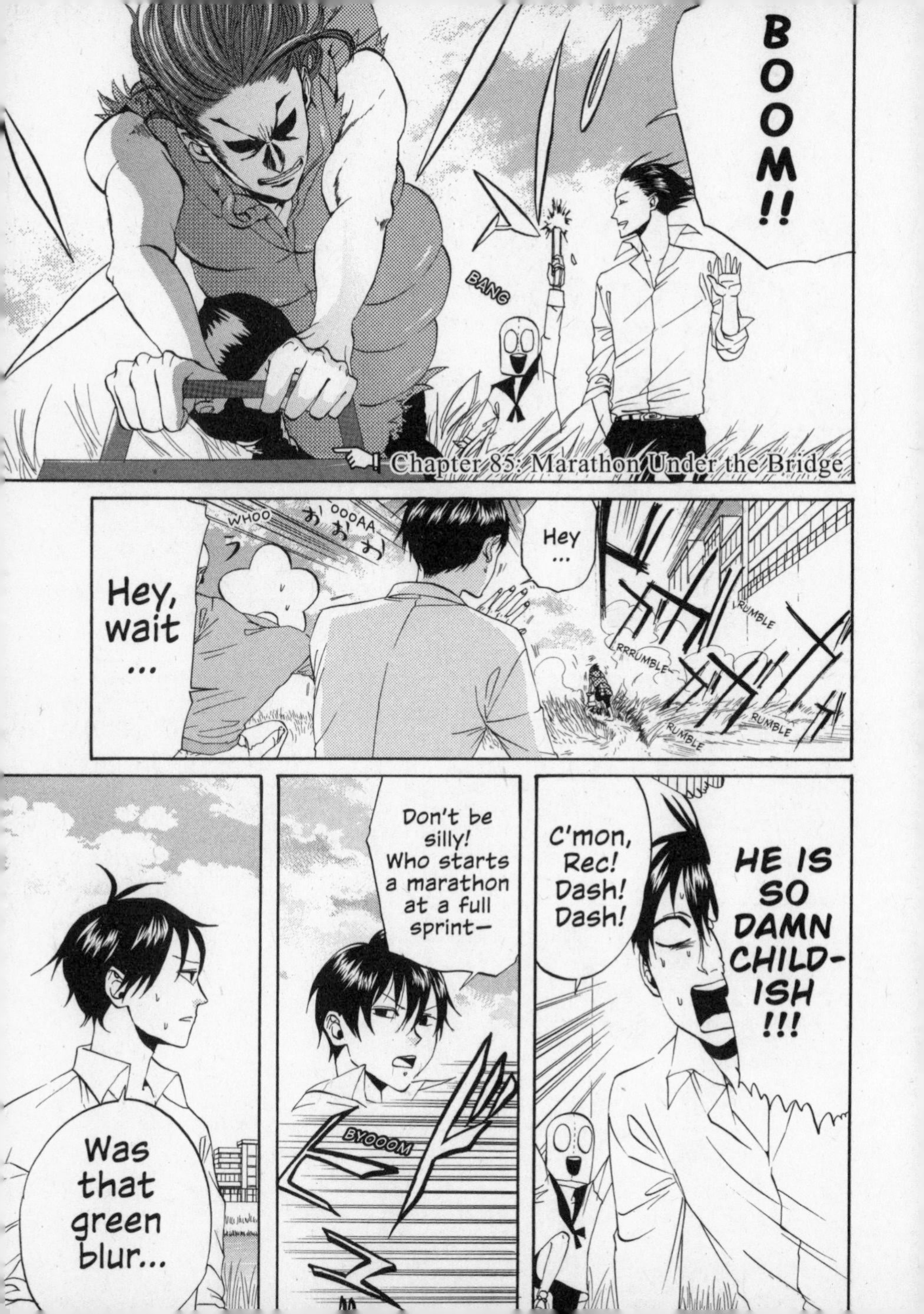
BOOM!!
BANG
Chapter 85: Marathon Under the Bridge
RUMBLE
RRRUMBLE
RUMBLE
RUMBLE
Hey ...
WHOO OOOAA
Hey, wait ...
HE IS SO DAMN CHILD-ISH !!!
C'mon, Rec! Dash! Dash!
Don't be silly! Who starts a marathon at a full sprint—
BYOOOM
Was that green blur...

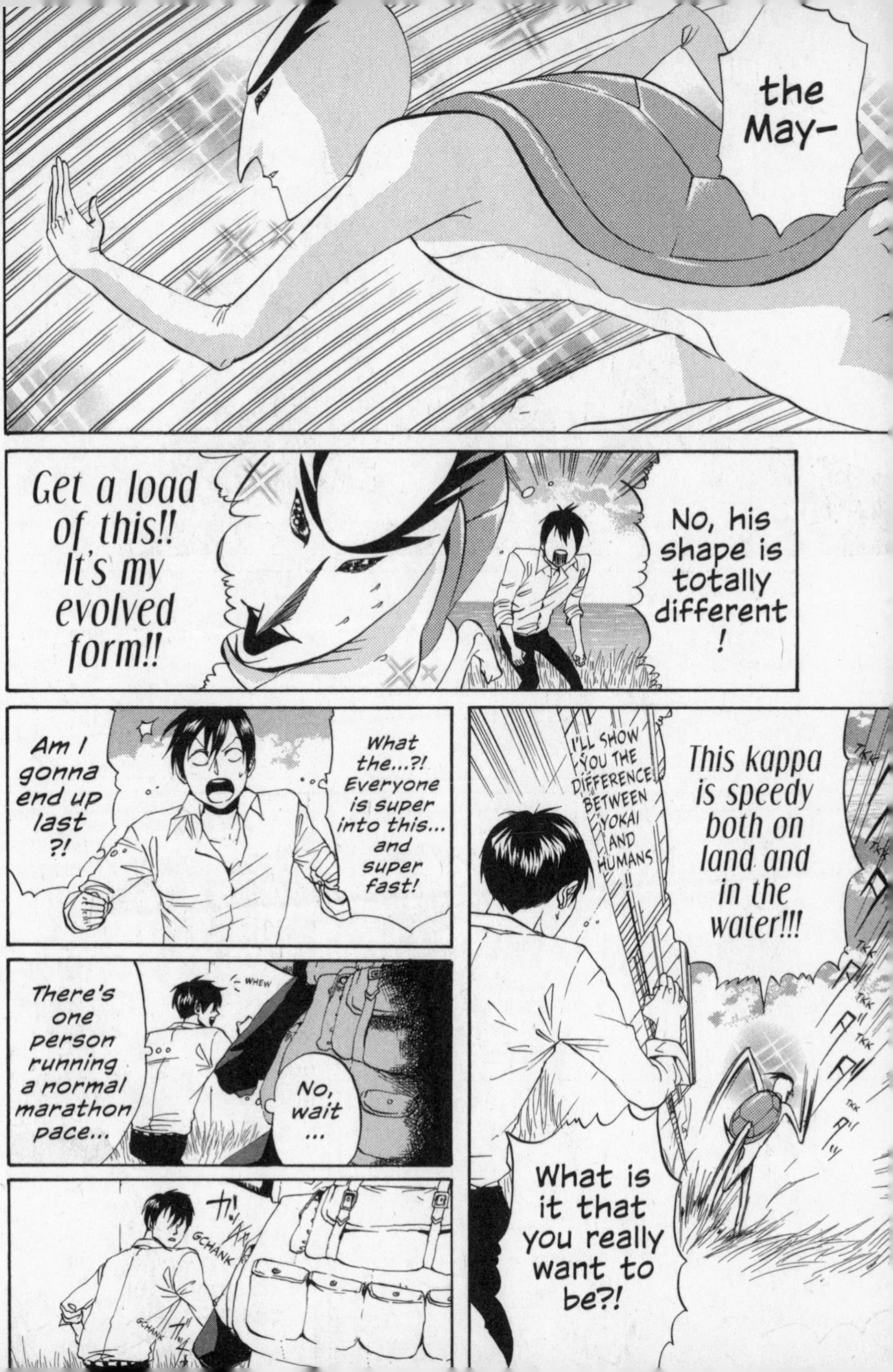
the May-
No, his shape is totally different!
Get a load of this!! It's my evolved form!!
This kappa is speedy both on land and in the water!!!
I'LL SHOW YOU THE DIFFERENCE BETWEEN YOKAI AND HUMANS!!
TKK
TKK
TKK
TKK
TKK
What is it that you really want to be?!
What the...?! Everyone is super into this... and super fast!
Am I gonna end up last?!
WHEW
No, wait...
There's one person running a normal marathon pace...
GCHANK
GCHANK

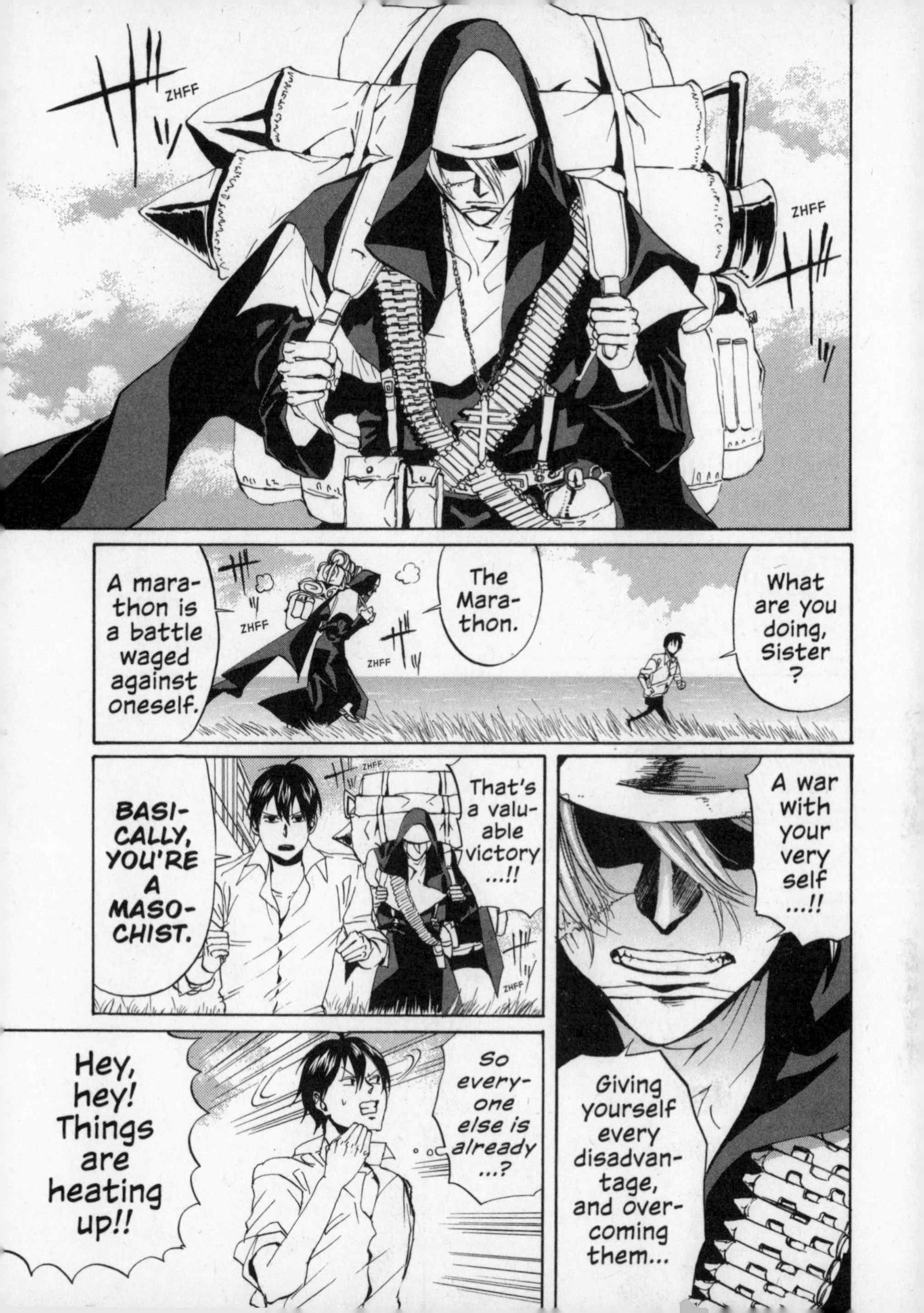
ZHFF
ZHFF
What are you doing, Sister?
The Mara-thon.
ZHFF
ZHFF
A mara-thon is a battle waged against oneself.
A war with your very self ...!!
Giving yourself every disadvan-tage, and over-coming them...
That's a valu-able victory ...!!
ZHFF
BASI-CALLY, YOU'RE A MASO-CHIST.
ZHFF
So every-one else is already ...?
Hey, hey! Things are heating up!!

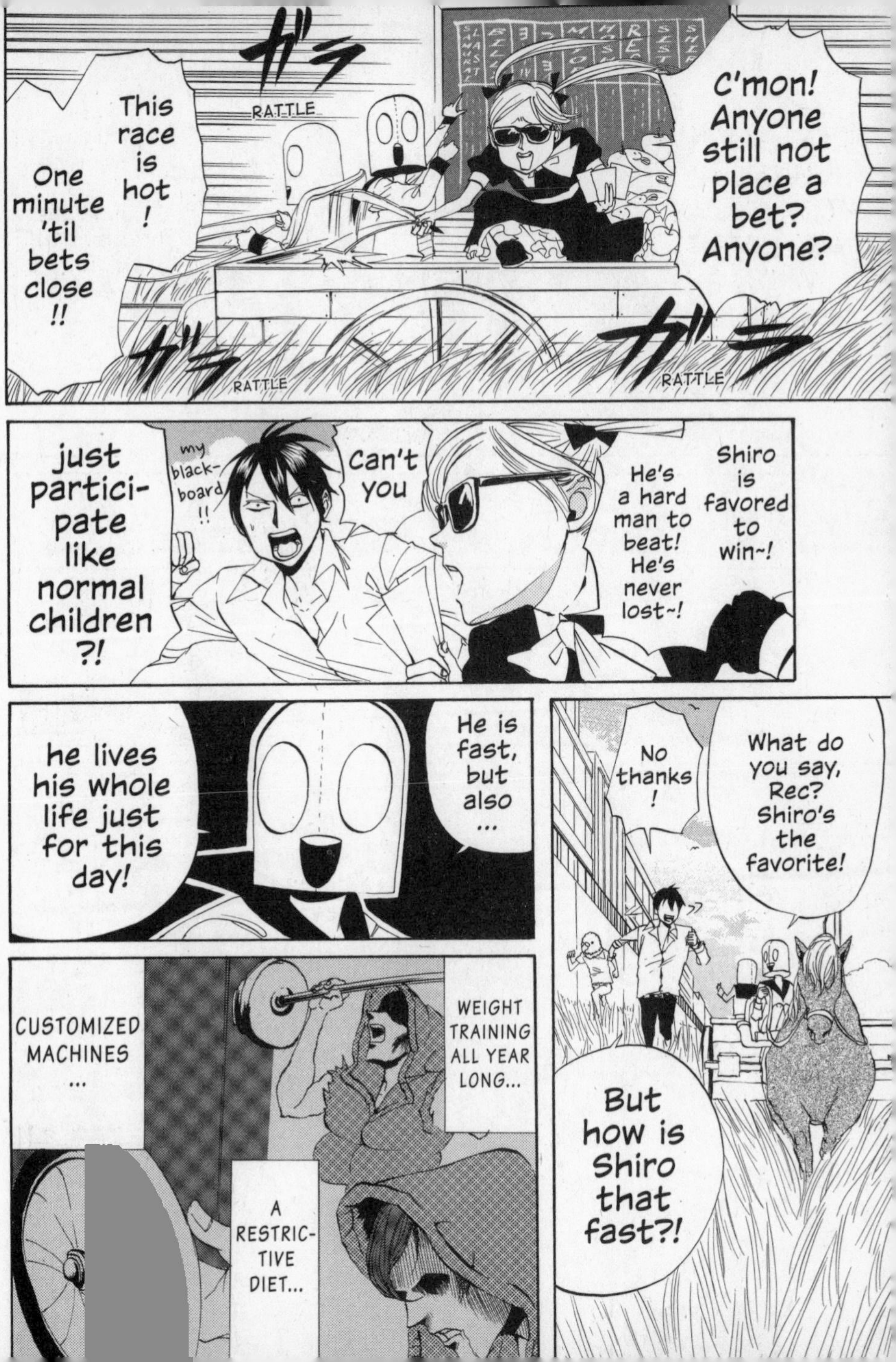
C'mon! Anyone still not place a bet? Anyone?
ガラ
RATTLE
ガラ
RATTLE
This race is hot!
One minute 'til bets close!!
ガラ
RATTLE
Shiro is favored to win~!
He's a hard man to beat! He's never lost~!
Can't you
my blackboard!!
just participate like normal children?!
What do you say, Rec? Shiro's the favorite!
No thanks!
But how is Shiro that fast?!
He is fast, but also...
he lives his whole life just for this day!
WEIGHT TRAINING ALL YEAR LONG...
CUSTOMIZED MACHINES...
A RESTRICTIVE DIET...

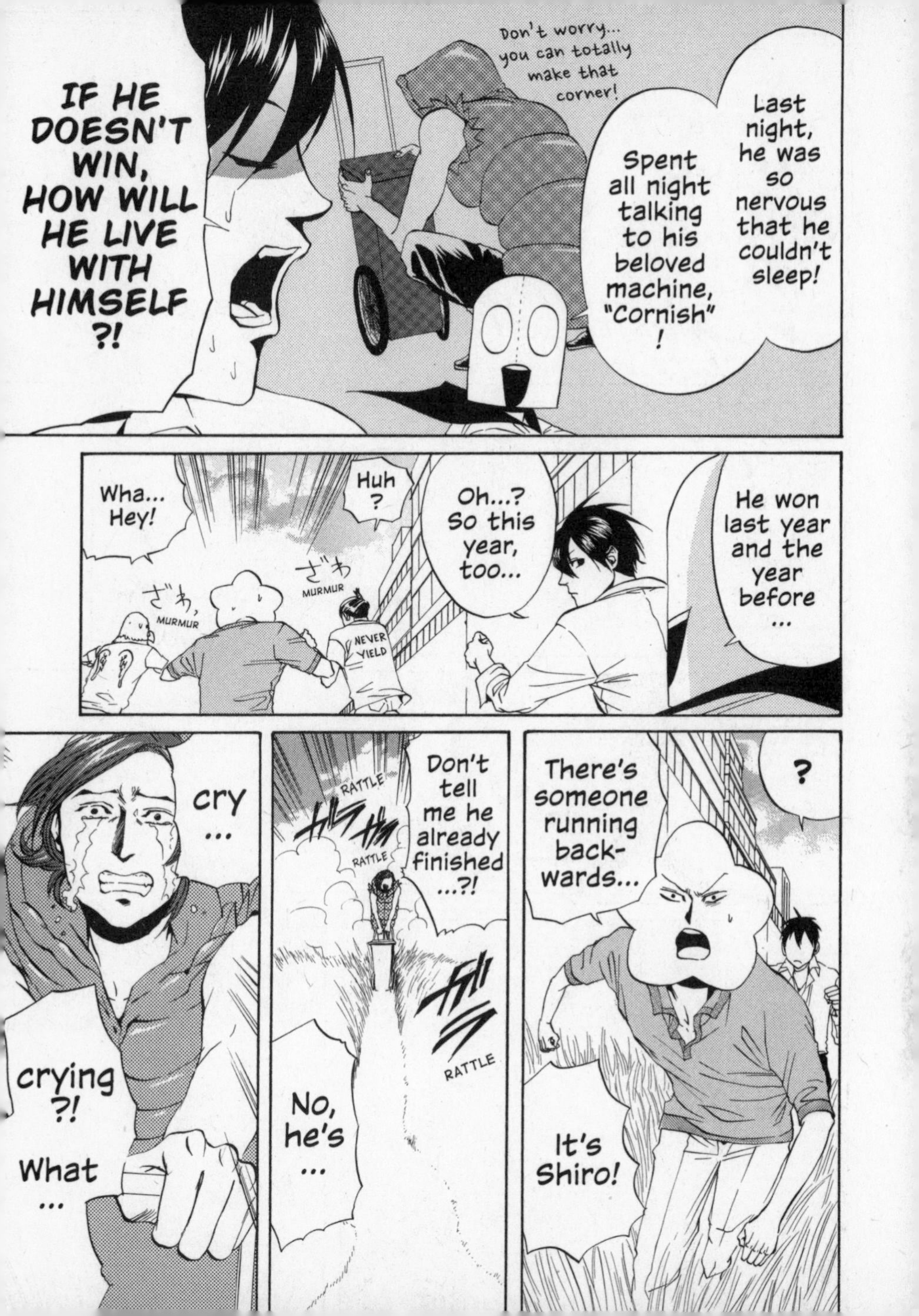
Last night, he was so nervous that he couldn't sleep!
Spent all night talking to his beloved machine, "Cornish"!
Don't worry... you can totally make that corner!
IF HE DOESN'T WIN, HOW WILL HE LIVE WITH HIMSELF?!
He won last year and the year before...
Oh...? So this year, too...
Huh?
ざわ MURMUR
NEVER YIELD
Wha... Hey!
ざわ, MURMUR
?
There's someone running backwards...
It's Shiro!
Don't tell me he already finished...?!
RATTLE
RATTLE
RATTLE
No, he's...
cry...
crying?!
What...

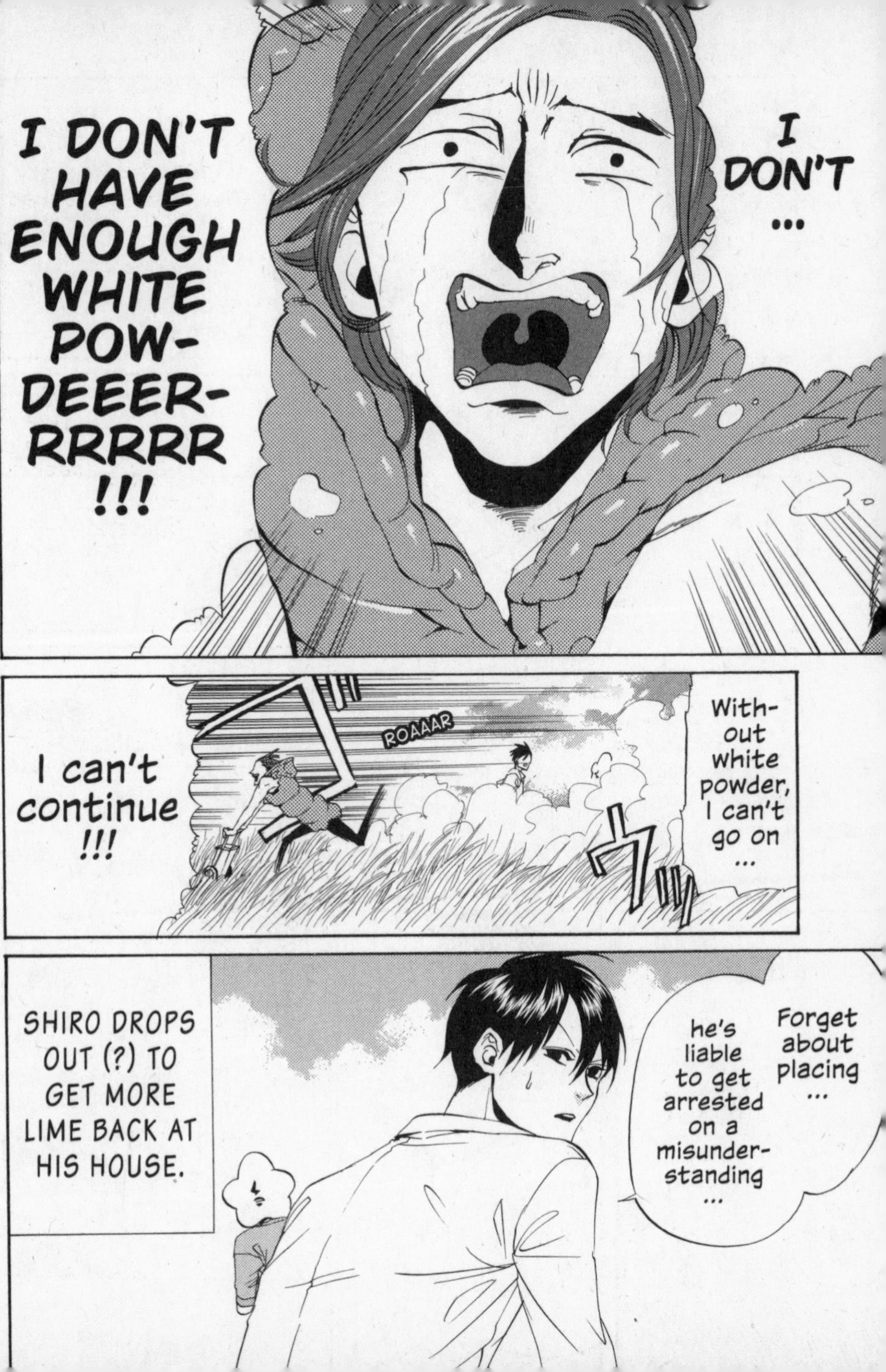

I DON'T ...
I DON'T HAVE ENOUGH WHITE POW-DEEER-RRRRR!!!
Without white powder, I can't go on ...
ウッ
ROAAAR
I can't continue!!!
Forget about placing ...
he's liable to get arrested on a misunderstanding ...
SHIRO DROPS OUT (?) TO GET MORE LIME BACK AT HIS HOUSE.

Chapter 86: Like the Wind... Like the Clouds...

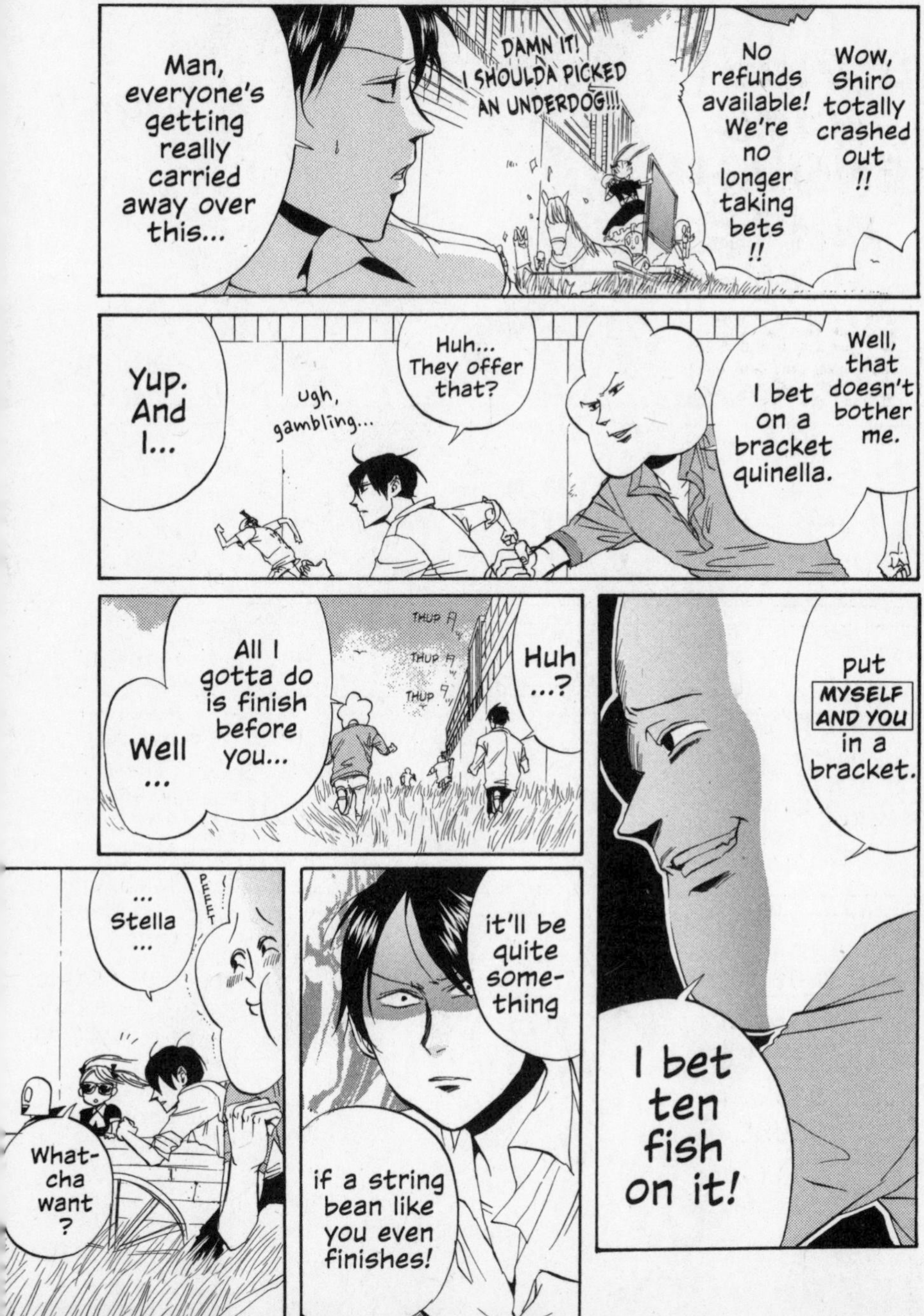

Wow, Shiro totally crashed out !!
No refunds available! We're no longer taking bets !!
DAMN IT! I SHOULDA PICKED AN UNDERDOG!!!
Man, everyone's getting really carried away over this...
Well, that doesn't bother me.
I bet on a bracket quinella.
Huh... They offer that?
ugh, gambling...
Yup. And I...
put MYSELF AND YOU in a bracket.
I bet ten fish on it!
Huh ...?
THUP
THUP
THUP
All I gotta do is finish before you...
Well ...
it'll be quite something
if a string bean like you even finishes!
... Stella ...
PFEET
What-cha want ?

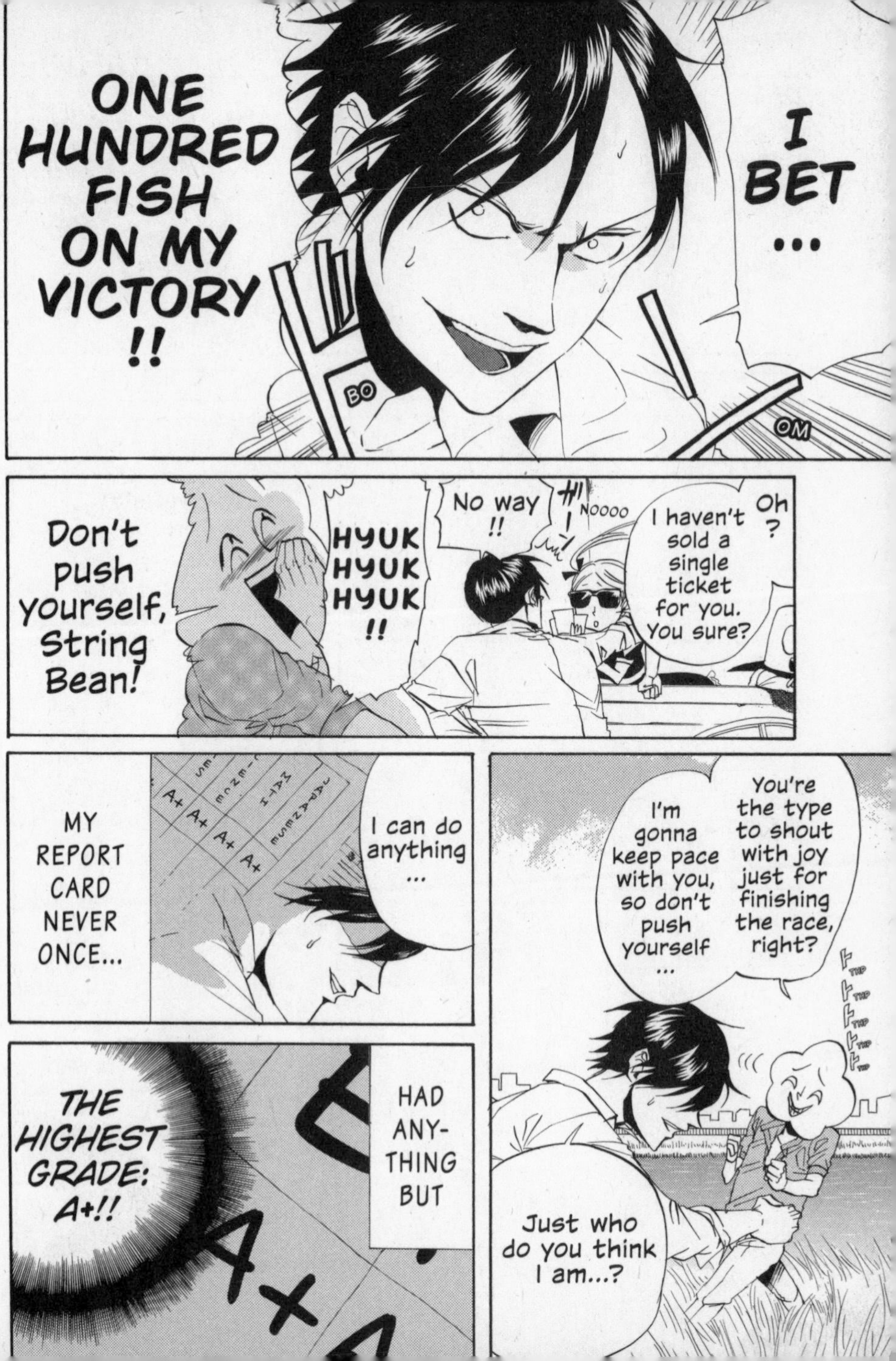
I BET...
ONE HUNDRED FISH ON MY VICTORY!!
BO
OM
Oh?
I haven't sold a single ticket for you. You sure?
NOOOO
No way!!
HYUK HYUK HYUK!!
Don't push yourself, String Bean!
You're the type to shout with joy just for finishing the race, right?
I'm gonna keep pace with you, so don't push yourself...
THP THP THP THP THP
Just who do you think I am...?
I can do anything...
MY REPORT CARD NEVER ONCE...
A+ A+ A+ A+
HAD ANYTHING BUT
THE HIGHEST GRADE: A+!!
A+

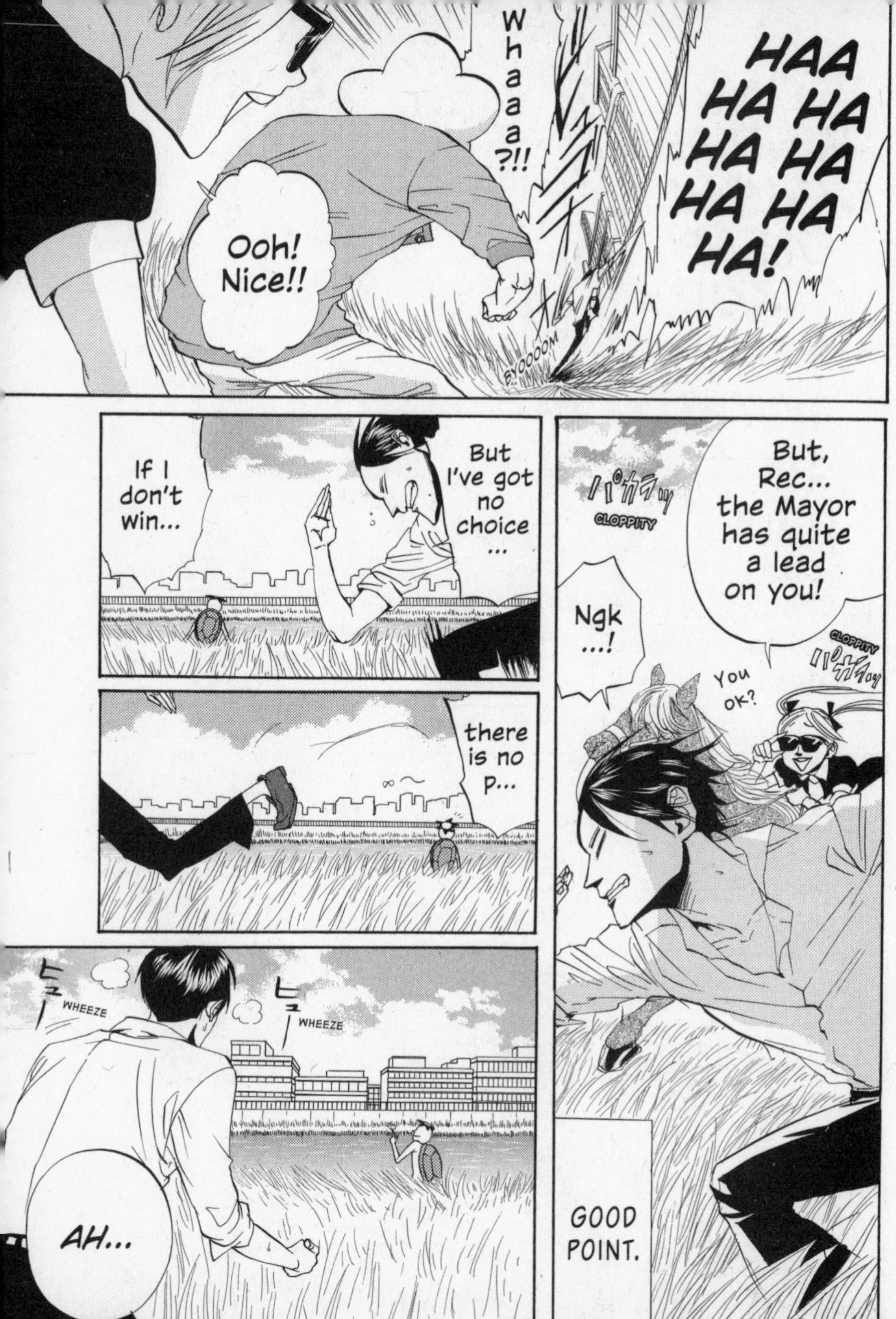
HAA HA HA HA HA HA HA HA!
Whaaaa?!!
Ooh! Nice!!
BYOOOOM
But, Rec... the Mayor has quite a lead on you!
CLOPPITY
Ngk ...!
CLOPPITY
You ok?
GOOD POINT.
But I've got no choice ...
If I don't win...
there is no p...
WHEEZE
WHEEZE
AH...

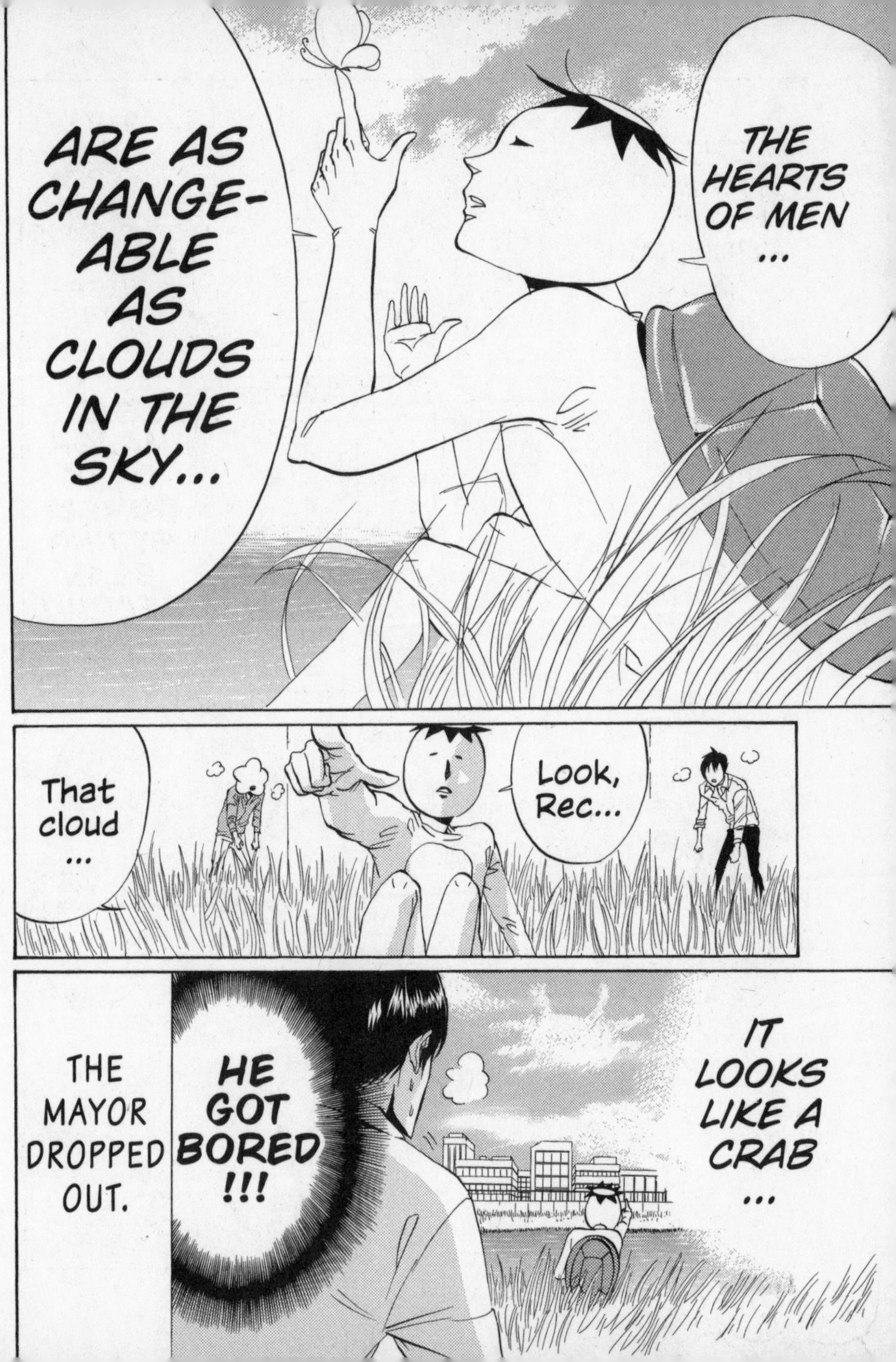
THE HEARTS OF MEN ...
ARE AS CHANGE-ABLE AS CLOUDS IN THE SKY...
Look, Rec...
That cloud ...
IT LOOKS LIKE A CRAB ...
HE GOT BORED !!!
THE MAYOR DROPPED OUT.

Chapter 87: Last Run

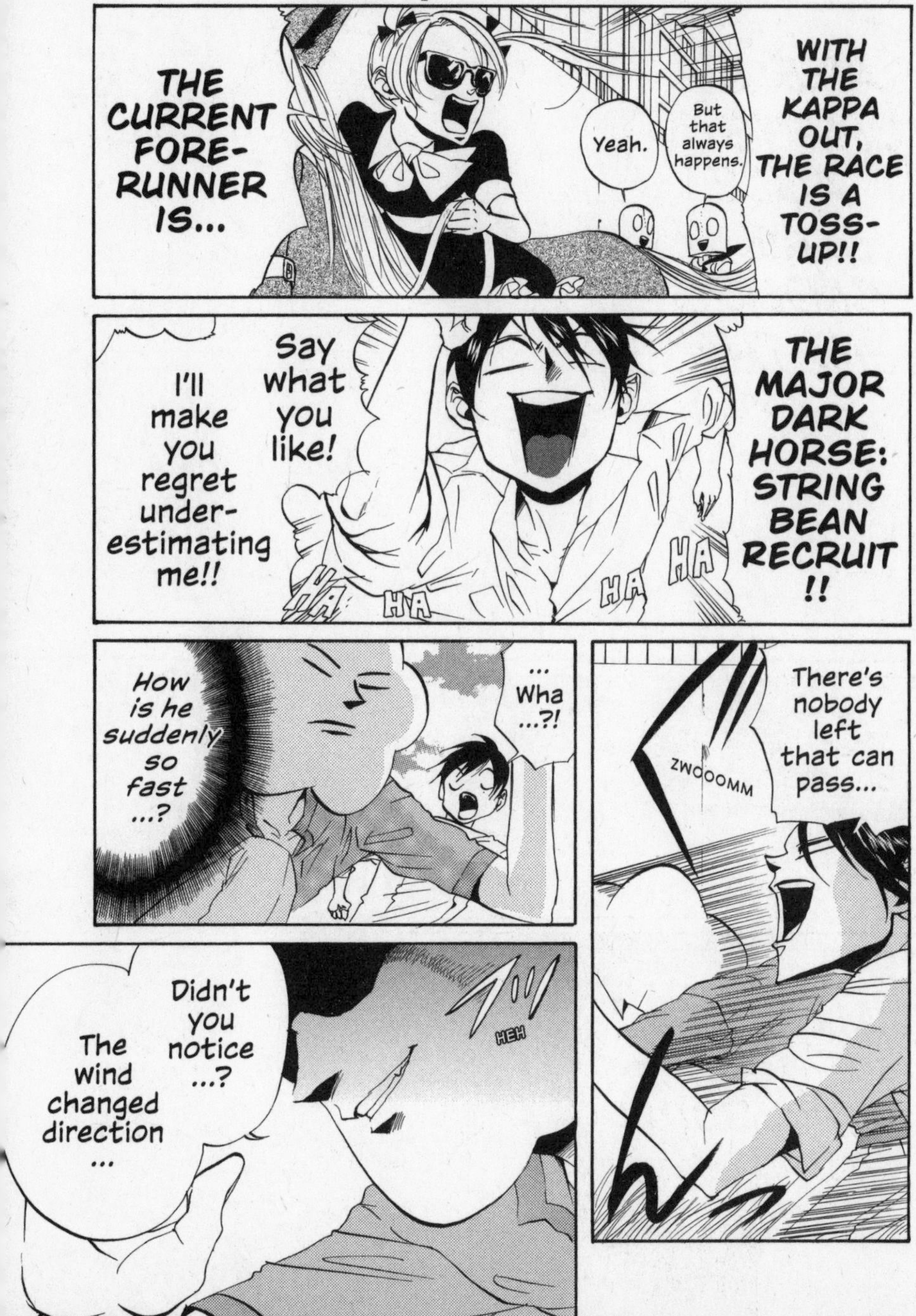
WITH THE KAPPA OUT, THE RACE IS A TOSS-UP!!
But that always happens.
Yeah.
THE CURRENT FORE-RUNNER IS...
THE MAJOR DARK HORSE: STRING BEAN RECRUIT!!
HA HA HA HA
Say what you like!
I'll make you regret under-estimating me!!
There's nobody left that can pass...
ZWOOOMM
...Wha...?!
How is he suddenly so fast...?
HEH
Didn't you notice...?
The wind changed direction...

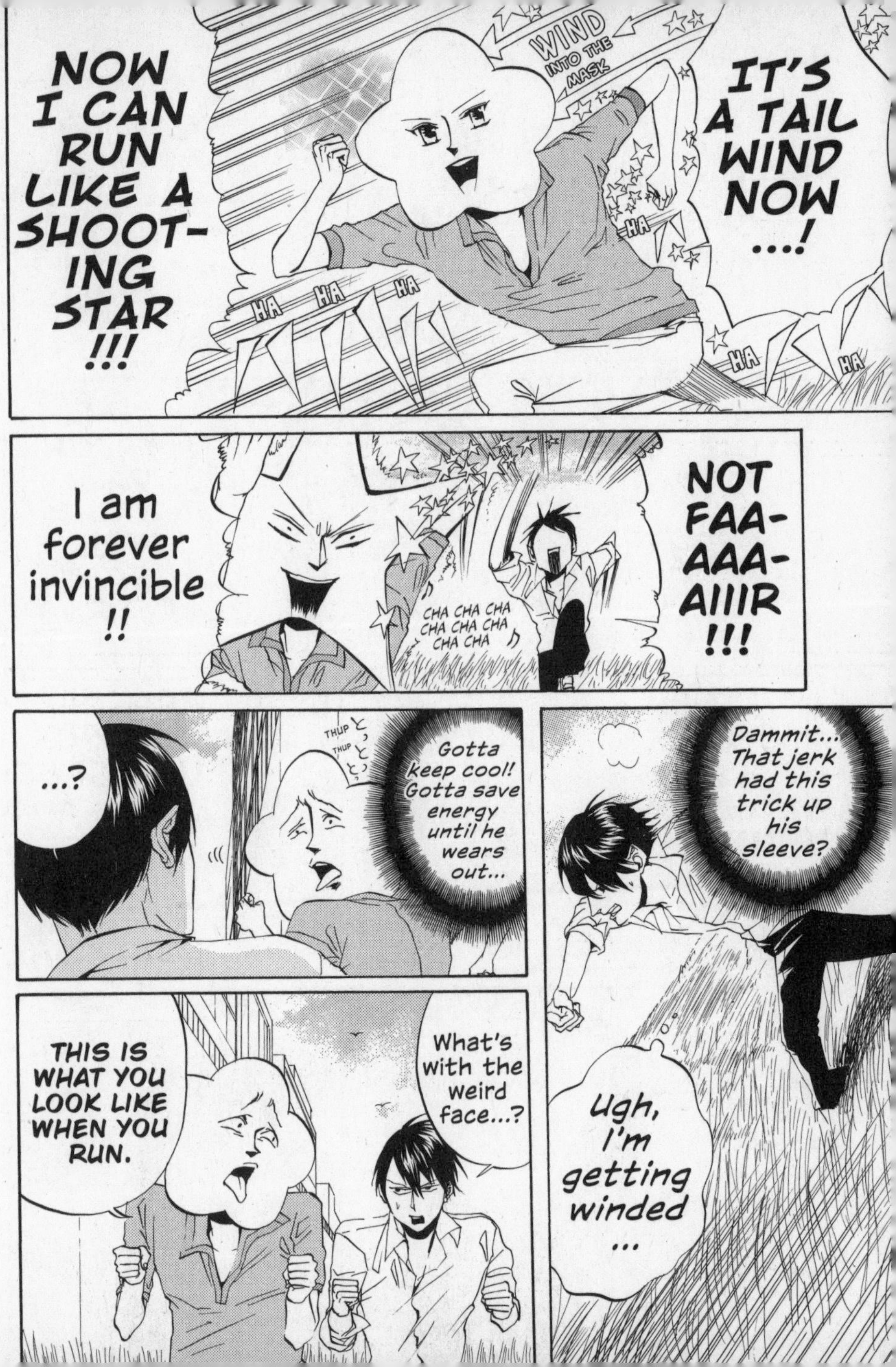
IT'S A TAIL WIND NOW ....!
WIND INTO THE MASK
HA
HA
NOW I CAN RUN LIKE A SHOOTING-STAR !!!
HA HA HA
NOT FAAAAAAIIIR !!!
CHA CHA CHA CHA CHA CHA CHA CHA
I am forever invincible !!
Dammit... That jerk had this trick up his sleeve?
Ugh, I'm getting winded ...
Gotta keep cool! Gotta save energy until he wears out...
THUP THUP
...?
What's with the weird face...?
THIS IS WHAT YOU LOOK LIKE WHEN YOU RUN.

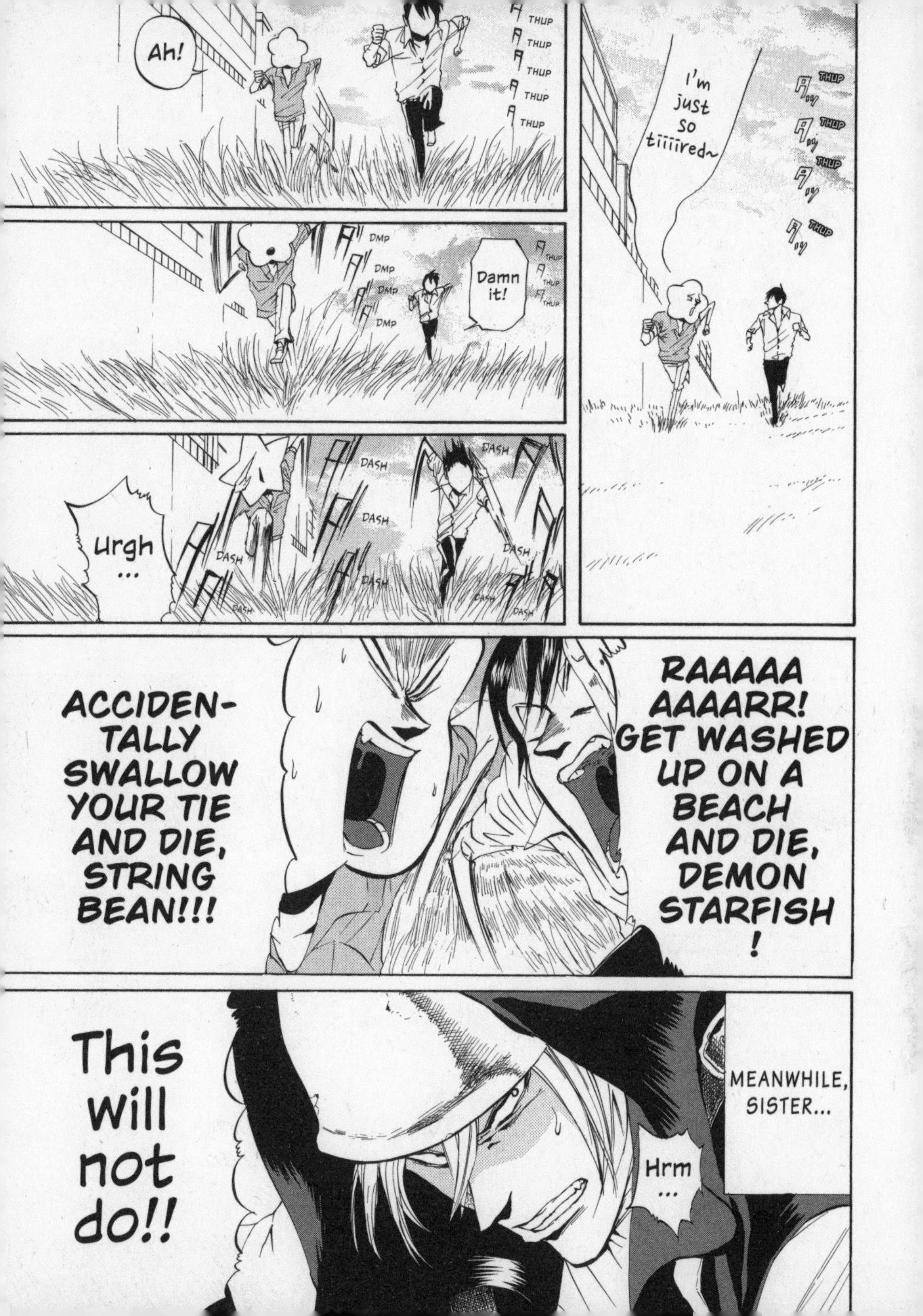
I'm just so tiiiired~
THUP THUP THUP THUP THUP
Ah!
THUP THUP THUP THUP THUP
Damn it!
THUP THUP THUP
DMP DMP DMP DMP
DASH DASH DASH DASH DASH DASH DASH DASH
Urgh...
RAAAAAAAAAARR! GET WASHED UP ON A BEACH AND DIE, DEMON STARFISH!
ACCIDENTALLY SWALLOW YOUR TIE AND DIE, STRING BEAN!!!
MEANWHILE, SISTER...
Hrm...
This will not do!!

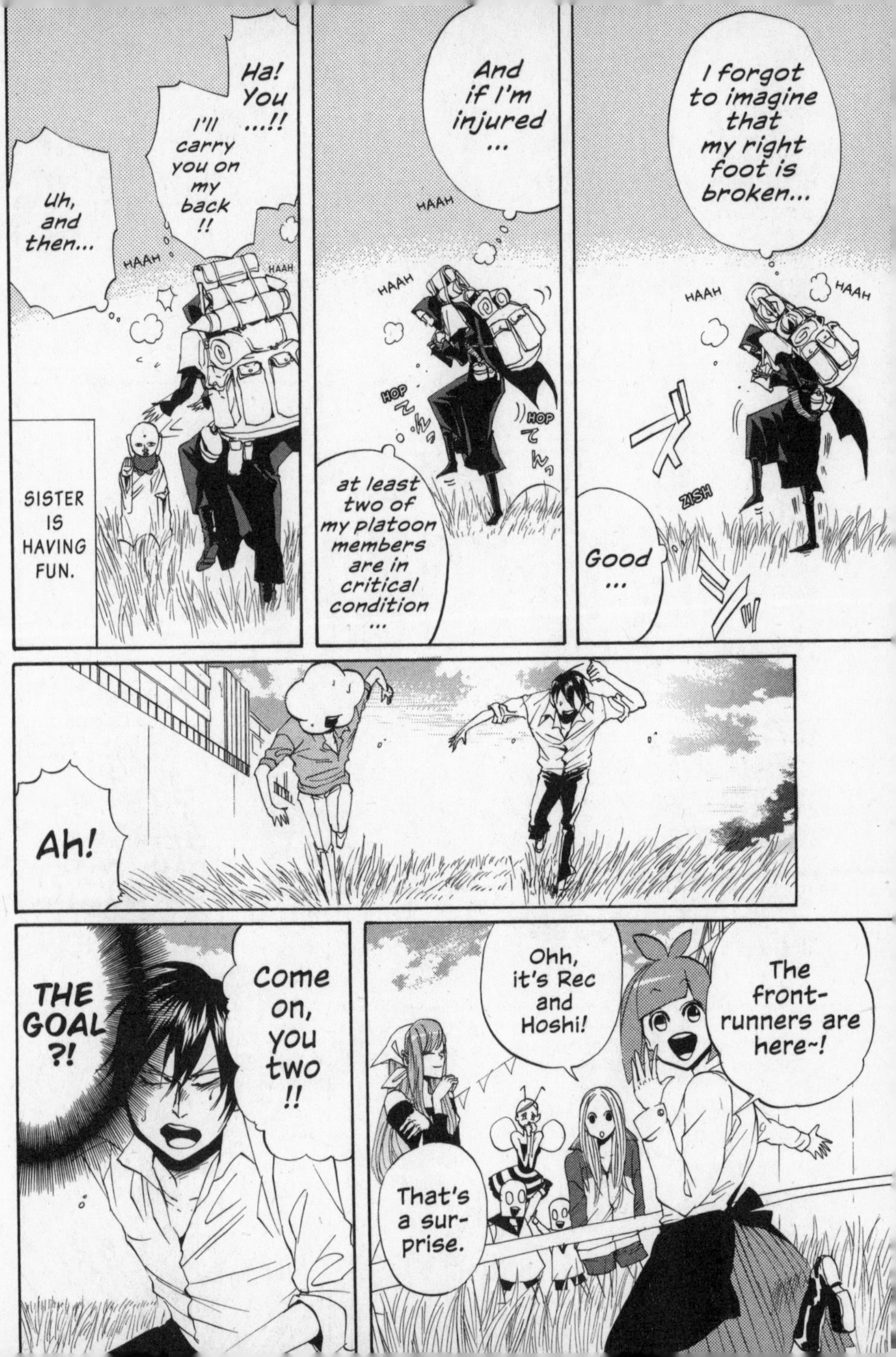
I forgot to imagine that my right foot is broken...
HAAH
HAAH
ZISH
Good ...
And if I'm injured ...
HAAH
HAAH
HOP
HOP
at least two of my platoon members are in critical condition ...
Ha! You ...!!
I'll carry you on my back !!
Uh, and then...
HAAH
HAAH
SISTER IS HAVING FUN.
Ah!
The front-runners are here~!
Ohh, it's Rec and Hoshi!
That's a surprise.
Come on, you two !!
THE GOAL ?!

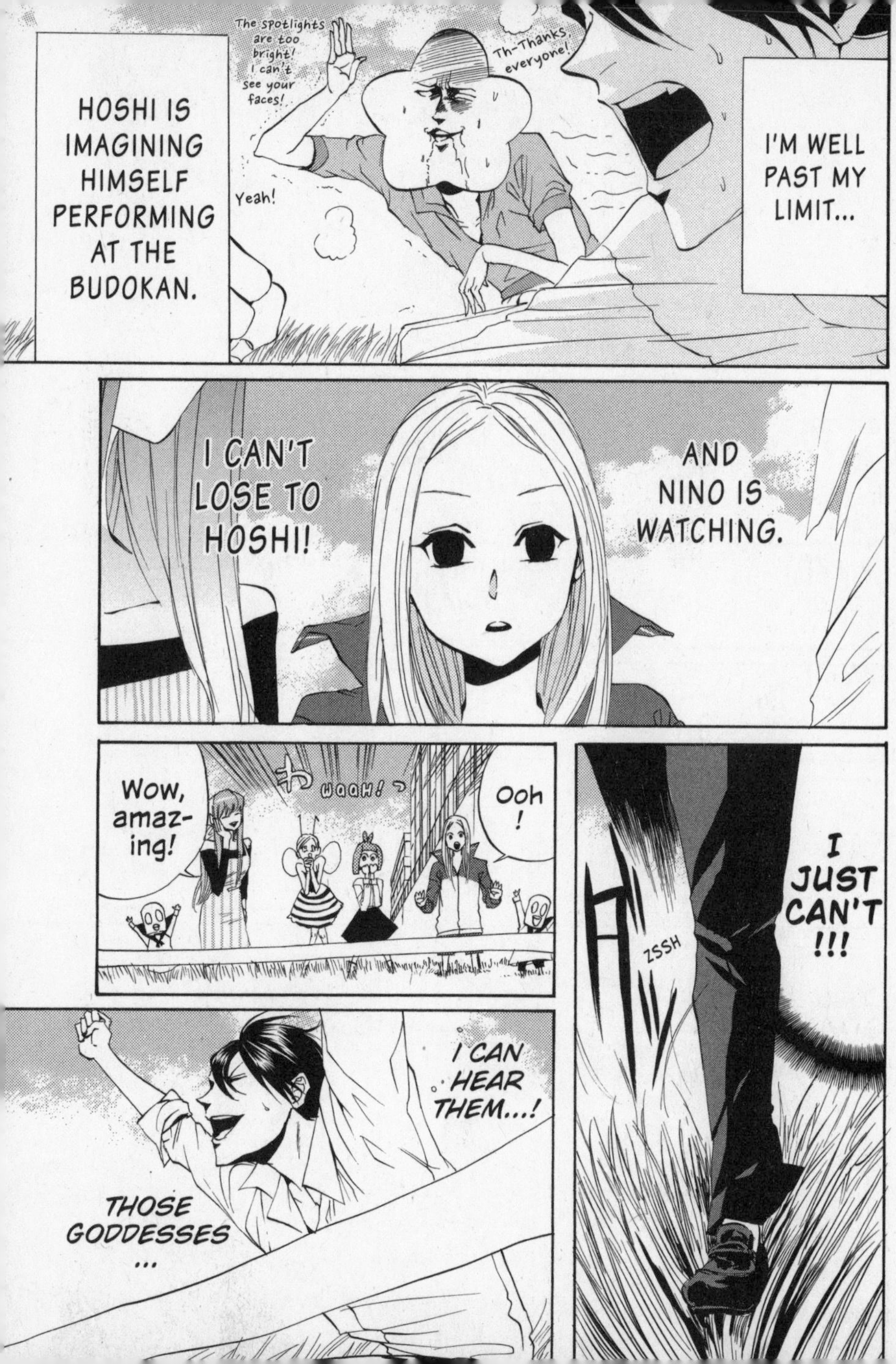
I'M WELL PAST MY LIMIT...
Th-Thanks, everyone!
The spotlights are too bright! I can't see your faces!
HOSHI IS IMAGINING HIMSELF PERFORMING AT THE BUDOKAN.
Yeah!
AND NINO IS WATCHING.
I CAN'T LOSE TO HOSHI!
I JUST CAN'T !!!
ZSSH
Ooh!
WAAH!
Wow, amazing!
I CAN HEAR THEM...!
THOSE GODDESSES ...

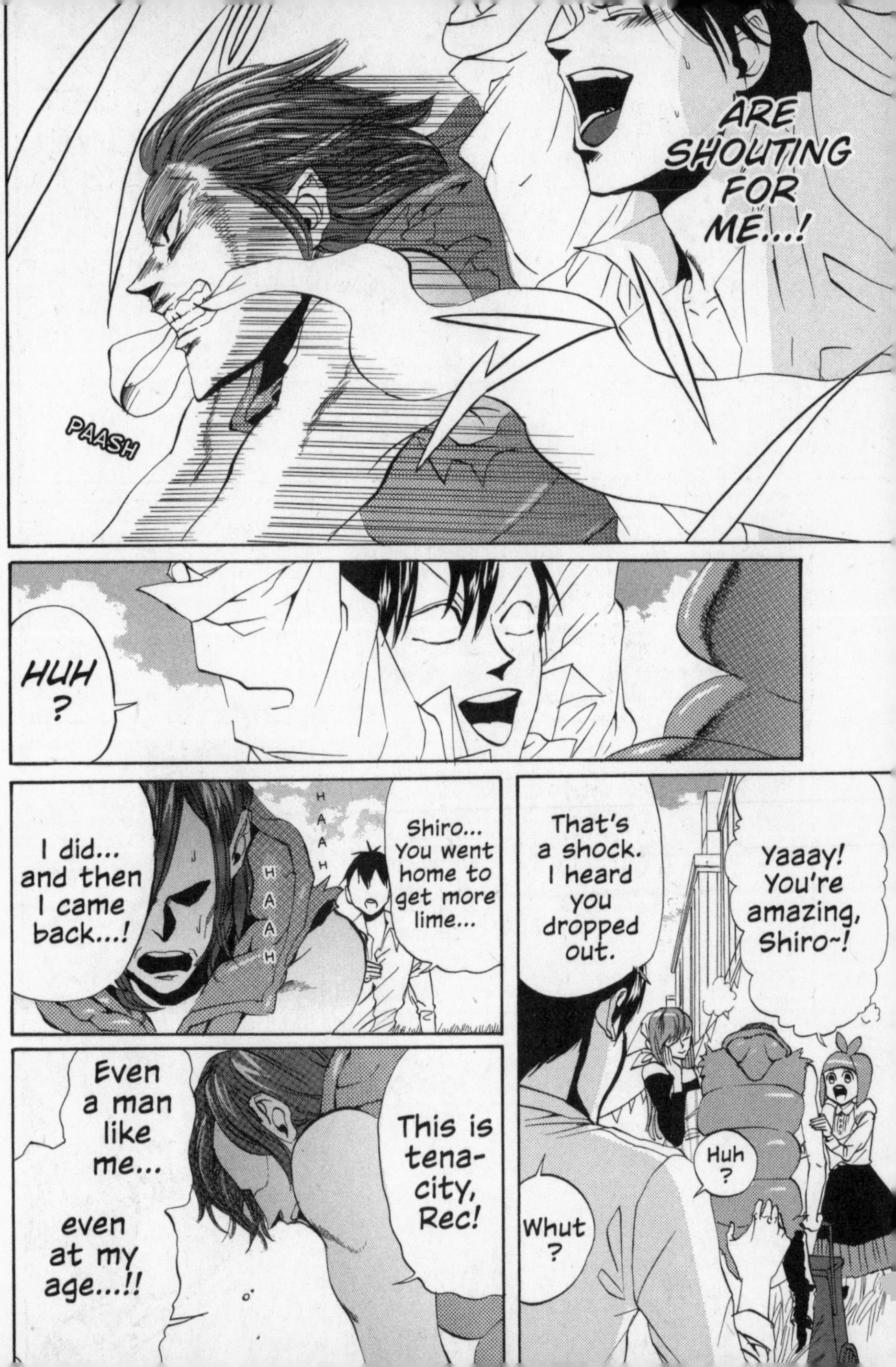
ARE SHOUTING FOR ME...!
PAASH
HUH ?
Yaaay! You're amazing, Shiro~!
That's a shock. I heard you dropped out.
Huh ?
Whut ?
Shiro... You went home to get more lime...
HAAAH HAAAH
I did... and then I came back...!
This is tena-city, Rec!
Even a man like me... even at my age...!!

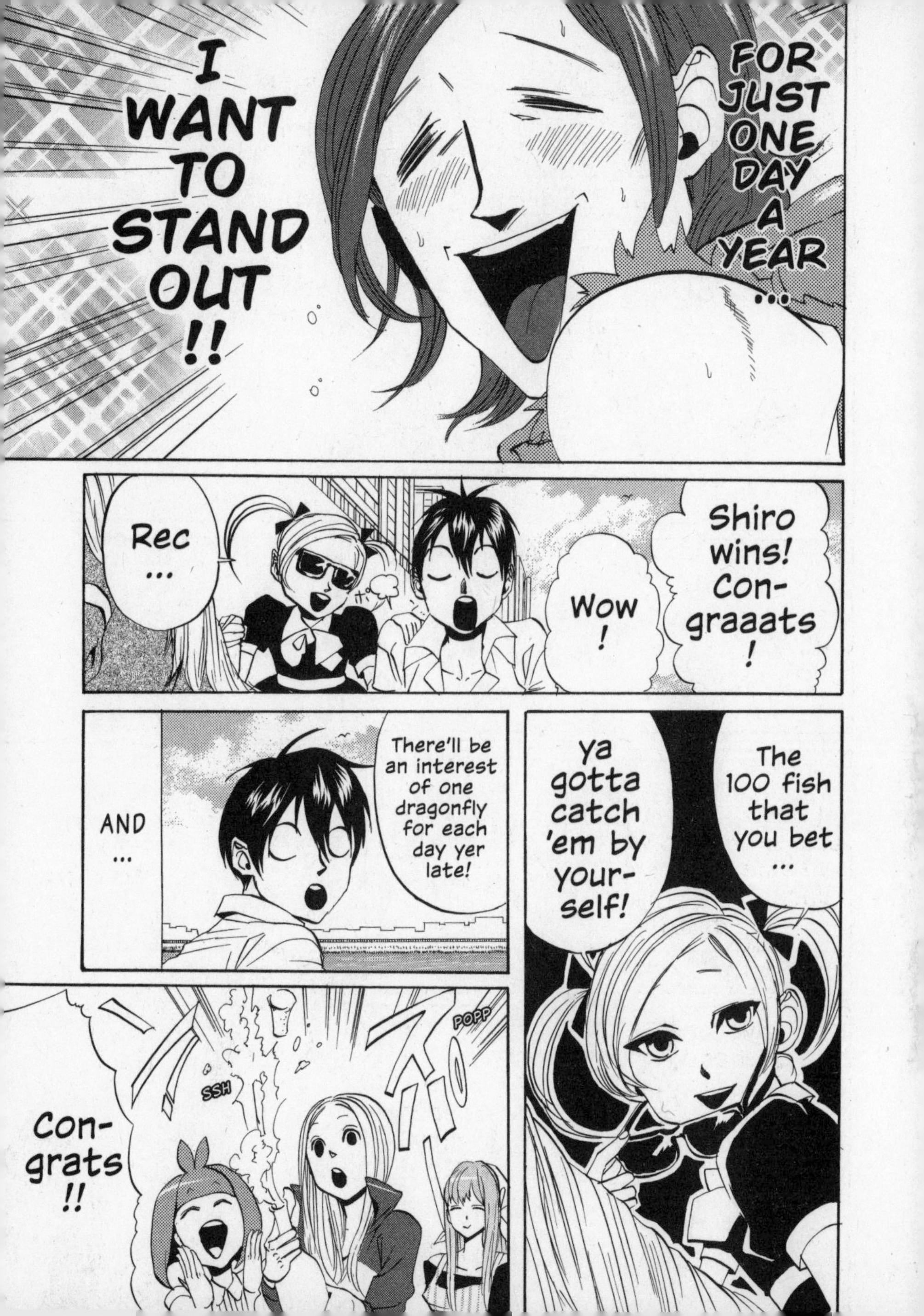
FOR JUST ONE DAY A YEAR...
I WANT TO STAND OUT!!
Shiro wins! Con-graaats!
Wow!
Rec...
The 100 fish that you bet...
Ya gotta catch 'em by your-self!
AND...
There'll be an interest of one dragonfly for each day yer late!
POPP
SSH
Con-grats!!

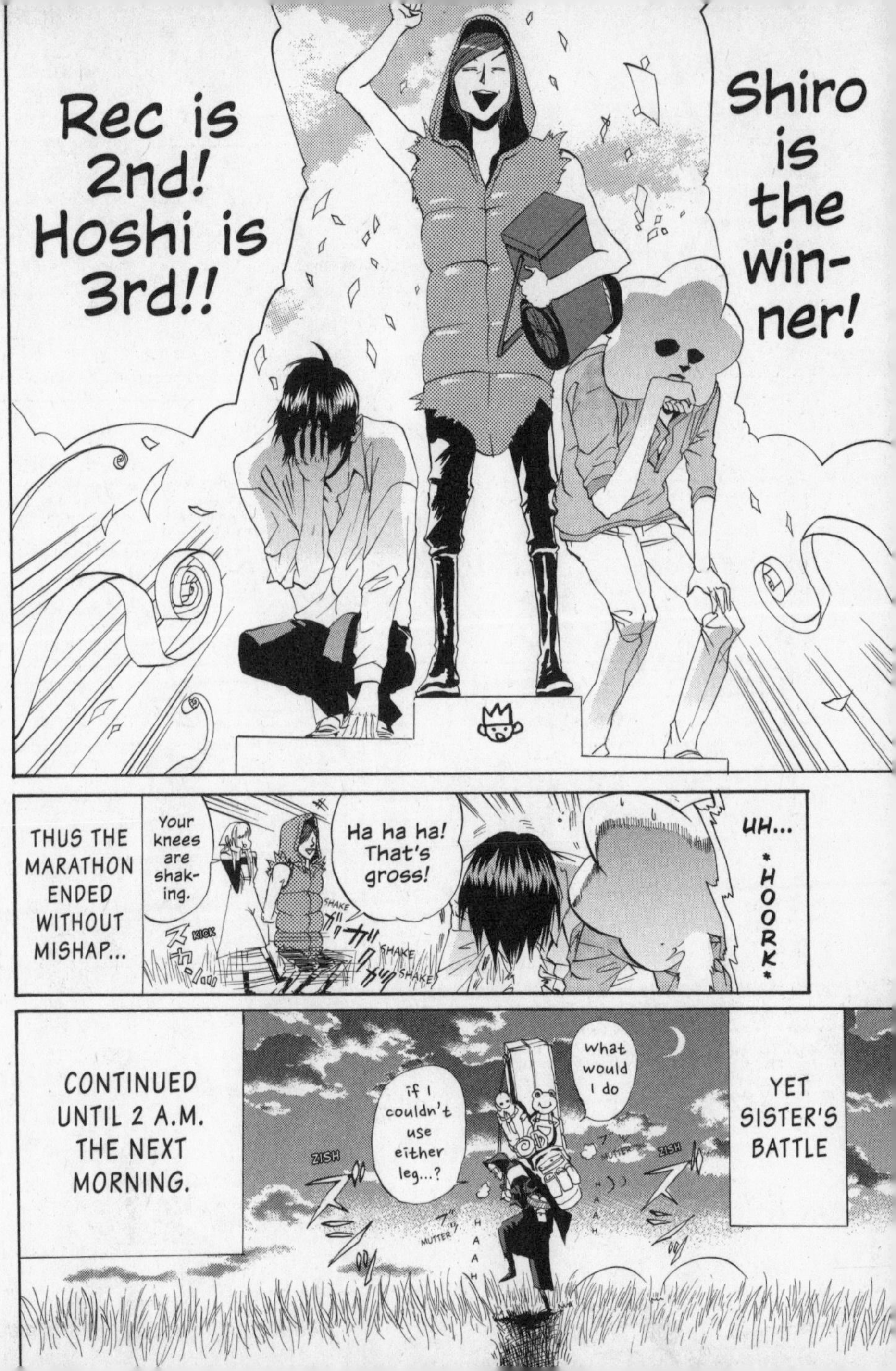
Shiro is the win-ner!
Rec is 2nd! Hoshi is 3rd!!
UH...
HOORK
Ha ha ha! That's gross!
SHAKE
SHAKE
SHAKE
Your knees are shak-ing.
KICK
THUS THE MARATHON ENDED WITHOUT MISHAP...
YET SISTER'S BATTLE
ZISH
MUTTER
HAAH
What would I do
if I couldn't use either leg...?
ZISH
MUTTER
HAAH
CONTINUED UNTIL 2 A.M. THE NEXT MORNING.

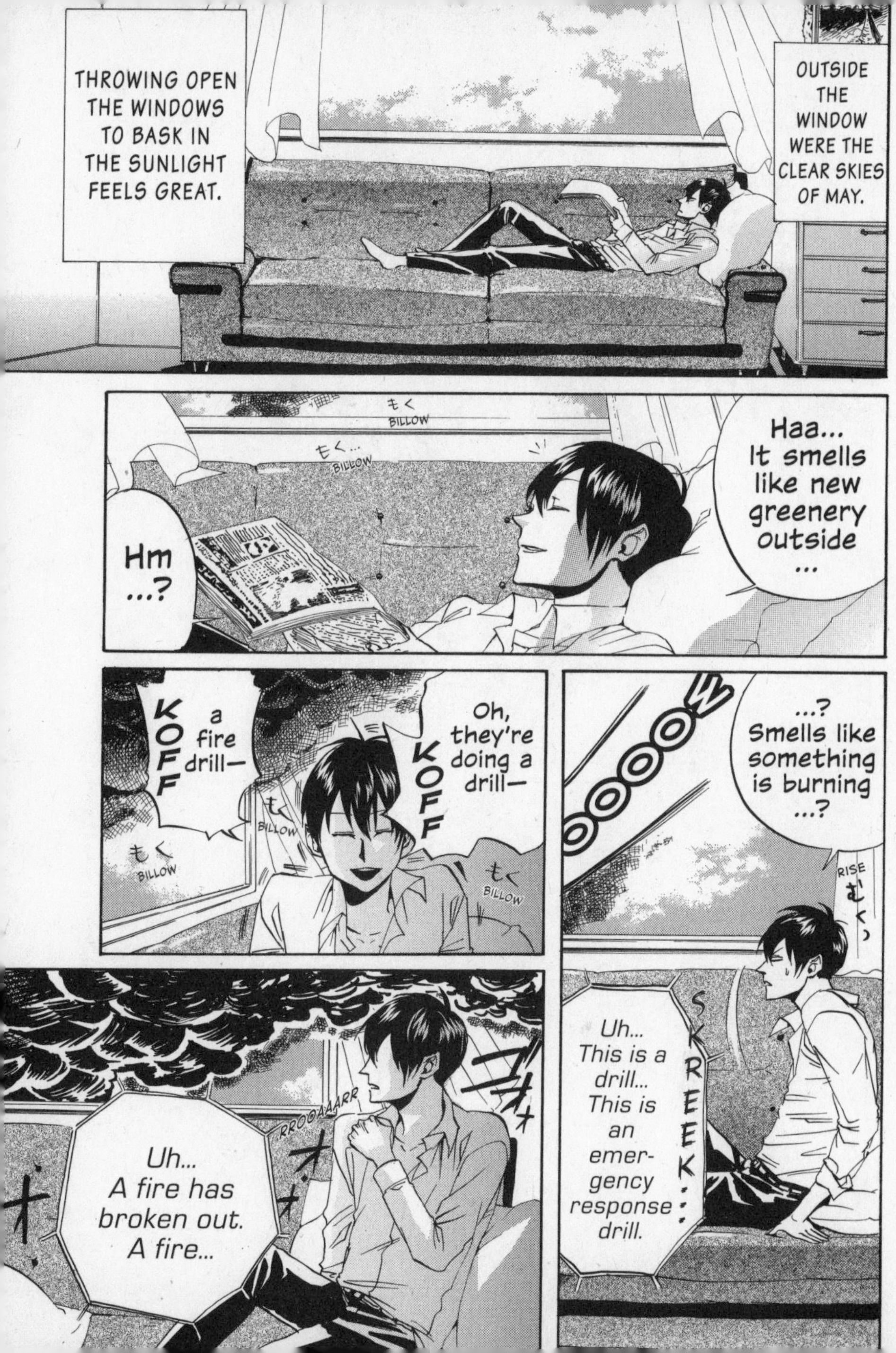
OUTSIDE THE WINDOW WERE THE CLEAR SKIES OF MAY.
THROWING OPEN THE WINDOWS TO BASK IN THE SUNLIGHT FEELS GREAT.
Haa... It smells like new greenery outside ...
もく BILLOW
もく... BILLOW
Hm ...?
...? Smells like something is burning ...?
OOOOOOW
RISE むくっ
Oh, they're doing a drill—
KOFF
a fire drill—
KOFF
もく BILLOW
もく BILLOW
もく BILLOW
Uh... This is a drill... This is an emergency response drill.
SKREEK...
RROOAAARR
Uh... A fire has broken out. A fire...

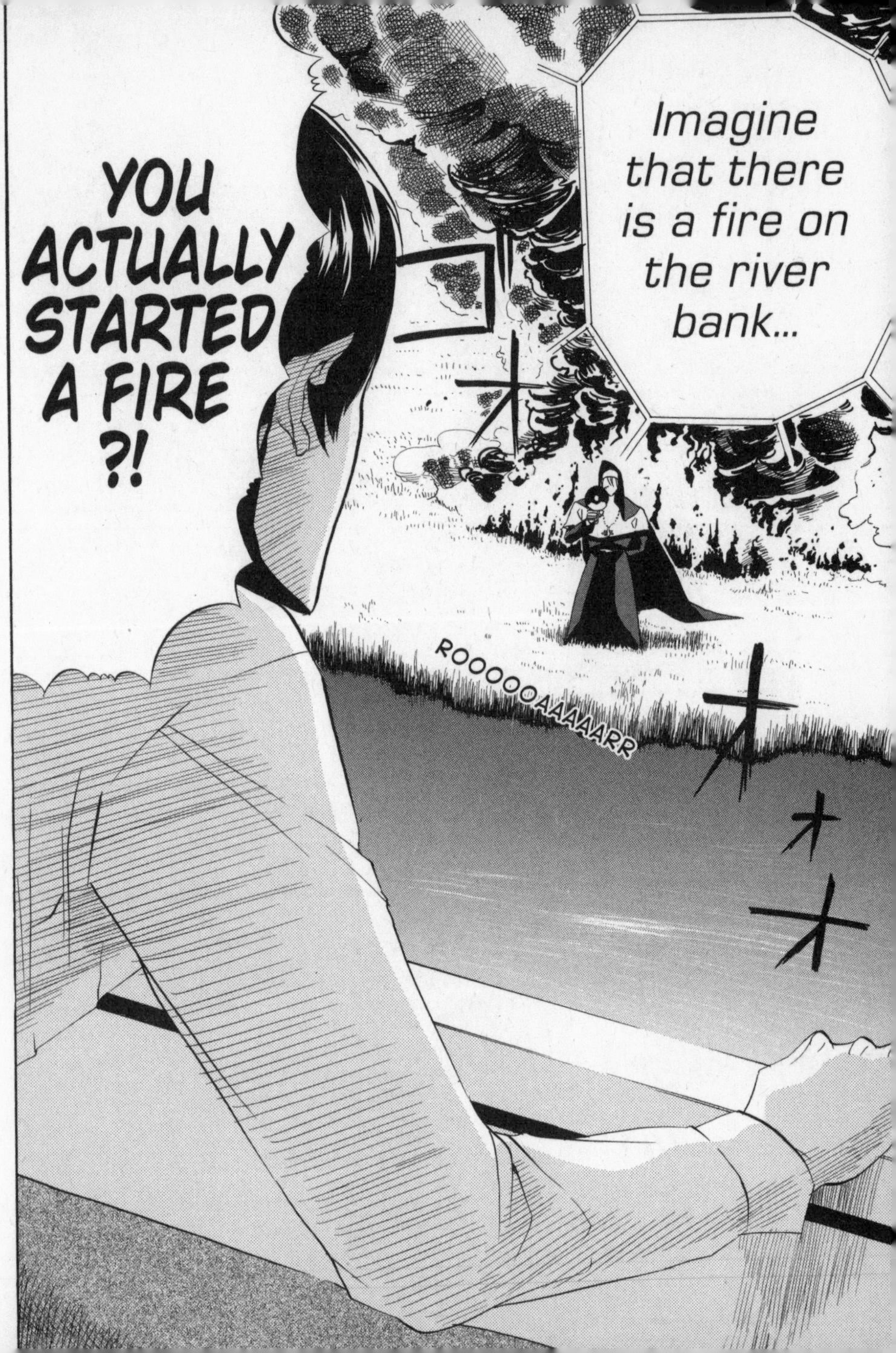
Imagine that there is a fire on the river bank...
YOU ACTUALLY STARTED A FIRE ?!
ROOOOOOAAAAAARR

Chapter 88: Fire Drill

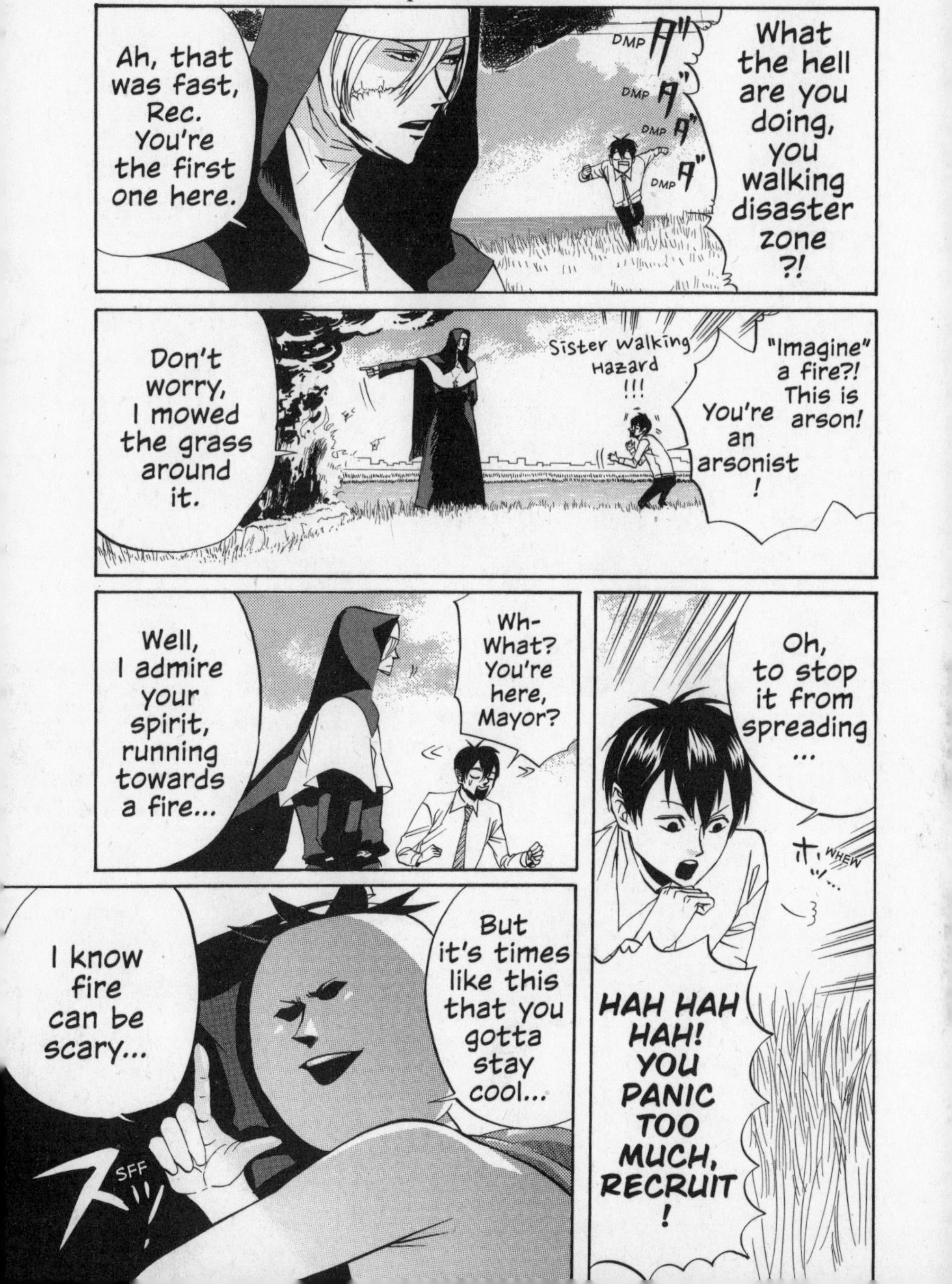
What the hell are you doing, you walking disaster zone?!
DMP
DMP
DMP
DMP
Ah, that was fast, Rec. You're the first one here.
"Imagine" a fire?! This is arson!
You're an arsonist!
Sister Walking Hazard!!!
Don't worry, I mowed the grass around it.
Oh, to stop it from spreading...
WHEW
HAH HAH HAH! YOU PANIC TOO MUCH, RECRUIT!
Wh-What? You're here, Mayor?
Well, I admire your spirit, running towards a fire...
But it's times like this that you gotta stay cool...
I know fire can be scary...
SFF

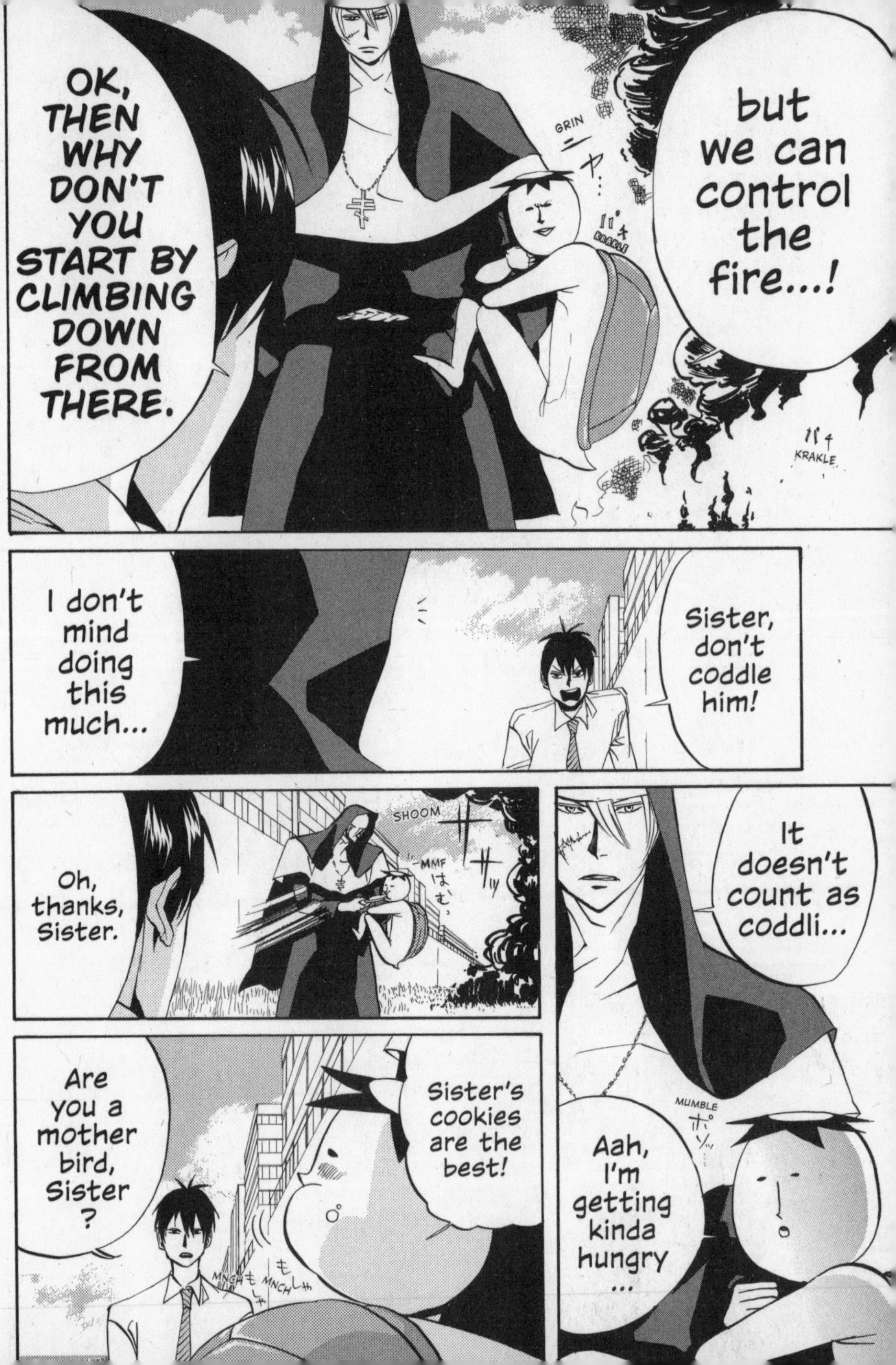

but we can control the fire...!
GRIN
KRAKLE
KRAKLE
OK, THEN WHY DON'T YOU START BY CLIMBING DOWN FROM THERE.
Sister, don't coddle him!
I don't mind doing this much...
It doesn't count as coddli...
MUMBLE
Aah, I'm getting kinda hungry...
SHOOM
MMF
Oh, thanks, Sister.
Sister's cookies are the best!
MNCH
MNCH
Are you a mother bird, Sister?

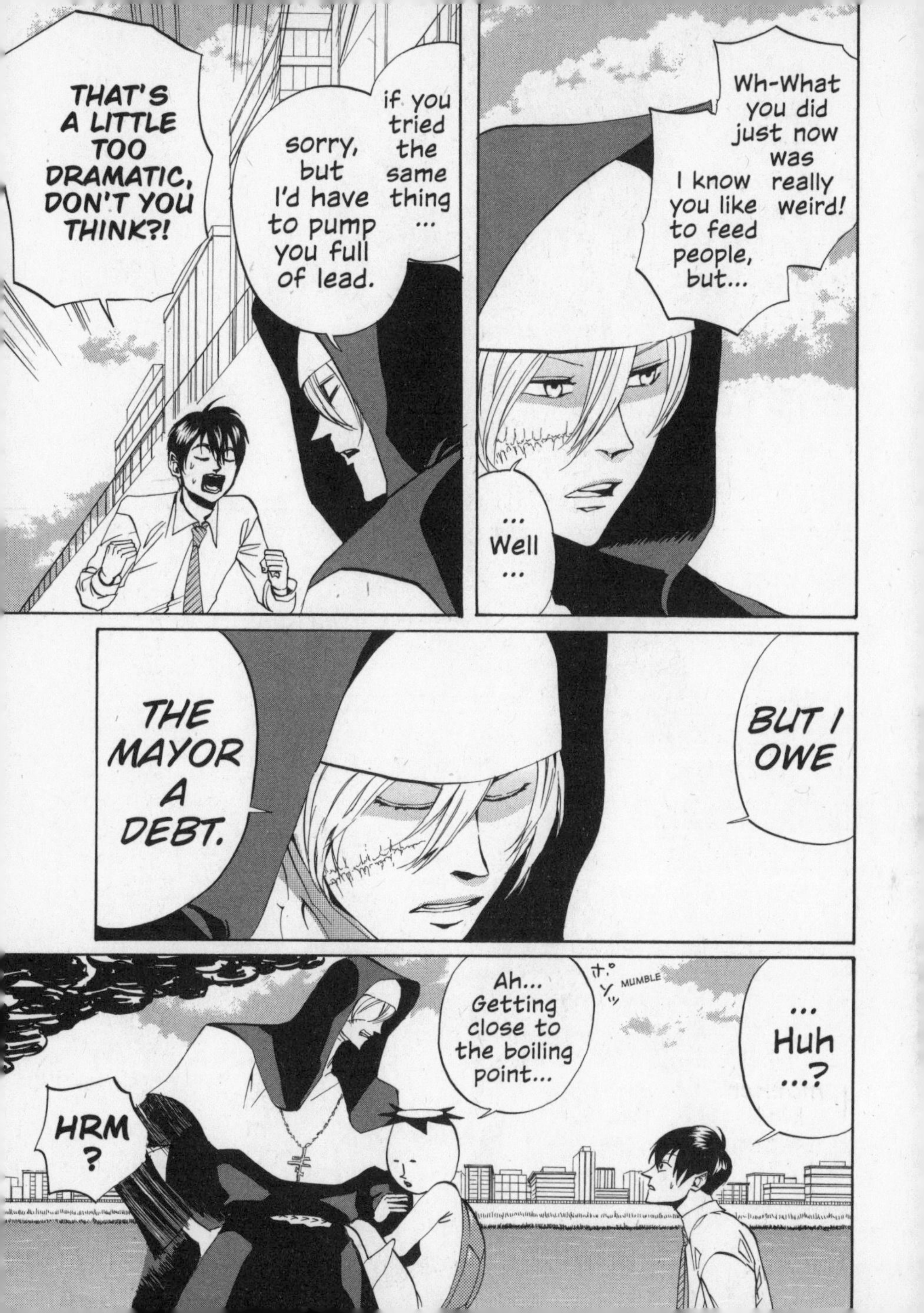
Wh-What you did just now was really weird! I know you like to feed people, but...
... Well ...
if you tried the same thing ... sorry, but I'd have to pump you full of lead.
THAT'S A LITTLE TOO DRAMATIC, DON'T YOU THINK?!
BUT I OWE
THE MAYOR A DEBT.
... Huh ...?
ボソッ MUMBLE
Ah... Getting close to the boiling point...
HRM ?

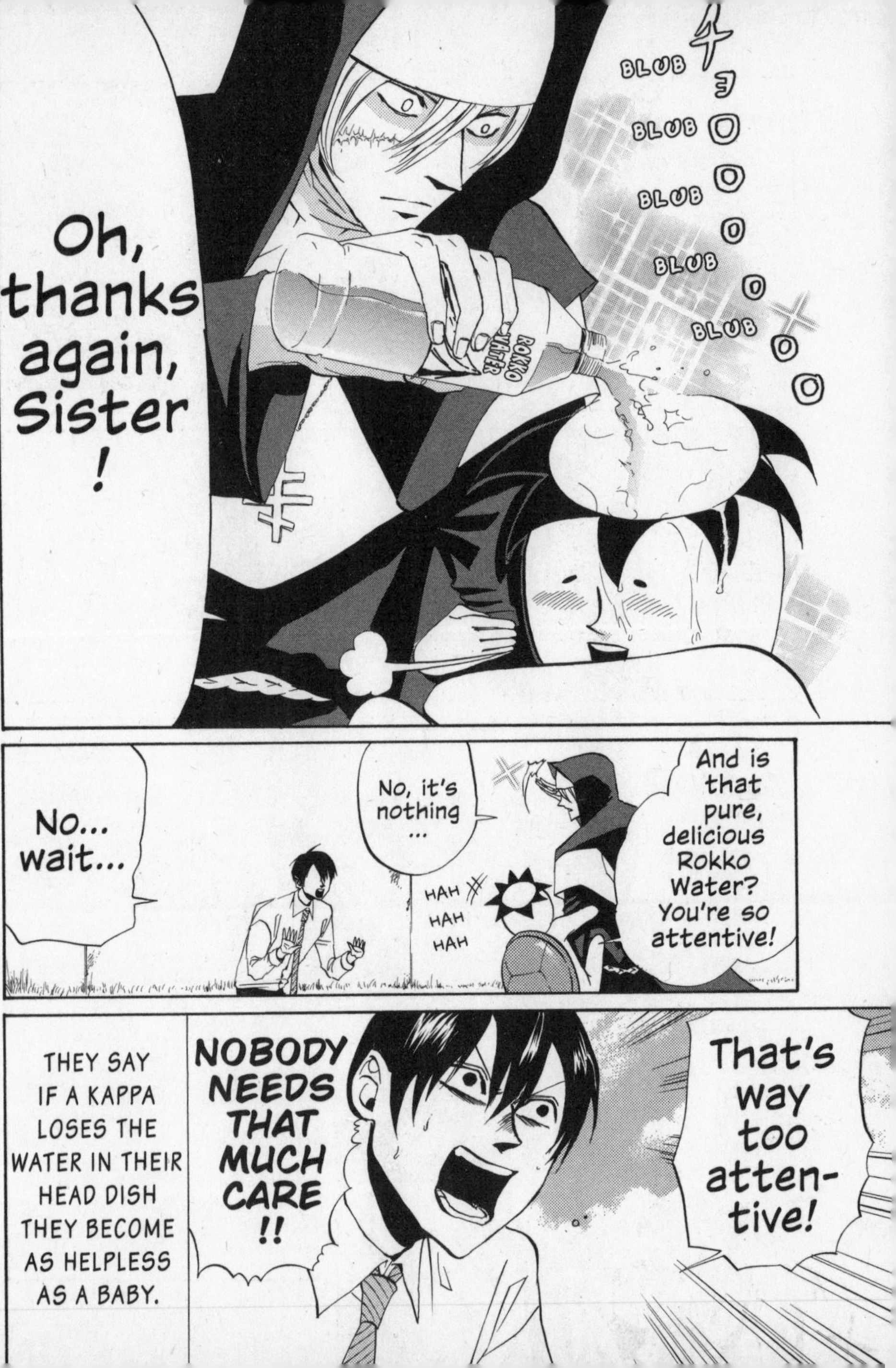
BLUB
BLUB
BLUB
BLUB
BLUB
ROKKO WATER
Oh, thanks again, Sister!
And is that pure, delicious Rokko Water? You're so attentive!
HAH HAH HAH
No, it's nothing...
No... wait...
That's way too atten-tive!
NOBODY NEEDS THAT MUCH CARE!!
THEY SAY IF A KAPPA LOSES THE WATER IN THEIR HEAD DISH THEY BECOME AS HELPLESS AS A BABY.

Chapter 89: Teamwork

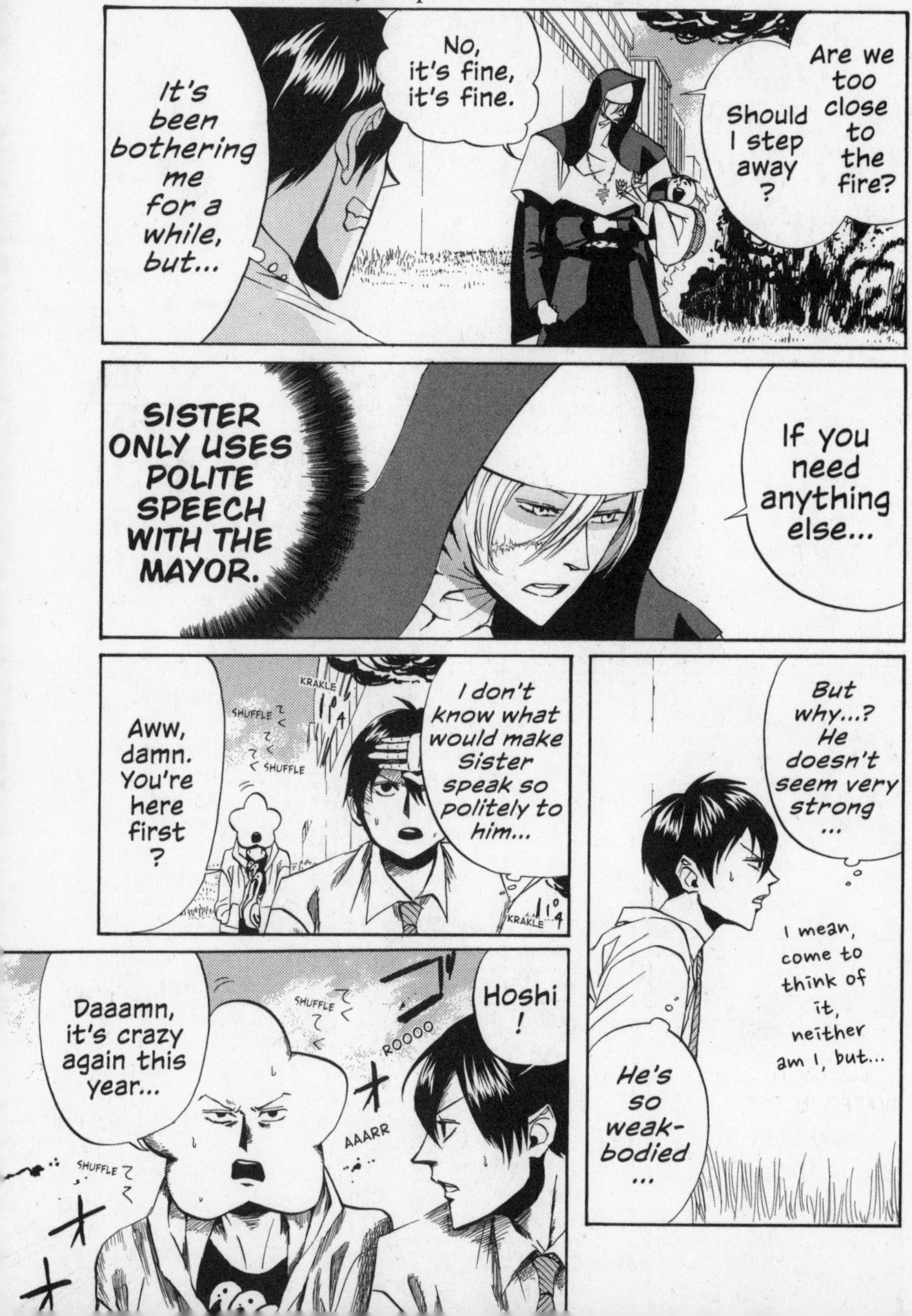
Are we too close to the fire?
Should I step away?
No, it's fine, it's fine.
It's been bothering me for a while, but...
If you need anything else...
SISTER ONLY USES POLITE SPEECH WITH THE MAYOR.
But why...? He doesn't seem very strong...
I mean, come to think of it, neither am I, but...
He's so weak-bodied...
KRAKLE
I don't know what would make Sister speak so politely to him...
SHUFFLE
SHUFFLE
Aww, damn. You're here first?
KRAKLE
Hoshi!
SHUFFLE
ROOOO
Daaamn, it's crazy again this year...
AAARR
SHUFFLE

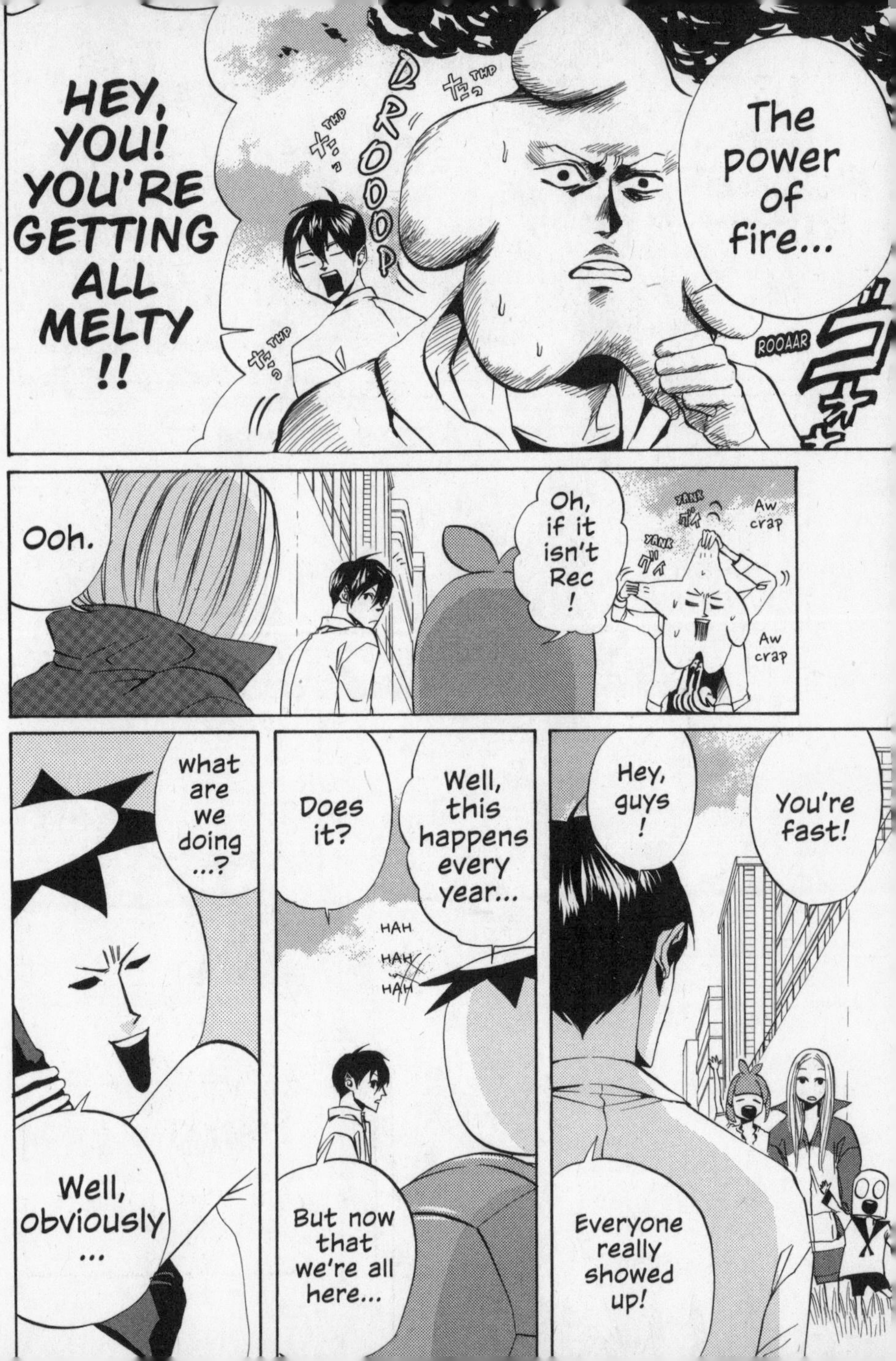

The power of fire...
ROOAAR
THP
DROOOP
THP
HEY, YOU! YOU'RE GETTING ALL MELTY !!
THP
Aw crap
YANK
Oh, if it isn't Rec!
YANK
Aw crap
Ooh.
You're fast!
Hey, guys!
Everyone really showed up!
Well, this happens every year...
Does it?
HAH
HAH
HAH
But now that we're all here...
what are we doing...?
Well, obviously...

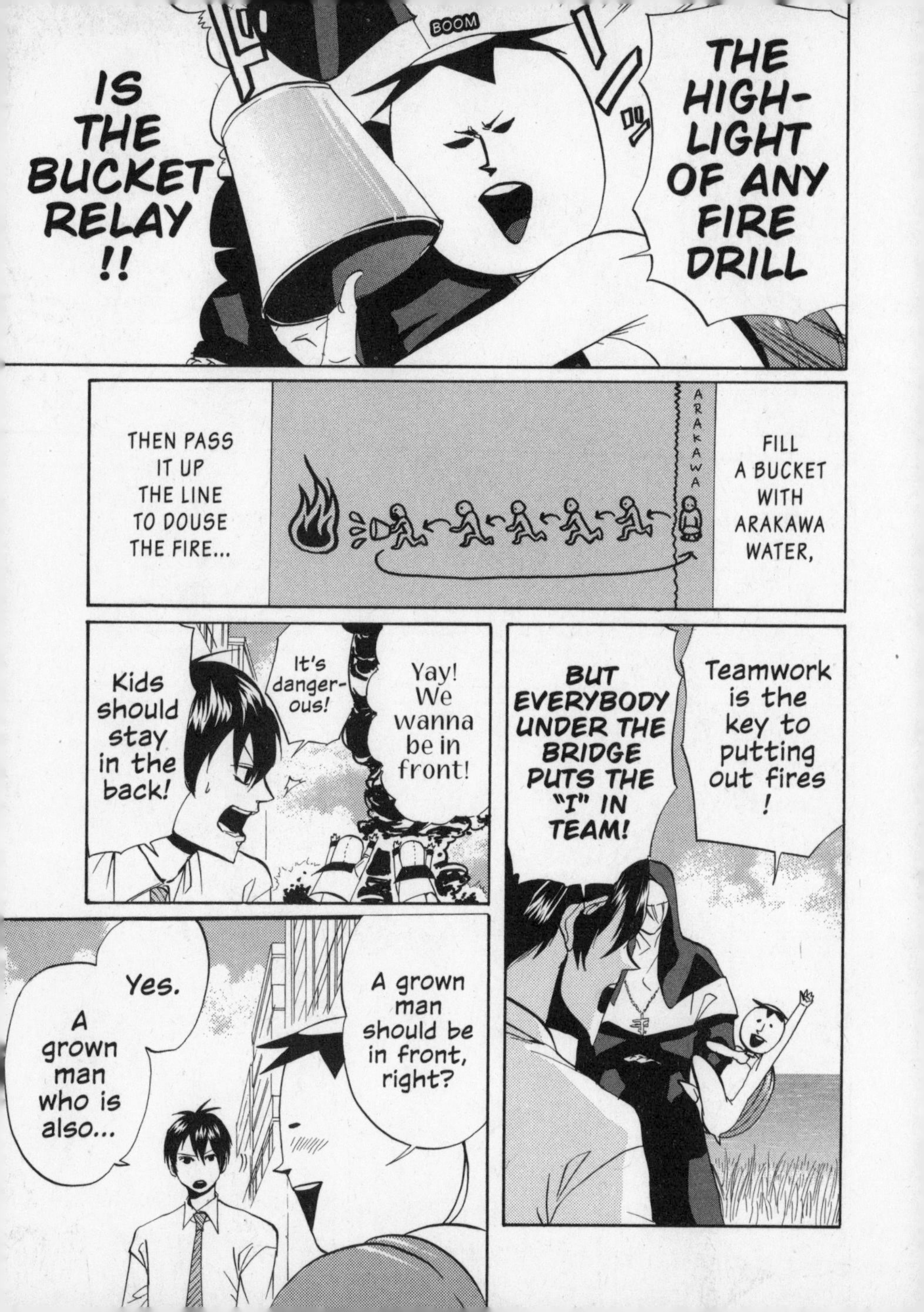
BOOM
THE HIGH-LIGHT OF ANY FIRE DRILL
IS THE BUCKET RELAY !!
FILL A BUCKET WITH ARAKAWA WATER,
ARAKAWA
THEN PASS IT UP THE LINE TO DOUSE THE FIRE...
Teamwork is the key to putting out fires!
BUT EVERYBODY UNDER THE BRIDGE PUTS THE "I" IN TEAM!
Yay! We wanna be in front!
It's danger-ous!
Kids should stay in the back!
A grown man should be in front, right?
Yes.
A grown man who is also...

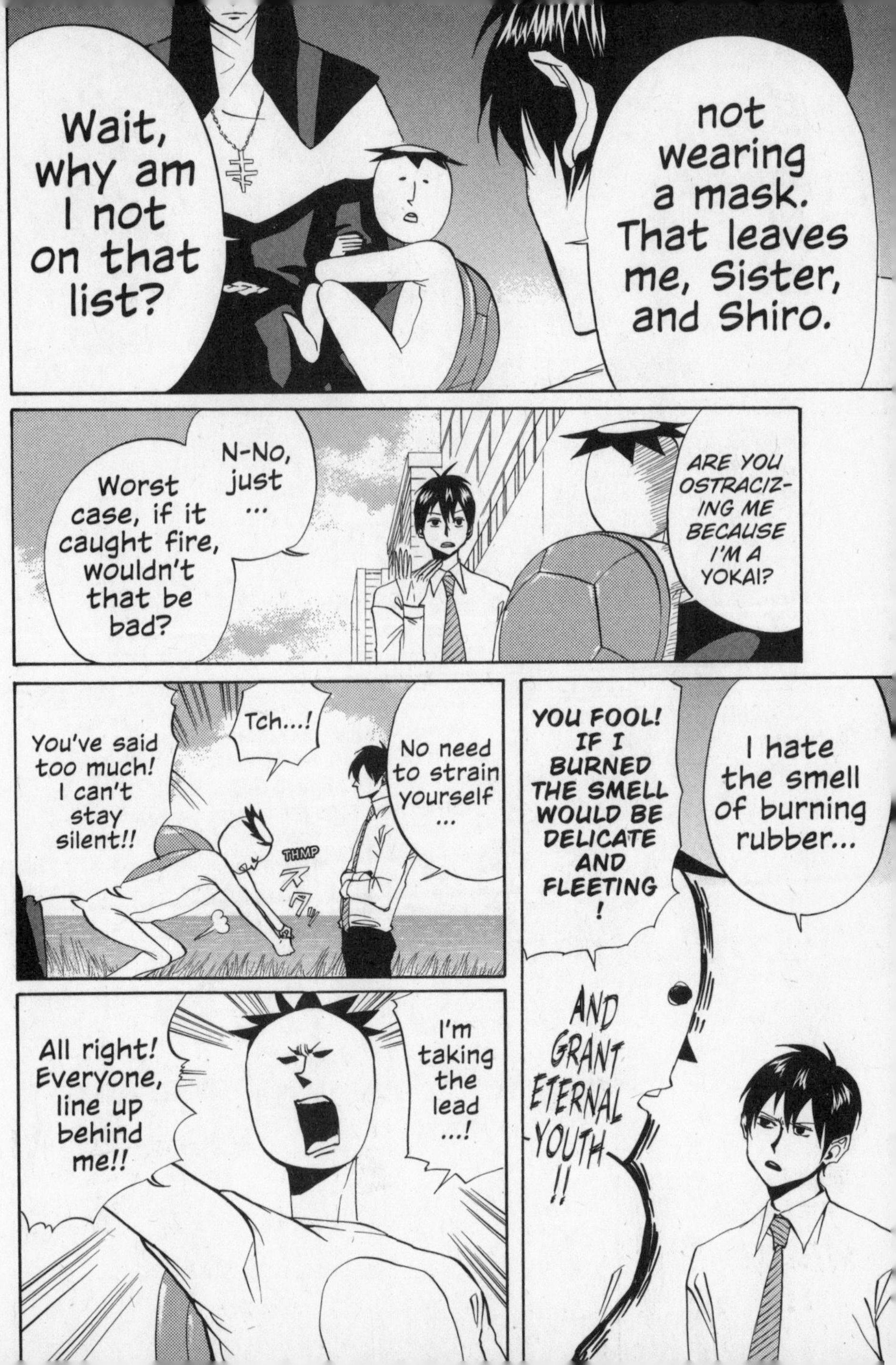
not wearing a mask. That leaves me, Sister, and Shiro.
Wait, why am I not on that list?
ARE YOU OSTRACIZING ME BECAUSE I'M A YOKAI?
N-No, just ...
Worst case, if it caught fire, wouldn't that be bad?
I hate the smell of burning rubber...
YOU FOOL! IF I BURNED THE SMELL WOULD BE DELICATE AND FLEETING!
AND GRANT ETERNAL YOUTH!!
No need to strain yourself ...
Tch...!
You've said too much! I can't stay silent!!
THMP
I'm taking the lead ...!
All right! Everyone, line up behind me!!

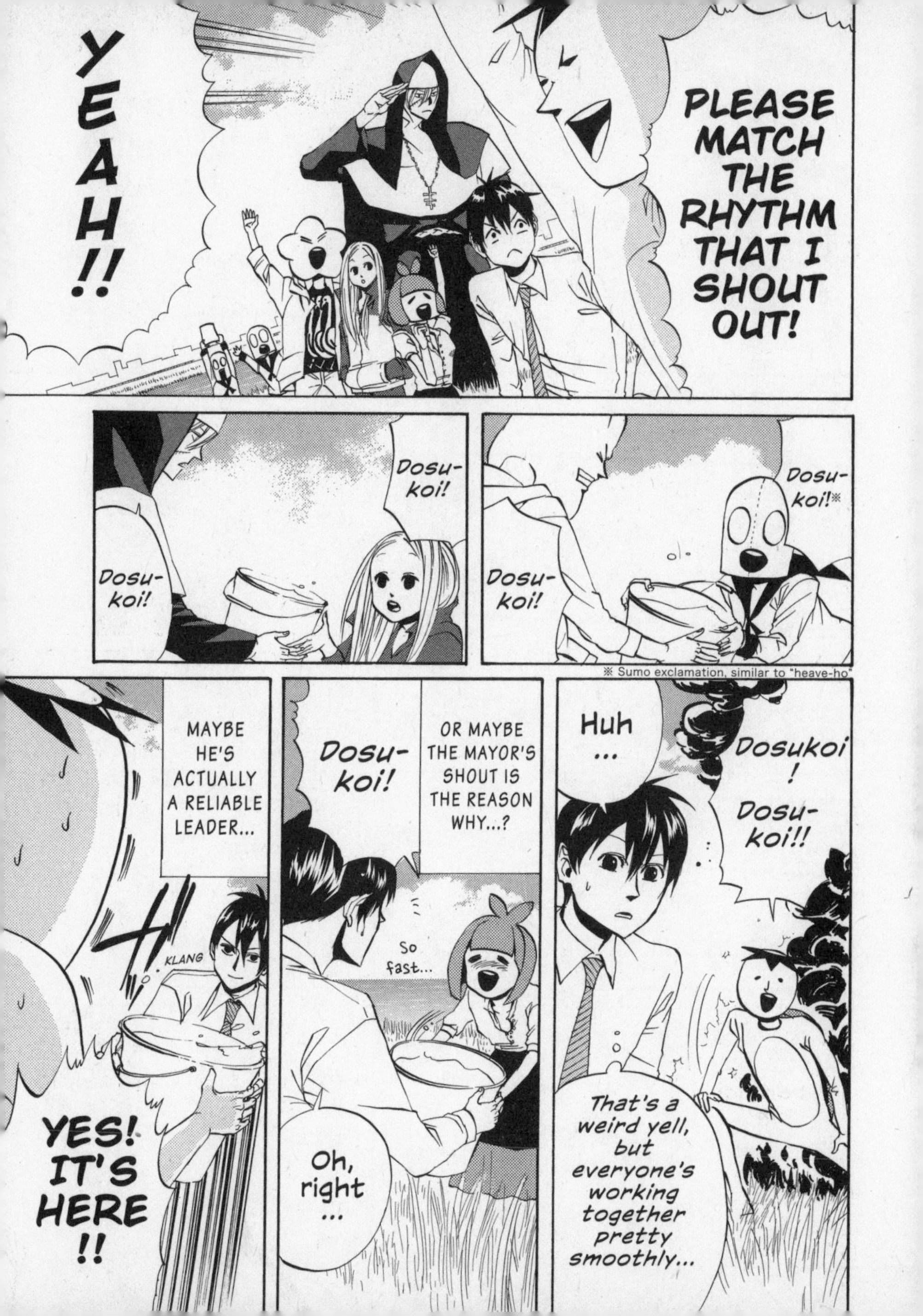
PLEASE MATCH THE RHYTHM THAT I SHOUT OUT!
YEAH!!
Dosu-koi!※
Dosu-koi!
Dosu-koi!
Dosu-koi!
Huh ...
Dosukoi! Dosu-koi!!
That's a weird yell, but everyone's working together pretty smoothly...
OR MAYBE THE MAYOR'S SHOUT IS THE REASON WHY...?
Dosu-koi!
So fast...
Oh, right ...
MAYBE HE'S ACTUALLY A RELIABLE LEADER...
KLANG
YES! IT'S HERE!!

※ Sumo exclamation, similar to "heave-ho"

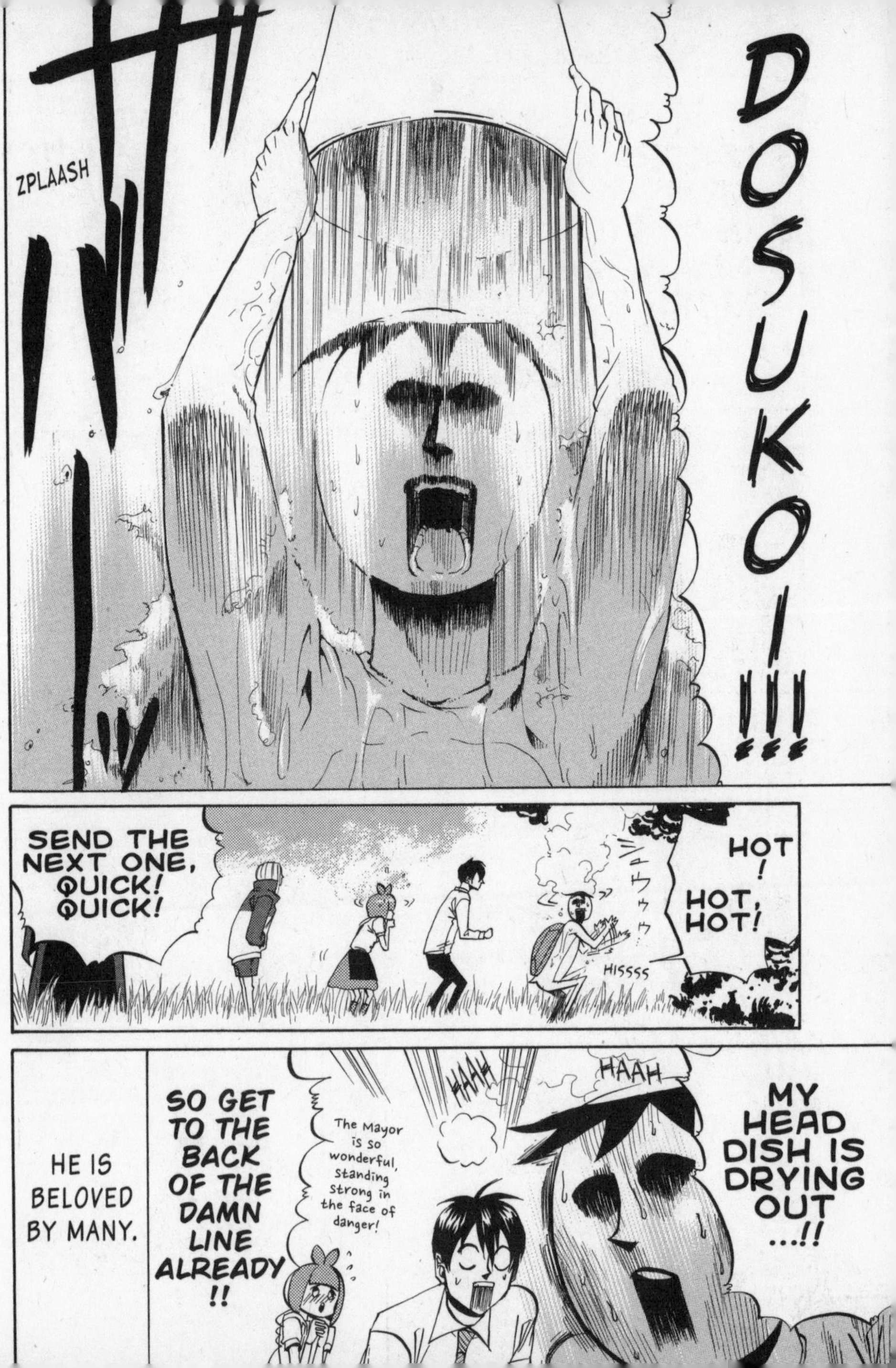
DOSUKOI!!!
ZPLAASH
HOT! HOT, HOT!
HISSSS
SEND THE NEXT ONE, QUICK! QUICK!
MY HEAD DISH IS DRYING OUT...!!
HAAH
HAAH
The Mayor is so wonderful, standing strong in the face of danger!
SO GET TO THE BACK OF THE DAMN LINE ALREADY!!
HE IS BELOVED BY MANY.

Chapter 90: Mayor Under the Bridge

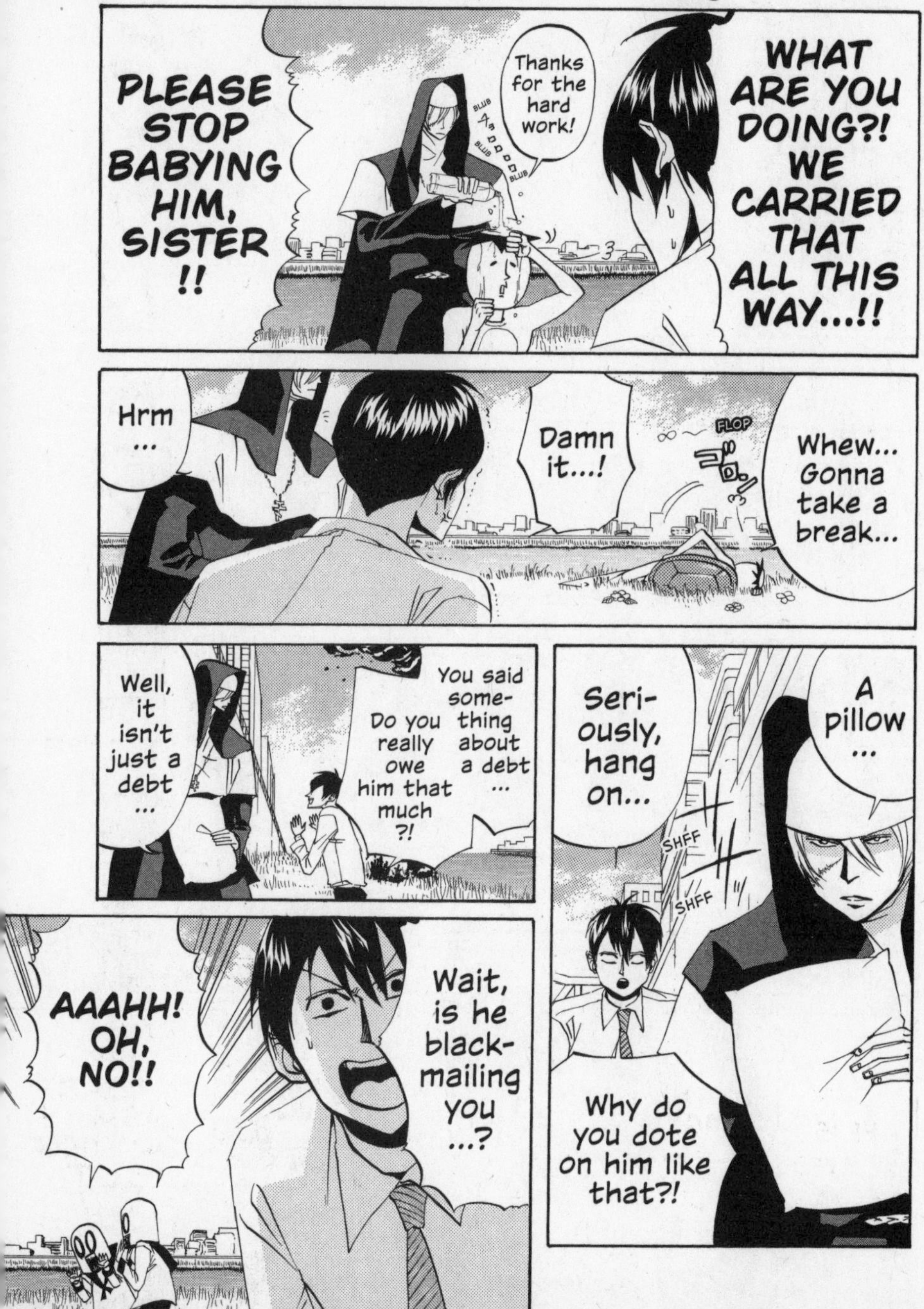

WHAT ARE YOU DOING?! WE CARRIED THAT ALL THIS WAY...!!
Thanks for the hard work!
BLUB
BLUB
BLUB
PLEASE STOP BABYING HIM, SISTER!!
Whew... Gonna take a break...
FLOP
Damn it...!
Hrm...
A pillow...
Seriously, hang on...
SHFF
SHFF
Why do you dote on him like that?!
You said something about a debt...
Do you really owe him that much?!
Well, it isn't just a debt...
Wait, is he blackmailing you...?
AAAHH! OH, NO!!

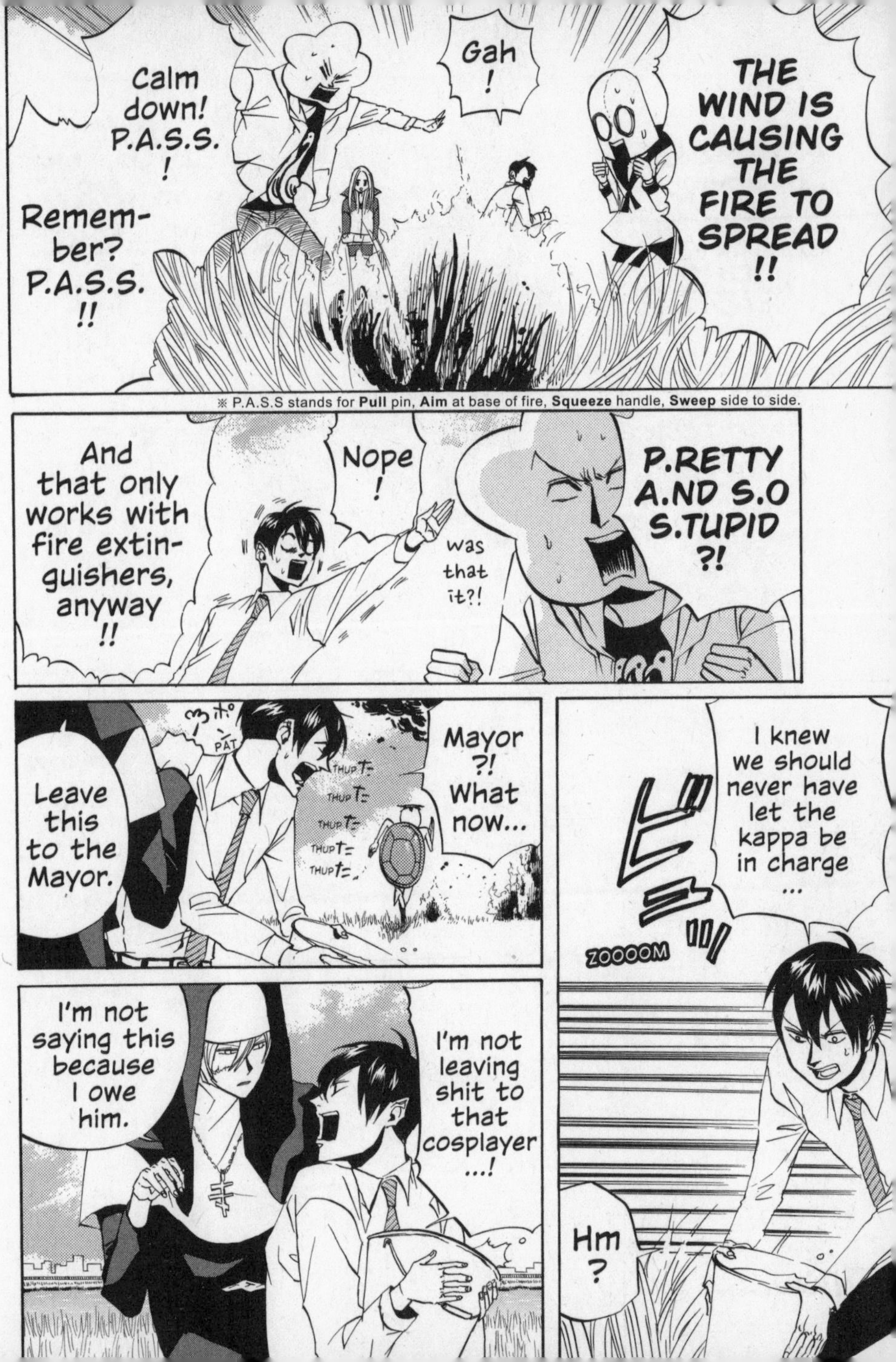
THE WIND IS CAUSING THE FIRE TO SPREAD!!
Gah!
Calm down! P.A.S.S.!
Remember? P.A.S.S.!!
P.RETTY A.ND S.O S.TUPID?!
was that it?!
Nope!
And that only works with fire extinguishers, anyway!!
I knew we should never have let the kappa be in charge...
ZOOOOM
Hm?
Mayor?! What now...
THUP THUP THUP THUP THUP
PAT
Leave this to the Mayor.
I'm not leaving shit to that cosplayer...!
I'm not saying this because I owe him.

※ P.A.S.S stands for **Pull** pin, **Aim** at base of fire, **Squeeze** handle, **Sweep** side to side.

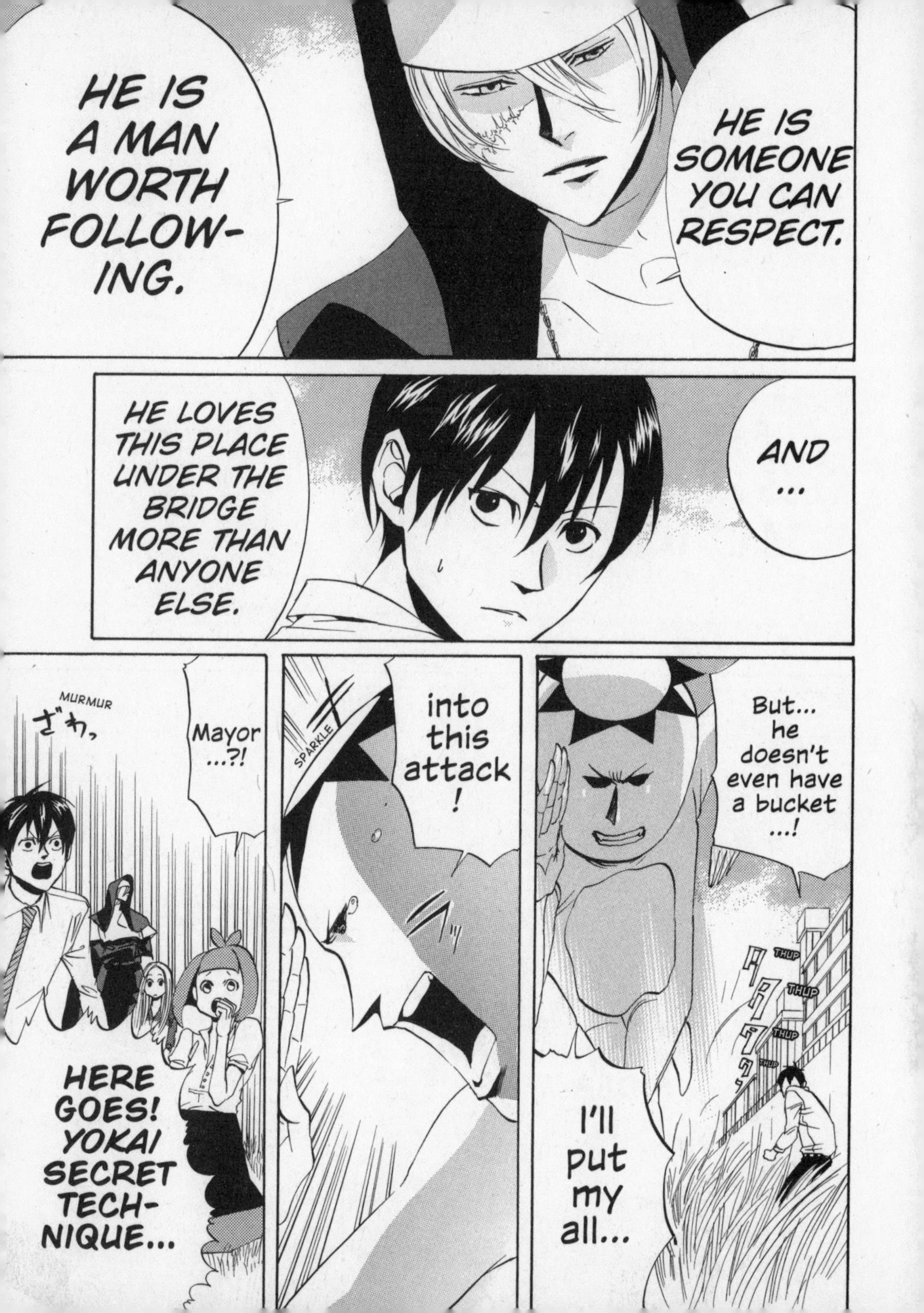
HE IS SOMEONE YOU CAN RESPECT.
HE IS A MAN WORTH FOLLOW-ING.
AND ...
HE LOVES THIS PLACE UNDER THE BRIDGE MORE THAN ANYONE ELSE.
But... he doesn't even have a bucket ...!
THUP
THUP
THUP
THUP
I'll put my all...
SPARKLE
into this attack!
MURMUR
ざわっ
Mayor ...?!
HERE GOES! YOKAI SECRET TECH-NIQUE...

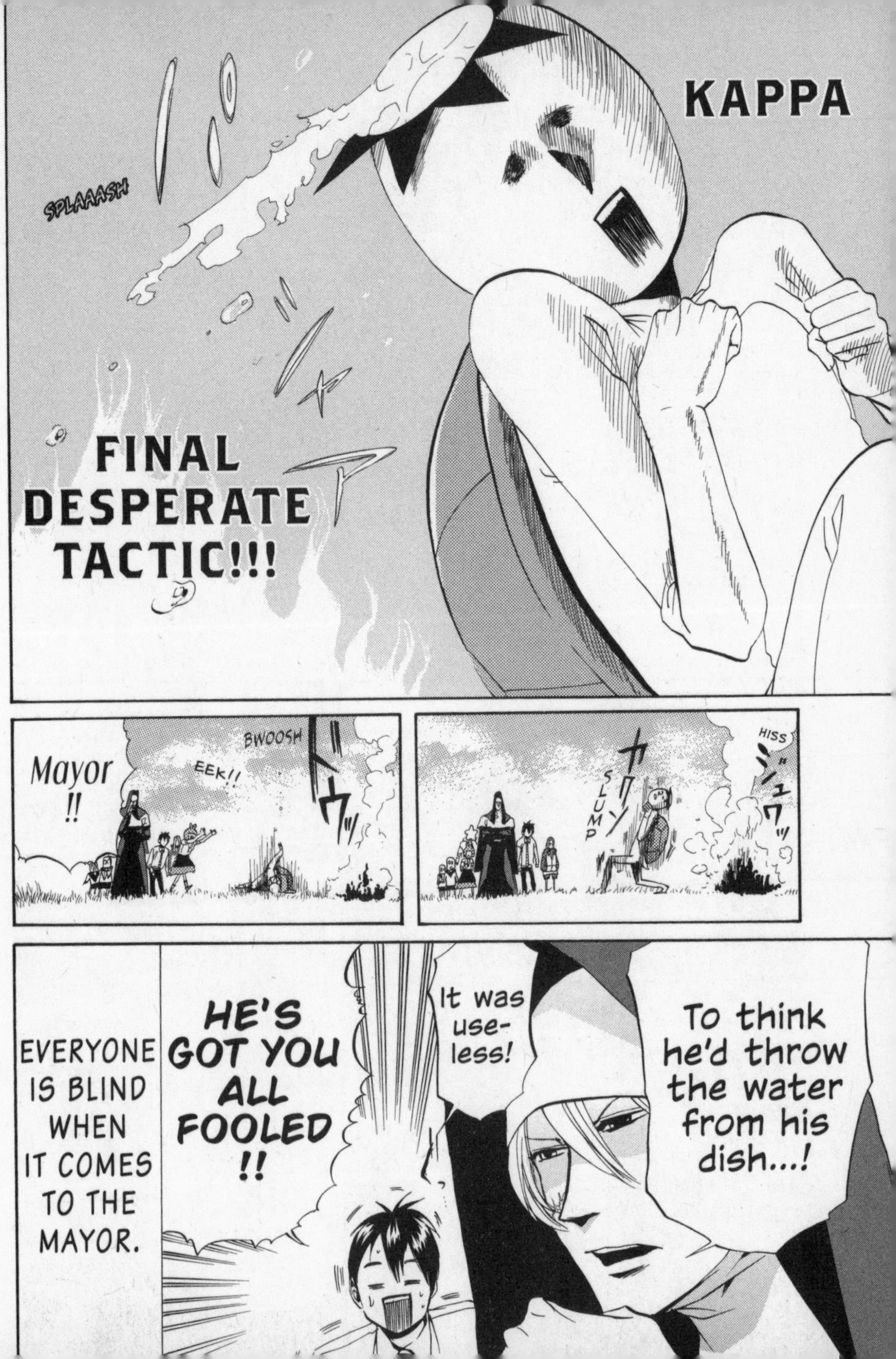
KAPPA
SPLAAASH
FINAL DESPERATE TACTIC!!!
HISS
SLUMP
Mayor!!
BWOOSH
EEK!!
To think he'd throw the water from his dish...!
It was useless!
HE'S GOT YOU ALL FOOLED!!
EVERYONE IS BLIND WHEN IT COMES TO THE MAYOR.

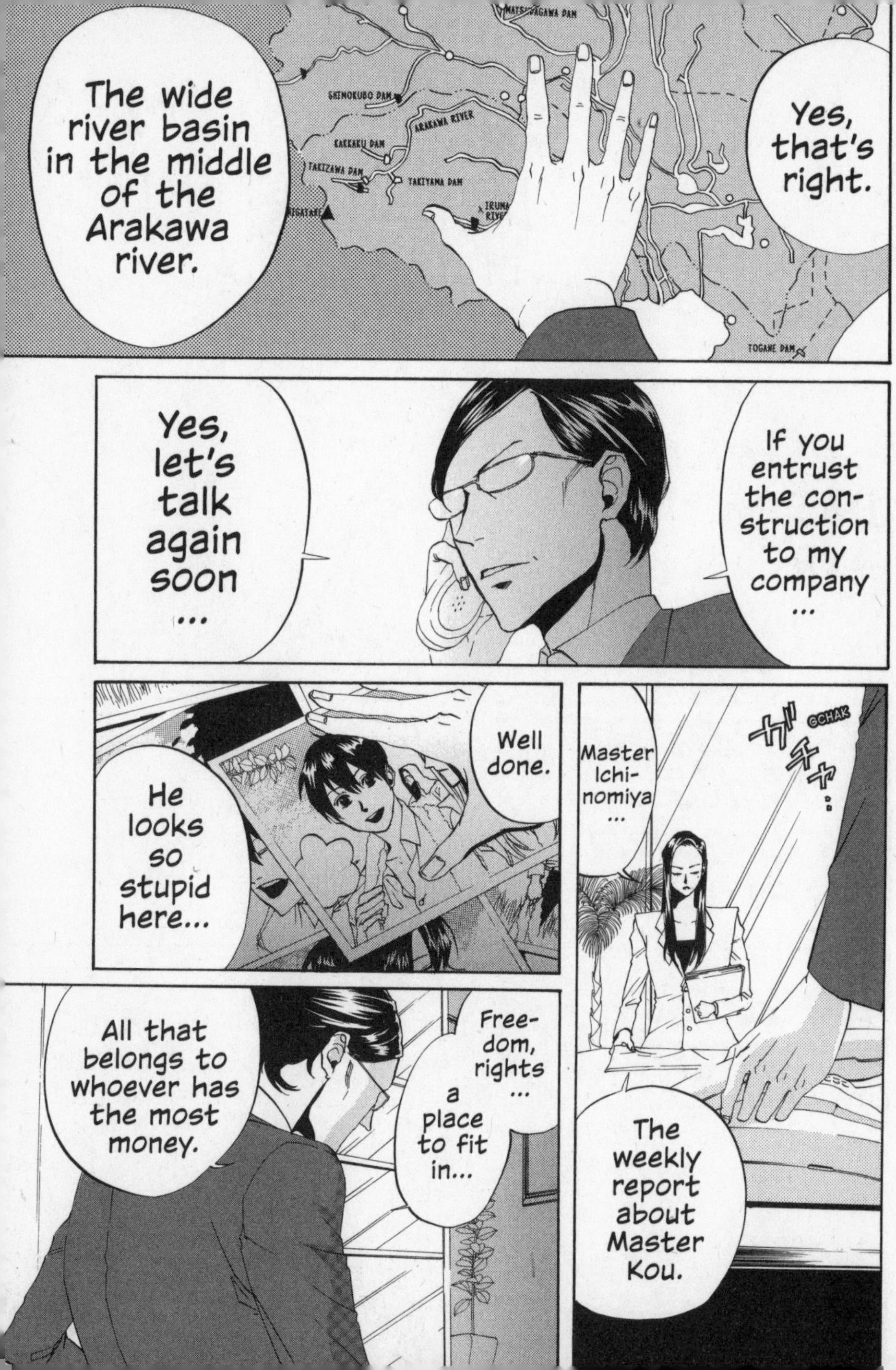
SHIMOKUBO DAM
ARAKAWA RIVER
KAKKAKU DAM
TAKIZAWA DAM
TAKIYAMA DAM
TOGANE DAM
Yes, that's right.
The wide river basin in the middle of the Arakawa river.
If you entrust the con-struction to my company ...
Yes, let's talk again soon ...
ガチャ
GCHAK
Master Ichi-nomiya ...
The weekly report about Master Kou.
Well done.
He looks so stupid here...
Free-dom, rights ...
a place to fit in...
All that belongs to whoever has the most money.

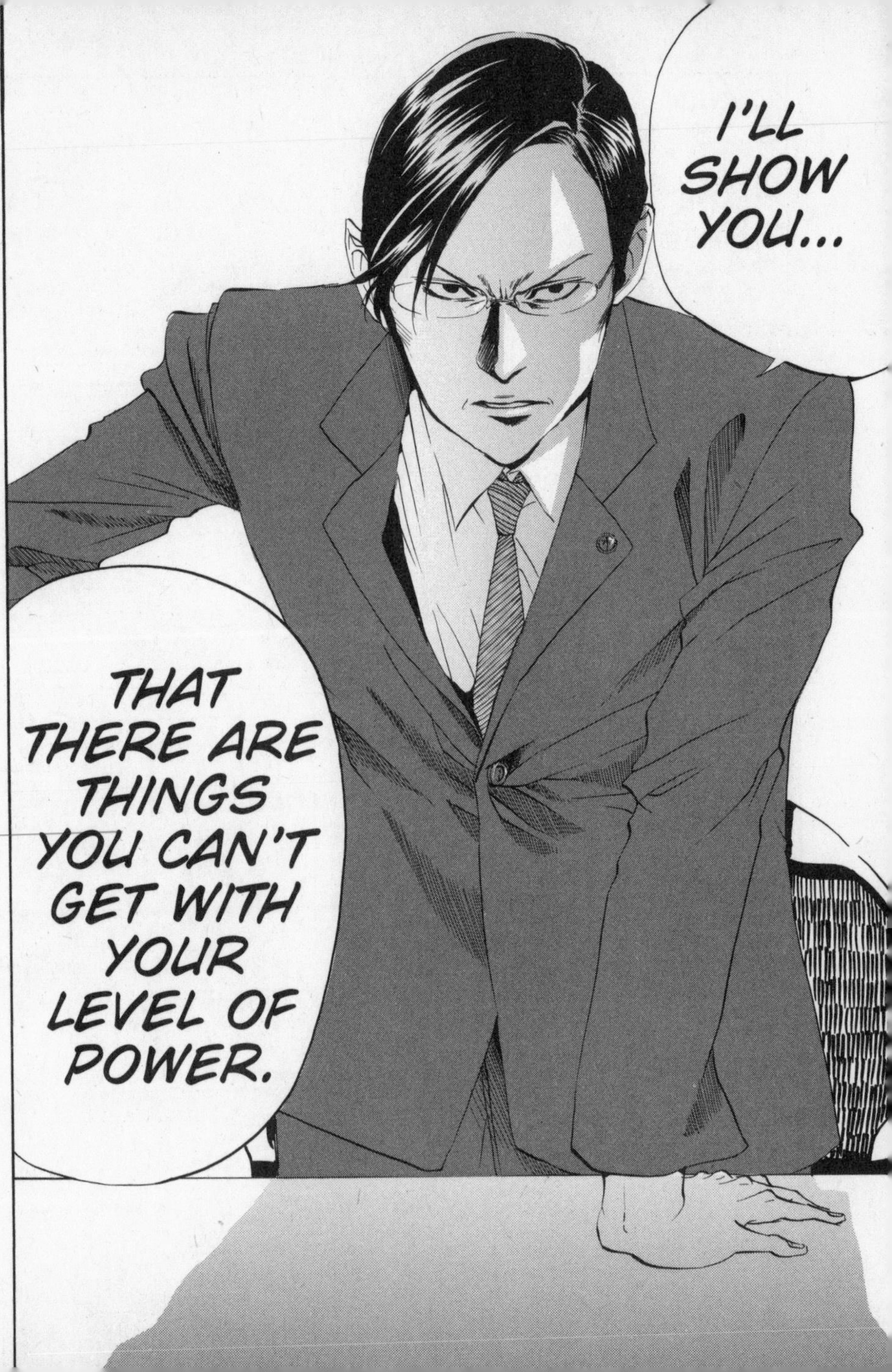
I'LL SHOW YOU...
THAT THERE ARE THINGS YOU CAN'T GET WITH YOUR LEVEL OF POWER.

Chapter 91: Enlightenment

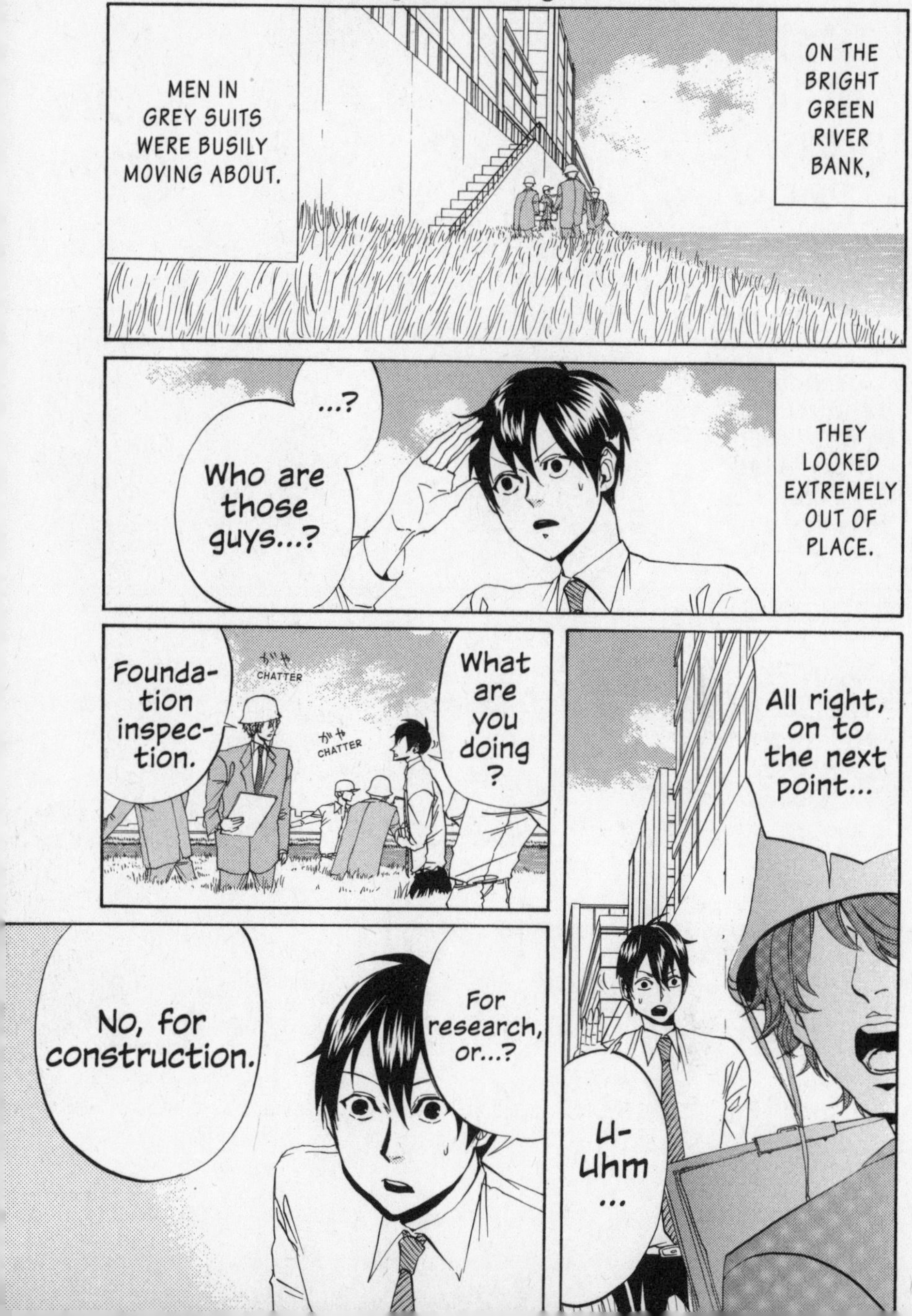
ON THE BRIGHT GREEN RIVER BANK,
MEN IN GREY SUITS WERE BUSILY MOVING ABOUT.
THEY LOOKED EXTREMELY OUT OF PLACE.
...?
Who are those guys...?
All right, on to the next point...
U-Uhm...
What are you doing?
CHATTER
CHATTER
Foundation inspection.
For research, or...?
No, for construction.

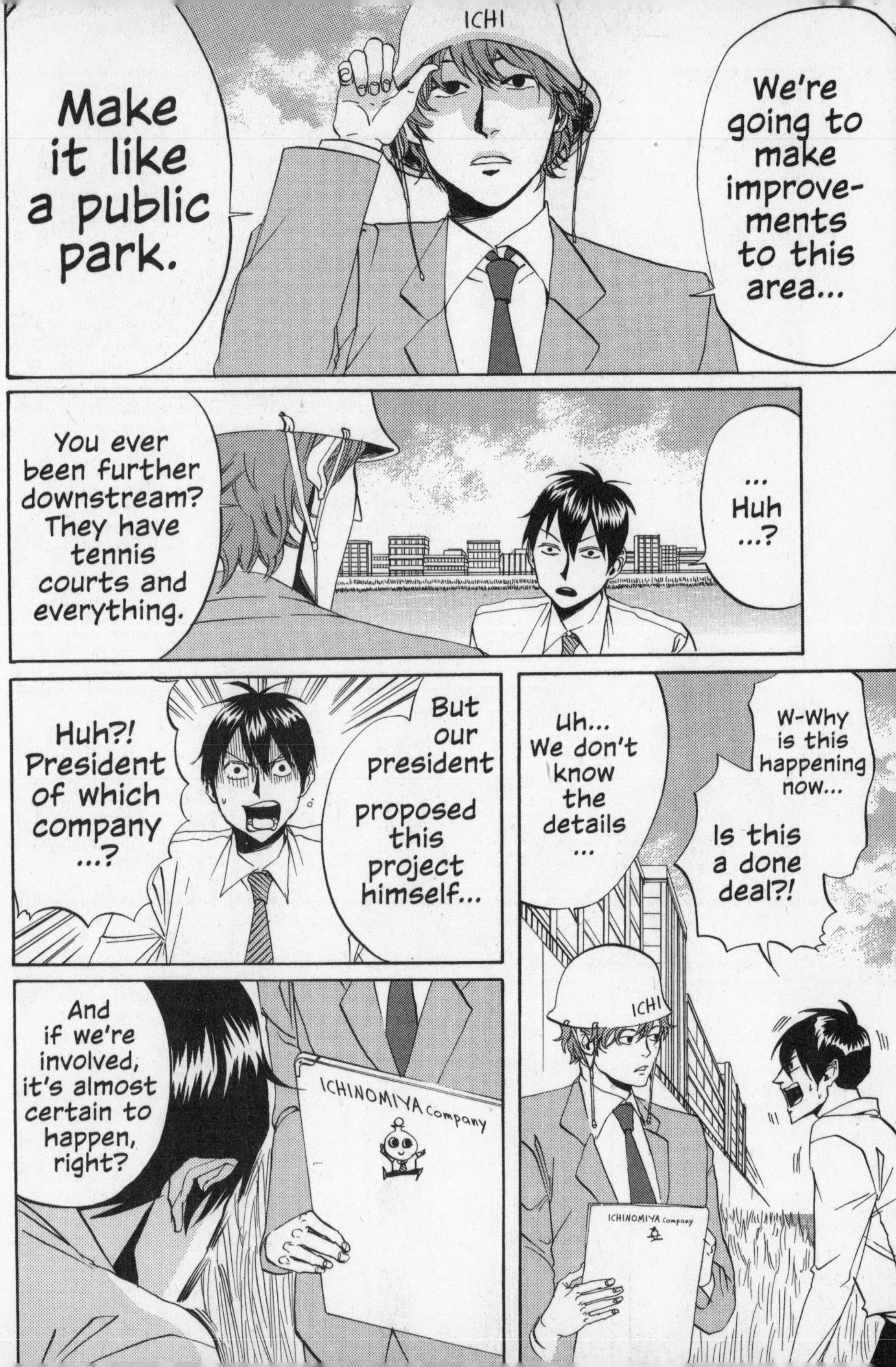
ICHI
We're going to make improvements to this area...
Make it like a public park.
... Huh ...?
You ever been further downstream? They have tennis courts and everything.
W-Why is this happening now...
Is this a done deal?!
Uh... We don't know the details ...
ICHI
ICHINOMIYA Company
But our president proposed this project himself...
Huh?! President of which company ...?
And if we're involved, it's almost certain to happen, right?
ICHINOMIYA Company

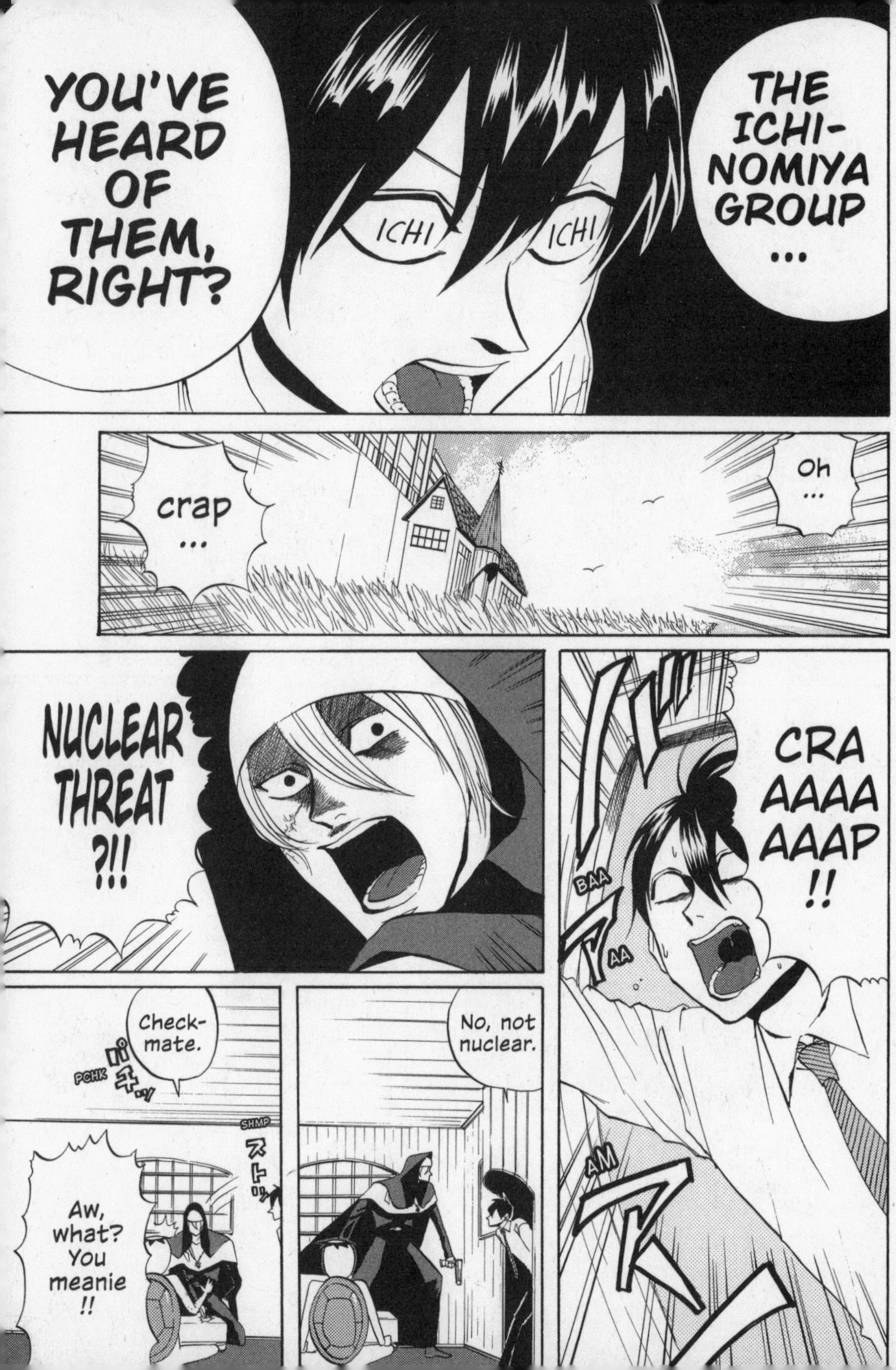
THE ICHI-NOMIYA GROUP ...
ICHI
ICHI
YOU'VE HEARD OF THEM, RIGHT?
Oh ...
crap ...
CRA AAAA AAAP !!
BAA
AA
AM
NUCLEAR THREAT ?!!
No, not nuclear.
SHMP
Check-mate.
PCHK
Aw, what? You meanie !!

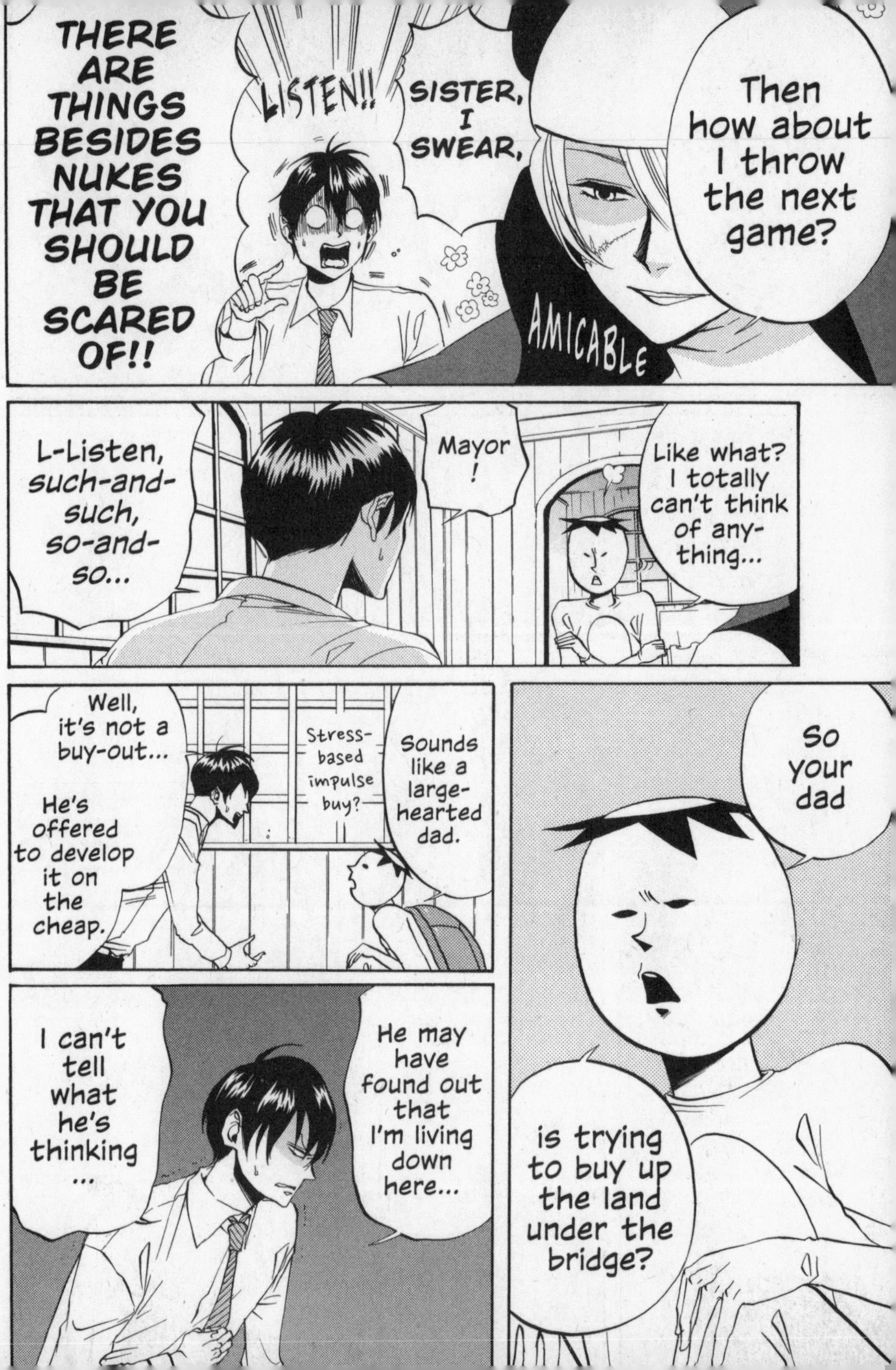
Then how about I throw the next game?
AMICABLE
SISTER, I SWEAR,
LISTEN!!
THERE ARE THINGS BESIDES NUKES THAT YOU SHOULD BE SCARED OF!!
Like what? I totally can't think of any-thing...
Mayor!
L-Listen, such-and-such, so-and-so...
So your dad
is trying to buy up the land under the bridge?
Sounds like a large-hearted dad.
Stress-based impulse buy?
Well, it's not a buy-out...
He's offered to develop it on the cheap.
He may have found out that I'm living down here...
I can't tell what he's thinking...

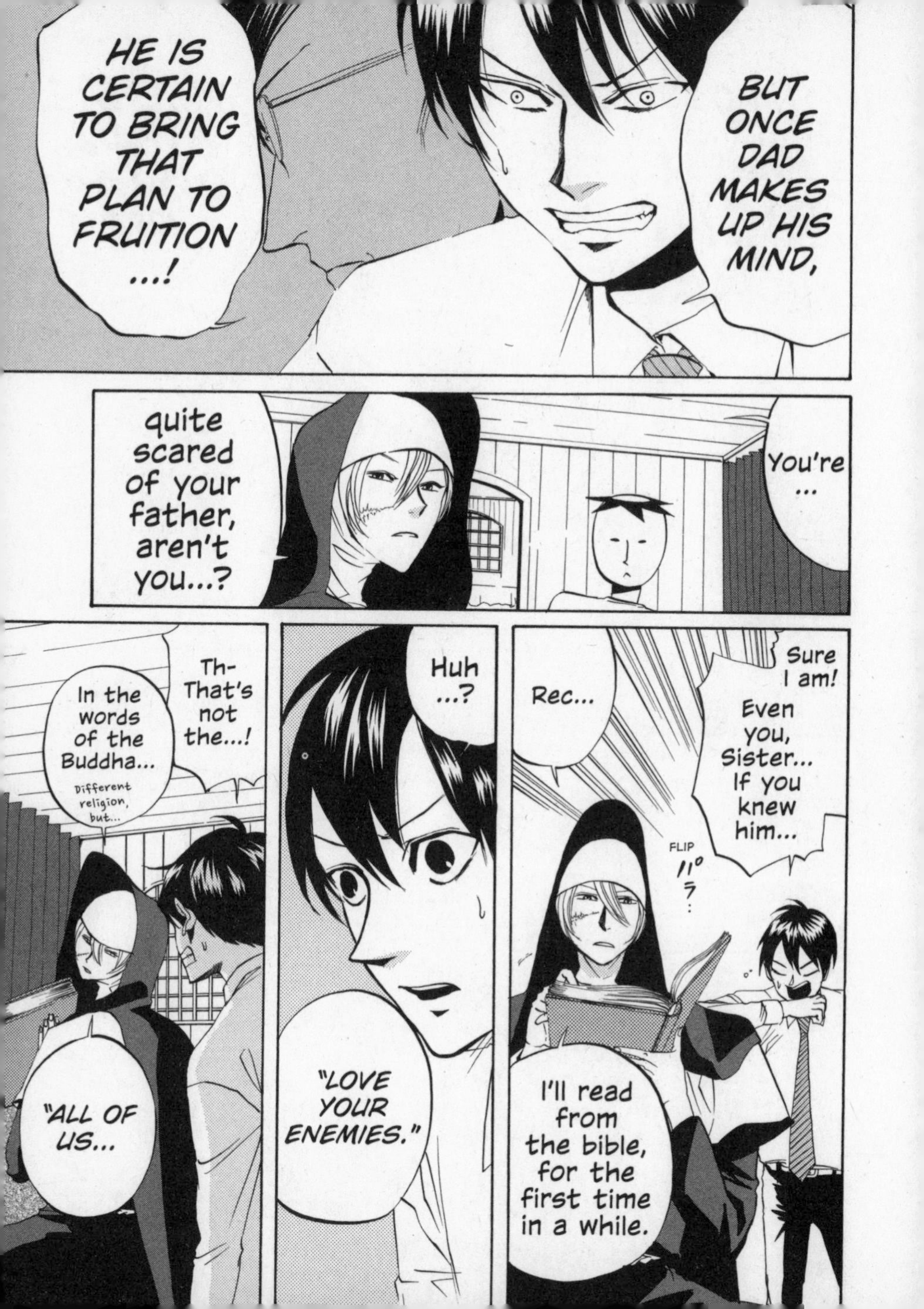
BUT ONCE DAD MAKES UP HIS MIND,
HE IS CERTAIN TO BRING THAT PLAN TO FRUITION ...!
You're ...
quite scared of your father, aren't you...?
Sure I am! Even you, Sister... If you knew him...
Rec...
FLIP
パラ
I'll read from the bible, for the first time in a while.
Huh ...?
"LOVE YOUR ENEMIES."
Th- That's not the...!
In the words of the Buddha...
Different religion, but...
"ALL OF US...

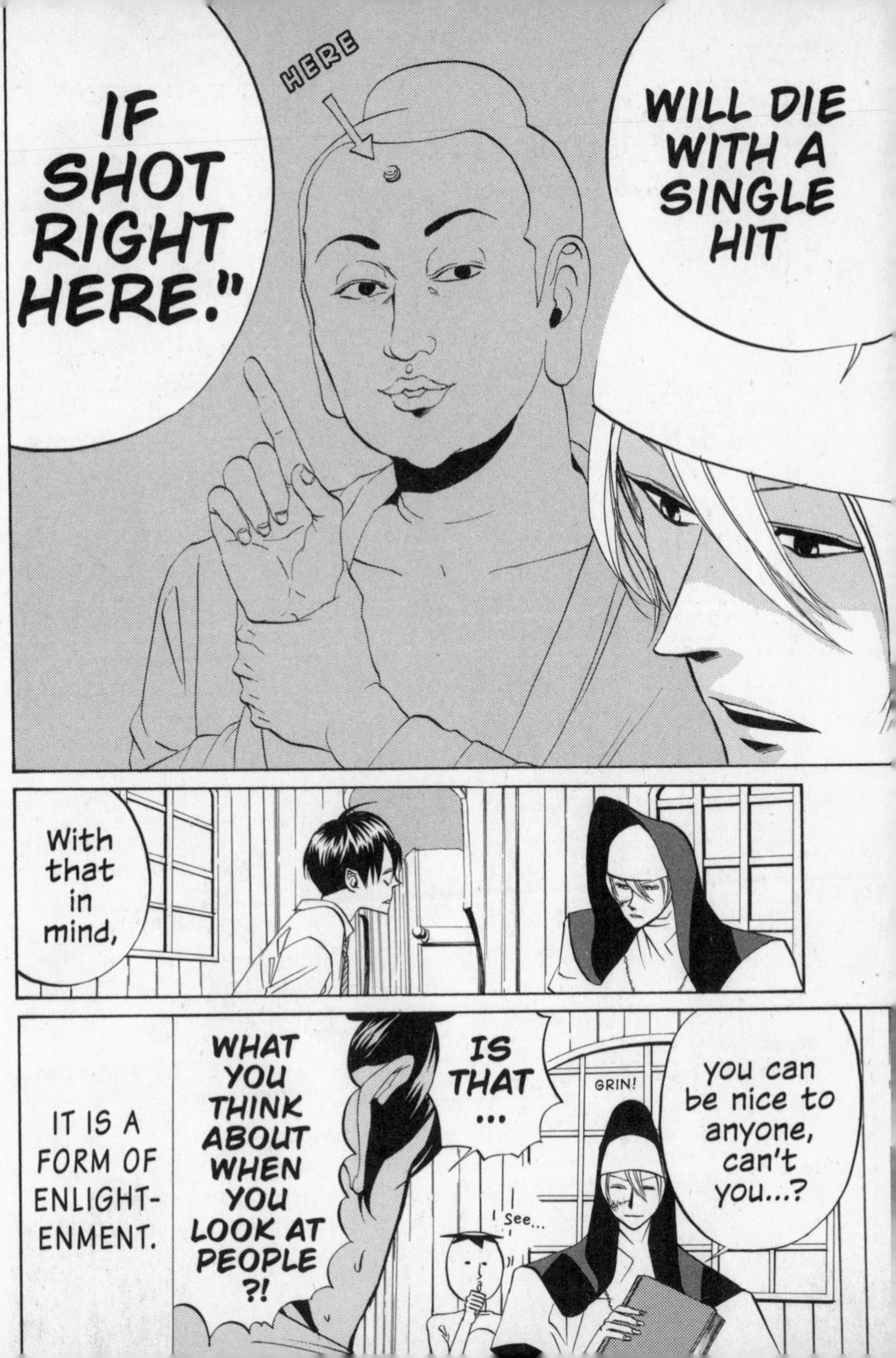
WILL DIE WITH A SINGLE HIT
HERE
IF SHOT RIGHT HERE."
With that in mind,
you can be nice to anyone, can't you...?
GRIN!
IS THAT ...
See...
WHAT YOU THINK ABOUT WHEN YOU LOOK AT PEOPLE ?!
IT IS A FORM OF ENLIGHT-ENMENT.

Chapter 92: Emergency

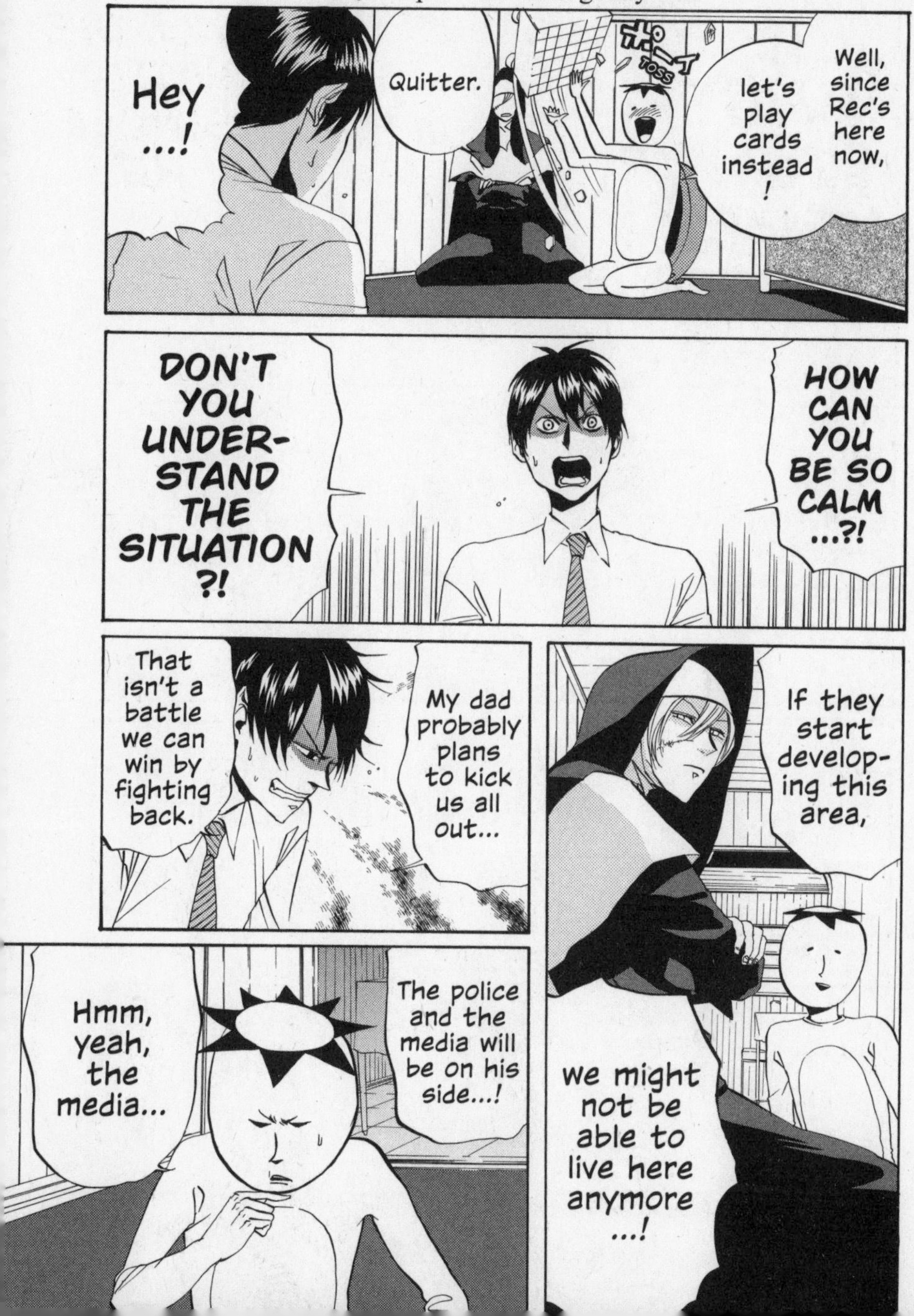
Well, since Rec's here now, let's play cards instead!
TOSS
Quitter.
Hey...!
HOW CAN YOU BE SO CALM...?!
DON'T YOU UNDERSTAND THE SITUATION?!
If they start developing this area,
we might not be able to live here anymore...!
My dad probably plans to kick us all out...
That isn't a battle we can win by fighting back.
The police and the media will be on his side...!
Hmm, yeah, the media...

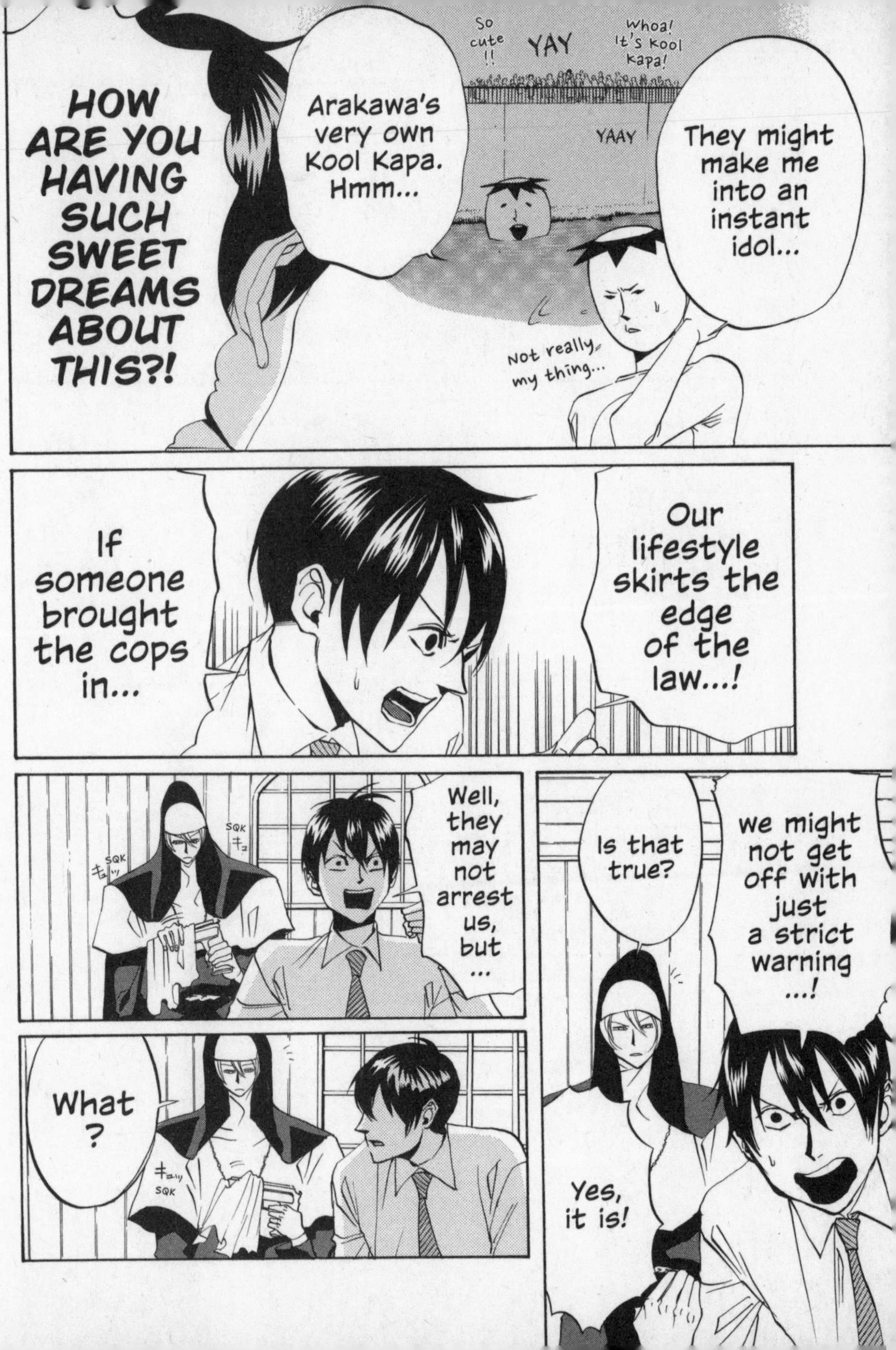
Whoa! It's Kool Kapa!
YAY
So cute !!
They might make me into an instant idol...
Arakawa's very own Kool Kapa. Hmm...
YAAY
Not really my thing...
HOW ARE YOU HAVING SUCH SWEET DREAMS ABOUT THIS?!
Our lifestyle skirts the edge of the law...!
If someone brought the cops in...
we might not get off with just a strict warning ...!
Is that true?
Yes, it is!
Well, they may not arrest us, but ...
SQK
SQK
What ?
SQK

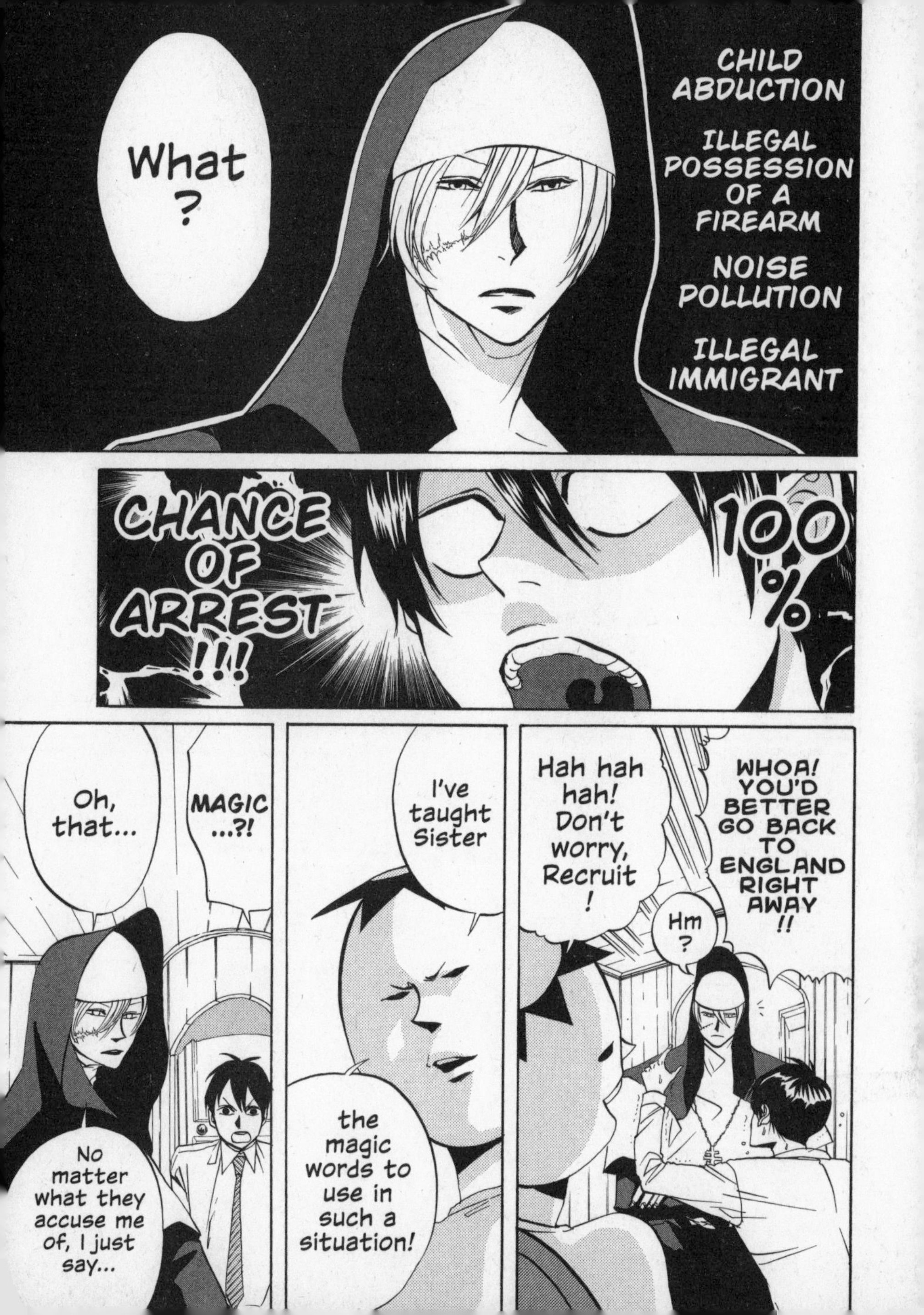
CHILD ABDUCTION
ILLEGAL POSSESSION OF A FIREARM
NOISE POLLUTION
ILLEGAL IMMIGRANT
What ?
100 %
CHANCE OF ARREST !!!
WHOA! YOU'D BETTER GO BACK TO ENGLAND RIGHT AWAY !!
Hah hah hah! Don't worry, Recruit !
Hm ?
I've taught Sister
the magic words to use in such a situation!
MAGIC ...?!
Oh, that...
No matter what they accuse me of, I just say...

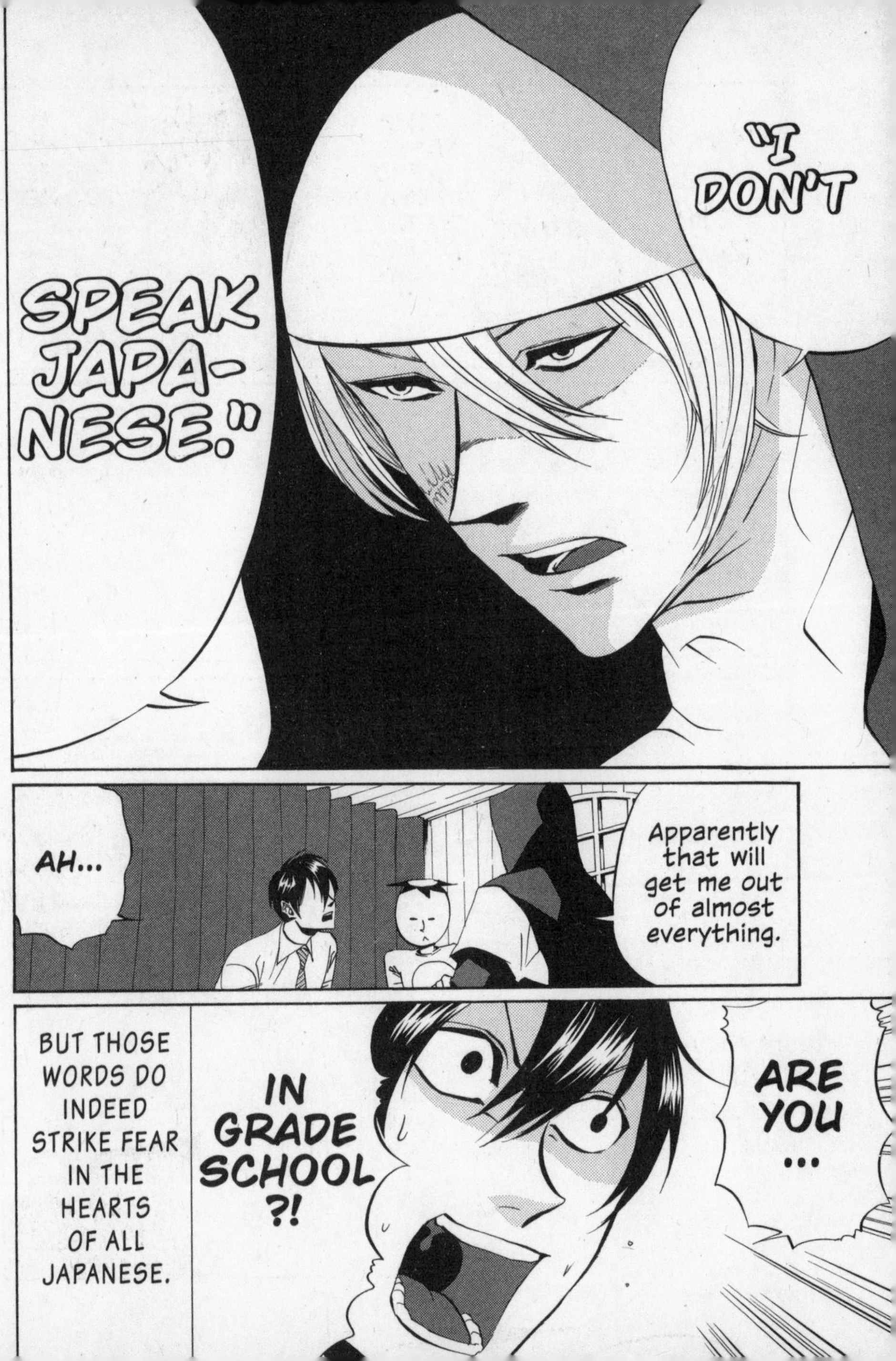
"I DON'T
SPEAK JAPA-NESE."
Apparently that will get me out of almost everything.
AH...
ARE YOU ...
IN GRADE SCHOOL ?!
BUT THOSE WORDS DO INDEED STRIKE FEAR IN THE HEARTS OF ALL JAPANESE.

Chapter 93: No Worries

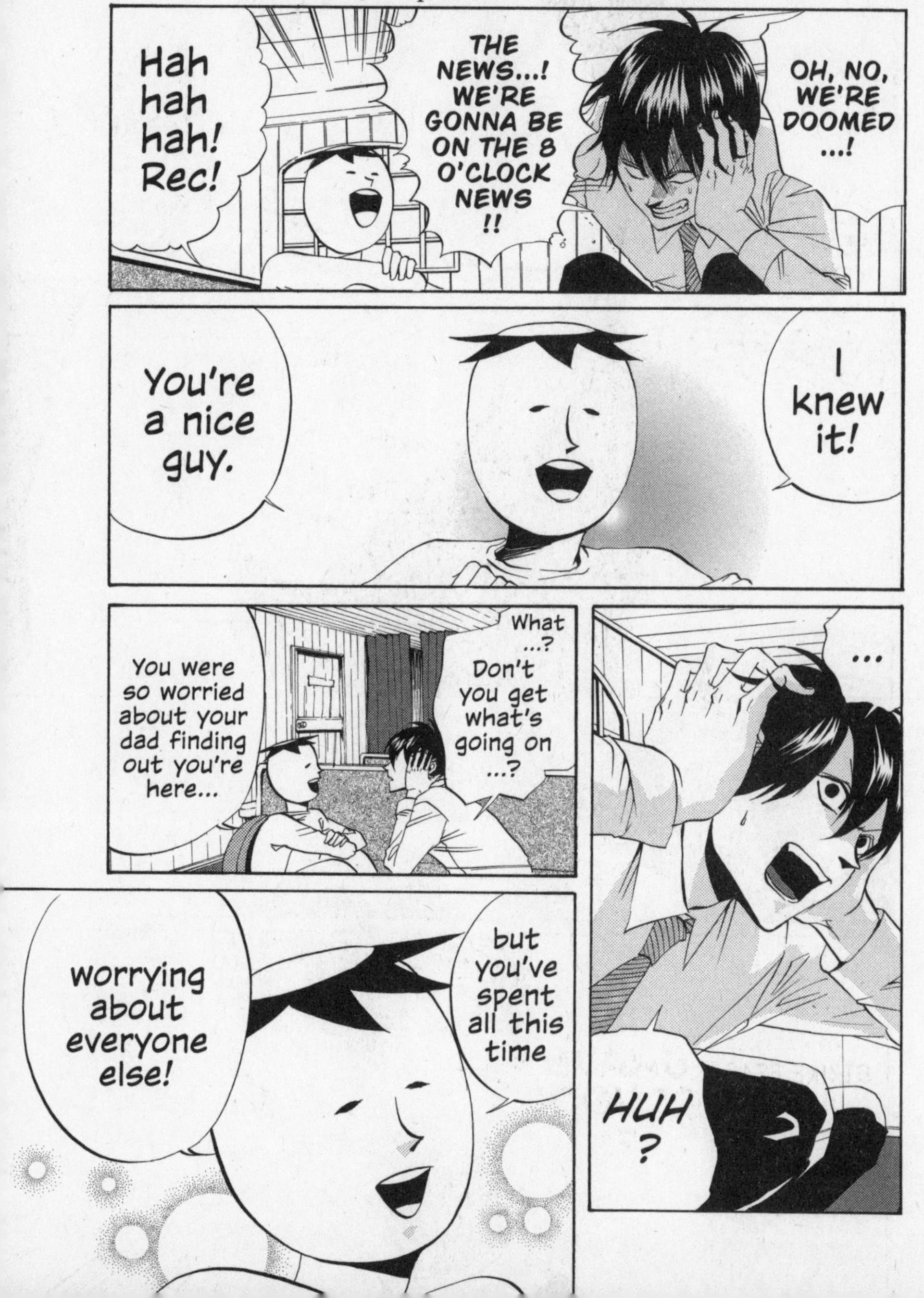
OH, NO, WE'RE DOOMED ...!
THE NEWS...! WE'RE GONNA BE ON THE 8 O'CLOCK NEWS !!
Hah hah hah! Rec!
I knew it!
You're a nice guy.
...
HUH ?
What ...? Don't you get what's going on ...?
You were so worried about your dad finding out you're here...
but you've spent all this time
worrying about everyone else!

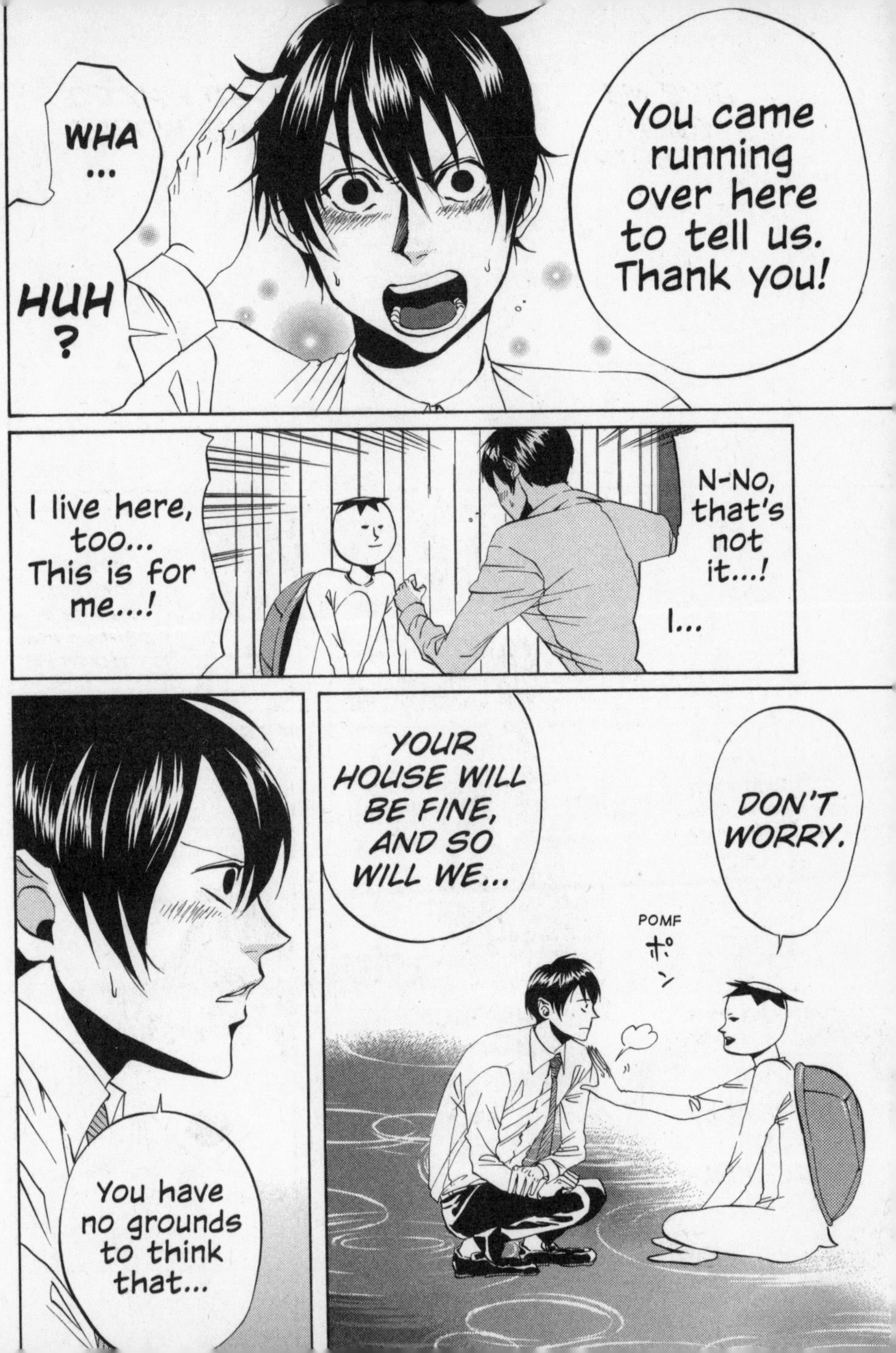
You came running over here to tell us. Thank you!
WHA ...
HUH ?
N-No, that's not it...!
I...
I live here, too... This is for me...!
DON'T WORRY.
YOUR HOUSE WILL BE FINE, AND SO WILL WE...
POMF
ポン
You have no grounds to think that...

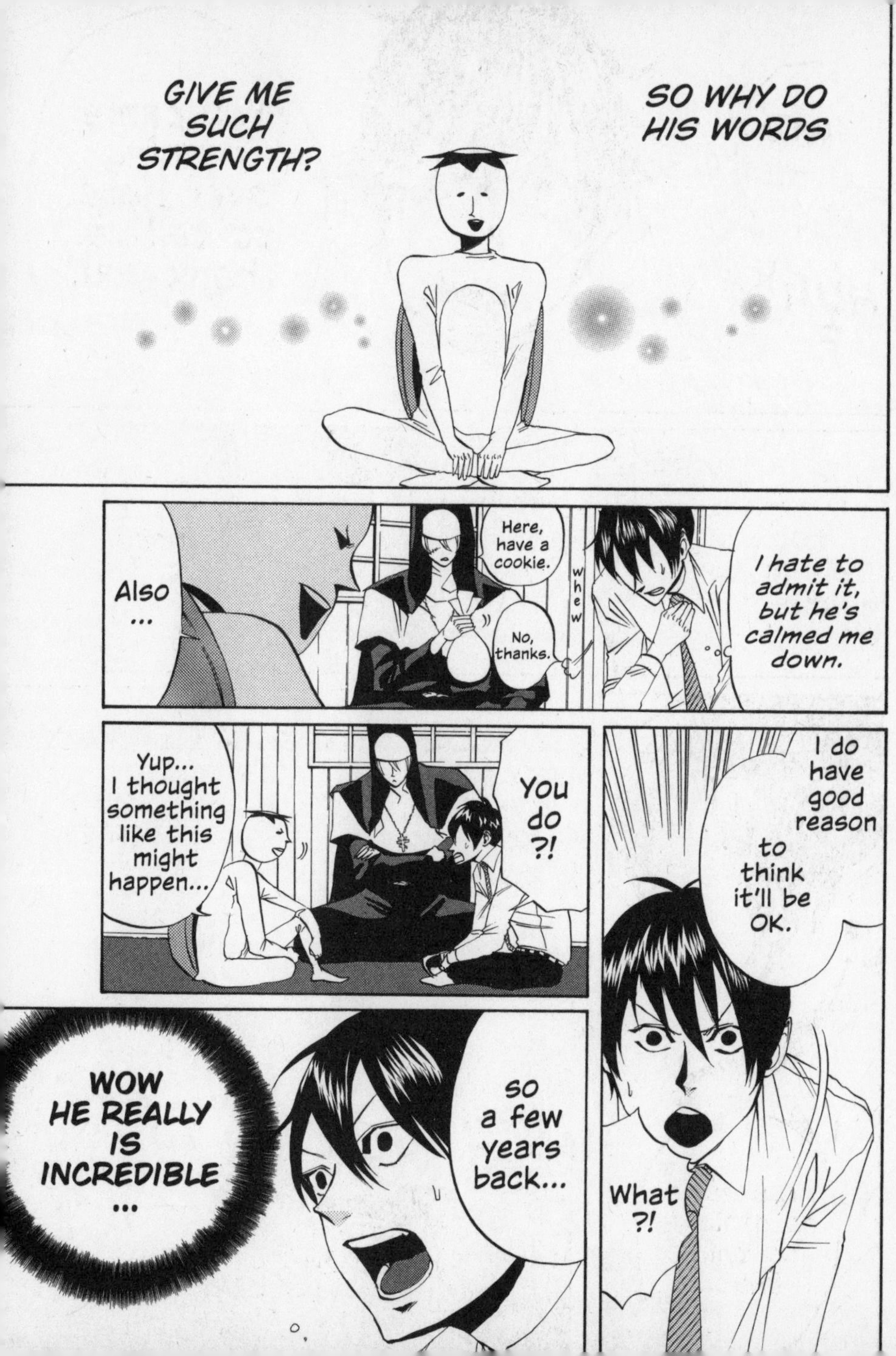
SO WHY DO HIS WORDS
GIVE ME SUCH STRENGTH?
I hate to admit it, but he's calmed me down.
whew
Here, have a cookie.
No, thanks.
Also ...
I do have good reason to think it'll be OK.
What ?!
You do ?!
Yup... I thought something like this might happen...
so a few years back...
WOW HE REALLY IS INCREDIBLE ...

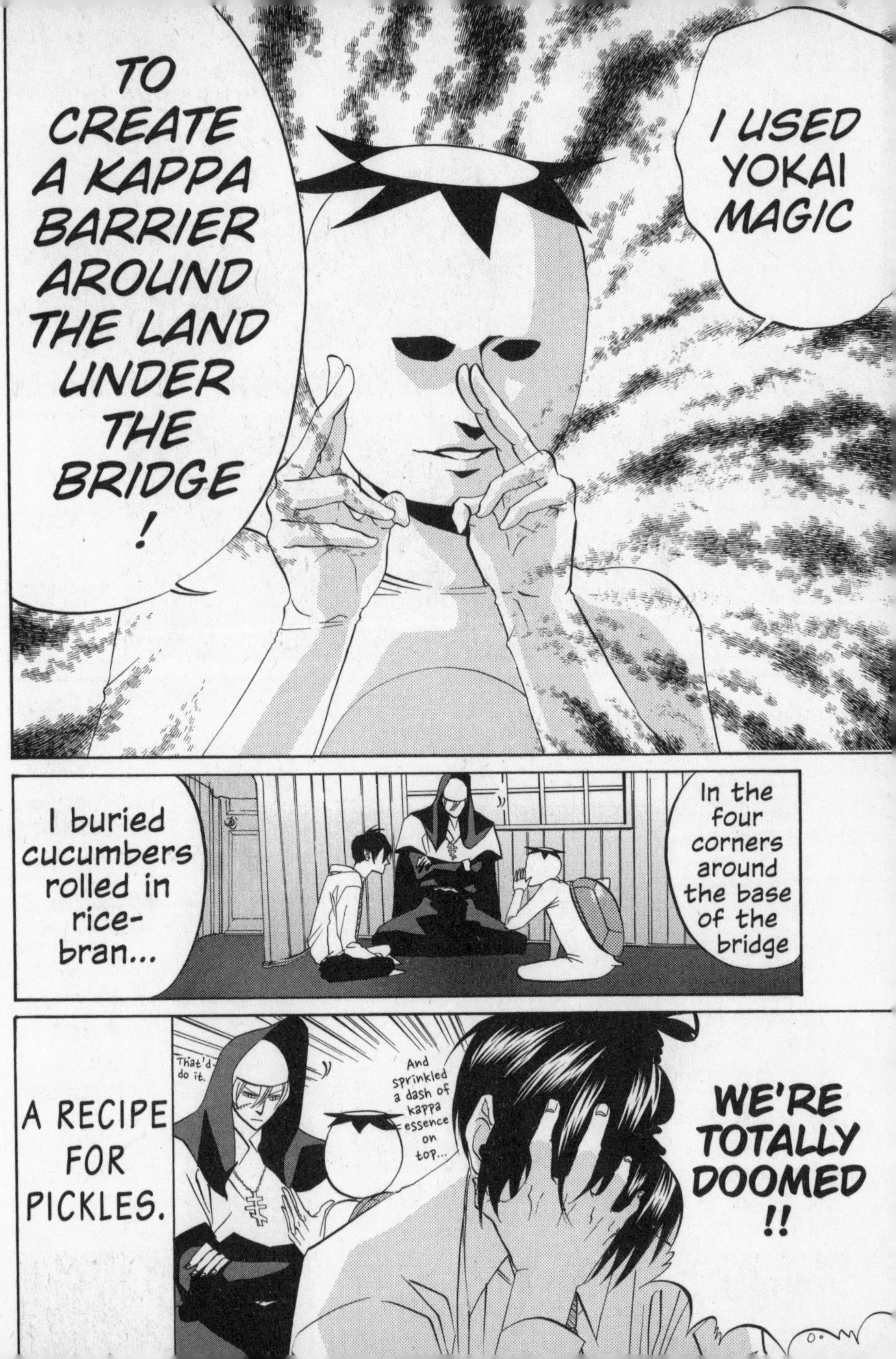
I USED YOKAI MAGIC
TO CREATE A KAPPA BARRIER AROUND THE LAND UNDER THE BRIDGE!
In the four corners around the base of the bridge
I buried cucumbers rolled in rice-bran...
WE'RE TOTALLY DOOMED!!
And sprinkled a dash of kappa essence on top...
That'd do it.
A RECIPE FOR PICKLES.

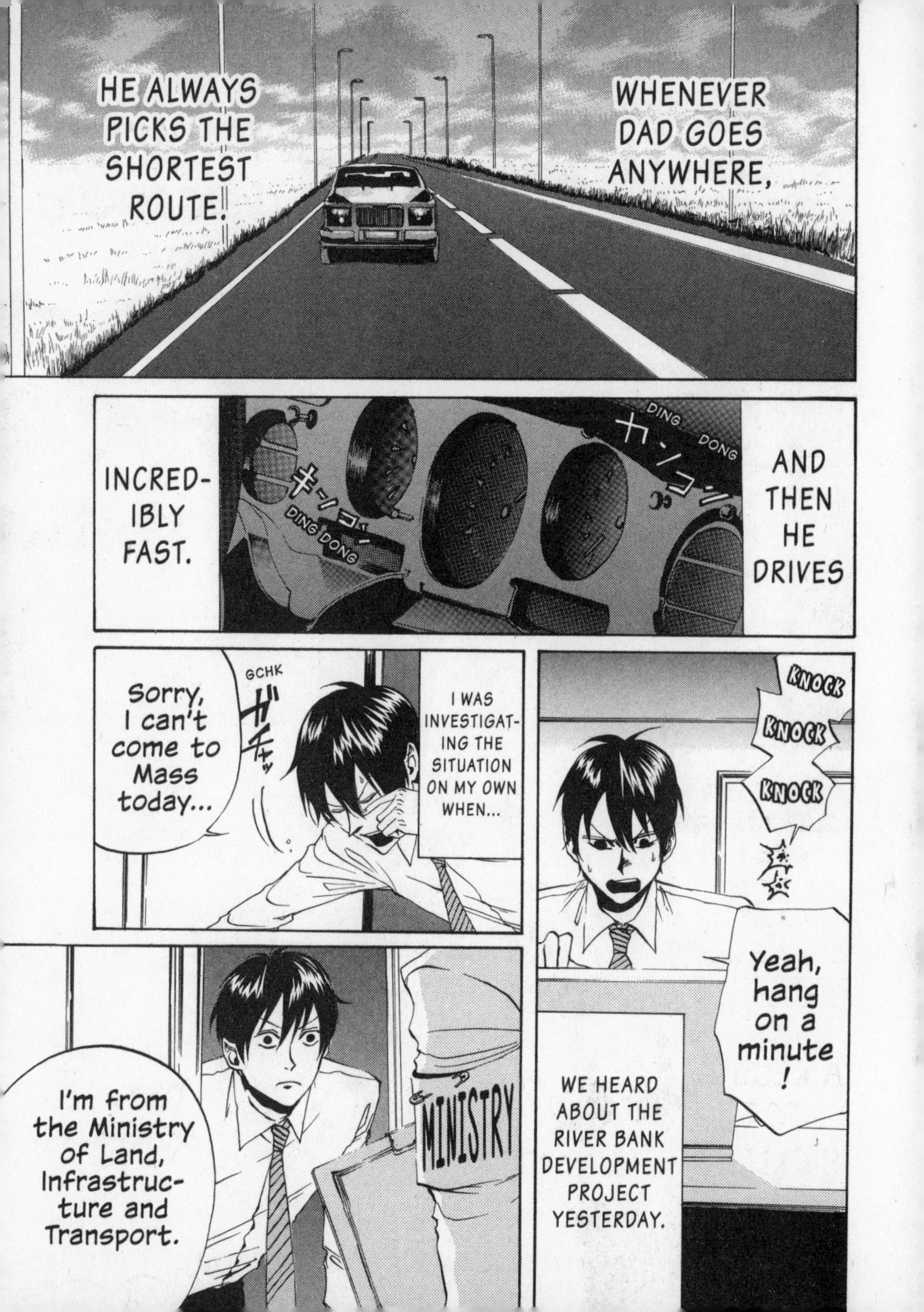
WHENEVER DAD GOES ANYWHERE,
HE ALWAYS PICKS THE SHORTEST ROUTE!
AND THEN HE DRIVES
DING DONG
DING DONG
INCRED-IBLY FAST.
KNOCK
KNOCK
KNOCK
Yeah, hang on a minute!
I WAS INVESTIGAT-ING THE SITUATION ON MY OWN WHEN...
GCHK
Sorry, I can't come to Mass today...
WE HEARD ABOUT THE RIVER BANK DEVELOPMENT PROJECT YESTERDAY.
MINISTRY
I'm from the Ministry of Land, Infrastruc-ture and Transport.

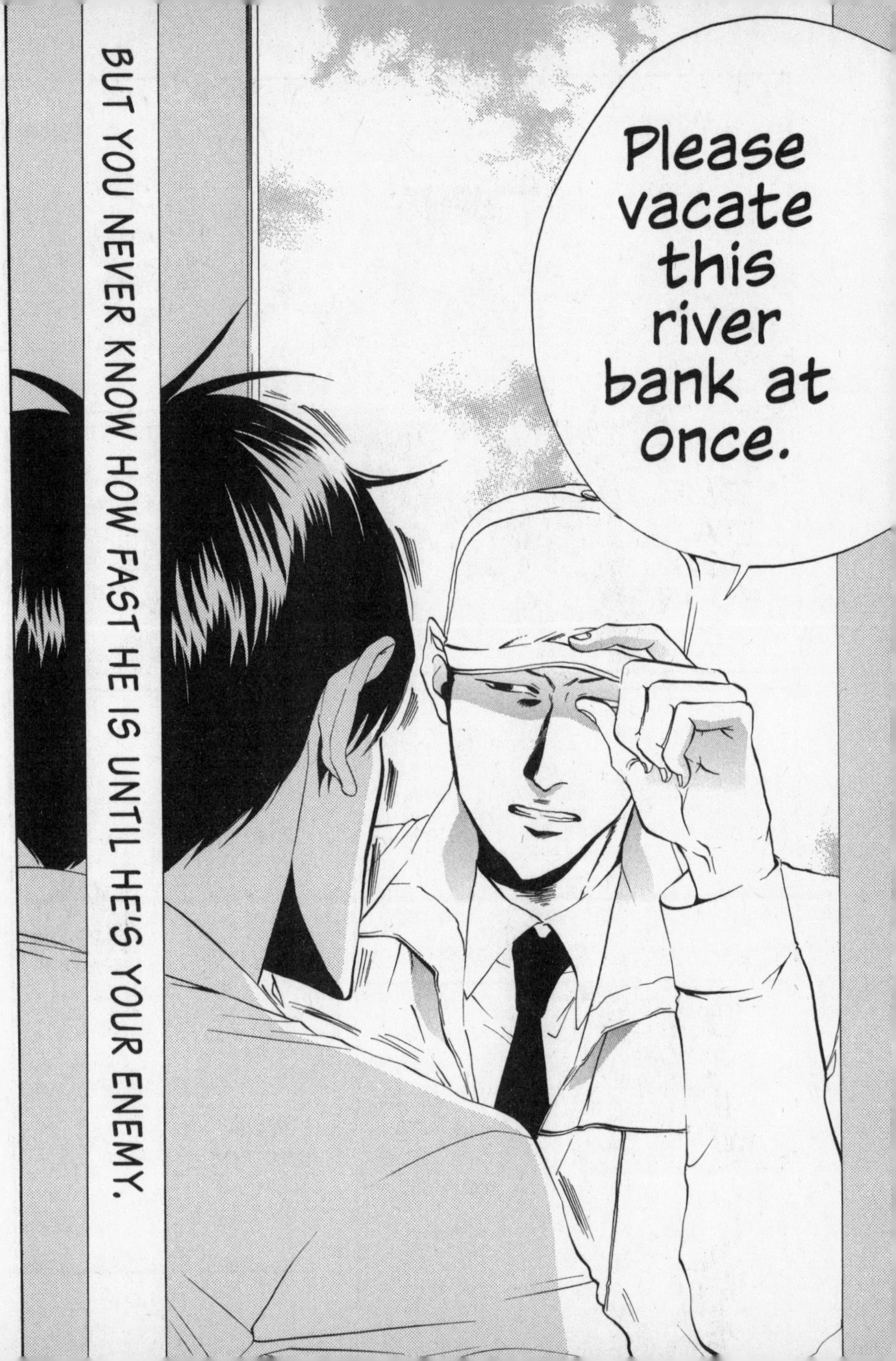
Please vacate this river bank at once.
BUT YOU NEVER KNOW HOW FAST HE IS UNTIL HE'S YOUR ENEMY.

Chapter 94: Official

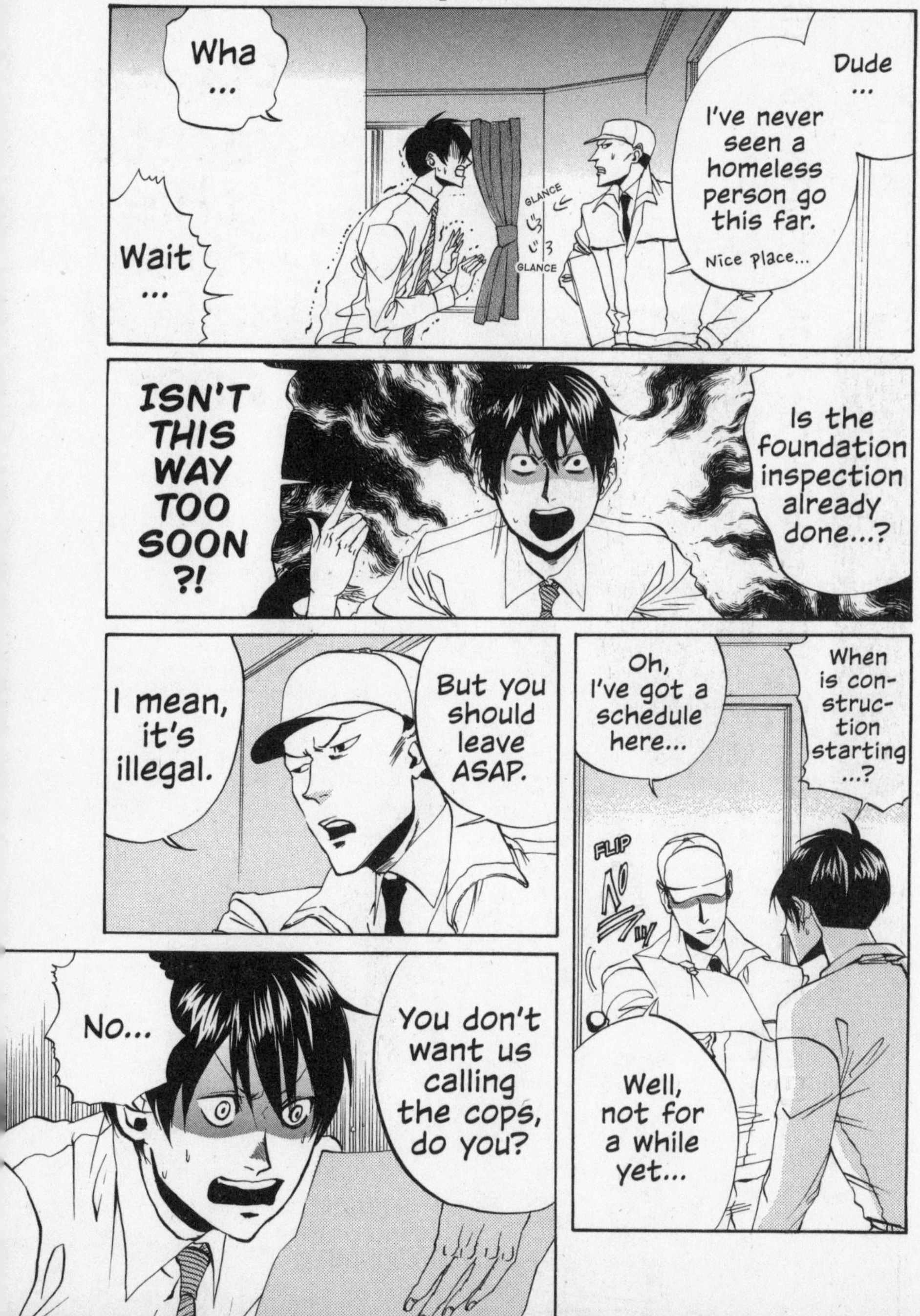
Dude... I've never seen a homeless person go this far.
Nice place...
GLANCE
GLANCE
Wha...
Wait...
Is the foundation inspection already done...?
ISN'T THIS WAY TOO SOON?!
When is construction starting...?
Oh, I've got a schedule here...
FLIP
Well, not for a while yet...
But you should leave ASAP.
I mean, it's illegal.
You don't want us calling the cops, do you?
No...

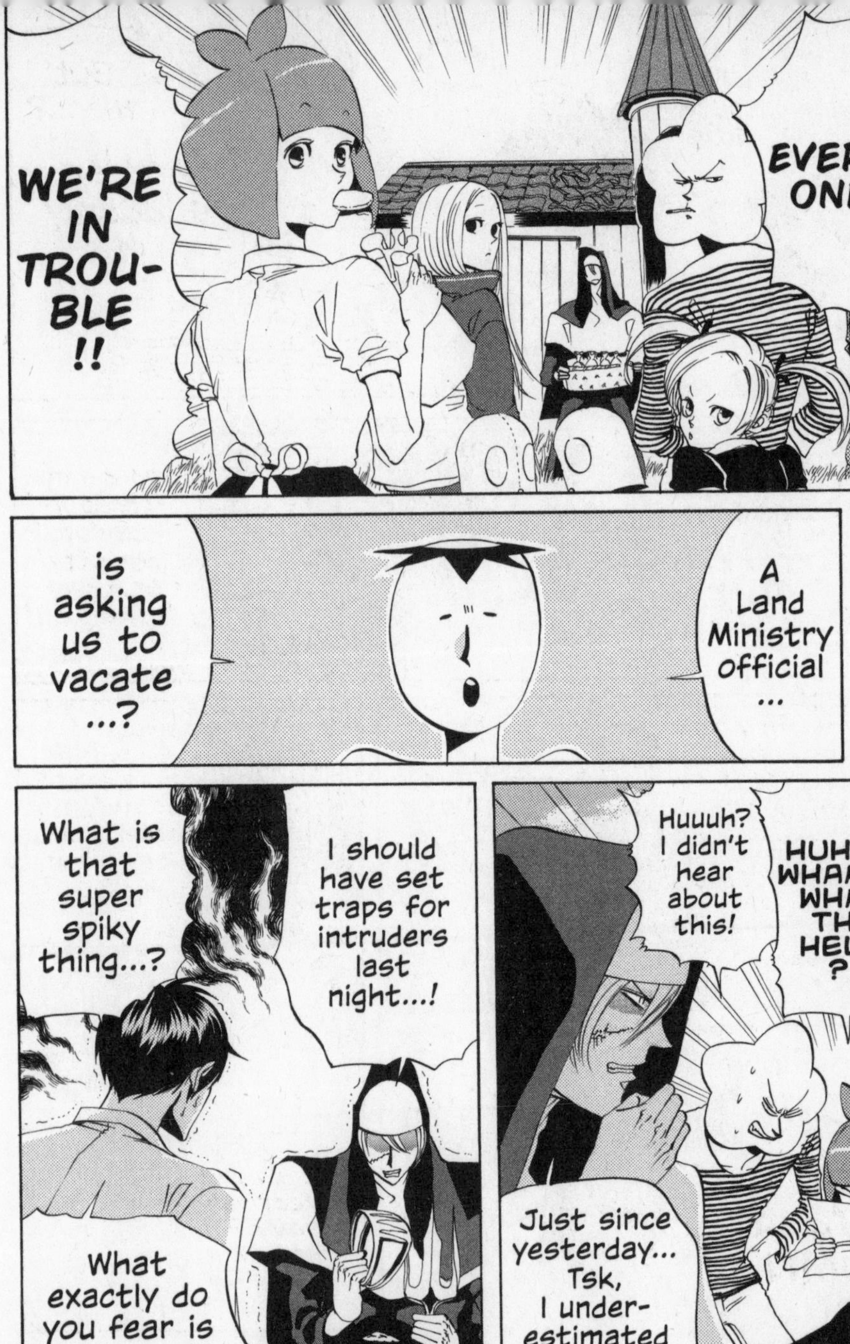
EVERY-ONE!
WE'RE IN TROU-BLE!!
A Land Ministry official...
is asking us to vacate...?
HUH...? WHAAT? WHAT THE HELL?!
Huuuh? I didn't hear about this!
Just since yesterday... Tsk, I under-estimated them...!
I should have set traps for intruders last night...!
What is that super spiky thing...?
What exactly do you fear is intruding?!

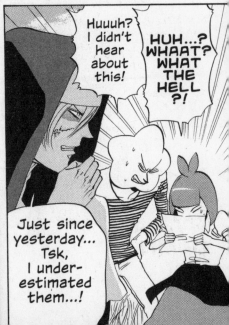

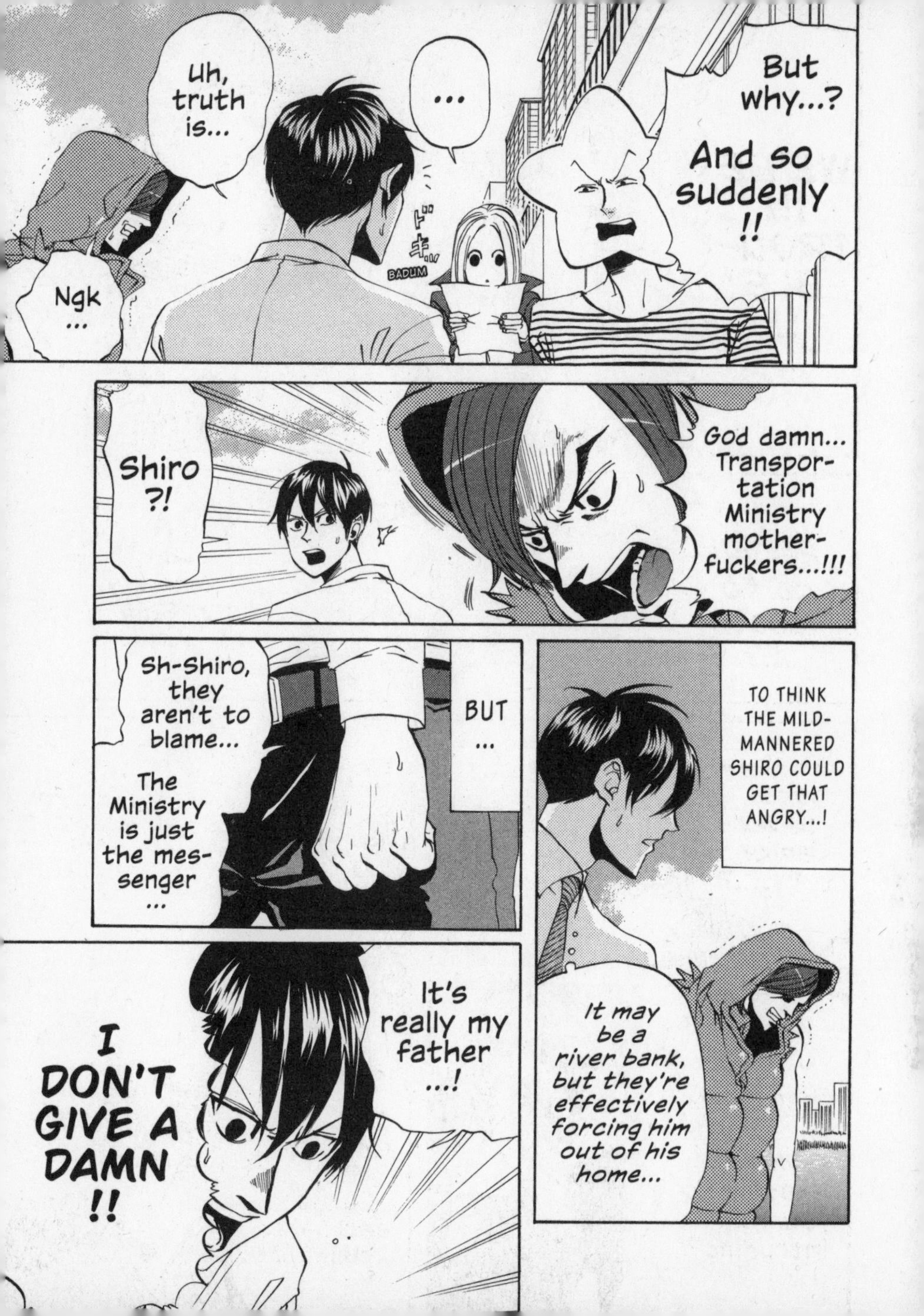
But why...?
And so suddenly !!
...
Uh, truth is...
BADUM
Ngk ...
God damn... Transportation Ministry motherfuckers...!!!
Shiro ?!
TO THINK THE MILD-MANNERED SHIRO COULD GET THAT ANGRY...!
It may be a river bank, but they're effectively forcing him out of his home...
BUT ...
Sh-Shiro, they aren't to blame...
The Ministry is just the messenger ...
It's really my father ...!
I DON'T GIVE A DAMN !!

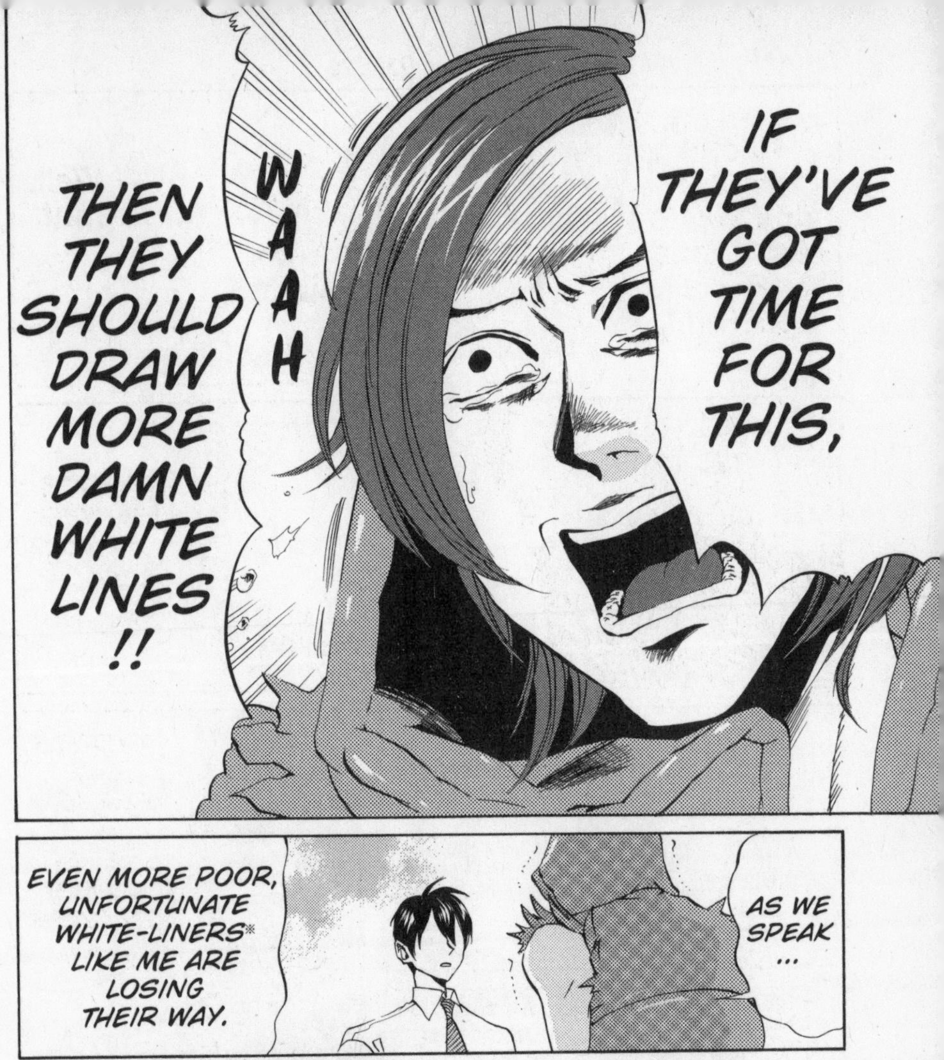
IF THEY'VE GOT TIME FOR THIS,
WAAH
THEN THEY SHOULD DRAW MORE DAMN WHITE LINES!!
AS WE SPEAK...
EVEN MORE POOR, UNFORTUNATE WHITE-LINERS※ LIKE ME ARE LOSING THEIR WAY.

※ People who only walk on white lines.

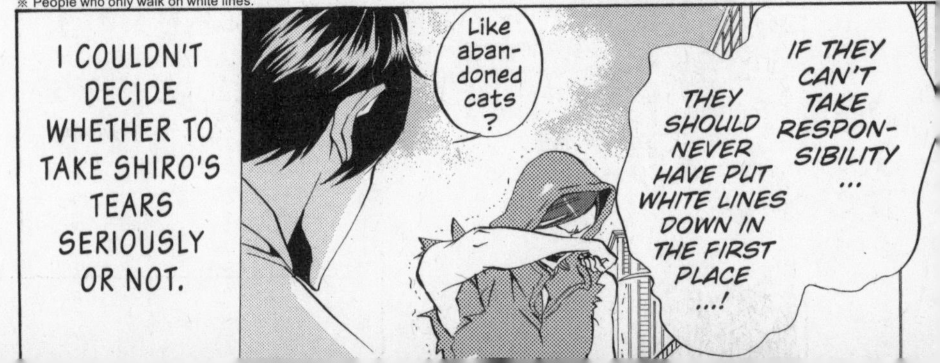
IF THEY CAN'T TAKE RESPONSIBILITY...
THEY SHOULD NEVER HAVE PUT WHITE LINES DOWN IN THE FIRST PLACE...!
Like abandoned cats?
I COULDN'T DECIDE WHETHER TO TAKE SHIRO'S TEARS SERIOUSLY OR NOT.

Chapter 95: Pig

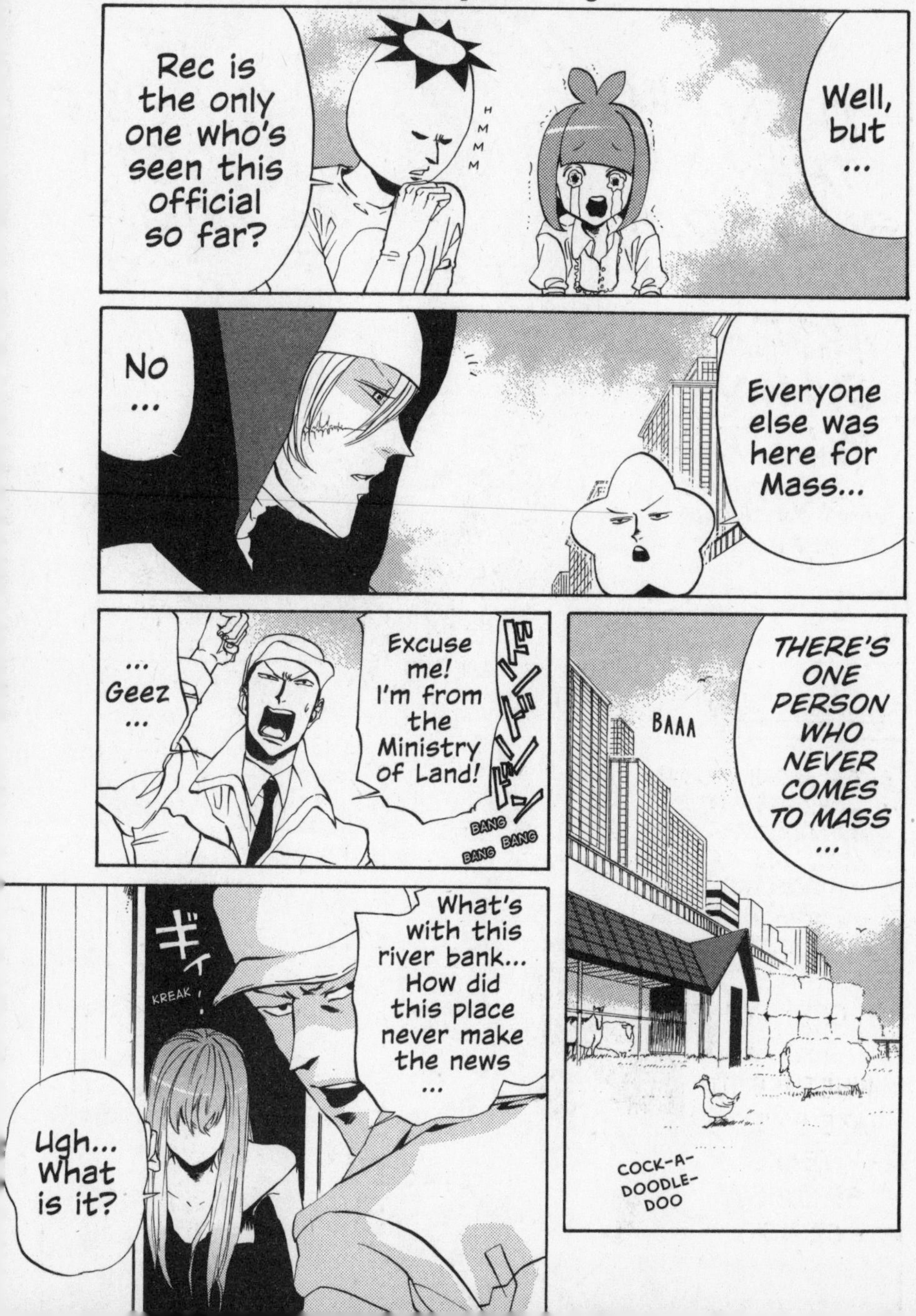
Well, but ...
Rec is the only one who's seen this official so far?
HMMM
Everyone else was here for Mass...
No ...
THERE'S ONE PERSON WHO NEVER COMES TO MASS ...
BAAA
COCK-A-DOODLE-DOO
Excuse me! I'm from the Ministry of Land!
BANG BANG BANG
... Geez ...
What's with this river bank... How did this place never make the news ...
ギィ
KREAK
Ugh... What is it?

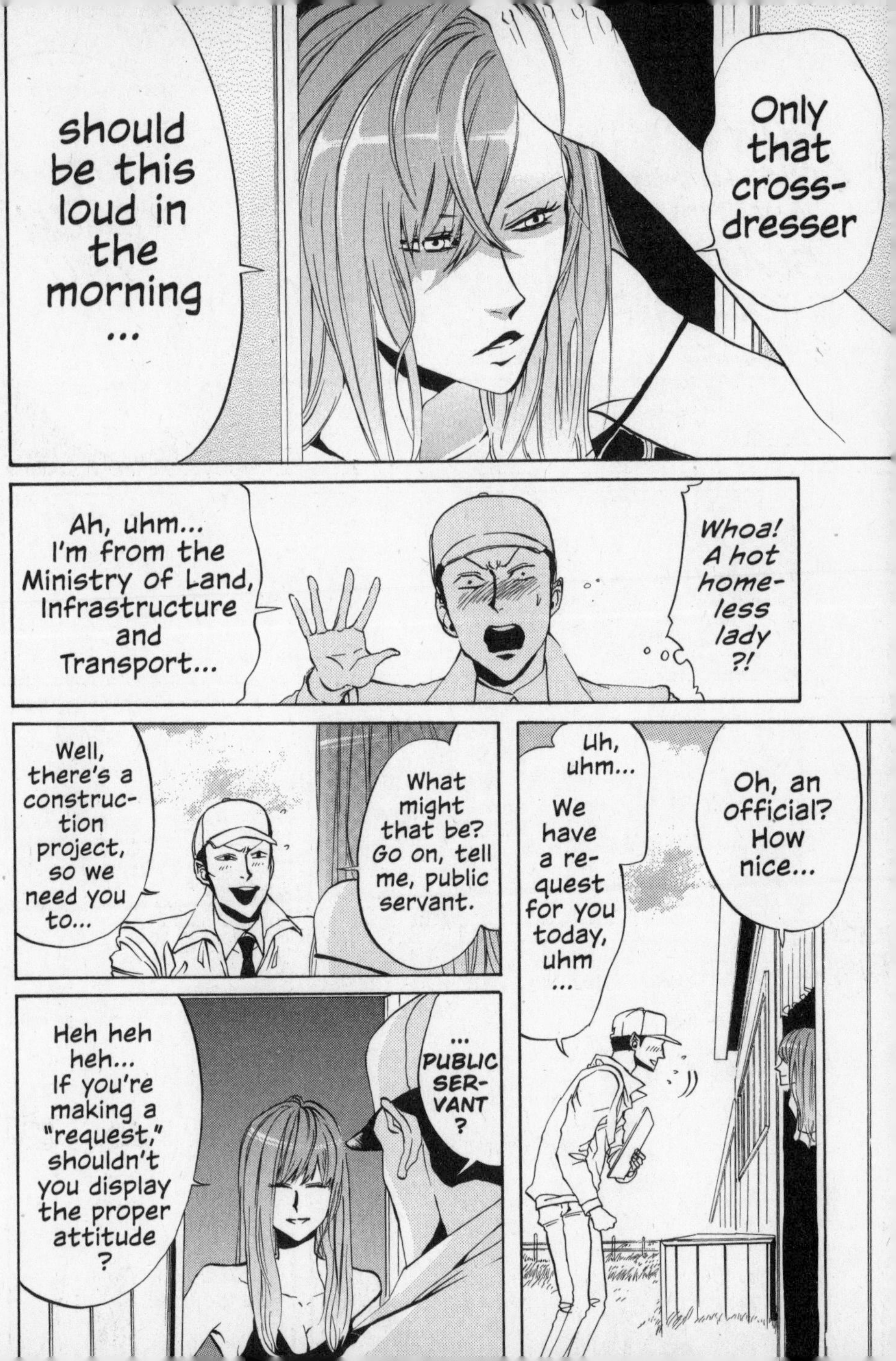
Only that cross-dresser
should be this loud in the morning...
Whoa! A hot homeless lady?!
Ah, uhm... I'm from the Ministry of Land, Infrastructure and Transport...
Oh, an official? How nice...
Uh, uhm... We have a request for you today, uhm...
What might that be? Go on, tell me, public servant.
Well, there's a construction project, so we need you to...
...PUBLIC SERVANT?
Heh heh heh... If you're making a "request," shouldn't you display the proper attitude?

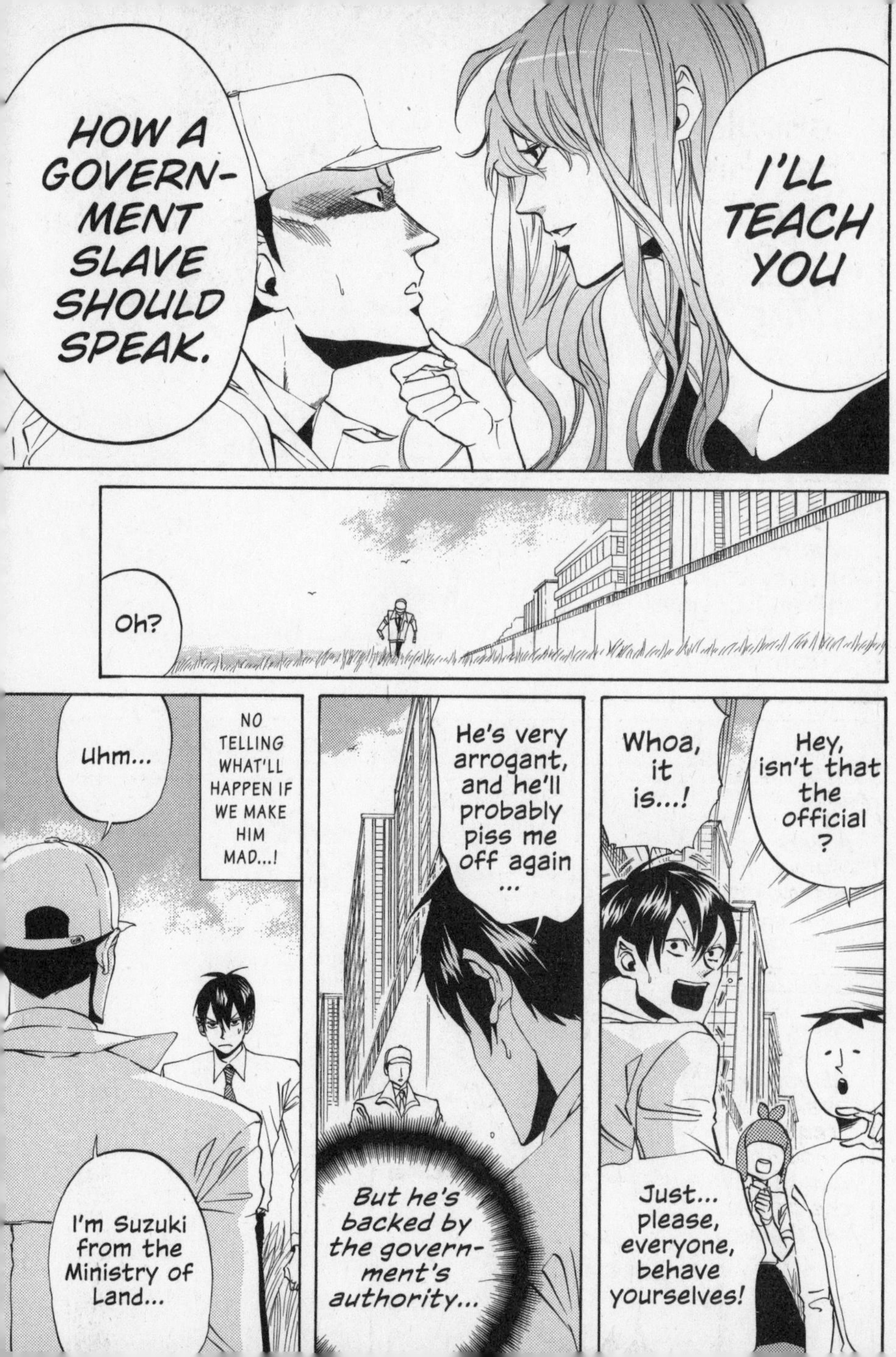
I'LL TEACH YOU
HOW A GOVERN-MENT SLAVE SHOULD SPEAK.
Oh?
Hey, isn't that the official?
Whoa, it is...!
Just... please, everyone, behave yourselves!
He's very arrogant, and he'll probably piss me off again ...
But he's backed by the govern-ment's authority...
NO TELLING WHAT'LL HAPPEN IF WE MAKE HIM MAD...!
Uhm...
I'm Suzuki from the Ministry of Land...

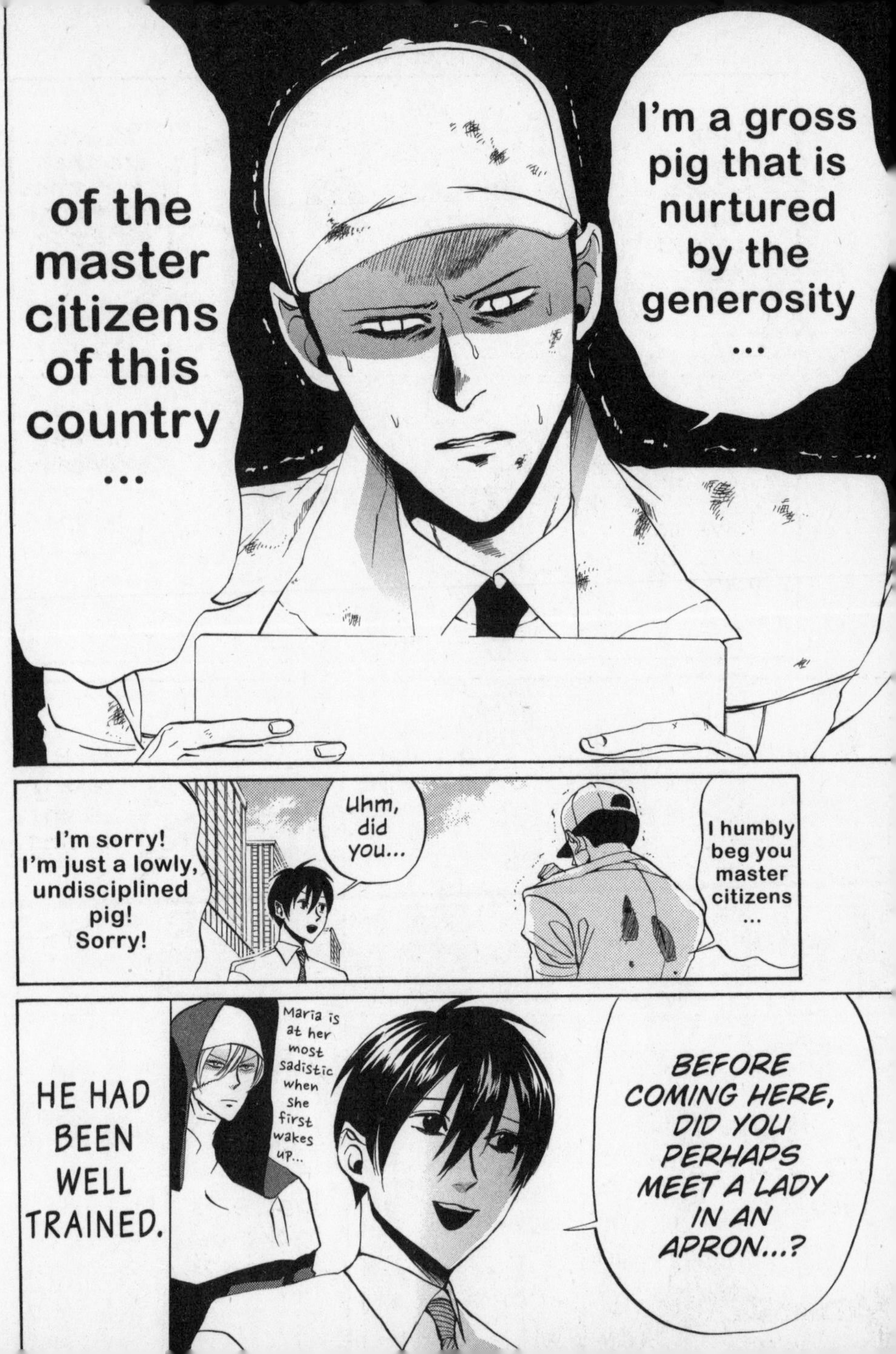
I'm a gross pig that is nurtured by the generosity ...
of the master citizens of this country ...
I humbly beg you master citizens ...
Uhm, did you...
I'm sorry! I'm just a lowly, undisciplined pig! Sorry!
BEFORE COMING HERE, DID YOU PERHAPS MEET A LADY IN AN APRON...?
Maria is at her most sadistic when she first wakes up...
HE HAD BEEN WELL TRAINED.

Chapter 96: Vow

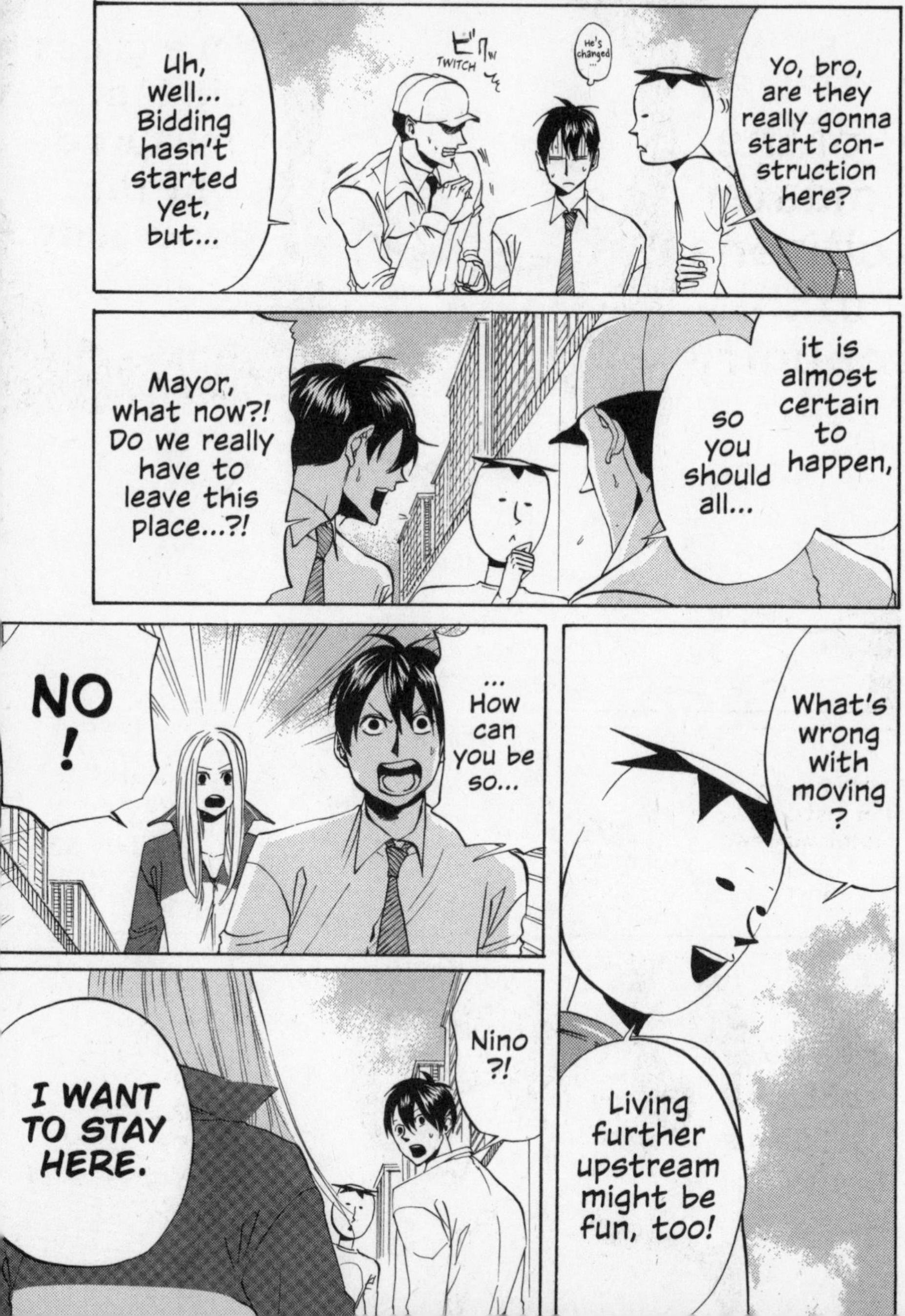
Yo, bro, are they really gonna start con-struction here?
He's changed...
TWITCH
Uh, well... Bidding hasn't started yet, but...
it is almost certain to happen,
so you should all...
Mayor, what now?! Do we really have to leave this place...?!
What's wrong with moving?
Living further upstream might be fun, too!
... How can you be so...
NO!
Nino?!
I WANT TO STAY HERE.

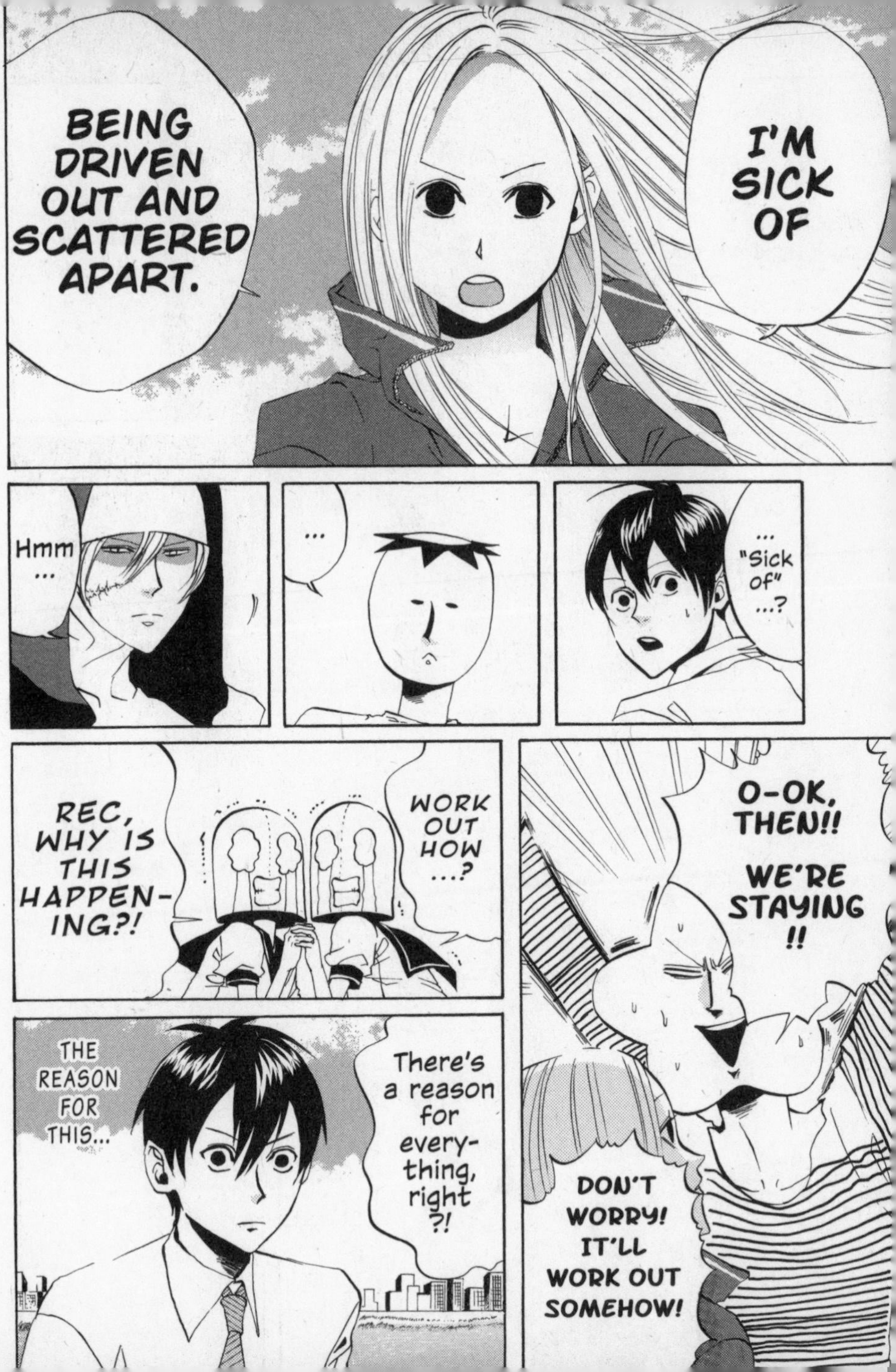
I'M SICK OF
BEING DRIVEN OUT AND SCATTERED APART.
... "Sick of" ...?
...
Hmm ...
O-OK, THEN!!
WE'RE STAYING!!
DON'T WORRY! IT'LL WORK OUT SOMEHOW!
WORK OUT HOW ...?
REC, WHY IS THIS HAPPEN-ING?!
There's a reason for every-thing, right?!
THE REASON FOR THIS...

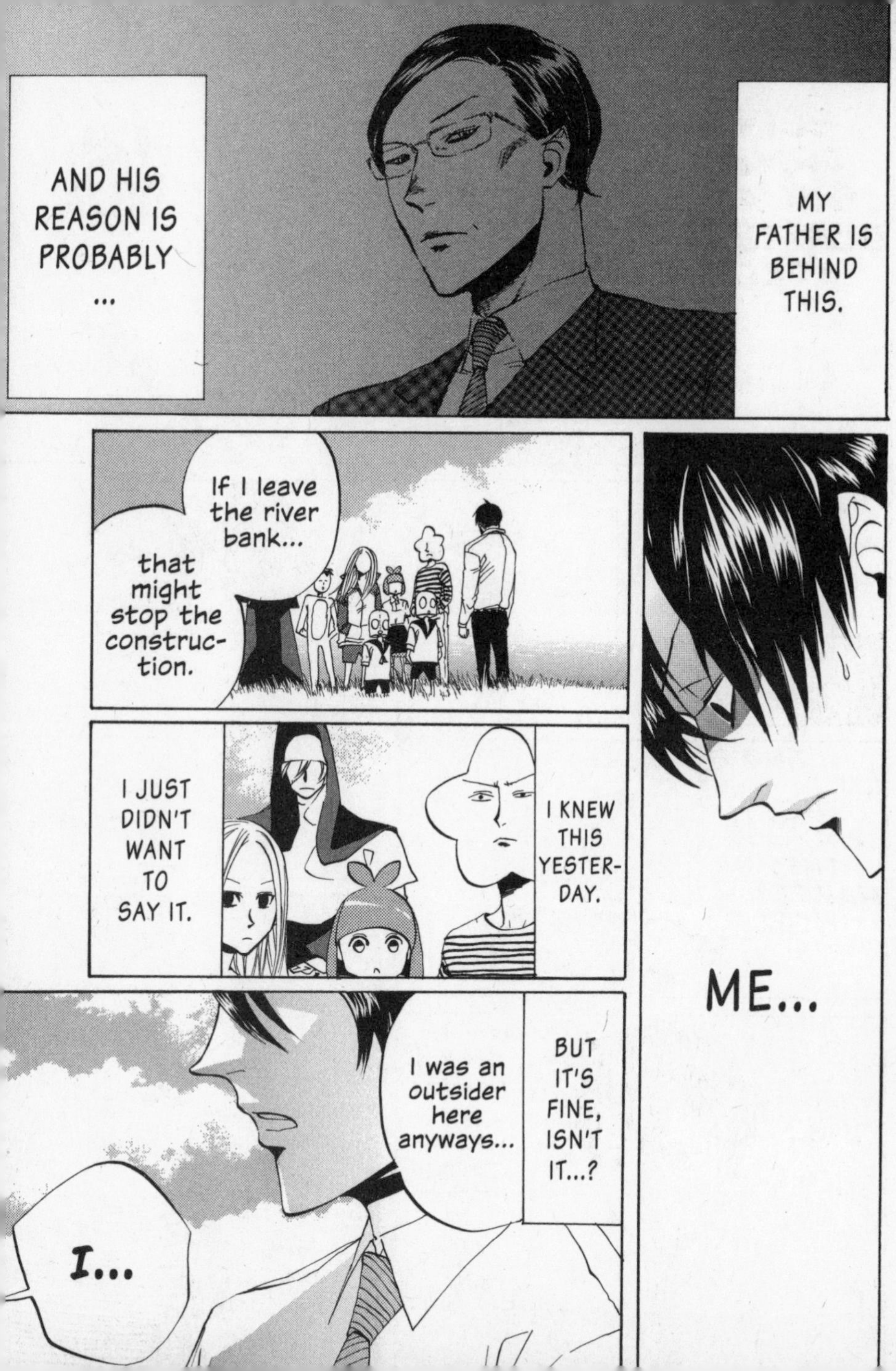
MY FATHER IS BEHIND THIS.
AND HIS REASON IS PROBABLY ...
ME...
If I leave the river bank...
that might stop the construction.
I KNEW THIS YESTERDAY.
I JUST DIDN'T WANT TO SAY IT.
BUT IT'S FINE, ISN'T IT...?
I was an outsider here anyways...
I...

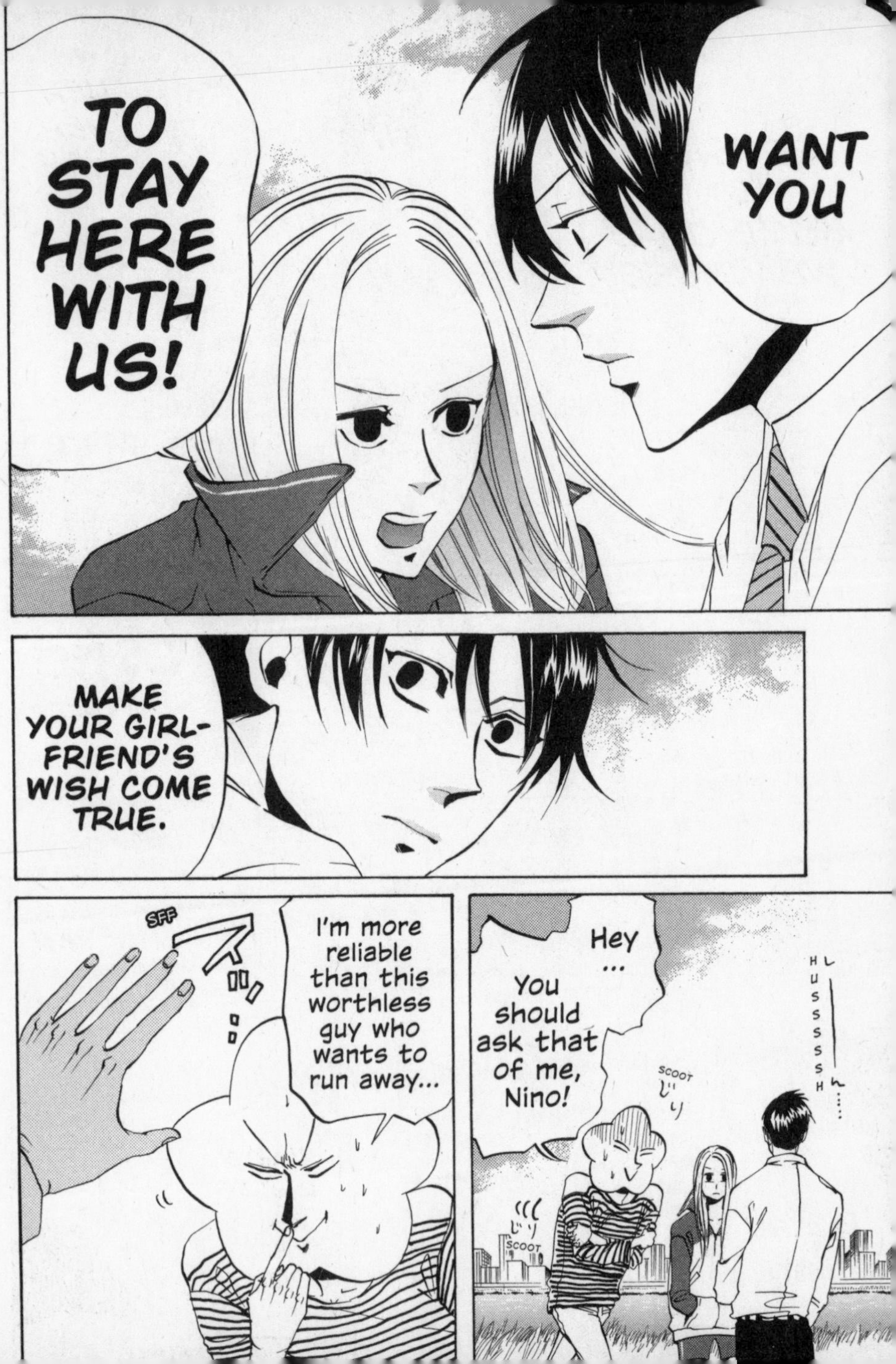
WANT YOU
TO STAY HERE WITH US!
MAKE YOUR GIRL-FRIEND'S WISH COME TRUE.
HUSSSSSH
Hey ...
You should ask that of me, Nino!
SCOOT
SCOOT
I'm more reliable than this worthless guy who wants to run away...
SFF

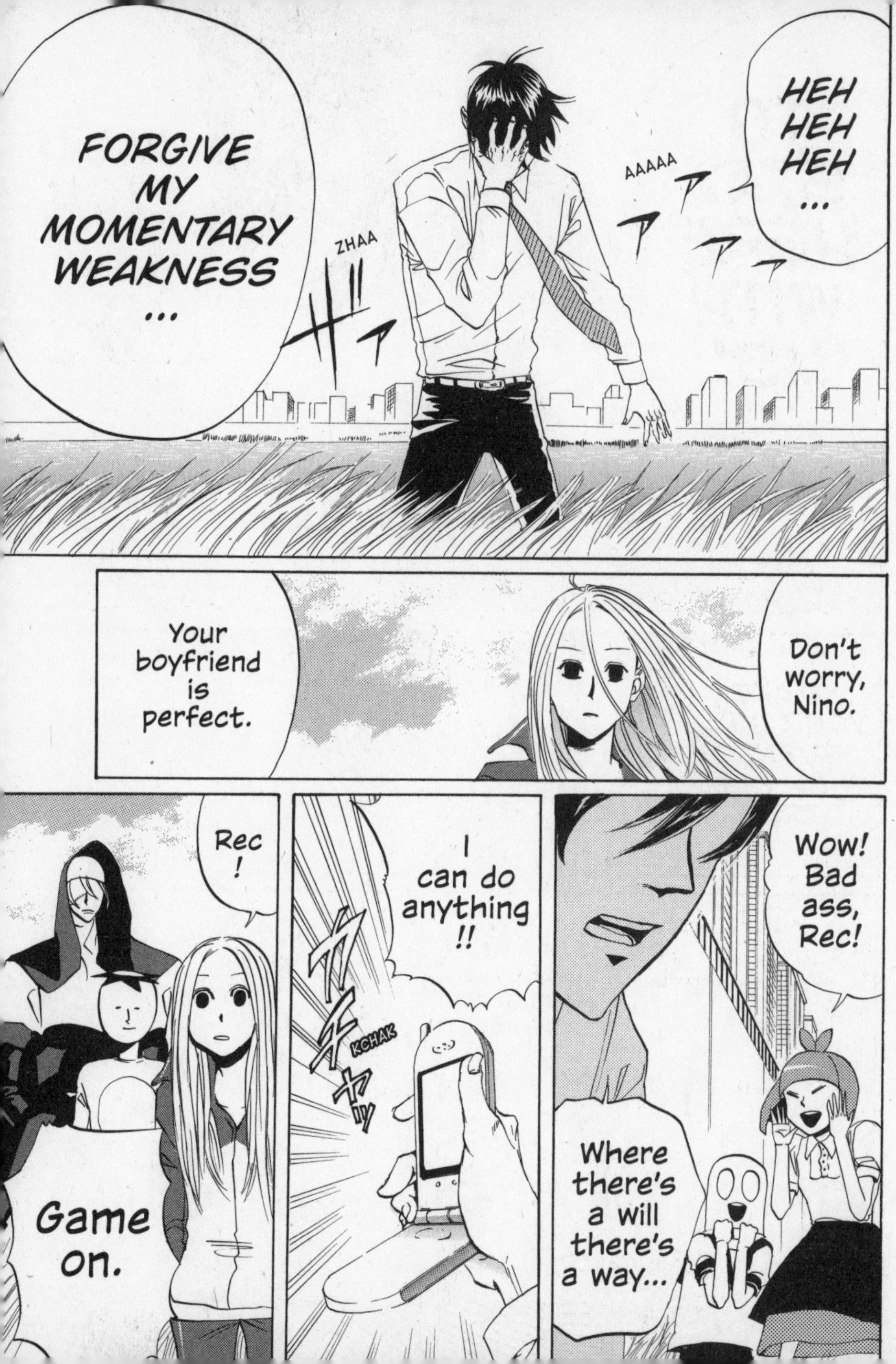
HEH HEH HEH ...
AAAAA
ZHAA
FORGIVE MY MOMENTARY WEAKNESS ...
Don't worry, Nino.
Your boyfriend is perfect.
Wow! Bad ass, Rec!
Where there's a will there's a way...
I can do anything !!
KCHAK
Rec !
Game on.

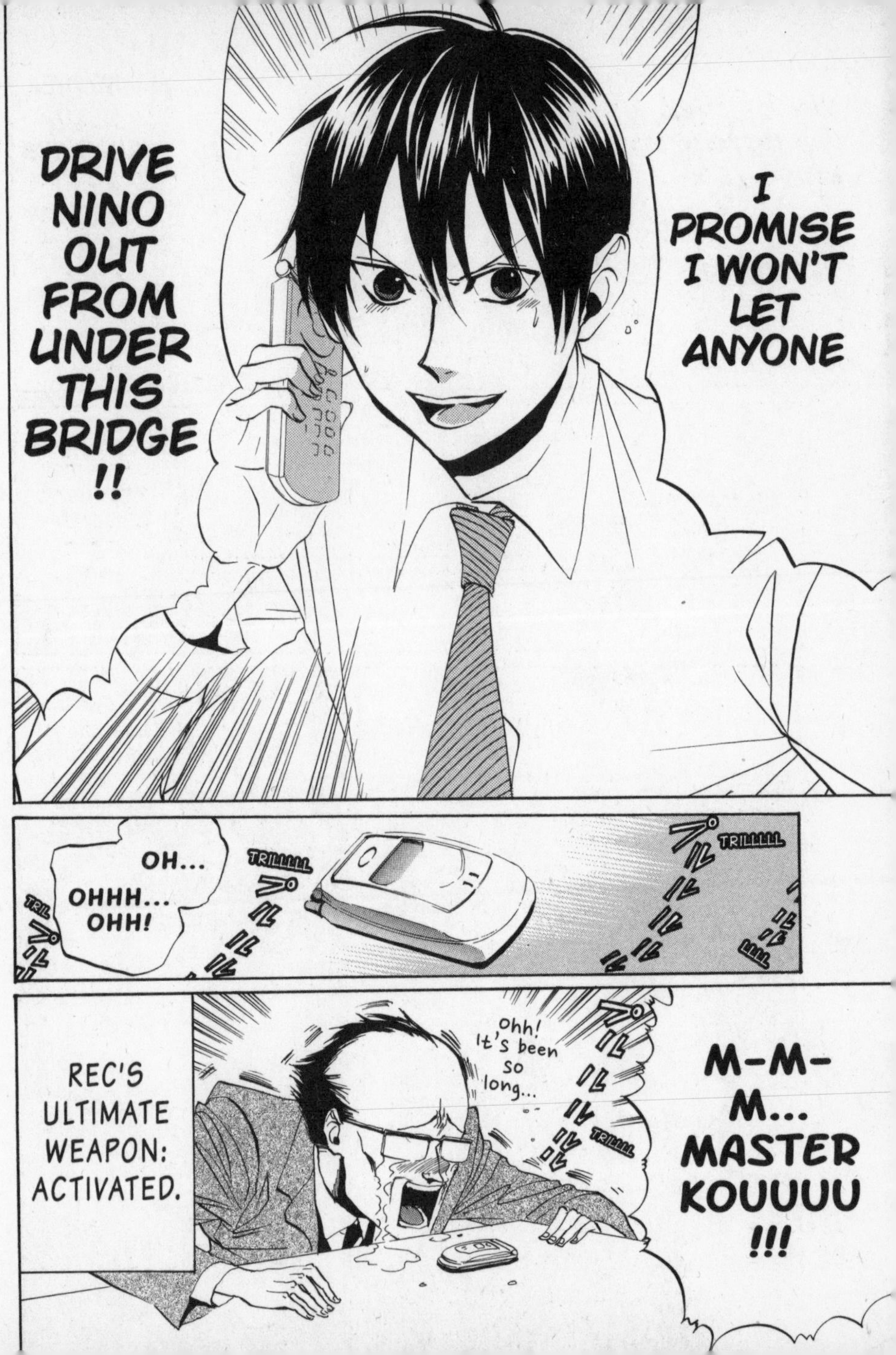
I PROMISE I WON'T LET ANYONE
DRIVE NINO OUT FROM UNDER THIS BRIDGE !!
TRILLLLL
TRILLLLL
OH... OHHH... OHH!
TRIL
M-M-M... MASTER KOUUUU !!!
TRILLLL
Ohh! It's been so long...
REC'S ULTIMATE WEAPON: ACTIVATED.

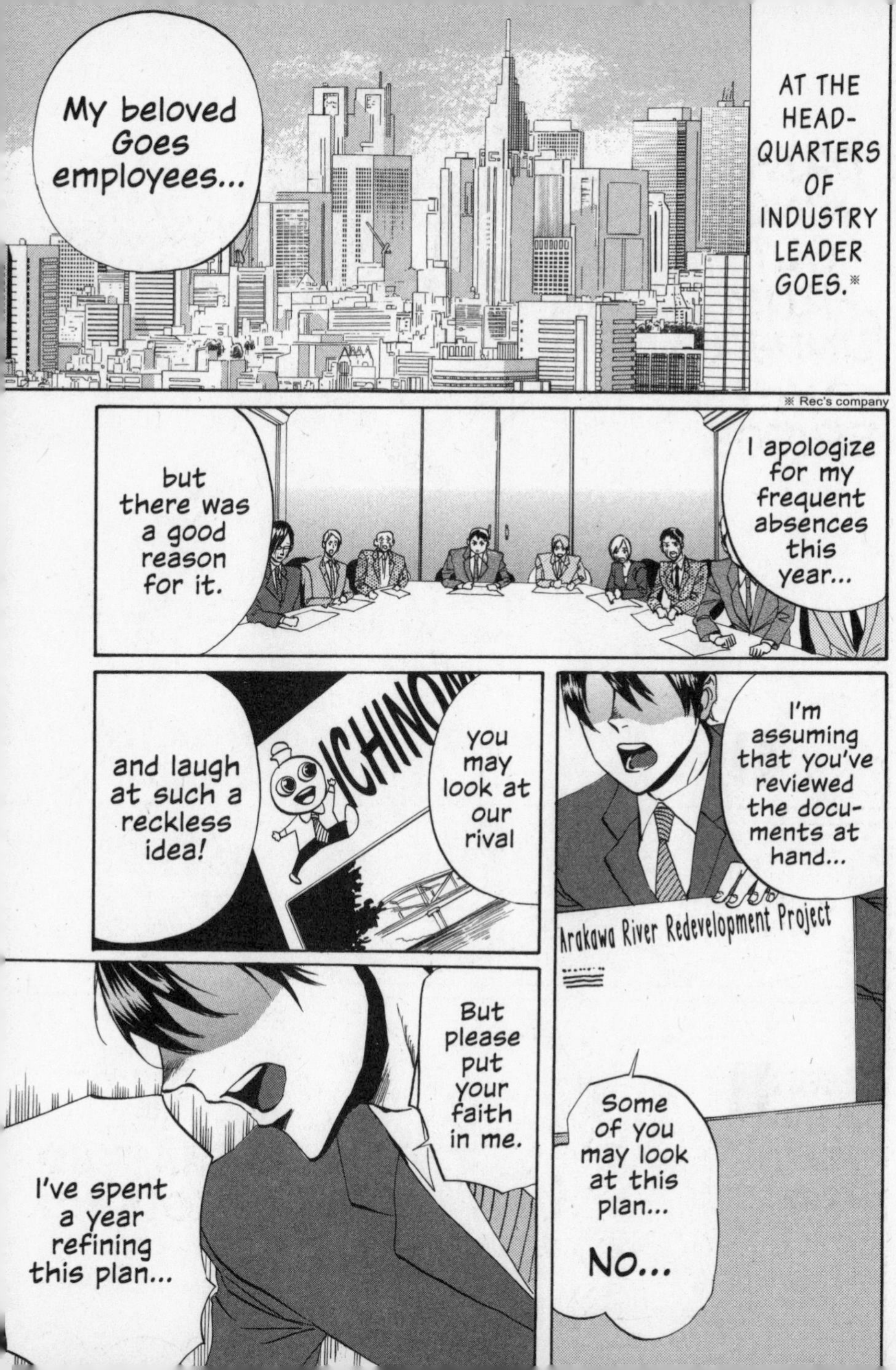
AT THE HEAD-QUARTERS OF INDUSTRY LEADER GOES.※
My beloved Goes employees...
※ Rec's company
I apologize for my frequent absences this year...
but there was a good reason for it.
I'm assuming that you've reviewed the documents at hand...
Arakawa River Redevelopment Project
Some of you may look at this plan...
NO...
you may look at our rival
and laugh at such a reckless idea!
But please put your faith in me.
I've spent a year refining this plan...

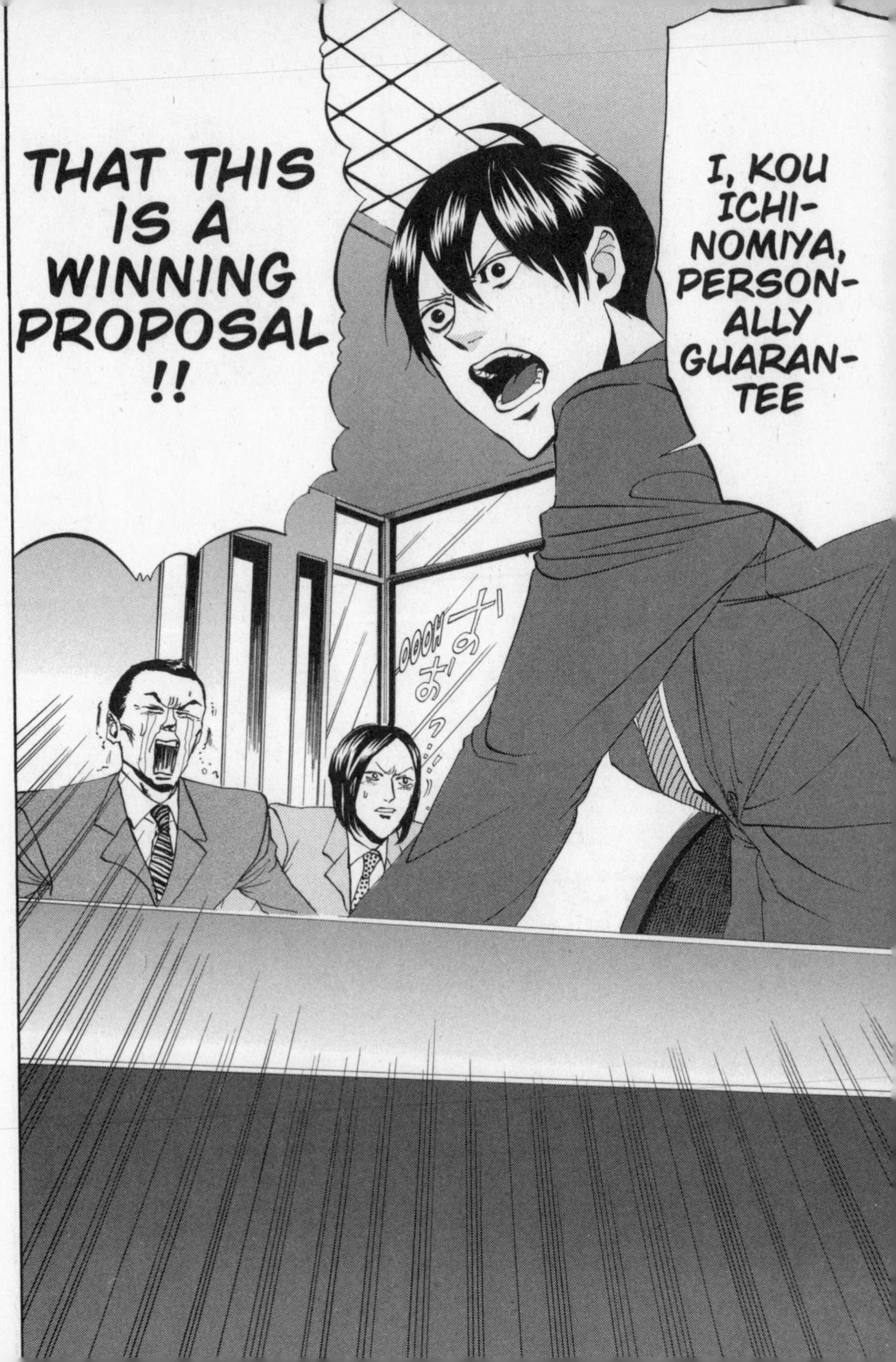
I, KOU ICHI-NOMIYA, PERSON-ALLY GUARAN-TEE
THAT THIS IS A WINNING PROPOSAL !!

Chapter 97: Boss Aura

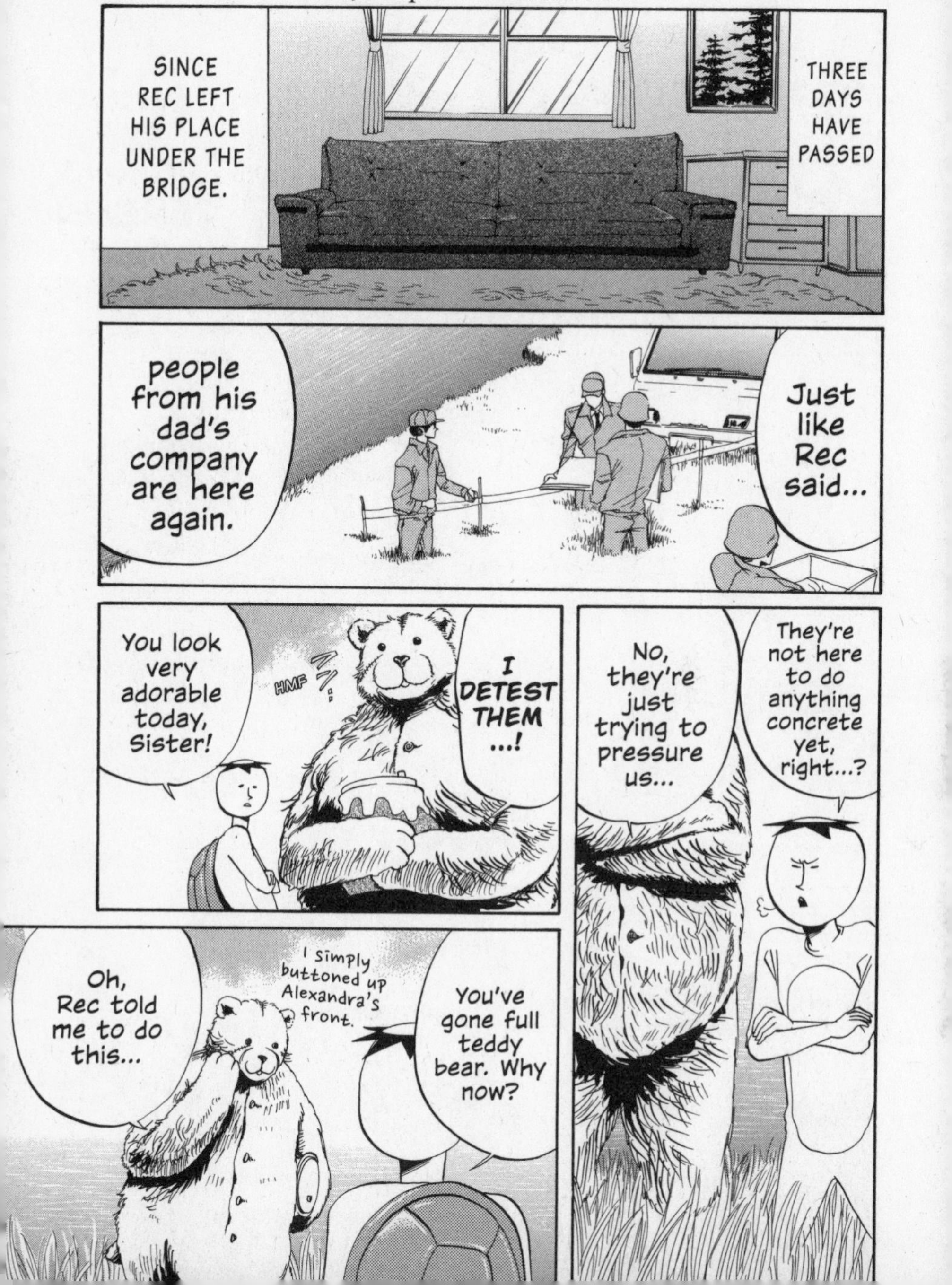
THREE DAYS HAVE PASSED
SINCE REC LEFT HIS PLACE UNDER THE BRIDGE.
Just like Rec said...
people from his dad's company are here again.
They're not here to do anything concrete yet, right...?
No, they're just trying to pressure us...
I DETEST THEM ...!
HMF
You look very adorable today, Sister!
You've gone full teddy bear. Why now?
I simply buttoned up Alexandra's front.
Oh, Rec told me to do this...

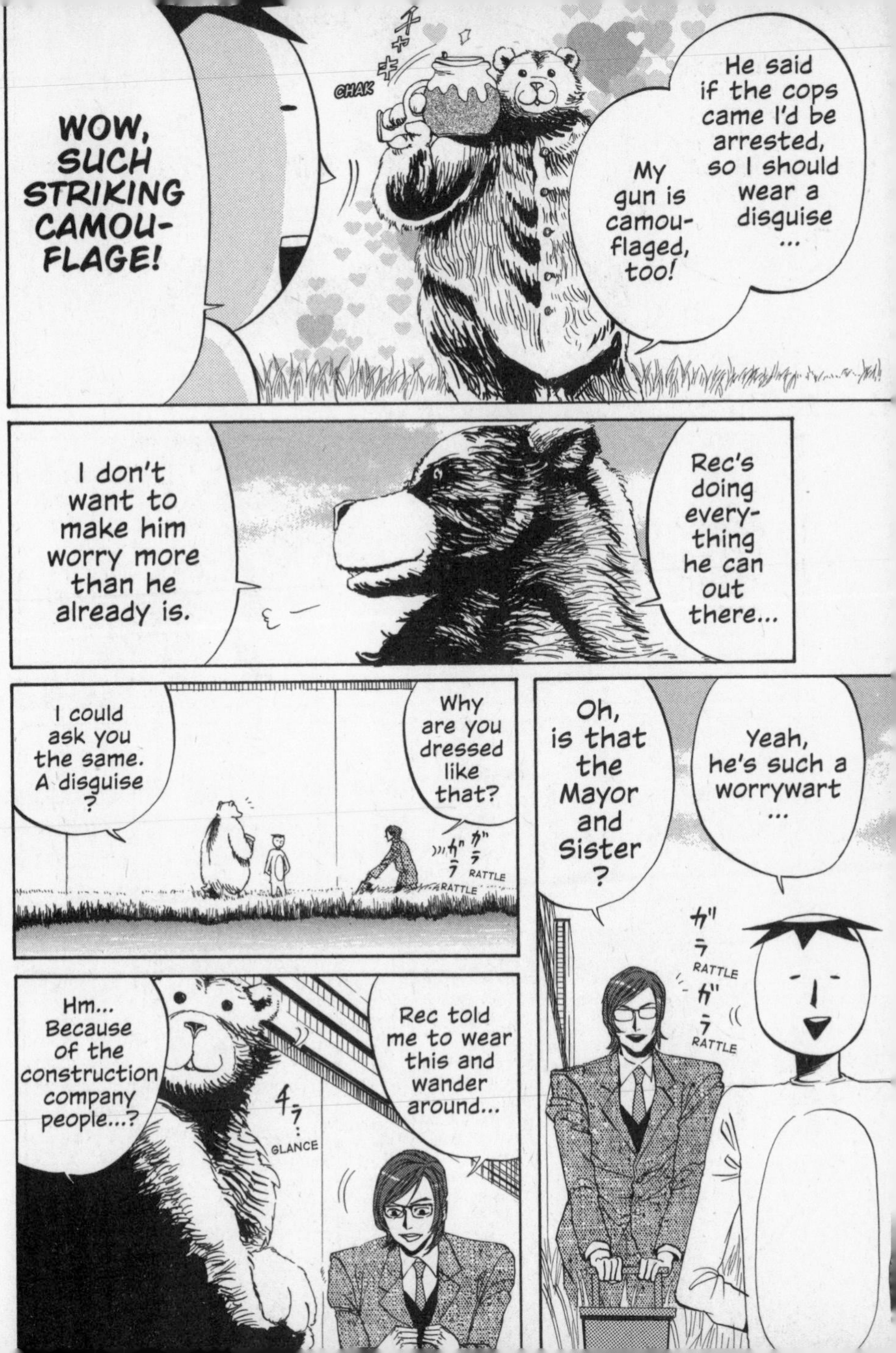
He said if the cops came I'd be arrested, so I should wear a disguise ...
My gun is camouflaged, too!
CHAK
WOW, SUCH STRIKING CAMOUFLAGE!
Rec's doing everything he can out there...
I don't want to make him worry more than he already is.
Yeah, he's such a worrywart ...
Oh, is that the Mayor and Sister ?
RATTLE
RATTLE
Why are you dressed like that?
RATTLE
RATTLE
I could ask you the same. A disguise ?
Rec told me to wear this and wander around...
GLANCE
Hm... Because of the construction company people...?

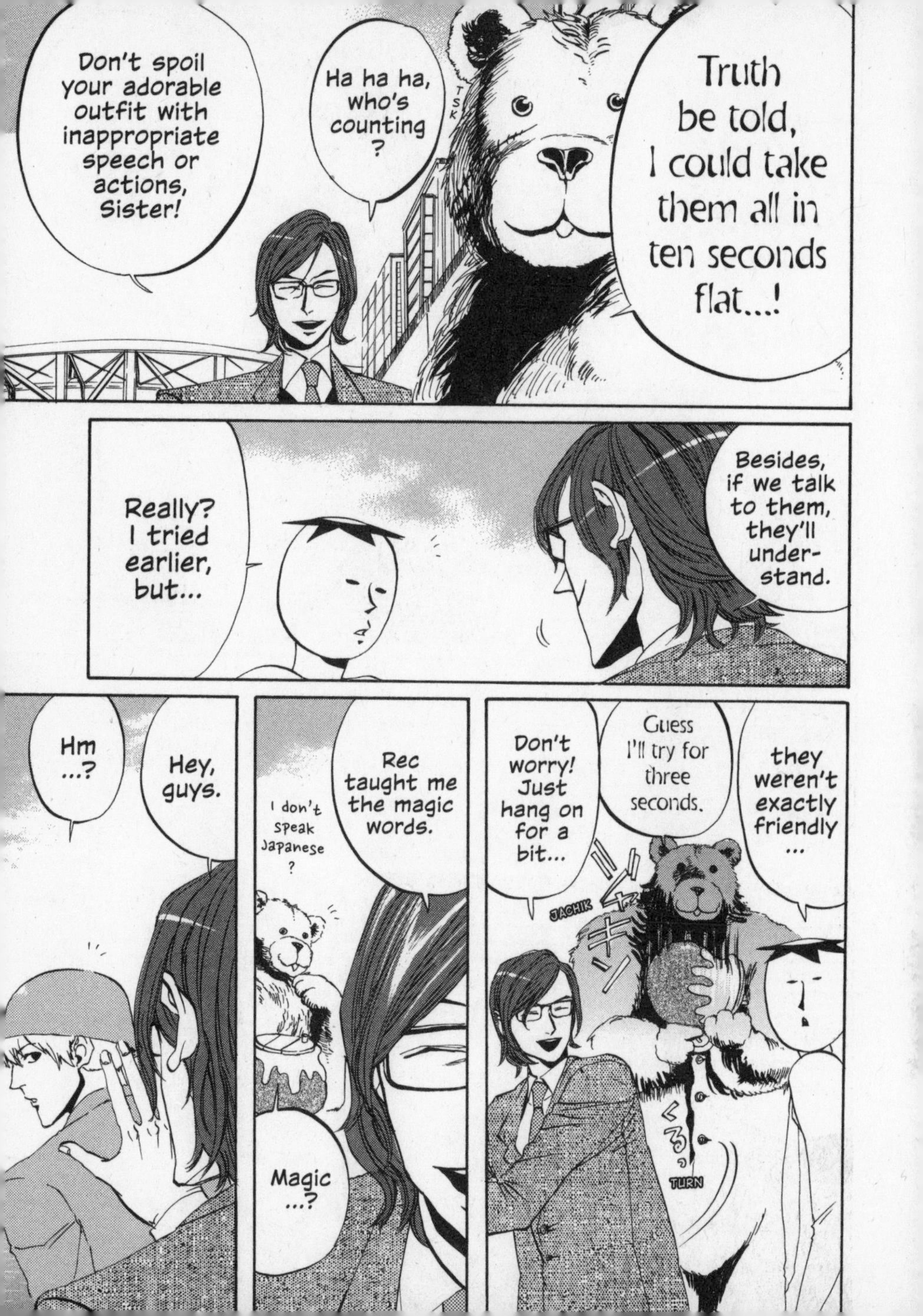
Truth be told, I could take them all in ten seconds flat...!
TSK
Ha ha ha, who's counting?
Don't spoil your adorable outfit with inappropriate speech or actions, Sister!
Besides, if we talk to them, they'll under-stand.
Really? I tried earlier, but...
they weren't exactly friendly ...
Guess I'll try for three seconds.
Don't worry! Just hang on for a bit...
JACHIK
TURN
Rec taught me the magic words.
I don't speak Japanese?
Magic ...?
Hey, guys.
Hm ...?

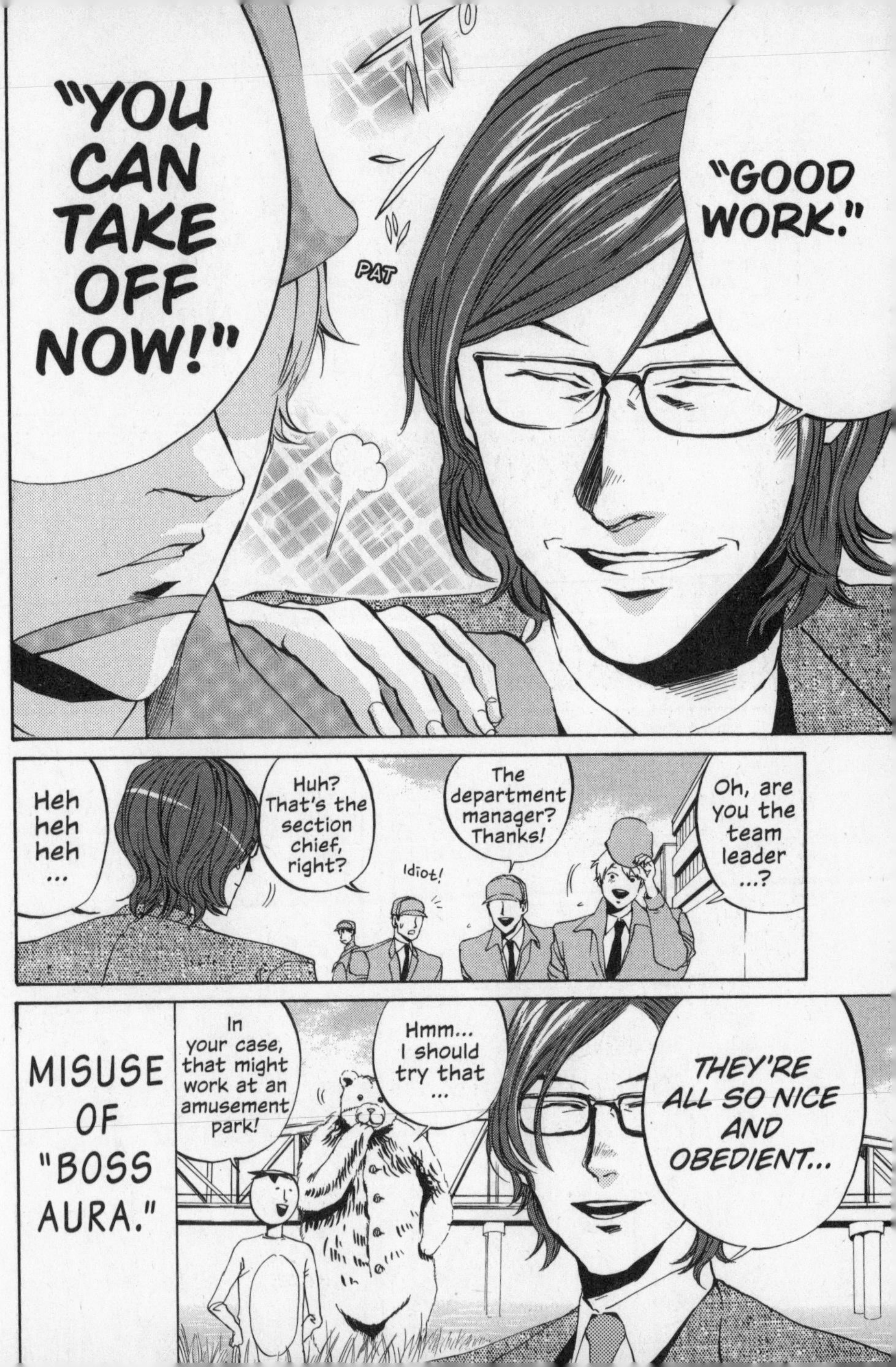
"GOOD WORK."
PAT
"YOU CAN TAKE OFF NOW!"
Oh, are you the team leader ...?
The department manager? Thanks!
Idiot!
Huh? That's the section chief, right?
Heh heh heh ...
THEY'RE ALL SO NICE AND OBEDIENT...
Hmm... I should try that ...
In your case, that might work at an amusement park!
MISUSE OF "BOSS AURA."

Chapter 98: Under the Bridge Without Rec

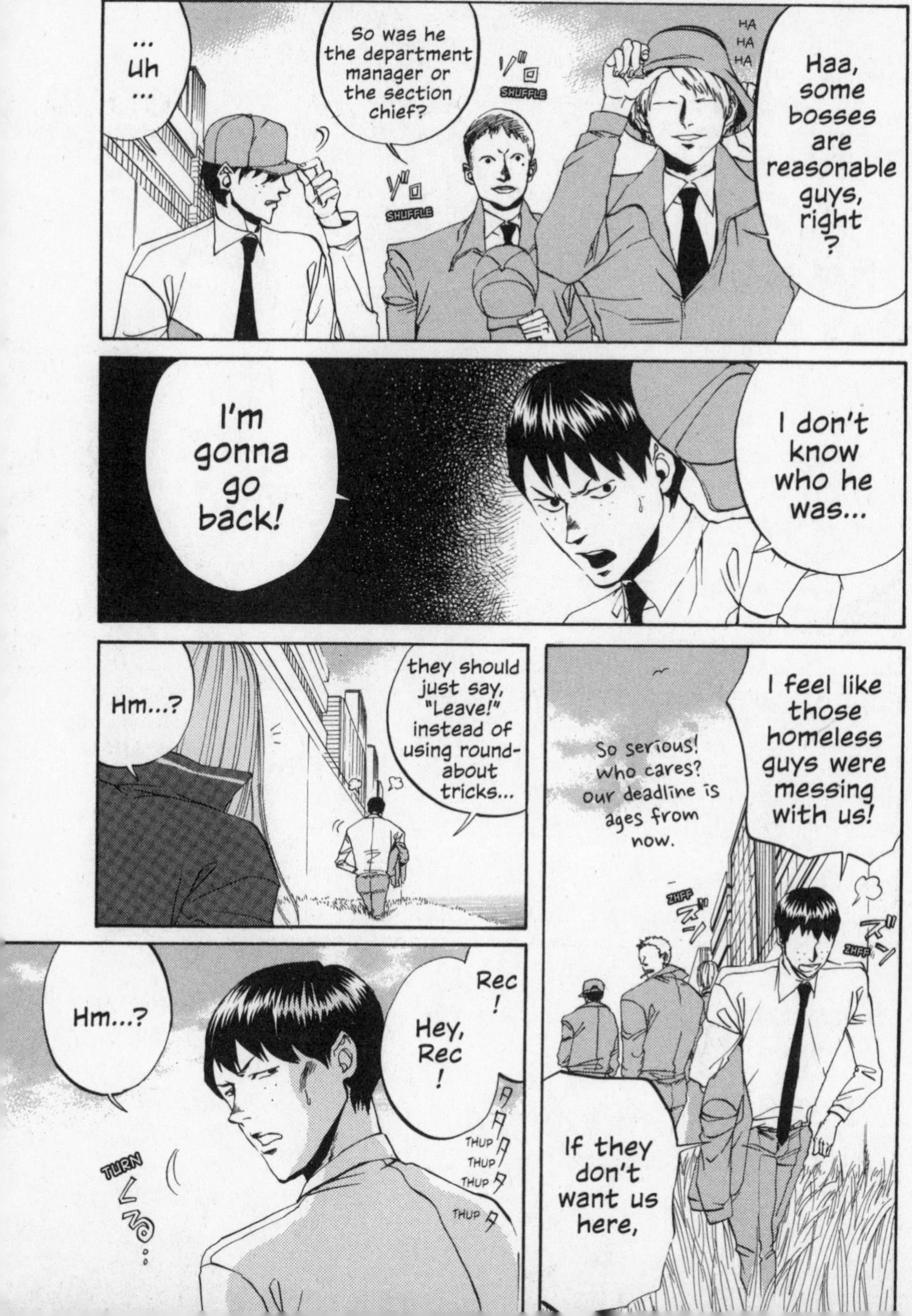
HA HA HA
Haa, some bosses are reasonable guys, right?
SHUFFLE
So was he the department manager or the section chief?
SHUFFLE
... uh ...
I don't know who he was...
I'm gonna go back!
I feel like those homeless guys were messing with us!
So serious! Who cares? our deadline is ages from now.
ZHFF
ZHFF
If they don't want us here,
they should just say, "Leave!" instead of using round-about tricks...
Hm...?
Rec!
Hey, Rec!
THUP THUP THUP THUP
Hm...?
TURN

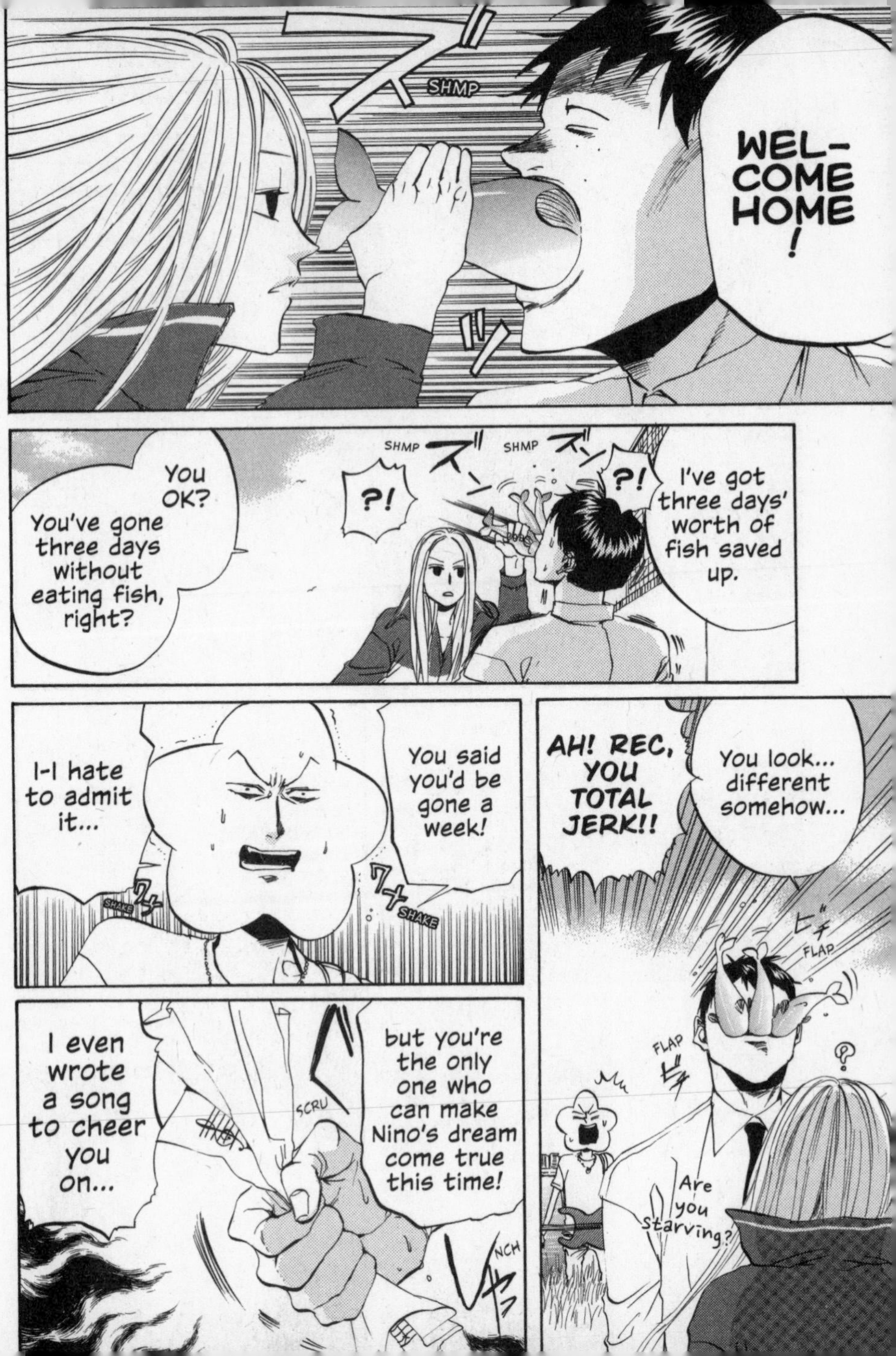
WEL-COME HOME!
SHMP
I've got three days' worth of fish saved up.
?!
SHMP
SHMP
?!
You OK? You've gone three days without eating fish, right?
You look... different somehow...
AH! REC, YOU TOTAL JERK!!
FLAP
FLAP
Are you starving?
You said you'd be gone a week!
SHAKE
I-I hate to admit it...
SHAKE
but you're the only one who can make Nino's dream come true this time!
NCH
SCRU
I even wrote a song to cheer you on...

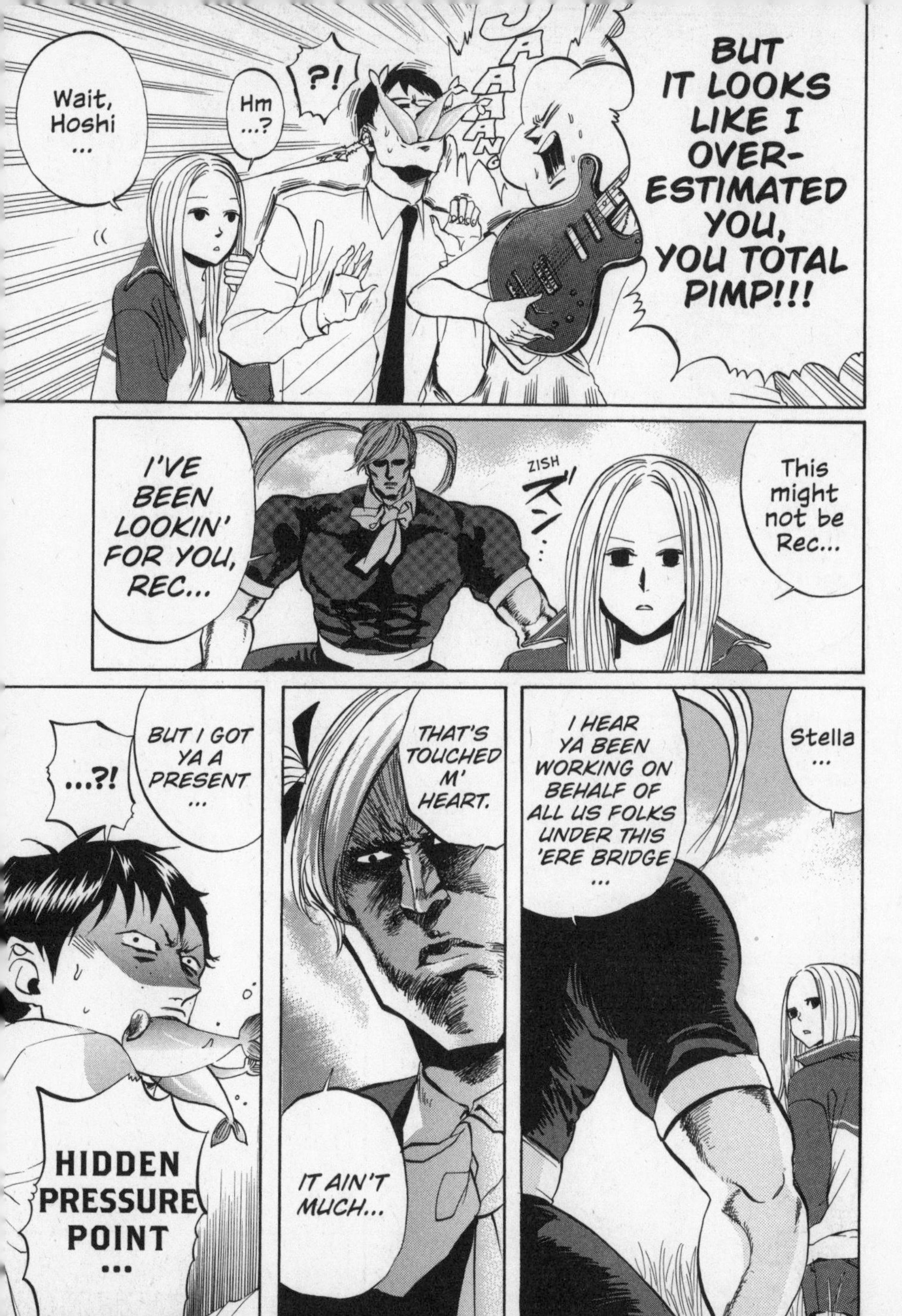
BUT IT LOOKS LIKE I OVER-ESTIMATED YOU, YOU TOTAL PIMP!!!
JAAAANG
?!
Hm ...?
Wait, Hoshi ...
This might not be Rec...
ZISH
I'VE BEEN LOOKIN' FOR YOU, REC...
Stella ...
I HEAR YA BEEN WORKING ON BEHALF OF ALL US FOLKS UNDER THIS 'ERE BRIDGE ...
THAT'S TOUCHED M' HEART.
IT AIN'T MUCH...
BUT I GOT YA A PRESENT ...
...?!
HIDDEN PRESSURE POINT ...

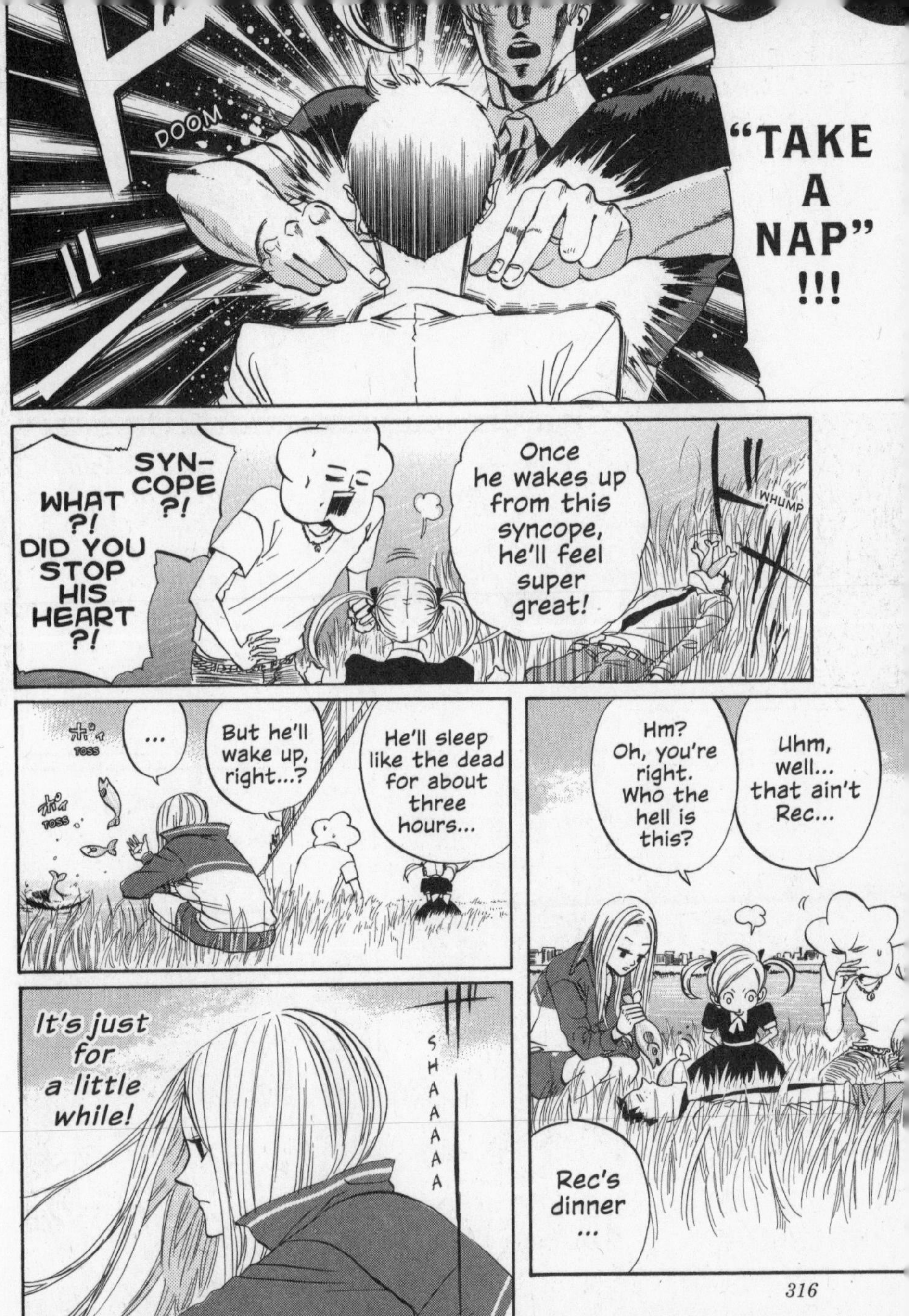
"TAKE A NAP" !!!
DOOM
WHUMP
Once he wakes up from this syncope, he'll feel super great!
SYN-COPE ?!
WHAT ?! DID YOU STOP HIS HEART ?!
Uhm, well... that ain't Rec...
Hm? Oh, you're right. Who the hell is this?
Rec's dinner ...
He'll sleep like the dead for about three hours...
But he'll wake up, right...?
...
TOSS
TOSS
SHAAAAA
It's just for a little while!

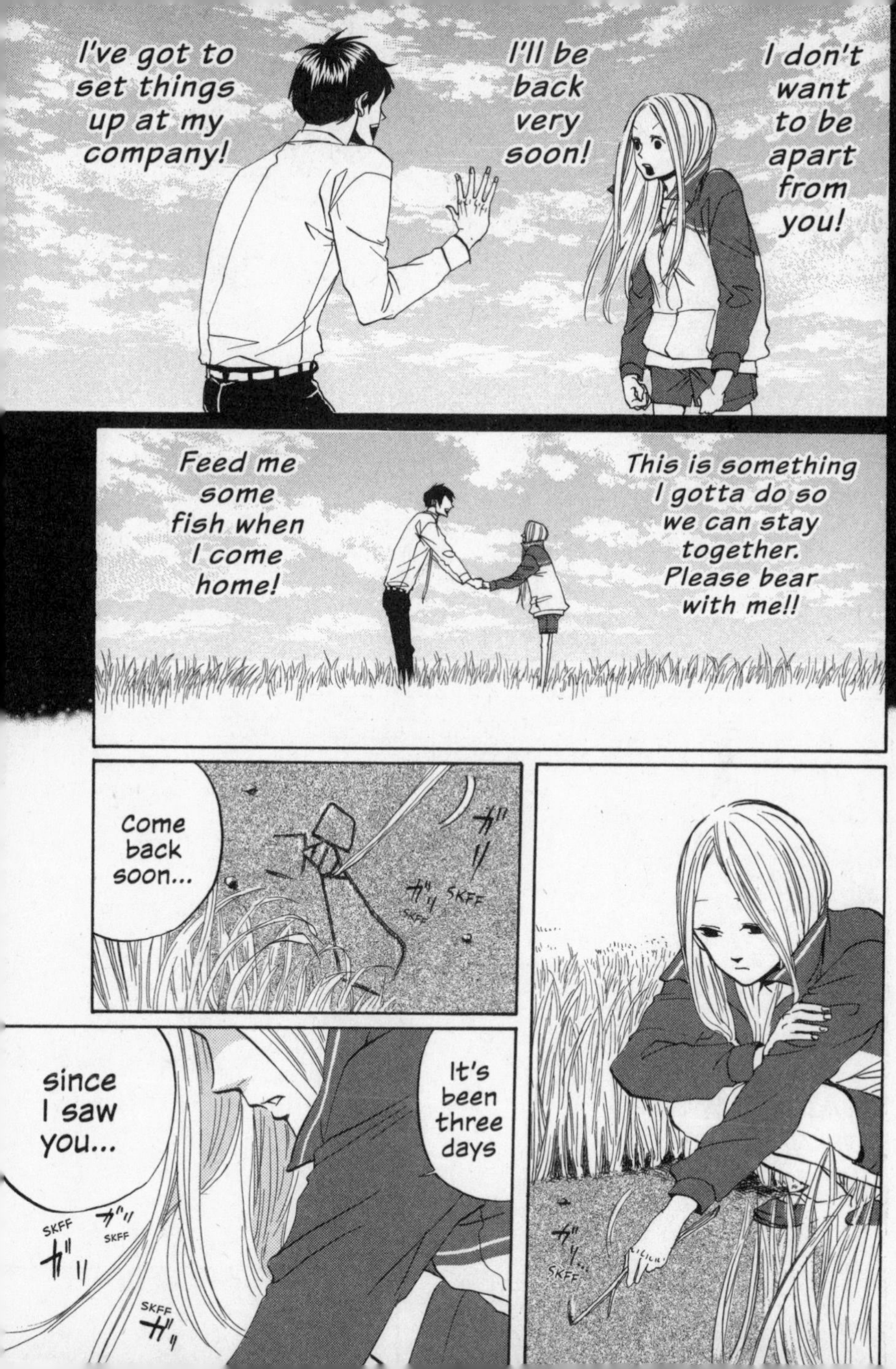
I don't want to be apart from you!
I'll be back very soon!
I've got to set things up at my company!
This is something I gotta do so we can stay together. Please bear with me!!
Feed me some fish when I come home!
ガリ... SKFF
ガリ SKFF
ガリ SKFF
Come back soon...
It's been three days
since I saw you...
SKFF ガリ
SKFF ガリ
SKFF ガリ

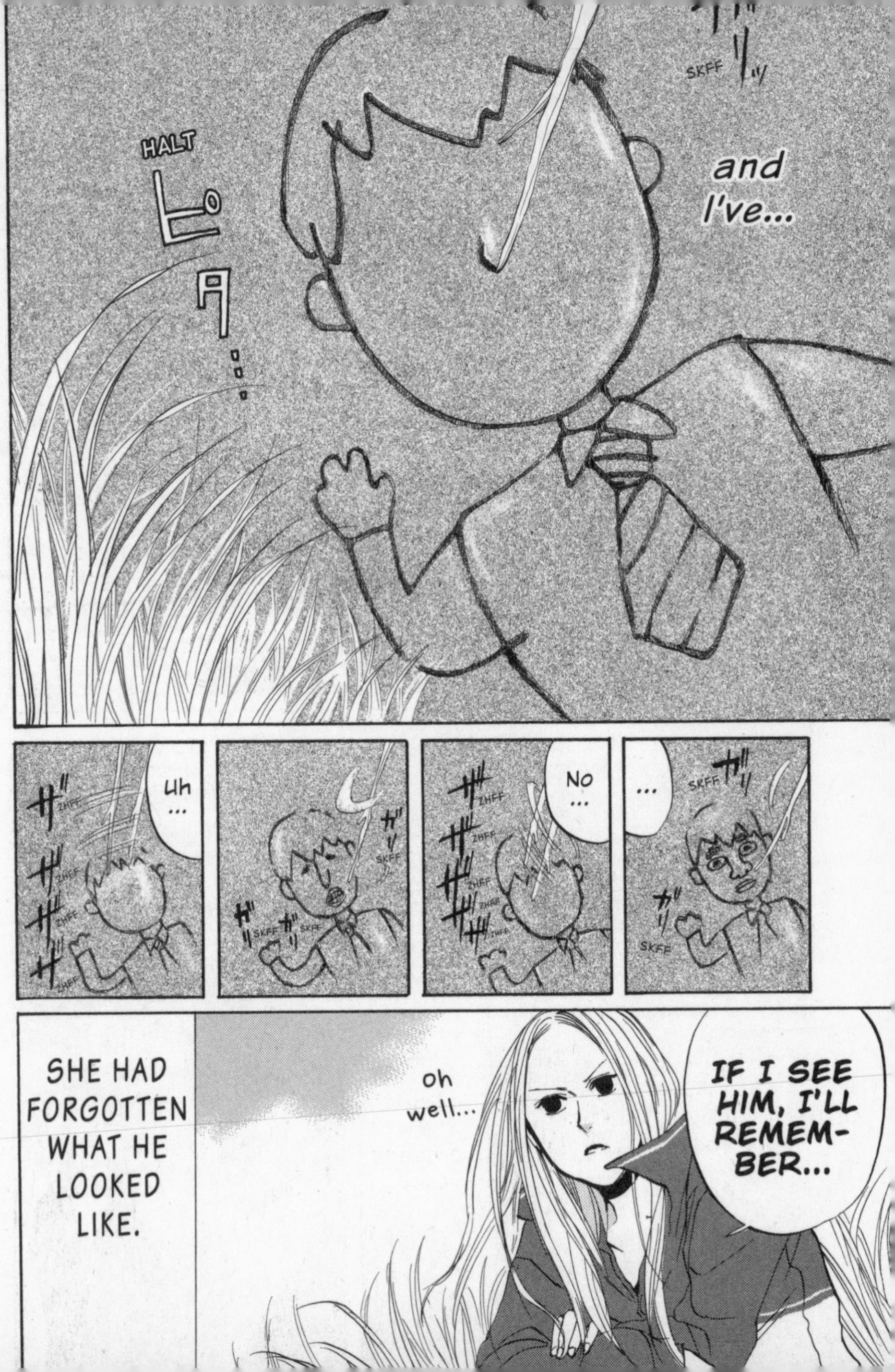
SKFF
and I've...
HALT
...
SKFF
SKFF
No ...
ZHFF
ZHFF
ZHFF
ZHFF
ZHFF
SKFF
SKFF
SKFF
uh ...
ZHFF
ZHFF
ZHFF
ZHFF
IF I SEE HIM, I'LL REMEMBER...
oh well...
SHE HAD FORGOTTEN WHAT HE LOOKED LIKE.

Chapter 99: Father and Son

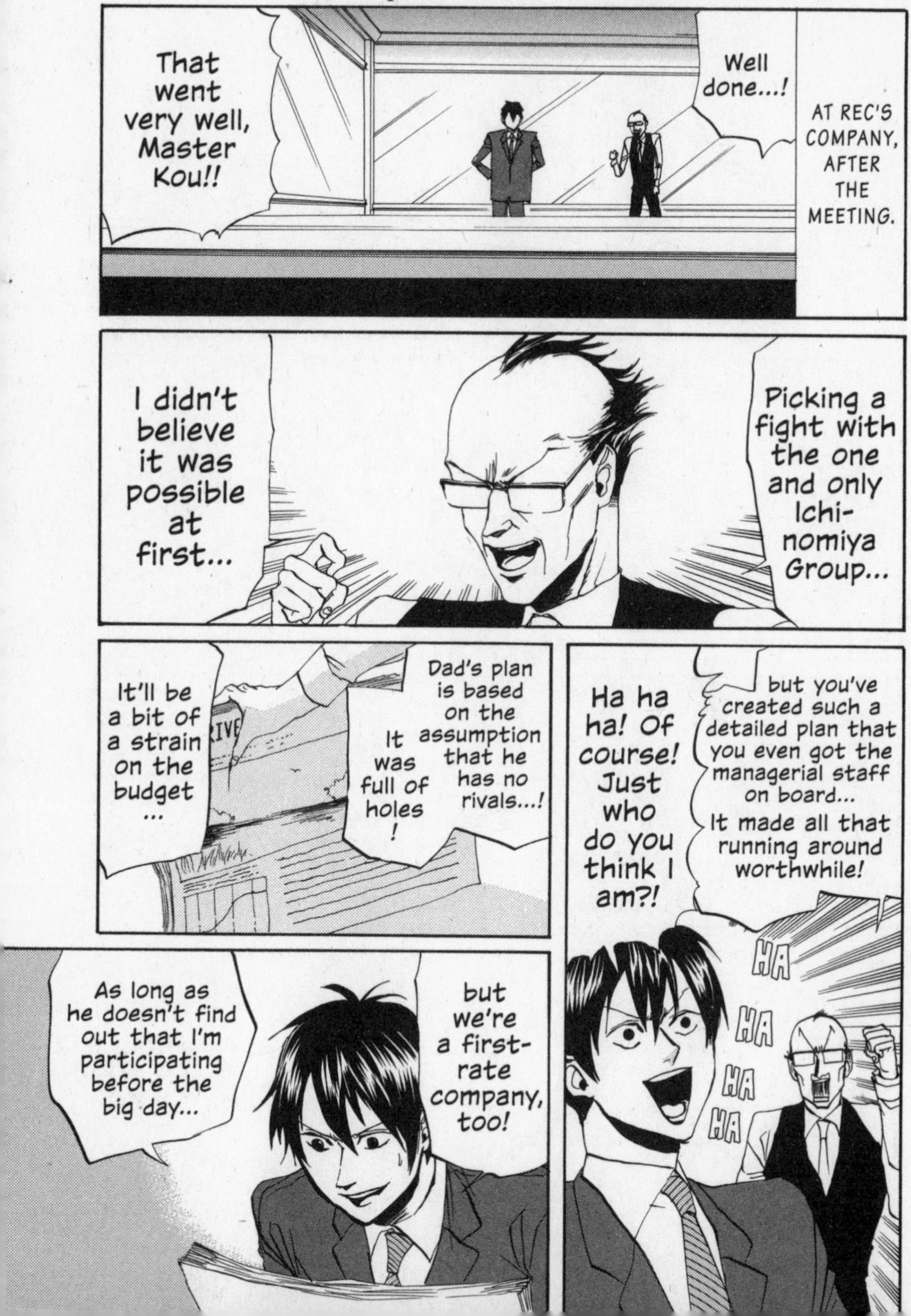

AT REC'S COMPANY, AFTER THE MEETING.
Well done...!
That went very well, Master Kou!!
Picking a fight with the one and only Ichi-nomiya Group...
I didn't believe it was possible at first...
but you've created such a detailed plan that you even got the managerial staff on board...
It made all that running around worthwhile!
Ha ha ha! Of course! Just who do you think I am?!
Dad's plan is based on the assumption that he has no rivals...!
It was full of holes!
It'll be a bit of a strain on the budget...
HA
HA
HA
HA
but we're a first-rate company, too!
As long as he doesn't find out that I'm participating before the big day...

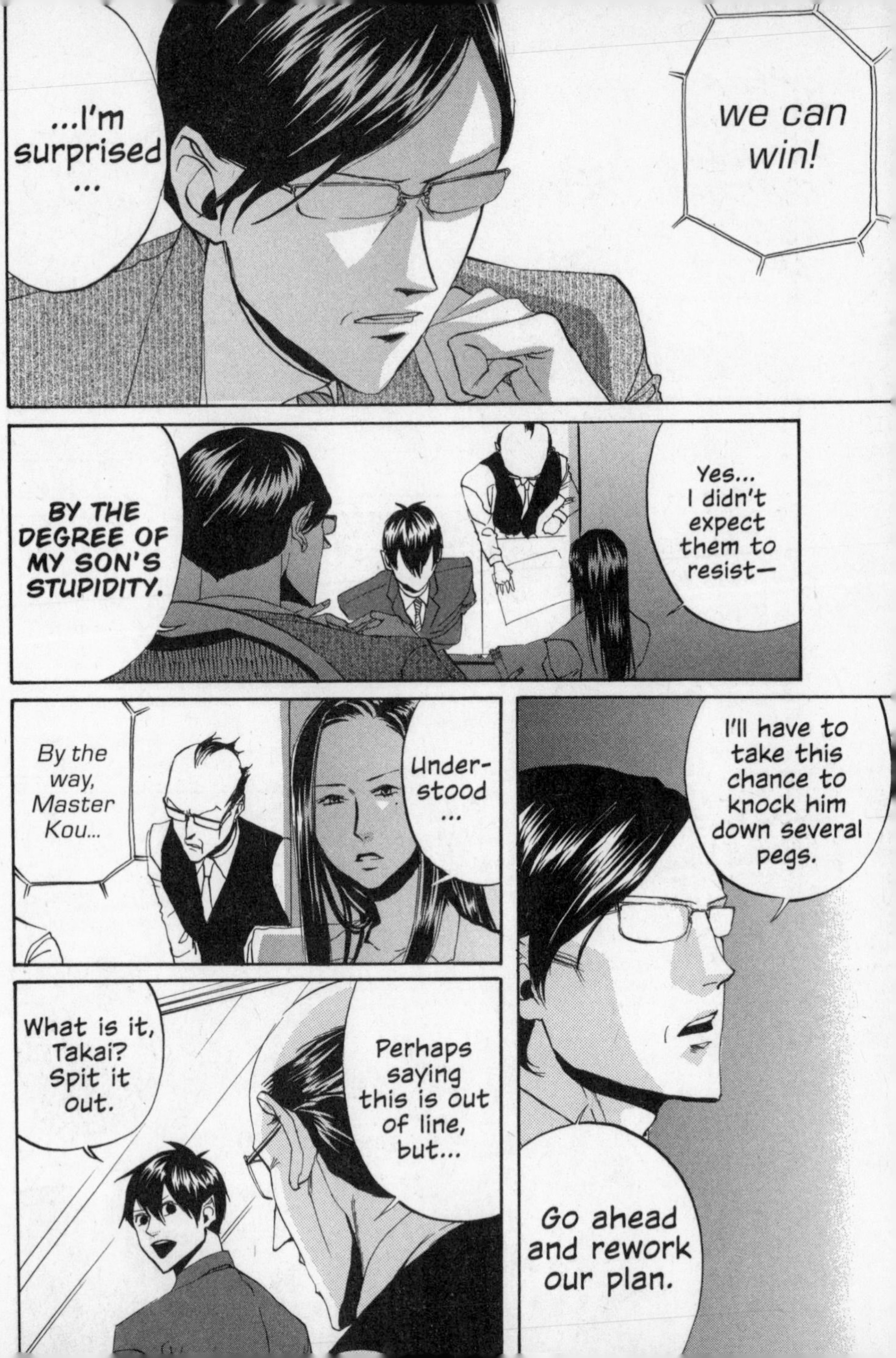
we can win!
...I'm surprised ...
Yes... I didn't expect them to resist—
BY THE DEGREE OF MY SON'S STUPIDITY.
I'll have to take this chance to knock him down several pegs.
Go ahead and rework our plan.
Under-stood ...
By the way, Master Kou...
Perhaps saying this is out of line, but...
What is it, Takai? Spit it out.

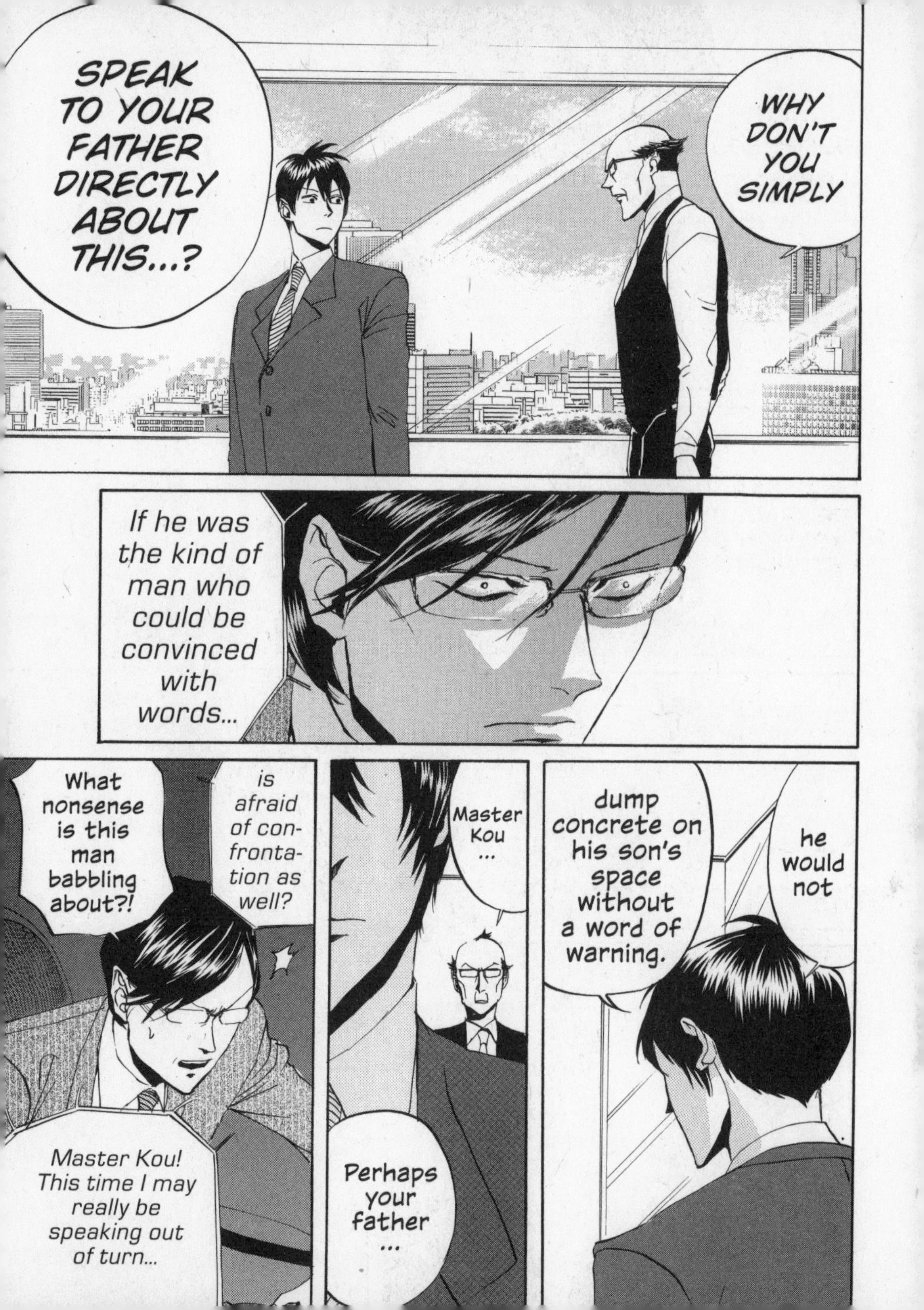
WHY DON'T YOU SIMPLY
SPEAK TO YOUR FATHER DIRECTLY ABOUT THIS...?
If he was the kind of man who could be convinced with words...
he would not
dump concrete on his son's space without a word of warning.
Master Kou ...
Perhaps your father ...
is afraid of con-frontation as well?
What nonsense is this man babbling about?!
Master Kou! This time I may really be speaking out of turn...

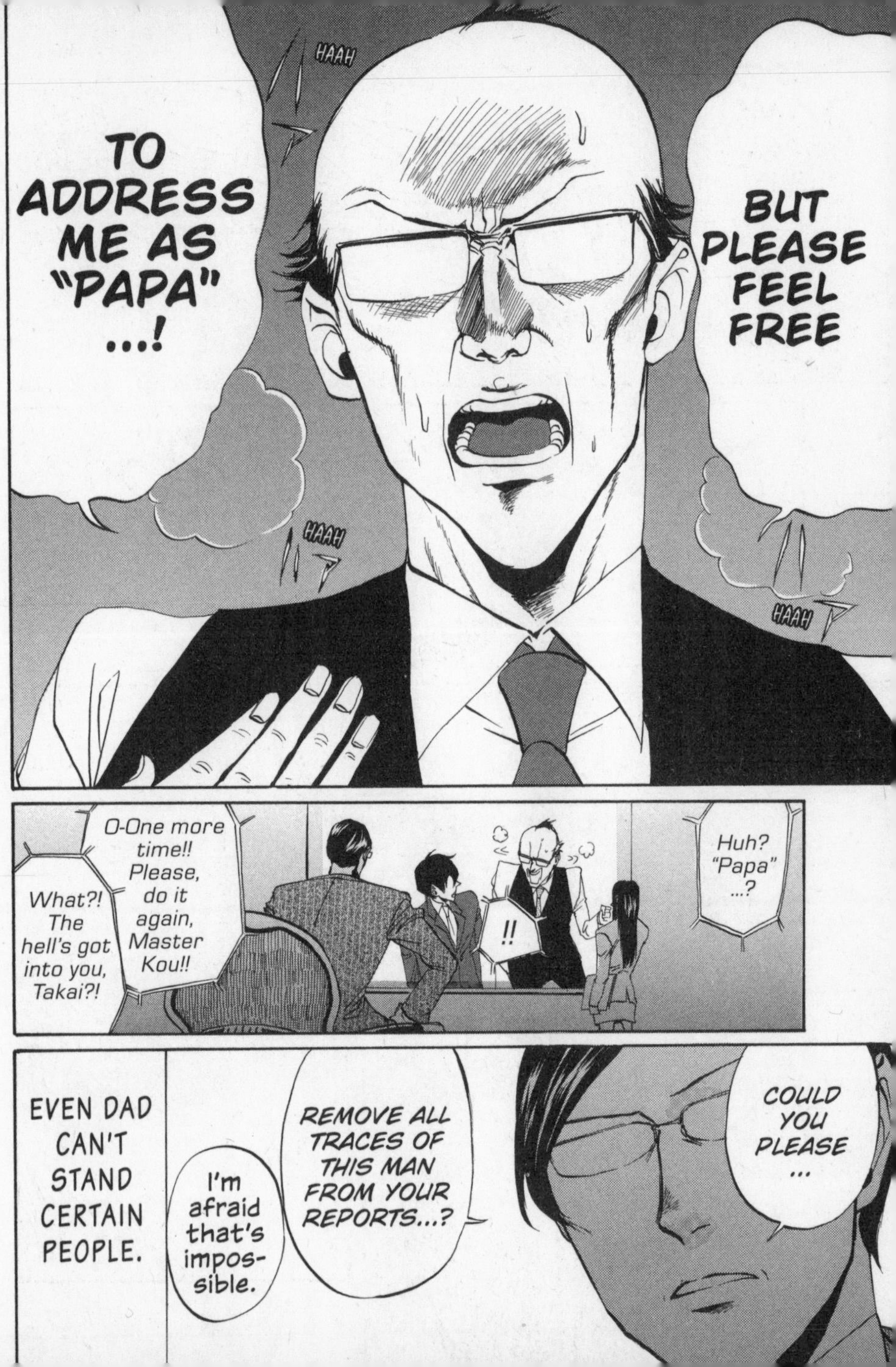
HAAH
BUT PLEASE FEEL FREE
TO ADDRESS ME AS "PAPA" ...!
HAAH
HAAH
Huh? "Papa" ...?
!!
O-One more time!! Please, do it again, Master Kou!!
What?! The hell's got into you, Takai?!
COULD YOU PLEASE ...
REMOVE ALL TRACES OF THIS MAN FROM YOUR REPORTS...?
I'm afraid that's impos-sible.
EVEN DAD CAN'T STAND CERTAIN PEOPLE.

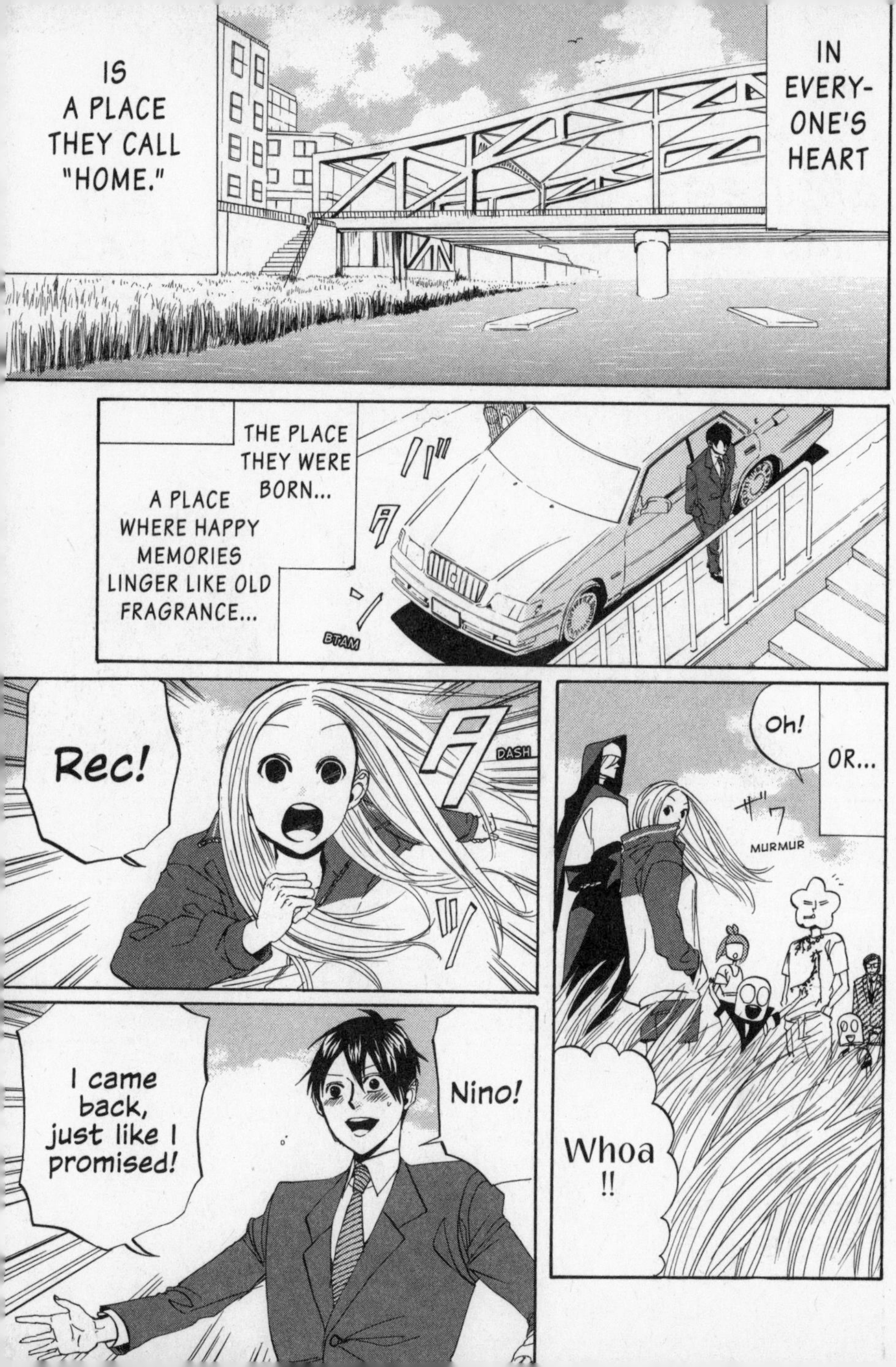
IN EVERY-ONE'S HEART
IS A PLACE THEY CALL "HOME."
THE PLACE THEY WERE BORN...
A PLACE WHERE HAPPY MEMORIES LINGER LIKE OLD FRAGRANCE...
BTAM
OR...
Oh!
MURMUR
Whoa !!
Rec!
DASH
Nino!
I came back, just like I promised!

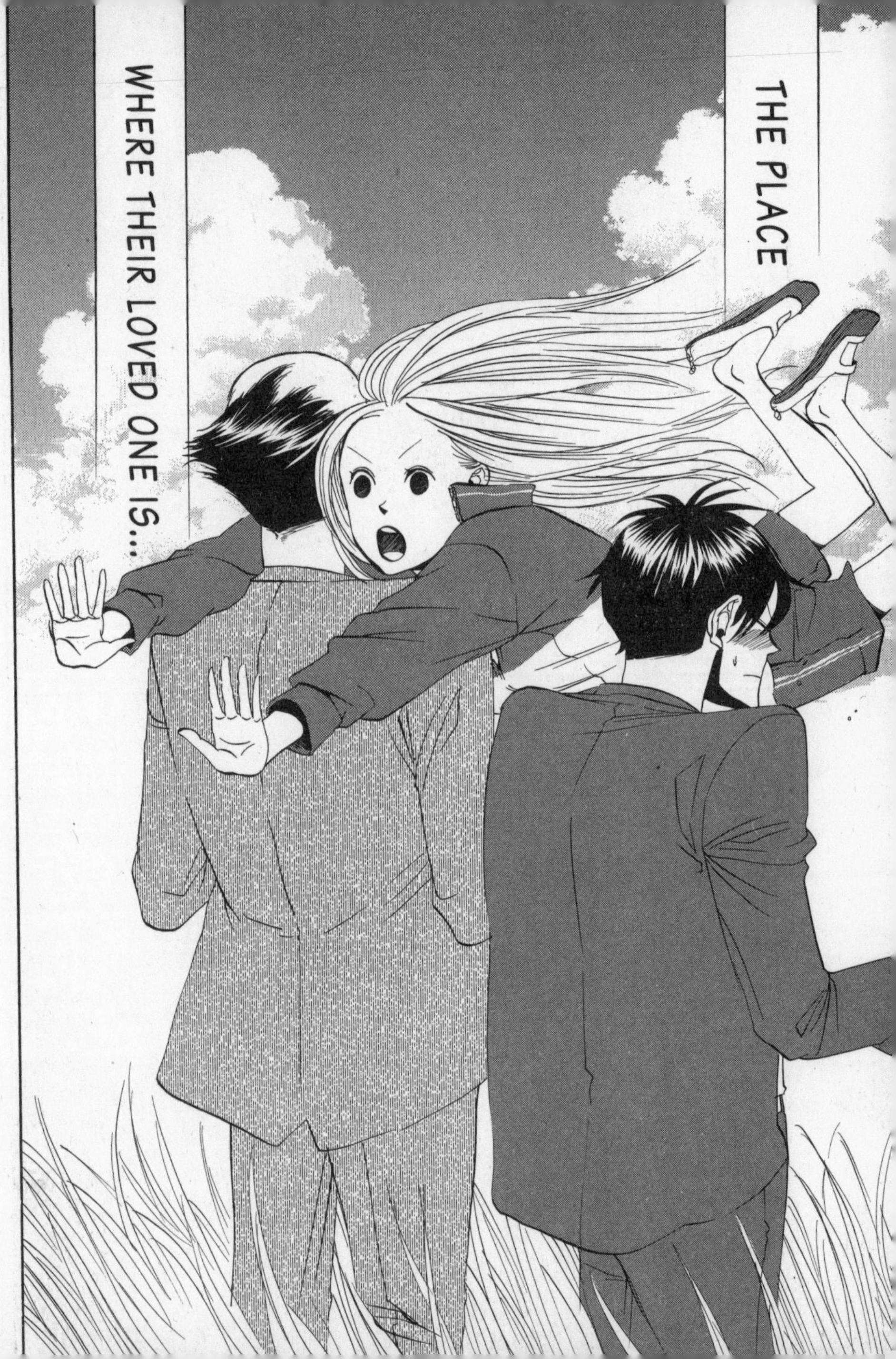
THE PLACE
WHERE THEIR LOVED ONE IS...

Chapter 100: Plan

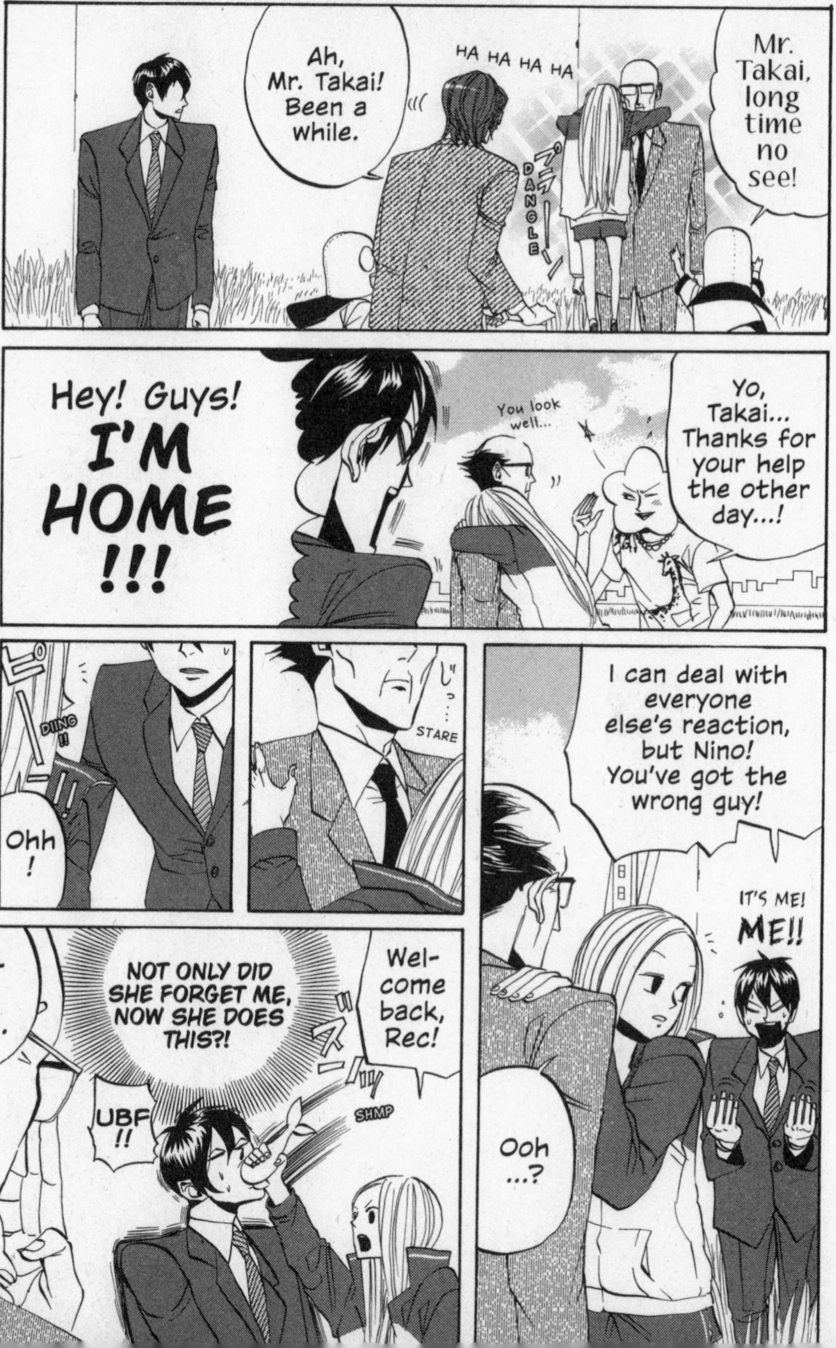

Mr. Takai, long time no see!
HA HA HA HA
DANGLE
Ah, Mr. Takai! Been a while.
Yo, Takai... Thanks for your help the other day...!
You look well...
Hey! Guys! I'M HOME!!!
I can deal with everyone else's reaction, but Nino! You've got the wrong guy!
IT'S ME! ME!!
Ooh ...?
STARE
DIING !!
Ohh !
Wel-come back, Rec!
NOT ONLY DID SHE FORGET ME, NOW SHE DOES THIS?!
SHMP
UBF !!
Mas-ter Kou...

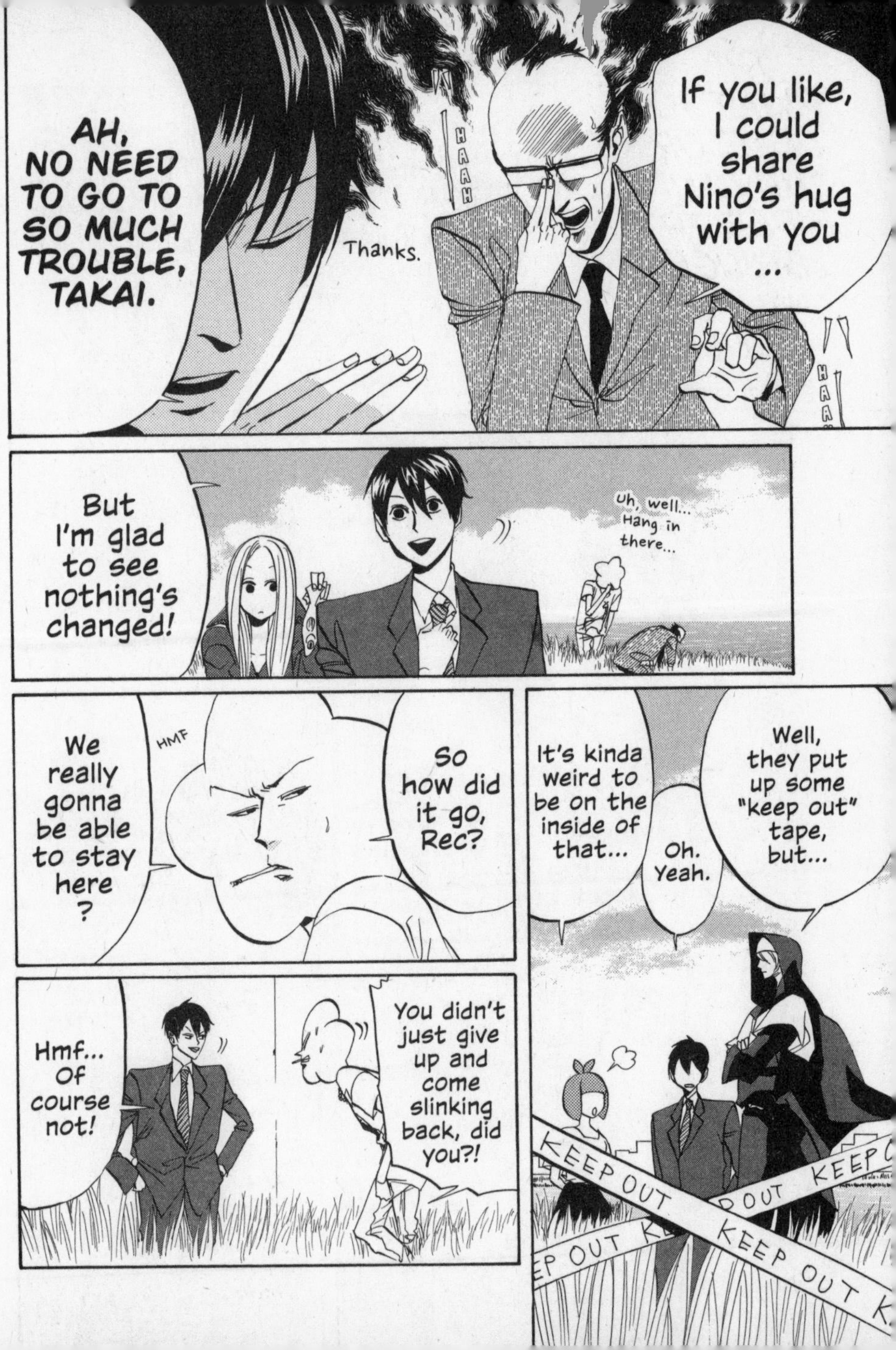
If you like, I could share Nino's hug with you ...
HAAAH
HAAAH
Thanks.
AH, NO NEED TO GO TO SO MUCH TROUBLE, TAKAI.
Uh, well... Hang in there...
But I'm glad to see nothing's changed!
Well, they put up some "keep out" tape, but...
Oh. Yeah.
It's kinda weird to be on the inside of that...
KEEP OUT
KEEP OUT
KEEP OUT
So how did it go, Rec?
HMF
We really gonna be able to stay here?
You didn't just give up and come slinking back, did you?!
Hmf... Of course not!

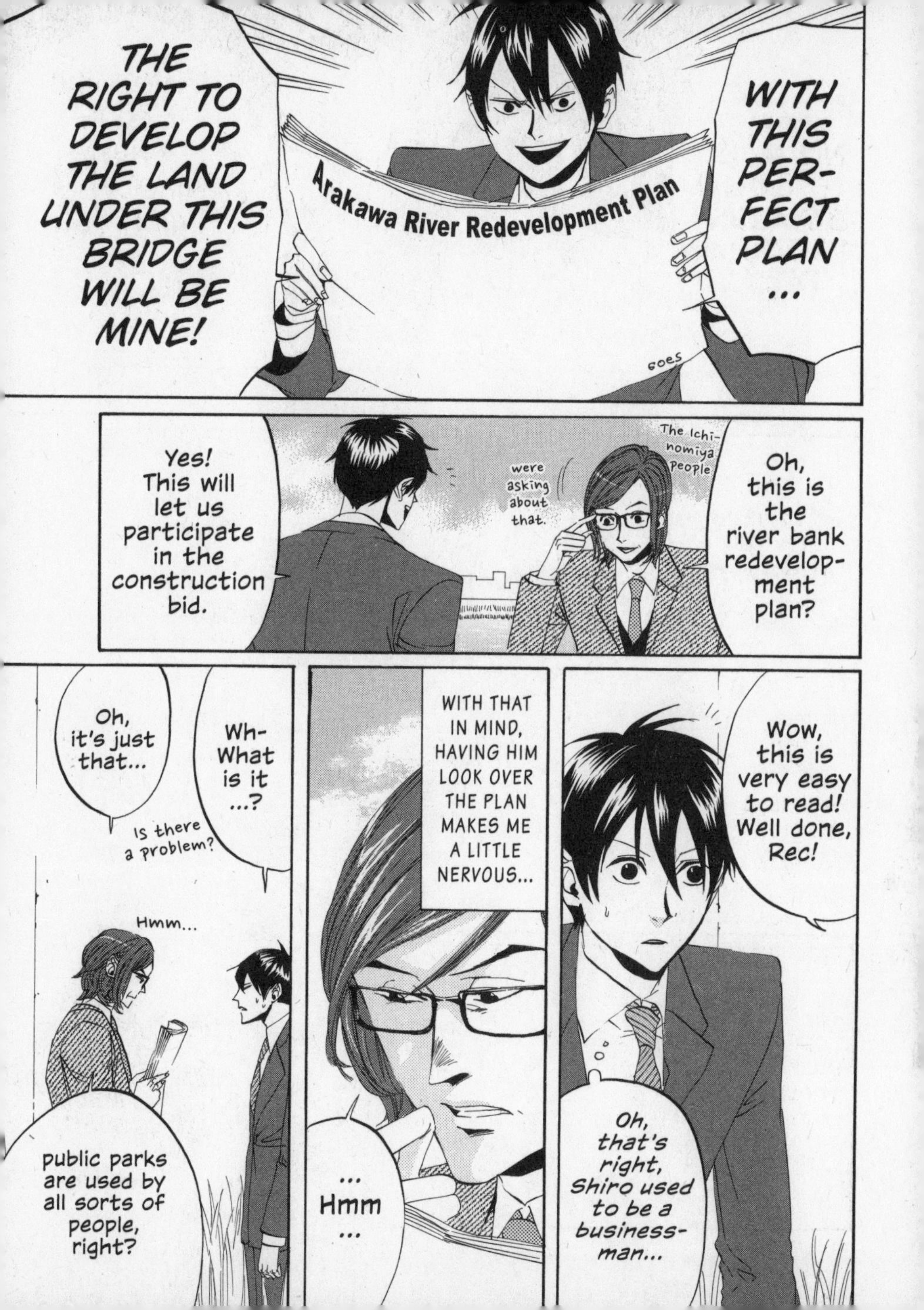
WITH THIS PER-FECT PLAN ...
THE RIGHT TO DEVELOP THE LAND UNDER THIS BRIDGE WILL BE MINE!
Arakawa River Redevelopment Plan
goes
Oh, this is the river bank redevelop-ment plan?
The Ichi-nomiya people were asking about that.
Yes! This will let us participate in the construction bid.
Wow, this is very easy to read! Well done, Rec!
Oh, that's right, Shiro used to be a business-man...
WITH THAT IN MIND, HAVING HIM LOOK OVER THE PLAN MAKES ME A LITTLE NERVOUS...
... Hmm ...
Wh- What is it ...?
Is there a problem?
Oh, it's just that...
Hmm...
public parks are used by all sorts of people, right?

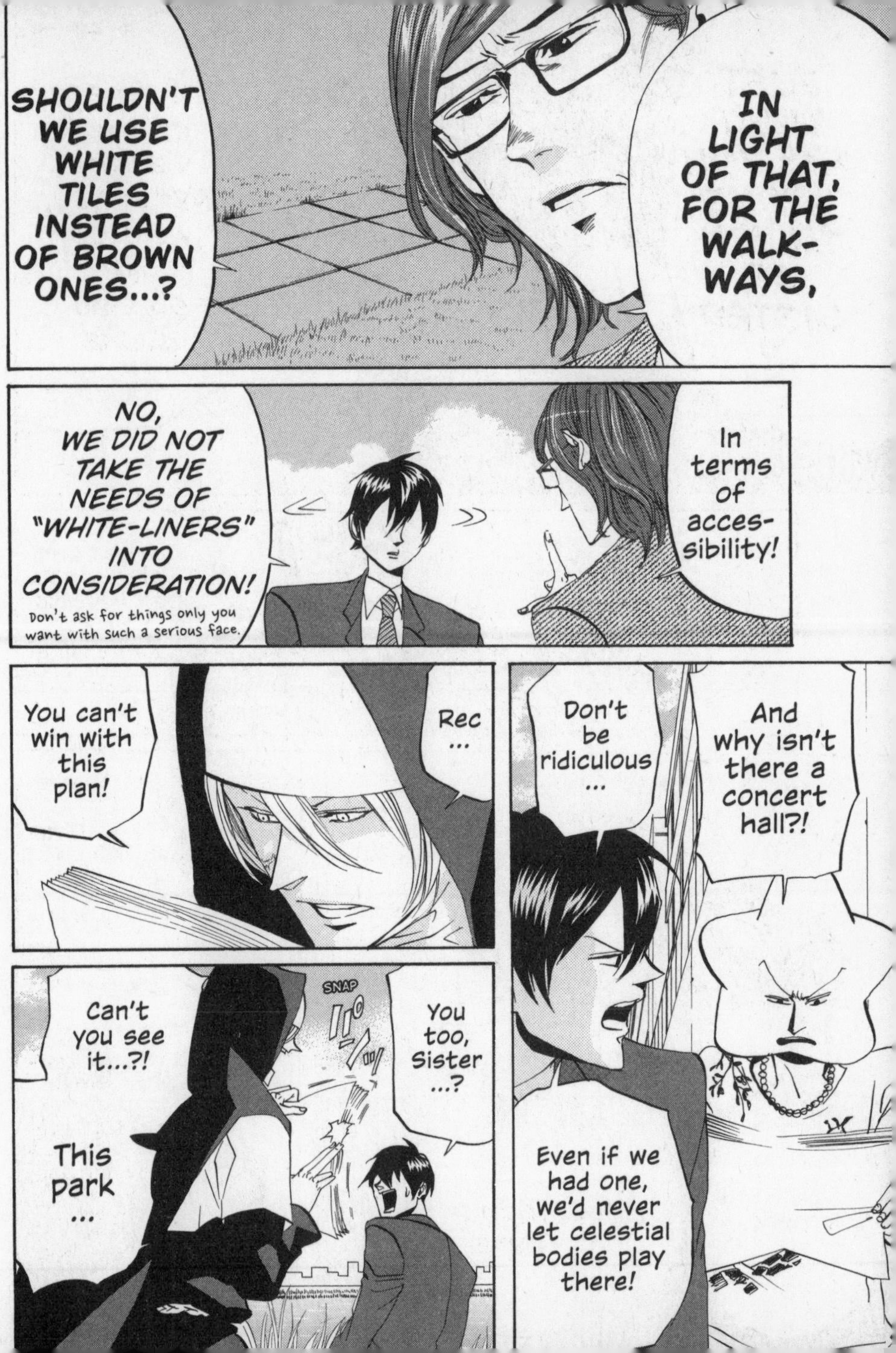
IN LIGHT OF THAT, FOR THE WALK-WAYS,
SHOULDN'T WE USE WHITE TILES INSTEAD OF BROWN ONES...?
In terms of acces-sibility!
NO, WE DID NOT TAKE THE NEEDS OF "WHITE-LINERS" INTO CONSIDERATION!
Don't ask for things only you want with such a serious face.
And why isn't there a concert hall?!
Don't be ridiculous ...
Even if we had one, we'd never let celestial bodies play there!
Rec ...
You can't win with this plan!
SNAP
You too, Sister ...?
Can't you see it...?!
This park ...

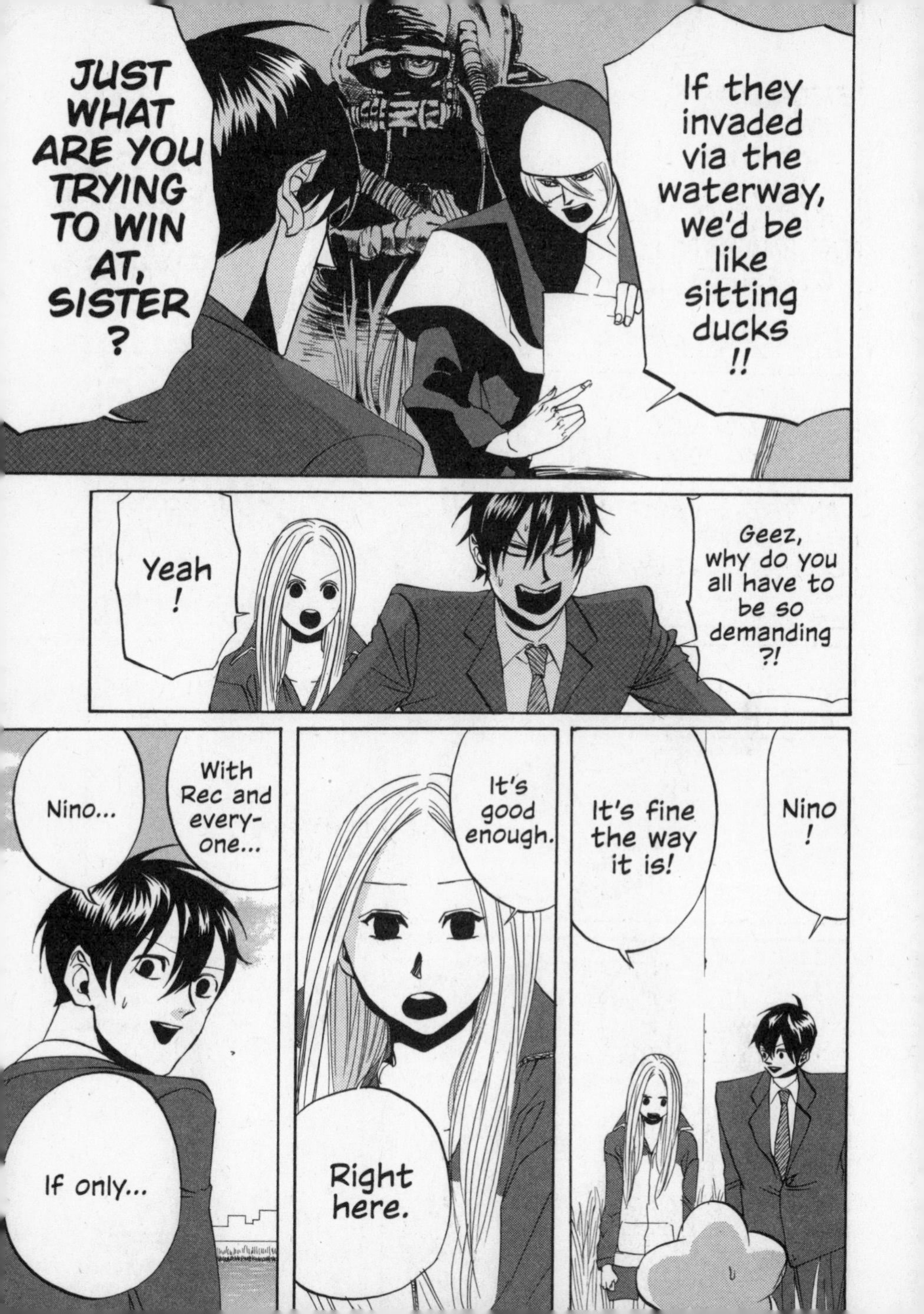
If they invaded via the waterway, we'd be like sitting ducks!!
JUST WHAT ARE YOU TRYING TO WIN AT, SISTER?
Geez, why do you all have to be so demanding?!
Yeah!
Nino!
It's fine the way it is!
It's good enough.
Right here.
With Rec and every-one...
Nino...
If only...

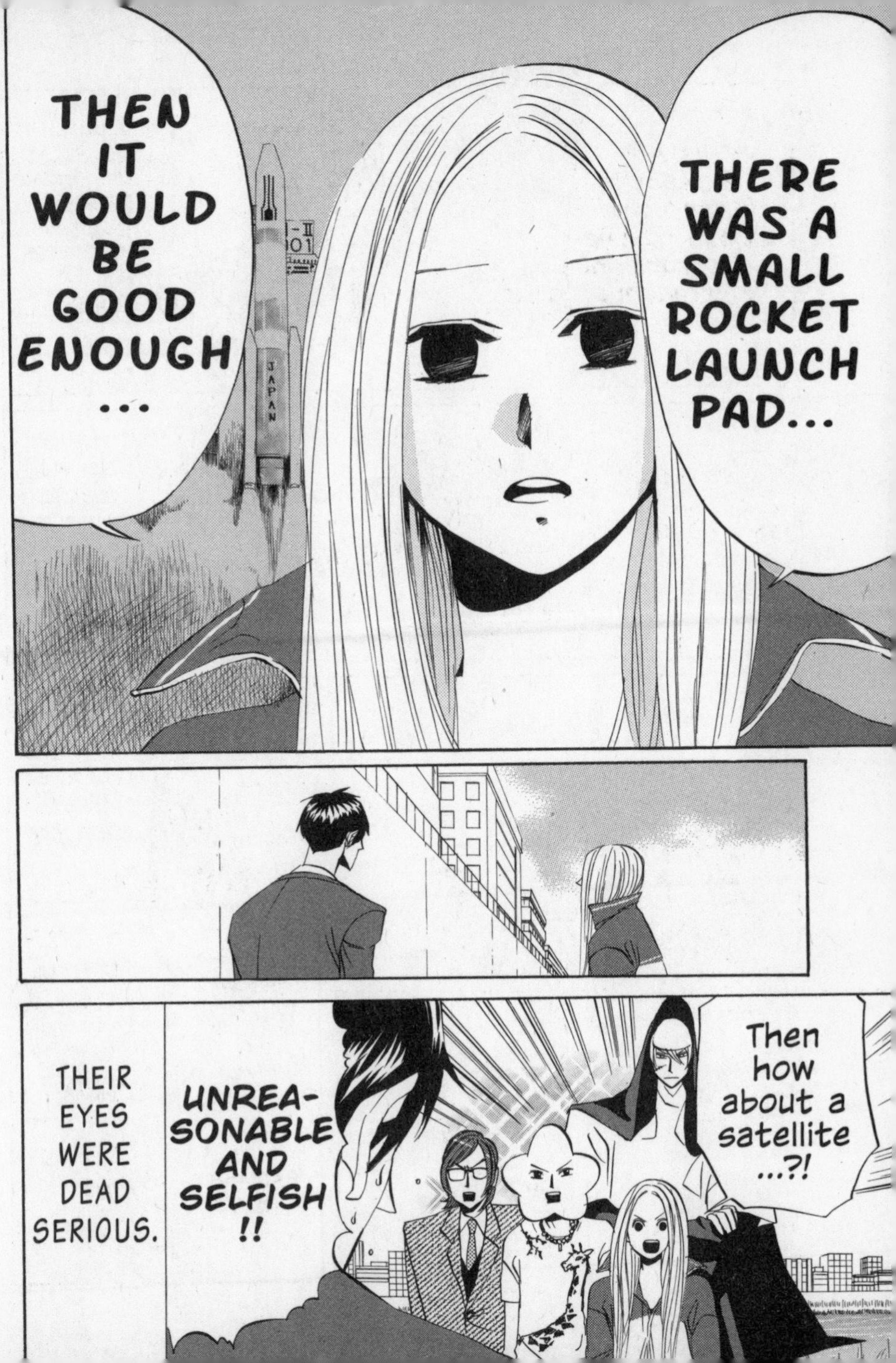
THERE WAS A SMALL ROCKET LAUNCH PAD...
JAPAN
THEN IT WOULD BE GOOD ENOUGH...
Then how about a satellite ...?!
UNREA-SONABLE AND SELFISH!!
THEIR EYES WERE DEAD SERIOUS.

Chapter 101: Ichinomiya Power

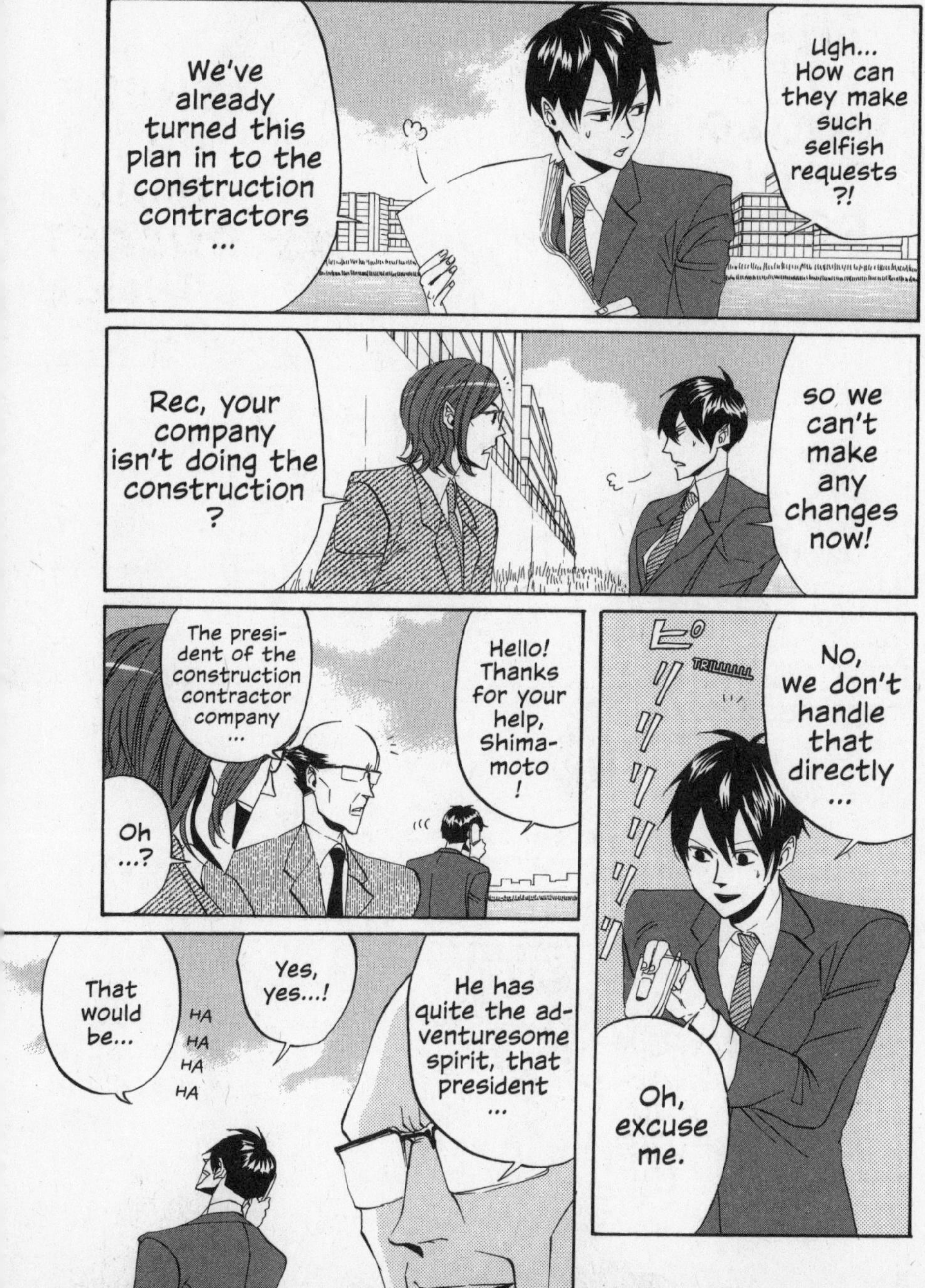
Ugh... How can they make such selfish requests?!
We've already turned this plan in to the construction contractors...
so we can't make any changes now!
Rec, your company isn't doing the construction?
TRILLLLLL
No, we don't handle that directly...
Oh, excuse me.
Hello! Thanks for your help, Shimamoto!
The president of the construction contractor company...
Oh...?
He has quite the adventuresome spirit, that president...
Yes, yes...!
HA HA HA HA
That would be...

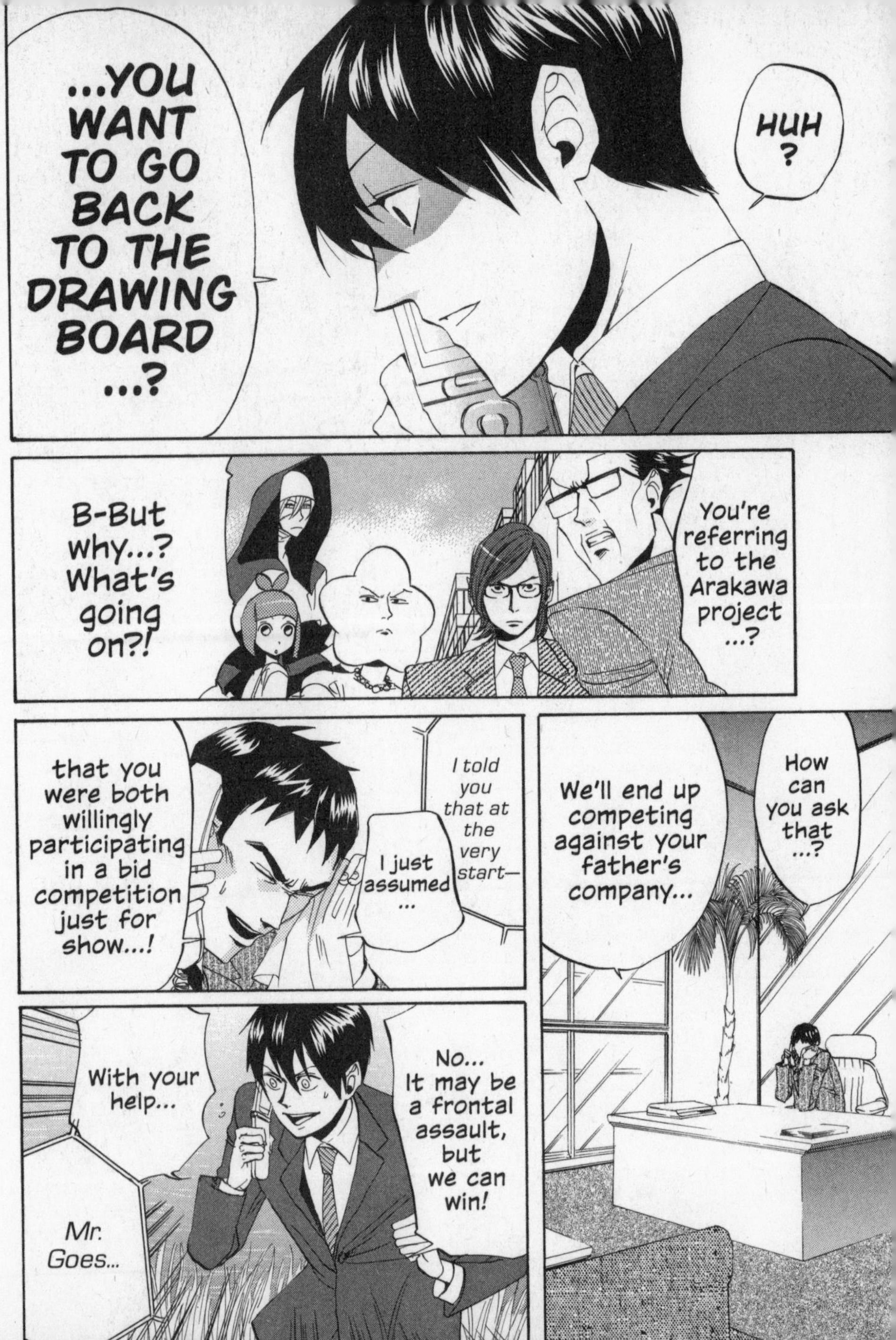
HUH?
...YOU WANT TO GO BACK TO THE DRAWING BOARD...?
You're referring to the Arakawa project...?
B-But why...? What's going on?!
How can you ask that...?
We'll end up competing against your father's company...
I told you that at the very start—
I just assumed...
that you were both willingly participating in a bid competition just for show...!
No... It may be a frontal assault, but we can win!
With your help...
Mr. Goes...

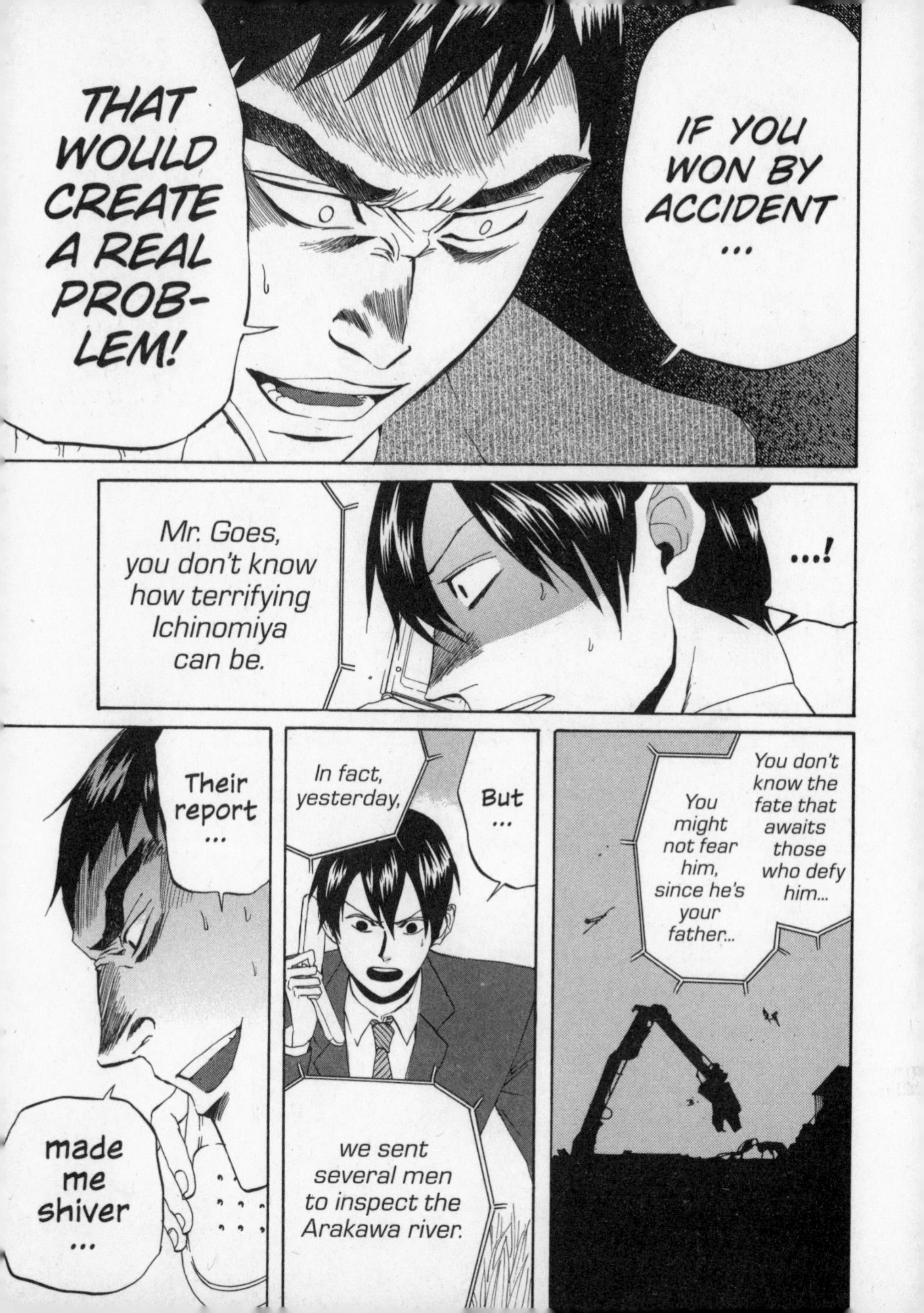
IF YOU WON BY ACCIDENT ...
THAT WOULD CREATE A REAL PROB-LEM!
...!
Mr. Goes, you don't know how terrifying Ichinomiya can be.
You don't know the fate that awaits those who defy him...
You might not fear him, since he's your father...
But ...
In fact, yesterday,
we sent several men to inspect the Arakawa river.
Their report ...
made me shiver ...

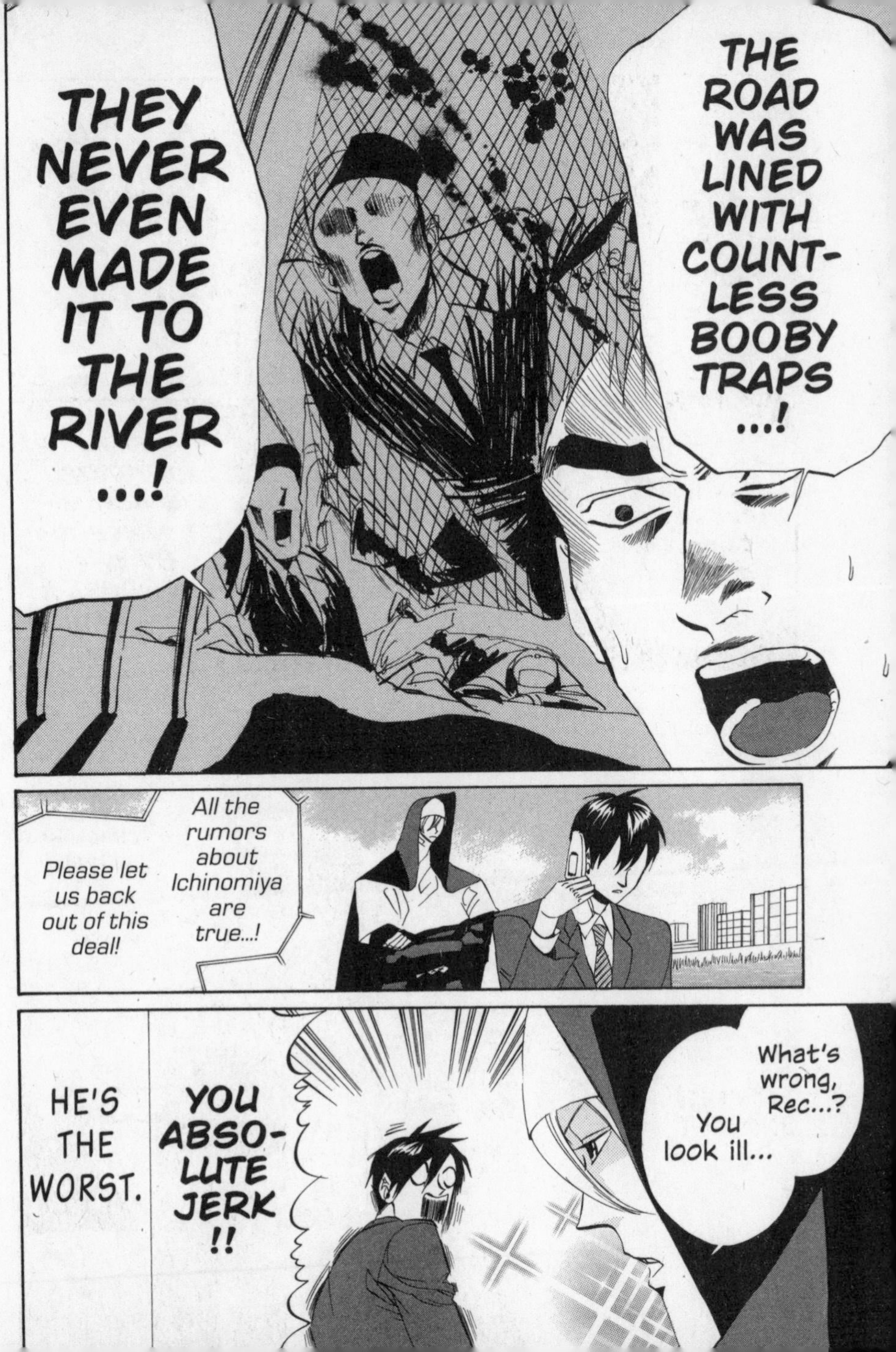
THE ROAD WAS LINED WITH COUNT-LESS BOOBY TRAPS ...!
THEY NEVER EVEN MADE IT TO THE RIVER ...!
All the rumors about Ichinomiya are true...!
Please let us back out of this deal!
What's wrong, Rec...? You look ill...
YOU ABSO-LUTE JERK !!
HE'S THE WORST.

Chapter 102: Phone Call

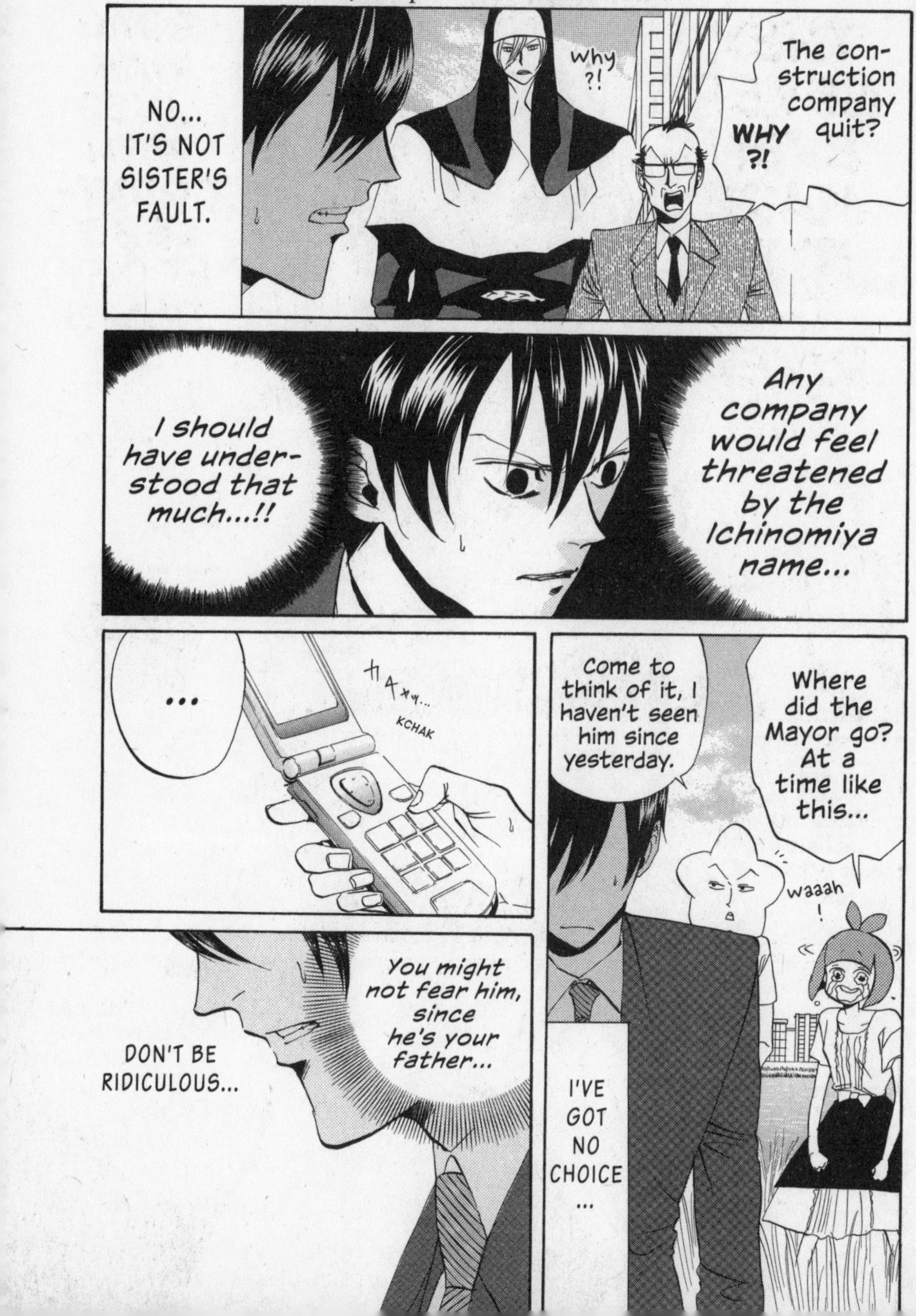

The con-struction company quit?
WHY ?!
Why ?!
NO... IT'S NOT SISTER'S FAULT.
Any company would feel threatened by the Ichinomiya name...
I should have under-stood that much...!!
Where did the Mayor go? At a time like this...
Come to think of it, I haven't seen him since yesterday.
waaah !
I'VE GOT NO CHOICE ...
...
KCHAK
You might not fear him, since he's your father...
DON'T BE RIDICULOUS...

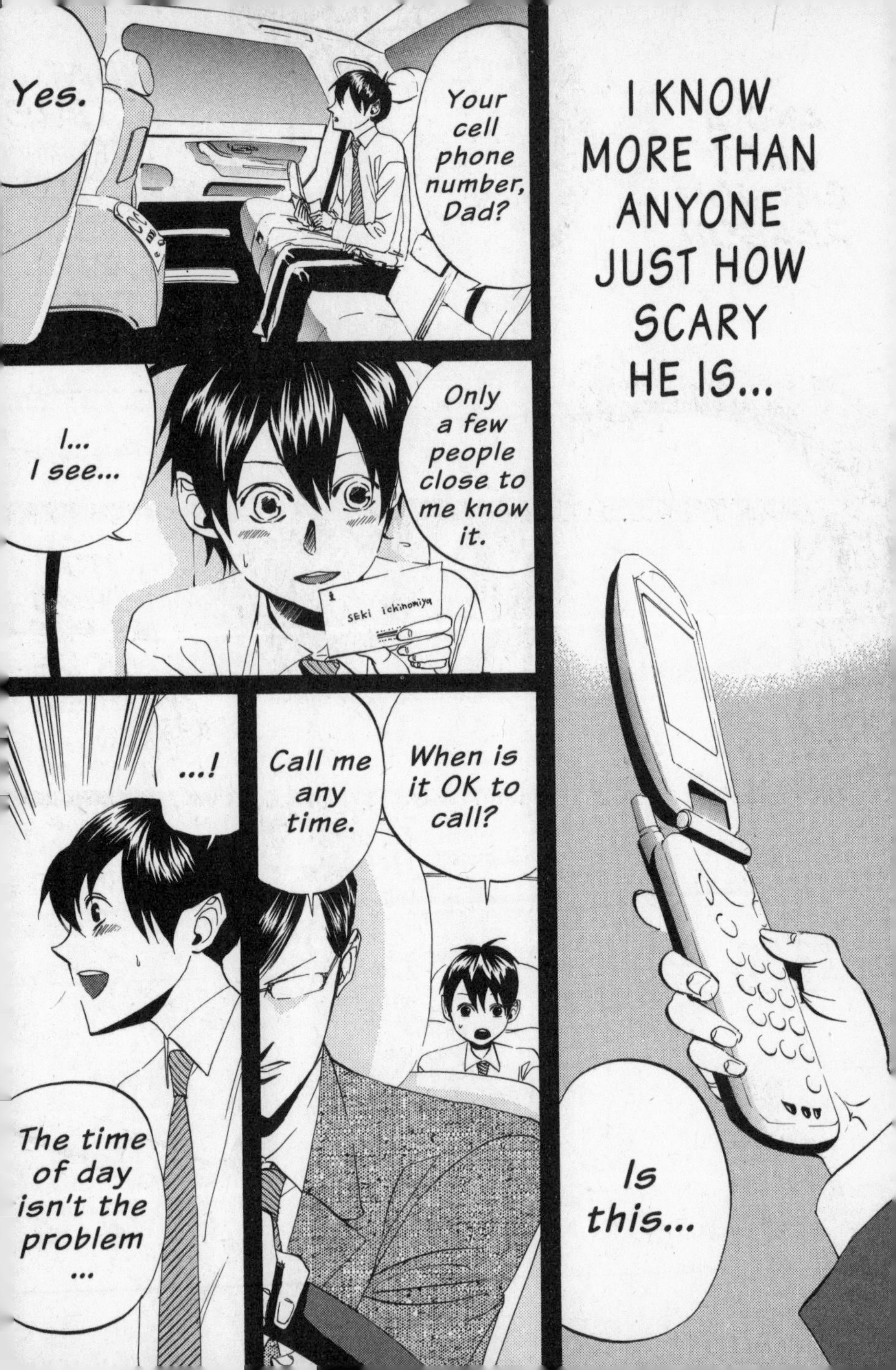
I KNOW MORE THAN ANYONE JUST HOW SCARY HE IS...
Is this...
Your cell phone number, Dad?
Yes.
Only a few people close to me know it.
I... I see...
SEKi ichinomiya
When is it OK to call?
Call me any time.
...!
The time of day isn't the problem ...

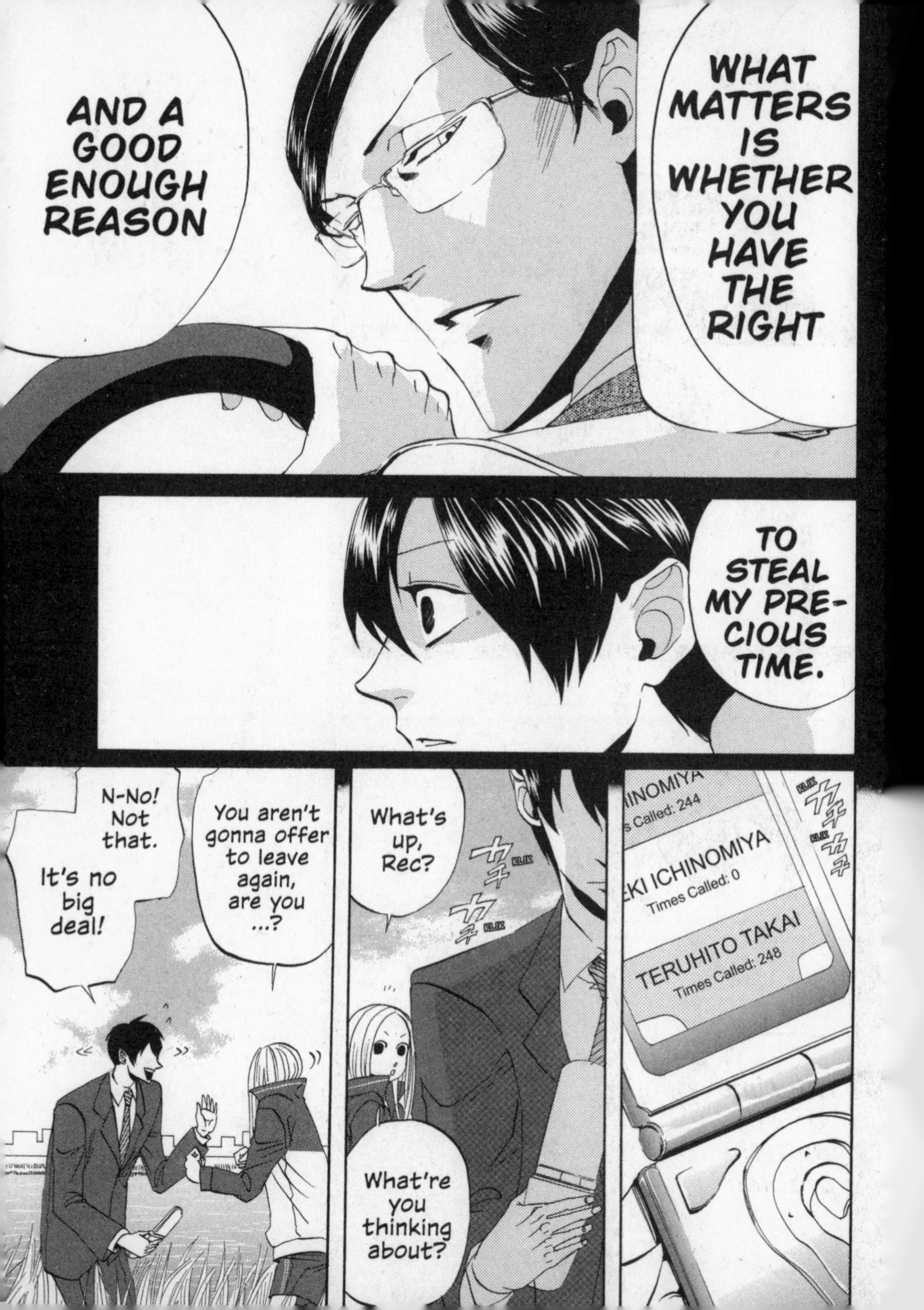
WHAT MATTERS IS WHETHER YOU HAVE THE RIGHT
AND A GOOD ENOUGH REASON
TO STEAL MY PRECIOUS TIME.
KLIK
KLIK
INOMIYA
Called: 244
ICHINOMIYA
Times Called: 0
TERUHITO TAKAI
Times Called: 248
What's up, Rec?
KLIK
KLIK
What're you thinking about?
You aren't gonna offer to leave again, are you ...?
N-No! Not that.
It's no big deal!

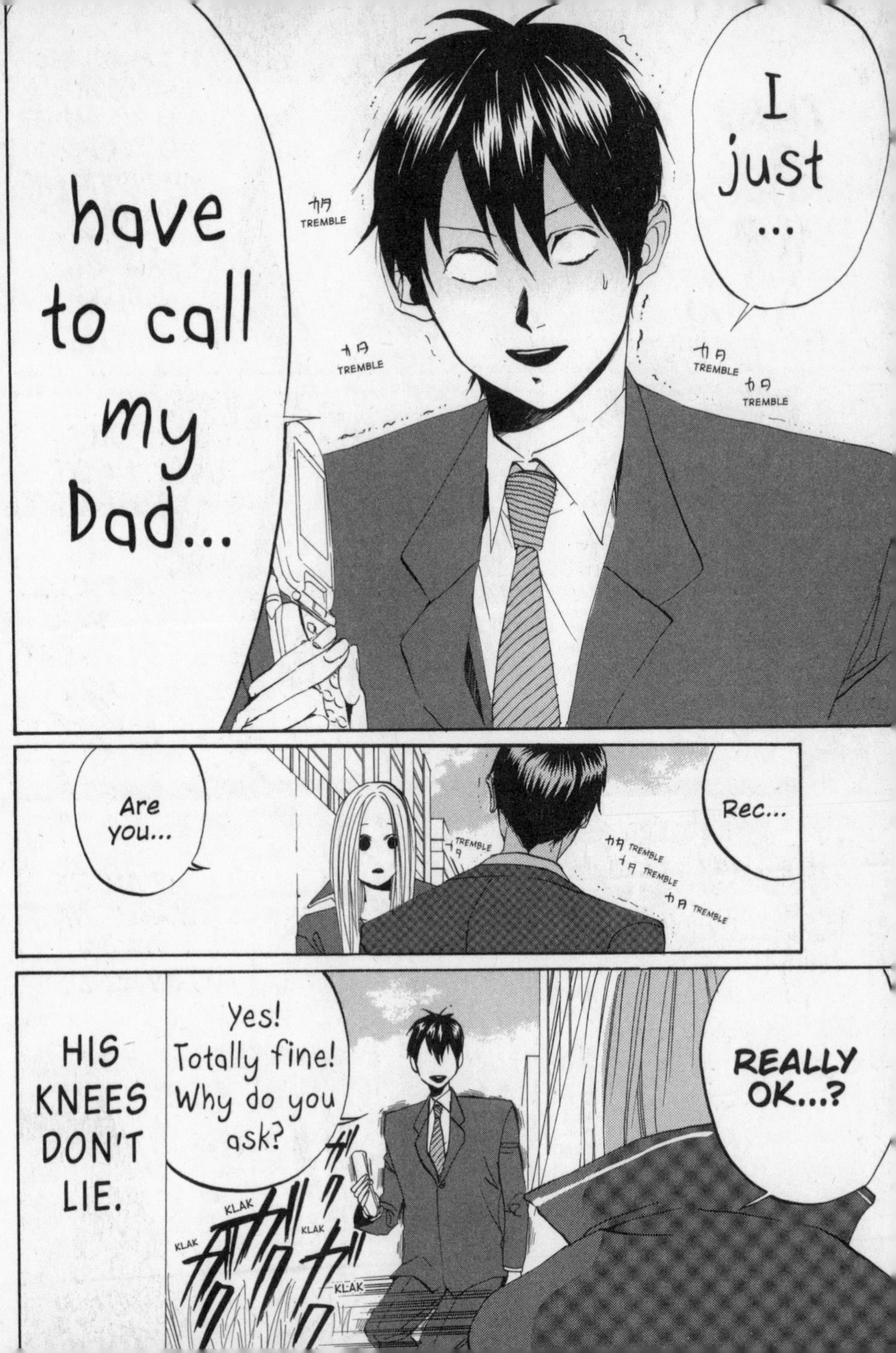
I just ...
have to call my Dad...
カタ TREMBLE
カタ TREMBLE
カタ TREMBLE
カタ TREMBLE
Rec...
カタ TREMBLE
カタ TREMBLE
カタ TREMBLE
カタ TREMBLE
Are you...
REALLY OK...?
Yes! Totally fine! Why do you ask?
KLAK
KLAK
KLAK
KLAK
HIS KNEES DON'T LIE.

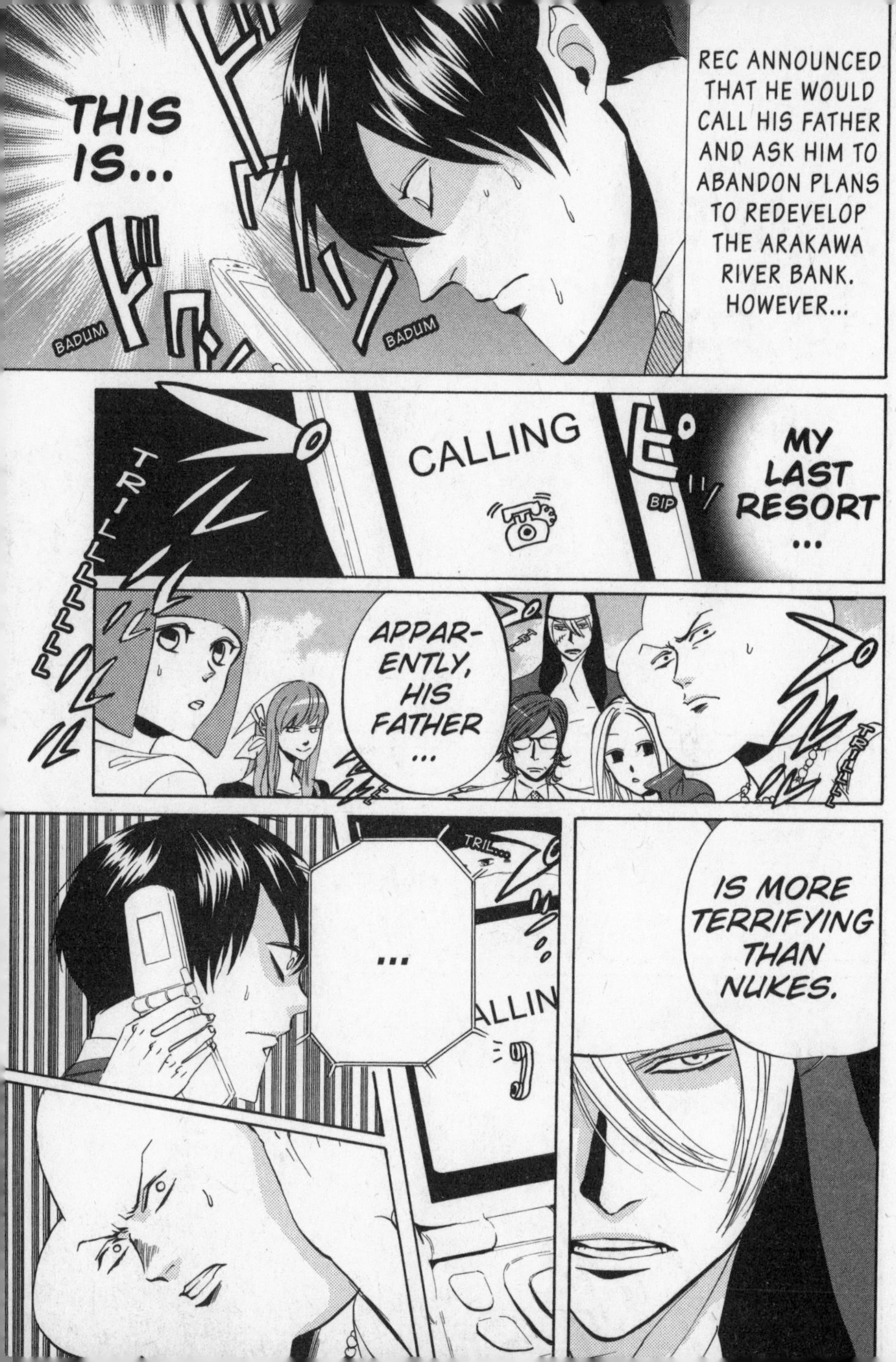
REC ANNOUNCED THAT HE WOULD CALL HIS FATHER AND ASK HIM TO ABANDON PLANS TO REDEVELOP THE ARAKAWA RIVER BANK. HOWEVER...
THIS IS...
BADUM
BADUM
MY LAST RESORT ...
BIP
CALLING
TRILLLLLLL
TRILL
APPAR-ENTLY, HIS FATHER ...
IS MORE TERRIFYING THAN NUKES.
TRIL...
...
ALLIN

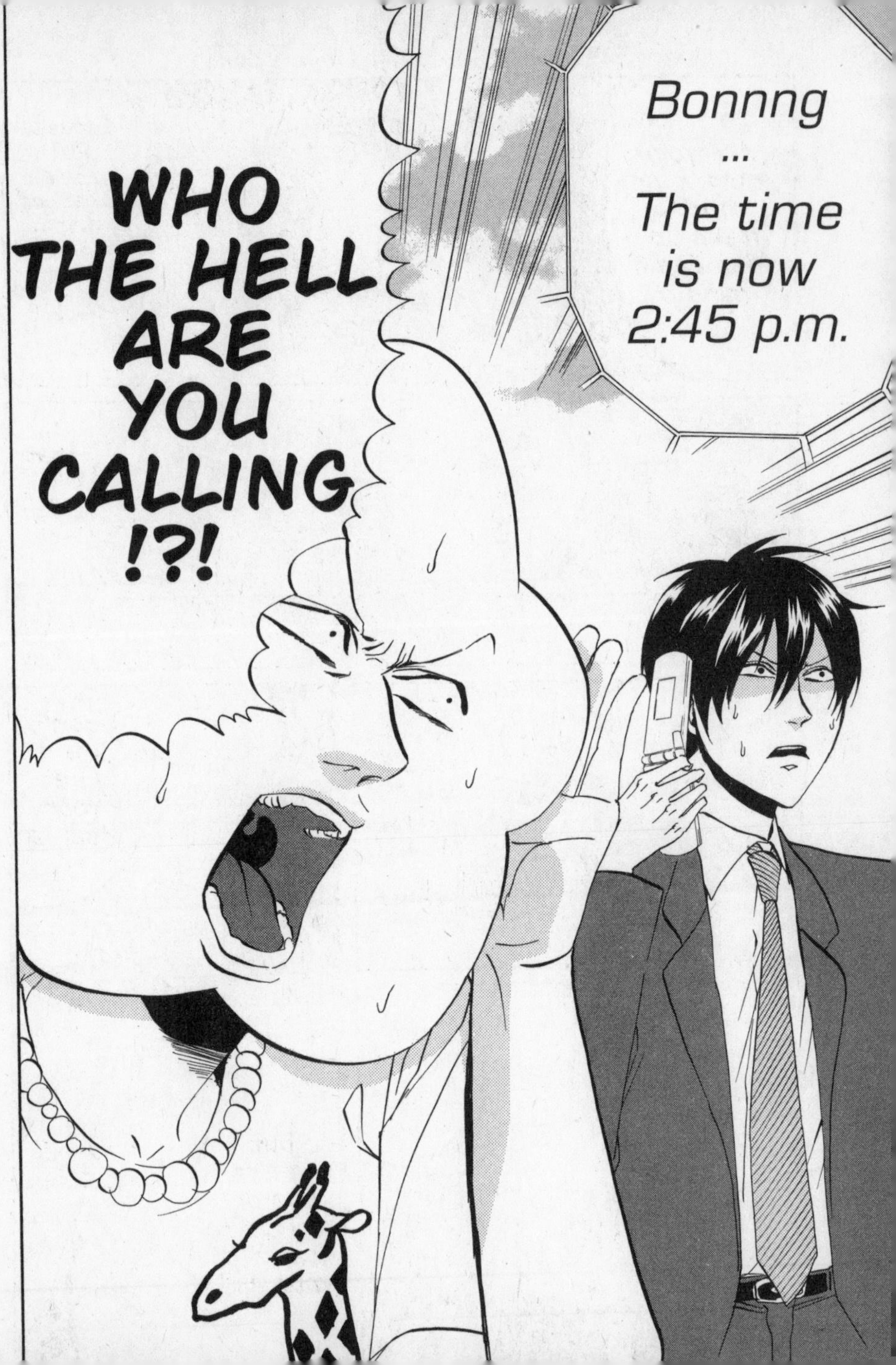
Bonnng
...
The time is now 2:45 p.m.
WHO THE HELL ARE YOU CALLING !?!

Chapter 103: Wish Upon a Star

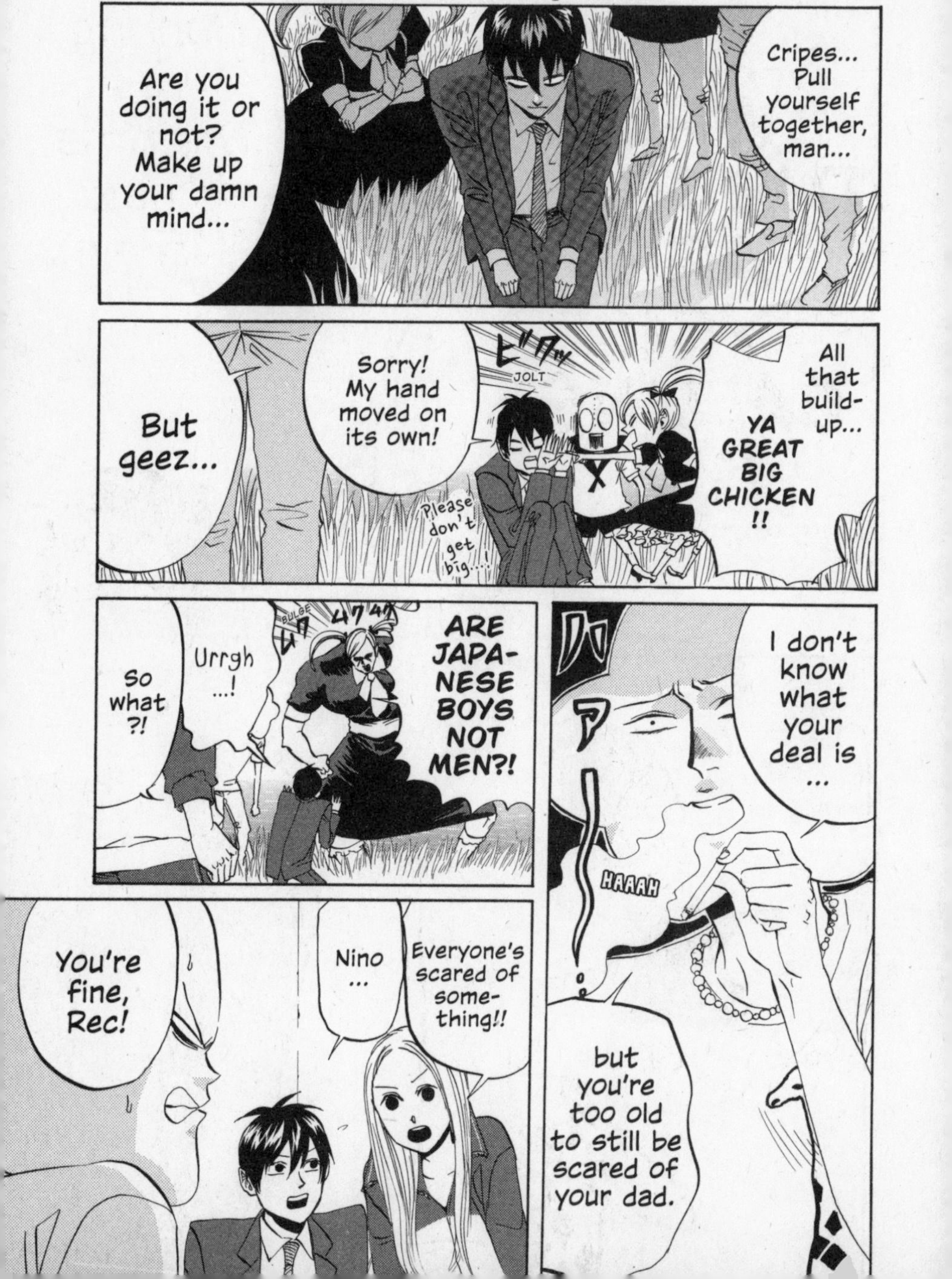
Cripes... Pull yourself together, man...
Are you doing it or not? Make up your damn mind...
All that build-up... YA GREAT BIG CHICKEN!!
JOLT
Sorry! My hand moved on its own!
Please don't get big...!
But geez...
I don't know what your deal is ...
HAAAH
but you're too old to still be scared of your dad.
ARE JAPANESE BOYS NOT MEN?!
BULGE
Urrgh ...!
So what ?!
Everyone's scared of something!!
Nino ...
You're fine, Rec!

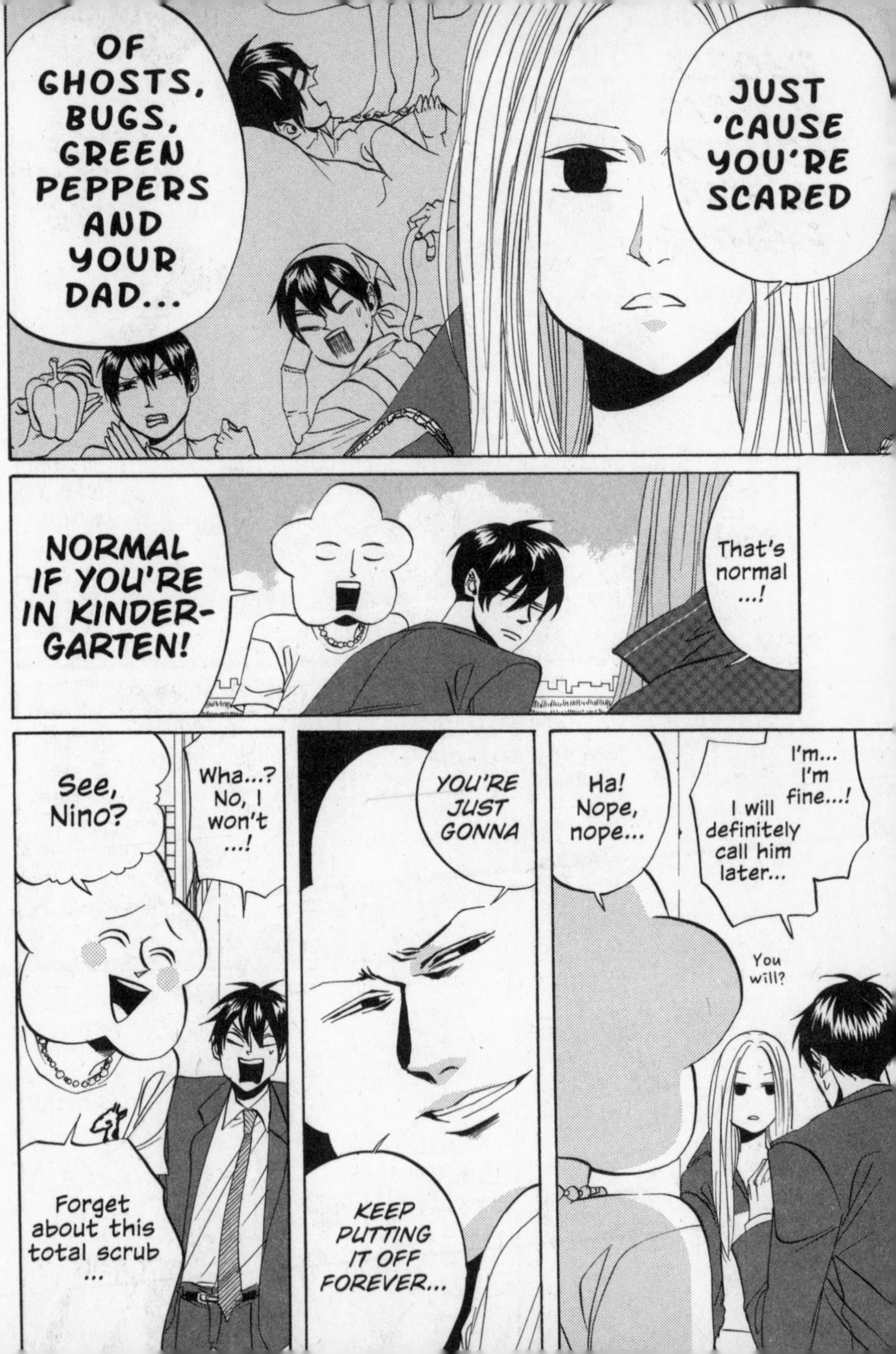
JUST 'CAUSE YOU'RE SCARED
OF GHOSTS, BUGS, GREEN PEPPERS AND YOUR DAD...
That's normal ...!
NORMAL IF YOU'RE IN KINDER-GARTEN!
I'm... I'm fine...!
I will definitely call him later...
You will?
Ha! Nope, nope...
YOU'RE JUST GONNA
KEEP PUTTING IT OFF FOREVER...
Wha...? No, I won't ...!
See, Nino?
Forget about this total scrub ...

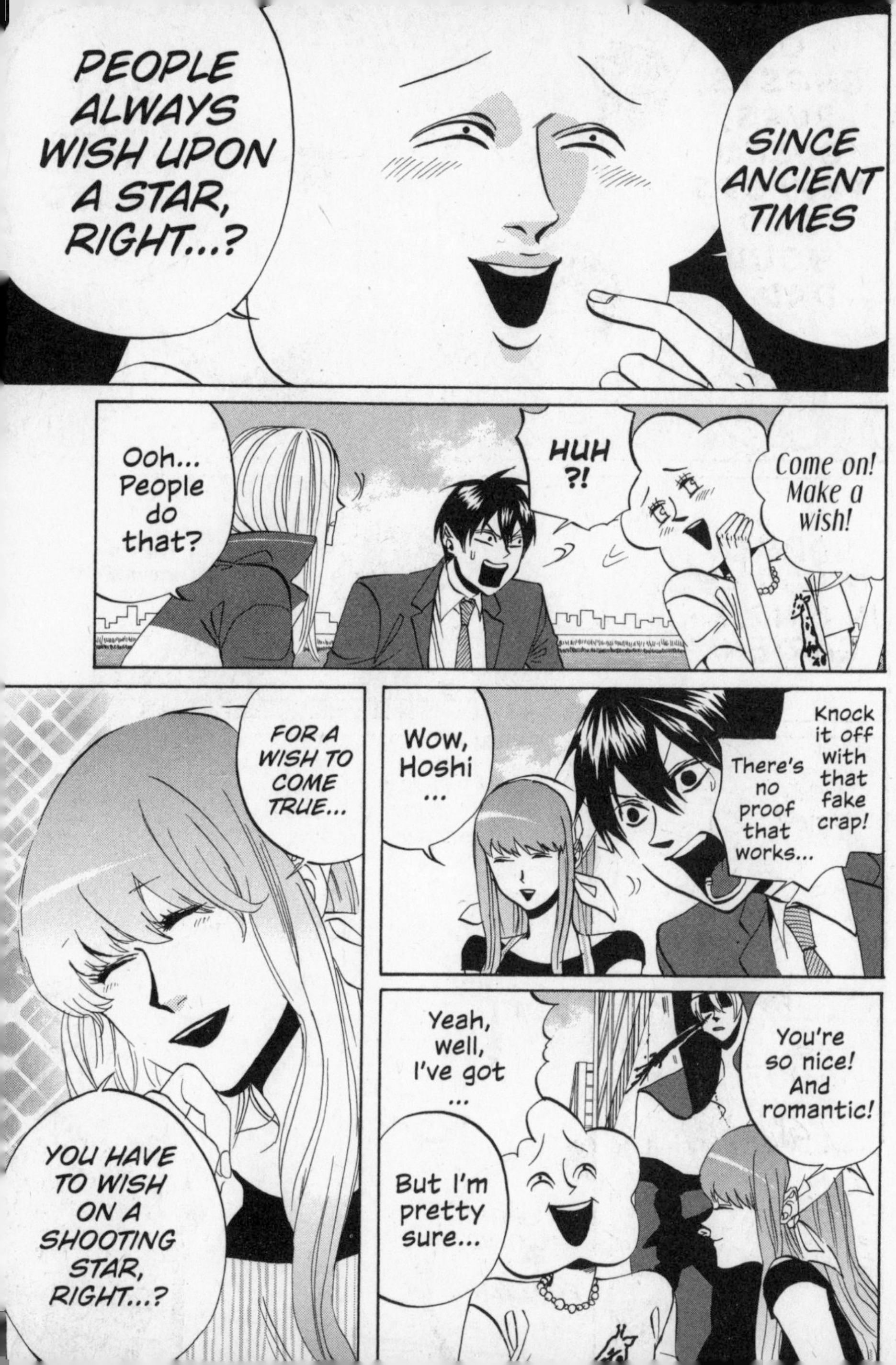
SINCE ANCIENT TIMES
PEOPLE ALWAYS WISH UPON A STAR, RIGHT...?
Come on! Make a wish!
HUH ?!
Ooh... People do that?
Knock it off with that fake crap!
There's no proof that works...
Wow, Hoshi ...
You're so nice! And romantic!
Yeah, well, I've got ...
But I'm pretty sure...
FOR A WISH TO COME TRUE...
YOU HAVE TO WISH ON A SHOOTING STAR, RIGHT...?

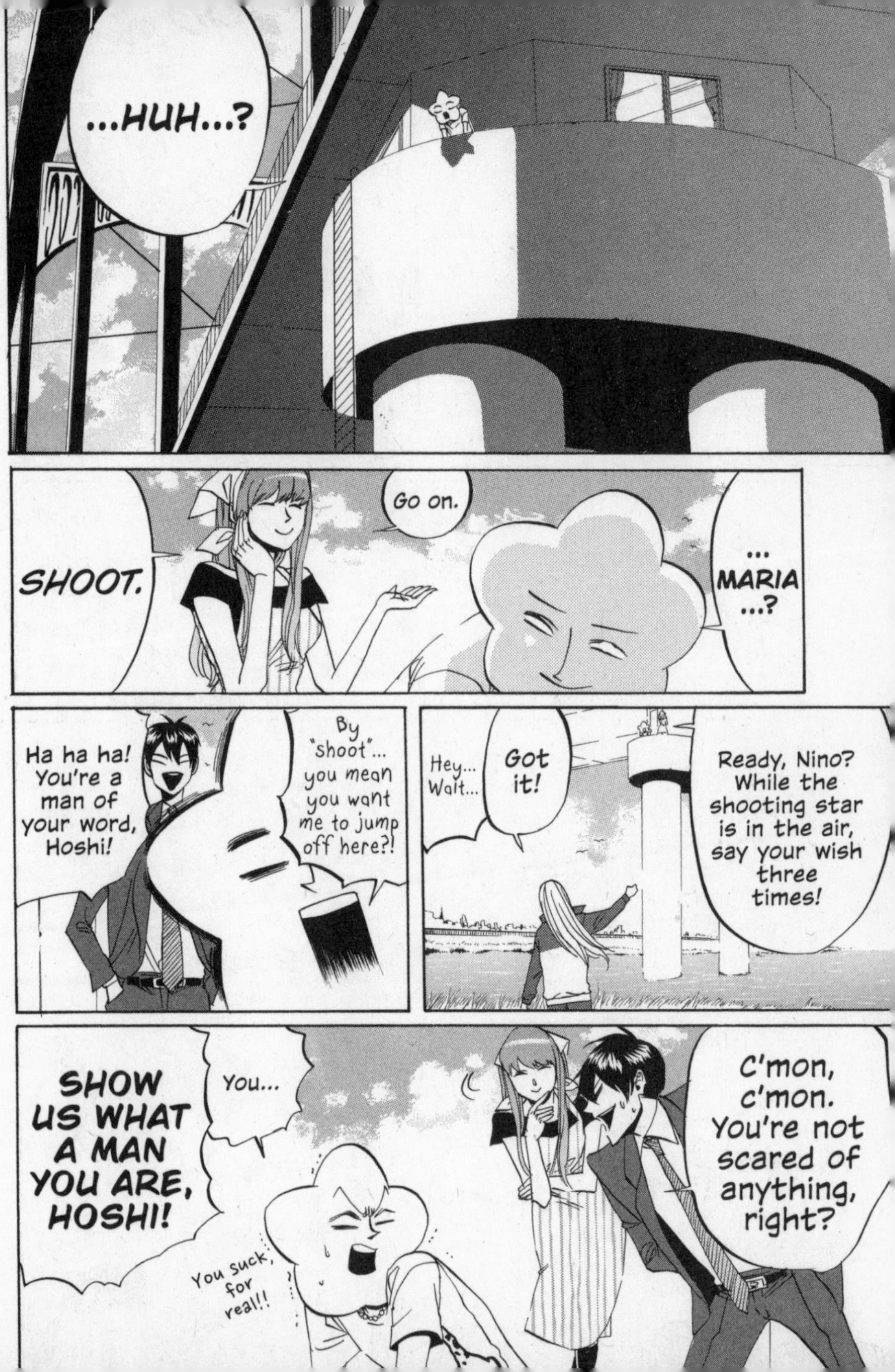
...HUH...?
... MARIA ...?
Go on.
SHOOT.
Ready, Nino? While the shooting star is in the air, say your wish three times!
Got it!
Hey... Wait...
By "shoot"... you mean you want me to jump off here?!
Ha ha ha! You're a man of your word, Hoshi!
C'mon, c'mon. You're not scared of anything, right?
You...
SHOW US WHAT A MAN YOU ARE, HOSHI!
You suck, for real!!

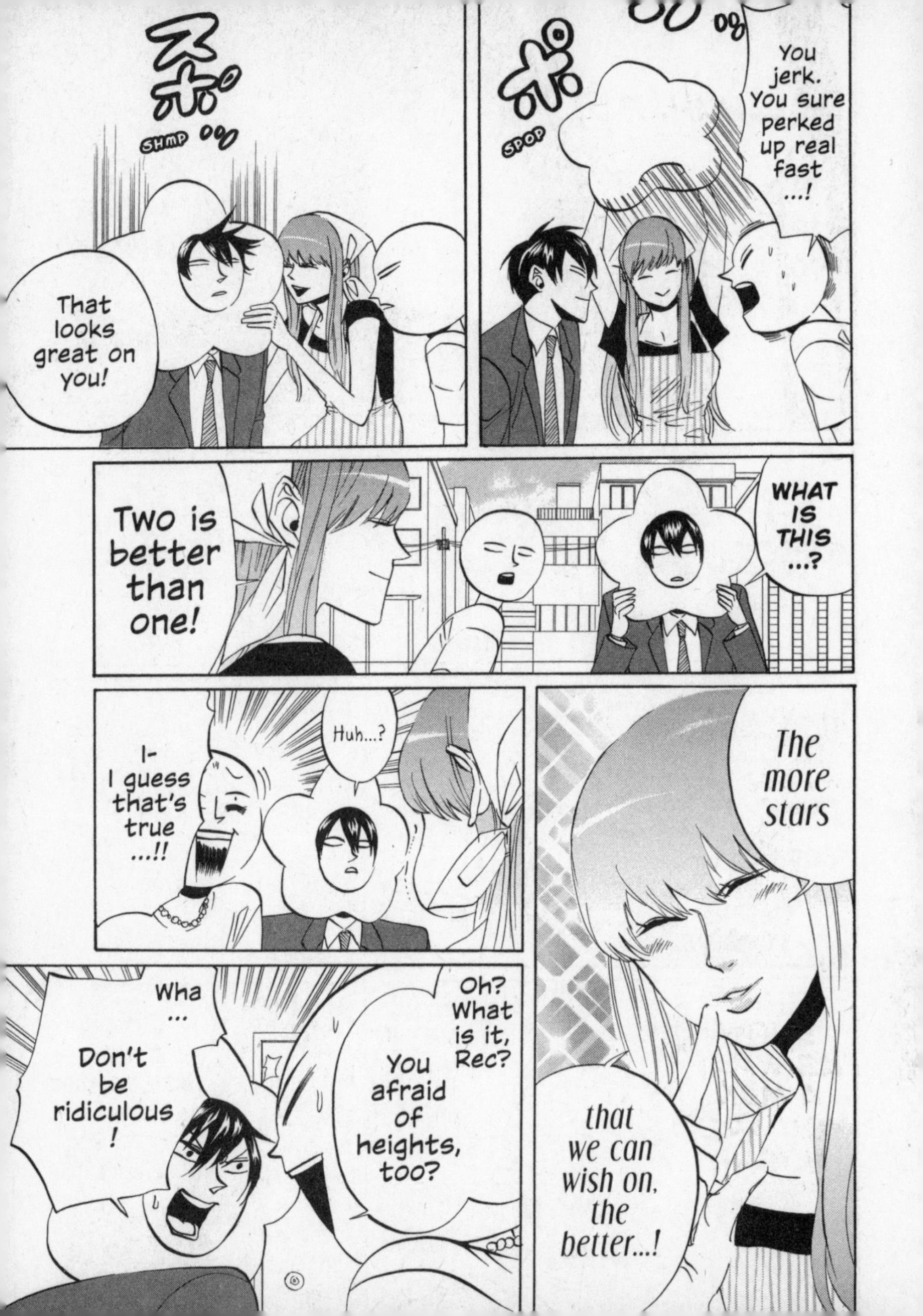
ポ
SPOP
You jerk. You sure perked up real fast ...!
ズボ
SHMP
That looks great on you!
WHAT IS THIS ...?
Two is better than one!
The more stars
that we can wish on, the better...!
Huh...?
I- I guess that's true ...!!
Oh? What is it, Rec?
You afraid of heights, too?
Wha ...
Don't be ridiculous !

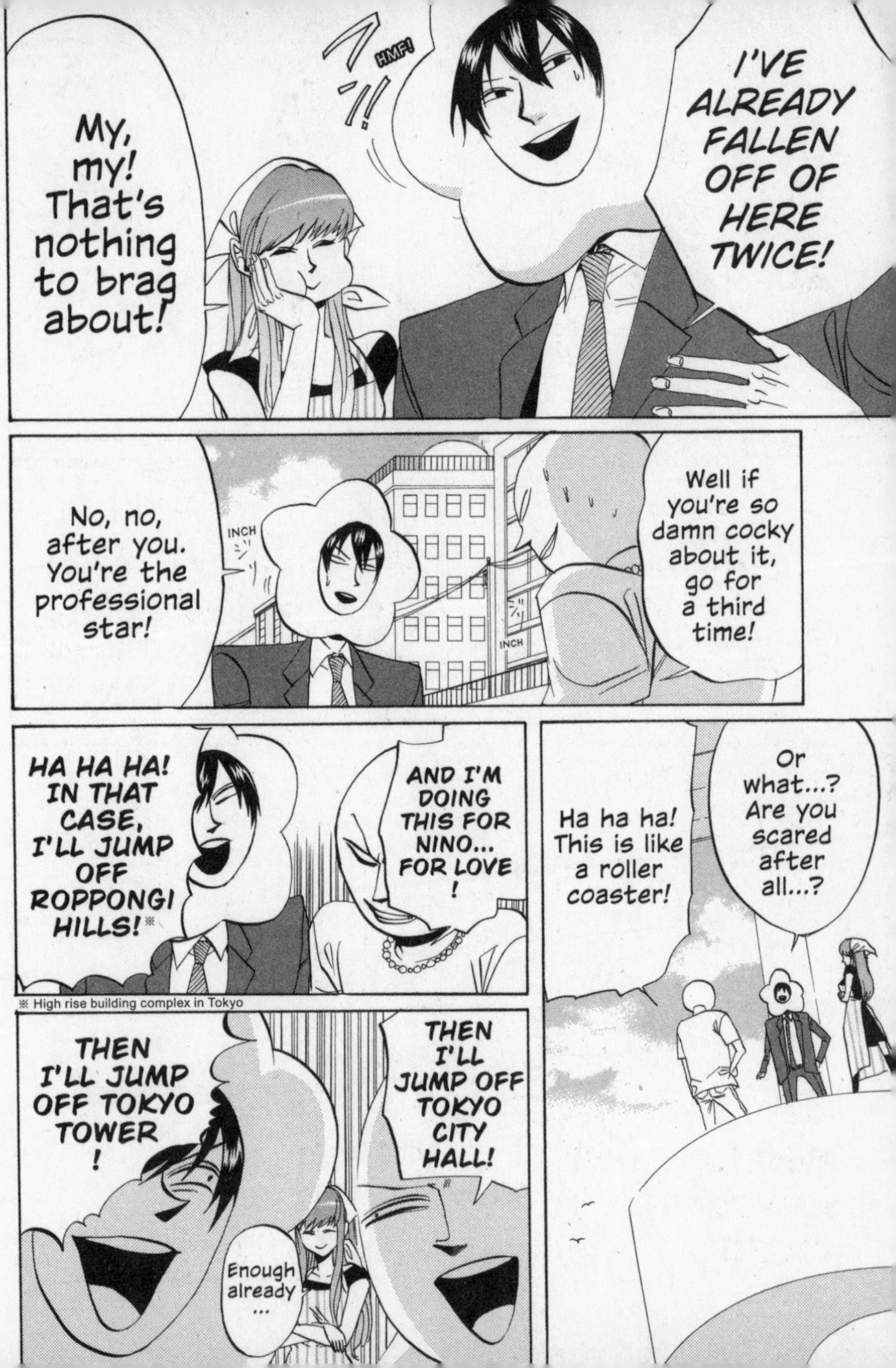
I'VE ALREADY FALLEN OFF OF HERE TWICE!
HMF!
My, my! That's nothing to brag about!
Well if you're so damn cocky about it, go for a third time!
INCH
INCH
No, no, after you. You're the professional star!
Or what...? Are you scared after all...?
Ha ha ha! This is like a roller coaster!
AND I'M DOING THIS FOR NINO... FOR LOVE!
HA HA HA! IN THAT CASE, I'LL JUMP OFF ROPPONGI HILLS!※
THEN I'LL JUMP OFF TOKYO CITY HALL!
THEN I'LL JUMP OFF TOKYO TOWER!
Enough already...

※ High rise building complex in Tokyo

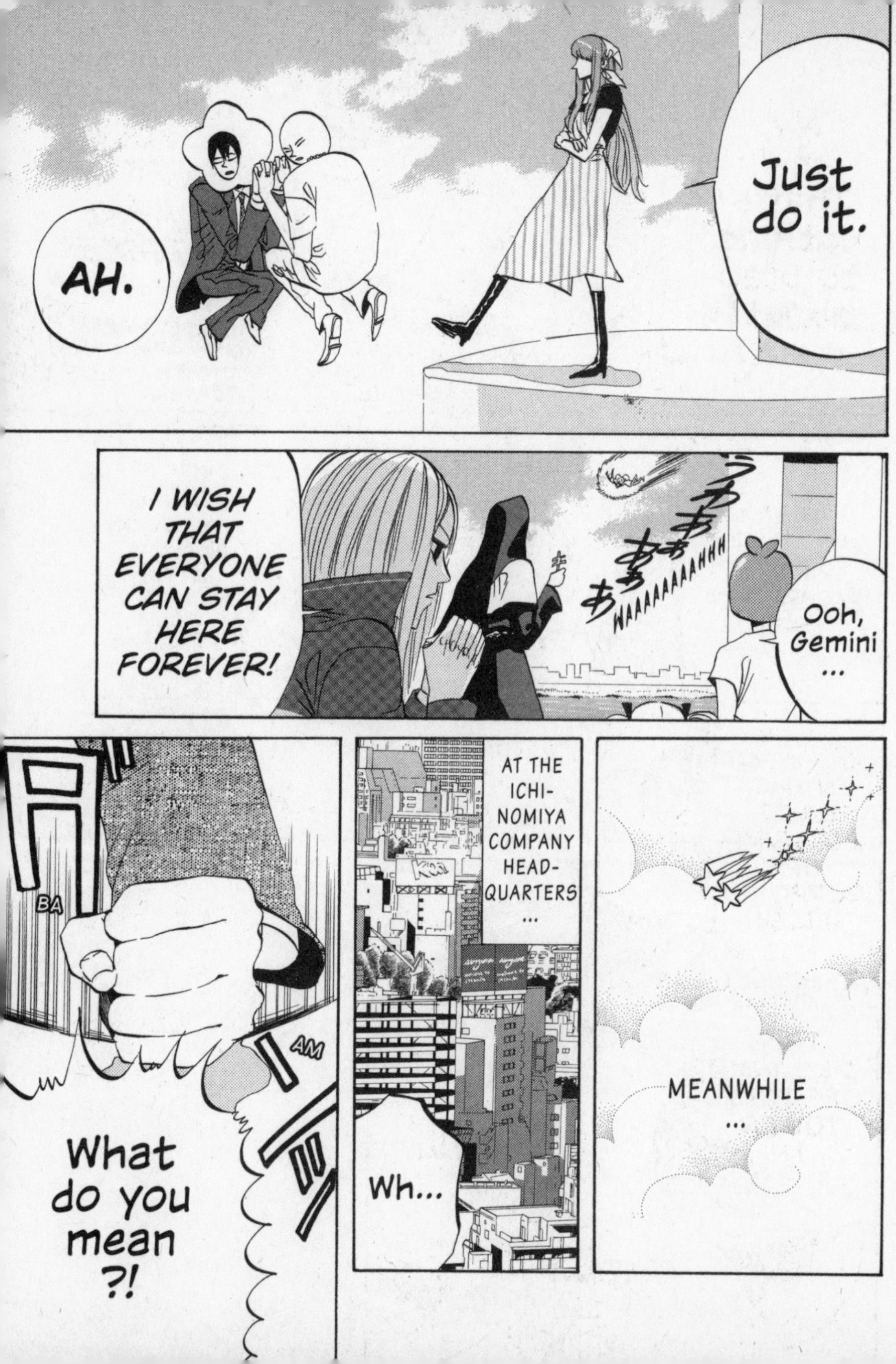
Just do it.
AH.
Ooh, Gemini ...
WAAAAAAAAHHH
I WISH THAT EVERYONE CAN STAY HERE FOREVER!
MEANWHILE ...
AT THE ICHI-NOMIYA COMPANY HEAD-QUARTERS ...
Wh...
BA
AM
What do you mean ?!

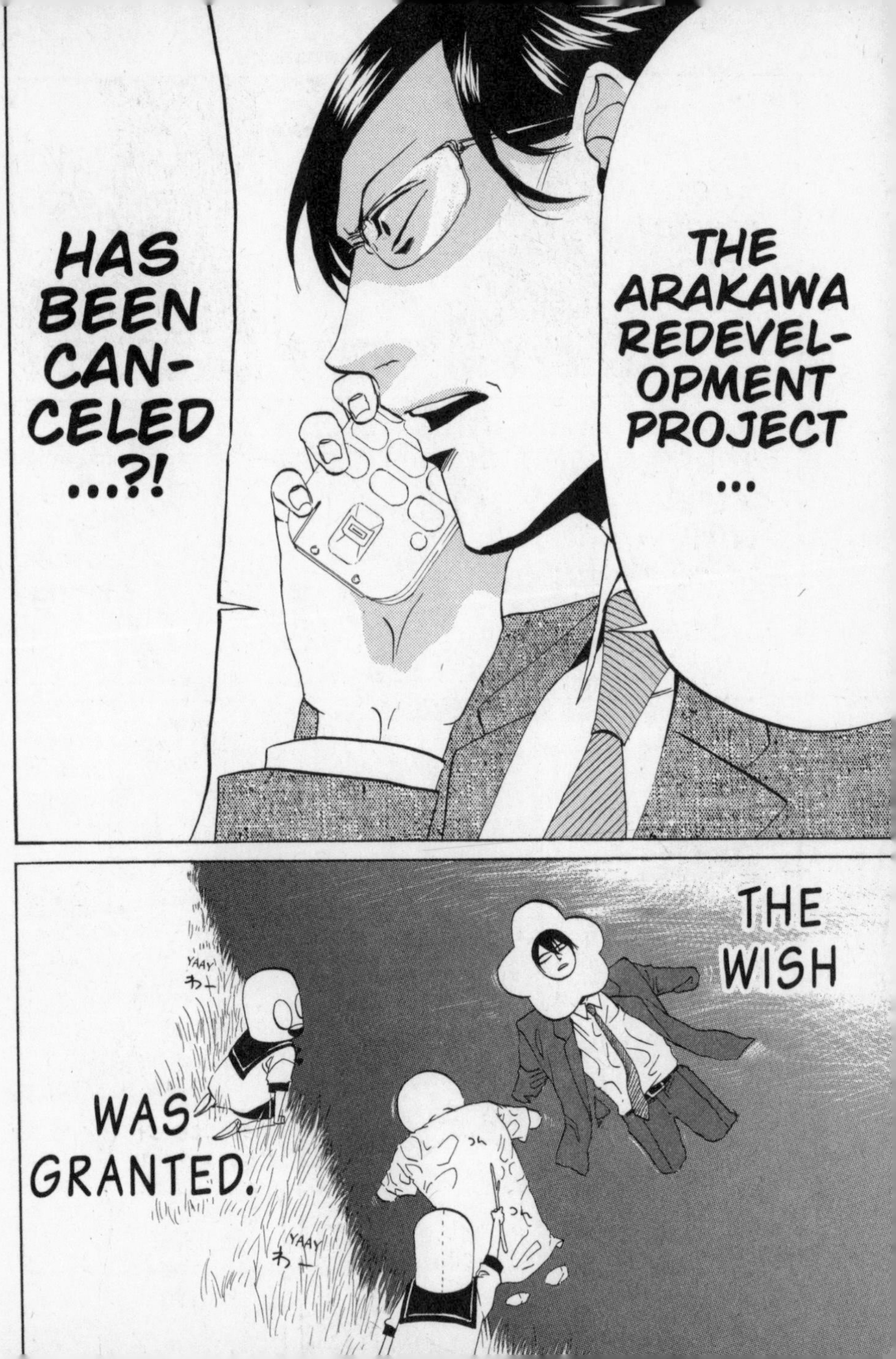
THE ARAKAWA REDEVEL-OPMENT PROJECT ...
HAS BEEN CAN-CELED ...?!
THE WISH
WAS GRANTED.
YAAY わー
YAAY わー

Chapter 104: Disturbance

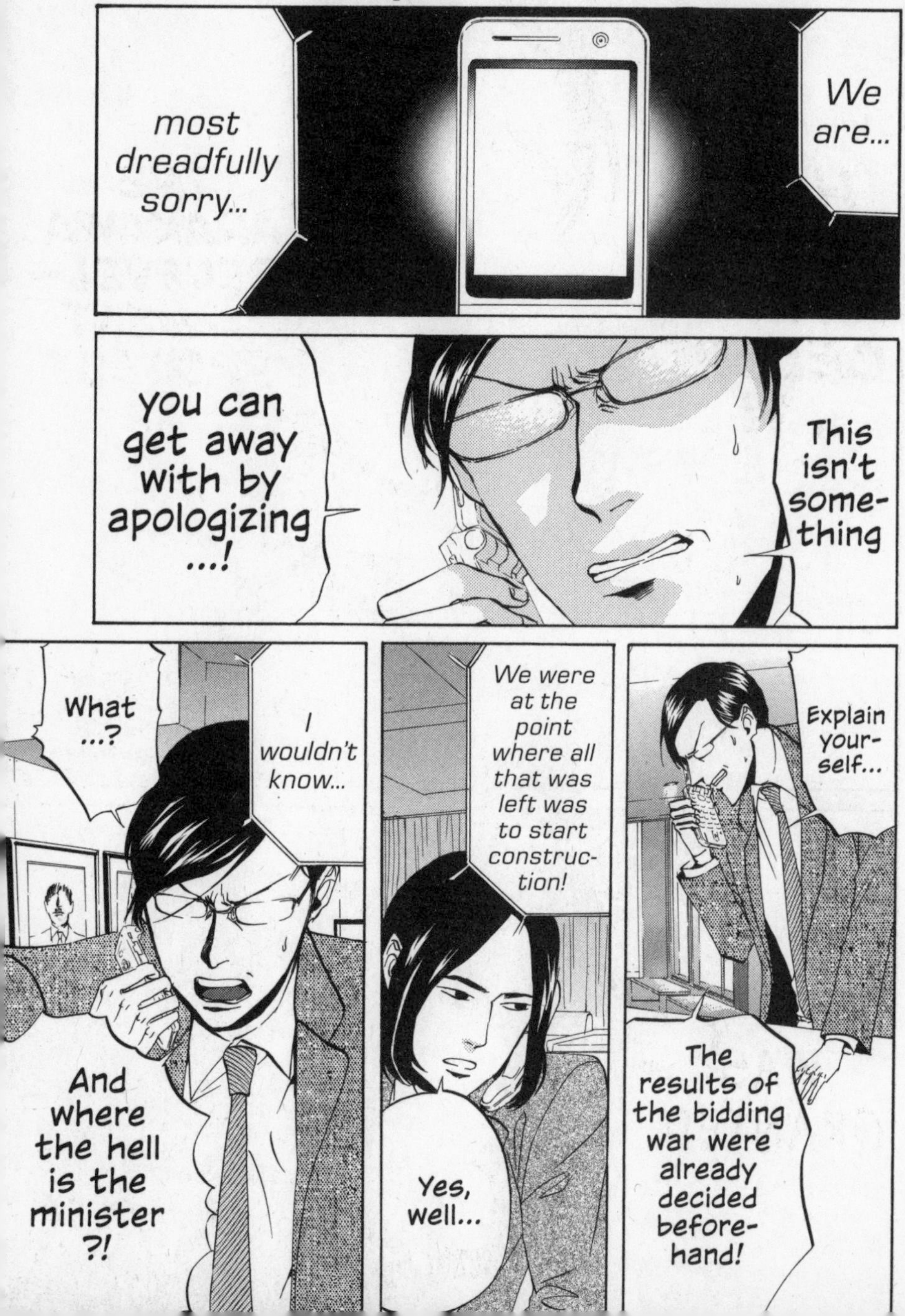
We are...
most dreadfully sorry...
This isn't something
you can get away with by apologizing ...!
Explain yourself...
The results of the bidding war were already decided beforehand!
We were at the point where all that was left was to start construction!
Yes, well...
I wouldn't know...
What ...?
And where the hell is the minister ?!

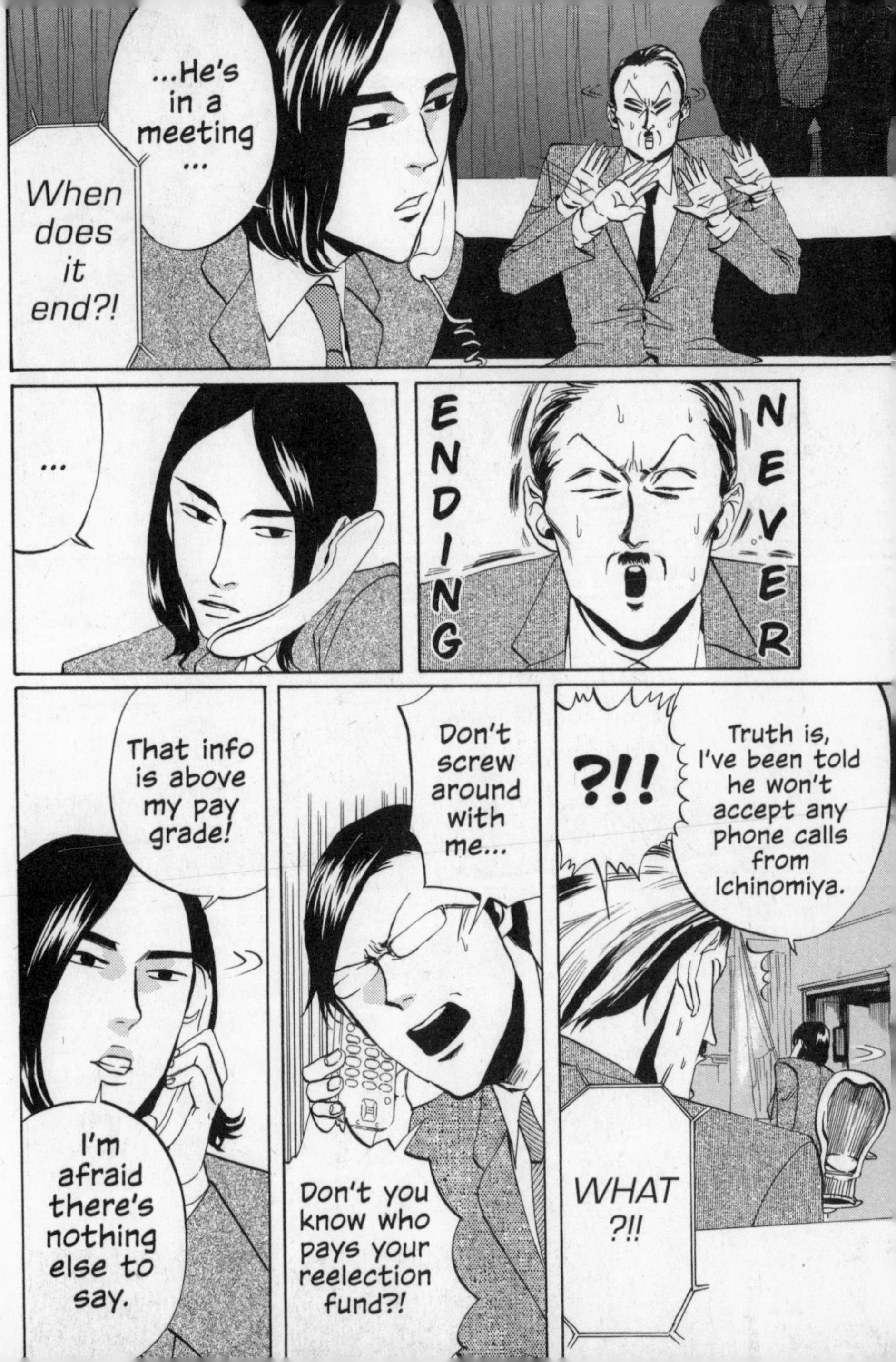
...He's in a meeting ...
When does it end?!
NEVER
ENDING
...
Truth is, I've been told he won't accept any phone calls from Ichinomiya.
?!!
WHAT ?!!
Don't screw around with me...
Don't you know who pays your reelection fund?!
That info is above my pay grade!
I'm afraid there's nothing else to say.

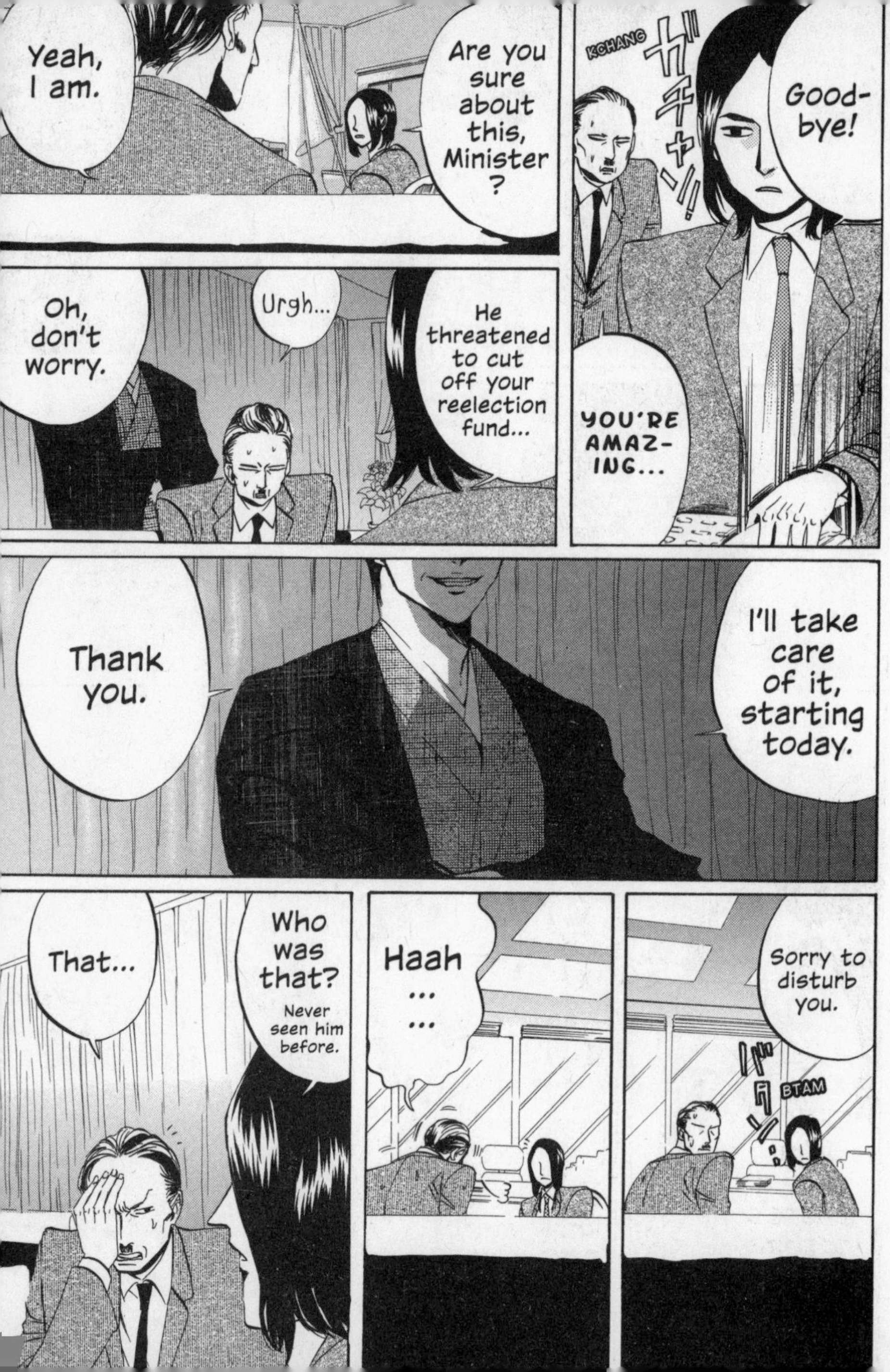
Good-bye!
KCHANG
YOU'RE AMAZ-ING...
Are you sure about this, Minister?
Yeah, I am.
He threatened to cut off your reelection fund...
Urgh...
Oh, don't worry.
I'll take care of it, starting today.
Thank you.
Sorry to disturb you.
BTAM
Haah... ...
Who was that?
Never seen him before.
That...

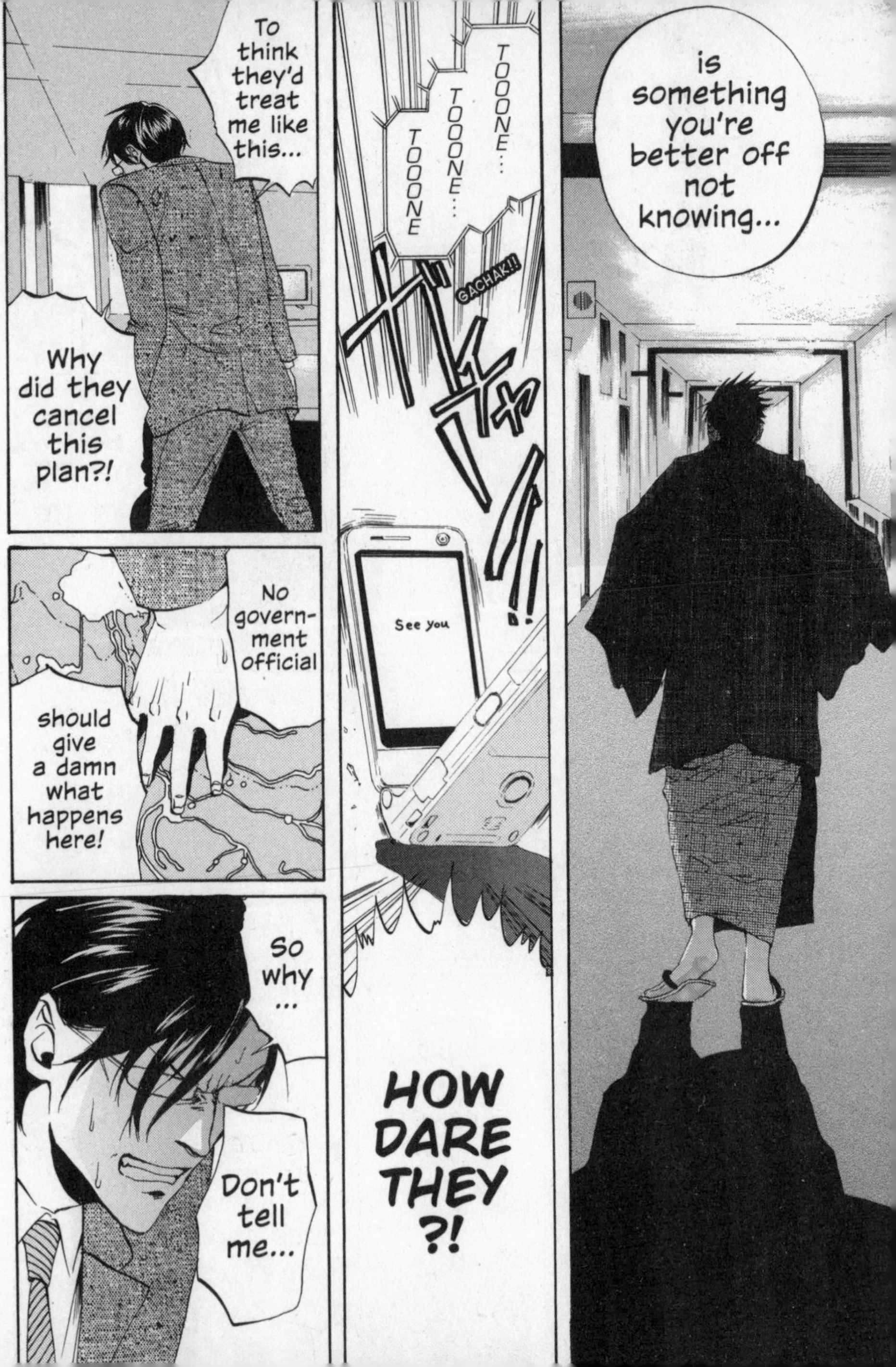
is something you're better off not knowing...
TOOONE...
TOOONE...
TOOONE
GACHAK!!
See you
HOW DARE THEY?!
To think they'd treat me like this...
Why did they cancel this plan?!
No government official
should give a damn what happens here!
So why...
Don't tell me...

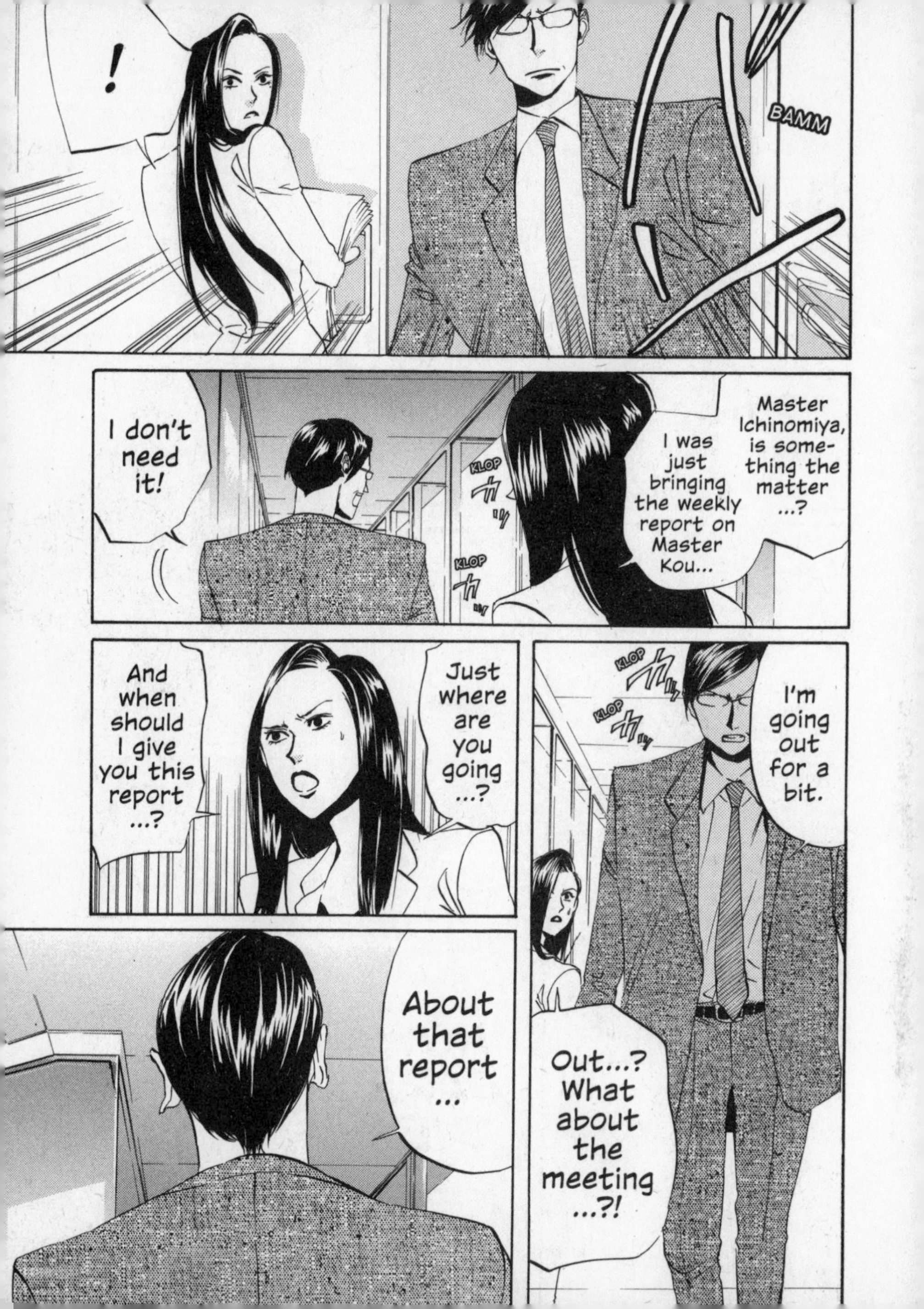
BAMM
!
Master Ichinomiya, is something the matter ...?
I was just bringing the weekly report on Master Kou...
KLOP
KLOP
I don't need it!
KLOP
KLOP
I'm going out for a bit.
Out...? What about the meeting ...?!
Just where are you going ...?
And when should I give you this report ...?
About that report ...

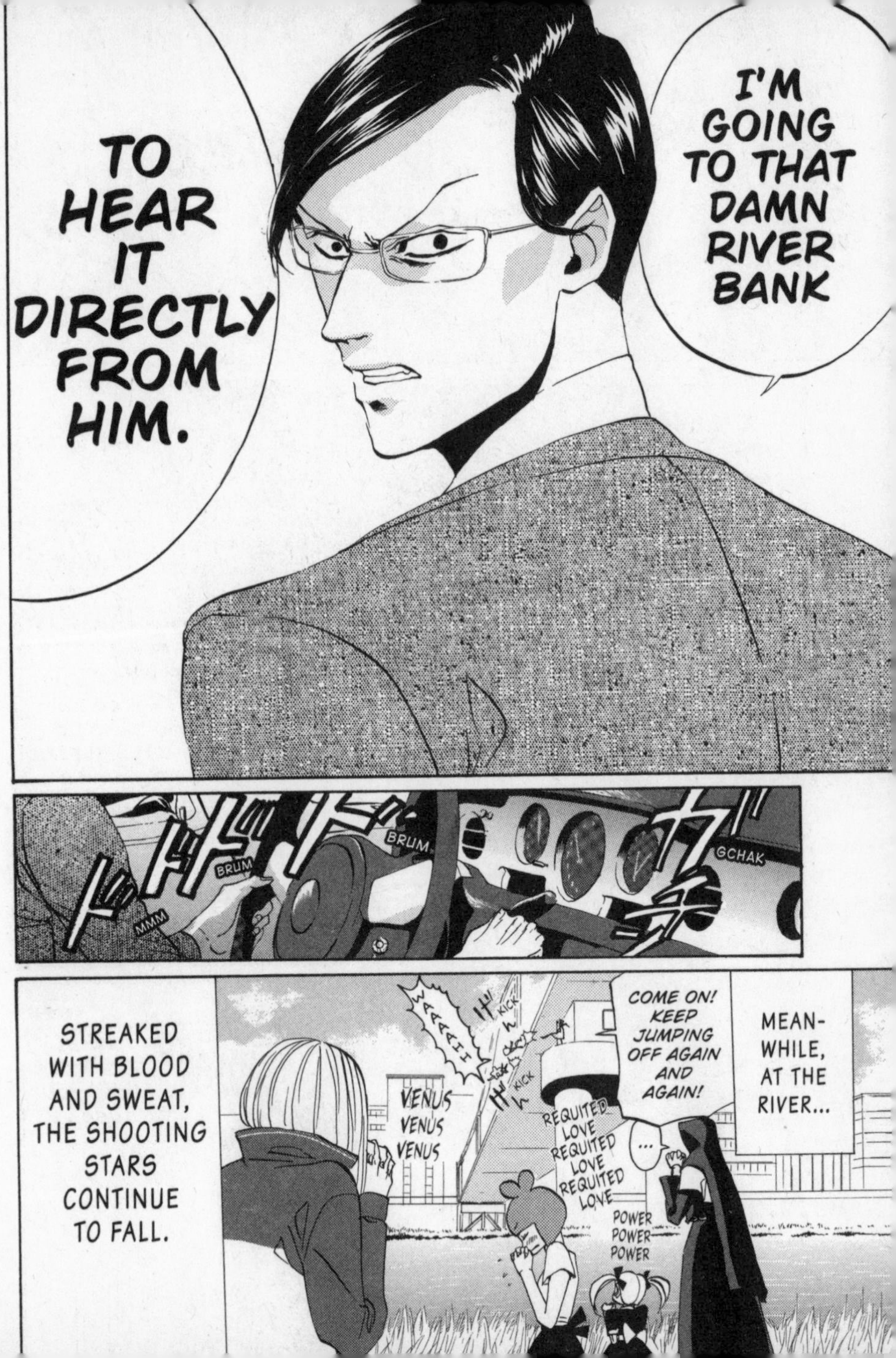
I'M GOING TO THAT DAMN RIVER BANK
TO HEAR IT DIRECTLY FROM HIM.
GCHAK
BRUM
BRUM
MMM
MEAN-WHILE, AT THE RIVER...
COME ON! KEEP JUMPING OFF AGAIN AND AGAIN!
...
KICK
KICK
REQUITED LOVE REQUITED LOVE REQUITED LOVE
POWER POWER POWER
VENUS VENUS VENUS
STREAKED WITH BLOOD AND SWEAT, THE SHOOTING STARS CONTINUE TO FALL.

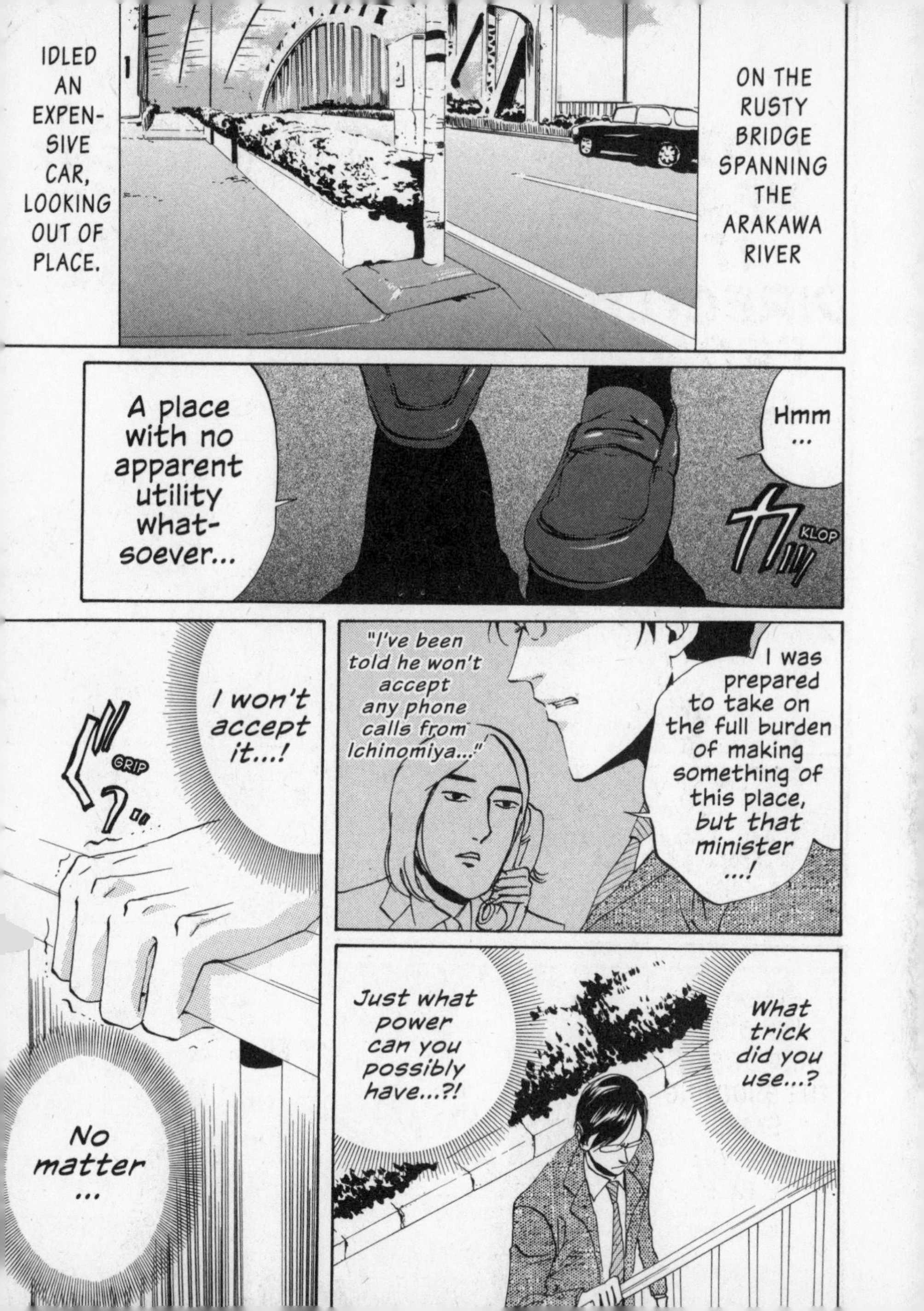
ON THE RUSTY BRIDGE SPANNING THE ARAKAWA RIVER
IDLED AN EXPEN-SIVE CAR, LOOKING OUT OF PLACE.
Hmm ...
KLOP
A place with no apparent utility what-soever...
I was prepared to take on the full burden of making something of this place, but that minister ...!
"I've been told he won't accept any phone calls from Ichinomiya..."
What trick did you use...?
Just what power can you possibly have...?!
I won't accept it...!
GRIP
No matter ...

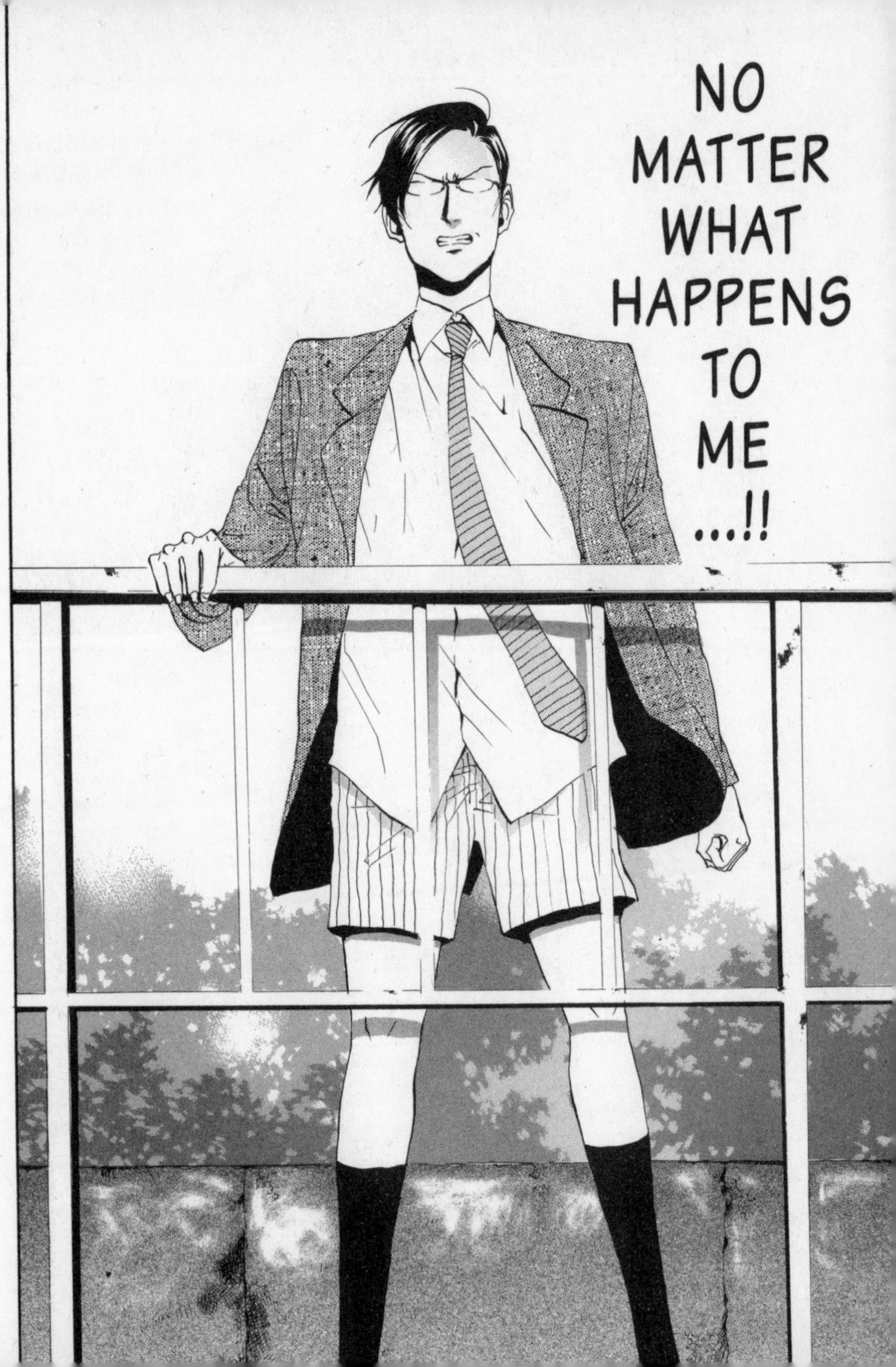
NO MATTER WHAT HAPPENS TO ME ...!!

Chapter 105: Father of the Man Who Owes No One

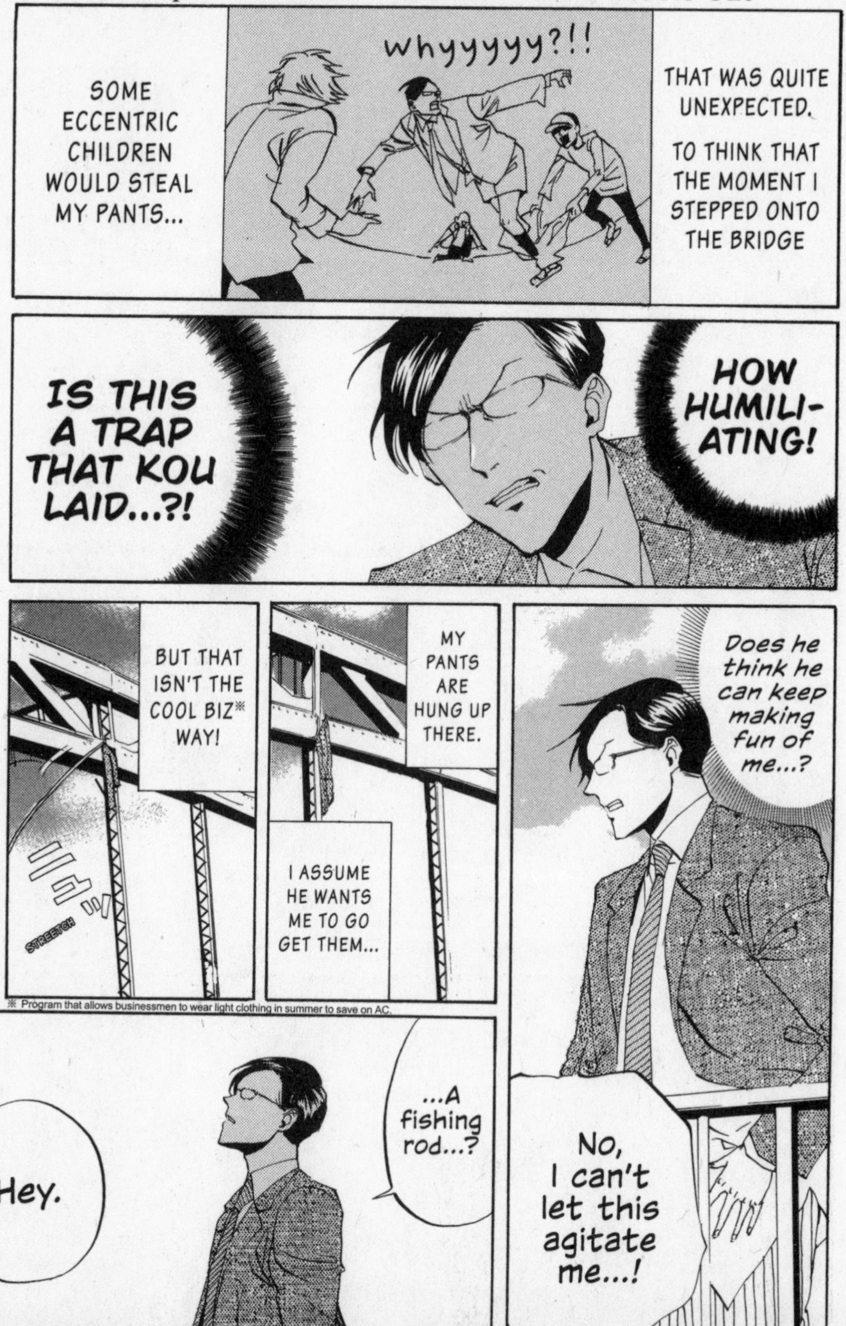
THAT WAS QUITE UNEXPECTED.
TO THINK THAT THE MOMENT I STEPPED ONTO THE BRIDGE
Whyyyyy?!!
SOME ECCENTRIC CHILDREN WOULD STEAL MY PANTS...
HOW HUMILI-ATING!
IS THIS A TRAP THAT KOU LAID...?!
Does he think he can keep making fun of me...?
No, I can't let this agitate me...!
MY PANTS ARE HUNG UP THERE.
I ASSUME HE WANTS ME TO GO GET THEM...
BUT THAT ISN'T THE COOL BIZ※ WAY!
STREETCH
...A fishing rod...?
Hey.

※ Program that allows businessmen to wear light clothing in summer to save on AC.

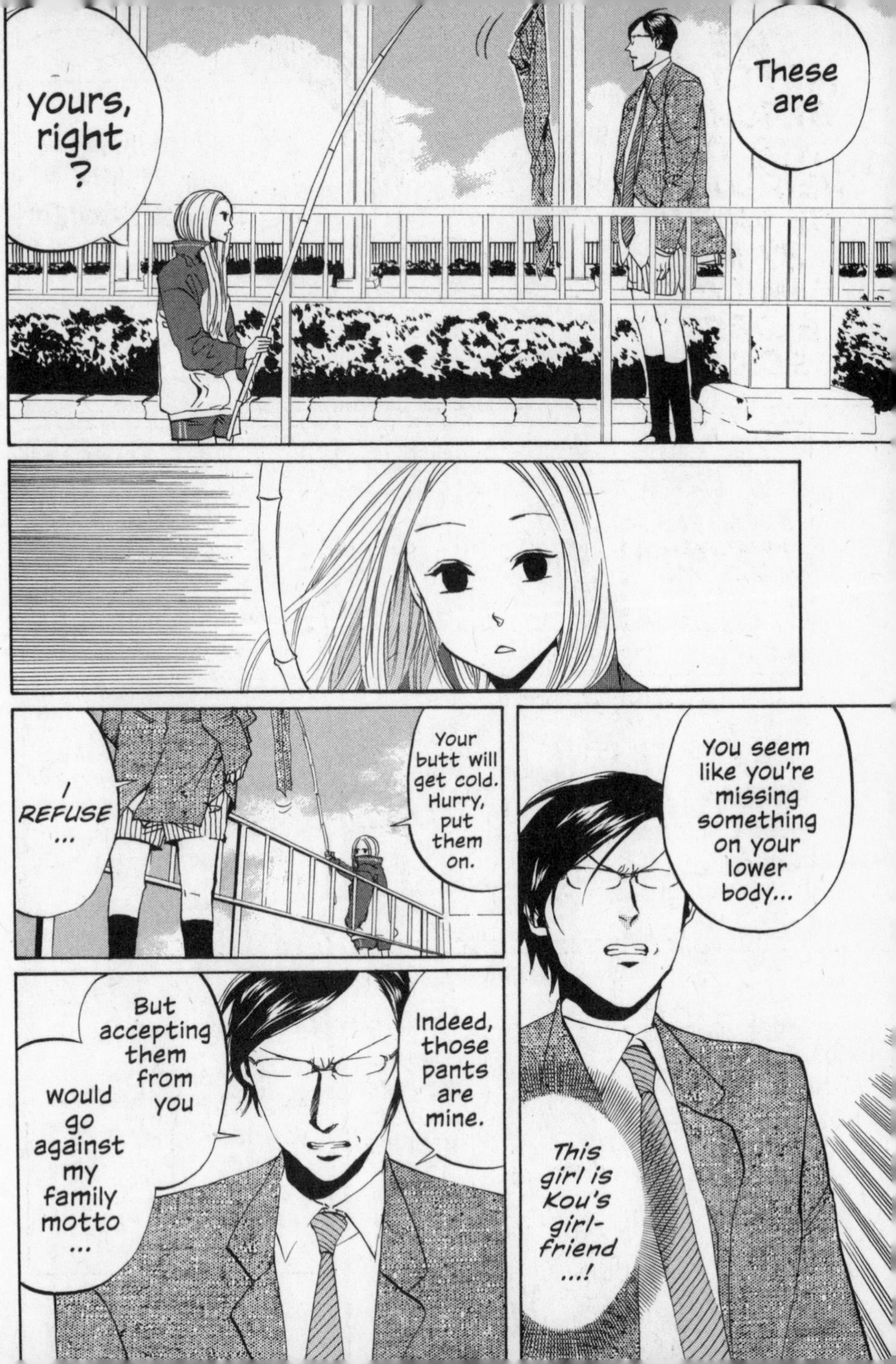
These are
yours, right?
You seem like you're missing something on your lower body...
This girl is Kou's girlfriend...!
Your butt will get cold. Hurry, put them on.
I REFUSE...
Indeed, those pants are mine.
But accepting them from you would go against my family motto...

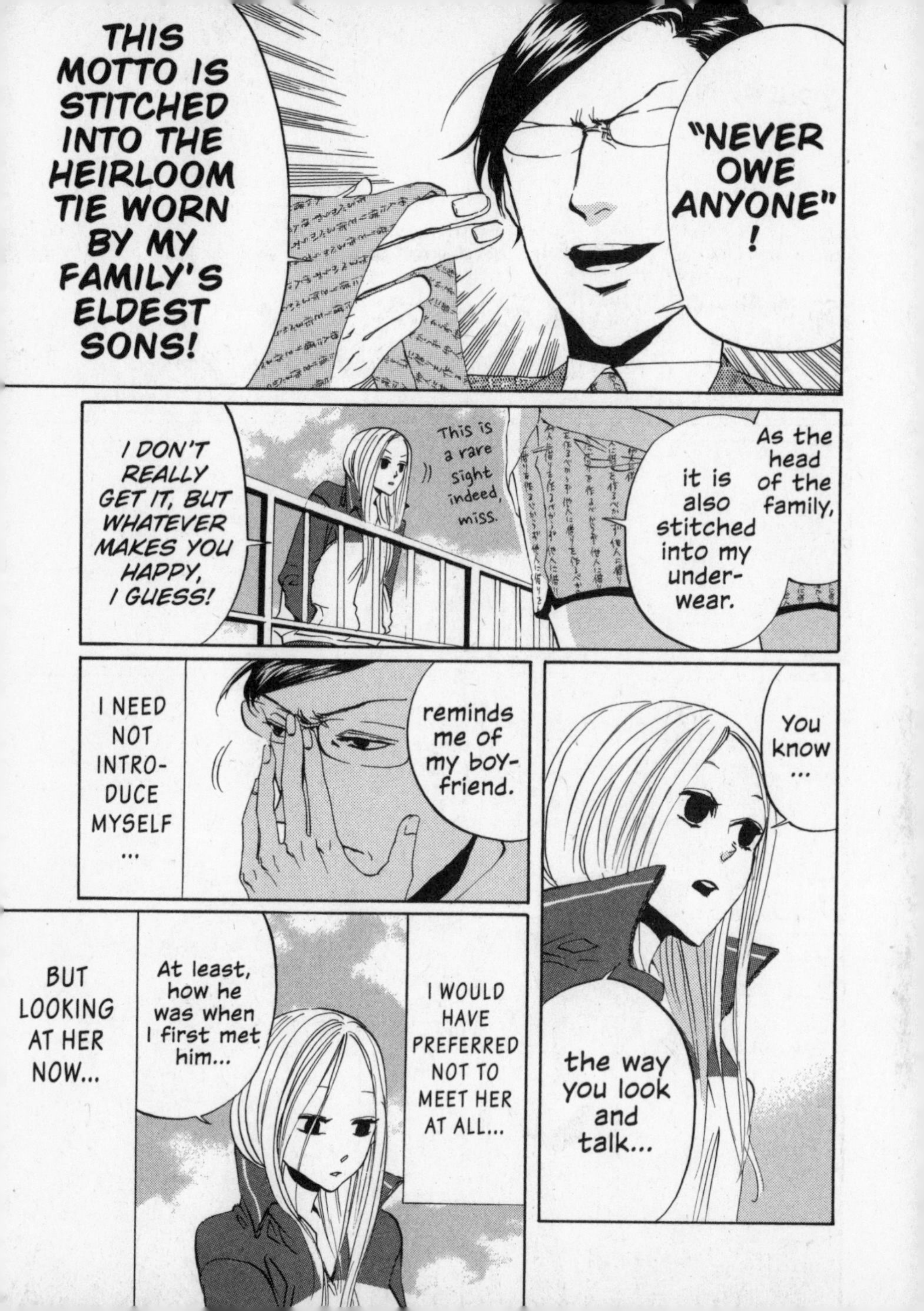
"NEVER OWE ANYONE"!
THIS MOTTO IS STITCHED INTO THE HEIRLOOM TIE WORN BY MY FAMILY'S ELDEST SONS!
As the head of the family,
it is also stitched into my under-wear.
This is a rare sight indeed, miss.
I DON'T REALLY GET IT, BUT WHATEVER MAKES YOU HAPPY, I GUESS!
You know ...
the way you look and talk...
reminds me of my boy-friend.
I NEED NOT INTRO-DUCE MYSELF ...
I WOULD HAVE PREFERRED NOT TO MEET HER AT ALL...
At least, how he was when I first met him...
BUT LOOKING AT HER NOW...

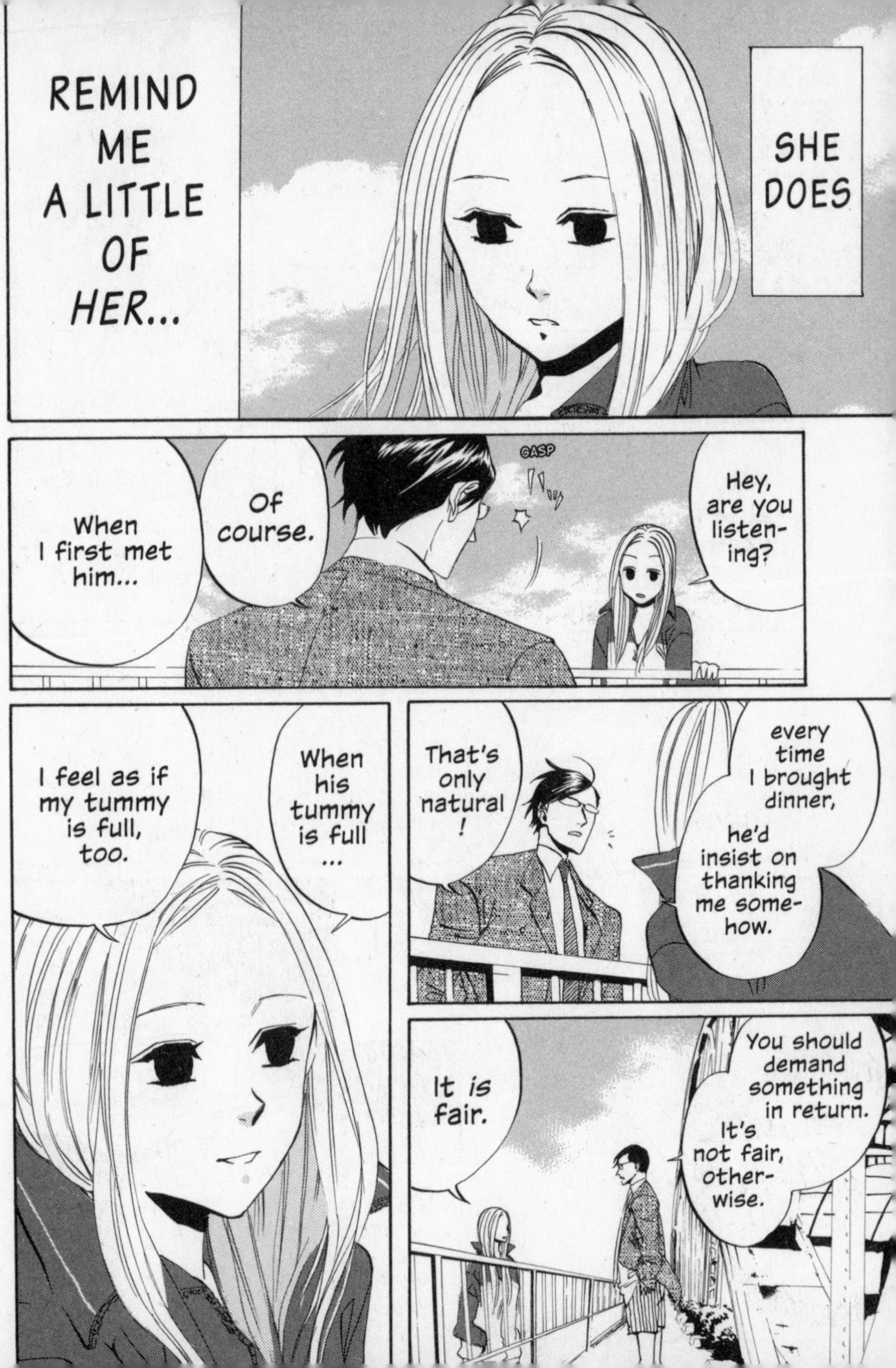
SHE DOES
REMIND ME A LITTLE OF HER...
Hey, are you listen-ing?
GASP
Of course.
When I first met him...
every time I brought dinner,
he'd insist on thanking me some-how.
That's only natural!
You should demand something in return.
It's not fair, other-wise.
It is fair.
When his tummy is full ...
I feel as if my tummy is full, too.

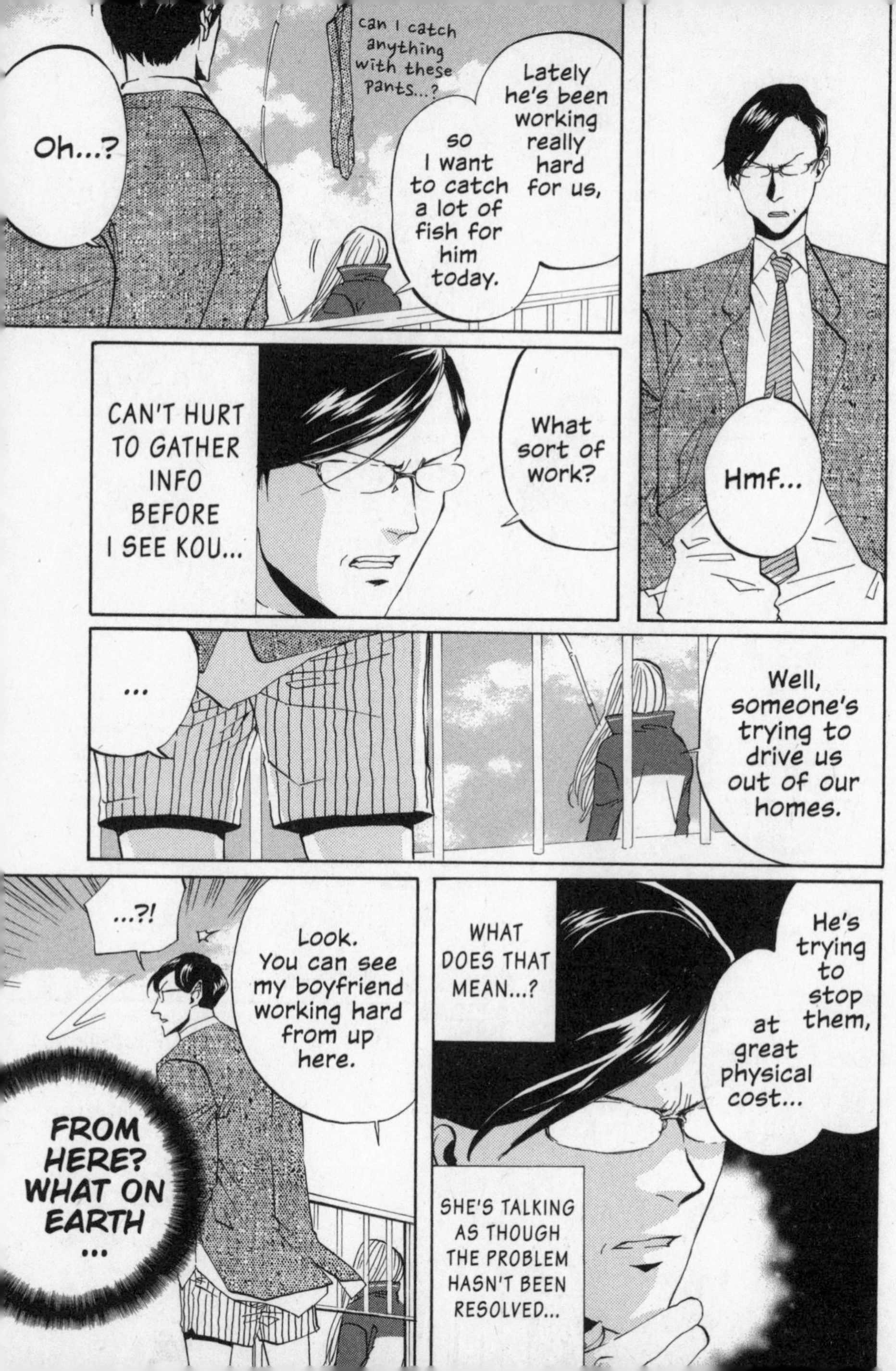
Hmf...
can I catch anything with these pants...?
Lately he's been working really hard for us,
so I want to catch a lot of fish for him today.
Oh...?
What sort of work?
CAN'T HURT TO GATHER INFO BEFORE I SEE KOU...
Well, someone's trying to drive us out of our homes.
...
He's trying to stop them,
at great physical cost...
WHAT DOES THAT MEAN...?
SHE'S TALKING AS THOUGH THE PROBLEM HASN'T BEEN RESOLVED...
Look. You can see my boyfriend working hard from up here.
...?!
FROM HERE? WHAT ON EARTH ...

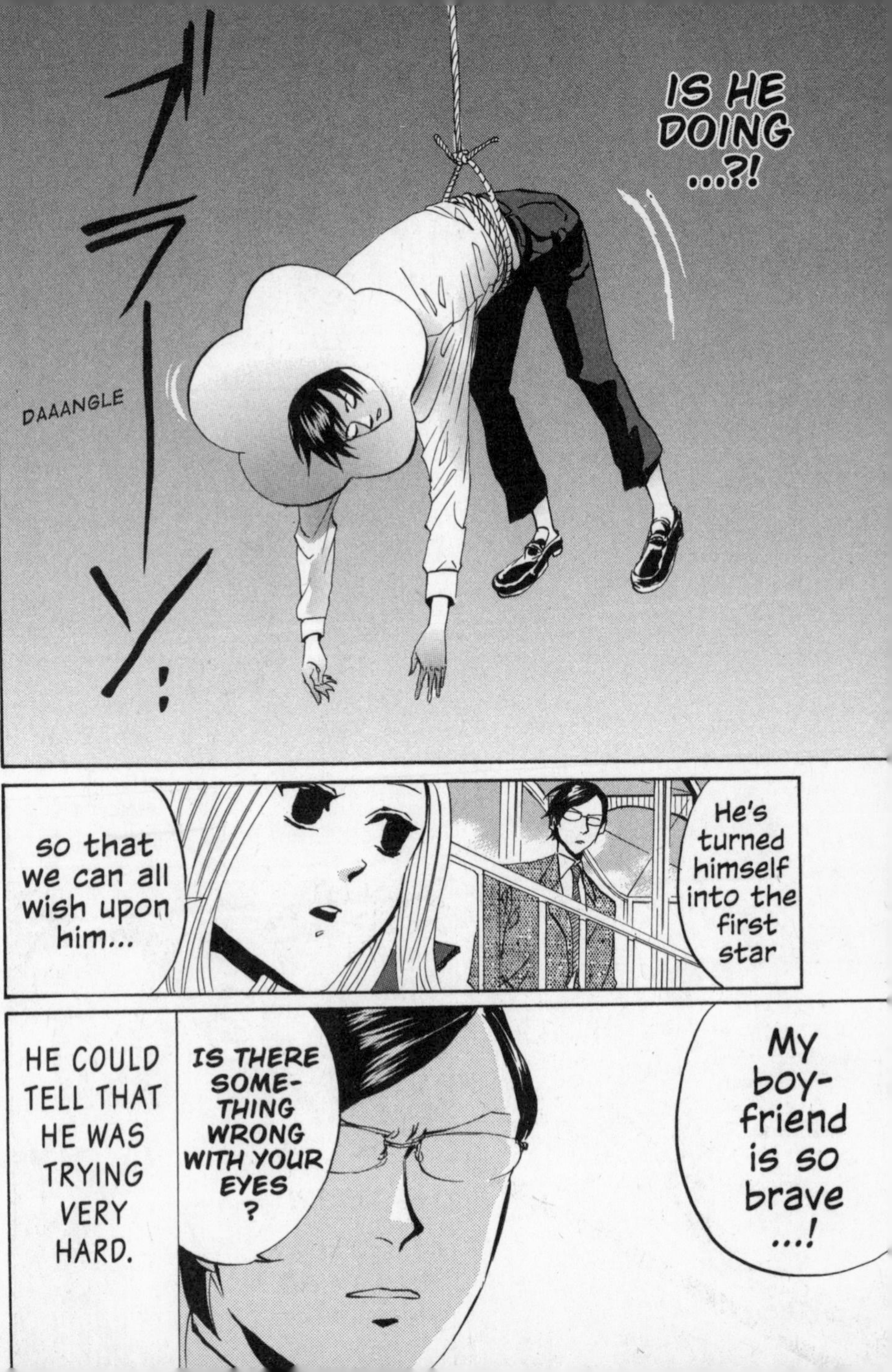
IS HE DOING ...?!
DAAANGLE
He's turned himself into the first star
so that we can all wish upon him...
My boy-friend is so brave ...!
IS THERE SOME-THING WRONG WITH YOUR EYES ?
HE COULD TELL THAT HE WAS TRYING VERY HARD.

☜ Chapter 106: A Father's Feelings

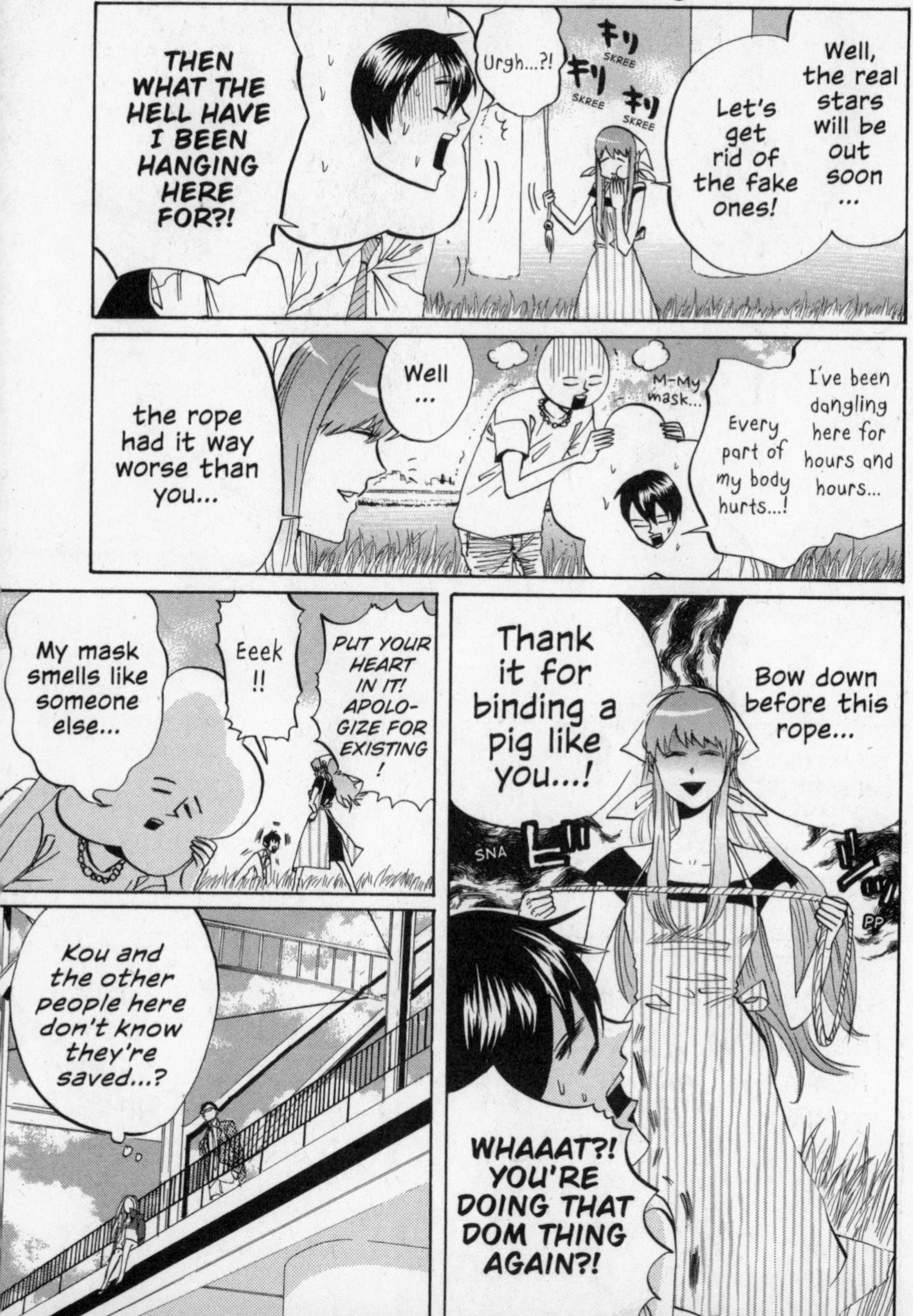
Well, the real stars will be out soon ...
Let's get rid of the fake ones!
キリ
SKREE
キリ
SKREE
キリ
SKREE
Urgh...?!
THEN WHAT THE HELL HAVE I BEEN HANGING HERE FOR?!
I've been dangling here for hours and hours...
Every part of my body hurts...!
M-My mask...
Well ...
the rope had it way worse than you...
Bow down before this rope...
Thank it for binding a pig like you...!
ッ
PP
ビ
SNA
WHAAAT?! YOU'RE DOING THAT DOM THING AGAIN?!
PUT YOUR HEART IN IT! APOLOGIZE FOR EXISTING!
Eeek !!
My mask smells like someone else...
Kou and the other people here don't know they're saved...?

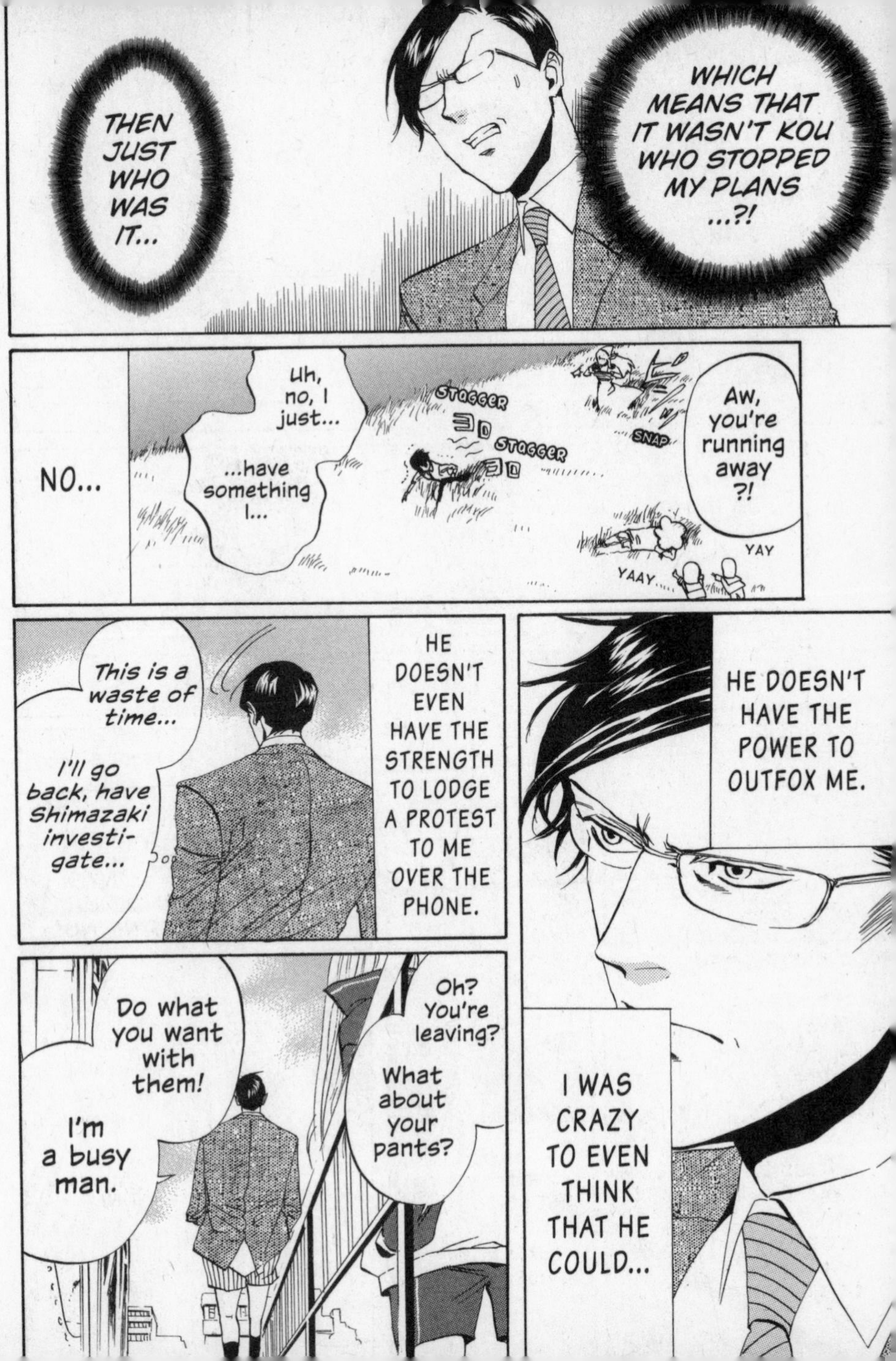
WHICH MEANS THAT IT WASN'T KOU WHO STOPPED MY PLANS ...?!
THEN JUST WHO WAS IT...
Aw, you're running away?!
YAY
YAAY...
SNAP
STAGGER
STAGGER
Uh, no, I just...
...have something I...
NO...
HE DOESN'T HAVE THE POWER TO OUTFOX ME.
I WAS CRAZY TO EVEN THINK THAT HE COULD...
HE DOESN'T EVEN HAVE THE STRENGTH TO LODGE A PROTEST TO ME OVER THE PHONE.
This is a waste of time...
I'll go back, have Shimazaki investi-gate...
Oh? You're leaving?
What about your pants?
Do what you want with them!
I'm a busy man.

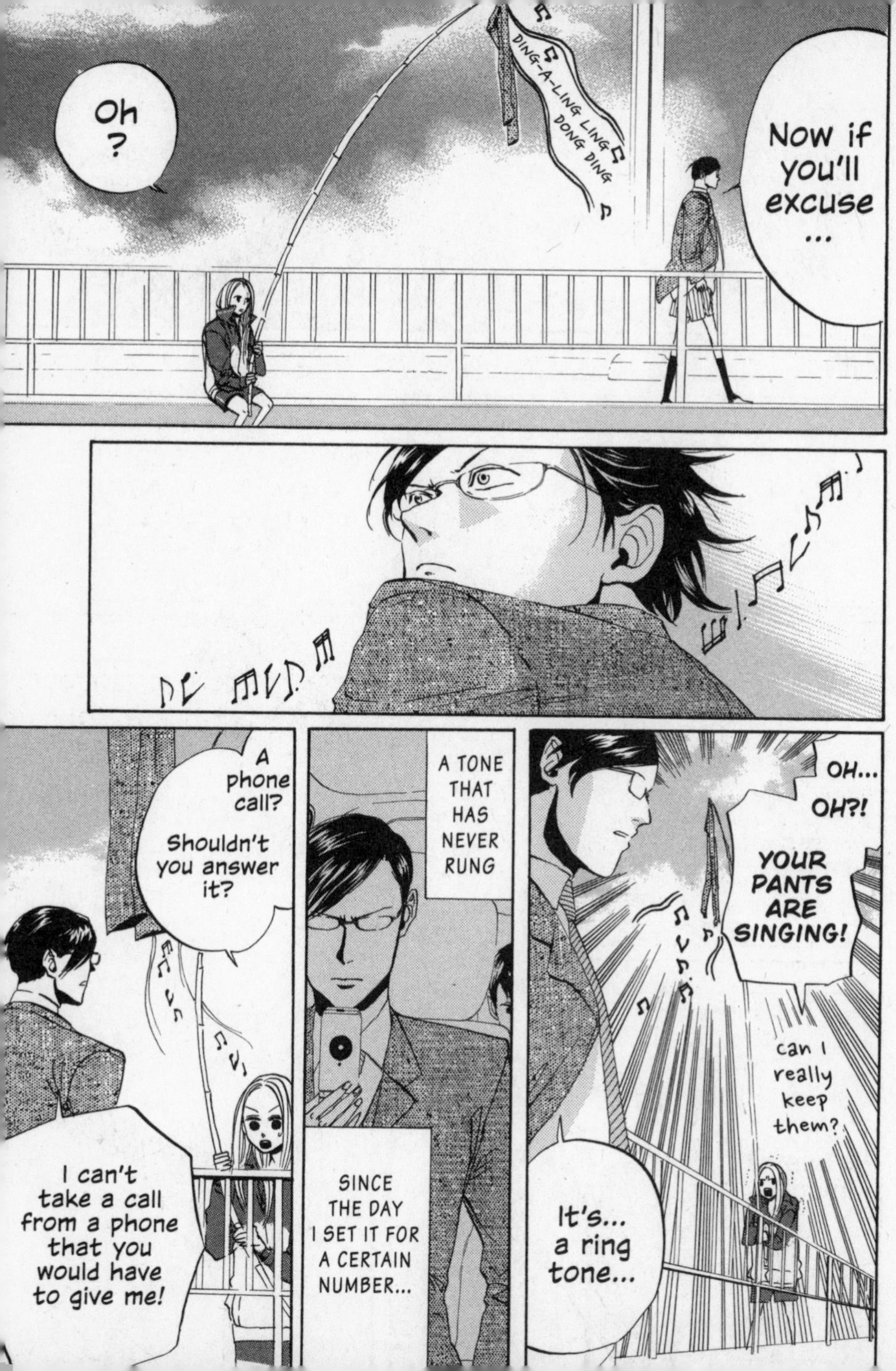
Now if you'll excuse ...
DING-A-LING LING DONG DING
Oh ?
OH... OH?!
YOUR PANTS ARE SINGING!
can I really keep them?
It's... a ring tone...
A TONE THAT HAS NEVER RUNG
SINCE THE DAY I SET IT FOR A CERTAIN NUMBER...
A phone call?
Shouldn't you answer it?
I can't take a call from a phone that you would have to give me!

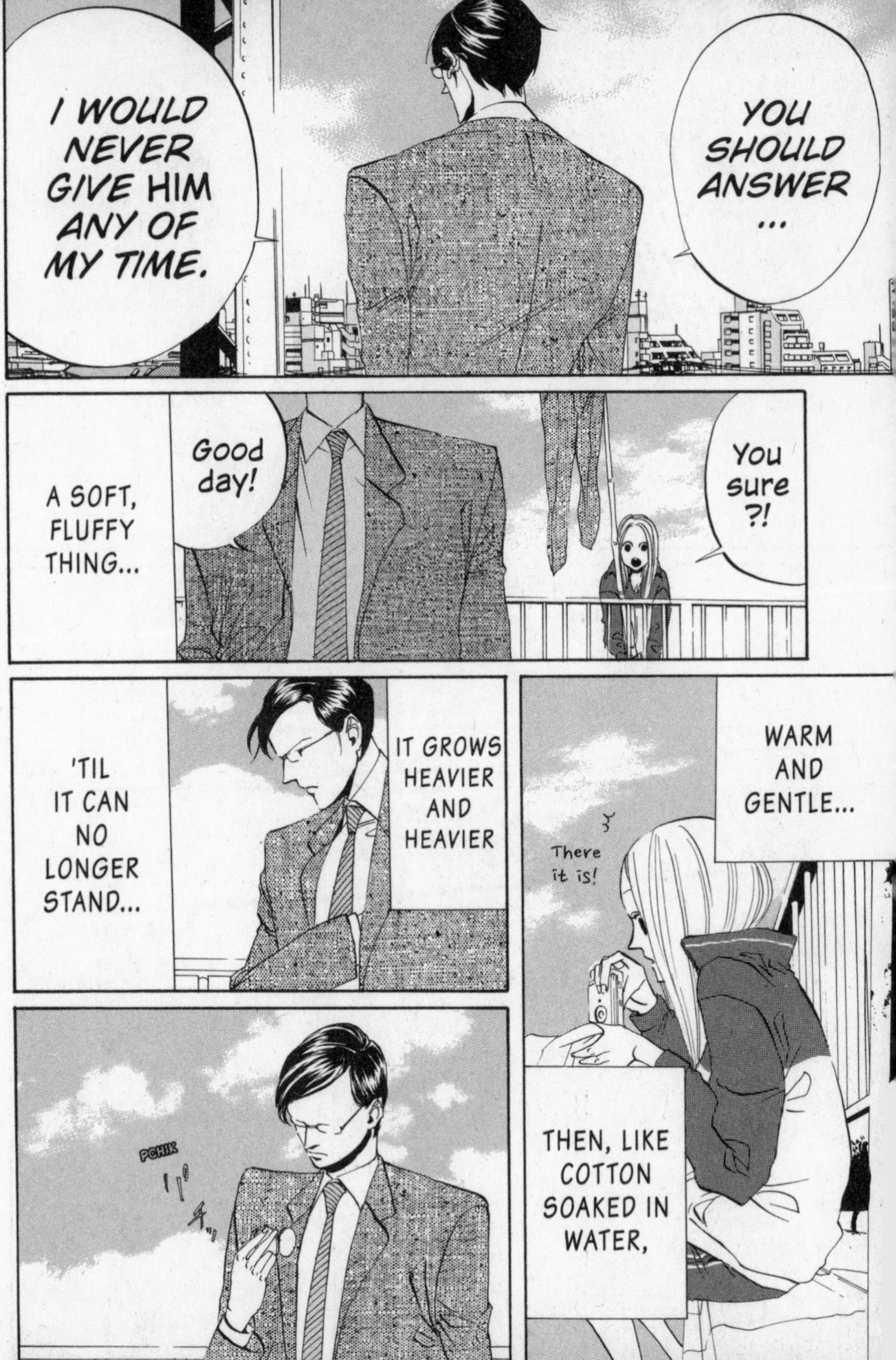
YOU SHOULD ANSWER...
I WOULD NEVER GIVE HIM ANY OF MY TIME.
You sure?!
Good day!
A SOFT, FLUFFY THING...
WARM AND GENTLE...
There it is!
THEN, LIKE COTTON SOAKED IN WATER,
IT GROWS HEAVIER AND HEAVIER
'TIL IT CAN NO LONGER STAND...
PCHIK

KEEP THAT UP UNTIL THE VERY END?

CAN YOU

if you think you can.

Do it ...

KLOP

KLOP

KLAK

YOU CAN DO WHAT I COULD NOT...

YOU THINK

IF...

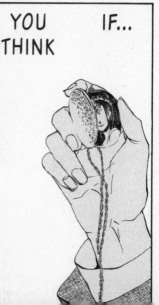

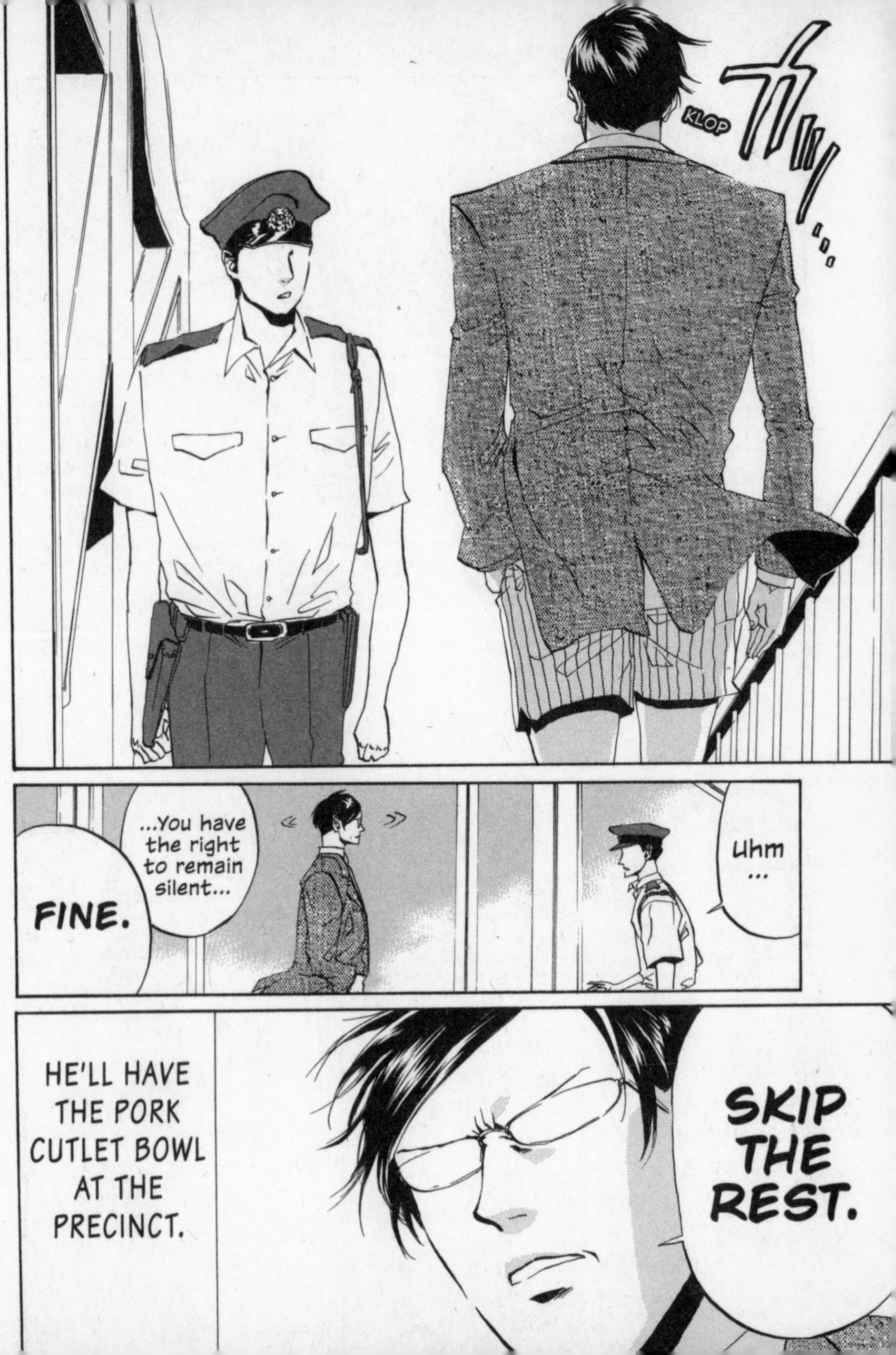
KLOP
Uhm ...
...You have the right to remain silent...
FINE.
SKIP THE REST.
HE'LL HAVE THE PORK CUTLET BOWL AT THE PRECINCT.

Chapter 107: Conclusion

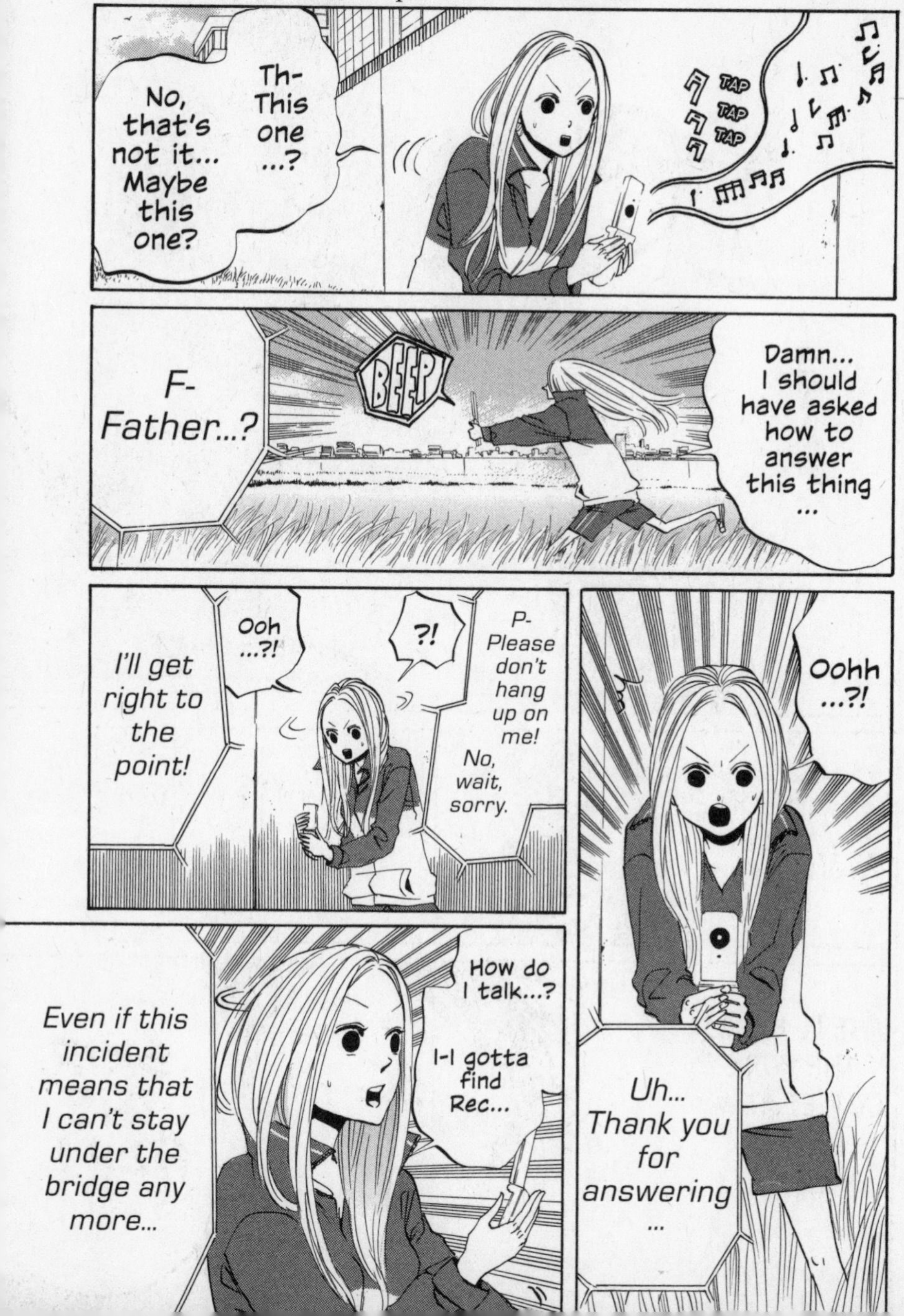
TAP
TAP
TAP
Th- This one ...?
No, that's not it... Maybe this one?
Damn... I should have asked how to answer this thing ...
BEEP
F- Father...?
Oohh ...?!
Uh... Thank you for answering ...
P- Please don't hang up on me!
No, wait, sorry.
?!
Ooh ...?!
I'll get right to the point!
How do I talk...?
I-I gotta find Rec...
Even if this incident means that I can't stay under the bridge any more...

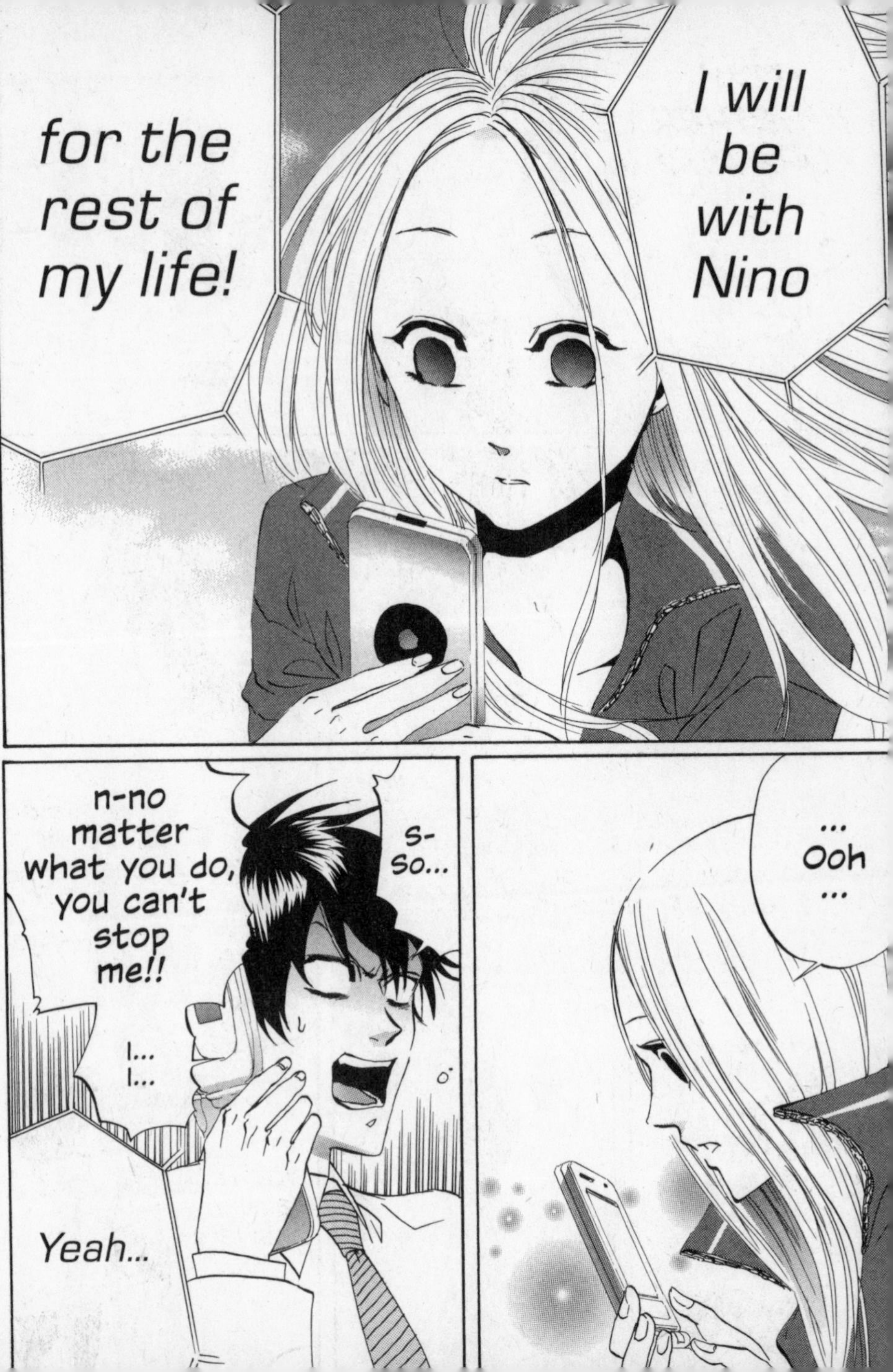
I will be with Nino
for the rest of my life!
... Ooh ...
s- so...
n-no matter what you do, you can't stop me!!
I... I...
Yeah...

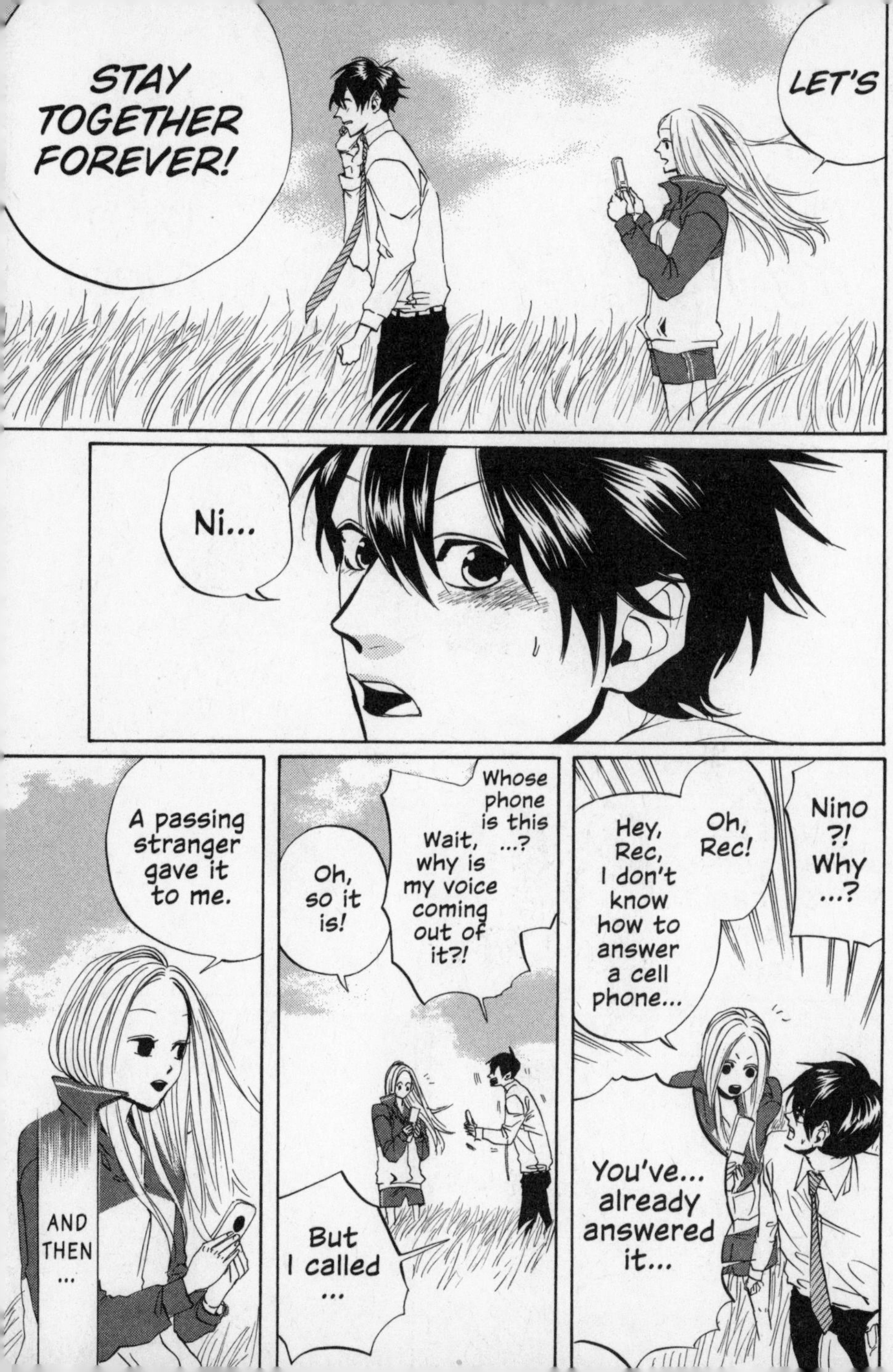
LET'S
STAY TOGETHER FOREVER!
Ni...
Nino ?! Why ...?
Oh, Rec!
Hey, Rec, I don't know how to answer a cell phone...
You've... already answered it...
Whose phone is this ...?
Wait, why is my voice coming out of it?!
Oh, so it is!
But I called ...
A passing stranger gave it to me.
AND THEN ...

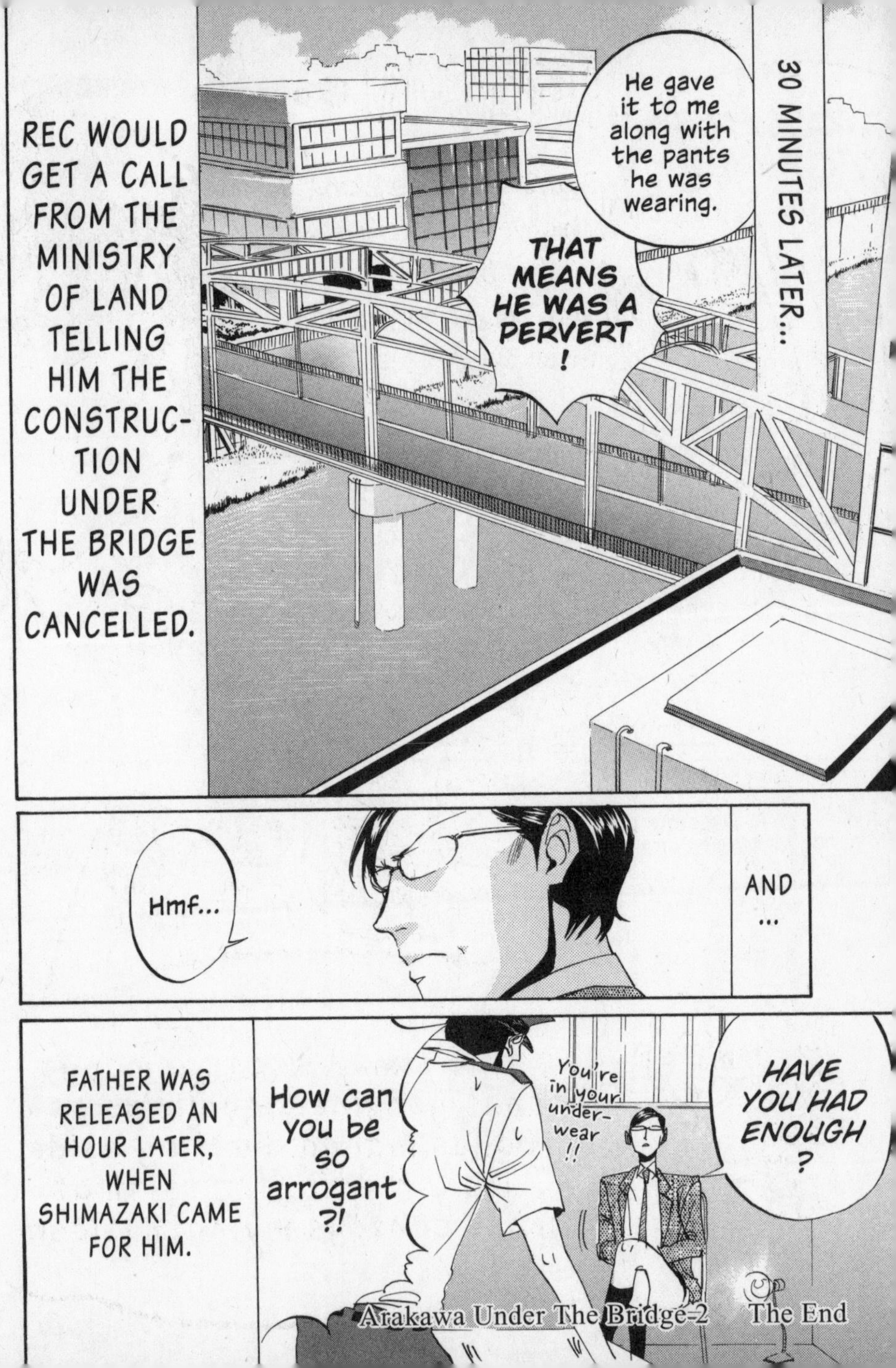

30 MINUTES LATER...
He gave it to me along with the pants he was wearing.
THAT MEANS HE WAS A PERVERT!
REC WOULD GET A CALL FROM THE MINISTRY OF LAND TELLING HIM THE CONSTRUCTION UNDER THE BRIDGE WAS CANCELLED.
AND ...
Hmf...
HAVE YOU HAD ENOUGH?
You're in your underwear!!
How can you be so arrogant?!
FATHER WAS RELEASED AN HOUR LATER, WHEN SHIMAZAKI CAME FOR HIM.
Arakawa Under The Bridge 2 The End

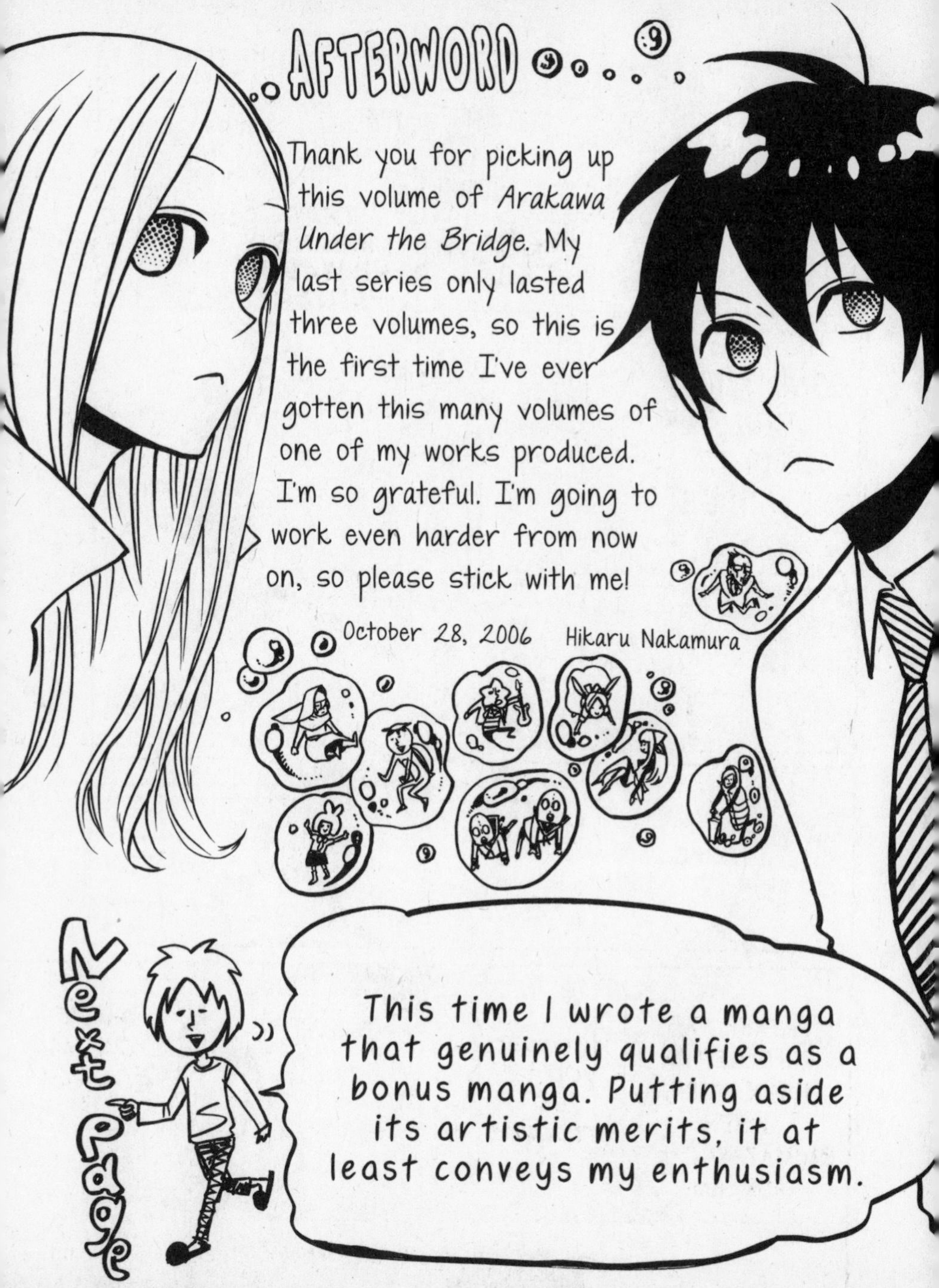
AFTERWORD
Thank you for picking up this volume of *Arakawa Under the Bridge*. My last series only lasted three volumes, so this is the first time I've ever gotten this many volumes of one of my works produced. I'm so grateful. I'm going to work even harder from now on, so please stick with me!
October 28, 2006 Hikaru Nakamura
This time I wrote a manga that genuinely qualifies as a bonus manga. Putting aside its artistic merits, it at least conveys my enthusiasm.
Next Page

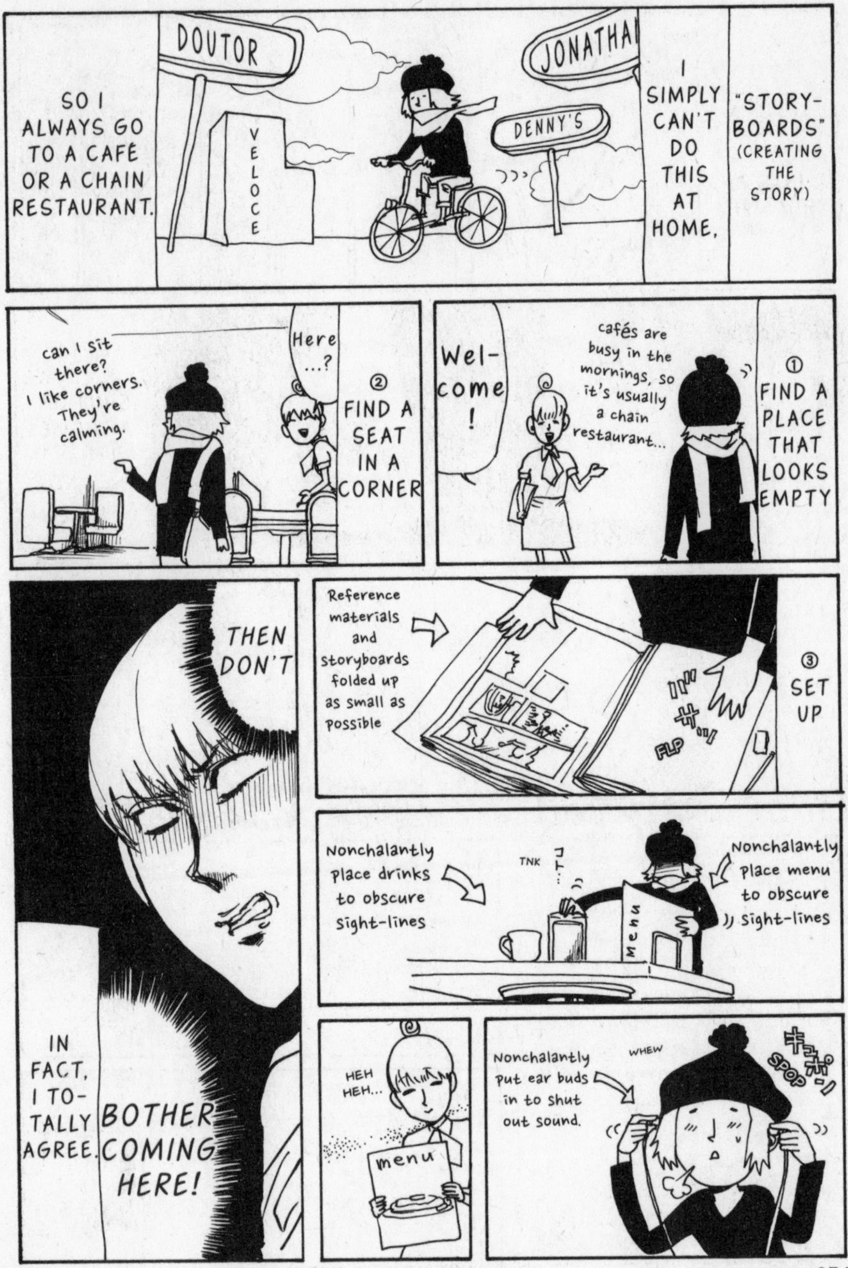

"STORY-BOARDS" (CREATING THE STORY)
I SIMPLY CAN'T DO THIS AT HOME,
JONATHAN
DENNY'S
DOUTOR
VELOCE
SO I ALWAYS GO TO A CAFÉ OR A CHAIN RESTAURANT.
① FIND A PLACE THAT LOOKS EMPTY
cafés are busy in the mornings, so it's usually a chain restaurant...
Wel-come!
② FIND A SEAT IN A CORNER
Here ...?
can I sit there? I like corners. They're calming.
③ SET UP
FLP
Reference materials and storyboards folded up as small as possible
Nonchalantly place menu to obscure sight-lines
Menu
TNK
Nonchalantly place drinks to obscure sight-lines
SPOP
WHEW
Nonchalantly put ear buds in to shut out sound.
HEH HEH...
menu
THEN DON'T
BOTHER COMING HERE!
IN FACT, I TO-TALLY AGREE.

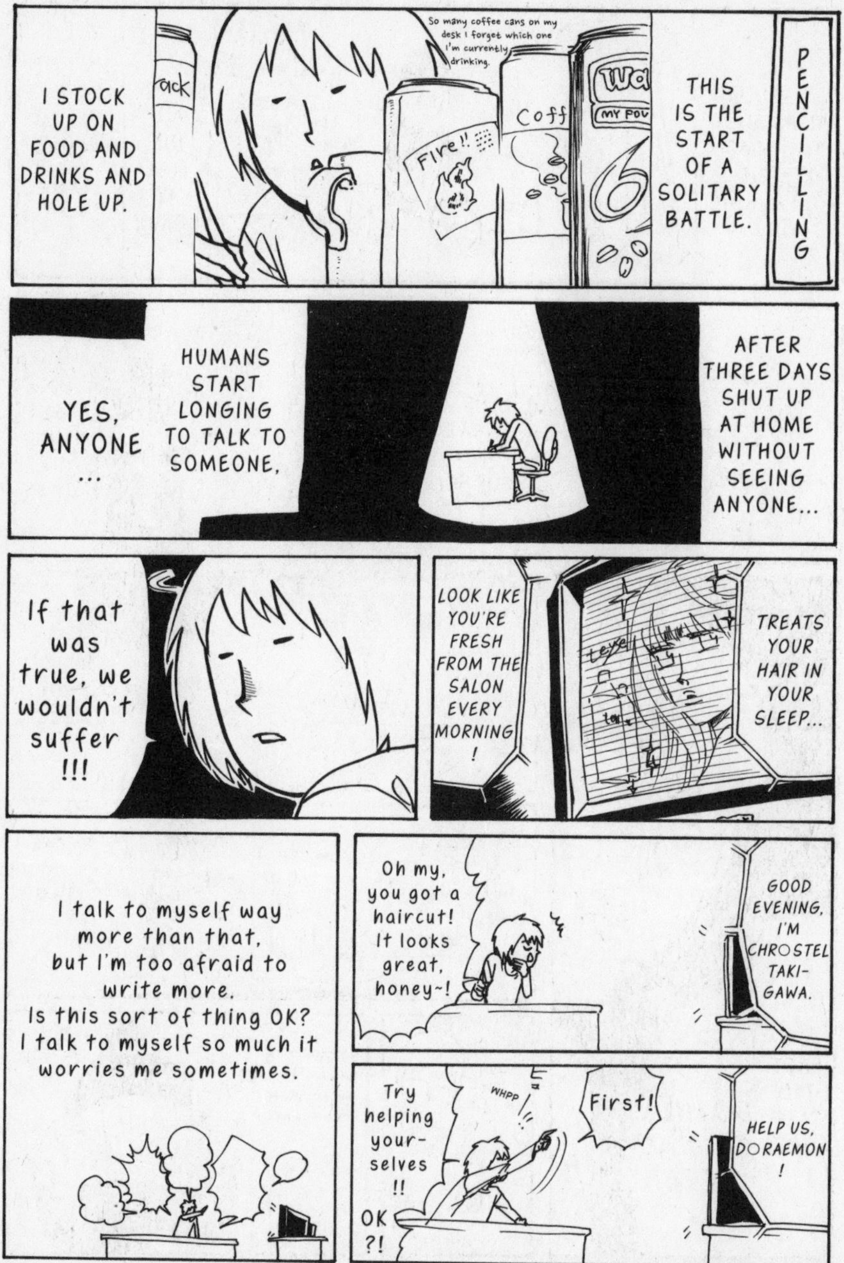
PENCILLING
THIS IS THE START OF A SOLITARY BATTLE.
So many coffee cans on my desk I forget which one I'm currently drinking.
Fire!!
I STOCK UP ON FOOD AND DRINKS AND HOLE UP.
AFTER THREE DAYS SHUT UP AT HOME WITHOUT SEEING ANYONE...
HUMANS START LONGING TO TALK TO SOMEONE,
YES, ANYONE ...
TREATS YOUR HAIR IN YOUR SLEEP...
LOOK LIKE YOU'RE FRESH FROM THE SALON EVERY MORNING !
If that was true, we wouldn't suffer !!!
GOOD EVENING, I'M CHROSTEL TAKI-GAWA.
Oh my, you got a haircut! It looks great, honey~!
HELP US, DORAEMON !
First!
WHPP
Try helping your-selves !!
OK ?!
I talk to myself way more than that, but I'm too afraid to write more. Is this sort of thing OK? I talk to myself so much it worries me sometimes.

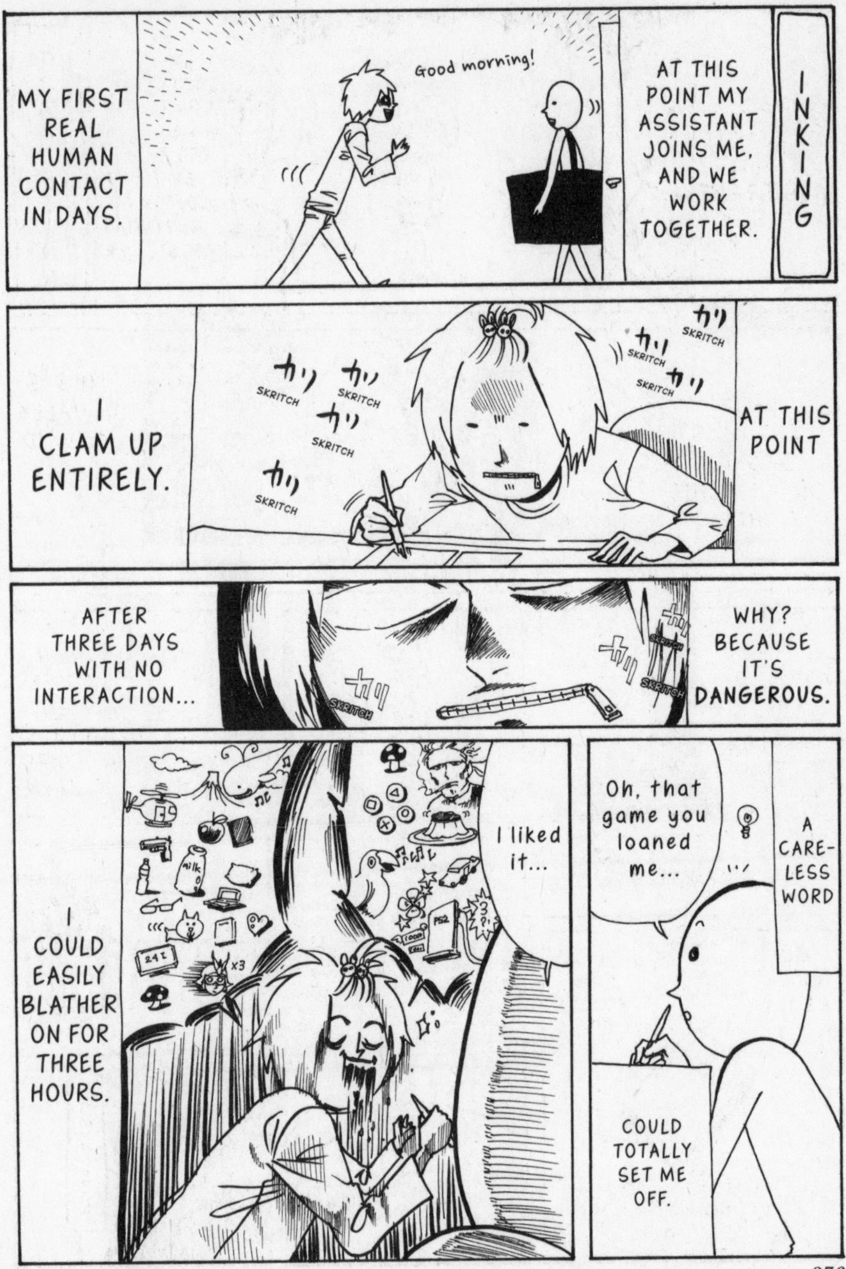
INKING
AT THIS POINT MY ASSISTANT JOINS ME, AND WE WORK TOGETHER.
Good morning!
MY FIRST REAL HUMAN CONTACT IN DAYS.
AT THIS POINT
カリ SKRITCH
カリ SKRITCH
カリ SKRITCH
カリ SKRITCH
カリ SKRITCH
カリ SKRITCH
カリ SKRITCH
I CLAM UP ENTIRELY.
WHY? BECAUSE IT'S DANGEROUS.
カリ SKRITCH
カリ SKRITCH
カリ SKRITCH
AFTER THREE DAYS WITH NO INTERACTION...
A CARE-LESS WORD
Oh, that game you loaned me...
COULD TOTALLY SET ME OFF.
I liked it...
I COULD EASILY BLATHER ON FOR THREE HOURS.

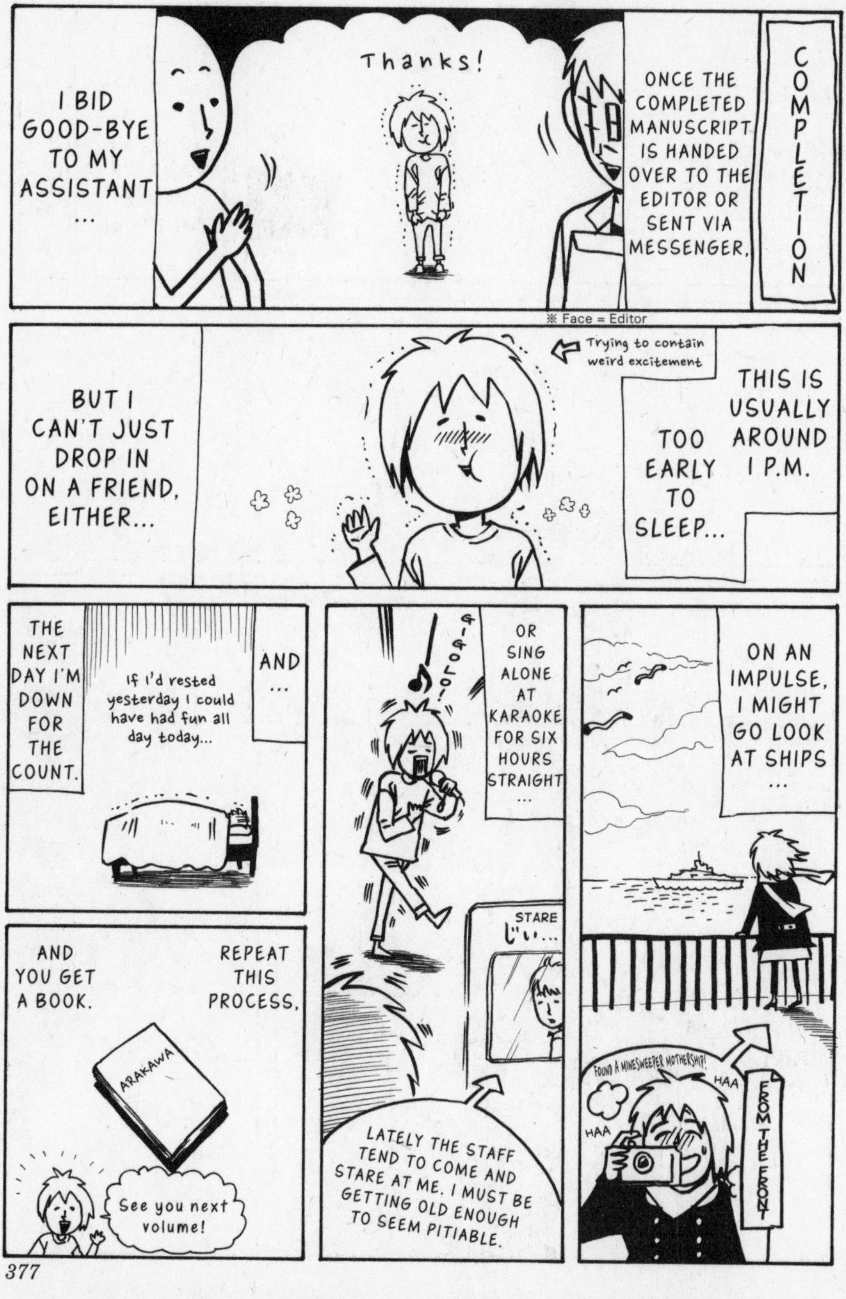
COMPLETION
ONCE THE COMPLETED MANUSCRIPT IS HANDED OVER TO THE EDITOR OR SENT VIA MESSENGER,
Thanks!
I BID GOOD-BYE TO MY ASSISTANT ...
※ Face = Editor
THIS IS USUALLY AROUND 1 P.M.
TOO EARLY TO SLEEP...
Trying to contain weird excitement
BUT I CAN'T JUST DROP IN ON A FRIEND, EITHER...
ON AN IMPULSE, I MIGHT GO LOOK AT SHIPS ...
FOUND A MINESWEEPER MOTHERSHIP!
HAA
FROM THE FRONT
HAA
OR SING ALONE AT KARAOKE FOR SIX HOURS STRAIGHT ...
GIGOLO!
STARE
じぃ...
LATELY THE STAFF TEND TO COME AND STARE AT ME. I MUST BE GETTING OLD ENOUGH TO SEEM PITIABLE.
AND ...
If I'd rested yesterday I could have had fun all day today...
THE NEXT DAY I'M DOWN FOR THE COUNT.
REPEAT THIS PROCESS,
AND YOU GET A BOOK.
ARAKAWA
See you next volume!

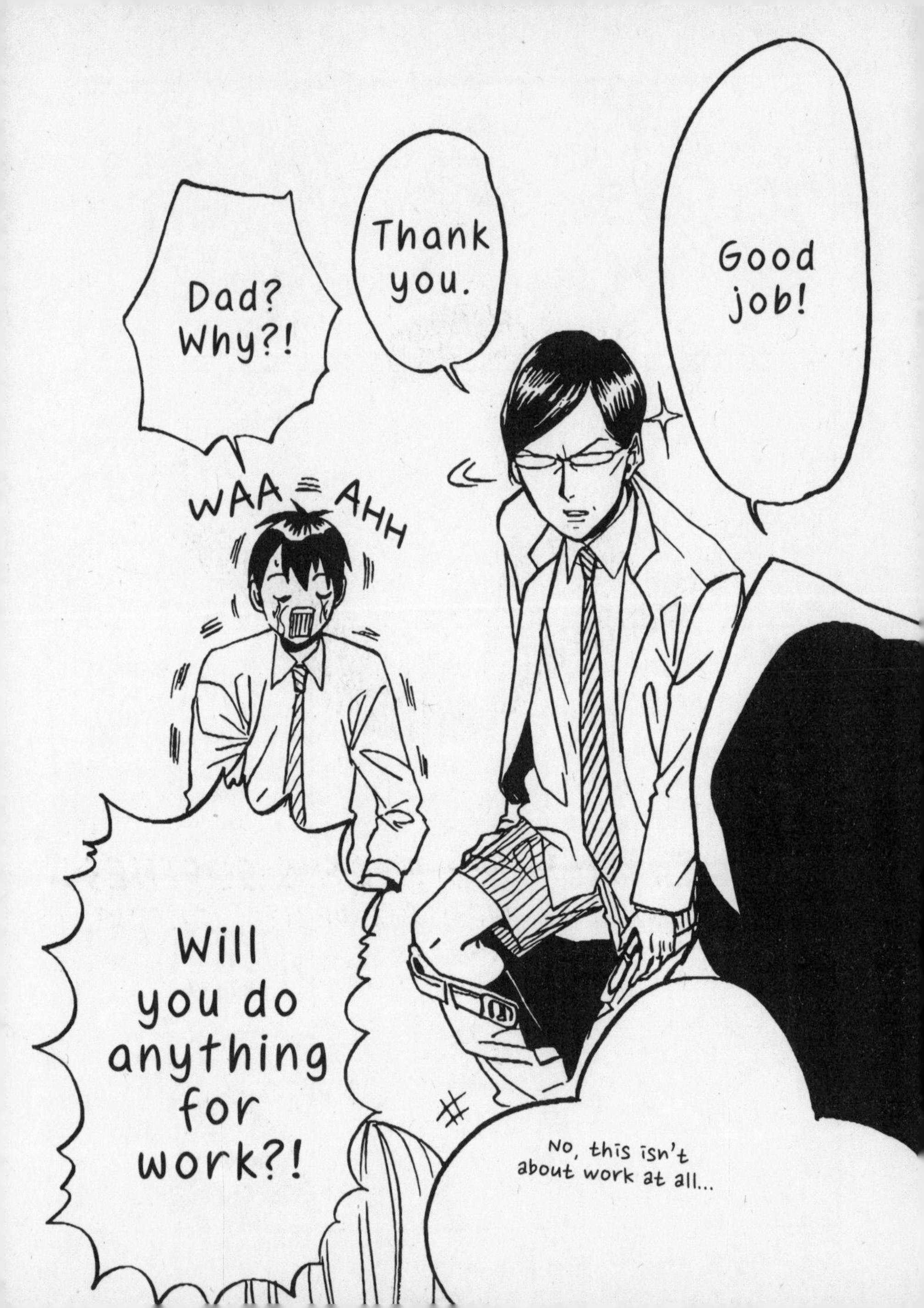
Good job!
Thank you.
Dad? Why?!
WAA AHH
Will you do anything for work?!
No, this isn't about work at all...

MEMORY FOAM'S SOFTNESS
WILL PROVIDE YOU WITH UNEXPECTED COMFORT...

ARAKAWA UNDER THE BRIDGE 2

Hikaru Nakamura

Translation: Andrew Cunningham
Production: Risa Cho
          Tomoe Tsutsumi

ARAKAWA UNDER THE BRIDGE Vol. 3 & 4
© 2006, 2007 Hikaru Nakamura / SQUARE ENIX CO., LTD.
First Published in Japan in 2006, 2007 by SQUARE ENIX CO., LTD.
Translation rights arranged with SQUARE ENIX CO., LTD. and Vertical, Inc.
through Tuttle-Mori Agency, Inc. Translation © 2018 by SQUARE ENIX CO., LTD.

Translation provided by Vertical Comics, 2018
Published by Vertical, Inc., New York

Originally published in Japanese as *Arakawa Andaa Za Burijji 3 & 4*
by SQUARE ENIX Co., Ltd., 2006, 2007
Arakawa Andaa Za Burijji first serialized in *Young Gangan*, SQUARE ENIX Co.,
Ltd., 2004-2015

This is a work of fiction.

ISBN: 978-1-945054-42-6

Manufactured in Canada

First Edition

Vertical, Inc.
451 Park Avenue South
7th Floor